Management

Revised Edition

Management

Revised Edition

Peter F. Drucker

with Joseph A. Maciariello

Collins
An Imprint of HarperCollinsPublishers

MANAGEMENT: TASKS, RESPONSIBILITIES, PRACTICES. Copyright © 1973, 1974 by Peter F. Drucker and MANAGEMENT, REVISED EDITION. Copyright © 2008 by the Peter F. Drucker Literary Trust. Foreword copyright © 2008 by Jim Collins. All rights reserved. Printed in the United States of America. No part of this book may be used or reproduced in any manner whatsoever without written permission except in the case of brief quotations embodied in critical articles and reviews. For information, address HarperCollins Publishers, 10 East 53rd Street, New York, NY 10022.

HarperCollins books may be purchased for educational, business, or sales promotional use. For information, please write: Special Markets Department, HarperCollins Publishers, 10 East 53rd Street, New York, NY 10022.

FIRST HARPER COLOPHON EDITION PUBLISHED 1985.
FIRST HARPERBUSINESS EDITION PUBLISHED 1993.

Designed by Level C

Library of Congress Cataloging-in-Publication Data

Drucker, Peter F. (Peter Ferdinand), 1909–2005.
   Management / Peter F. Drucker, with Joseph A. Maciariello. — Rev. ed.
      p. cm.
   Originally published New York: Harper & Row, [1974].
   Includes bibliographical references and index.
   ISBN 978-0-06-125266-2
   1. Management.   I. Maciariello, Joseph A.   II. Title.
   HD31.D773   2008
   658—dc22   2007036934

08   09   10   11   12   WBC/QWF   10   9   8   7   6   5   4   3   2   1

Peter F. Drucker was asked in early 1999, "What do you consider to be your most important contribution?" His answer:

* That I early on—almost sixty years ago—realized that **management** has become the constitutive organ and function of the *Society of Organizations*;

* That **management** is not "Business Management"—though it first attained attention in business—but the governing organ of *all* institutions of Modern Society;

* That I established the study of **management** as a discipline in its own right; and

* That I focused this discipline on People and Power; on Values, Structure, and Constitution; *and above all,* on responsibilities—that is, focused the Discipline of Management on **management** as a truly liberal art.

—Peter F. Drucker,
January 18, 1999

Source: The Drucker Institute
Claremont Graduate University
Claremont, California 91711

Contents

Contents

Peter Drucker's Legacy

During a discussion in graduate school, a professor challenged my first-year class: managers and leaders—are they different? The conversation unfolded something like this:

"Leaders set the vision; managers just figure out how to get there," said one student.

"Leaders inspire and motivate, whereas managers keep things organized," said another.

"Leaders elevate people to the highest values. Managers manage the details."

The discussion revealed an underlying worship of "leadership" and a disdain for "management." Leaders are inspired. Leaders are large. Leaders are the kids with black leather jackets, sunglasses, and sheer unadulterated cool. Managers, well, they're the somewhat nerdy kids, decidedly less interesting, lacking charisma. And of course, we all wanted to be *leaders,* and leave the drudgery of management to others.

We could not have been more misguided and juvenile in our thinking. As Peter Drucker shows right here, in these pages, *the very best leaders are first and foremost effective managers.* Those who seek to lead but fail to manage will become either irrelevant or dangerous, not only to their organizations, but to society.

Business and social entrepreneur Bob Buford once observed that Drucker contributed as much to the triumph of free society as any other individual. I agree. For free society to function we must have high-performing, self-governed institutions in every sector, not just in business, but equally in the social sectors. Without that, as Drucker himself pointed out, the only workable alternative is totalitarian tyranny. Strong institutions, in turn, depend directly on excellent management, and no individual had a greater impact on the practice of management and no single book captures its essence better than his seminal text, *Management.*

My first encounter with Drucker's impact came at Stanford in the early 1990s, when Jerry Porras and I researched the great corporations of the twentieth century. The more we dug into the formative stages and inflection points of companies like General Electric, Johnson & Johnson, Procter & Gamble, Hewlett-Packard, Merck

and Motorola, the more we saw Drucker's intellectual fingerprints. David Packard's notes and speeches from the foundation years at HP so mirrored Drucker's
writings that I conjured an image of Packard giving management sermons with a
classic Drucker text in hand. When we finished our research, Jerry and I struggled
to name our book, rejecting more than 100 titles. Finally in frustration I blurted,
"Why don't we just name it *Drucker Was Right,* and we're done!" (We later named
the book *Built to Last.*)

What accounts for Drucker's enormous impact? I believe the answer lies not
just in his specific ideas, but in his entire *approach* to ideas, composed of four elements:

1. He looked out the window, not in the mirror

2. He started first—and always—with results

3. He asked audacious questions

4. He infused all his work with a concern and compassion for the individual.

I once had a conversation with a faculty colleague about the thinkers who had
influenced us. I mentioned Drucker. My colleague wrinkled his nose, and said:
"Drucker? But he's so *practical.*" Drucker would have loved that moment of disdain, reveling in being criticized for the fact that his ideas worked. They worked
because he derived them by precise observation of empirical facts. He pushed always to look *out there*, in the world, to derive ideas, challenging himself and his
students to "Look out the window, not in the mirror!" Drucker falls in line with
thinkers like Darwin, Freud and Taylor—empiricists all. Darwin wrote copious
notebooks, pages and pages about pigeons and turtles. Freud used his therapeutic
practice as a laboratory. Taylor conducted empirical experiments, systematically
tracking thousands of details. Like them, Drucker immersed himself in empirical
facts and then asked, "What underlying principle explains these facts, and how
can we harness that principle?"

Drucker belonged to the church of results. Instead of starting with an almost
religious belief in a particular category of answers—a belief in leadership, or culture, or information, or innovation, or decentralization, or marketing, or strategy,
or any other category—Drucker began first with the question "what accounts for
superior results?" and *then* derived answers. He started with the outputs—the
definitions and markers of success—and worked to discover the inputs, not the
other way around. And then he preached the religion of results to his students and
clients, not just to business corporations but equally to government and the social
sectors. The more noble your mission, the more he demanded: what will define

superior performance? "Good intentions," he would seemingly yell without ever raising his voice, "are no excuse for incompetence."

And yet while practical and empirical, Drucker never became technical or trivial, nor did he succumb to the trend in modern academia to answer (in the words of the late John Gardner) "questions of increasing irrelevance with increasing precision." By remaining a professor of management—not as a science, but as a liberal art—he gave himself the freedom to pursue audacious questions. My first reading of Drucker came on vacation in Monterey, California. My wife and I embarked on one of our adventure walks through a used book store, treasure hunting for unexpected gems. I came across a beaten-up, dog-eared copy of *Concept of the Corporation,* expecting a tutorial on how to build a company. But within a few pages, I realized that it asked a much bigger question: what is the proper role of the corporation at this stage of civilization? Drucker had been invited to observe General Motors from the inside, and the more he saw, the more disturbed he became. "General Motors . . . can be seen as the triumph and the failure of the technocrat manager," he later wrote. "In terms of sales and profits [GM] has succeeded admirably. . . . But it has also failed abysmally—in terms of public reputation, of public esteem, of acceptance by the public." Drucker passionately believed in management not as a technocratic exercise, but as a profession with a noble calling, just like the very best of medicine and law.

Drucker could be acerbic and impatient, a curmudgeon. But behind the prickly surface, and behind every page in his works, stands a man with tremendous compassion for the individual. He sought not just to make our economy more productive, but to make all of society more productive *and* more humane. To view other human beings as merely a means to an end, rather than as ends in themselves, struck Drucker as profoundly immoral. And as much as he wrote about institutions and society, I believe that he cared most deeply about the individual.

I personally experienced Drucker's concern and compassion in 1994, when I found myself at a crossroads, trying to decide whether to jettison a traditional path in favor of carving my own. I mentioned to an editor for *Industry Week* that I admired Peter Drucker. "I recently interviewed Peter," he said, "and I'd be happy to ask if he'd be willing to spend some time with you."

I never expected anything to come of it, but one day I got a message on my answering machine. "This is Peter Drucker"—slow, deliberate, in an Austrian accent—"I would be very pleased to spend a day with you, Mr. Collins. Please give me a call." We set a date for December, and I flew to Claremont, California. Drucker welcomed me into his home, enveloping my extended hand into two of his. "Mr. Collins, so very pleased to meet you. Please come inside." He invested the better part of a day sitting in his favorite wicker chair, asking questions, teaching, guiding, and challenging. I made a pilgrimage to Claremont seeking wisdom from the greatest management thinker, and I came away feeling that I'd met a compassionate and generous human being who—almost as a side benefit—was a prolific genius.

There are two ways to change the world: the pen (the use of ideas) and the sword (the use of power). Drucker chose the pen, and thereby rewired the brains of thousands who carry the sword. Those who choose the pen have an advantage over those who wield the sword: the written word never dies. If you never had the privilege to meet Peter Drucker during his lifetime, you can get to know him in these pages. You can converse with him. You can write notes to him in the margins. You can argue with him, be irritated by him, and inspired. He can mentor you, if you let him, teach you, challenge you, change you—and through you, the world you touch.

Peter Drucker shined a light in a dark and chaotic world, and his words remain as relevant today as when he banged them out on his cranky typewriter decades ago. They deserve to be read by every person of responsibility, now, tomorrow, ten years from now, fifty and a hundred. That free society triumphed in the twentieth century guarantees nothing about its triumph in the twenty-first; centralized tyranny remains a potent rival, and the weight of history is not on our side. When young people ask, "What can I do to make a difference?" one of the best answers lies right here in this book. Get your hands on an organization aligned with your passion, if not in business, then in the social sectors. If you can't find one, start one. And then lead it—through the practice of management—to deliver extraordinary results and to make such a distinctive impact that you multiply your own impact by a thousand-fold.

Jim Collins
Boulder, Colorado
December, 2007

Introduction to the Revised Edition of *Management: Tasks, Responsibilities, Practices*

The original edition of *Management: Tasks, Responsibilities, Practices* was published in 1973. Peter Drucker continued to write, teach, and act as a consultant to management for thirty-two years after the publication of the book. This revised edition updates the original edition by integrating it with the work published on this subject by Peter Drucker from 1974 to 2005. All of the sources used to revise this book, except for the content of this chapter, are from materials housed at The Drucker Institute, Claremont, California, and are copyrighted by Peter F. Drucker.

My task was one of synthesizing this new material with the original material, always replacing the old with the new. In addition, I eliminated obsolescent material from the original edition and updated specific examples whenever possible.

HOW TO USE THIS BOOK

This book, like the original, is a comprehensive treatment of management. It describes in detail the three *responsibilities* of management: the *performance of the institution* for which managers work, *making work productive* and *the worker achieving*, and *managing social impacts* and *social responsibilities*. It goes on to describe the *tasks* and *practices* that a manager must acquire to fulfill his or her responsibilities.

Parts 1 through 5 of the book are devoted both to the *responsibilities* of managers and to the *responsibilities* of the leadership group of an organization. Parts 6 through 9 are devoted to the numerous, interrelated *tasks* and *practices* managers must acquire to fulfill their responsibilities. Part 10 describes in detail the new demands placed on managers and management by the *information revolution* and by the advent of the *knowledge society*. These new demands were foreshadowed but not fully addressed in the original edition.

The revised edition follows the original in that it addresses a number of audiences. Experienced executives and consultants may want to use this as a reference to consult when facing a specific problem or issue. The most effective way to use an insight from this book is to put it into practice. This is how one acquires maximum value from management principles.

A new manager should try to relate each of the issues in this book to his or her position or organization. Here one must be careful. These principles have all been worked out over a period of sixty-five years in actual organizations. Therefore, a principle will make much more sense to you when you can relate it to actual practice. So, new managers should think through each chapter in light of their specific responsibilities. Parts 6 through 9 may be of immediate relevance for the new manager.

Students of management and of the liberal arts can also use Peter Drucker's companion book, *Management Cases,* to learn how to apply the principles in this book to actual management problems. When possible, they should also try to process the material in each of the chapters by relating principles to actual organizations with which they are familiar. Some material may be truly effective only once the reader has real-world experience with the issue.

The systems perspective contained in figure 1 and described in the remainder of this introduction may be absorbed immediately by the experienced executive or consultant to integrate the entire contents of this book into a cohesive whole. Figure 1 and this introduction may also be used as a reference guide for relating each of Peter Drucker's dozen or so major management concepts to one another.

The material in this introduction has been successfully used as a reference guide for teaching this book to undergraduate and graduate students, and to executives. When used this way, it has been of greatest utility when used continuously from the beginning to the end of a course.

MANAGEMENT AS A SYSTEM OF INTERRELATED ELEMENTS (FIGURE 1)

Peter Drucker's writings on management are extensive and varied. Yet through all of his work a definite vision of what management is and how leaders and managers should operate does emerge. Management is a *discipline* and a *practice*. It is polycentric—it has many centers and interrelated elements. It is, therefore, very difficult to master this subject by mastering individual chapters in a linear way. One must integrate the elements into a working framework, as the whole is greater and different than the sum of its parts. Each of the ten parts of this book is related to one or more other parts. Each chapter is a part of the whole—the "words"—but the "music," if you will, comes from seeing management as an organic whole.

Figure 1
Systems View: Management as a Whole

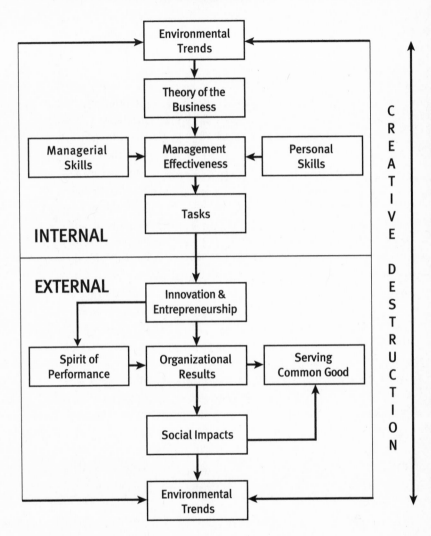

This introduction describes these interrelated elements of management as a system. Figure 1 provides a road map that relates each element to the whole subject. Each element is the subject of one or more chapters in this book. Seek to understand and apply the subject of *management as an organic whole* and not merely as a set of isolated elements. This portrayal of management as an organic whole is consistent with the view expressed in the original text where Peter Drucker explains the nature of organizations and management:

> There is one fundamental insight underlying all management science. It is that the business enterprise is a *system* of the highest order: a system the parts of which are human beings contributing voluntarily of their knowledge, skill, and dedication to a joint venture. And one thing characterizes all genuine systems, whether they be mechanical, like the control of a missile, biological like a tree, or social like the business enterprise: it is interdependence. The whole of a system is not necessarily improved if one particular function or part is improved or made more efficient. In fact, the: system may well be damaged thereby, or even destroyed. In some cases the best way to strengthen the system may be to weaken a part—to make it less precise or less efficient. For what matters in any system is the performance of the whole; this is the result of growth and of dynamic balance, adjustment, and integration rather than of mere technical efficiency (p. 508, *Management: Tasks, Responsibilities, Practices*).

Figure 1 provides a systems view of this revised edition. The diagram and the material in this chapter will help you navigate, absorb, and apply the material contained in this book. The elements and chapters in the book are most effectively viewed as an organic whole, an interrelated system of elements that encompass responsibilities, tasks, and practices. These elements taken together create the basis for the practice of management.

THE SPIRIT OF PERFORMANCE (CHAPTER 27)

The Spirit of Performance (lower left in figure 1) is at the core of Drucker's work on leadership and management. Organizations that exhibit a high spirit of performance are led by managers who are committed to *doing the right thing* and to *getting the right things done*.

Managers should focus on creating organizations that have a high spirit of performance. To attain such a spirit of performance, managers must

- Exhibit high levels of integrity in their moral and ethical conduct

- Focus on results

- Build on strengths—one's own and others'

- Meet at least the minimum requirements of major stakeholders such as customers, employees, and stockholders

- Lead beyond borders by meeting certain additional social needs that contribute to the common good

Managers committed to a high Spirit of Performance possess integrity of character, have a vision for the purpose of their organization, focus on opportunities and results, are change leaders, and follow the essential tasks, responsibilities, and practices of management.

THE THEORY OF THE BUSINESS (CHAPTER 8)

Leading a business begins by formulating a valid "theory of the business."

The theory of the business is the way an organization intends to create value for its customers, and the concept is therefore applicable to all organizations, not just business organizations. Formulating the theory requires answers to the following questions:

- What is our mission?

- What are our core competencies?

- Who are our customers and noncustomers?

- What do we consider results for the enterprise?

- What should our theory be? (This in turn requires managers to look for opportunities for innovation.)

The theory of a business is often not obvious, nor can it be formulated without controversy. Formulating a theory of business requires that executives look beyond the walls of the organization to the *external environment*. The environment is not limited to where the enterprise is currently operating, but also includes other "environments," such as those where noncustomers are being served and where future customers are likely to be served. Formulating a theory of the business must be a forward-looking exercise. It requires creating a *mission,* which in turn compels the organization to systematically evaluate emerging trends, future changes in its environments, and current or emerging social problems that may be turned into opportunities.

In determining core competencies, an organization's managers must ask, "What are we really good at?" And, "What should we be doing?"

Assumptions about mission, core competencies, and customers must not only fit reality, but also be consistent with each other. It is for this reason that an organization's theory must be constantly tested and updated, since, for example, one does not want to be selling only mainframe computers, as IBM once did, when one's customers are shifting their preferences to personal computers.

If the theory of the business is different from an organization's current business, then the practices of *abandonment* and of *innovation* and *change* become necessary. Leaders must be able to recognize when to give up products, processes, and customers and reallocate resources toward more promising opportunities.

In summary, the theory of the business sets direction; it should be used to communicate to the organization's members where the organization is going, provide the rationale for why it is going down a given path, and align the activities of its members.

IDENTIFYING ENVIRONMENTAL TRENDS AND THE FUTURE THAT HAS ALREADY HAPPENED (CHAPTERS 4–7, 10, PART 4)

Current and soon-to-be-upon-us trends do not change the need for a theory of the business, for management practices, for skills and tasks, and for managing social impacts and the other elements in figure 1, but they do shift the opportunity set based on known and projected trends that are evident in the environment.

Given the growing importance of knowledge work, for example, managers will have to focus much more attention on making knowledge-work productive and knowledge-workers achieving. This requires attention to building on strengths and to increasing the productivity of knowledge workers, but also to integrating these specialists into a performing whole. This integration of specialists is becoming the very essence of management in knowledge societies.

Demographic changes in the developed world include a population that is getting older, accompanied by a birthrate in many developed countries that is below the level required to maintain the size of the population. Consequently, the traditional workforce in these places is shrinking. Such demographic changes mean that an enterprise's marketing strategies and theory of the business may have to change. Split markets in which both the younger and older generations make up the population dictate very different value propositions and marketing strategies. "What is value?" to customers will have to be viewed through two different generational value systems (e.g., that of the millennium generation and that of the baby boom generation).

SOCIAL IMPACTS AND SOCIAL RESPONSIBILITIES (CHAPTERS 20–21)

The ethical rule that managers should live by when pursuing their organization's mission is *primum non nocere*: "above all, not knowingly to do harm." Organizations are public institutions, and their actions have impacts on society. Their codes of professional ethics must include to not knowingly do harm. Legal and ethical violations should be met with stiff penalties for those who break the law or otherwise knowingly do harm.

There are two different types of social impact in this context (bottom center of figure 1):

- Those negative ones that an organization creates

- Social ills that may be converted to business opportunities

Both types of impact are important and must be managed, since the first deals with what an organization does to harm society, and the second with what an organization can do to help society.

An organization's social impact is defined as activities or results of activities that derive from an organization's pursuit of its mission. Each institution must be dedicated to a social impact or purpose. For example, a hospital should heal the sick, a business should satisfy economic wants, and a church, synagogue, or mosque should nourish people spiritually. Detrimental impacts to society created in this process must be minimized, because they are harmful to the common good and are also outside of the proper mission of an organization.

There also needs to be a balance between cleaning up after one's negative impacts and, in doing so, incurring costs that create a competitive disadvantage for the organization within its industry. In the latter case, it is in the interest of executives in an industry (e.g., the accounting profession) to agree on regulations (i.e., to avoid auditing scandals such as those involving Enron, WorldCom, and so on) that minimize negative impacts.

Organizations must focus on their missions, minimize negative social impacts, and take proactive interest in the common good. Institutions are organs of society. As such, they are significantly dependent upon the welfare of society for their own welfare. To this end, when executive insiders know that substantial negative social impacts are present, management must work to obtain appropriate regulations so as to level the competitive playing field within its industry.

The difficulty and expense that executives are now incurring as they comply with the requirements of the Sarbanes-Oxley Act of 2002 (enacted as a result of the public outcry over numerous accounting scandals of the 1990s) were preventable. All that was needed was self-regulation by members of the accounting profession as represented by the American Institute of Certified Public Accountants and the Financial Accounting Standards Board. Such self-regulation would have led to far more effective legislation for preventing accounting abuses, because it would have been developed by the professional groups best informed to propose

xxii   **Introduction to the Revised Edition**

the regulation to Congress and to later enforce the regulation among their members.

The second type of social impact, social ills or dysfunctions, should be thought of as challenges and treated as potential business opportunities. Organizations should aggressively pursue activities that turn the elimination of social dysfunctions into business opportunities (e.g., Branch Rickey, general manager of the Brooklyn Dodgers, breaking the color line by bringing Jackie Robinson into major league baseball).

Another example of turning social ills into business opportunities is the recent emphasis by General Electric on "17 clean-technology businesses" and its expectation that the new emphasis will expand sales of products supported by these "green" technologies "from $10 billion in sales in 2004 to $20 billion by 2010, with more ambitious targets thereafter," which is indicative of the potential opportunities created by the global increase in greenhouse gases (GHG). In addition, GE has established for each business unit different targets for reducing emissions of carbon dioxide and overall GHG.*

Finally, management must also support the common good by helping community organizations financially and personally, through corporate donations and by encouraging employees to donate money and to volunteer their time. Management should also lend their executive expertise to help community groups address major social problems (in one example, the revitalization of downtown Cleveland, Ohio, was aided by the executive expertise of local CEOs). Executives should remember that a business cannot prosper in a dying society. Yet, in the process of seeking to promote the common good, executives should never lose sight of their principal mission, for if they lose sight of their principal mission, they will be of little use to society.

CREATIVE DESTRUCTION AND INNOVATION AND ENTREPRENEURSHIP (PART 8)

The Internet provides everyone with equal access to information and eliminates distance in the world economy. Globalization and outsourcing have intensified competition in labor, product, and capital markets. The rate of change is becoming torrid, and one can react to it, adapt to it, or become proactive and lead it—thus influencing future environmental trends. A highly spirited organization consists of executives who are proactive in leading change by discerning the "future that has already happened."

By taking advantage of these emerging trends, these executives embrace the

---

* "Special Report: The Greening of General Electric," *The Economist*, December 10, 2005, pp. 77–78.

ongoing process of creative destruction that is characteristic of free and global markets and, by doing so, these executives become change leaders. They recognize that an organization that seeks to maintain the status quo is already in decline.*

Change leaders formulate entrepreneurial strategies and look for opportunities to apply these strategies. They also create an internal culture and set of management systems that encourage and reward innovation and entrepreneurship.

The most effective way to seize opportunities to manage the future that has already happened is to be proactive, take advantage of emerging trends, embrace change, and become a change leader. Management practices must change to fit these new realities of the global, knowledge-based information society.

MANAGERIAL SKILLS, MANAGERIAL TASKS, AND PERSONAL SKILLS

The corporation of tomorrow will be far more complex than that of today. It will constitute a web of partnerships, joint ventures, alliances, outsourcing contractors, and various other kinds of associates or affiliates that is unprecedented in the current breadth and intricacy. Each aspect of the corporation may have its own management, but the relationships among entities will certainly have to be coordinated and made to perform. This complexity requires of the manager advanced skills and practices, both in his or her role as manager and as individual professional.

Management effectiveness requires three interconnected skills and practices, as shown in figure 1.

- Specific skills managers must acquire to be effective as leaders

- Particular tasks that managers must perform to lead their organizations to effectiveness

- Personal skills and practices that make individuals effective both in life and in managerial practice

---

* The process of "creative destruction" was described fully by the great Austrian economist Joseph A. Schumpeter. The most accessible explanation of the process by Schumpeter is in chapter 7 of his *Capitalism, Socialism and Democracy* (New York: Harper & Row Publishers, 1942, pp. 81–110). For example, "The opening up of new markets, foreign or domestic, and the organizational development from craft shop and factory floor to such concerns as U.S. Steel, illustrate the same process of industrial mutation . . . that incessantly revolutionizes the economic structure from within, incessantly destroying the old one, incessantly creating a new one. This process of Creative Destruction is the essential fact about capitalism. It is what capitalism consists in and what every capitalist concern has got to live with" (p. 83). And, "competition of the kind we have in mind acts not only when in being but also when it is an ever present threat. It disciplines before it attacks" (p. 85).

MANAGERIAL SKILLS (CHAPTERS 28–33)

To be effective, managers must acquire skills in six areas:

- Decision making

- People decisions

- Communications

- Budgeting

- Measurement and controls

- Information literacy

Effective managers make effective decisions. There are six steps of effective decision making and five characteristics of effective decisions. First, and by far the most important step, effective decision makers define and classify the problem. It is much easier to fix a wrong solution to a problem if the problem has been defined correctly than it is to fix a "correct" solution to a problem that has been defined incorrectly. If a problem has been defined incorrectly, no solution to that problem can be found. Conversely, if a problem is defined correctly, then an incorrect solution will provide useful feedback information, leading the executive closer to the right solution. The remaining five steps of effective decision making are

1. Ask, "Is this problem generic or unique?" Decisions that are generic ought to be solved by finding and applying a rule that someone else has used to solve the problem. For problems that are unique, the decision maker must next determine the *boundary conditions* that must be satisfied in order for the decision to be effective.

2. Establishing boundary conditions requires an answer to the question, "What does the decision have to accomplish to be effective in solving the problem?"

3. Next, the decision maker asks, "What is the right solution, given these conditions?"

4. Then—and this is where a great many decisions fail—the decision maker must convert the decision into action by assigning to one or more persons the responsibility for carrying out the decision and by eliminating any barriers faced by those who must act.

5. Finally, the effective decision maker follows up on the decision, obtains feedback on what actually happened as a result of the decision, and compares this with the intended or desired results.

As for the characteristics of an effective decision-making process, decision makers first ask, "Is a decision necessary at all?" If it is, they explore alternatives by soliciting opinions from those closest to the problem. Next, they ask the proponents of decisions to test their "hypothesis" against the facts to determine if the facts support their opinions (in other words, What would the facts have to be for a specific opinion to be correct?).

Effective decision makers encourage *dissent* on alternatives and then act on the chosen alternative if the potential benefits of doing so outweigh the costs and risks. Dissent, properly carried out, taps the imaginations of the parties involved in the search for an appropriate decision and leads to a more complete understanding of what the problem is all about. And if a decision fails to meet the boundary conditions after vigorous debate, the decision maker will now have a better understanding of the possible causes of failure, having considered other alternatives.

Finally, effective decision making takes courage, since, as with many effective medicines, effective decisions can sometimes have side effects or unintended outcomes.

People decisions are a special case of decision making requiring their own rules. These decisions are among the most important decisions made by managers, because they have the greatest impact on the performance of the organization. And many of these decisions turn out to be ineffective.

There are five steps in making effective people decisions:

1. Carefully think through the assignment.

2. Look at three to five qualified people.

3. Consider each candidate's strengths.

4. Discuss each candidate with his or her colleagues and bosses.

5. Make sure the appointee understands the job and what it requires, and reports back on what it requires once he or she is in the job.

In addition to the five steps, there are other considerations for the decision maker. Accept responsibility for any people decision you make, such as placement or promotion that fails. Accept also that people who do not perform must be removed. However, just because a person does not perform in the job does not mean that the person is a bad worker whom the organization should let go.

Newcomers are best put in an established position where the expectations are known and help is available. Finally and most fundamentally, it is the manager's responsibility to try to make the right people decision every time.

Next we turn to a discussion of the remaining four areas of managerial skills that executives must acquire to carry out their tasks.

1. First, managers must learn to be good *communicators.* Effective executives must engage in upward communication, a two-way process in which communication is initiated by the recipient as well as received. This helps ensure that the recipient understands what is being communicated—because unless the recipient "hears," communication has not taken place. Information and communication are different. Communication has not taken place unless the emitter is sure that the receiver understands what action is to be taken as a result of, say, a conversation or a memo. The most effective way to ensure that real communication has taken place is to ask the receiver to describe what he or she has heard from the conversation, including the demands for required action, and to make sure it is what the emitter wanted to convey.

2. *Budgeting* is the most widely used tool of management. Budgets are revenue-and-expenditure plans developed for each unit to help management decide where to apply the financial and human resources of an organization. In estimating revenues and expenses, executives are able to establish communication with each part of the organization and integrate each part's objectives, plans, and expenditures with the whole of the organization. Budgets, correctly understood and used, are thus major tools for integrating the plans and performance of the organization—upward, downward, and sideways. By holding each unit responsible for the plans and expenditures in the budget, the budgeting process provides a framework for achieving accountability for performance for each unit and person in the organization. Budgeting is thus crucial to the process of managing an organization.

   The budget process provides a forum for evaluating existing markets, products, processes, and programs for continuation. Activities that would not be supported if not already in place are prime candidates for abandonment. So as not to cause chaos each period, a periodic review (sometimes called a zero-based review) of the activities for each unit should be established well in advance. *This helps to institutionalize a systematic process of abandonment within the organization.*

3. Creating appropriate *measurements* and maintaining *control* are other skills that effective executives must acquire. An organization's choice of controls indicates to people what is valued and what is desired. Controls are therefore not neutral. They reflect the values of the organization, and they direct behavior. Consequently, controls must focus on results. They should be easy to understand and be considered a *resource* for the person who is responsible for the work that is being controlled. Controls must also be timely and congruent with goals.

4. Organizing *information* for decision making is a skill that managers must acquire. Managers and organizations increasingly must rely on technology to support and guide their organization (e.g., the creation of performance dashboards, or comprehensive metrics, for each position is now not uncommon). The blizzard of data will have to be converted into information that is pertinent for each knowledge worker and executive. This will enhance the ability of managers to expand output per hour for both service and knowledge workers.

   Most important, management, to be effective, must obtain information external to the enterprise. Many, if not most, changes that have transformed enterprises have originated *outside* the specific industry of the enterprise. This information is not contained in the computers of organizations in a specific industry.

   Creating data networks and knowledge management systems will also be important in order to link databases and create direct access to relevant information across global supply chains.

   Information has to be organized to challenge a company's strategy. It has to test the company's assumptions, its theory of the business. This includes testing the company's assumptions about the environment: society and its structure, the market, the customer, and technology. And information on the environment, where the major threats and opportunities are likely to arise, has become increasingly urgent.

MANAGEMENT TASKS (CHAPTERS 9–11, 24–26, PART 9, CHAPTER 45)

The five tasks of the manager are aimed at implementing the Theory of the Business. The effectiveness with which these tasks are carried out depends on the acquisition of managerial and personal skills.

1. The theory of the business (THOB) is the starting point for setting objectives. Management by objectives (MBO) is a well-defined method of setting objectives to achieve the mission of the organization, as defined in the THOB. MBO involves setting goals and objectives to balance short-range and long-range

objectives. These objectives become the basis for organizing the human and capital resources of the firm and for making work assignments.

The MBO process brings together aspects of the management process. For example, to determine mission and objectives, an executive must determine an organization's theory of the business. And to make sure that an organization is properly implementing its THOB, managers must engage in a communication process, make decisions, use measurements, and use tools of information technology. But management by objectives is not only a technique that executives should learn; it is a genuine philosophy of management.

MBO embodies a process that supports and facilitates teamwork. Communication—upward, downward, and sideways—is essential to setting and accomplishing objectives. Upward communication must be used to ensure that each executive has a clear picture of where the organization is going and how his or her objectives fit into the whole. Most important, when properly employed, MBO relies on a process of self-control and seeks to achieve alignment between individual needs and the goals of the organization. MBO thus seeks to meld *individual freedom and responsibility* with *organizational performance and results*. It rests on a high concept of human motivation and behavior. It is the underpinning for a highly-spirited organization.

2. An executive's responsibility to organize would appear simple on its surface; however, organizing requires analytical skill in order to understand the activities, decisions, and relationships required if the organization is to achieve its mission. Organizing requires that managers classify activities and place them in the organization's structure according to their contribution to results. Organizing should result in minimizing the number of relationships required for each position to achieve desired performance.

The organization's structure should allow decisions to be made at the lowest level possible, consistent with minimizing the number of people that must be consulted to make each decision. Managers should seek clarity, simplicity, and economy in their structures, and they should keep to a minimum the number of layers required, because each layer in an organization is a communication link that adds complexity and noise to the decision process.

3. A manager must also motivate and communicate. This requires social skills, trust, a focus on results, and other conditions for a highly spirited organization, which includes providing equitable rewards that balance the merits of the individual with the needs and stability of the group. Motivation comes from thoughtful people decisions, job design, high expectations for performance, and sound decisions on compensation and rewards.

4. To ensure that efforts in the organization are directed toward objectives, a manager must establish yardsticks of performance. Performance in each position is

measured in relation to the objectives of the person and those of the organization. Establishing controls and appropriate reporting mechanisms facilitate the process of self-control as well as the processes of developing oneself and others.

5. Managing oneself and one's career and developing others are becoming more important with the advent of knowledge work, the knowledge economy, and competition brought about by the forces of globalization. Managing oneself requires the individual to establish a process for determining what one is good at (in other words, one's strengths) and for determining where one's efforts in one's work will be the most fruitful, that is, will make the greatest contribution.

Managers must also take responsibility for developing the abilities of subordinates and coworkers around them. This is a key result area for the manager. This process is crucial for cultivating future leaders of an enterprise and for helping employees acquire *personal skills* that will prepare them for the future. Development is, however, a double-edged process. One cannot develop oneself unless one is actively engaged in the development of others.

PERSONAL SKILLS (PART 10)

Managing oneself requires that the knowledge worker take responsibility for managing his or her career. This requires self-knowledge and self-development.

Knowledge workers face significant *new demands*.

1. They have to ask, "Who am I? What are my strengths? How do I work?"

2. They have to ask, "Where do I belong?"

3. They have to ask, "What is my contribution?"

4. They have to take responsibility for their relationships, up and down and sideways.

If one were to take a poll, it is likely that few people would identify themselves as ever having considered topics such as: Am I a listener or reader? How do I learn most effectively? Is my job aligned with my values? What is my plan for continuous learning and self-revitalization? What is my plan for the second half of my life? What do I want to be remembered for?

But these are important issues to settle in order to set the direction of one's career and one's life. One must determine where one belongs—in a large or small organization; as a freelancer; in a corporation, government, or a social-sector institution; or perhaps as an executive or a technologist.

People and communication skills are going to be increasingly important for managers of the future as they navigate and negotiate their way through their organizations' complex system, network, and cellular structures.[*]

The increased use of technology will have an impact on the productivity of managers and professionals, thus requiring an expansion of personal skills—including the ability to take full advantage of technology tools such as the Internet, mobile electronic devices, and videoconferencing. These skills can enhance one's ability to collaborate among colleagues and to network across the globe.

SUMMARY

Figure 1 presents a systems view of Drucker on management. It summarizes Drucker's teachings on management as an organic whole. Managerial skills, personal skills, and managerial tasks must be combined into principles of managerial effectiveness to implement an enterprise's theory of the business. These principles include the discipline of innovation and entrepreneurship. Management principles must be directed toward developing and maintaining a high spirit of performance, achieving organizational results, and managing social impacts to serve the common good.

Each element of figure 1 is described in this book. Unless otherwise indicated, all chapters in this book are adapted from the works of Peter Drucker and are contained in his numerous books and articles. This book draws upon his entire body of knowledge, which is housed at The Drucker Institute (http://www.thedrucker-institute.com).

---

[*] See Malcolm Gladwell, "The Cellular Church," *The New Yorker,* September 12, 2005, pp. 60–67. Gladwell is the author of *The Tipping Point* and *Blink*.

Preface

What will future historians consider the most important event of the twentieth century: The two World Wars? The atomic bomb? The rise of Japan to be the first non-Western great economic power? The information revolution? The *demographic revolutions* that occurred in the twentieth century—revolutions that have profoundly changed the world's human landscape and that have no precedents. And I mean not only the *quantitative change:* the explosive growth of population in the twentieth century and the equally explosive extension of life spans resulting in an aging population in all developed and in most emerging countries. Equally important, indeed perhaps more important, was the *qualitative change:* the unprecedented transformation of the workforce in all developed countries, from one doing largely unskilled, manual work, to one doing knowledge work.

At the beginning of the twentieth century, ninety out of every hundred people in the working population in every country were manual workers, farmers and their hired hands, domestic servants, factory workers, miners, or construction workers. And life expectancies, especially work-life expectancies, were so low that a majority of working people were disabled well before they reached what was then the threshold of old age, that is, age fifty.

But while the life expectancy of the individual and especially the individual knowledge worker has risen beyond anything anybody could have foretold at the beginning of the twentieth century, the life expectancy of the employing institution has been going down, and is likely to keep going down. Or rather, the number of years has been shrinking during which an employing institution—and especially a business enterprise—can expect to stay successful. This period was never very long. Historically, very few businesses were successful for as long as thirty years in a row. To be sure, not all businesses ceased to exist when they ceased to do well. But the ones that survived beyond thirty years usually entered into a long period of stagnation—and only rarely did they turn around again and once more become successful growth businesses.

Thus, while the life expectancies and especially the working-life expectancies of the individual and especially of the knowledge worker have been expanding very rapidly, the life expectancy of the employing organizations has actually been going down. And—in a period of very rapid technological change, of increasing competition because of globalization, of tremendous innovation—the successful life-expectancies of employing institutions are almost certain to continue to go down. More and more people, and especially knowledge workers, can therefore expect to outlive their employing organizations and to have to be prepared to develop new careers, new skills, new social identities, new relationships, for the second half of their lives.

And now the largest single group in the workforce in all developed countries is knowledge workers rather than manual workers. At the beginning of the twentieth century, knowledge workers in any country, even the most highly developed ones, were very scarce. I doubt that there was any country in which they exceeded 2 or 3 percent of the working population. Now, in the United States, they account for around 33 percent of the working population. By the year 2020, they will account for about the same proportion in Japan and in Western Europe. They are something we have never seen before. These knowledge workers own their means of production, for they own their knowledge. And their knowledge is portable; it is between their ears.

For untold millennia, there were no choices for the overwhelming majority of people in any country. A farmer's son became a farmer. A craftsman's son became a craftsman, and a craftsman's daughter married a craftsman; a factory worker's son or daughter went to work in a factory. Whatever mobility there was was downward mobility. In the 250 years of Tokugawa rule in Japan, for instance, very few people advanced from being commoners to being samurai—that is, privileged warriors. An enormous number of samurai, however, lost their status and became commoners, that is, moved down. The same was true all over the world. Even in the most mobile of countries, the early twentieth-century United States, upward mobility was still the exception. We have figures from the early 1900s until 1950 or 1955. They show conclusively that at least nine out of every ten executives and professionals were themselves the sons of executives and professionals. Only one out of every ten executives or professionals came from the "lower orders" (as they were then called).

The business enterprise, as it was invented around 1860 or 1870—and it was an invention that had little precedent in history—was such a radical innovation precisely because there was upward mobility within it for a few people. This was the reason why the business enterprise ruptured the old communities—the rural village, the small town, or the craft guild.

But even the business enterprise, as it was first developed, tried to become a traditional community. It is commonly believed—in Japan as well as in the West—that the large Japanese company with its lifetime employment is something that exists only in Japan and expresses specific Japanese values. Apart from the fact that this is historical nonsense—lifetime employment in Japan even for white collar, salaried employees was a twentieth-century invention and did not exist before the end of Meiji (that is, before the twentieth century)—the large business enterprise in the West was not very different. Anyone who worked as a salaried employee for a large company in Germany, Great Britain, the United States, Switzerland, and so on had, in effect, lifetime employment. And even a salaried employee above the entry level in such a company considered himself "a company man" and identified himself with the company. He—and of course in those days they were all men—was a "Siemens Man" in Germany or a "General Electric Man" in the United States. Most of the big companies all over the West, just like the Japanese companies, hired people for only the entrance positions, and they expected them to stay until they died or retired. In fact, the Germans, with their passion for codifying everything, even created a category for such people. They were called "private civil servants" (*Privatbeamte*). Socially, they ranked below civil servants. But legally, they had the same job security and, in effect, lifetime employment—with the implicit assumption that they, in turn, would be committed to their employer for their entire working life and career. The Japanese company as it was finally formulated in the 1950s or early 1960s was, in other words, simply the most highly structured and most visible expression of the large business enterprise as it had been first developed in the late nineteenth-century and then reached full maturity in the first half of the twentieth century.

The early nineteenth-century business—and even the mid-nineteenth-century business—derived success from low costs. Successfully managing a business meant being able to produce the same commodities everybody else produced but at lower cost. In the twentieth century this then changed to what we now call "strategy" or analysis for the purpose of creating competitive advantage. I may claim to have been the first one to point this out, in a 1964 book called *Managing for Results*. But by that time a shift was already underway to another basic foundation: knowledge. [I had realized that in 1959—and the first result of this realization was my book *The Effective Executive* (1966). It was in that book that the shift to the knowledge worker was foreshadowed and its implication for the business first analyzed.]

The knowledge worker, to repeat, differs from any earlier worker in two major aspects. First, the knowledge worker owns the means of production and they are portable. Second, he or she is likely to outlive any employing organization. Add to this that knowledge work is very different in character from earlier forms of work. It is effective only if highly specialized. What makes a brain surgeon effective is that he is a specialist in brain surgery. By the same token, however, he probably could not repair a damaged knee. And he certainly would be helpless if confronted with a tropical parasite in the blood.

This is true for all knowledge work. "Generalists"—and this is what the traditional business enterprise, including the Japanese companies, tried to develop—are of limited use in a knowledge economy. In fact, they are productive only *if they themselves become specialists in managing knowledge and knowledge workers.* This, however, also means that knowledge workers, no matter how much we talk about "loyalty," will increasingly and of necessity see their knowledge area—that is, their specialization rather than the employing organization—as what identifies and characterizes them. Their community will increasingly be people who share the same highly specialized knowledge, no matter where they work or for whom.

In the United States, as late as the 1950s or 1960s, when meeting somebody at a party and asking him what he did, one would get the answer, "I work for General Electric" or "for Citibank"—or for some other employing organization. In other words, one would get exactly the same kind of answer in Germany, in Great Britain, in France, and in any other developed country. Today, in the United States, if one asks someone whom one meets at a party, "What do you do?" the answer is likely to be, "I am a metallurgist" or "I am a tax specialist" or "I am a software designer." In other words, in the United States, at least, knowledge workers no longer identify themselves with an employer. They identify themselves with a knowledge area. The same is increasingly true in Japan, certainly among the younger people.

This is more likely to change the organization of the future, and especially the business enterprise, than technology, information, or e-commerce.

Since 1959, when I first realized that this change was about to happen, I consciously worked at thinking through the meaning of this tremendous change, and especially the meaning for individuals. For not only is it individuals who will have to convert this change into opportunity for themselves, for their careers, for their achievement, for their identification and fulfillment. It is the individual knowledge worker who, in large measure, will determine what the organization of the future will look like and which kind of organization of the future will be successful.

There is as a consequence only one satisfactory definition of management, whether we talk of a business, a government agency, or a nonprofit organization: *to make human resources productive.* It will increasingly be the only way to gain competitive advantage. Of the traditional resources of the economist—land, labor, and capital—none anymore truly confers a competitive advantage. To be sure, not to be able to use these resources as well as anyone else is a tremendous competitive *disadvantage.* But every business has access to the same raw materials at the same price. Access to money is worldwide. And manual labor, the traditional third resource, has become a relatively unimportant factor in most enterprises. Even in traditional manufacturing industries, labor costs are no more than 12 or 13 percent of total costs, so that even a very substantial advantage in labor costs (say a 5 percent advantage) results in a negligible competitive advantage except in a very small and shrinking number of highly labor-intensive industries (e.g., knitting woolen sweaters). The only meaningful competitive advantage is the productivity of the knowledge worker. And that is very largely in the hands of the knowledge worker rather than in the hands of management. Knowledge workers will increasingly determine the shape of the successful employing organizations.

What this implies is basically the topic of this book. These are very new *demands*. To satisfy them will increasingly be the key to success and survival for the individual and enterprise alike. To enable its readers to be among the successes—as executives in their organization, in managing themselves and others—is the primary aim of the revised edition of this book.

I suggest you read one chapter at a time—it is a long book. And then first ask, "What do these issues, these challenges, mean for our organization and for me as a knowledge worker, a professional, an executive?" Once you have thought this through, ask, "What action should our organization and I, the individual knowledge worker and/or executive, take to make the challenges of this chapter into opportunities for our organization and me?"

1

Introduction: Management and Managers Defined

Management may be the most important innovation of the twentieth century—and the one most directly affecting the young, educated people in colleges and universities who will be tomorrow's "knowledge workers" in managed institutions, and their managers the day after tomorrow. But what is management? Why management? How do you define "managers"? What are their tasks, their responsibilities? And how has the study and discipline of management developed to its present state?

When the first business schools in the United States opened around the turn of the twentieth century, they did not offer a single course in management. At about that same time, the word "management" was first popularized by Frederick Winslow Taylor to describe what he had formerly (and more accurately) called "work study" or "task study"; we call it "industrial engineering" today. But when Taylor talked about what we now call "management" and "managers," he said "the owners" and "their representatives."

The roots of the discipline of management go back approximately 200 years (see "Note: The Roots and History of Management," later in this chapter). But management as a function, management as a distinct work, management as a discipline and area of study—these are all products of the twentieth century. And most people became aware of management only after World War II.

Within the life span of today's old-timers, our society has become a "knowledge society," a "society of organizations," and a "networked society." In the twentieth century, the major social tasks came to be performed in and through organized institutions—business enterprises, large and small; school systems; colleges and universities; hospitals; research laboratories; governments and government agencies of all kinds and sizes; and many others. And each of them in turn is entrusted to "managers" who practice "management."

WHAT IS MANAGEMENT?

Management and managers are the specific need of all institutions, from the smallest to the largest. They are the specific organ of every institution. They are what holds it together and makes it work. None of our institutions could function without managers. And managers do their own job—they do not do it by delegation from the "owner." The need for management does not arise just because the job has become too big for any one person to do alone. Managing a business enterprise or a public-service institution is inherently different from managing one's own property or from running a practice of medicine or a solo law or consulting practice.

Of course, many a large and complex enterprise started from a one-man shop. But beyond the first steps, growth soon entails more than a change in size. At some point (and long before the organization becomes even "fair-sized"), size turns into complexity. At this point "owners" no longer run "their own" businesses even if they are the sole proprietors. They are then in charge of a business enterprise— and if they do not rapidly become managers, they will soon cease to be "owners" and be replaced, or the business will go under and disappear. For at this point, the business turns into an organization and requires for its survival different structure, different principles, different behavior, and different work. It requires managers and management.

Legally, management in the business enterprise is still seen as a delegation of ownership. But the doctrine that already determines practice, even though it is still only evolving in law, is that *management precedes and even outranks ownership*. The owner has to subordinate himself to the enterprise's need for management and managers. There are, of course, many owners who successfully combine both roles, that of owner-investor and that of top management. But if the enterprise does not have the management it needs, ownership itself is worthless. And in enterprises that are big or that play such a crucial role as to make their survival and performance matters of national concern, public pressure or governmental action will take control away from an owner who stands in the way of management. Thus the late Howard Hughes was forced by the United States government in the 1950s to give up control of his wholly owned Hughes Aircraft Company, which produced electronics crucial to U.S. defense. Managers were brought in because he insisted on running the company as "owner." Similarly the German government in the 1960s put the faltering Krupp company under autonomous management, even though the Krupp family owned 100 percent of the stock.

The change from a business that the *owner-entrepreneur* can run with "helpers" to a business that requires *management* is a sweeping change. It requires the application of basic concepts, basic principles, and individual vision to the enterprise.

One can compare the two kinds of business to two different kinds of organism: the insect, which is held together by a tough, hard skin, and the vertebrate animal, which has a skeleton. Land animals that are supported by a hard skin cannot grow beyond a few inches in size. To be larger, animals must have a skeleton. Yet the skeleton has not evolved out of the hard skin of the insect; for it is a different organ with different antecedents. Similarly, management becomes necessary when an organization reaches a certain size and complexity. But management, while it replaces the "hard-skin" structure of the owner-entrepreneur, is not its successor. It is, rather, its *replacement*.

When does a business reach the stage at which it has to shift from "hard skin" to "skeleton"? The line lies somewhere between 300 and 1,000 employees in size. More important, perhaps, is the increase in complexity. When a *variety* of tasks all have to be performed in *cooperation, synchronization,* and *communication,* an organization needs managers and management. One example would be a small research lab in which twenty to twenty-five scientists from a number of disciplines work together. Without management, things go out of control. Plans fail to turn into action. Or worse, different parts of the plans get going at different speeds, different times, and with different objectives and goals. The favor of the "boss" becomes more important than performance. At this point the product may be excellent, the people able and dedicated. The boss may be—and often is—a person of great ability and personal power. But the enterprise will begin to flounder, stagnate, and soon go downhill unless it shifts to the "skeleton" of managers and management structure.

The word "management" is centuries old. Its application to the governing organ of an institution and particularly to a business enterprise is American in origin. "Management" denotes both a function and the people who discharge it. It denotes a social position and authority, but also a discipline and a field of study.

Even in American usage, "management" is not an easy term, for institutions other than business do not always speak of management or managers. Universities or government agencies have *administrators,* as have hospitals. Armed services have *commanders.* Other institutions speak of *executives,* and so on.

Yet all these institutions have in common the *management function,* the management task, and the management work. All of them require management. And in all of them, management is the effective, the active organ.

Without the institution, there would be no management. But without management, there would be only a mob rather than an institution. The institution is itself an organ of society and exists only to contribute a needed result to society, the economy, and the individual. Organs, however, are never defined by what they do, let alone by how they do it. They are defined by their *contribution.* And it is management that enables the institution to contribute.

Management is *tasks*. Management is a *discipline*. But management is also *people*. Every achievement of management is the achievement of a manager. Every failure is a failure of a manager. *People manage* rather than "forces" or "facts." The vision, dedication, and integrity of managers determine whether there is management or mismanagement.

· WHO ARE THE MANAGERS?

Most people when asked what they mean by "manager" will reply, "a boss." But when the sign over the shoeshine stand in an airport reads "John Smith, Manager," everybody knows that this means that Mr. Smith is not the boss, but a hired hand with a minimum of authority and a salary just above that of the workers who shine the shoes.

Early in the history of management a manager was defined as someone who is *"responsible for the work of other people."* This definition distinguished the manager's function from that of the owner. It made clear that managing was a specific kind of work that could be analyzed, studied, and improved systematically. The definition focused on the essentially new, large, and permanent organization emerging to perform the economic tasks of society.

Yet, the definition is not at all satisfactory. In fact, it never was. From the beginning, there were people in the enterprise, often in responsible positions, who were clearly management and yet did not "manage," that is, were not responsible for the work of other people. The treasurer of a company, the person responsible for the supply and use of money in the business, may have subordinates and in that sense be a manager in terms of the traditional definition. But clearly, the treasurer alone does most of the treasurer's job—working with the company's underwriters, with the financial community, and so on. The treasurer is an "individual contributor" rather than a manager. But treasurers are executives in that they contribute directly to the results of the enterprise and they are members of top management. Also, the definition focuses on the tools for a task rather than on the task itself. The person in charge of market research in a company may have a large number of subordinates and is thus a manager in the traditional sense. But it really makes no difference to his or her function and contribution whether there is a large staff, a small staff, or no staff at all. The same contribution, in terms of market research and market analysis, can well be made by a person to whom no one reports.

In fact, the market researcher may even make a greater contribution when not forced to spend a great deal of time with subordinates and on their work. He or she may thus make market research more effective in the business, better understood by management associates, and more firmly built into the company's basic business decisions.

The most rapidly growing group in today's organizations is composed of people who are management in the sense of being responsible for contribution to and results of the enterprise but who are not responsible for the work of other people. They are individual professional contributors of all kinds who work by themselves (perhaps with an assistant and a secretary) and yet have an impact on the company's wealth-producing capacity, the direction of its business, and its performance. They are executives, because they bear executive responsibility, yet they are not responsible for the work of other people.

Such people are not to be found only in technical research work, though it was here that they first emerged as a distinct group. The senior chemist in the laboratory has major responsibility and makes major decisions, many of them irreversible in their impact. But so does the person who works out and thinks through the company's organizational structure and designs managerial jobs. Here also belongs the senior cost accountant who determines the definition and allocation of costs. By defining the measurements for management, he or she, in effect, largely decides whether a certain product will be kept or will be abandoned. Other people in this same category are the people charged with the development and maintenance of quality standards for a company's products, the woman working on the distributive system through which the company's products are being brought to the market, and the advertising director, who may be responsible for the basic promotion policy of a company, its advertising message, the media it uses, and the measurements of advertising effectiveness.

The traditional definition of "management" is responsible for the fact that the individual professional contributor presents a problem within the structure and a problem to himself. His or her title, pay, function, and career opportunities are confused, ambiguous, and a cause of dissatisfaction and friction. Yet the number of these career professionals is increasing fast.

THE NEW DEFINITION OF A MANAGER

What really defines a manager? Who should be considered management? The first attempt at answering these questions, made in the early 1950s, merely supplemented the old definition of the manager by recognizing the "individual professional contributor" and calling for "parallel paths of opportunity" for both. This made it possible to pay properly for advanced "professional" work rather than have higher pay dependent on promotion into a position of responsibility for the work of others.

Yet this formula has not fully solved the problem. The organizations that have adopted it report that individual professional contributors are only slightly less dissatisfied than they were before. They remain convinced that true opportunities for advancement still exist primarily within the administrative structure, and that one has to become a "boss" to "get ahead." Above all, the separation of the managerial world into two groups serves to emphasize the inferiority of those who do their own work as compared with those responsible for the work of others. The emphasis is still on *power* and *authority* rather than on *responsibility* and *contribution*.

Any analysis that does not start out from the traditional definition but instead looks at the work itself will come to the conclusion that the traditional definition of a manager as "one responsible for the work of others" emphasizes a secondary, rather than a primary, characteristic.

As we will see a little later, one can divide the work of a manager into planning, organizing, integrating, measuring, and developing people. Career professionals, knowledge workers—for example, a market researcher who works alone or a senior cost accountant—also have to plan, to organize, and to measure results against objectives and expectations. What they do and how they do it has a considerable impact on how people develop, especially if they also act as teachers to others in the organization. Career professionals also have to integrate their work with the work of other people in the organization. Above all, if they are to have results, they have to integrate "sideways," that is, with people in other areas and functions who have to put their work to use.

The traditional definition of the manager focuses on "integrating downward," that is, on integrating the work of subordinates. But even for managers who have subordinates, "sideways" relationships with people over whom they have no supervisory authority are usually at least as important in the work and are usually more important in terms of decision and information. The district sales manager has to work closely with the operations scheduler, sales analyst, and cost accountant—and they, in turn, have to work closely with the district sales manager. Most of the day-to-day decisions these people have to make are decisions that affect their "peers" rather than their subordinates. Integrating, in other words, is important because people work in organizations and with other people rather than because they have subordinates.

The essence of the job of the first-line supervisor in plant or office—the supervisor on the assembly line or the supervisor of the processing room for policies in the insurance company—is indeed the management of people. But then, the first-line supervisor is only marginally a "manager"—which is the reason why first-line supervision presents so many "problems." First-line supervisors, whether in the factory or in the office, are not commonly expected to plan and to organize, or to take much responsibility for their contribution and results. Thus they are not managers. They are expected to deliver according to objectives set for them by others. In the typical mass-production plant, this is all the supervisor possibly can or should do.

It would, therefore, seem appropriate to stress that the first criterion in identifying those people within an organization who have management responsibility is not command over people. *It is responsibility for contribution. Function rather than power has to be the distinctive criterion and the organizing principle.*

But what should these people be called? Many organizations have experimented with new definitions or have tried to give old terms a new meaning. Perhaps the best thing is not to coin a new term but to follow popular usage that speaks of the "management group," *all of whom have executive responsibility for contribution.* Within the management group there will be people whose function includes the traditional managerial function, responsibility for the work of others. There will be others who do not carry this responsibility within their specific assignment. And there will be a third group, somewhat ambiguous and in between: people whose job is that of a team leader or task-force captain, or people who combine the function of adviser to top management with supervisory and administrative responsibilities over a staff in a given area. Managers will move into situations where they are not superiors, and career professionals will sometimes serve as task-force leaders.

This is not a neat, let alone a perfect, solution. In every organization there are people who are true specialists and who, though they are anything but rank-and-file workers, do not see themselves as part of management either. Their allegiance is to their technical or professional skill, rather than to their organization. The psychologist within a human resources department would prefer to be thought of as a professional—that is, a member of the world of a particular academic specialty—rather than as an *executive of this or that organization* (or even as a faculty member of this or that university). And so does the software design specialist.

Nevertheless, this definition enables us to call "manager" all the people who perform management tasks, whether or not they have power over others.

WHAT DO MANAGERS DO?

Most managers spend most of their time on things that are not "managing." A sales manager makes a statistical analysis or handles an important customer. A manufacturing manager designs a new plant layout or tests new materials. A company president works through the details of a bank loan or negotiates a big contract—or spends hours presiding at a dinner in honor of longtime-service employees. All these pertain to a particular function. All are necessary and have to be done well. But they are apart from the work that is common to all managers, whatever their function or activity, rank or position. We can apply to the *job* of manager the systematic analysis of "scientific management." We can isolate that which a person does because he or she is a manager. We can divide the work into its constituent operations. And everybody can improve his or her performance as a manager by improving performance of these activities.

There are five basic operations in the work of the manager. Together they result in the integration of resources into a viable, growing organism.

A manager, in the first place, *sets objectives*. He or she determines what the objectives should be. She determines what the goals in each area of objective should be. She decides what has to be done to reach these objectives. She makes the objectives effective by communicating them to the people whose performance is needed to attain them.

Second, a manager *organizes*. He or she analyses the activities, decisions, and relations needed. He classifies the work. He divides it into manageable activities and further divides the activities into manageable jobs. He groups these units and jobs into an organization structure. He or she selects people for the management of these units and for the jobs to be done.

Third, a manager *motivates and communicates*. He makes a team out of the people that are responsible for various jobs. He does that in his own relations to the people with whom he works. He does it through his "people decisions" on pay, placement, and promotion. And he does it through constant communication, to and from his subordinates, and to and from his superior, and to and from his colleagues. This is the manager's integrating function.

The fourth basic element in the work of the manager is *measurement*. The manager establishes targets and yardsticks—and few factors are as important to the performance of the organization and of every person in it. He or she sees to it that each person has measurements available that are focused on the performance of the whole organization and that, at the same time, focus on the work of the individual. The manager analyzes, appraises, and interprets performance. As in all other areas of this work, he or she communicates the meaning of the measurements and their findings to subordinates, superiors, and colleagues.

Fifth, and finally, a manager *develops people*, including himself or herself. This task, which in this age of knowledge takes on even greater importance, occupies an entire section in this book.

Every one of these categories can be divided further into subcategories, and each of the subcategories could be discussed in a book of its own. Moreover, every category requires different qualities and qualifications.

Setting objectives, for instance, is a problem of achieving balances: a balance between organization results and realization of the principles one believes in; a balance between the immediate needs of the business and those of the future; a balance between desirable ends and available means. Setting objectives clearly requires analytical and synthesizing ability.

Organizing, too, requires analytical ability. For it demands the most economical use of scarce resources. But it deals with human beings and, therefore, stands under the principle of justice and requires integrity. Both analytical ability and integrity are similarly required for the development of people, but there is also a need for human perception and insight.

The skill needed for motivation and communication is primarily social. Instead of analysis, integration and synthesis are needed. Justice dominates as the principle; economy is secondary. And integrity is of much greater importance than analytical ability.

Measuring requires, first and foremost, analytical ability. But it also demands that measurement be used to make self-control possible, rather than abused to control people from the outside and above—that is, to dominate them. It is the common violation of this principle that largely explains why measurement is the weakest area in the work of the manager today. For example, measurements are sometimes used as a weapon of an internal secret police that supplies audits and critical appraisals of a manager's performance to the boss without even sending a copy to the appraised manager. As long as measurements are abused as a tool of control, measuring will remain the weakest area in the manager's performance.

Setting objectives, organizing, motivating and communicating, measuring, and developing people are formal, classifying categories. Only a manager's experience can bring them to life and make them concrete and meaningful. But because they are formal, they apply to every manager and to everything he or she does as a manager. They can, therefore, be used by all managers to appraise their own skill and performance and to work systematically on improving themselves and their performance.

Being able to set objectives does not make a manager, any more than the ability to tie a small knot in a confined space makes a surgeon. But without the ability to set objectives, a person cannot be an adequate manager; just as no one can do good surgery without tying small knots. And as a surgeon becomes a better surgeon by improving the knot-tying skill, so a manager becomes a better manager by improving skill and performance in all categories of the work.

THE MANAGER'S RESOURCE: PEOPLE

The manager works with a specific resource: *people*. And the human being is a unique resource, requiring particular qualities in whoever attempts to work with it.

"Working" with the human being always means developing him or her. The direction that this development takes decides whether the human being—both as a person and as a resource—will become more productive or cease, ultimately, to be productive at all. This applies, as cannot be emphasized too strongly, not alone to the person who is being managed but also to the manager. Whether he or she develops subordinates in the right direction, helps them to grow and become bigger and richer persons, will directly determine whether he or she will develop, will grow or wither, become richer or become impoverished, improve or deteriorate.

One can learn certain skills in managing people—for instance, the skill to lead a conference or to conduct an interview. One can set down practices that aid development—in the structure of the relationship between manager and subordinate, in a promotion system, in the rewards and incentives of an organization. But when all is said and done, developing people still requires a basic quality in the manager that cannot be created by supplying skills or by emphasizing the importance of the task. It requires *integrity of character.*

There is tremendous stress these days on liking people, helping people, getting along with people, as qualifications for a manager. These alone are never enough. In every successful organization there are bosses who do not like people, who do not help them, and who do not get along with them. Cold, unpleasant, demanding, they often teach and develop more people than anyone else. They command more respect than the most likable person ever could. They demand exacting workmanship of themselves and other people. They set high standards and expect that they will be lived up to. They consider only what is right and never who is right. And though often themselves persons of brilliance, they never rate intellectual brilliance above integrity in others. The manager who lacks these qualities of character—no matter how likable, helpful, or amiable, no matter, even, how competent or brilliant—is a menace who is unfit to be a manager.

What a manager does can be analyzed systematically. What a manager has to be able to do can be learned. But there is one qualification the manager cannot acquire but must bring to the task. It is not genius: it is character.

MANAGEMENT: A PRACTICE, NOT A SCIENCE

During the years since the 1930s, every developed country has become a society of institutions. Every major social task—whether economic performance or health care, education or the protection of the environment, the pursuit of new knowledge or defense—is today being entrusted to organizations, designed for long life and managed by their own managements. *On the performance of these institutions, the performance of modern society—if not the very survival of its members—increasingly depends. The performance and the survival of the institution depend on the performance of management.*

The individual has a direct stake in the performance of managers and management. Nine out of every ten of the people who go to college beyond high school go to work as employees in organizations. Their effectiveness and performance, their satisfaction, their achievement, and their growth as human beings largely depend on the performance of management in the employing institution. And a good many of these "knowledge workers" will themselves become managers, so their own capacity to perform and to achieve will depend on their knowledge of management and on their skill as practitioners of management.

In view of this, it would be comforting to be able to speak of management as a "science." But, in fact, we can only do harm by believing that management can ever fully be a science.

To be sure, the work of the manager can be systematically analyzed and classified. There are, in other words, distinct professional features and a scientific aspect to management. Management is not just a matter of experience, hunch, or native ability. Its elements and requirements can be analyzed, organized systematically, and learned by anyone with normal intelligence. Altogether this entire book is based on the proposition that the days of the "intuitive" manager are numbered. This book assumes that managers can improve their performance in all areas of management and at all levels of management—from the trainee position to the level of the chief executive officer of the giant multinational corporation—through the systematic study of principles, the acquisition of organized knowledge, and the continuing analysis of performance in all areas of work. Nothing can contribute so much to skill, to effectiveness, and to performance as a manager. And underlying this theme is the conviction that the impact of the manager on modern society and its citizens is so great as to require of the manager the self-discipline and the high service standards of the true professional.

And yet, the ultimate test of management is *performance*. Achievement rather than knowledge remains, of necessity, both aim and proof. Management is a *practice* rather than a *science* or a *profession,* though containing elements of both. Only damage to society and the economy could result from the attempt to "professionalize" management by limiting access to management to people with a special academic degree. The end would be the replacement of managers by bureaucrats and the stifling of innovation, entrepreneurship, and creativity.

Anyhow, we still know far too little to put management into the straitjacket of a "science" or to make the practice of management into a licensed professional monopoly. For the study of management is no older than management itself—and that means that it has barely begun.

But we do know a good deal—though, as this book will make clear, the areas of ignorance and searching exceed the areas in which we have truly firm, truly tested knowledge, and the "right answer."

We know, first, a good many things that, however plausible they may seem, do not work in the practice of management. We further know that management is not confined to one country or to one culture. Indeed, over a century ago when the first managed institutions arose—the transcontinental railroad in America, for instance—management as a practice and management as a discipline were tackled by people of many nationalities. In the years following World War II it sometimes seemed to many observers that management was an American invention. This was a mistake—and shortly proven to be such by the rapid recovery of Western Europe and Japan. The management function, the work of management, its tasks and its dimensions, are universal and do not vary from country to country. But the way the work is done is strongly influenced by national traits, national traditions, national history—and sometimes determined by them, as in such important areas as the relationship between government and business, the dos and don'ts in managing people, or the structure of top management.

Management is a social function, embedded both in a tradition of values, customs, and beliefs, and in governmental and political systems. Management is—and should be—culture-conditioned; in turn, management and managers shape culture and society. Thus, although management is an organized body of knowledge and, as such, applicable everywhere, it is also *culture*. It is not "value-free" science.

Above all we know that managers practice management. They do not practice economics. They do not practice quantification. They do not practice behavioral science. These are tools for managers. But they no more practice economics than a physician practices blood testing. They no more practice behavioral science than a biologist practices the microscope. They no more practice quantification than a lawyer practices precedents. Managers practice management.

Thus, there are specific managerial skills that pertain to management, rather than to any other discipline. One of these is communication within organizations. Another is the making of decisions under conditions of uncertainty. And there is also a specific entrepreneurial skill: strategic planning.

As a specific discipline, management has its own basic problems, its own specific approaches, its own distinct concerns. A manager who understands the discipline of management will still be an effective—perhaps even first-rate—manager with no more than minimum competence in managerial skills and tools. A person who knows only the skills and techniques, without understanding the fundamentals of management, is not a manager but merely a technician.

Management is a practice rather than a science. In this, it is comparable to medicine, law, and engineering. It is not knowledge but performance. Furthermore, it is not the application of common sense, or leadership, let alone financial manipulation. Its practice is based both on knowledge and on responsibility.

NOTE: THE ROOTS AND HISTORY OF MANAGEMENT

Some recent writings on management give the impression that their authors consider management to be an invention of the years since World War II, and an American invention at that. True, before World War II interest in and study of management was confined to small groups—the popular interest in management as a discipline and a field of study is fairly recent. But management, both as a practice and as a field of study, has a respectable history, in many different countries, going back almost two centuries.

When the early economists—from Adam Smith (1723–1790) to Karl Marx (1818–1883)—did their work, management did not exist. To them, the economy was impersonal and governed by objective economic forces. As a modern spokesman for the classical tradition, the Anglo-American Kenneth Boulding (1910–1993), phrased it: "Economics deals with the behavior of commodities, rather than with the behavior of men." Or, as with Marx, impersonal laws of history were seen to dominate. Humanity can only adapt. It can, at best, optimize what the economy makes possible; at worst, it impedes the forces of the economy and wastes resources. The last of the great English classical economists, Alfred Marshall (1842–1924), did add management to the factors of production, land, labor, and capital. But this was a halfhearted concession. Management was still not a central factor.

From the beginning there was, however, a different approach that put the manager into the center of the economy and that stressed the managerial task of making resources productive. J. B. Say (1767–1832), the brilliant French economist, was an early follower of Adam Smith. But in his own works, the pivot is not the factors of production. It is the entrepreneur—a word Say coined—who directs resources from less productive into more productive investments and who thereby creates wealth. Say was followed by the "utopian socialists" of the French tradition, notably Francois Fourier (1772–1837) and that eccentric genius the Comte de Saint-Simon (1760–1825). At that time there were no large organizations and no managers, but both Fourier and Saint-Simon anticipated developments and "discovered" management before it actually came into being. Saint-Simon, in particular, saw the emergence of organization. And he saw the task of making resources productive and of building social structures. He saw managerial tasks.

It is for their stress on management as a separate and distinct force, and one that can act independently of the factors of production as well as the laws of history, that Marx vehemently denounced the French. But it is the French—and above all Saint-Simon—who, in effect, laid down the basic approaches and the basic concepts on which every socialist economy has actually been designed. No matter how much the socialists today invoke the name of Marx, their spiritual ancestor is Saint-Simon.

In America, too, management was early seen as central. Alexander Hamilton (1757–1804), in his famous "Report on Manufactures," started out with Adam Smith, but then Hamilton gave emphasis to the constructive, purposeful, and systematic role of management. He saw in management, rather than in economic forces, the engine of economic and social development; and in organization, the carrier of economic advance. Following him, Henry Clay (1777–1852), with his famous "American system," produced what might be called the first blueprint for systematic economic development.

A little later, an industrialist in Scotland, Robert Owen (1771–1858), actually became the first manager. In his textile mill, Owen, in the 1820s, first tackled the problems of productivity and motivation, or the relationship of worker to work or worker to enterprise and of worker to management—to this day key questions in management. With Owen, the manager emerges as a real person. But it was a long time before Owen had successors.

THE EMERGENCE OF LARGE-SCALE ORGANIZATION

What had to happen first was the rise of large-scale organization. This occurred simultaneously—around 1870—in two places. In North America the transcontinental railroad emerged as a managerial problem. On the continent of Europe, the "universal bank"—entrepreneurial in aim, national in scope, and with multiple headquarters—made obsolescent traditional structures and concepts and required management.

One response was given by Henry Towne (1844–1924) in the United States, especially in his paper *The Engineer as Economist*. Towne outlined what might be called the first program for management. He raised basic questions: effectiveness as against efficiency; organization of the work as against the organization of workers; value set in the marketplace and by the customer as against technical accomplishment. With Towne begins the systematic concern with the relationship between the tasks of management and the work of management.

At roughly the same time, in Germany, Georg Siemens (1839–1901), in building the Deutsche Bank into the leading financial institution of continental Europe, first designed an effective top management, first thought through the top-management tasks, and first tackled the basic problems of communications and information in the large organization.

In Japan, Eiichi Shibusawa (1840–1931), a statesman turned business leader, in the 1870s and 1880s first raised fundamental questions regarding the relationship between business enterprise and national purpose, and between business needs and individual ethics. He tackled management education systematically. Shibusawa first envisioned the professional manager. Japan's rise to economic leadership in this century is largely founded on Shibusawa's thought and work.

A few decades later, in the years before and after the turn of the twentieth century, all the major approaches to modern management were fashioned. Again the developments occurred independently in many countries.

In the 1880s, Frederick Winslow Taylor (1856–1915), a self-taught American engineer, began the study of work. It is fashionable today to look down on Taylor for his outdated psychology, but Taylor was the first person in history who did not take work for granted, but looked at it and studied it. His approach to work is still the basic foundation. And, although Taylor in his approach to the worker was clearly a man of the nineteenth century, he started out with social rather than engineering or profit objectives. What led Taylor to his work and provided his motivation throughout was, first, the desire to free the worker from the burden of heavy toil, destructive of body and soul. And then it was the hope to make it possible to give the laborer a decent livelihood through increasing the productivity of work.

Around the same time in France, Henri Fayol (1841–1925), head of a coal mine that for its time was a very large company, first thought through organization structure and developed the first rational approach to the organization of enterprise: the functional principle. In Germany, Walter Rathenau (1867–1922), whose early training had been in a large company, asked, "What is the place of the large enterprise in a modern society and in a modern nation? What impact does it have on both? And what are its fundamental contributions and its fundamental responsibilities?" Most of the present questions concerning the social responsibilities of business were first raised and thought through by Rathenau in the years before World War I. Also in Germany, at the same time, the new discipline of *Betriebswissenschaft* (literally, the science of enterprise) was developed by such men as Eugen Schmalenbach (1873–1955). The management sciences developed since—managerial accounting, operations research, decision theory, and so on—are largely extentions (though, in the main, unconscious ones) of the *Betriebswissenschaft* of those years before World War I. And in America, German-born Hugo Muensterberg (1863–1916) first tried to apply the social and behavioral sciences, and especially psychology, to modern organization and management.

THE FIRST MANAGEMENT BOOM

After World War I there came what might be called the first management boom. It was sparked primarily by two of the most highly respected statesmen of the period, the American Herbert Hoover (1874–1964) and the Czech Thomas G. Masaryk (1850–1937). Hoover, a Quaker engineer, had vaulted to worldwide prominence by applying principles of management to the first massive foreign-aid operation in history. He planned the feeding of hundreds of thousands of starving people: first, before America's entry into World War I, in his Belgian Relief Operation, and then, after the end of World War I, in the relief operations in Central and Eastern Europe. But it was Masaryk, a historian who had become the first president of the new Czech Republic, who conceived the idea that management would be able to restore the economies of Europe after their destruction by war—an idea that then found its realization twenty-five years later in the Marshall Plan after World War II. These two men founded the international management movement and tried to mobilize management as a major social force.

But the period between the two World Wars was not congenial to such an idea. It was a period of stagnation, a period in which the highest goal that any national government or any economy—except that of the United States—could conceive was a return to what had been. It rapidly became a world in which mounting political, social, and economic tensions paralyzed will as well as vision.

THE WORK OF THE 1920s AND 1930s

The first management boom fizzled out. Its high hopes were replaced by frustration. Yet behind the apparent stagnation, work went on. It was in those years that the foundations for the sweeping management boom of the post–World War II period were put in place.

In the early 1920s, Pierre S. du Pont (1870–1954) at the Du Pont Company, followed by Alfred P. Sloan, Jr., (1875–1966) at General Motors, first developed the organization principle for the new "big business"—the principle of decentralization. Du Pont and, even more, Sloan also first developed systematic approaches to business objectives, to business strategy, and to strategic planning. Also, in the United States, Sears, Roebuck and Company—led first by Julius Rosenwald (1862–1932) and then by Robert E. Wood (1879–1969)—built the first business to be based on the marketing approach. In Europe shortly thereafter, the architects of the Dutch-English merger that resulted in the Unilever companies designed what may well be to this day the most advanced structure for the multinational corporation and also came to grips with the problem of multinational business planning and multinational marketing.

The discipline of management was also further developed. In the United States there were the successors to Taylor, the husband-and-wife team of Frank and Lillian Gilbreth (1868–1924, 1878–1972) and Henry L. Gantt (1861–1919). In Great Britain, Ian Hamilton (1853–1947), reflecting on his experiences as a military leader during World War I, realized the need to balance formal structure with policies that give "soul" to an organization. Two Americans, Mary Parker Follett (1868–1933) and Chester Barnard (1886–1961), first studied the process of decision making in organizations, the relationships between formal and informal organizations, and the role and function of the executive. Cyril Burt (1883–1972) in England and the Australian Elton Mayo (1880–1949), working at Harvard, developed the disciplines of, respectively, industrial psychology and human relations and applied each to enterprise and management.

Management as a discipline also began to be taught in the interwar years. The Harvard Business School first began in the 1930s to teach courses in management—though still mainly in production management. And at the same time, the Massachusetts Institute of Technology started advanced management work with young executives in mid-career.

The American James McKinsey (1889–1937) and the Englishman Lyndall F. Urwick (1891–1983) started management consulting, that is, consulting no longer confined to technical problems but dealing with fundamental management concerns, such as business policy and management organization. Urwick also classified and codified the work on the structure of management and on the function of the executive that had been done until that time.

SUMMARY

In the twentieth century our society became a society of organizations. Organizations depend on managers—are built by managers, directed and held together by managers, and made to perform by managers. Once an organization grows beyond a very small size, it needs managers who practice professional management. This means management grounded in a discipline and informed by the objective needs of the organization and of its people, rather than management based on ownership or on political appointment. Every organization needs people managers who do the specific work of management: planning, organizing, integrating, measuring, and developing people. It needs managers who take responsibility for contribution. *Responsibility for contribution,* rather than rank or title or command over people, defines the manager. And integrity rather than genius is the manager's basic requirement.

2

Management as a Social Function and Liberal Art

In the 1850s, when Karl Marx was beginning to work on *Das Kapital* the phenomenon of management was unknown. So were the enterprises that managers run. The largest manufacturing company around was a Manchester, England, cotton mill employing fewer than 300 people and owned by Marx's friend and collaborator, Friedrich Engels. And in Engels's mill—one of the most profitable businesses of its day—there were no "managers," only "charge hands" who, themselves workers, enforced discipline over a handful of fellow "proletarians."

Rarely in human history has any institution emerged as quickly as management or had as great an impact so fast. In less than 150 years, management has transformed the social and economic fabric of the world's developed countries. It has created a global economy and set new rules for countries that would participate in that economy as equals. And it has itself been transformed. Few executives are aware of the tremendous impact management has had. Indeed, a good many are like M. Jourdain, the character in *Le Bourgeois Gentilhomme,* the Molière play, who did not know that he spoke prose. They barely realize that they practice—or mispractice—management. As a result, they are ill-prepared for the tremendous challenges that now confront them. The truly important problems managers face do not come from technology or politics. They do not originate outside management and enterprise. They are problems caused by the very success of management itself.

To be sure, the fundamental task of management remains the same: to make people capable of joint performance through common goals, common values, the right structure, and the training and development they need to perform and to respond to change. But the very meaning of this task has changed, if only because the performance of management has converted the workforce from one composed largely of unskilled laborers to one of highly educated knowledge workers.

MANAGEMENT AS THE AGENT OF TRANSFORMATION

On the threshold of World War I, a few thinkers were just becoming aware of management's existence. But few people, even in the most advanced countries, had anything to do with "management." Now the largest single group in the labor force, more than one-third of the total, are people whom the U.S. Bureau of the Census calls "managerial and professional." Management has been the main agent of this transformation.

Management explains why, for the first time in human history, we can employ large numbers of knowledgeable, skilled people in productive work. No earlier society could do this. Indeed, no earlier society could support more than a handful of such people. Until quite recently, no one knew how to put people with different skills and knowledge together to achieve common goals.

Eighteenth-century China was the envy of contemporary Western intellectuals because it supplied more jobs for educated people than did all of Europe—some 20,000 per year. Today the United States, with about the same population China then had, graduates more than one million college students a year, few of whom have the slightest difficulty finding well-paid employment. Management enables us to employ them.

Knowledge, especially advanced knowledge, is always specialized. By itself it produces nothing. Yet a modern business, and not only the largest ones, may employ up to 10,000 highly knowledgeable people who represent up to sixty different knowledge areas. Engineers of all sorts, designers, marketing experts, economists, statisticians, psychologists, planners, accountants, human resources people—all working together in a joint venture. None would be effective without the managed enterprise.

There is no point in asking which came first: the educational explosion of the last hundred years or the management that put this knowledge to productive use. Modern management and modern enterprise could not exist without the knowledge base that developed societies have built. But equally it is management, and management alone, that makes effective all this knowledge and these knowledgeable people. The emergence of management has converted knowledge from social ornament and luxury into the true capital of any economy.

Not many business leaders could have predicted this development back in 1870, when large enterprises were first beginning to take shape. The reason was not so much lack of foresight as lack of precedent. At that time, the only large permanent organization around was the army. Not surprisingly, therefore, its command-and-control structure became the model for the men who were putting together transcontinental railways, steel mills, modern banks, and department stores. The command model, with a very few at the top giving orders and a great many at the bottom obeying them, remained the norm for nearly one hundred years. But it was never as static as its longevity might suggest. On the contrary, it began to change almost at once, as specialized knowledge of all sorts poured into enterprise.

The first university-trained engineer in manufacturing industry was hired by Siemens in Germany in 1867; his name was Friedrich von Hefner-Alteneck. Within five years he had built a research department. Other specialized departments followed suit. By World War I the standard functions of a manufacturer had been developed: research and engineering, manufacturing, sales, finance and accounting, and, a little later, human resources (or personnel).

Even more important for its impact on enterprise—and on the world economy in general—was another management-directed development that took place at this time. That was the *application of management to manual work* in the form of training. The child of wartime necessity, training has propelled the transformation of the world economy in the last sixty years because it allows low-wage countries to do something that traditional economic theory had said could never be done: to become efficient—and yet still low-wage—competitors almost overnight.

Adam Smith reported that it took several hundred years for a country or region to develop a tradition of labor and the expertise in manual and managerial skills needed to produce and market a given product, whether cotton textiles or violins.

During World War I, however, large numbers of unskilled, preindustrial people had to be made productive workers in practically no time. To meet this need, businesses in the United States and the United Kingdom began to apply "scientific management"—developed by Frederick W. Taylor between 1885 and 1910 and outlined in his book of that title—to the systematic training of blue-collar workers on a large scale. They analyzed tasks and broke them down into individual, unskilled operations that could then be learned quite quickly. Further developed in World War II, training was then picked up by the Japanese and, twenty years later, by the South Koreans, who made it the basis for their countries' phenomenal development.

During the 1920s and 1930s, management was applied to many more areas and aspects of the manufacturing business. Decentralization, for instance, arose to combine the advantages of bigness and the advantages of smallness within one enterprise. Accounting went from "bookkeeping" to analysis and control. Planning grew out of the "Gantt charts" designed in 1917 and 1918 to plan war production, and so did the use of analytical logic and statistics, which use quantification to convert experience and intuition into definitions, information, and diagnosis. Marketing evolved as a result of applying management concepts to distribution and selling. Moreover, as early as the mid 1920s and early 1930s, some American management pioneers—Thomas Watson, Sr., at the fledgling IBM, Robert E. Wood at Sears, Roebuck, and Elton Mayo at the Harvard Business School among them—began to question the way manufacturing was organized. They concluded that the assembly line was a short-term compromise. Despite its tremendous productivity, it was poor economics because of its inflexibility, poor use of human resources, even poor engineering. They began the thinking and experimenting that eventually led to "automation" as the way to organize the manufacturing process, and to teamwork, quality circles, and the information-based organization as the way to manage human resources. Every one of these managerial innovations represented *the application of knowledge to work*—the substitution of system and information for guesswork, brawn, and toil. Every one, to use Frederick Taylor's terms, replaced "working harder" with "working smarter."

The powerful effect of these changes became apparent during World War II. To the very end, the Germans were by far the better strategists. Having much shorter interior lines, they needed fewer support troops and could match their opponents in combat strength. Yet the Allies won—their victory achieved by management. The United States had one-fifth the population of all the other belligerents together and almost the same proportion of men in uniform, yet it produced more war materiel than all the others taken together. It managed to transport the stuff to fighting fronts as far apart as China, Russia, India, Africa, and Western Europe. No wonder, then, that by the war's end almost all the world had become management-conscious. Or that management had emerged as a recognizably distinct kind of work, one that could be studied and developed into a discipline—as happened in each country that has enjoyed economic leadership during the postwar period.

After World War II we began to see that management is not *business* management. It pertains to every human effort that brings together in one organization people of diverse knowledge and skills. It needs to be applied to all social sector institutions, such as hospitals, universities, churches, arts organizations, and social-service agencies, which since World War II have grown faster in the United States than either business or government. For even though the need to manage volunteers or raise funds may differentiate nonprofit managers from their for-profit peers, many more of their responsibilities are the same—among them defining the right strategy and goals, developing people, measuring performance, and marketing the organization's services. *Management, world-wide, has become the new social function.*

MANAGEMENT AND ENTREPRENEURSHIP

One important advance in the discipline and in the practice of management is that both now embrace entrepreneurship and innovation. A sham fight these days pits "management" against "entrepreneurship" as adversaries, if not as mutually exclusive. That's like saying that the fingering hand and the bow hand of the violinist are "adversaries" or "mutually exclusive." Both are always needed and at the same time. And both have to be coordinated and work together. Any *existing* organization, whether a business, a church, a labor union, or a hospital, goes down fast if it does not innovate. Conversely, any *new* organization, whether a business, a church, a labor union, or a hospital, collapses if it does not manage. *Not to innovate* is the single largest reason for the *decline of existing organizations. Not to know how to manage* is the single largest reason for the failure of *new ventures.*

Yet few management books paid attention to entrepreneurship and innovation. One reason was that during the period after World War II when most of these books were written, managing the existing, rather than innovating the new and different, was the dominant task. During this period most institutions developed along lines laid down clearly thirty or fifty years earlier. This has now changed dramatically. We have again entered an era of innovation, and it is by no means confined to "high tech" or even to technology generally. In fact, social innovation— as this book tries to make clear—may be of greater importance and may have a much greater impact than any scientific or technical invention. Furthermore we now have a "discipline" of entrepreneurship and innovation (on this see my book *Innovation and Entrepreneurship* [1985]). This discipline is clearly a part of management and indeed rests on well-known and tested management principles. It applies to both existing organizations and new ventures, and to both business and non-business institutions, including government.

THE ACCOUNTABILITY OF MANAGEMENT

Management books tend to focus on the function of management inside its organizations. Few yet accept its social function. But it is precisely because management has become so pervasive as a social function that it faces its most serious challenge. To whom is management accountable? And for what? On what does management base its power? What gives it legitimacy? These are not business questions or economic questions. They are *political* questions. Yet they underlie *the* most serious assault on management in its history, a far more serious assault than any mounted by Marxists or labor unions: *the takeover.* An American phenomenon at first, it has spread throughout the noncommunist developed world. What made it possible was the emergence of employee pension funds as controlling shareholders of publicly owned companies. The pension funds, while legally "owners," are economically "investors"—and, indeed, often "speculators." They have no interest in the enterprise or its welfare. In fact, in the United States, at least, they are "trustees" and are not supposed to consider anything but immediate pecuniary gain. What underlies the takeover bid is the postulate that the enterprise's sole function is to provide the largest possible *immediate* gain to the shareholder. In the absence of any other justification for management and enterprise, the takeover firms with their attractive bids prevail—and only too often dismantle or loot the going concern, sacrificing long-range, wealth-producing capacity to short-term gains.

Management—and not only in the business enterprise—has to be accountable for performance. But how is performance to be defined? How is it to be measured? How is it to be enforced? And to *whom* should management be accountable? That these questions can be asked is itself a measure of the success and importance of management. That they need to be asked is, however, also an indictment of managers. They have not yet faced up to the fact that they represent power—and power has to be accountable, has to be legitimate. They have not yet faced up to the fact that they matter.

WHAT IS MANAGEMENT?

But what is management? Is it a bag of techniques and tricks? A bundle of analytical tools like those taught in business schools? These are important, to be sure, just as a thermometer and anatomy are important to the physician. But the evolution and history of management—its successes as well as its problems—teach that management is, above all else, a very few, essential principles. To be specific:

1. Management is about *human beings*. Its task is to make people capable of joint performance, to make their strengths effective and their weaknesses irrelevant. This is what organization is all about, and it is the reason that management is the critical, determining factor. These days practically all of us, especially educated people, are employed by managed institutions, large and small, business and non-business. We depend on management for our livelihoods. And our ability to contribute to society also depends as much on the management of the organization in which we work as it does on our own skills, dedication, and effort.

2. Because management deals with the integration of people in a common venture, it is deeply embedded in *culture*. What managers do in West Germany, in Britain, in the United States, in Japan, or in Brazil is exactly the same. How they do it may be quite different. Thus one of the basic challenges managers in a developing country face is to find and identify those parts of their own tradition, history, and culture that can be used as management building blocks. The difference between Japan's economic success and India's relative backwardness is largely explained by the fact that Japanese managers were able to plant imported management concepts in their own cultural soil and make them grow.

3. Every enterprise requires commitment to common *goals and shared values*. Without such commitment, there is no enterprise. There is only a mob. The enterprise must have simple, clear, and unifying objectives. The mission of the organization has to be clear enough and big enough to provide common vision. The goals that embody it have to be clear, public, and constantly reaffirmed.

Management's first job is to *think through, set,* and *exemplify* those objectives, values, and goals.

4. Management must also enable the enterprise and each of its members to grow and develop as needs and opportunities change. Every enterprise is a *learning and teaching institution.* Training and development must be built into it on all levels—training and development that never stop.

5. Every enterprise is composed of people with different skills and knowledge doing many different kinds of work. It must be built on *communication* and on *individual responsibility.* All members need to think through what they aim to accomplish—and make sure that their associates know and understand that aim. All have to think through what they owe to others—and make sure that others understand. All have to think through what they, in turn, need from others—and make sure that others know what is expected of them.

6. Neither the quantity of output nor the "bottom line" is by itself an adequate measure of the *performance* of management and enterprise. Market standing, innovation, productivity, development of people, quality, financial results—all are crucial to an organization's performance and to its survival. Nonprofit institutions, too, need measurements in a number of areas specific to their mission. Just as a human being needs a diversity of measures to assess its health and performance, an organization needs a diversity of measures to assess its health and performance. Performance has to be built into the enterprise and its management; it has to be measured—or at least judged—and it has to be continuously improved.

7. Finally, the single most important thing to remember about any enterprise is that *results exist only on the outside.* The result of a business is a satisfied customer. The result of a hospital is a healed patient. The result of a school is a student who has learned something and puts it to work ten years later. Inside an enterprise, there are only costs.

Managers who understand these principles and manage themselves in their light will be achieving, accomplished managers.

MANAGEMENT AS A LIBERAL ART

Thirty years ago, the English scientist and novelist C. P. Snow talked of the "two cultures" of contemporary society. Management, however, fits neither Snow's "humanist" nor his "scientist." It deals with action and application; and its test is its results. This makes it a technology. But management also deals with people, their values, their growth and development—and this makes it a humanity. So does its concern with and impact on social structure and the community. Indeed, as has been learned by everyone who, like this author, has been working with managers of all kinds of institutions for long years, management is deeply involved in spiritual concerns—the nature of man, good and evil.

Management is thus what tradition used to call a liberal art: "liberal" because it deals with the fundamentals of knowledge, self-knowledge, wisdom, and leadership; "art" because it is practice and application. Managers draw on all the knowledge and insights of the humanities and the social sciences—on psychology and philosophy, on economics and history, on ethics as well as on the physical sciences. But they have to focus this knowledge on effectiveness and results—on healing a sick patient, teaching a student, building a bridge, designing and selling a "user-friendly" software program.

For these reasons, management will increasingly be the discipline and the practice through and in which the "humanities" will again acquire recognition, impact, and relevance.

SUMMARY

Managers have been agents of transformation, converting the workforce in developed countries from one of manual workers to one of highly educated knowledge workers. This has been accomplished by applying knowledge to work. Management brings human effort from all disciplines together in a single organization and therefore has become a new social function. As such the discipline and practice of management is important to the effectiveness of all of society's institutions. In carrying out its function, management relies on knowledge from the humanities, social sciences, and technology. As such, management is a liberal art in the truest sense and a discipline wherein the liberal arts find relevance and usefulness.

3

The Dimensions
of Management

Business enterprises and public-service institutions as well are organs of society. They do not exist for their own sake, but to fulfill a specific social purpose and to satisfy a specific need of society, community, or individual. They are not ends in themselves, but means. The right question to ask in respect to them is not What are they? but What are they supposed to be doing and what are their tasks?

Management, in turn, is the organ of the institution.

The question What is management? comes second. First we have to define management in and through its tasks.

There are three tasks—equally important but essentially different—that face the management of every institution:

- To think through and define the *specific purpose* and *mission* of the institution, whether business enterprise, hospital, or university

- To make *work productive* and the *worker achieving*

- To manage *social impacts* and *social responsibilities*

These might be called the dimensions of management.

MISSION

An institution exists for a specific purpose and mission, a specific social function. In the business enterprise, this means economic performance.

With respect to this first task, the task of specific performance, business and nonbusiness institutions differ. In respect to every other task, they are similar. But only business has economic performance as its specific mission. It is the definition of a business that it exists for the sake of economic performance. In all other institutions—hospital, church, university, or armed services—economics is a restraint. In those institutions, the budget sets limits to what the institution and the manager can do. In business enterprise, economic performance is the rationale and purpose.

Business management must always, in every decision and action, put economic performance first. It can justify its existence and its authority only by the economic results it produces. A business management has failed if it fails to produce economic results. It has failed if it does not supply goods and services desired by the consumer at a price the consumer is willing to pay. It has failed if it does not improve, or at least maintain, the wealth-producing capacity of the economic resources entrusted to it. And this, whatever the economic or political structure or ideology of a society, means responsibility for profitability.

But business management is no different from the management of other institutions in one crucial respect: it has to *manage*. And managing is not just passive, adaptive behavior; it means taking action to make the desired results come to pass.

The early economist conceived of the businessman's behavior as purely passive; success in business meant rapid and intelligent adaptation to events occurring outside, in an economy shaped by impersonal, objective forces that were neither controlled by the businessman nor influenced by his reaction to them. We may call this the concept of the "trader." Even if he was not considered a parasite, his contributions were seen as purely mechanical: the shifting of resources to more productive use. Today's economist sees the businessman as choosing rationally between alternatives of action. This is no longer a mechanistic concept; obviously the choice has a real impact on the economy. But still, the economist's "businessman"—the picture that underlies the prevailing economic "theory of the firm" and the theorem of the "maximization of profits"—reacts to economic developments. The businessperson is still passive, still adaptive—though with a choice among various ways to adapt. Basically, this is a concept of the "investor" or the "financier" rather than of the *manager*.

Of course, it is always important to adapt to economic changes rapidly, intelligently, and rationally. But managing implies responsibility for attempting to *shape* the economic environment; for planning, initiating, and carrying through changes in that economic environment; for constantly pushing back the limitations of economic circumstances on the enterprise's ability to contribute. What is possible—the economist's "economic conditions"—is therefore only one pole in managing a business. What is desirable in the interest of economy and enterprise is the other. And while humanity can never really "master" the environment, while we are always held within a tight vise of possibilities, it is management's specific job to make what is desirable first possible and then actual. Management is not just a creature of the economy; it is a creator as well. And only to the extent to which it masters the economic circumstances, and alters them by consciously directed action, does it really manage. To manage a business means, therefore, to *manage by objectives*.

PRODUCTIVE WORK AND WORKER ACHIEVEMENT

The second task of management is to make work productive and the worker achieving. Business enterprise (or any other institution) has only one true resource: *people*. It performs by making human resources productive. It accomplishes its performance through work. To make work productive is, therefore, an essential function. But at the same time, these institutions in today's society are increasingly the means through which individual human beings find their livelihood, find their access to social status, to community, and to individual achievement and satisfaction. To make the worker achieving is, therefore, more and more important and is a measure of the performance of an institution. It is increasingly a task of management.

Organizing work according to its own logic is only the first step. The second and far more difficult one is making work suitable for human beings—and their logic is radically different from the logic of work. Making the worker achieving implies consideration of the human being as an organism having peculiar physiological and psychological properties, abilities, and limitations.

The enterprise, by definition, must be capable of producing more or better than all the resources that comprise it. It must be a genuine whole: greater than—or at least different from—the sum of its parts, with its output larger than the sum of all inputs.

The enterprise cannot, therefore, be a mechanical assemblage of resources. To make an enterprise out of resources it is not enough to put them together in logical order and then throw the switch of capital, as the nineteenth-century economists firmly believed (and as many of their successors among academic economists still believe). What is needed is a change of the resources into a more productive form. This requires management.

But it is also clear that the "resources" capable of enlargement can only be human resources. All other resources stand under the laws of mechanics. They can be better utilized or worse utilized, but they can never have an output greater than the sum of the inputs. People, alone of all resources, can grow and develop. Only the directed, focused, united effort of free human beings can produce a real whole. When we speak of growth and development, we imply that the human being himself determines what he contributes.

Yet, we habitually define rank-and-file workers—as distinguished from managers—as people who do as they are directed, without responsibility or share in the decisions concerning their own work. This indicates that we consider workers in the same light as other material resources and, as far as their contribution to the enterprise is concerned, as standing under the laws of mechanics. This is a serious misunderstanding. The misunderstanding, however, is not in the definition of rank-and-file work, but rather in the failure to see that rank-and-file jobs are potentially managerial, or would be more productive if made so.

Human resources acquire the capacity to grow, to develop, to contribute through management. We speak of "organization"—the formal structure of the enterprise. But what we mean is the organization of managers and of the functions they manage; neither brick and mortar nor rank-and-file workers are the stuff of organization structure. We speak of "leadership" and of the "spirit" of an organization. But leadership is given by managers and effective primarily within management; and the spirit is made by the spirit within the management group. We talk of "objectives" for the company and of its performance. But the objectives are goals for management people; the performance is management performance. And if an enterprise fails to perform, we rightly hire not different workers but a new president.

SOCIAL RESPONSIBILITIES

The third task of management is managing the social impacts and the social responsibilities of the enterprise. None of our institutions exists by itself and as an end in itself. Every one is an organ of society and exists for the sake of society. Business is no exception. "Free enterprise" cannot be justified as being good for business. It can be justified only as being good for society.

Every one of our institutions today exists to contribute outside of itself, to supply and satisfy nonmembers. Business exists to supply goods and services to customers and economic surplus to society, rather than to supply jobs to workers and managers, or even dividends to shareholders. Jobs and dividends are necessary means but not ends. The hospital exists not for the sake of doctors and nurses, but for the sake of the patients whose one and only desire is to leave the hospital cured and never come back. The school exists not for the sake of teachers, but for the students. For a management to forget this is mismanagement.

To discharge its job, to produce economic goods and services, the business enterprise has to have impacts on people, on communities, and on society. It has to have power and authority over people, for example, employees, whose own ends and purposes are not defined by and within the enterprise. It has to have impact on the community as a neighbor, as the source of jobs and tax revenue but also of waste products and pollutants. And, increasingly, in our pluralist society of organizations, it has to add to its fundamental concern for the quantities of life (economic goods and services) a concern for the quality of life, for the physical, human, and social environment of modern man and modern community.

WHICH TASK IS MOST IMPORTANT?

Managing these three tasks always has to be done at the same time and within the same managerial action. It cannot even be said that one of the three tasks predominates or requires greater skill or competence. True, economic performance comes first—it is the aim of the enterprise and the reason for its existence. But if work and worker are grossly mismanaged, there will be no economic performance, no matter how good the chief executive may be in managing the business. Economic performance achieved by mismanaging work and workers is illusory and actually destructive of capital, even in the fairly short run. Such performance will raise costs to the point where the enterprise ceases to be competitive. It will, by creating class hatred and class warfare, make it impossible in the end for the enterprise to operate at all. And mismanaging social impacts eventually will destroy society's support for the enterprise—and with it the enterprise as well.

Each of these three dimensions has a primacy of its own. Managing a business has primacy because the enterprise is an economic institution; but making work productive and workers achieving has importance precisely because society is not an economic institution and looks to management for the realization of basic beliefs and values. Managing the enterprise's social impacts has importance because no organ can survive the body that it serves; and the enterprise is an organ of society and community.

THE TIME DIMENSION

One complexity is ever present in every management problem, every decision, every action—not, properly speaking, a fourth task of management, and yet an additional dimension: time.

Management always has to consider both; the present and the future; both the short run and the long run. A management problem is not solved if immediate profits are purchased by endangering the long-range health, perhaps even the survival, of the company. A management decision is irresponsible if it risks disaster this year for the sake of a grandiose future. The all too common case of the great man in management who produces startling economic results as long as he runs the company but leaves behind nothing but a sinking hulk is an example of irresponsible managerial action and of failure to balance present and future. The immediate economic results are actually fictitious and are achieved by destroying capital. In every case where present and future are not both satisfied, where their requirements are not harmonized, or at least balanced, capital—that is, wealth-producing resource—is endangered, damaged, or destroyed.

There are two reasons why the time dimension is of particular importance in management's job, and of particular difficulty. In the first place, through economic and technological progress, the time span for the fruition and proving out of a decision is steadily lengthening. Thomas Edison, in the 1880s, needed two years or so between the start of laboratory work on an idea and the start of pilot-plant operations. Today it may well take Edison's successors fifteen years. A human organization, such as a sales force or a management group, may take even longer to build and to pay for itself.

The second peculiar characteristic of the time dimension is that management has to live always in both present and future. It must keep the enterprise performing in the present—or else there will be no enterprise capable of performing in the future. And it has to make the enterprise capable of performance, growth, and change in the future. Otherwise it has destroyed capital—that is, the capacity of resources to produce wealth tomorrow.

For the manager the future is *discontinuity*. And yet the future, however different, can be reached only from the present. The greater the leap into the unknown, the stronger the foundation for the takeoff has to be. The time dimension gives the managerial decision its special characteristics.

ADMINISTRATION AND ENTREPRENEURSHIP

Managers always have to administer, to manage and improve, what already exists and is already known. But there is another dimension to managerial performance. Managers also have to be entrepreneurs. They have to redirect resources from areas of low or diminishing results to areas of high or increasing results. They have to slough off yesterday and to make obsolete what already exists and is already known. They have to create tomorrow.

In the ongoing business markets, technologies, products, and services exist. Facilities and equipment are in place. Capital has been invested and has to be serviced. People are employed and are in specific jobs, and so on. The administrative job of the manager is to *optimize the yield from these resources.*

This means *efficiency,* that is, doing better what is already being done. It means focus on costs. But the optimizing approach should focus on *effectiveness*. It focuses on opportunities to produce revenue, to create markets, and to change the economic characteristics of existing products and markets. It asks not, How do we do this or that better? It asks, Which of the products really produce extraordinary economic results or are capable of producing them? Which of the markets and/or end uses are capable of producing extraordinary results? It then asks, To what results should, therefore, the resources and efforts of the business be allocated so as to produce extraordinary results rather than the "ordinary" ones, which is all efficiency can possibly produce?

Of course efficiency is important. Even the healthiest business, the business with the greatest effectiveness, can die of poor efficiency. But even the most efficient business cannot survive, let alone succeed, if it is efficient in doing the wrong things, that is, if it lacks effectiveness. No amount of efficiency would have enabled the manufacturer of buggy whips to survive.

Effectiveness is the foundation of success—efficiency is a minimum condition for survival after success has been achieved. *Efficiency is concerned with doing things right. Effectiveness is doing the right things.*

Efficiency concerns itself with the input of effort into all areas of activity. Effectiveness, however, starts out with the realization that in business, as in any other social organism, 10 or 15 percent of the phenomena—such as products, orders, customers, markets, or people—produce 80 to 90 percent of the results. The other 85 to 90 percent of the phenomena, no matter how efficiently taken care of, produce nothing but costs.

The first administrative job of the manager is, therefore, to make effective the very small core of worthwhile activities that is capable of being effective. At the same time, he or she neutralizes (or abandons) the very large number of ordinary transactions—products or staff activities, research work or sales efforts—that, no matter how well done, will not yield extraordinarily high results.

The second administrative task is to bring the business all the time a little closer to the full realization of its potential. Even the most successful business works at a low performance as measured against its potential—the economic results that could be obtained were efforts and resources marshaled to produce the maximum yield they are inherently capable of.

This task is not innovation; it actually takes the business as it is today and asks, What is its theoretical optimum? What prevents us from attaining it? Where (in other words) are the limiting and restraining factors that hold back the business and deprive it of the full return on its resources and efforts?

At the same time, inherent in the managerial task is entrepreneurship: making the business of tomorrow. Inherent in this task is innovation.

Making the business of tomorrow starts out with the conviction that the business of tomorrow will be and must be different. But it also starts out—of necessity—with the business of today. Making the business of tomorrow cannot be a flash of genius. It requires systematic analysis and hard, rigorous work today—and that means by people in today's business and operating within it.

Success cannot, one might say, be continued forever. Businesses are, after all, human creations, which have no true permanence. Even the oldest businesses are creations of recent centuries. But a business enterprise must continue beyond the lifetime of the individual or of the generation to be capable of producing its contributions to economy and to society. The perpetuation of a business is a central entrepreneurial task—and ability to do so may well be the most definitive test of a management.

SUMMARY

There are three basic tasks—they might be called dimensions—in management. There is the first task of thinking through and defining the specific purpose and mission of the organization—whether business enterprise, hospital, school, or government agency. There is the second task of making work productive and the worker achieving. There is finally the task of managing social impacts and social responsibilities. In respect to the second and third tasks, all institutions are alike. It is the first task that distinguishes the business from the hospital, school, or government agency. And the specific purpose and mission of business enterprise is economic performance. To discharge it, managers always have to balance the present against an uncertain and risky future, have to perform for the short run and make their business capable of performance over the long run. Managers always have to be stewards of what already exists; they have to be administrators. They also have to create what is to be; they have to be entrepreneurs, risk takers, and innovators. For a modern business can produce results, both for society and for its own people, only if it can survive beyond the life span of a person and perform in a new and different future.

Part I

Management's New Realities

There is no doubt that in the developed world, and in emerging countries as well, the environment is becoming quite different from the environment of the late twentieth century. Much of it is unprecedented. And most of it is already here, or is rapidly emerging.

Against that background, the next four chapters seek to answer three questions: What can and should managements *do now* to be ready for the new realities? What other big changes may lie ahead of which we are as yet unaware? What are the *new management paradigms* emerging out of these new realities?

4

Knowledge Is All

The new reality is that knowledge is the key resource in society and knowledge workers are the dominant group in the workforce. The three main characteristics of knowledge economy are

- Borderlessness, because knowledge travels even more effortlessly than money.

- Upward mobility, available to everyone through easily acquired formal education.

- The potential for failure as well as success. Anyone can acquire the "means of production"—that is, the knowledge required for the job—but not everyone can win.

These three characteristics are making the knowledge society a highly competitive one, for organizations and individuals alike. Information technology, although only one of many new features of the new realities, is already having one hugely important effect: it is allowing knowledge to spread nearly instantly, and making it accessible to everyone. Given the ease and speed at which information travels, every institution in the knowledge society—not only businesses, but also schools, universities, hospitals, and increasingly government agencies too—has to be globally competitive, even though most organizations will continue to be local in their activities and in their markets. This is because the Internet will increasingly keep customers everywhere informed on what is available anywhere in the world, and at what price.

This new knowledge economy relies heavily on knowledge workers. At present, this term is widely used to describe people with considerable theoretical knowledge and learning: doctors, lawyers, teachers, accountants, chemical engineers. But the most striking growth will be in "knowledge technologists": computer technicians, software designers, analysts in clinical labs, manufacturing technologists, paralegals. These people are as much manual workers as they are knowledge workers; in fact, they usually spend far more time working with their hands than with their brains. But their manual work is based on a substantial amount of theoretical knowledge that can be acquired only through formal education, not through an apprenticeship. They are not, as a rule, much better paid than traditional skilled workers, but they see themselves as "professionals." Just as unskilled manual workers in manufacturing were the dominant social and political force in the twentieth century, knowledge technologists are likely to become the dominant social—and perhaps also political—force over the next decades.

THE NEW WORKFORCE

A century ago, the overwhelming majority of people in developed countries worked with their hands: on farms, in domestic service, in small craft shops, and (at that time still a small minority) in factories. Fifty years later, the proportion of manual workers in the American labor force had dropped to around half, and factory workers had become the largest single section of the workforce, making up 35 percent of the total. Now, another fifty years later, less than a quarter of American workers make their living from manual jobs. Factory workers still account for the majority of the manual workers, but their share of the total workforce is down to around 15 percent.

Of all the big developed countries, America now has the smallest proportion of factory workers in its labor force. Britain is not far behind. In Japan and Germany, their share is still around a quarter, but it is shrinking steadily.

Before World War I there was not even a word for people who made their living other than by manual work. The term "service worker" was coined around 1920, but it has turned out to be rather misleading. These days, fewer than half of all nonmanual workers are actually service workers. The only fast-growing group in the workforce, in America and in every other developed country, is "knowledge workers"—people whose jobs require formal and advanced schooling. They now account for a full third of the American workforce, outnumbering factory workers by two to one. In another fifteen years or so, they are likely to make up close to two-fifths of the workforce of all rich countries.

The terms *knowledge industries, knowledge work* and *knowledge worker* are nearly fifty years old. They were coined around 1960, simultaneously but independently—the first by a Princeton economist, Fritz Machlup, the second and third by this writer. Now everyone uses them, but as yet hardly anyone understands their implications for human values and human behavior, for managing people and making them productive, for economics, and for politics. What is already clear, however, is that the emerging knowledge society and knowledge economy will be radically different from the society and economy of the late twentieth century, in the following ways.

The knowledge workers, collectively, are the new capitalists. Knowledge has become the key resource, and the only scarce one. This means that knowledge workers collectively own the means of production. But as a group, they are also capitalists in the old sense: through their stakes in pension funds and mutual funds, they have become majority shareholders and owners of many large businesses in the knowledge society.

Effective knowledge is specialized. That means knowledge workers need access to an organization—a collective that brings together an array of knowledge workers and applies their specialties to a common end-product. The most gifted mathematics teacher in a secondary school is effective only as a member of the faculty. The most brilliant consultant on product development is effective only if there is an organized and competent business to convert her advice into action. The greatest software designer needs a hardware producer. But in turn, the high school needs the mathematics teacher, the business needs the expert on product development, and the PC manufacturer needs the software programmer. Knowledge workers therefore see themselves as equal to those who retain their services, as "professionals" rather than as "employees." The knowledge society is a society of seniors and juniors rather than of bosses and subordinates.

HIS AND HERS

All this has important implications for the role of women in the labor force. Historically, women's participation in the world of work has always equaled men's. The lady of leisure sitting in her parlor was the rarest of exceptions even in a wealthy nineteenth-century society. A farm, a craftsman's business, or a small shop had to be run by a couple to be viable. As late as the beginning of the twentieth century, a doctor could not start a practice until he had got married; he needed a wife to make appointments, open the door, take patients' histories, and send out the bills.

But although women have always worked, since time immemorial the jobs they have done have usually been different from men's. There was men's work and there was women's work. Countless women in the Bible go to the well to fetch water, but not one man. Knowledge work, on the other hand, is "unisex," not because of feminist pressure but because it can be done equally well by both sexes. That said, the first modern knowledge jobs were designed for only one sex or the other. Teaching as a profession was invented in 1794, the year the École Normale was founded in Paris, and was seen as strictly a man's job. Sixty years later, during the Crimean War of 1853–56, Florence Nightingale founded the second new knowledge profession, nursing. This was considered as exclusively women's work. But by 1850 teaching everywhere had become unisex, and in 2000 two-fifths of America's students at nursing school were men.

There were no women doctors in Europe until the 1890s. But one of the earliest European women to get a medical doctorate, the great Italian educator Maria Montessori, reportedly said, "I am not a woman doctor; I am a doctor who happens to be a woman." The same logic applies to all knowledge work. Knowledge workers, whatever their sex, are professionals, applying the same knowledge, doing the same work, governed by the same standards, and judged by the same results.

High-knowledge workers such as doctors, lawyers, scientists, clerics, and teachers have been around for a long time, although their number has increased exponentially in the past one hundred years. The largest group of knowledge workers, however, barely existed until the start of the twentieth century, and its numbers took off only after World War II. They are knowledge technologists—people who do much of their work with their hands (and to that extent are the successors to skilled workers), but whose pay is determined by the knowledge between their ears, acquired in formal education rather than through apprenticeship. They include X-ray technicians, physiotherapists, ultrasound specialists, psychiatric case workers, dental technicians, and scores of others. Since the early 1970s medical technologists have been the fastest-growing segment of the labor force in America, and probably in Britain as well.

In the next fifteen or twenty-five years the number of knowledge technologists in computers, manufacturing, and education is likely to grow even faster. Office technologists such as paralegals are also proliferating. And it is no accident that yesterday's "secretary" is rapidly turning into an "assistant," having become the manager of the boss's office and the boss's work. Within two or three decades, knowledge technologists will become the dominant group in the workforce in all developed countries, occupying the same position of importance that unionized factory workers held at the peak of their power in the 1950s and 1960s.

The most important thing about these knowledge workers is that they do not identify themselves as "workers" but as "professionals." Many of them spend a good deal of their time doing largely unskilled work, for example, straightening out patients' beds, answering the telephone, or filing. However, what identifies them in their own and in the public's mind is that part of their job that involves putting their formal knowledge to work. It is what makes them full-fledged knowledge workers.

Such workers have two main needs: formal education that enables them to enter knowledge work in the first place, and continuing education throughout their working lives to keep their knowledge up to date. For the old high-knowledge professionals such as doctors, clerics, and lawyers, formal education has been available for many centuries. But for knowledge technologists, only a few countries so far provide systematic and organized preparation. Over the next few decades, educational institutions to prepare knowledge technologists will grow rapidly in all developed and emerging countries, just as new institutions to meet new requirements have always appeared in the past. What is different this time is the need for the continuing education of already well-trained and highly knowledgeable adults. Schooling traditionally stopped when work began. In the knowledge society, it never stops.

Knowledge is unlike traditional skills, which change very slowly. A museum near Barcelona in Spain contains a vast number of the hand tools used by the skilled craftsmen of the late Roman Empire, which any craftsman today would instantly recognize, because they are very similar to the tools still in use. For the purposes of skill training, therefore, it was reasonable to assume that whatever had been learned by age seventeen or eighteen would last for a lifetime.

Conversely, knowledge rapidly becomes obsolete, and knowledge workers regularly have to go back to school. Continuing education of already highly educated adults will therefore become a big growth area in the next society. But most of it will be delivered in nontraditional ways, ranging from weekend seminars to on-line training programs, and in any number of places, from a traditional university to the student's home. The information revolution, which is expected to have an enormous impact on education and on traditional schools and universities, will probably have an even greater effect on the continuing education of knowledge workers.

Knowledge workers of all kinds tend to identify themselves with their knowledge. They introduce themselves by saying, "I am an anthropologist" or "I am a physiotherapist." They may be proud of the organization they work for, be it a company, a university, or a government agency, but they "work at" the organization; they do not "belong to" it. Most of them probably feel that they have more in common with someone who practices the same specialty in another institution than with their colleagues at their own institution who work in a different knowledge area.

Although the emergence of knowledge as an important resource increasingly means specialization, knowledge workers are highly mobile within their specialty. They think nothing of moving from one university, one company, or one country to another, as long as they stay within the same field of knowledge. There is a lot of talk about trying to restore knowledge workers' loyalty to their employing organization, but such efforts will get nowhere. Knowledge workers may have an attachment to an organization and feel comfortable with it, but their primary allegiance is likely to be to their specialized branch of knowledge.

Knowledge is nonhierarchical. Either it is relevant in a given situation or it is not. An open-heart surgeon may be much better paid than, say, a speech therapist and enjoy a much higher social status, yet if a particular situation requires the rehabilitation of a stroke victim, then in that instance the speech therapist's knowledge is greatly superior to that of the surgeon. This is why knowledge workers of all kinds see themselves not as subordinates but as professionals, and expect to be treated as such.

Money is as important to knowledge workers as to anybody else, but they do not accept it as the ultimate yardstick, nor do they consider money as a substitute for professional performance and achievement. In sharp contrast to yesterday's workers, to whom a job was first of all a living, most knowledge workers see their job as a life.

EVER UPWARD

The knowledge society is the first human society where upward mobility is potentially unlimited. Knowledge differs from all other means of production in that it cannot be inherited or bequeathed. It has to be acquired anew by every individual, and everyone starts out with the same total ignorance.

Knowledge has to be put in a form in which it can be taught, which means it has to become public. It is always universally accessible, or quickly becomes so. All this makes the knowledge society a highly mobile one. Anyone can acquire any knowledge at a school, through a codified learning process, rather than by serving as an apprentice to a master.

Until 1850 or perhaps even 1900, there was little mobility in any society. The Indian caste system, in which birth determines not only an individual's status in society but his occupation as well, was only an extreme case. In most other societies too, if the father was a peasant, the son was a peasant, and the daughters married peasants. By and large, the only mobility was downward, caused by war or disease, personal misfortune or bad habits such as drinking or gambling.

Even in America, the land of unlimited opportunities, there was far less upward mobility than is commonly believed. The great majority of professionals and managers in America in the first half of the twentieth century were still the children of professionals and managers rather than the children of farmers, small shopkeepers, or factory workers. What distinguished America was not the amount of upward mobility but, in sharp contrast to most European countries, the way it was welcomed, encouraged, and cherished.

The knowledge society takes this approval of upward mobility much further: it considers every impediment to such mobility a form of discrimination. This implies that everybody is now expected to be a "success"—an idea that would have seemed ludicrous to earlier generations. Naturally, only a tiny number of people can be outstanding successes; but a very large number are expected to be adequately successful.

In 1958, John Kenneth Galbraith first wrote about "The Affluent Society." This was not a society with many rich people, or in which the rich were richer, but one in which the majority could feel financially secure. In the knowledge society, a large number of people, perhaps even a majority, have something even more important than financial security: social standing, or "social affluence."

THE PRICE OF SUCCESS

The upward mobility of the knowledge society, however, comes at a high price: the psychological pressures and emotional traumas of the rat race. There can be winners only if there are losers. This was not true of earlier societies. The son of the landless laborer who became a landless laborer himself was not a failure. In the knowledge society, however, he is not only a personal failure but a failure of society as well.

Japanese youngsters suffer sleep deprivation because they spend their evenings at a crammer to help them pass their exams. Otherwise they will not get into the prestige university of their choice, and thus into a good job. These pressures create hostility to learning. They also threaten to undermine Japan's prized economic equality and turn the country into a plutocracy, because only well-off parents can afford the prohibitive cost of preparing their youngsters for university. Other countries, such as America, Britain, and France, are also allowing their schools to become viciously competitive. That this has happened over such a short time—no more than thirty or forty years—indicates how much the fear of failure has already permeated the knowledge society.

Given this competitive struggle, a growing number of highly successful knowledge workers of both sexes—business managers, university teachers, museum directors, doctors—"plateau" in their forties. They know they have achieved all they will achieve. If their work is all they have, they are in trouble. Knowledge workers therefore need to develop, preferably while they are still young, a noncompetitive life and community of their own, and some serious outside interest—be it working as a volunteer in the community, playing in a local orchestra, or taking an active part in a small town's local government. This outside interest will give them the opportunity for personal contribution and achievement.

SUMMARY

Knowledge industries, knowledge work, and the knowledge societies have been emerging steadily since the 1950s. They are now realities in developed countries. And this has a number of implications for managers. The expansion of knowledge work corresponds to the decline in manufacturing employment. A rapidly growing segment of knowledge work consists of knowledge technicians, a trend that should continue.

The long-term trend in manufacturing employment is following the long-term decline in employment in agriculture. Participation rates of women in the workforce have been steadily trending up because knowledge work is unisex, unlike most manufacturing employment, which is dominated by men.

Knowledge workers tend to identify at least as much with their knowledge discipline as they do with the organization in which they are employed. This creates new challenges for managers, because knowledge workers are highly mobile and more difficult to integrate into the mission of the organization.

5

New Demographics

By 2030, people over sixty-five in Germany, the world's third-largest economy, will account for almost half the adult population, compared with one-fifth now. And unless the country's birth rate recovers from its present low of 1.3 per woman, over the same period its population of under-thirty-fives will shrink about twice as fast as the older population will grow. The net result will be that the total population, now 82 million, will decline to 70 to 73 million. The number of people of working age will fall by a full quarter, from 40 million today to 30 million.

The German demographics are far from exceptional. In Japan, the world's second-largest economy, the population is peaking about now (2007), at around 128 million. By 2050, according to the more pessimistic government forecasts, the population will have shrunk to around 95 million. Long before that, around 2030, the share of the over-sixty-fives in the adult population will have grown to about half. And the birth rate in Japan, as in Germany, is down to 1.3 per woman.

The figures are much the same for most other developed countries—Italy, France, Spain, Portugal, the Netherlands, Sweden—and for a good many emerging ones, including China. In some regions, such as central Italy, southern France, or southern Spain, birth rates are even lower than in Germany or Japan.

Life expectancy—and with it the number of older people—has been going up steadily for three hundred years. But the decline in the number of young people is something new. The only developed country that has so far avoided this fate is America. But even here the birth rate is below replacement level, and the proportion of older people in the adult population will rise steeply in the next thirty years.

This means that winning the support of older people will become a political imperative in every developed country. Pensions have already become a regular election issue in these places. There is also a growing debate about the desirability of immigration to maintain a country's population and workforce. Together these two issues are transforming the political landscape in every developed country.

By 2030 at the latest, the age at which full retirement benefits start will have

risen to the mid-seventies in all developed countries, and benefits for healthy pen-
sioners will be substantially lower than they are today. Indeed, fixed retirement
ages for people in reasonable physical and mental condition may have been abolished to prevent the pension's burden on the working population from becoming
unbearable. Already young and middle-aged people at work suspect that there
will not be enough pension money to go around when they themselves reach traditional retirement age. But politicians everywhere continue to pretend that they
can save the current pensions system.

NEEDED BUT UNWANTED

Immigration is certain to be an even hotter issue. The respected DIW research
institute in Berlin estimates that by 2020 Germany will have to import 1 million
immigrants of working age each year simply to maintain its workforce. Other rich
European countries are in the same boat. And in Japan there is talk of admitting
500,000 Koreans each year—and sending them home five years later. For all big
countries but America, immigration on such a scale is unprecedented.

The political implications are already being felt. In 1999, fellow Europeans
were shocked by the electoral success in Austria of a xenophobic, right-wing party
whose main plank was "no immigration." Similar movements are growing in
Flemish-speaking Belgium, in traditionally liberal Denmark, and in northern
Italy. Even in America, immigration is upsetting long-established political align-
ments. American trade unions' opposition to large-scale immigration has put
them in the antiglobalization camp that organized violent protests during the
Seattle meeting of the World Trade Organization in 1999. A future Democratic
candidate for the American presidency may have to choose between getting the
union vote by opposing immigration or getting the vote of Latinos and other newcomers by supporting it. Equally, a future Republican candidate may have to
choose between the support of business, which is clamoring for workers, and the
vote of a white middle class that increasingly opposes immigration.

Even so, America's experience of immigration should give it a lead in the developed world for several decades to come. Since the 1970s, it has been admitting
large numbers of immigrants, either legally or illegally. Most immigrants are
young, and the birth rates of first-generation immigrant women tend to be higher
than those of other women of their adopted country. This means that for the next
thirty or forty years America's population will continue to grow, albeit slowly,
whereas in some other developed countries it will fall.

A COUNTRY OF IMMIGRANTS

But it is not numbers alone that will give America an advantage. Even more important,
the country is culturally attuned to immigration, and long ago learned to integrate

immigrants into its society and economy. In fact, recent immigrants, whether Latinos or Asians, may be integrating faster than ever. One-third of all recent Latino immigrants, for instance, are reported to be marrying non-Latinos and nonimmigrants. The one big obstacle to the full integration of recent immigrants in America is the poor performance of American public schools (see chapter 14).

Among developed countries, only Australia and Canada have a tradition of immigration similar to America's. Japan has resolutely kept foreigners out, except for a spate of Korean immigrants in the 1920s and 1930s, whose descendants are still being discriminated against. The mass migrations of the nineteenth century were either into empty, unsettled spaces (such as the United States, Canada, Australia, Brazil) or from farm to city within the same country. By contrast, immigration in the twenty-first century is by foreigners—in nationality, language, culture, and religion—who move into settled countries. European countries have so far been less than successful at integrating such foreigners.

The biggest effect of the demographic changes may be to split hitherto homogeneous societies and markets. Until the 1920s or 1930s, every country had a diversity of cultures and markets. They were sharply differentiated by class, occupation, and residence, for example, "the farm market" or "the carriage trade," both of which disappeared some time between 1920 and 1940. Yet since World War II, all developed countries have had only one mass culture and one mass market. Now that demographic forces in all the developed countries are pulling in opposite directions, will that homogeneity survive?

The markets of the developed world have been dominated by the values, habits, and preferences of the young population. Some of the most successful and most profitable businesses of the past half-century, such as Coca-Cola and Procter & Gamble in America, Unilever in Britain, and Henkel in Germany, owe their prosperity in large measure to the growth of the young population and to the high rate of family formation between 1950 and 2000. The same is true of the car industry over that period.

THE END OF THE SINGLE MARKET

Now there are signs that the market is splitting. In financial services, perhaps America's fastest-growing industry over the past twenty-five years, it has split already. The bubble market of the late 1990s, with its frantic day-trading in high-tech stocks, belonged mainly to the under-forty-fives. But the customers in the markets for such investments as mutual funds or deferred annuities tend to be over fifty, and that market has also been growing apace. The fastest-growing industry in any developed country may turn out to be the continuing education of already well-educated adults, which is based on values that are all but incompatible with those of the youth culture.

But it is also conceivable that some youth markets will become exceedingly lu-
crative. In the coastal cities of China, where the government was able to enforce its
one-child policy, middle-class families are now reported to spend more on their
one child than earlier middle-class families spent on their four or five children together. This seems to be true in Japan too. Many American middle-class families
are spending heavily on the education of their single child, mainly by moving into
expensive suburban neighborhoods with good schools. But this new luxury youth
market is quite different from the homogeneous mass market of the post–Korean
War era. That mass market is rapidly weakening because of the decline in the
number of young people reaching adulthood.

In the future there will almost certainly be two distinct workforces, broadly
made up of the under-fifties and the over-fifties respectively. These two workforces
are likely to differ markedly in their needs and behavior, and in the jobs they do.
The younger group will need a steady income from a permanent job, or at least a
succession of full-time jobs. The rapidly growing older group will have much more
choice and will be able to combine traditional jobs, nonconventional jobs, and leisure in whatever proportion suits them best.

The split into two workforces is likely to start with female knowledge technologists. A nurse, a computer technologist, or a paralegal can take fifteen years out to
look after her children and then return to full-time work. Women, who now outnumber men in American higher education, increasingly look for work in the new
knowledge technologies. Such jobs are the first in human history to be well
adapted to the special needs of women as childbearers, and to their increasing longevity. That longevity is one of the reasons for the split in the job market. A fifty-
year working life—unprecedented in human history—is simply too long for one
kind of work.

The second reason for the split is a shrinking life expectancy for businesses and
organizations of all kinds. In the past, employing organizations have outlived employees. In the future, employees, and especially knowledge workers, will increasingly outlive even successful organizations. Few businesses or even government
agencies or programs last for more than thirty years. Historically, the working life
span of most employees has been less than thirty years, because most manual
workers simply wore out. But knowledge workers who enter the labor force in their
twenties are likely to be still in good physical and mental shape fifty years later.

"Second career" and "second half of one's life" have already become buzzwords
in America. Increasingly, employees there take early retirement as soon as their
pension and Social Security rights are guaranteed for the time when they reach
traditional retirement age; but they do not stop working. Instead, their "second
career" often takes an unconventional form. They may work freelance (and often
forget to tell the tax man about their work, thus boosting their net income), or

part-time, or as "temporaries," or for an outsourcing contractor, or as contractors themselves. Such "early retirement to keep on working" is particularly common among knowledge workers, who are still a minority among people now reaching fifty or fifty-five, but will become the largest single group of older people in America from about 2030.

BEWARE DEMOGRAPHIC CHANGES

Population predictions for the next fifteen years can be made with some certainty because everybody who will be in the workforce in 2020 is already alive. But, as American experience in the past couple of decades has shown, demographic trends can change quite suddenly and unpredictably, with fairly immediate effects. The American baby boom of the late 1940s, for instance, triggered the housing boom of the 1950s.

In the mid-1920s, America had its first "baby bust." Between 1925 and 1935 the birth rate declined by almost half, dipping below the replacement rate of 2.2 live births per woman. In the late 1930s, President Franklin Roosevelt's Commission on American Population (consisting of the country's most eminent demographers and statisticians) confidently predicted that America's population would peak in 1945 and would then start declining. But an exploding birth rate in the late 1940s proved it wrong. Within ten years, the number of live births per woman doubled from 1.8 to 3.6. Between 1947 and 1957, America experienced an astonishing "baby boom." The number of babies born rose from 2.5 million to 4.1 million.

Then, in 1960–61, the opposite happened. Instead of the expected second-wave baby boom as the first boomers reached adulthood, there was a big bust. Between 1961 and 1975, the birth rate fell from 3.7 to 1.8. The number of babies born went down from 4.3 million in 1960 to 3.1 million in 1975. The next surprise was the "baby boom echo" in the late 1980s and early 1990s. The number of live births went up quite sharply, surpassing even the numbers of the first baby boom's peak years. With the benefit of hindsight, it is now clear that this echo was triggered by large-scale immigration into America, beginning in the early 1970s. When the girls born to these early immigrants started having children of their own in the late 1980s, their birth rates were still closer to those of their parents' country of origin than to those of their adopted country. Fully one-fifth of all children of school age in California in the first decade of this century have at least one foreign-born parent.

But nobody knows what caused the two baby busts, or the baby boom of the 1940s. Both busts occurred when the economy was doing well, which, in theory, should have encouraged people to have lots of children. And the baby boom should never have happened, because historically birth rates have always gone down after a big war. The truth is that we simply do not understand what determines birth rates in modern societies. So not only will demographics be the most important factor in the next society, it will also be the least predictable and least controllable one.

SUMMARY

Demographic trends are having significant political and economic effects in developed countries. Low birth rates in these countries are escalating political tensions over immigration policies and favor those countries, such as the United States, that have a culture of easily assimilating immigrants. Yet even in the United States, immigration is increasing political tensions among various groups: employers who need immigrant workers, unions who fear the impact of new immigrants on wages and employment of their members, and large existing immigrant populations, such as the Latino population, which strongly favor lenient policies toward both legal and illegal immigrants.

The aging of the population in developed countries is straining existing social pension systems, leading to pressure to increase the traditional retirement age. Knowledge workers are likely to reenter labor markets as part-time employees after retirement in order to supplement their pensions. Increased life expectancies, especially among knowledge workers, should make second and parallel careers possible and desirable. This should continue to change the structure of the workforce.

As the population ages, so will the demand for financial services among the post-fifty-years-old segment of the population. This is also the segment that is likely to increase its demand for continuing education. Continuing education, health care, and financial services are likely to continue to be among the growth markets of the future.

6

The Future of the Corporation and the Way Ahead

For most of the time since the corporation was invented around 1870, the following five basic points have been assumed to apply:

1. The corporation is the "master," the employee is the "servant." Because the corporation owns the means of production without which the employee cannot make a living, the employee needs the corporation more than vice versa.

2. The great majority of employees work full-time for the corporation. The pay they get for the job is their only income and provides their livelihood.

3. The most efficient way to produce anything is to bring together under one management as many as possible of the activities needed to turn out the product.

The theory underlying the latter was not developed until after World War II, by Ronald Coase (b. 1910), an Anglo-American economist, who argued that bringing together activities into one company lowers "transactional costs," and especially the cost of communications (for which theory he received the 1991 Nobel Prize in economics). But the concept itself was discovered and put into practice seventy or eighty years earlier by John D. Rockefeller, Sr. He saw that to put exploration, production, transport, refining, and selling into one corporate structure resulted in the most efficient and lowest-cost petroleum operation. On this insight he built the Standard Oil Trust, probably the most profitable large enterprise in business history. The concept was carried to an extreme by Henry Ford in the early 1920s. The Ford Motor Company not only produced all parts of the automobile and assembled it, but made its own steel, its own glass, and its own tires. It owned the plantations in the Amazon that grew the rubber trees, owned and ran the railroad that carried supplies to the plant and carried the finished cars from it, and planned eventually to sell and service Ford cars too (though it never did).

4. Suppliers and especially manufacturers have market power because they have information about a product or a service that the customer does not and cannot have, and does not need if he or she can trust the brand. This explains the profitability of brands.

5. To any one particular technology pertains one, and only one, industry, and conversely, to any one particular industry pertains one, and only one, technology. This means that all technology needed to make steel is peculiar to the steel industry; and conversely, that whatever technology is being used to make steel comes out of the steel industry itself. The same applies to the paper industry, to agriculture, or to banking and commerce.

EVERYTHING IN ITS PLACE

Similarly, everybody took it for granted that every product or service had a specific application, and that for every application there was a specific product or material. So beer and milk were sold only in glass bottles, car bodies were made only from steel, working capital for a business was supplied by a commercial bank through a commercial loan, and so on. Competition therefore took place mainly within an industry. By and large, it was obvious what the business of a given company was and what its markets were.

Every one of these assumptions remained valid for a whole century, but from 1970 onward every one of them has been turned upside down. The list now reads as follows:

1. The means of production is knowledge, which is owned by knowledge workers and is highly portable. This applies equally to high-knowledge workers such as research scientists and to knowledge technologists such as physiotherapists, computer technicians, and paralegals. Knowledge workers provide "capital" just as much as do those who provide money. The two are dependent on each other. This makes the knowledge worker an equal—an associate or a partner.

2. Many employees, perhaps a majority, will still have full-time jobs with a salary that provides their only or main income. But a growing number of people who work for an organization will not be full-time employees but be part-timers, temporaries, consultants, or contractors. Even of those who do have a full-time job, a large and growing number may not be employees of the organization for which they work, but employees of, for example, an outsourcing contractor.

3. There always were limits to the importance of transactional costs. Henry Ford's all-inclusive Ford Motor Company proved unmanageable and became a disaster. But now the traditional axiom that an enterprise should aim for maximum integration has become almost entirely invalidated. One reason is that the knowledge needed for any activity has become highly specialized. It is therefore increasingly expensive, and also increasingly difficult, to maintain enough critical mass for every major task within an enterprise. And because knowledge rapidly deteriorates unless it is used constantly, maintaining within an organization an activity that is used only intermittently guarantees incompetence.

The second reason why maximum integration is no longer needed is that communications costs have come down so fast as to become insignificant. This decline began well before the information revolution. Perhaps its biggest cause has been the *growth and spread of business literacy*. When Rockefeller built his Standard Oil Trust, he had great difficulty finding people who knew even the most elementary bookkeeping or had heard of the most common business terms. At the time, there were no business textbooks or business courses, so the transactional costs of making oneself understood were extremely high. Sixty years later, by 1950 or 1960, the large oil companies that succeeded the Standard Oil Trust could confidently assume that their more senior employees were business literate.

By now the new information technology—Internet and e-mail—has practically eliminated the physical costs of communications. This has meant that the most productive and most profitable way to organize is to *disintegrate*. This is being extended to more and more activities. Outsourcing the management of an institution's information technology, data processing, and computer system has become routine. In the early 1990s, most American computer firms, for example, Apple, even outsourced the production of their hardware to manufacturers in Japan or Singapore. In the late 1990s, practically every Japanese consumer-electronics company repaid the compliment by outsourcing the manufacturing of its products for the American market to American contract manufacturers.

In the past decade the entire human-resources management of more than 2 million American workers—hiring, firing, training, benefits, and so on—has been outsourced to professional employee organizations (PEOs) and business processing organizations (BPOs). This sector, which ten years ago barely existed, is now growing at a rate of 30 percent a year. It originally concentrated on small and medium-sized companies, but the biggest of the firms, Exult, a BPO, founded only in 1998, now manages the full spectrum of employee processes, such as payroll, recruiting and staffing, training administration, employee data management, relocation, and severance administration for a number of Global Fortune 500 companies. Their ever-growing client list includes British Petroleum, Bank of America, International Paper, Prudential Financial, Circuit City, McKesson, Universal Entertainment, Unisys, and Bank of Montreal.

4. The customer now has the information. Whoever has the information has the power. Power is thus shifting to the customer, be it another business or the ultimate consumer. Specifically, that means the supplier, for example, the manufacturer, will cease to be a seller and instead become a buyer for the customer. This is already happening.

5. Lastly, there are few unique technologies anymore. Increasingly, the knowledge needed in a given industry comes out of some totally different technology with which, very often, the people in the industry are unfamiliar. No one in the telephone industry knew anything about fiberglass cables. They were developed by

a glass company, Corning. Conversely, more than half of the important inventions developed since World War II by the most productive of the great research labs, the Bell Laboratories (now Lucent), have been applied mainly outside the telephone industry. (On this topic see extended discussion in chapter 7.)

WHO NEEDS A RESEARCH LAB?

Research directors, as well as high-tech industrialists, now tend to believe that the company-owned research lab, that proud nineteenth-century invention, has become obsolete. This explains why, increasingly, development and growth of a business is taking place not inside the corporation itself but through partnerships, joint ventures, alliances, minority participation, and know-how agreements with institutions in different industries and with a different technology. Something that only fifty years ago would have been unthinkable is becoming common: alliances between institutions of a totally different character—say, a profit-making company and a university department, or a city or state government and a business that contracts for a specific service such as cleaning the streets or running prisons.

Practically no product or service any longer has either a single specific end-use or application, or its own market. Commercial paper, short-term unsecured debt issued by corporations and financial institutions, competes with the banks' commercial loans. Cardboard, plastic, and aluminum compete with glass for the bottle market. Glass is replacing copper in cables. Steel is competing with wood and plastic in providing the studs around which the American one-family home is constructed. The deferred annuity is pushing aside traditional life insurance—but, in turn, insurance companies rather than financial-service institutions are becoming the managers of commercial risks.

A "glass company" may, therefore, have to redefine itself by *what it is good at doing* rather than by the material in which it has specialized in the past. One of the world's largest glassmakers, Corning, sold its profitable business making traditional glass products to become the number one producer and supplier of high-tech materials. Merck, America's largest pharmaceutical company, diversified from making drugs into wholesaling every kind of pharmacy product, most of them not even made by Merck and a good many made by competitors.

The same sort of thing is happening in the nonbusiness sectors of the economy. One example is the freestanding "birthing center" run by a group of obstetricians that competes with the American hospital's maternity ward. And Britain, long before the Internet, created the Open University, which allows people to get a university education and obtain a degree without ever setting foot in a classroom or attending a lecture.

THE NEXT COMPANY

One thing is almost certain: in the future there will be, not one kind of corporation, but several different ones. The modern company was invented simultaneously but independently in three countries: America, Germany, and Japan. It was a complete novelty and bore no resemblance to the economic organization that had been the "economic enterprise" for millennia: the small, privately owned, and personally run firm. As late as 1832, England's McLane Report—the first statistical survey of business— found that nearly all firms were privately owned and had fewer than ten employees. The only exceptions were quasi-governmental organizations such as the Bank of England and the East India Company. Forty years later, a new kind of organization with thousands of employees had appeared on the scene, for example, the American railroads, built with federal and state support, and Germany's Deutsche Bank.

Wherever the corporation went, it acquired some local national characteristics and adapted to each country's different legal rules. Moreover, very large corporations everywhere are run quite differently from the small owner-managed kind. And there are substantial internal differences in culture, values, and rhetoric between corporations in different industries. Banks everywhere are very much alike, and so are retailers or manufacturers. But banks everywhere are different from retailers or manufacturers. Otherwise, however, the differences between corporations everywhere are more of style than of substance. The same is true of all other organizations in modern society: government agencies, armed forces, hospitals, universities, and so on.

The tide turned around 1970, first with the emergence of new institutional investors such as pension funds and mutual trusts as the new owners, then—more decisively—with the emergence of knowledge workers as the economy's big new resource and the society's representative class. The result has been a fundamental change in the corporation.

A bank in the next society will still not look like a hospital, nor be run like one. But different banks may be quite different from one another, depending on how each of them responds to the changes in its *workforce, technology,* and *markets.* A number of different models are likely to emerge, especially of organization and structure, but perhaps also different models of recognition and reward.

The same legal entity—for example, a business, a government agency, or a large not-for-profit organization—may well contain several different human organizations that interlock but are managed separately and differently. One of these is likely to be a traditional organization of full-time employees. Yet there may also be a closely linked but separately managed human organization made up mainly of older people who are not employees but associates or affiliates. And there are likely to be "perimeter" groups, such as the people who work for the organization, even full-time, but as employees of an outsourcing contractor or of a contract manufacturer. These people have no contractual relationship with the business they work for, which in turn has no control over them. They may not have to be "managed," but they have to be made productive. They will, therefore, have to be deployed where their specialized knowledge can make the greatest contribution.

Just as important, the people in every one of these organizational categories will have to be satisfied. Attracting them and holding them will become the central task of people management. We already know what does not work: bribery. In the past ten or fifteen years many businesses in America have used bonuses or stock options to attract and keep knowledge workers. It always fails.

Of course knowledge workers need to be satisfied with their pay, because dissatisfaction with income and benefits is a powerful disincentive. The incentives, however, are different. The management of knowledge workers should be based on the assumption that the corporation needs them more than they need the corporation. They know they can leave. They have both mobility and self-confidence. This means they have to be treated and managed as volunteers, in the same way as volunteers who work for not-for-profit organizations (on the treatment of volunteers in the not-for-profit organization, see chapter 13). The first thing such people want to know is what the company is trying to do and where it is going. Next, they are interested in personal achievement and personal responsibility—which means they have to be put in the right job. Knowledge workers expect continuous learning and continuous training. Above all, they want respect, not so much for themselves but for their area of knowledge. In that regard, they have moved several steps beyond traditional workers, who used to expect to be told what to do, although later they were increasingly expected to "participate." Knowledge workers, in contrast, expect to make the decisions in their own area.

FROM CORPORATION TO CONFEDERATION

The first example of the corporation as a confederation is General Motors which, in the 1920s, first developed both the organizational concepts and the organizational structure upon which today's large corporations everywhere are based. And it was based for seventy-five of those eighty years on two basic principles: we own as much as possible of whatever we manufacture, and we own everything we do.

Now it is experimenting with becoming the minority partner in competing companies—Saab in Sweden, Suzuki and Isuzu in Japan.

At the same time, it has divested itself of 70 to 80 percent of what it manufactures, but at the same time it is turning itself into a merchant, buying for the customers through its dealership but also directly, finding the car the customer wants.

THE TOYOTA WAY

The second example of a corporation as a confederation goes exactly the other way. Toyota, which since the 1980s, has been the most successful automotive company and is the now the largest. It is restructuring itself around its core competency—manufacturing. It is moving away from having multiple suppliers of parts and accessories to having only one or two everywhere. At the same time, it uses its manufacturing competence to manage these suppliers. They remain independent companies, but they are basically part of Toyota in terms of management.

This is not a new idea. Sears, Roebuck did the same for its suppliers in the 1920s and 1930s. Britain's Marks & Spencer was the world's most successful retailer for fifty years, maintaining its preeminence largely by keeping an iron grip on its suppliers. It is rumored in Japan that Toyota intends ultimately to market its manufacturing consultancy to non-car companies, turning its manufacturing core competence into a separate big business.

Yet another approach is being explored by a large manufacturer of branded and packaged consumer goods. Some 60 percent of the company's products are sold in the developed countries through some 150 retail chains. The company plans to create a worldwide Web site that will take orders from customers in all countries, either to be picked up in the retail store nearest to them or to be delivered by that store to their home. But—and this is the true innovation—the Web site will also take orders for noncompeting packaged and branded consumer products made by other, and especially smaller, firms. Such firms have great difficulty in getting their wares on to increasingly crowded supermarket shelves. The multinational's Web site could offer them direct access to customers and delivery through an established large retailer. The pay-off for the multinational and the retailer would be that both get a decent commission without having to invest any money of their own, without risk, and without sacrificing shelf space to slow-moving items.

There are already a good many variations on this theme: the already mentioned American contract manufacturers, who now make the products for half a dozen competing Japanese consumer-electronics firms; a few independent specialists who design software for competing information-hardware makers; the independent specialists who design credit cards for competing American banks and also often market and clear the cards for the bank (all the bank does is the financing).

All these approaches, however different, still take the traditional corporation as their point of departure. But there are some new ideas that do away with the corporate model altogether. One example is a "syndicate" being tested by several noncompeting manufacturers in the European Union. Each of the constituent companies is medium-sized, family-owned, and owner-managed. Each is a leader in a narrow, highly engineered product line. Each is heavily export-dependent. The individual companies intend to remain independent and to continue to design their products separately. They will also continue to make them in their own plants for their main markets and to sell them in these markets. But for other markets, and especially for emerging or less developed countries, the syndicate will arrange for the making of the products, either in syndicate-owned plants producing for several of the members or by local contract manufacturers. The syndicate will handle the delivery of all members' products and service them in all markets. Each member will own a share of the syndicate, and the syndicate, in turn, will own a small share of each member's capital. If this sounds familiar, it is because the model is the nineteenth-century farmers' cooperative.

As the corporation moves toward a confederation or a syndicate, it will increasingly need a top management that is separate, powerful, and accountable. This top management's responsibilities will cover the entire organization's direction, planning, strategy, values, and principles; its structure and its relationship among its various members; its alliances, partnerships, and joint ventures; and its research, design, and innovation. Top management will have to take charge of the management of the two resources common to all units of the organization: *key people* and *money*. It will represent the corporation to the outside world and maintain relationships with governments, the public, the media, and organized labor.

LIFE AT THE TOP

An equally important task for top management in the next society's corporation will be to balance the three dimensions of the corporation: as an *economic* organization, as a *human* organization, and as an increasingly important *social* organization. Each of the three models of the corporation developed in the past half century stressed one of these dimensions and subordinated the other two. The German model of the "social market economy" put the emphasis on the social dimension; the Japanese one, on the human dimension; and the American one ("shareholder sovereignty"), on the economic dimension.

None of the three is adequate on its own. The German model achieved both economic success and social stability, but at the price of high unemployment and dangerous labor-market rigidity. The Japanese model was strikingly successful for twenty years, but faltered at the first serious challenge; indeed, it has become a major obstacle to Japan's recovery from its most recent deep recession. The "shareholder sovereignty" model is also bound to flounder. It is a fair-weather model that works well only in times of prosperity. Obviously, the enterprise can fulfill its human and social functions only if it prospers as a business. But now that knowledge workers are becoming the key employees, a company also needs to be a desirable employer to be successful.

Crucially, the claim that made shareholder sovereignty possible, the absolute primacy of business gains, has also highlighted the importance of the corporation's social function. The new shareholders whose emergence since 1960 or 1970 produced shareholder sovereignty are not "capitalists." They are employees who own a stake in the business through their retirement and pension funds. By 2000, pension funds and mutual funds had come to own the majority of the share capital of America's large companies. This has given shareholders the power to demand short-term rewards. But the need for a secure retirement income will increasingly focus people's minds on the future value of the investment. Corporations, therefore, will have to pay attention to both their short-term business results and their long-term performance, as providers of retirement benefits. The two are not irreconcilable, but they are different, and they will have to be balanced.

In the last half-century after World War II, the business corporation has proven itself brilliantly as an economic organization—a creator of wealth and jobs. In the next society, the biggest challenge for the large company may be its social legitimacy: *its values, its mission, its vision.* In their different ways, the top people at all of these German, Japanese, and American companies were trying to do the same thing: to establish their organization's unique personality.

Will the corporation survive? Yes, after a fashion. Something akin to a corporation will have to coordinate the next society's economic resources. Legally and perhaps financially, it may even look much the same as today's corporation. But instead of there being a single model adopted by everyone, there will be a range of models to choose from.

THE WAY AHEAD: THE TIME TO GET READY FOR
THE NEW REALITIES IS NOW

The next society has developed far enough for action to be considered in the following areas:

The future corporation. Enterprises—including a good many nonbusinesses, such as universities—should start experimenting with new corporate forms and conducting a few pilot studies, especially in working with alliances, partners, and joint ventures, and in defining new structures and new tasks for top management. New models are also needed for geographical and product diversification for multinational companies, and for balancing concentration and diversification.

People policies. The way people are managed almost everywhere assumes that the workforce is still largely made up of people who are employed by the enterprise and work full-time for it until they are fired, quit, retire, or die. Yet already in many organizations as many as two-fifths of the people who work there are not employees and do not work full-time.

Today's human-resources managers also still assume that the most desirable and least costly employees are young ones. In America, especially, older people, and particularly older managers and professionals, have been pushed into early retirement to make room for younger people who are believed to cost less or to have more up-to-date skills. The results of this policy have not been encouraging. Generally speaking, after two years wage costs per employee for the younger recruits tend to be back where they were before the "oldies" were pushed out, if not higher. The number of salaried employees seems to be going up at least as fast as production or sales, which means that the new young hires are no more productive than the old ones were. But in any event, demography will make the present policy increasingly self-defeating and expensive.

The first need is for a people policy that covers all those who work for an enterprise, whether they are employed by it or not. After all, the performance of every single one of them matters. So far, no one seems to have devised a satisfactory solution to this problem. Second, enterprises must attract, hold, and make productive people who have reached official retirement age, have become independent outside contractors, or are not available as full-time permanent employees. For example, highly skilled and educated older people, instead of being retired, might be offered a choice of continuing relationships that convert them into long-term "inside outsiders," preserving their skill and knowledge for the enterprise and yet giving them the flexibility and freedom they expect and can afford.

There is a model for this, but it comes from academia rather than business: the professor emeritus, who has vacated his chair and no longer draws a salary. He remains free to teach as much as he wants, but gets paid only for what he or she does. Many emeriti do retire altogether, but perhaps as many as half continue to teach part-time, and many continue to do full-time research. A similar arrangement might well suit senior professionals in a business. A big American corporation is currently trying out such an arrangement for older top-level people in its law and tax departments, in research and development, and in staff jobs. But for people in operating work, for example, sales or manufacturing, something different needs to be developed.

Outside information. Perhaps surprisingly, it can be argued that the information revolution has caused managements to be less well informed than they were before. They have more data, to be sure, but most of the information made so readily available through information technology is about internal company matters. As this chapter has shown, though, the most important changes affecting an institution today are likely to be outside ones, about which present information systems offer few clues.

One reason is that information about the outside world is not usually available in computer-useable form. It is not codified, nor is it usually quantified. This is why information technology people, and their executive customers, tend to scorn information about the outside world as "anecdotal." Moreover, far too many managers assume, wrongly, that the society they have known all their lives will remain the same forever.

Outside information is becoming available on the Internet. It is now possible for managements to ask what outside information they need, as a first step toward devising a proper information system for collecting relevant information about the outside world. (On converting data to information, see chapter 33.)

Change agents. To survive and succeed, every organization will have to turn itself into a change agent. *The most effective way to manage change successfully is to create it.* But experience has shown that grafting innovation onto a traditional enterprise does not work. The enterprise has to become a change agent. This requires the organized abandonment of things that have been shown to be unsuccessful, and the organized and continuous improvement of every product, service, and process within the enterprise (which the Japanese call *kaizen*). It requires the exploitation of successes, especially unexpected and unplanned-for ones, and it requires systematic innovation. The point of becoming a change agent is that it changes the mindset of the entire organization. Instead of seeing change as a threat, its people will come to consider it as an opportunity.

AND THEN?

So much for getting ready for the future that we can already see taking shape. But what about future trends and events we are not even aware of yet? If there is one thing that can be forecast with confidence, it is that the future will turn out in unexpected ways.

Take, for example, the information revolution. Almost everybody is sure of two things about it: first, that it is proceeding with unprecedented speed; and second, that its effects will be more radical than anything that has gone before. Wrong, and wrong again. Both in its speed and its impact, the information revolution uncannily resembles its two predecessors within the past two hundred years—the *first industrial revolution* of the later eighteenth and early nineteenth centuries, and the *second industrial revolution* in the late nineteenth century.

The first industrial revolution, triggered by James Watt's improved steam engine in the mid-1770s, immediately had an enormous impact on the West's imagination, but it did not produce many social and economic changes until the invention of the railroad, in 1829, and of prepaid postal service and of the telegraph, in the decade thereafter. Similarly, the invention of the computer in the mid-1940s, the information revolution's equivalent of the steam engine, stimulated people's imagination, but it was not until forty years later, with the spread of the Internet in the 1990s, that the information revolution began to bring about big economic and social changes.

Equally, today we are puzzled and alarmed by the growing inequality in income and wealth and by the emergence of the "superrich," such as Microsoft's Bill Gates. Yet the same sudden and inexplicable growth in inequality and the same emergence of the "superrich" of their day, characterized both the first and the second industrial revolutions. Those earlier superrich were a good deal richer, relative to the average income and average wealth of their time and country, than a Bill Gates is, relative to today's average income and wealth in America.

These parallels are close enough and striking enough to make it almost certain that, as in the earlier industrial revolutions, *the main effects of the information revolution on the next society still lie ahead.* The decades of the nineteenth century following the first and second industrial revolutions were the most innovative and most fertile periods since the sixteenth century for the creation of new institutions and new theories. The first industrial revolution turned the factory into the central production organization and the main creator of wealth. Factory workers became the first new social class since the appearance of knights in armor more than one thousand years earlier. The house of Rothschild, which emerged as the world's dominant financial power after 1810, was not only the first investment bank but also the first multinational company since the fifteenth-century Hanseatic League and the Medici family. The first industrial revolution brought forth, among many other things, intellectual property, universal incorporation, limited liability, the trade union, the cooperative, the technical university, and the daily newspaper. The second industrial revolution produced the modern civil service and the modern corporation, the commercial bank, the business school, and the first nonmenial jobs outside the home for women.

The two industrial revolutions also bred new theories and new ideologies. *The Communist Manifesto* was a response to the first industrial revolution; the political theories and theorists that together shaped the twentieth-century democracies—Otto von Bismarck's welfare state, Britain's Christian Socialism and Fabian Society, America's regulation of business—were all responses to the second one. So was

Frederick Winslow Taylor's *scientific management* (starting in 1881), with its productivity explosion.

BIG IDEAS

Following the information revolution, once again we see the emergence of new institutions and new theories. The new economic regions—the European Union, NAFTA (North American Free Trade Agreement) and the proposed Free-Trade Area of the Americas—are neither traditionally free-trade nor traditionally protectionist. They attempt a new balance between the two and between the economic sovereignty of the national state and supranational economic decision making. Equally, there is no real precedent for the Citigroups, Goldman Sachses, or ING Barings that have come to dominate world finance. They are not multinational but *transnational*. The money they deal in is almost totally beyond the control of any country's government or central bank.

And then there is the upsurge in interest in the Austro-American economist Joseph Schumpeter's postulates of *dynamic disequilibrium* as the economy's only stable state, of the innovator's *creative destruction* as the economy's driving force, and of new technology as the main, if not the only, economic change agent—the very antitheses of earlier economic theories based on the idea of equilibrium as a healthy economy's norm, monetary and fiscal policies as the drivers of a modern economy, and technology as exogenous.

All of this suggests that the greatest changes are almost certainly still ahead of us. We can also be sure that the society of 2030 will be very different from that of today. It will not be dominated or even shaped by information technology. Information technology will, of course, be important, but it will be only one of several important new technologies. The central features of the next society, as of its predecessors, will be new institutions and new theories, ideologies, and problems.

SUMMARY

A number of key assumptions on which the corporation was invented are now being reversed. Some of these assumptions will be discussed further in chapter 7. Two are especially important to summarize. First, the *specialized nature of knowledge,* the *reduction in communications costs,* and the *crisscross of technology* are having a profound impact on reversing the century trend toward integrating the separate activities of the corporation into a hierarchy. Second, development and growth of a business is increasingly taking place, not inside the corporation itself, but through partnerships, joint ventures, alliances, minority participation, and know-how agreements with institutions in different industries and with different technologies. Thus the process of "integration" is being reversed by the process of "disintegration." Attracting and holding these diverse groups will become the central tasks of people management in the new corporation. The people in these groups do not have permanent relationships with the business. They may not have to be managed, but they have to be made productive. They will, therefore, have to be deployed where their specialized knowledge can make the greatest contribution. And they will have to be satisfied.

7

Management's New Paradigm

INTRODUCTION

Basic assumptions about reality are the *paradigms* of a social science, such as management. They are usually subconsciously held by the scholars, the writers, the teachers, the practitioners in the field. Yet those assumptions largely determine what the discipline—scholars, writers, teachers, practitioners—assumes to be *reality*.

The discipline's basic assumptions about reality determine what it focuses on. They determine what a discipline considers "facts" and, indeed, what it considers the discipline itself to be all about. The assumptions also largely determine what is being disregarded in a discipline or is being pushed aside as an "annoying exception." They decide in a given discipline both what is being paid attention to and what is neglected or ignored.

Yet, despite their importance, the assumptions are rarely analyzed, rarely studied, rarely challenged—indeed rarely even made explicit.

For a social discipline such as management the assumptions are actually a good deal more important than are the paradigms for a natural science. The paradigm—that is, the prevailing general theory—has no impact on the natural universe. Whether the paradigm states that the sun rotates around the earth or, on the contrary, that the earth rotates around the sun has no effect on sun and earth. A natural science deals with the behavior of *objects*. But a social discipline such as management deals with the behavior of *people* and *human institutions*. Practitioners will, therefore, tend to act and to behave as the discipline's assumptions tell them to. Even more important, the reality of a natural science, the physical universe and its laws, do not change (or if they do, only over eons rather than over centuries, let alone over decades). The social universe has no *natural laws* of this kind. It is thus subject to continuous change. And this means that assumptions that were valid yesterday can, in no time at all, become invalid and, indeed, totally misleading.

What matter most in a social discipline such as management are, therefore, the basic assumptions. And a *change* in the basic assumptions matters even more. Since the study of management first began—and it truly did not emerge until the 1930s—*two sets* of assumptions regarding the *realities* of management have been held by most scholars, most writers, and most practitioners.

One set of assumptions underlies the *discipline* of management:

1. Management is *business* management.

2. There is—or there must be—*one* right organization structure.

3. There is—or there must be—*one* right way to manage people.

Another set of assumptions underlies the *practice* of management:

1. Technologies, markets, and end-uses are given.

2. Management's scope is legally defined.

3. Management is internally focused.

4. The economy as defined by national boundaries is the "ecology" of enterprise and management.

MANAGEMENT IS *BUSINESS* MANAGEMENT

To most people, inside and outside management, this assumption is self-evident. Indeed, management writers, management practitioners, and the laity do not even hear the lone word "management"; they automatically hear *business management*.

This assumption regarding the universe of management is of fairly recent origin. Before the 1930s, the few writers and thinkers who concerned themselves with management—beginning with Frederick Winslow Taylor around the turn of the century and ending with Chester Barnard just before World War II—all assumed that business management was just a subspecies of general management and basically no more different from the management of any other organization than one breed of dog is from another breed of dog.

What led to the identification of *management* with *business management* was the Great Depression and with it a hostility to business and contempt for business executives. In order not to be tarred with the business brush, management in the public sector was rechristened *public administration* and proclaimed a separate discipline—with its own university departments, its own terminology, its own career ladder. At the same time—and for the same reason—what had begun as a study of management in the rapidly growing hospital (e.g., by Raymond Sloan, the younger brother of GM's Alfred Sloan) was split off as a separate discipline and christened *hospital administration*.

Not to refer to *management* was, in other words, *political correctness* in the Depression years.

In the postwar period, however, the fashion turned. By 1950, *business* had become a good word—largely as the result of the performance during World War II of American business management—and then very soon *business management* became politically correct, as a field of study, above all. And ever since, management has remained identified, in the public mind as well as in academia, with *business management*.

Now we are beginning to unmake this seventy-year-old mistake—as witness the renaming of so many "business schools" as "schools of management," the rapidly growing offerings in "nonprofit management" by these schools, the emergence of executive management programs recruiting both business and nonbusiness executives, or the emergence of departments of pastoral management in divinity schools.

But the assumption that management is *business* management still persists. It is therefore important to assert, and to do so loudly, that *Management* is **not** *Business Management*—any more than, say, *medicine* is *obstetrics*.

There are, of course, differences in management among different organizations—*mission* defines *strategy*, after all, and *strategy* defines *structure*. There surely are differences between managing a chain of retail stores and managing a Catholic diocese (though amazingly fewer than either chain stores or bishops believe); between managing an air base, a hospital, and a software company. But the greatest differences are in the terms that individual organizations use. Otherwise *the differences are mainly in application rather than in principles*. There are not even tremendous differences in tasks and challenges.

The first conclusion of this analysis of the *assumptions* that must underlie management to make productive both its study and its practice is therefore: ***Management is the specific and distinguishing organ of any and all organizations***.

THE ONE RIGHT ORGANIZATION

Concern with management and its study began with the sudden emergence of large organizations—business, governmental civil service, the large standing army (which was the novelty of late nineteenth-century society). And from the very beginning more than a century ago, the study of organization has rested on one assumption: *There is—or there must be—one right organization.*

What is presented as the one right organization has changed more than once. But the search for the one right organization has continued and continues today.

It was World War I that made clear the need for a formal organization structure. But it was also World War I that showed that Henri Fayol's (and Andrew Carnegie's) functional structure was not the one right organization. Immediately after World War I, first Pierre S. du Pont (1870–1954) and then Alfred P. Sloan (1875–1966) developed *decentralization*. And now, in the last few years, we have come to tout the "team" as the one right organization for pretty much everything.

By now, however, it should have become clear that there is no such thing as the one right organization. There are only organizations, each of which has distinct strengths, distinct limitations, and specific applications. Organization is not an absolute. It is a tool for making people productive in working together. As such, a given organization structure fits certain tasks in certain conditions and at certain times.

One hears a great deal today about "the end of hierarchy." This is blatant nonsense. In any institution there has to be a final authority, that is, a "boss"—someone who can make the final decisions and who can expect them to be obeyed. In a situation of common peril—and every institution is likely to encounter it sooner or later—the survival of all depends on clear command. If the ship goes down, the captain does not call a meeting, the captain gives an order. And if the ship is to be saved, everyone must obey the order, must know exactly where to go and what to do, and do it without "participation" or argument. "Hierarchy," and the unquestioning acceptance of it by everyone in the organization, is the only hope in a crisis.

Other situations within the same institution require deliberation. Others still require teamwork—and so on. In any one enterprise—probably even in Fayol's "typical manufacturing company"—there is the need for a number of different organization structures coexisting side by side.

Managing foreign currency exposure is an increasingly critical—and increasingly difficult—task in a world economy. It requires total centralization. No one unit of the enterprise can be permitted to handle its own foreign currency exposures. But in the same enterprise, servicing the customer, especially in high-tech areas, requires almost complete local autonomy—going way beyond traditional decentralization. Each of the individual service people has to be the "boss," with the rest of the organization taking its direction from them.

Certain forms of research require a strict functional organization, with all specialists "playing their instrument" by themselves. Other kinds of research, however, especially research that involves decision making at an early stage (e.g., some pharmaceutical research), require teamwork from the beginning. And the two kinds of research often occur side by side and in the same research organization.

The belief that there must be one right organization is closely tied to the fallacy that management is *business* management. If earlier students of management had not been blinkered by this fallacy but had looked at nonbusinesses, they would have soon found that there are vast differences in organization structure, according to the nature of the task.

A Catholic diocese is organized very differently from an opera. A modern army is organized very differently from a hospital.

There are, indeed, some *principles of organization*.

One is surely that organization has to be transparent. People have to know and have to understand the organization structure they are supposed to work in. This sounds obvious—but it is far too often violated in most institutions (even in the military).

Another principle has already been mentioned: Someone in the organization must have the authority to make the final decision in a given area. And someone must clearly be in command in a *crisis*. It also is a sound principle that *authority be commensurate with responsibility*.

It is a sound principle that one person in an organization should have only one "master." There is wisdom to the old proverb of the Roman law that a slave who has three masters is a free man. It is a very old principle of human relations that no one should be put into a conflict of loyalties—and having more than one master creates such a conflict (which, by the way, is the reason that the *jazz combo* team, so popular now, is so difficult—every one of its members has two masters, the head of the specialty function, e.g., engineering, and the team leader). It is a sound structural principle to have the fewest layers, that is, to have an organization that is as *flat* as possible—if only because, as information theory tells us, *every relay doubles the noise and cuts the message in half.*

But these principles do not tell us *what to do.* They only tell us what not to do. They do not tell us what will work. They tell us what is unlikely to work. These principles are not too different from the ones that inform an architect's work. They do not tell him what kind of building to build. They tell him what the restraints are. And this is pretty much what the various principles of organization structure do.

One implication: *Individuals will have to be able to work at one and the same time in different organization structures.* For one task they will work in a team. But for another task they will have to work—and at the same time—in a command-and-control structure. The same individual who is a "boss" within his or her own organization is a "partner" in an alliance, minority participation, a joint venture, and so on. Organizations, in other words, will have to become part of the executive's toolbox.

Even more important: We need to go to work on studying the strengths and the limitations of different organizations (see chapters 38–42). For what tasks are what organizations most suitable? For what tasks are what organizations least suitable? And when, in the performance of a task, should we switch from one kind of organization to another? This analysis is perhaps most needed for the currently politically correct organization: *the team.*

One area in which research and study are particularly needed is the *organization of top management.* Yet I doubt that anyone would assert that we really know how to organize the top management job, whether in a business, a university, a hospital, or even a modern church. One clear sign is the growing disparity between our rhetoric and our practice: we talk incessantly about teams—and every study comes to the conclusion that the top management job does, indeed, require a team—yet we now practice, not only in American industry, the most extreme *personality cult of CEO supermen.* And no one seems to pay the slightest attention, in our present worship of these larger-than-life CEOs, to the question of how and by what process they are to be succeeded. Yet, succession has always been the ultimate test of any top management of any institution.

There is, in other words, an enormous amount of work to be done in organizational theory and organization practice—even though both are the oldest areas of organized work and organized practice in management.

The pioneers of management a century ago were right, *organizational structure is needed.* The modern enterprise—whether business, civil service, university, hospital, large church, or large military—needs organization, just as any biological organization beyond the amoeba needs structure. But the pioneers were wrong in their assumption that there is—or should be—one right organization. Just as there are a great number of different structures for biological organizations, so there are a number of organizations for the social organism that is the modern institution. Instead of searching for the right organization, management needs to learn to look for, to develop, to test: **The organization that fits the task.**

THE ONE RIGHT WAY TO MANAGE PEOPLE

In no other area are the basic traditional assumptions held as firmly—though mostly subconsciously—as in respect to people and their management. And in no other area are they so totally at odds with reality and so totally counterproductive.

There is one right way to manage people—or at least there should be. This assumption underlies practically every book or paper on the management of people. Its most quoted exposition is Douglas McGregor's book *The Human Side of Enterprise* (1960), which asserted that managements have to choose between two and only two different ways of managing people, "Theory X" and "Theory Y," and which then asserted that Theory Y is the only sound one. (A little earlier I had said pretty much the same thing in my 1954 book *The Practice of Management.*) A few years later, Abraham H. Maslow (1908–1970) showed in his *Eupsychian Management* (1965; new edition 1995, entitled *Maslow on Management*) that both McGregor and I were wrong. He showed conclusively that different people have to be managed differently.

I became an immediate convert—Maslow's evidence is overwhelming. But to date, very few people have paid much attention.

On this fundamental assumption that there is—or at least should be—one and only one right way to manage people rest all the other assumptions about people in organizations and their management.

One of these assumptions is that the people who work for an organization are employees of the organization, working full-time and dependent on the organization for their livelihood and their careers. Another such assumption is that the people who work for an organization are subordinates. Indeed, it is assumed that the great majority of these people have either no skill or low skills and do what they are being assigned to do.

Decades ago, when these assumptions were first formulated, during and at the end of World War I, they conformed closely enough to reality to be considered valid. Today every one of them has become untenable. The majority of people who work for an organization may still be *employees* of the organization. But a very large and steadily growing minority—though working for the organization—are no longer its employees, let alone its full-time employees (as was described in chapter 6). They work for an outsourcing contractor—for example, the outsourcing firm that provides maintenance in a hospital or a manufacturing plant, or the outsourcing firm that runs the data processing system for a government agency or a business. They are temps or part-timers. Increasingly, they are individual contractors working on a retainer or for a specific contractual period.

Even if employed full-time by the organization, fewer and fewer people are "subordinates"—even in fairly low-level jobs. Increasingly they are "knowledge workers." And knowledge workers are not *subordinates;* they are "associates." For, once beyond the apprentice stage, knowledge workers must know more about their job than their boss does—or else they are no good at all. In fact, that they know more about their job than anybody else in the organization is part of the definition of knowledge workers.

In addition, today superiors usually have not held the jobs their subordinates hold—as they did only a few short decades ago and as it is still widely assumed they do. A regimental commander in the army, only a few decades ago, had held every one of the jobs of his subordinates—battalion commander, company commander, platoon commander. The only difference in these respective jobs—between the lowly platoon commander and the lordly regimental commander—was in the number of people each commands; the work was exactly alike. To be sure, today's regimental commanders have commanded troops earlier in their careers—but often for only a short period. They have also advanced through captain and major. But for most of their careers they have held very different assignments—staff jobs, research jobs, teaching jobs, attached to an embassy abroad, and so on. They simply can no longer assume that they know what their subordinate, the captain in charge of a company, is doing or trying to do—they have been captains, of course, but they may have never commanded a company.

Similarly, the vice president of marketing may have come up the sales route. He or she knows a great deal about selling. But he or she knows nothing about market research, pricing, packaging, service, sales forecasting. The marketing vice president, therefore, cannot possibly tell the experts in the marketing department what they should be doing, or how. Yet these people are supposed to be the marketing vice president's subordinates—and the marketing vice president is definitely responsible for their performance and for their contribution to the company's marketing efforts.

The same is true for the hospital administrator or the hospital's medical director in respect to the trained knowledge workers in the clinical laboratory or in physical therapy.

To be sure, these associates are subordinates in that they depend on the boss when it comes to being hired or fired, promoted, appraised, and so on. But in his or her own job the superior can perform only if these so-called subordinates take responsibility for *educating him* or *her,* that is, for making the superior understand what market research or physical therapy can do and should be doing, and what *results* are in their respective areas. In turn, these "subordinates" depend on the superior for direction; they depend on the superior to tell them what the *score* is.

Their relationship, in other words, is far more like that between the conductor of an orchestra and the instrumentalist than it is like the traditional superior-subordinate relationship. The superior in an organization employing knowledge workers cannot, as a rule, do the work of the supposed subordinate any more than the conductor of an orchestra can play the tuba. In turn, the knowledge worker is dependent on the superior to give direction and, above all, to define what the score is for the entire organization—that is, what are the *standards* and *values, performance* and *results.* And just as an orchestra can sabotage even the ablest conductor—and certainly even the most autocratic one—a knowledge organization can easily sabotage even the ablest, let alone the most autocratic, superior.

Altogether, an increasing number of people who are full-time employees have to be managed as if they were volunteers. They are paid, to be sure. But knowledge workers have mobility. They can leave. They own their *means of production,* which is their knowledge. What motivates—and especially what motivates knowledge workers—is what motivates volunteers. Volunteers, we know, have to get more satisfaction from their work than paid employees, precisely because they do not get a paycheck. They need, above all, challenge. They need to know the organization's mission and to believe in it. They need continuous training. They need to see results.

Implicit in this is that different groups in the work population have to be managed differently, and that the same group in the work population has to be managed differently at different times. Increasingly, *employees* have to be managed as *part-*

ners—and it is the definition of a partnership that all partners are equal. It is also the definition of a partnership that partners cannot be ordered. They have to be persuaded. Increasingly, therefore, the management of people is a *marketing job*. And in marketing one does not begin with the question, "What do we want?" One begins with the question, "What does the other party want? What are its values? What are its goals? What does it consider results?" And this is neither "Theory X" nor "Theory Y," nor any other specific theory of managing people.

Maybe we will have to redefine the task altogether. It may not be "managing the work of people." The starting point, both in theory and in practice, may have to be "managing for performance." The starting point may be a definition of results—just as the starting points of both the orchestra conductor and the football coach are the *score*.

The *productivity* of the knowledge worker is likely to become the center of the management of people, just as the work on the productivity of the manual worker became the center of managing people a hundred years ago, that is, since Frederick W. Taylor. This will require, above all, very different assumptions about people in organizations and their work:

One does not "manage" people. The task is to lead people.

And the goal is to make productive the specific strengths and knowledge of each individual.

TECHNOLOGIES AND END-USERS ARE FIXED AND GIVEN

Four major assumptions, as said at the beginning of this chapter, have been underlying the *practice* of management all along—in fact, for much longer than there has been a *discipline* of management.

The assumptions about technology and end-users underlie, to a very large extent, the rise of modern business and of the modern economy altogether. They go back to the very early days of the Industrial Revolution. When the textile industry first developed, out of what had been cottage industries, it was assumed—and with complete validity—that the textile industry had its own unique technology. The same was true in respect to coal mining and any of the other industries that arose in the late eighteenth century and the first half of the nineteenth century. The first one to understand this and to base a major enterprise on it was also one of the first men to develop what we would today call a modern business, the German Werner Siemens (1816–1892). It led him, in 1869, to hire the first university-trained scientist to start a modern research lab—devoted exclusively to what we would now call electronics, and based on a clear understanding that electronics (in those days called "low-voltage") was distinct and separate from all other industries and had its distinct and separate technology.

Out of the insight that technologies and their end-uses are distinct, grew not only Siemens's own company with its own research lab, but also the German chemical industry, which assumed worldwide leadership because it based itself on the assumption that chemistry—and especially organic chemistry—had its own unique technology. Out of it then grew the other major leading companies the world over—the American electrical and chemical companies, the automobile companies, the telephone companies, and so on. Out of this insight also grew more of what may well be the most successful invention of the nineteenth century, the research laboratory—the last one, almost a century after Siemens's, the 1950 lab of IBM. At around the same time the research labs of the major pharmaceutical companies emerged as a worldwide industry after World War II.

By now, though, the assumptions underlying these successes have become untenable. The best example of this is in the pharmaceutical industry, which increasingly has come to depend on technologies that are fundamentally different from the technologies on which the pharmaceutical research lab is based: genetics, microbiology, molecular biology, medical electronics, and so on.

In the nineteenth century and throughout the first half of the twentieth century, it could be taken for granted that technologies outside one's own industry had no, or at least only minimal, impact on it. *Now the assumption to start with is that the technologies that are likely to have the greatest impact on a company and an industry are technologies outside its own field.*

The original assumption was, of course, that one's own research lab would and could produce everything the company—or the company's industry—needed. And, in turn, the assumption was that everything that this research lab produced would be used in and by the industry that it served.

Today's technologies, unlike the nineteenth-century technologies, no longer run in parallel. They constantly *crisscross,* as discussed briefly in chapter 6. Technology that people in their given industries have barely heard of (just as the people in the pharmaceutical industry had never heard of genetics, let alone medical electronics) revolutionizes those industries. Such outside technologies force industries to learn, to acquire, to adapt, to change their very mind-set, not to mention their technical knowledge.

A second assumption that was equally important to the rise of nineteenth- and twentieth-century industry and companies was: *End-uses are fixed and given.* For example, for the end-use of putting beer into containers, there is now extreme competition among various suppliers of containers. But at one time all of them were glass companies, and there was only one way of putting beer into containers—put it in a glass bottle. Fixed end-use was accepted as obvious, not only by business, industry, and the consumer, but by governments as well. The American regulation of business rests on the assumptions that to every industry there pertains a unique technology and that to every end-use there pertains a specific and unique product or service. These are the assumptions on which antitrust was based. And to this day antitrust law concerns itself with the domination of the market in glass bottles and pays little attention to the fact that beer increasingly is put not into glass bottles but into cans or plastic bottles.

But since World War II end-uses are no longer uniquely tied to a certain product or service. The plastics, of course, were the first major exception to the rule. But by now it is clear that it is not just one material moving in on what was considered the "turf" of another one. Increasingly, the same want is being satisfied by very different means. It is the want that is unique, and not the means to satisfy it.

As late as the beginning of World War II, dissemination of news was basically the monopoly of the printed newspaper—an eighteenth-century invention that saw its biggest growth in the early years of the twentieth century. Now there are many competing deliverers of news: the radio, the television, still the printed newspaper, increasingly the same newspaper delivered online through the Internet, separate news organizations that operate only electronically—(as is increasingly the case with economic and business news), and quite a few additional ones.

And then there is the new "basic resource" *information*. It differs radically from all other commodities in that it does not stand under the *scarcity* theorem. On the contrary, it stands under an *abundance* theorem. If I sell a thing—for example, a book—I no longer have the book. If I impart information, I still have it. And in fact, information becomes more valuable the more people have it. What this means for economics is well beyond the scope of this chapter, though it is clear that it will force us to radically revise basic economic theory. But it also means a good deal for management. Increasingly, basic assumptions will have to be changed. Information does not pertain exclusively to any industry or to any business. Information also does not have any one end-use, nor does any end-use require or depend upon one particular kind of information.

Therefore, management now has to start out with the assumption that there is no one technology that pertains to an industry and that, on the contrary, all technologies are capable—and indeed likely—to be of major importance to any industry and to have impact on any industry. Similarly, management has to start with the assumption that there is no one given end-use for any product or service and that, conversely, no end-use is going to be linked solely to any one product or service.

One implication of this is that increasingly the *noncustomers* of an enterprise—whether a business, a university, a church, a hospital—are as important as the customers, if not more important.

Even the biggest enterprise (other than a government monopoly) has many more noncustomers than it has customers. There are very few institutions that supply as large a percentage of a market as 30 percent. There are, therefore, few institutions where the noncustomers do not amount to at least 70 percent of the potential market. And yet very few institutions know anything about the noncustomers—very few of them even know that they exist, let alone know who they are. And even fewer know why they are not customers. Yet, it is with the noncustomers that changes always start.

The starting point has to be what customers consider value. The starting point has to be the assumption—an assumption amply proven by all our experience—that the customer never buys what the supplier sells. What is value to the customer is always something quite different from what is value or quality to the supplier. This applies as much to a business as to a university or to a hospital.

Management, in other words, will increasingly have to be based on the assumption that neither technology nor end-use is a foundation for management policy. They are limitations. The foundations have to be customer values and customer decisions on the distribution of their disposable income. It is with those that management policy and management strategy increasingly will have to start.

MANAGEMENT'S SCOPE IS LEGALLY DEFINED

Management, both in theory and in practice, deals with a legal entity, the individual enterprise—whether the business corporation, the hospital, the university, and so on. The scope of management is thus legally defined. This has been—and still is—the almost universal assumption.

One reason for this assumption is the traditional concept of management as being based on command and control. Command and control are indeed legally defined. The chief executive of a business, the bishop of a diocese, the administrator of a hospital, have no command-and-control authority beyond the legal confines of their institution.

Almost a hundred years ago it first became clear that the legal definition was not adequate to manage a major enterprise.

The Japanese are usually credited with the invention of the *keiretsu,* the management concept in which the suppliers to an enterprise are tied together with their main customer, for example, Toyota, for planning, product development, cost control, and so on. But actually the keiretsu is much older and an American invention. It goes back to around 1910 and to the man who first saw the potential of the automobile to become a major industry, William C. Durant (1861–1947). It was Durant who created General Motors by buying up small but successful automobile manufacturers such as Buick and merging them into one big automobile company. A few years later Durant then realized that he needed to bring the main suppliers into his corporation. He began to buy up and merge into General Motors one parts-and-accessories maker after the other, finishing in 1920 by buying Fisher

Body, the country's largest manufacturer of automobile bodies. With this purchase General Motors had come to own the manufacturers of 70 percent of everything that went into its automobiles—and had become by far the world's most integrated large business. It was this prototype keiretsu that gave General Motors the decisive advantage, both in cost and in speed, that made it within a few short years both the world's largest and the world's most profitable manufacturing company, and the unchallenged leader in an exceedingly competitive American automobile market. In fact, for some thirty-odd years, General Motors enjoyed a 30 percent cost advantage over all its competitors, including Ford and Chrysler.

But the Durant keiretsu was still based on the belief that management means command and control—this was the reason that Durant bought all the companies that became part of General Motors' keiretsu. And this eventually became the greatest weakness of GM. Durant had carefully planned to ensure the competitiveness of the GM-owned accessory suppliers. Each of them (except Fisher Body) had to sell 50 percent of its output outside of GM, that is, to competing automobile manufacturers, and thus had to maintain competitive costs and competitive quality. But after World War II the competing automobile-parts market disappeared— and with them the check on the competitiveness of GM's wholly owned accessory divisions. Also, with the unionization of the automobile industry, in 1936–1937, the high labor costs of automobile assembly plants were imposed on General Motors' accessory divisions, which put them at a cost disadvantage that, to this day, they have not been able to overcome. In other words, that Durant based his keiretsu on the assumption that management means command and control largely explains the decline of General Motors in the last twenty-five years and the company's inability to turn itself around.

This was clearly realized in the 1920s and 1930s by the builder of the next keiretsu, Sears, Roebuck. As Sears became America's largest retailer, especially of appliances and hardware, it too realized the necessity of bringing together its main suppliers into one group, so as to make possible joint planning, joint product development and product design, and cost control across the entire economic chain. But instead of buying these suppliers, Sears bought small minority stakes in them— more as a token of its commitment than as an investment—and based the relationship otherwise on contract. And the next keiretsu builder—and probably the most successful one so far (even more successful than the Japanese)—was Marks & Spencer in England, which, beginning in the early 1930s, integrated practically all its suppliers into its own management system, but exclusively through contracts, rather than through ownership stakes or ownership control.

It is the Marks & Spencer model that the Japanese, quite consciously, copied in the 1960s.

In every single case, beginning with General Motors, the keiretsu—that is, the integration, into one management system, of enterprises that are linked economically rather than controlled legally—has given a cost advantage of at least 25 percent and more often 30 percent. In every single case, it has given dominance in the industry and in the marketplace.

And yet the keiretsu is not enough. It is still based on power. Whether it is General Motors and the small, independent accessory companies that Durant bought between 1915 and 1920, or Sears, Roebuck, or Marks & Spencer, or Toyota—the central company has overwhelming economic power. *The keiretsu is not based on a partnership of equals. It is based on the dependence of the suppliers.*

Increasingly, however, the economic chain brings together genuine partners, that is, institutions in which there is equality of power and genuine independence. This is true of the partnership between a pharmaceutical company and the biology faculty of a major research university. This is true of the joint ventures through which American industry got into Japan after World War II. This is true of the partnerships today between chemical or pharmaceutical companies and companies in genetics, molecular biology, or medical electronics.

These companies in the new technologies may be quite small—and very often are—and badly in need of capital. But they own independent technology. Therefore, they are the senior partners when it comes to technology. They, rather than the much bigger pharmaceutical or chemical company, have a choice about whom to ally themselves with. The same is largely true in information technology, and also in finance. Then, neither the traditional keiretsu nor command and control work.

What is needed, therefore, is a redefinition of the scope of management. *Management has to encompass the entire process.* For business, this by and large means the economic process.

The new assumption on which management, both as a discipline and as a practice, will increasingly have to base itself is that the scope of management is not legal. It has to be operational. It has to embrace the entire process. It has to be focused on results and performance across the entire economic chain.

MANAGEMENT'S SCOPE IS POLITICALLY DEFINED

It is still generally assumed in the discipline of management—and very largely still taken for granted in the practice of management—that the domestic economy, as defined by national boundaries, is the ecology of enterprise and management—and of nonbusinesses as much as of businesses.

This assumption underlies the traditional "multinational." As is well known, before World War I, as large a share of the world's production of manufactured goods and of financial services was multinational as it is now. The 1913 leading company in any industry, whether in manufacturing or in finance, derived as large a share of its sales from selling outside its own country as it did by selling inside its own country. But insofar as it produced outside its own national boundaries, it produced within the national boundaries of another country.

One example of this was Fiat. The largest supplier of war materiel to the Italian army during World War I was a young but rapidly growing company in Turin called Fiat—it made all the automobiles and trucks for the Italian army. The largest supplier of war materiel to the Austo-Hungarian army in World War I was also a company called Fiat—in Vienna. It supplied all the automobiles and trucks to the Austro-Hungarian army. It was two to three times the size of its parent company. For Austria-Hungary was a much larger market than Italy, partly because it had a much larger population, and partly because it was more highly developed, especially in its western parts. Fiat-Austria was wholly owned by Flat-Italy. But except for the designs that came from Italy, Fiat-Austria was a separate company. Everything it used was made or bought in Austria. All products were sold in Austria. And every employee up to and including the CEO was an Austrian. When World War I came, and Austria and Italy became enemies, all the Austrians had had to do, therefore, was change the bank account of Fiat-Austria—it kept on working as it had all along.

Even traditional industries like the automotive industry or insurance are no longer organized that way.

Post–World War II industries such as the pharmaceutical industry or the information industries are increasingly not even organized in "domestic" and "international" units, as GM and Allianz, the global financial services company, still are. They are run as a worldwide system in which individual tasks—whether research, design, engineering, development, testing, or, increasingly, manufacturing and marketing—are each organized *transnationally.*

One large pharmaceutical company has seven labs in seven different countries, each focusing on one major area (e.g., antibiotics) but all run as one "research department" and all reporting to the same research director in headquarters. The same company has manufacturing plants in eleven countries, each highly specialized and producing one or two major product groups for worldwide distribution and sale. It has one medical director who decides in which of five or six countries a new drug is to be tested. But managing the company's foreign exchange exposure is totally centralized in one location for the entire system.

In the traditional multinational, economic reality and political reality were congruent. The country was the "business unit," to use today's term. In today's transnational—but also, increasingly, in the old multinationals, as they are forced to transform themselves—the country is only a cost center. It is a complication rather than the unit for organization or the unit of business, of strategy, of production, and so on. Management and national boundaries are no longer congruent. The scope of management can no longer be politically defined. National boundaries will continue to be important. But the new assumption has to be:

National boundaries are important primarily as restraints. The practice of management—and by no means for businesses only—will increasingly have to be defined operationally rather than politically.

THE INSIDE IS MANAGEMENT'S DOMAIN

All the traditional assumptions led to one conclusion: The inside of the organization is the domain of management.

This assumption explains the otherwise totally incomprehensible distinction between management and entrepreneurship.

In actual practice, this distinction makes no sense whatever. An enterprise, whether a business or any other institution, that does not innovate and does not engage in entrepreneurship will not survive long.

It should have been obvious from the beginning that management and entrepreneurship are only two different dimensions of the same task. An entrepreneur who does not learn how to manage will not last long. A management that does not learn to innovate will not last long. In fact, as chapter 8 argues in detail, business—and every other organization today—has to be designed for change as the norm and has to create change rather than just react to it.

But entrepreneurial activities start with the *Outside* and are focused on the *outside*. They therefore do not fit within the traditional assumptions of management's domain—which explains why the two activities have so commonly come to be regarded as different, if not incompatible. Any organization, however, that actually believes that management and entrepreneurship are different, not to mention incompatible, will soon find itself out of business.

The inward focus of management has been greatly aggravated in the last decades by the rise of information technology. Information technology may, so far, have actually done more damage to management than helped it, as is discussed in greater depth in chapter 33.

The traditional assumption that the inside of the organization is the domain of management includes the idea that management concerns itself with efforts, if not costs only. For effort is the only thing that exists within an organization. And, similarly, everything inside an organization is a cost center.

But the results of any institution exist only on the outside.

It is understandable that management *began* as a concern for the inside of the organization. When the large organizations first arose—with the business enterprise, around 1870, being the first and by far the most visible one—managing the inside was the new challenge. Nobody had ever done it before. But while the assumption that management's domain is the inside of the organization originally made sense—or can at least be explained—its continuation makes no sense whatever. It contradicts the very function and nature of organization.

Management must focus on the results and performance of the organization. Indeed, the first task of management is to *define what results and performance are in a given organization*—and this, as anyone who has worked on this task can testify, is in itself one of the most difficult, one of the most controversial, but also one of the most important tasks. It is, therefore, the specific function of management to organize the resources of the organization *for results outside the organization.*

The new assumption—and the basis for the new paradigm on which management, both as a discipline and as a practice has to be based—is therefore:

Management exists for the sake of the institution's results. It has to start with the intended results and has to organize the resources of the institution to attain these results. It is the organ to make the institution—whether business, church, university, hospital, or a battered women's shelter—capable of producing results outside of it.

This chapter has not tried to give answers—intentionally so. It has tried to raise questions and to pull together various strains from earlier chapters into six new paradigms for management. But underlying all of these is one insight: *Management is the specific tool, the specific function, the specific instrument, to make institutions capable of producing results.*

This, however, requires a *final* new management paradigm:

Management's concern and management's responsibility are everything that affects the performance of the institution and its results—whether inside or outside, whether under the institution's control or totally beyond it.

SUMMARY

Prevailing assumptions about the realities of management determine what scholars, teachers, and executives assume to be reality. This chapter challenges three assumptions underlying the *discipline* of management: management is *business* management, there is one right organization, and there is one right way to manage people. Also challenged are four assumptions underlying the *practice* of management: technologies and end-users are fixed and given, management's scope is legally defined, and the inside is management's domain.

The new paradigms that supersede the three *disciplinary* assumptions of management are

1. Management is the specific and distinguishing organ of any and all organizations.

2. Management must look for the organization that fits the task.

3. One does not "manage" people. The task is to lead people and make productive the specific strengths and knowledge of each individual.

The new paradigms that supersede the four *practice* assumptions of management are

1. Neither technology nor end-use of a product is the correct foundation for management policy. Management must start with customer values and customer decisions as the basis for its strategy.

2. The scope of management is not legal; it is operational, covering the entire economic chain.

3. The practice of management will have to be defined operationally rather than by political boundaries.

4. Finally, the results of any institution exist only on the outside.

Part II

Business Performance

We do not yet have an integrated *discipline of business management*. But we know what a business is and what its key functions are. We understand the functions of profit and the requirements of productivity. Any business needs to think through the question, *What is our business and what should it be?* From the definition of its mission and purpose, a business must derive objectives in a number of key areas, and it must balance these objectives against each other and against the competing demands of today and tomorrow. A business needs to convert objectives into concrete strategies and to concentrate resources on them. Finally, it needs to think through its strategic planning, the decisions of today that will make the business of tomorrow.

8

The Theory of the Business

Not in a very long time—not, perhaps, since the late 1940s or early 1950s—have there been as many new major management techniques as there are today: downsizing, outsourcing, total quality management, six-sigma, activity-based costing, economic value analysis, benchmarking, reengineering. Each is a powerful tool. But, with the exceptions of outsourcing and reengineering, these tools are designed primarily to do differently what is already being done. They are "how to do" tools.

Yet *"what* to do" is increasingly becoming the central challenge facing managements, especially those of big companies that have enjoyed long-term success. The story is a familiar one: a company that was a superstar only yesterday finds itself stagnating and frustrated, in trouble, and, often, in a seemingly unmanageable crisis. This phenomenon is by no means confined to the United States. It has become common in Japan and Germany, the Netherlands and France, Italy and Sweden. And it occurs just as often outside business—in labor unions, government agencies, hospitals, museums, and churches. In fact, the phenomenon seems even less tractable in those areas.

The root cause of nearly every one of these crises is not that things are being done poorly. It is not even that the wrong things are being done. Indeed, in most cases, the right things are being done—but fruitlessly. What accounts for this apparent paradox? *The assumptions on which the organization has been built and is being run no longer fit reality.* These are the assumptions that shape any organization's behavior, dictate its decisions about what to do and what not to do, and define what the organization considers meaningful results. These assumptions are about markets. They are about identifying customers and competitors, their values and behavior. They are about technology and its dynamics, about a company's strengths and weaknesses. These assumptions are about what a company gets paid for. They are what I call a company's *theory of the business.*

Every organization, whether a business enterprise or not, has a theory of the business. Indeed, a valid theory that is clear, consistent, and focused is extraordinarily powerful. The theory of the business explains both the past successes of companies like General Motors and IBM, which dominated the U.S. economy for the latter half of the twentieth century, and the challenges they have faced since. In fact, what underlies the current malaise of so many large and successful organizations worldwide is that their theory of the business no longer works.

IBM AGILITY

Whenever a big organization gets into trouble—and especially if it has been successful for many years—people blame sluggishness, complacency, arrogance, mammoth bureaucracies. Plausible explanations? Yes. But rarely the relevant ones or correct. Consider the two most visible and widely reviled bureaucracies among large U.S. companies that have recently experienced trouble.

Since the earliest days of the computer, it had been an article of faith at IBM that the computer would go the way of electricity. The future, IBM knew, and could prove with scientific rigor, lay with the central station, the ever-more-powerful mainframe into which a huge number of users could plug. Everything—economics, the logic of information, technology—led to that conclusion. But then, suddenly, when it seemed as if such a central-station, mainframe-based information system was actually coming into existence, two young men came up with the first commercial personal computer. Every computer maker knew that the PC was absurd. It did not have the memory, the database, the speed, or the computing ability necessary to succeed. Indeed, every computer maker knew that the PC had to fail—a conclusion reached by Xerox only a few years earlier, when its research team had actually built the first PC. But when that misbegotten monstrosity—first the Apple, then the Macintosh— came on the market, people not only loved it, they bought it.

Every big, successful company throughout history, when confronted with such a surprise, has refused to accept it. Most mainframe makers responded in the same way. The list was long: Control Data, Univac, Burroughs, and NCR in the United States; Siemens, Nixdorf, Machines Bull, and ICL in Europe; Hitachi and Fujitsu in Japan. IBM—the overlord of mainframes, with as much in sales as all the other computer makers put together and with record profits—could have reacted in the same way. In fact, it *should* have. Instead, IBM immediately accepted the PC as the new reality. Almost overnight, it brushed aside all its proven and time-tested policies, rules, and regulations and set up not one but two competing teams to design an even simpler PC. A couple of years later, IBM had become the world's largest PC manufacturer and the industry standard setter.

There is absolutely no precedent for this achievement in all of business history; it hardly argues bureaucracy, sluggishness, or arrogance. Yet despite this unprecedented flexibility, agility, and humility, IBM was floundering a few years later in both the mainframe and the PC businesses. It was suddenly unable to move, to take decisive action, to change.

GM HAD STRENGTH

The case of GM is equally perplexing. In the early 1980s—the very years in which GM's main business, passenger automobiles, seemed almost paralyzed—the company acquired two large businesses: Hughes Electronics and Ross Perot's Electronic Data Systems. Analysts generally considered both companies to be mature and chided GM for grossly overpaying for them. Yet, within a few short years, GM had more than tripled the revenues and profits of the allegedly mature EDS. And ten years later, in 1994, EDS had a market value six times the amount that GM had paid for it and ten times its original revenues and profits.

Similarly, GM bought Hughes Electronics—a huge but profitless company involved exclusively in defense—just before the defense industry collapsed. Under GM management, Hughes actually increased its defense profits and became one of the few big defense contractors to move successfully into large-scale nondefense work. Remarkably, the same finance-oriented people who had been so ineffectual in the automobile business—thirty-year GM veterans who had never worked for any other company or, for that matter, outside of finance and accounting departments—were the ones who achieved these startling results. And in the two acquisitions, they simply applied policies, practices, and procedures that had already been used by GM.

This story is a familiar one at GM. Since the company's founding in a flurry of acquisitions in 1908, one of its core competencies has been to overpay for well-performing but mature businesses—as it did for Buick, AC Spark Plug, and Fisher Body in those early years—and then turn them into world-class champions. Very few companies have been able to match GM's performance in making successful acquisitions, and GM surely did not accomplish these feats by being bureaucratic, sluggish, or arrogant. Yet what worked so beautifully in those businesses that GM knew nothing about failed miserably in GM itself.

PARALYZED IBM

What can explain the fact that at both IBM and GM the policies, practices, and behaviors that worked for decades—and in the case of GM, are still working well when applied to something new and different—no longer work for the organization in which and for which they were developed? The realities that each organization actually faces today are quite dramatically different from those that each still assumes it lives with. Put another way, reality has changed, but the theory of the business has not changed with it.

Mainframe computers and PCs are no more one entity, in fact, than are electric generating stations and electric toasters. The latter, while different, are interdependent and complementary. In contrast, mainframe computers and PCs are primarily competitors. And in their basic definition of information, they actually contradict each other: for the mainframe, information means memory; for the PC, it means software. Building generating stations and making toasters must be run as separate businesses, but they can be owned by the same corporate entity, as General Electric did for decades. This was not the case for IBM.

IBM tried to combine mainframe computers and PCs. But because the PC was the fastest-growing part of the business, IBM could not subordinate it to the mainframe business while simultaneously competing successfully in the PC market. And because the mainframe was still the cash cow, IBM could not divest it in order to capture a leadership position in the PC market.

In the end, IBM shifted its strategy to one of providing information solutions and accepted the premise that "over time, the information technology industry would be service-led, not technology-led."*

PATCHING GM

GM had an even more powerful, and successful, theory of the business than IBM had, one that made GM the world's largest and most profitable manufacturing organization. The company did not have one setback in seventy years—a record unmatched in business history. GM's theory combined in one seamless web assumptions about markets and customers with assumptions about core competencies and organizational structure.

Since the early 1920s, GM assumed that the U.S. automobile market was homogeneous in its values and segmented by extremely stable income groups. The resale value of the "good" used car was the only independent variable under management's control. High trade-in values enabled customers to upgrade their new-car purchases to the next category—in other words, to cars with higher profit margins. According to this theory, frequent or radical changes in models could only depress trade-in values.

Internally, these market assumptions went hand in hand with assumptions about how production should be organized to yield the biggest market share and the highest profit. In GM's case, the answer was long runs of mass-produced cars with a minimum of changes each model year, resulting in the largest number of uniform yearly models on the market at the lowest fixed cost per car.

GM's management then translated these assumptions about market and production into a structure of semiautonomous divisions, each focusing on one income segment and each arranged so that its highest-priced model overlapped with the next division's lowest-priced model, thus almost forcing people to trade up, provided that used-car prices were high.

* Louis V. Gerstner, Jr. *Who Says Elephants Can't Dance?* HarperBusiness, New York, 2002, p. 123.

For seventy years, this theory worked like a charm. Even in the depths of the Depression, GM never suffered a loss while steadily gaining market share. But in the late 1970s, its assumptions about the market and about production became invalid. The market was fragmenting into highly volatile "lifestyle" segments. Income became one factor among many in the buying decision, not the only one. At the same time, *lean manufacturing* created an *economics of small scale*. It made short runs and variations in models less costly and more profitable than long runs of uniform products.

GM knew all this but simply could not believe it. (GM's union still doesn't.) Instead, the company tried to patch things over. It maintained the existing divisions based on income segmentation, but each division now offered a "car for every purse." It tried to compete with lean manufacturing's economics of small scale by automating the large-scale, long-run mass production (losing billions in the process). Contrary to popular belief, GM patched things over with prodigious energy, hard work, and lavish investments of time and money. But patching only confused the customer, the dealer, and the employees and management of GM itself. In the meantime, GM neglected its real growth market, where it had leadership and would have been almost unbeatable: light trucks and minivans.

THE THREE ASSUMPTIONS

A theory of the business has three parts. First, there are assumptions about the *environment of the organization:* society and its structure, the market, the customer, and technology.

Second, there are assumptions about the *specific mission of the organization.* Sears, Roebuck and Company, in the years during and following World War I, defined its mission for itself as being the informed buyer for the American family. A decade later, Marks & Spencer in Great Britain defined its mission as being the change agent in British society by becoming the first classless retailer. AT&T, again in the years during and immediately after World War I, defined its role as ensuring that every U.S. family and business have access to a telephone. An organization's mission need not be so ambitious. GM envisioned a far more modest role—as the leader in "terrestrial motorized transportation equipment," in the words of Alfred P. Sloan, Jr.

Third, there are assumptions about the *core competencies* needed to accomplish the organization's mission. For example, West Point, founded in 1802, defined its core competence as the ability to turn out leaders who deserve trust. Marks & Spencer, around 1930, defined its core competence as the ability to identify, design, and develop the merchandise it sold, instead of as the ability to buy. AT&T, around 1920, defined its core competence as technical leadership that would enable the company to improve service continuously while steadily lowering rates.

The assumptions about environment define what an organization is paid for. The assumptions about mission define what an organization considers to be meaningful results; in other words, they point to how it envisions itself making a difference in the economy and in the society at large. Finally, the assumptions about core competencies define where an organization must excel in order to maintain leadership.

Of course, all this sounds deceptively simple. It usually takes years of hard work, thinking, and experimenting to reach a clear, consistent, and valid theory of the business. Yet to be successful, every organization must work one out.

What are the specifications of a valid theory of the business? There are four.

THE FOUR SPECIFICATIONS

1. *The assumptions about environment, mission, and core competencies must fit reality.* When four penniless young men from Manchester, England, Simon Marks and his three brothers-in-law, decided in the early 1920s that a humdrum penny bazaar should become an agent of social change, World War I had profoundly shaken their country's class structure. It had also created masses of new buyers for good-quality, stylish, but cheap merchandise like lingerie, blouses, and stockings—Marks & Spencer's first successful product categories. Marks & Spencer then systematically set to work developing brand-new and unheard-of core competencies. Until then, the core competence of a merchant was the ability to buy well. Marks & Spencer decided that it was the *merchant, rather than the manufacturer, who knew the customer.* Therefore, the merchant, not the manufacturer, should design the products, develop them, and find producers to make the goods to his design, specifications, and costs. This new definition of the merchant took five to eight years to develop and make acceptable to traditional suppliers, who had always seen themselves as "manufacturers," not "subcontractors."

2. *The assumptions in all three areas have to fit one another.* This was perhaps GM's greatest strength in the long decades of its ascendancy. Its assumptions about the market and about the optimum manufacturing process were a perfect fit. GM decided in the mid-1920s that it also required new and as-yet-unheard-of core competencies: financial control of the manufacturing process and a theory of capital allocations. As a result, GM invented modern cost accounting and the first rational capital-allocation process.

3. *The theory of the business must be known and understood throughout the organization.* That is easy in an organization's early days. But as it becomes successful, an organization tends increasingly to take its theory for granted, becoming less and less conscious of it. Then the organization becomes sloppy. It begins to cut corners. It begins to pursue what is expedient rather than what is right. It stops thinking. It stops questioning. It remembers the answers but has forgotten the questions. The

theory of the business becomes "culture." But culture is no substitute for discipline, and the theory of the business is a discipline.

4. *The theory of the business has to be tested constantly.* It is not graven on tablets of stone. It is a hypothesis. And it is a hypothesis about things that are in constant flux—society, markets, customers, technology. And so, built into the theory of the business must be the ability to change itself.

PREVENTIVE CARE

Some theories of the business are so powerful that they last for a long time. But being human artifacts, they don't last forever, and indeed, today they rarely last for very long at all. Eventually every theory of the business becomes obsolete and then invalid. That is precisely what happened to those on which the great U.S. businesses of the 1920s were built. It happened to the GMs and the AT&Ts. It has happened to IBM. It is clearly happening today to Deutsche Bank and its theory of the universal bank. It is also clearly happening to the rapidly unraveling Japanese keiretsu.

The first reaction of an organization whose theory is becoming obsolete is almost always a defensive one. The tendency is to put one's head in the sand and pretend that nothing is happening. The next reaction is an attempt to patch, as GM did in the early 1980s or as Deutsche Bank is doing today. Indeed, the sudden and completely unexpected crisis of one big German company after another of which Deutsche Bank is the "house bank" indicates that its theory no longer works. That is, Deutsche Bank no longer does what it was designed to do: provide effective governance of the modern corporation.

But patching never works. Instead, when a theory shows the first signs of becoming obsolete, it is time to start thinking again, to ask again which assumptions about the environment, mission, and core competencies reflect reality most accurately—with the clear premise that our historically transmitted assumptions, those with which all of us grew up, no longer suffice.

What, then, needs to be done? There is a need for preventive care—that is, for building into the organization systematic monitoring and testing of its theory of the business. There is a need for early diagnosis. Finally, there is a need to rethink a theory that is stagnating and to take effective action in order to change policies and practices, bringing the organization's behavior in line with the new realities of its environment, with a new definition of its mission and with new core competencies to be developed and acquired.

There are only two preventive measures. But, if used consistently, they should keep an organization alert and capable of rapidly changing itself and its theory. The first measure is *abandonment*. Every three years, an organization should challenge every product, every service, every policy, every distribution channel with the question, *If we were not in it already, would we be going into it now?* By questioning accepted policies and routines, the organization forces itself to think about its theory. It forces itself to test assumptions. It forces itself to ask, Why didn't this work, even though it looked so promising when we went into it five years ago? Is it because we made mistakes? Is it because we did the wrong things? Or is it because the right things didn't work?

Without systematic and purposeful abandonment, an organization will be overtaken by events. It will squander its best resources on things it should never have been doing or should no longer do. As a result, it will lack the resources, especially capable people, needed to exploit the opportunities that arise when markets, technologies, and core competencies change. In other words, it will be unable to respond constructively to the opportunities that are created when its theory of the business becomes obsolete.

The failure to incorporate preventative care—to follow and continually update their theory of the business—led Marks & Spencer to become vulnerable to a takeover bid, one which the company did successfully defeat. Marks & Spencer had so completely moved into complacency and away from what made them successful that the business itself was threatened, both internally and by competitive pressures. It took this threat for the company to refocus on the customer, on providing quality, value, service, innovation, and trust. It took near-failure to reinvest themselves in their people, to shift from their former reliance on outside consultants and on a demoralizing strategy-hopping approach. To regain their focus, they had to evaluate all aspects of their theory of the business and incorporate systematic abandonment (for a complete account see "Back in Fashion: How We're Reviving a British Icon" *Harvard Business Review,* May 2007).

The second preventive measure is to study what goes on outside the business, and especially to study *noncustomers.* Walk-around management became fashionable a few years back. It is important. And so is knowing as much as possible about one's customers—the area, perhaps, where information technology is making the most rapid advances. But the first signs of fundamental change rarely appear within one's own organization or among one's own customers. Almost always they show up first among one's noncustomers. Noncustomers always outnumber customers. Wal-Mart, today's retail giant, has 20 percent of the U.S. consumer-goods market. That means 80 percent of the market is noncustomers.

In fact, the best recent example of the importance of the noncustomer is U.S. department stores. At their peak over thirty years ago, department stores served 30 percent of the U.S. nonfood retail market. They questioned their customers constantly, studied them, and surveyed them. But they paid no attention to the 70 percent of the market who were not their customers. They saw no reason why they should. Their theory of the business assumed that most people who could afford to shop in department stores did. Sixty years ago, that assumption fit reality. But when the baby boomers came of age, it ceased to be valid. For the dominant group among baby boomers—women in educated two-income families—it was not money that determined where to shop. Time was the primary factor, and this generation's women could not afford to spend their time shopping in department stores.

Today the department stores' prototypical customer has a paying job, if not a career. She has many occasions to choose or to make decisions, most of which are more interesting than what to cook for dinner. And even if she never leaves the house, she has unlimited access to the outside world through the telephone and computer screen. Shopping is no longer a satisfaction to her. It's a chore.

Because department stores looked only at their own customers, they did not recognize this change until a few years ago. By then, business was already drying up. And it was too late to get the baby boomers back. The department stores learned the hard way that although being customer driven is vital, it is not enough. An organization must be market driven too.

THE WARNING SIGNS

To diagnose problems early, managers must pay attention to the warning signs. A theory of the business always becomes obsolete when an organization *attains its original objectives*. Attaining one's objectives, then, is not cause for celebration; it is cause for new thinking. By the mid-1950s, AT&T accomplished its mission to give every U.S. family and business access to the telephone. Some executives then said it was time to reassess the theory of the business and, for instance, separate local service—where the objectives had been reached—from growing and future businesses, beginning with long-distance service and extending into global telecommunications. Their arguments went unheeded, and a few years later AT&T began to flounder, only to be rescued by an antitrust settlement, which did by fiat what the company's management had refused to do voluntarily.

Rapid growth is another sure sign of crisis in an organization's theory. Any organization that doubles or triples in size within a fairly short period of time has necessarily outgrown its theory. Even Silicon Valley has learned that beer bashes are no longer adequate for communication once a company has grown so big that people have to wear name tags. But such growth challenges much deeper assumptions, policies, and habits. To continue in health, let alone grow, the organization has to again ask itself the questions about its environment, mission, and core competencies.

There are two more clear signals that an organization's theory of the business is no longer valid. One is unexpected success—whether one's own or a competitor's. The other is unexpected failure—again, whether one's own or a competitor's.

At the same time that Japanese automobile imports had Detroit's Big Three on the ropes, Chrysler registered a totally unexpected success. Its traditional passenger cars were losing market share even faster than GM's and Ford's were. But sales of its Jeep and its new minivans—an almost accidental development—skyrocketed. At the time, GM was the leader of the U.S. light-truck market and unchallenged in the design and quality of its products, but it wasn't paying attention to its light-truck capacity. After all, minivans and light trucks had always been classified as commercial rather than passenger vehicles in traditional statistics, even though most of them are now being bought as passenger vehicles. However, had it paid attention to the success of its weaker competitor, Chrysler, GM might have realized much earlier that its assumptions about both its market and its core competencies were no longer valid. From the beginning, the minivan and light-truck market was not an income-class market and was little influenced by trade-in prices. And, paradoxically, light trucks were the one area in which GM, twenty-five years ago, had already moved quite far toward what we now call lean manufacturing.

Unexpected failure is as much a warning as unexpected success and should be taken as seriously as a sixty-year-old man's first "minor" heart attack. Seventy years ago, in the midst of the Depression, Sears decided that automobile insurance had become an "accessory" rather than a financial product and that selling it would therefore fit its mission of being the informed buyer for the American family. Everyone thought Sears was crazy. But automobile insurance became Sears's most profitable business almost instantly. Twenty years later, in the 1950s, Sears decided that diamond rings had become a necessity rather than a luxury, and the company became the world's largest—and probably most profitable—diamond retailer. It was only logical for Sears to decide in 1981 that investment products had become consumer goods for the American family. It bought Dean Witter and moved its offices into Sears's stores. The move was a total disaster. The U.S. public clearly did not consider its financial needs to be "consumer products." When Sears finally gave up and decided to run Dean Witter as a separate business outside Sears stores, Dean Witter at once began to blossom. In 1992, Sears sold it at a tidy profit.

Had Sears seen its failure to become the American family's supplier of investments as a failure of its theory and not as an isolated incident, it might have begun to restructure and reposition itself ten years earlier than it actually did, when it still had substantial market leadership. For Sears might then have seen that the Dean Witter failure threw into doubt the entire concept of market homogeneity—the very concept on which Sears and other mass retailers had based their strategy for years.

DECISIVE ACTION

Traditionally, we have searched for the miracle worker with a magic wand to turn an ailing organization around. To establish, maintain, and restore a theory, however, does not require a Genghis Khan or a Leonardo da Vinci in the executive suite. What is required is not genius; it is hard work. It is not being clever; it is being conscientious. It is what CEOs are paid for.

There are, indeed, quite a few CEOs who have successfully changed their theory of the business. The CEO who built Merck into the world's most successful pharmaceutical business by focusing solely on the research and development of patented, high-margin breakthrough drugs radically changed the company's theory by acquiring a large distributor of generic and nonprescription drugs. He did so without a "crisis," while Merck was ostensibly doing very well. Similarly, a few years ago, the new CEO of Sony, the world's best-known manufacturer of consumer electronic hardware, changed the company's theory of the business. He acquired a Hollywood movie-production company and, with that acquisition, shifted the organization's center of gravity from being a hardware manufacturer in search of software to being a software producer that creates a market demand for hardware.

But for every one of these apparent miracle workers, there are scores of equally capable CEOs whose organizations stumble. We can't rely on miracle workers to rejuvenate an obsolete theory of the business any more than we can rely on them to cure other types of serious illness. And when one talks to these supposed miracle workers, they deny vehemently that they act by charisma, vision, or, for that matter, the laying on of hands. They start out with diagnosis and analysis. They accept that attaining objectives and rapid growth demand a serious rethinking of the theory of the business. They do not dismiss unexpected failure as being the result of a subordinate's incompetence or as an accident but treat it as a symptom of "systems failure." They do not take credit for unexpected success but treat it as a challenge to their assumptions.

They accept that a theory's obsolescence is a degenerative and, indeed, life-threatening disease. And they know and accept the surgeon's time-tested principle, the oldest principle of effective decision making: a degenerative disease will not be cured by procrastination. It requires decisive action.

SUMMARY

A theory of the business has three parts:

1. Assumptions about the environment of the organization. These define what the organization expects it can be paid for.

2. Assumptions about the specific mission of the organization. These define how the organization intends to make a difference in society and what results are meaningful.

3. Assumptions about the core competencies needed to accomplish the mis-

sion. These define in which areas the organization must excel in order to achieve its mission.

These three assumptions must fit *one another* and *reality*. The theory of the business must be understood throughout the organization.

When an organization takes its theory for granted, it stops thinking and questioning the very premises of its existence. And every theory eventually becomes obsolete. Without systematic abandonment, an organization will squander its scarce resources on what it should not do and deprive itself of resources it needs to exploit opportunities.

One of the most effective ways to test the validity of a theory is to study the behavior of noncustomers.

9

The Purpose and Objectives of a Business

Asked what a business is, the typical businessman is likely to answer, "An organization to make a profit." The typical economist is likely to give the same answer, "to maximize profits." This answer is not only false, it is irrelevant.

The danger in the concept of profit maximization is that it makes profitability appear to be a myth. Profit and profitability are, however, crucial—for society even more than for the individual business. Yet profitability is, not the purpose of, but a limiting factor on business enterprise and business activity. Profit is not the explanation, cause, or rationale of business behavior and business decisions, but the test of their validity. If archangels instead of businessmen sat in directors' chairs, they would still have to be concerned with profitability, despite their total lack of personal interest in making profits.

The root of the confusion is the mistaken belief that the motive of a person—the so-called profit motive of the executive—is an explanation of his behavior or his guide to right action. Whether there is such a thing as a profit motive at all is highly doubtful. It was invented by the classical economists to explain the economic reality that their theory of static equilibrium could not explain. There has never been any evidence for the existence of the profit motive. We have long since found the true explanation for the phenomena of economic change and growth that the profit motive was first put forth to explain.

It is irrelevant for an understanding of business behavior, profit, and profitability whether there is a profit motive or not. That Jim Smith is in business to make a profit concerns only him and the Recording Angel. *It does not tell us what Jim Smith does and how he performs.* We do not learn anything about the work of a prospector hunting for uranium in the Nevada desert by being told that he is trying to make his fortune. We do not learn anything about the work of a heart specialist by being told that he is trying to make a livelihood, or even that he is trying to benefit humanity. The profit motive and its offspring maximization of profits are just as irrelevant to the function of a business, the purpose of a business, and the job of managing a business.

In fact, the concept is worse than irrelevant: it does harm. It is a major cause for the misunderstanding of the nature of profit in our society and for hostility to profit, which are among the most dangerous diseases of a society or organizations. It is largely responsible for the worst mistakes of public policy—in this country as well as in Western Europe—which are squarely based on the failure to understand the nature, function, and purpose of business enterprise. And it is in large part responsible for the prevailing belief that there is an inherent contradiction between profit and a company's ability to make a social contribution. Actually, a company can make a social contribution only if it is highly profitable.

To know what a business is, we have to start with its *purpose*. Its purpose must lie outside of the business itself. In fact, it must lie in society, since business enterprise is an organ of society. There is only one valid definition of business purpose: *to create a customer.*

Markets are not created by God, nature, or economic forces but by executives. The want a business satisfies may have been felt by the customer before he was offered the means of satisfying it. Like food in a famine, it may have dominated the customer's life and filled all his waking moments, but it remained a potential want until the action of businessmen converted it into effective demand. Only then is there a customer and a market. The want may have been unfelt by the potential customer; no one knew that he wanted a photocopier or a computer until these became available. There may have been no want at all until business action created it—by innovation, by credit, by advertising, or by salesmanship. In every case, it is business action that creates the customer.

It is the customer who determines what a business is. It is the customer alone whose willingness to pay for a good or for a service converts economic resources into wealth, things into goods. What the customer buys and considers value is never a product. It is always utility, that is, what a product or a service does for him.

THE PURPOSE OF A BUSINESS

Because its purpose is to create a customer, the business enterprise has two—and only these two—basic functions: *marketing* and *innovation*.

Despite the emphasis on marketing and the marketing approach, marketing is still rhetoric rather than reality in far too many businesses. *Consumerism* proves this. For what consumerism demands of business is that it actually market. It demands that business start out with the needs, the realities, the values of the customer. It demands that business define its goal as the satisfaction of customer needs. It demands that business base its reward on its contribution to the customer.

But consumerism is also the opportunity for organizations to adopt a customer focus through marketing. It forces businesses to become market-focused in their actions as well as in their pronouncements.

Above all, consumerism should dispel the confusion which largely explains why there has been so little real marketing. When managers speak of marketing, they usually mean the organized performance of all *selling* functions. This is still selling. It still starts out with "our products." It still looks for "our market." True marketing starts out the way Marks & Spencer starts out, with the customer, his demographics, his realities, his needs, his values. It does not ask, "What do we want to sell?" It asks, "What does the customer want to buy?" It does not say, "This is what our product or service does." It says, "These are the satisfactions the customer looks for, values and needs.

Indeed, selling and marketing are antithetical rather than synonymous or even complementary.

There will always be, one can assume, a need for some selling. But the aim of marketing is to make selling superfluous. *The aim of marketing is to know and understand the customer so well that the product or service fits him and sells itself.*

Marketing alone does not make a business enterprise. In a static economy, there are no business enterprises. There are not even executives. The middleman of a static society is a broker who receives his compensation in the form of a fee, or a speculator who creates no value. A business enterprise can exist only in an expanding economy, or at least in one that considers change both natural and acceptable. And business is the specific organ of *growth, expansion,* and *change.*

The second function of a business is, therefore, *innovation*—the provision of different economic satisfactions. It is not enough for the business to provide just any economic goods and services; it must provide better and more economic ones. It is not necessary for a business to grow bigger; but it is necessary that it constantly grow better.

Innovation may result in a lower price—the datum with which the economist has been most concerned, for the simple reason that it is the only one that can be handled by quantitative tools. But the result may also be a new and better product, a new convenience, or the definition of a new want.

The most productive innovation is a *different* product or service that creates a new potential of satisfaction, rather than an improvement. Typically this new and different product costs more—yet its overall effect is to make the economy more productive.

The antibiotic drug costs far more than the cold compress, which is all yesterday's physician had to fight pneumonia.

Innovation may be finding new uses for old products. A salesman who succeeds in selling refrigerators to Eskimos to prevent food from freezing would be as much of an innovator as he would have been had he developed brand-new processes or invented a new product. To sell Eskimos a refrigerator to keep food cold is finding *a new market;* to sell a refrigerator to keep food from getting *too* cold is actually creating *a new product.* Technologically there is, of course, only the same old product; but economically there is innovation.

Above all, "innovation" is not *invention.* It is a term of economics rather than of technology. Nontechnical innovations—social or economic innovations—are at least as important as technological ones.

In the organization of the business enterprise, innovation can no more be considered a separate function than can marketing. It is not confined to engineering or research but extends across all parts of the business, all functions, all activities. It cannot be confined to manufacturing. Innovation in distribution is as important as innovation in manufacturing; and so is innovation in an insurance company or in a bank.

Innovation can be defined as the task of endowing human and material resources with new and greater wealth-producing capacity.

Managers must convert society's needs into opportunities for profitable business. That, too, is a definition of innovation. It needs to be stressed today, when we are so conscious of the needs of society, schools, health-care systems, cities, and the environment.

Today's business enterprise (but also today's hospital and government agency) brings together a great many men and women of high knowledge and skill, at practically every level of the organization. But such high knowledge and skill impacts how the work is to be done and what work is actually tackled.

As a result, decisions affecting the entire business and its capacity to perform are made at all levels of the organization, even fairly low ones. Risk-taking decisions— what to do and what not to do, what to continue work on and what to abandon, what products, markets, or technologies to pursue with energy and which ones to ignore—are, in the reality of today's business enterprise (especially the large one), made every day by a host of people of subordinate rank, very often by people without a *traditional* managerial title or position (e.g., research scientists, design engineers, product planners, and tax accountants).

Every one of these executives bases his or her decisions on some theory, if only vague, of the business. Everyone, in other words, has an answer to the question, "What is our business and what should it be?" Unless, therefore, the business itself—and that means its top management—has thought through the question and formulated the answer or answers to it, the decision makers in the business, all the way up and down, will decide and act on the basis of different, incompatible, and conflicting theories of the business. They will pull in different directions without even being aware of their divergences. But they will also decide and act on the basis of wrong and misdirecting theories of the business.

Common vision, common understanding, and unity of direction and effort of the entire organization require definition of "what our business is and what it should be."

Nothing may seem simpler or more obvious than to know what a company's business is. A steel mill makes steel; a railroad runs trains to carry freight and passengers; an insurance company underwrites fire risks; a bank lends money. Actually, "What is our business?" is almost always a difficult question and the right answer is usually anything but obvious.

The answer to the question "What is our business?" is the first responsibility of top management. That business purpose and business mission are so rarely given adequate thought is perhaps the most important single cause of business frustration and business failure. Conversely, in outstanding businesses such as Procter & Gamble and Toyota, success always rests to a large extent on clearly and deliberately raising the question, "What is our business?," and answering it thoughtfully and thoroughly.

With respect to the definition of business purpose and business mission, there is only one such focus, one starting point. It is the customer. The customer defines the business. A business is not defined by the company's name, statutes, or articles of incorporation. It is defined by the want the customer satisfies when he buys a product or a service. To satisfy the customer is the mission and purpose of every business.

The question "What is our business?" can, therefore, be answered only by looking at the business from the outside, from the point of view of customer and market. All the customer is interested in is his own values, his own wants, his own reality. For this reason alone, any serious attempt to state "what our business is" must start with the customer, and her realities, situation, behavior, expectations, and values.

"Who is the customer?" is the first and the crucial question in defining business purpose and business mission. It is not an easy, let alone an obvious question. How it is answered determines, in large measure, how the business defines itself.

The consumer—that is, the ultimate user of a product or a service—is always a customer. But he is never *the* customer; there are usually at least two, sometimes more. Each customer defines a different business, has different expectations and values, buys something different.

Most businesses have at least two customers. The rug and carpet industry has both the contractor and the homeowner for its customers. Both have to buy if there is to be a sale. The manufacturers of branded consumer goods always have two customers at the very least: the housewife and the grocer. It does not do much good to have the housewife eager to buy if the grocer does not stock the brand. Conversely, it does not do much good to have the grocer display merchandise advantageously and give it shelf space if the housewife does not buy.

It is also important to ask, "Where is the customer?" One of the secrets of Sears's success in the 1920s was the discovery that its old customer was now in a different place: the farmer had become mobile and was beginning to buy in town.

The next question is, "What does the customer buy?" The Cadillac people say that they make an automobile, and their business is called the Cadillac Motor Car Company. But does the man who spends $50,000 on a new Cadillac buy transportation, or does he buy primarily prestige? Does the Cadillac compete with Chevrolet, Ford, and Volkswagen? Nicholas Dreystadt, the German-born service mechanic who took over Cadillac in the Depression years of the 1930s, answered, "Cadillac competes with diamonds and mink coats. The Cadillac customer does not buy "transportation" but "status." This answer saved Cadillac, which was about to go under. Within two years or so, it was a major growth business despite the Depression.

Most managements, if they ask the question at all, ask, "What is our business?" when the company is in trouble. Of course, then it *must* be asked. And asking the question then may, indeed, yield spectacular results and may even reverse what appears to be irreversible decline.

To wait until a business or an industry is in trouble is playing Russian roulette. It is irresponsible management. The question should be asked at the inception of a business—and particularly in the case of a business that has ambitions to grow.

The most important time to seriously ask, "What is our business?" is when a company has been successful. Success always obsoletes the very behavior that achieved it. It always creates new realities. It always creates, above all, its own and different problems. Only the fairy story ends "They lived happily ever after."

It is not easy for the management of a successful company to ask, "What is our business?" Everybody in the company then thinks that the answer is so obvious as not to deserve discussion. It is never popular to argue with success, never popular to rock the boat. Sooner or later, however, even the most successful answer to the question, "What is our business?" becomes obsolete.

In asking, "What is our business?" management therefore also needs to add, "And what *will* it be? What changes in the environment are already discernible that are likely to have a high impact on the characteristics, mission, and purpose of our business?" and "How do we *now* build these anticipations into our theory of the business, into its objectives, strategies, and work assignments?"

Again the market, its potential and its trends, is the starting point. How large a market can we project for our business in five or ten years, assuming no basic changes in customers, in market structure, or in technology? And, what factors could validate or disprove these projections?

The most important of these trends is one to which few businesses pay much attention: changes in population structure and population dynamics. Traditionally executives, following economists, have assumed that demographics are a constant.

Historically this has been a sound assumption. Populations used to change very slowly except as a result of catastrophic events, such as major war or famine. This is no longer true, however. Populations nowadays can and do change drastically, in developed as well as in developing countries.

The importance of demographics does not lie only in the impact population structure has on buying power and buying habits, and on the size and structure of the workforce. Population shifts are the only future events for which true prediction is possible.

Management needs to anticipate changes in market structure that result from changes in the economy, from changes in fashion or taste, from moves by competition. And competition must always be defined according to the customer's concept of what product or service he buys, and thus, it must include indirect as well as direct competition.

Finally, management has to ask, "Which of the consumer's wants are not adequately satisfied by the products or services offered to him today?" The ability to ask this question and to answer it correctly usually makes the difference between a growth company and one that depends for its development on the rising tide of the economy or of the industry. But whoever contents himself to rise with the tide will also fall with it.

"WHAT SHOULD OUR BUSINESS BE?"

"What *will* our business be?" aims at adaptation to anticipated changes. It aims at modifying, extending, developing the existing, ongoing business.

But there is need also to ask, "What *should* our business be?" What opportunities are opening up, or can be created, to fulfill the purpose and mission of the business by making it into a *different* business?

Businesses that fail to ask this question are likely to miss their major opportunity.

Next to changes in the society, the economy, and the market, as factors demanding consideration in answering "What should our business be?" comes, of course, innovation—one's own and that of others.

Just as important as the decision concerning what new and different things should be done is planned, systematic abandonment of the old that no longer fits the purpose and mission of the business, no longer conveys satisfaction to the customer or customers, no longer makes a superior contribution.

An essential step in deciding what our business is, what it will be, and what it should be is, therefore, systematic analysis of all existing products, services, processes, markets, end-uses, and distribution channels. Are they still viable? And are they likely to remain viable? Do they still give value to the customer? And are they likely to do so tomorrow? Do they still fit the realities of population and markets, of technology and economy? And if not, how can we best abandon them—or at least stop pouring in further resources and efforts? Unless these questions are being asked seriously and systematically, and unless managements are willing to act on the answers to them, the best definition of "what our business is, will be, and should be" will remain a pious platitude. Energy will be used up in defending yesterday. No one will have the time, resources, or will to work on exploiting today, let alone to work on making tomorrow.

Defining the purpose and mission of the business is difficult, painful, and risky. But it alone enables a business to set objectives, to develop strategies, to concentrate its resources, and to go to work. It alone enables a business to be managed for performance.

The basic definition of the business and of its purpose and mission have to be translated into *objectives*. Otherwise, they remain insight, good intentions, and brilliant epigrams that never become achievement.

1. Objectives must be derived from "what our business is, what it will be, and what it should be." They are not abstractions. They are the action commitments through which the mission of a business is to be carried out, and the standards against which performance is to be measured. *Objectives,* in other words, are the *fundamental strategy of a business.*

2. Objectives must be *operational.* They must be capable of being converted into specific targets and specific assignments. They must be capable of becoming the basis, as well as the motivation, for work and achievement.

3. Objectives must make possible *concentration* of resources and efforts. They must winnow out the fundamentals among the goals of a business so that the key resources of people, money, and physical facilities can be concentrated. They must, therefore, be selective rather than encompass everything.

4. There must be *multiple objectives* rather than a single objective. Much of today's lively discussion of management by objectives is concerned with the search for the "one right objective." This search is not only likely to be as unproductive as the quest for the philosopher's stone; it does harm and misdirects. To manage a business is to balance a variety of needs and goals, and this requires multiple objectives.

5. Objectives are needed in all areas on which the *survival* of the business depends. The specific targets, the goals in any objective area, depend on the strategy of the individual business. But the areas in which objectives are needed are the same for all businesses, for all businesses depend on the same factors for their survival.

A business must first be able to create a customer. There is, therefore, need for a *marketing objective.* Businesses must be able to innovate, or else their competitors will obsolesce them. There is need for an *innovation objective.* All businesses depend

on the three factors of production of the economist, that is, on *human resources,
capital resources,* and *physical resources.* There must be objectives for their supply,
their employment, and their development. The resources must be employed productively and their productivity has to grow if the business is to survive. There is
need, therefore, for *productivity objectives.* Business exists in society and community
and, therefore, has to discharge social responsibilities, at least to the point where it
takes responsibility for its impact upon the environment. Therefore objectives in
respect to the *social dimensions* of business are needed.

Finally, there is need for *profit*—otherwise none of the objectives can be attained. They all require effort, that is, cost. And they can be financed only out of
the profits of a business. They all entail risks; they all, therefore, require a profit to
cover the risk of potential losses. *Profit is not an objective,* but *it is a requirement* that
has to be objectively determined with respect to the individual business, its strategy, its needs, and its risks.

Objectives, therefore, have to be set in these eight key areas:

- Marketing

- Innovation

- Human Resources

- Financial Resources

- Physical Resources

- Productivity

- Social Responsibility

- Profit Requirements

Objectives are the basis for work and assignments. They determine the structure of the business, the key activities that must be discharged, and, above all, the
allocation of people to tasks. *Objectives are the foundation for designing both the structure
of the business and the work of individual units and individual managers.*

Objectives are always needed in all eight key areas. The area without specific
objectives will be neglected. Unless we determine what shall be measured and
what the yardstick of measurement in an area will be, the area itself will not be
seen. (On measurement, see chapter 31.)

The measurements available for the key areas of a business enterprise are still by
and large haphazard. We do not even have adequate concepts, let alone measurements,
except for market standing. For something as central as profitability we have only

a rubber yardstick, and we have no real tools at all to determine how much profitability is necessary. With respect to innovation and, even more, to productivity, we hardly know more than that something ought to be done. In the other areas, including physical and financial resources, we are reduced to statements of intentions; we do not possess goals and measurements for their attainment.

However, enough is known about each area to give at least a progress report. Enough is known for each business to go to work on objectives.

We know one more thing about objectives: *how to use them.*

If objectives are only good intentions, they are worthless. They must degenerate into work. And work is always specific, always has—or should have—clear, unambiguous, measurable results, a deadline, and a specific assignment of accountability. But objectives that become a straitjacket do harm. Objectives are always based on expectations. And expectations are, at best, informed guesses. Objectives express an appraisal of factors that are largely outside the business and not under its control. The world does not stand still.

The proper way to use objectives is the way an airline uses schedules and flight plans. The schedule provides for the 9:00 AM flight from Los Angeles to get to Boston by 5:00 PM. But if there is a blizzard in Boston that day, the plane will land in Pittsburgh instead and wait out the storm. The flight plan provides for flying at 30,000 feet and for flying over Denver and Chicago. But if the pilot encounters turbulence or strong headwinds, he will ask flight control for permission to go up another 5,000 feet and to take the Minneapolis-Montreal route. Yet no flight is ever operated without a schedule and flight plan. Any change is immediately fed back to produce a new schedule and flight plan. Unless 97 percent or so of its flights proceed on the original schedule and flight plan—or within a very limited range of deviation from either—a well-run airline gets another operations manager who knows his job.

Objectives are not fate; they are direction. They are not commands; they are commitments. They do not determine the future; they are a means to mobilize the resources and energies of the business for the making of the future.

MARKETING OBJECTIVES

Marketing and innovation are the foundation areas in objective setting. It is in these two areas that a business obtains its results. It is performance and contribution in these areas for which a customer pays.

It is somewhat misleading to speak of *a* marketing objective. Marketing performance requires a number of objectives:

- for existing products and services in existing and present markets;

- for abandonment of "yesterday" in product, services, and markets;

- for new products and services for existing markets;

- for new markets;

- for the distributive organization;

- for service standards and service performance;

- for credit standards and credit performance, and so on.

Many books have been written on every one of these areas. But it is almost never stressed that objectives in these areas can be set only after two key decisions have been made: the decision on *concentration,* and the decision on *market standing.*

Archimedes, one of the great scientists of antiquity, is reported to have said, "Give me a place to stand on, and I can lift the universe off its hinges." The place to stand on is the area of concentration. It is the area that gives a business the leverage that lifts the universe off its hinges. The concentration decision is, therefore, a crucial decision. In large measure, it converts the definition of "what our business is" into meaningful operational commitment.

The other major decision underlying marketing objectives is that on market standing. One common approach is to say, "We want to be the leader." The other one is to say, "We don't care what share of the market we have as long as sales go up." Both sound plausible, but both are wrong.

Obviously, not everybody can be the leader. One has to decide in which segment of the market, with what product, what services, what values, one should be the leader. It does not do much good for a company's sales to go up if it loses market share, that is, if the market expands much faster than the company's sales do.

A company with a *small share of the market* will eventually become marginal in the marketplace, and thereby exceedingly vulnerable.

Market standing, regardless of the sales curve, is therefore essential. The point at which a supplier becomes marginal varies from industry to industry. But to be a marginal producer is dangerous for long-term survival.

There is also a maximum market standing above which it may be unwise to go—even if there were no antitrust laws. Market domination tends to lull the leader to sleep; monopolists flounder on their own complacency rather than on public opposition. Market domination produces tremendous internal resistance against any innovation and thus makes adaptation to change dangerously difficult.

There is also well-founded resistance in the marketplace to dependence on one dominant supplier. Whether it is the purchasing agent of a manufacturing company, the procurement officer in the Air Force, or the housewife, no one likes to be at the mercy of the monopoly supplier.

Finally, the dominant supplier in a rapidly expanding, especially a new, market is likely to do less well than if he shared that market with one or two other major and competing suppliers. This may seem paradoxical—and most businessmen find it difficult to accept. But the fact is that a new market, especially a new major market, tends to expand much more rapidly when there are several suppliers rather than only one. It may be very flattering to a supplier's ego to have 80 percent of a market. But if as a result of domination by a single source, the market does not expand as it otherwise might, the supplier's revenues and profits are likely to be considerably lower than they would have been if two suppliers shared a fast-expanding market. Eighty percent of 100 is considerably less than 50 percent of 250. A new market that has only one supplier is likely to become static at 100. It will be limited by the imagination of the one supplier, who is likely to always know what his product or service cannot or should not be used for. If there are several suppliers, they are likely to uncover and promote markets and end-uses the single supplier never dreams of. And the market might grow rapidly to 250.

DuPont seems to have grasped this. In its most successful innovations, DuPont retains a sole-supplier position only until the new product has paid for the original investment. Then DuPont licenses the innovation and launches competitors deliberately. As a result, a number of aggressive companies start developing new markets and new uses for the product. Nylon would surely have grown much more slowly without DuPont-sponsored competition. Its markets are still growing, but without competition it would probably have begun to decline in the early 1950s, when newer synthetic fibers were brought on the market by Monsanto and Union Carbide in the U.S., Imperial Chemicals in Great Britain, and AKU in Holland.

The market standing to aim at is not the maximum but the *optimum*.

THE INNOVATION OBJECTIVE

The innovation objective is the objective through which a company makes operational its definition of "what our business should be."

There are essentially three kinds of innovation in every business: innovation in product or service, innovation in marketplace and consumer behavior and values, and innovation in the various skills and activities needed to make the products and services and to bring them to market. They might be called respectively *product innovation, social innovation* (e.g., installment credit), and *managerial innovation*.

The problem in setting innovation objectives is the difficulty of measuring the relative impact and importance of various innovations. But how are we to determine what weighs more: a hundred minor but immediately applicable improvements in packaging a product, or one fundamental chemical discovery that after ten more years of hard work may change the character of the business altogether?

A department store and a pharmaceutical company will answer this question differently, but so may two different pharmaceutical companies.

RESOURCES OBJECTIVES

A group of objectives deals with the resources a business needs to be able to perform—with their supply, their utilization, and their productivity.

All economic activity, economists have told us for two hundred years, requires three kinds of resources: land, that is, products of nature; labor, that is, human resources; and capital, that is, the means to invest in tomorrow. The business must be able to attract all three and put them to productive use.

A business that cannot attract the people and the capital it needs will not last long.

The first sign of the decline of an industry is its loss of appeal to qualified, able, and ambitious people. The American railroads, for instance, did not begin their decline after World War II—it only became obvious and irreversible then. The decline actually set in around the time of World War I. Before World War I, able graduates of American engineering schools looked for a railroad career. From the end of World War I on, for whatever reason, the railroads no longer appealed to young engineering graduates, or to any educated young people.

In the two areas of people and capital supply, genuine marketing objectives are therefore required. "What do our jobs have to be to attract and hold the kind of people we need and want? What is the supply available on the job market? And, what do we have to do to attract it?" Similarly, "What does the investment in our business have to be, in the form of bank loans, long-term debts, or equity, to attract and hold the capital we need?"

Resource objectives have to be set in a double process. One starting point is the anticipated needs of the business, which then have to be projected on the outside, that is, on the market for land, labor, and capital. But the other starting points are these "markets" themselves, which then have to be projected onto the structure, the direction, the plans of the business.

PRODUCTIVITY OBJECTIVES

Attracting resources and putting them to work is only the beginning. The task of a business is to make resources productive. Every business, therefore, needs productivity objectives with respect to each of the three major resources—people, capital, and products of nature—and with respect to overall productivity itself.

A productivity measurement is the best yardstick for comparing managements of different units within an enterprise, and for comparing managements of different enterprises.

All businesses have access to pretty much the same resources. Except for the rare monopoly situation, the only thing that differentiates one business from another in any given field is the quality of its management on all levels. The first measurement of this crucial factor is productivity, that is, the degree to which resources are utilized and their yield.

The continuous improvement of productivity is one of management's most important jobs. It is also one of the most difficult; for productivity is a balance between a diversity of factors, few of which are easily definable or clearly measurable.

Capital is one of the three factors of production. And if productivity of capital is accomplished by making the other resources less productive, there is actually a loss of productivity.

Productivity is a difficult concept, but it is central. Without productivity objectives, a business does not have direction. Without productivity measurements, it does not have control.

THE SOCIAL RESPONSIBILITY OBJECTIVES

Only a few years ago executives as well as economists considered the social dimension so intangible that performance objectives could not be set. We have now learned that the intangible can become very tangible indeed. Such lessons as the attacks on industry for the destruction of the environment are expensive ways to learn that business needs to think through its impacts and its responsibilities and to set objectives for both.

The social dimension is a survival dimension. An enterprise exists in society and the economy. Within an institution one always tends to assume that the institution exists by itself in a vacuum. And managers inevitably look at their business from the inside. But the business enterprise is a creature of society and the economy. Society or the economy can put any business out of existence overnight. The enterprise exists on sufferance and exists only as long as society and the economy believe that it does a job, and a necessary, useful, and productive one.

That such objectives need to be built into the strategy of a business, rather than be statements of good intentions, needs to be stressed here. These are not objectives that are needed because the manager has a responsibility to society. They are needed because the manager has a responsibility to the enterprise.

PROFIT: A NEED AND LIMITATION

Only after the objectives in the aforementioned seven key areas have been thought through and established can a business tackle the question "How much profitability do we need?" To attain any of these objectives entails high risks. It requires effort, and that means cost. Profit is, therefore, needed to pay for attainment of the objectives of the business. Profit is a condition of survival. It is the cost of the future, the cost of staying in business.

A business that obtains enough profit to satisfy its objectives in the key areas is a business that has the means of survival. A business that falls short of the profitability demands made by its key objectives is a marginal and endangered business.

Profit planning is necessary. But it is planning for a needed minimum profitability rather than for that meaningless shibboleth "profit maximization." The minimum needed may well turn out to be a good deal higher than the profit goals of many companies, let alone their actual profit results.

BALANCING OBJECTIVES

There are three kinds of balance needed in setting objectives. Objectives have to be balanced against attainable profitability. Objectives have to be balanced as to the demands of the immediate and the distant future. They have to be balanced against each other, and trade-offs have to be established between desired performance in one area and desired performance in others. In setting objectives, management always has to balance the immediate future against the long-range future. But if it sacrifices the long-range needs of "what our business will be" and "what our business should be" to immediate results, there will also be no business fairly soon.

Setting objectives always requires a decision on where to take the risks, a decision as to how immediate results should be sacrificed for the sake of long-range growth, or how long-range growth should be jeopardized for the sake of short-run performance. There is no formula for these decisions. They are risky, entrepreneurial, and uncertain—but they must be made.

Growth companies often promise both more sales and higher profits indefinitely. This alone is reason to distrust them. Every experienced manager should know that these two objectives are not normally compatible. To produce more sales almost always means to sacrifice immediate profit. To produce higher profit almost always means to sacrifice long-range sales.

There are few things that distinguish competent from incompetent management quite as sharply as performance in balancing objectives. There is no formula for doing the job. Each business requires its own balance—and it may require a different balance at different times. Balancing is not a mechanical job. It is a risk-taking decision that is made in the budgeting and priority-setting processes. (On the topic of budgeting, see chapter 32.)

FROM OBJECTIVES TO DOING

One final step remains: to convert objectives into doing. Action rather than knowledge is the purpose of asking, "What *is* our business, what *will* it be, what *should* it be?" and of thinking through objectives. The aim is to focus the energies and resources of the organization on the right results. The end products of business analysis, therefore, are work programs and specific and concrete work assignments with defined goals, with deadlines, and with clear accountability. Unless objectives are converted into action, they are not objectives; they are dreams.

SUMMARY

Marketing and innovation are the two result areas with which the setting of objectives has to begin. Both are likely to require a range of objectives rather than one target figure. Both also require prior decisions of high risk: on concentration and on market standing. And then there is the need for objectives with respect to all resources—people, capital, and key physical resources—their supply, their utilization, and their productivity. There is the need for objectives with respect to the social dimension of business, its social responsibilities and social impacts. In all these areas, the small business needs clear objectives just as much as the big one. Profit and profitability come at the end; they are survival needs of a business and therefore require objectives. But the needed profitability also establishes limitations on all the other objectives. Objectives have to be balanced—with each other, in terms of the different requirements of the short and the long term, and against available resources. Finally, action priorities have to be set.

10

Making the Future Today

We know only two things about the future:

- It cannot be known.

- It will be different from what exists now and from what we now expect.

These assertions are not particularly new or particularly striking. But they have far-reaching implications.

1. Any attempt to base today's actions and commitments on *predictions* of *future events* is futile. The best we can hope to do is to anticipate the *future effects of events* that have already irrevocably happened.

2. But precisely because the future is going to be different and cannot be predicted, it is possible to make the unexpected and unpredicted come to pass. *To try to make the future happen is risky; but it is a rational activity.* And it is less risky than coasting along on the comfortable assumption that nothing is going to change, less risky than following a prediction as to what "must" happen or what is "most probable."

Managers must accept the need to work systematically on making the future. But this does not mean the manager can work for the elimination of risks and uncertainties. That power is not given to mortal man. The one thing he or she can try to do is to find, and occasionally to create, *the right risk* and to *exploit uncertainty*. The purpose of the work on making the future is not to decide what should be done tomorrow, but what should be done today to have a tomorrow.

We are slowly learning how to do this work systematically and with direction and control. The starting point is the realization that there are two different, though complementary, approaches:

- Finding and exploiting the time lag between the appearance of a discontinuity in economy and society and its full impact—one might call this *anticipation of a future that has already happened.*

- Imposing on the, as yet, unborn future a new idea that tries to give direction and shape to what is to come. This one might call *making the future happen*.

THE FUTURE THAT HAS ALREADY HAPPENED

There is a time lag between a major social, economic, or cultural event and its full impact. A sharp rise or a sharp drop in the birthrate will not have an effect on the size of the available labor force for fifteen to twenty years. But the change has already happened. Only catastrophe—destructive war, famine, or pandemic—could alter its impact tomorrow.

These are the opportunities of the future that has already happened. They might therefore be called a *potential*. But the future that has already happened is not within the present organization; it is outside: a change in society, knowledge, culture, industry, or economic structure.

It is, moreover, a *major change* rather than a trend, a *break in the pattern* rather than a variation within it. There is, of course, considerable uncertainty and risk in committing resources to anticipation. But the risk is limited. We cannot really know how fast the impact will occur. But that it will occur, we can say with a high degree of assurance; and we can, to a useful extent, describe it.

Fundamental knowledge has to be available today to be able to serve us ten or fifteen years hence. In the mid-nineteenth century one could only speculate about the consequences for the economy of Michael Faraday's discoveries in electricity. A good many of the speculations were undoubtedly wide of the mark. But that this breakthrough into an entirely new field of energy would have major impact could be said with some certainty.

Major cultural changes, too, operate over a fairly long period. This is particularly true of the subtlest but most pervasive cultural change: a change in people's awareness. It is by no means certain that present underdeveloped countries will succeed in rapidly developing themselves. On the contrary, it is probable that only a few will succeed, and that even these few will go through difficult times and suffer severe crises. But that the peoples of Latin America, Asia, and Africa have become aware of the possibility of development and that they have committed themselves to it and to its consequences is a fact. It creates a momentum that only disaster could reverse. These countries may not succeed in industrializing themselves. But they will, for a historical period at least, give priority to industrial development—and hard times may only accentuate their new awareness of the possibility of, and need for, industrial development.

The changes that generate the future that has already happened can be found through *systematic search*. The first area to examine is always *demographics*. Population changes are the most fundamental—for the labor force, for the market, for social pressures, and economic opportunities. They are the least reversible in the normal course of events. They have a known minimum lead-time between change and impact: before a rise in the birthrate puts pressure on school facilities, at least five or six years will elapse—but then the pressure will come. And the consequences of population changes are most nearly predictable.

Another field that always should be searched for a future that has already happened is that of *knowledge*. This search should not, however, be confined to the present knowledge areas of the organization. In looking for the future, we assume that, say, the business will be different. And one of the major areas in which we may be able to anticipate a different business is that of the knowledge resource on which the specific excellence of a business is founded. We must, therefore, look at major knowledge areas, whether they have a direct relation to the present business or not. And wherever we find a fundamental change that has not yet had major impact, we should ask, "Are there opportunities here that we should and could anticipate?"

The behavioral sciences provide an example of a major change in a knowledge area, although few businesses would consider it directly relevant to them. *Learning theory* is one area in psychology where really new knowledge has been developed these last seventy-five years. Although this may seem rather remote to managers, the new knowledge is likely to have an impact not only on the form and content of education but on teaching and learning materials, school equipment, school design, and even on research organization and research management.

One also looks at other industries, other countries, other markets, with the question, *Has anything happened there that might establish a pattern for our industry, our country, our market?*

Next, one always asks, *Is anything happening in the structure of an industry that indicates a major change?*

One such change—well in progress throughout the entire industrial world—is the *materials revolution,* which erases or blurs the lines that traditionally separated different materials streams. Only a generation ago materials streams were separate from beginning to end. Paper, for instance, was the main manufactured material into which wood could be converted. Paper, in turn, had to be made from a tree. The same situation held for other major materials—aluminum and petroleum, steel and zinc. Most of the finished products coming out of these material streams had specific and unique end-uses. In other words, most substances determined end-uses, and most end-uses determined substances. Today, however, even the process is no longer unique. The paper industry increasingly incorporates into their processes techniques developed by the plastics manufacturers and converters; and the textile industry increasingly adapts paper industry processes.

Inside the business, also, there can usually be found clues to events that, while basic and irreversible, have not yet had their full impact.

Often one indication is internal friction within the company. Something is being introduced—and it becomes a source of dissension. Unwittingly, one has touched a sensitive spot—sensitive often because the new activity is in anticipation of future changes and, therefore, in contradiction to the accepted pattern.

For example, in an American company, when product development is introduced as a new function and as a specific kind of work, it creates friction. Usually this manifests itself in a long wrangle as to where the new activity belongs. Does it belong in marketing? Or does it belong in research and engineering? Actually, this is much less a dispute over the new function than it is *a dim first awareness that the marketing approach tends to make all functions secondary and that all functions are cost centers rather than producers of results.* This, however, must lead to fundamental changes in organization. It is the anticipation of these changes that makes people react violently to the symptom, "product development."

IT HAS HAPPENED

Two additional and related questions should be asked: *"What do the generally approved forecasts assert is likely to happen ten, fifteen, twenty years hence?" "Has it actually happened already?"* Most people can imagine only what they have already seen. If, therefore, a forecast meets with widespread acceptance, it is quite likely that it does not forecast the future, but in effect, reports on the recent past.

There is in American business history one famous illustration of the productivity of this approach. Around 1910, in the early years of Henry Ford's success, the first forecasts appeared that predicted the growth of the automobile into mass transportation. Most people at that time still considered this unlikely to happen before another thirty years or so. But William C. Durant, then a small manufacturer, asked, "Has this not already happened?" As soon as he asked the question, the answer was obvious: It had happened, though the main impact was yet to come. The public's awareness had changed from regarding the car as a toy of the rich to demanding a car for mass transportation. And this would require large automobile companies. On this insight, Durant imagined General Motors and began to pull together a number of small automobile manufacturers and small accessory companies into the kind of business that would be able to take advantage of this new market and its opportunity.

The final question should therefore be: *"What are our own assumptions regarding society and the economy, the market and customer, knowledge and technology? And are they still valid?"*

Looking for the future that has already happened and anticipating its impacts introduces a *new perception* in the beholder. The new event is easily visible, as the illustrations should have made clear. The need is to make oneself see it. What could or might then be done is usually not too difficult to discover. The opportunities, in other words, are neither remote nor obscure. The pattern, however, has to be recognized first.

As the examples should also have demonstrated, this is an approach of great power. But there is also a major danger: the temptation to see as a change that which we believe to be happening, or worse, what we believe should happen. This is so great a danger that, as a general rule, any finding should be distrusted for which there is enthusiasm within the company. If everybody shouts, "This is what we wanted all along," it is likely that wishes rather than facts are being reported.

For the power of this approach is that it *questions and ultimately overturns deeply entrenched assumptions, practices, and habits.* It leads to decisions to work toward change in the entire conduct, if not in the structure, of the business. It leads to the decision to make the business different.

THE POWER OF AN IDEA

It is futile to try to guess what products and processes the future will want. But it is possible to decide what idea one wants to make a reality in the future, and to build a different business on such an idea.

Making the future happen also means creating a different business. But what makes the future happen is always a business's embodiment of an idea of a different economy, a different technology, a different society. It need not be a big idea; but it must be one that differs from the norm of today.

The idea has to be an entrepreneurial one—an idea of wealth-producing potential and capacity, expressed in a going, working, producing business, and effective through business actions and behavior. It does not emerge from the question, "What should future society look like?"—the question of the social reformer, revolutionary, or philosopher. Underlying the entrepreneurial idea that makes the future is always the question, "What major change in the economy, the market, or knowledge would enable us to conduct business the way we would really like to do it, the way we would really obtain the best economic results?"

Because this seems so limited and self-centered an approach, historians tend to overlook it and to be blind to its impact. The great philosophical idea has, of course, more profound effects. But few philosophical ideas have any effect at all. While each business idea is more limited, a large proportion of business ideas are effective. Innovating managers have, therefore, had a good deal more impact as a group than the historians realize.

The very fact that an entrepreneurial idea does not encompass all of society or all of knowledge but encompasses just one narrow area makes it more viable. The people who have this idea may be wrong about everything else in the future economy or society. But that does not matter as long as they are approximately right with respect to their own business focus. All that they need to be successful is *one small, specific development.*

Thomas Watson, who founded and built IBM, did not see, at all, the development of technology. But he had the idea of data processing as a unifying concept on which to build a business. The business was, for a long time, fairly small and confined itself to such mundane work as keeping accounting ledgers and time records. But it was ready to jump when the technology came in—out of totally unrelated wartime work—that made data processing actually possible, the technology of the electronic computer. While Watson built a small and unspectacular business in the 1920s designing, selling, and installing punch-card equipment, the mathematicians and logicians of *logical positivism* (e.g., P. W. Bridgman in the United States and Rudolf Carnap in Austria) talked about and wrote a systematic methodology of quantification and universal measurements. It is most unlikely that they ever heard of the young, struggling IBM Company, and certain that they did not connect their ideas with it. Yet it was Watson's IBM and not their philosophical ideas that became operational when the new technology emerged in World War II.

The men who built Sears, Roebuck—Richard Sears, Julius Rosenwald, Albert Loeb, and, finally, General Robert E. Wood—had active social concerns and a lively social imagination. Yet not one of them thought of remaking the economy. I doubt even that the idea of a mass market—as opposed to the traditional class markets—occurred to them until long after the event. Yet, from its early beginnings, Sears, Roebuck had the idea that the poor man's money could be made to have the same purchasing power as the rich man's. This was not a particularly new idea. Social reformers and economists had bandied it about for decades. The cooperative movement in Europe largely grew out of it. But Sears was the first business built on the idea in the United States. It started out with the question, *"What would make the farmer a customer for a retail business?"* The answer was simply, "He needs to be sure of getting goods of the same dependable quality as do city people at the same low price." At the time, this was an innovative idea of considerable audacity.

Great entrepreneurial innovations have been achieved by converting an existing *theoretical proposition* into an effective business. The entrepreneurial innovation that has had a great impact on economic development converted the theoretical proposition of the French social philosopher Comte de Saint-Simon into a bank. Saint-Simon, starting from J. B. Say's concept of the entrepreneur, developed a philosophical system around the creative role of capital. The idea became effective, however, through a banking business, the famous Crédit Mobilier, which his disciples, the brothers Pereire, founded in Paris in the middle of the nineteenth century. The Crédit Mobilier was to be the conscious developer of industry through the direction of the liquid resources of the community. It became the prototype for the entire banking system of the then underdeveloped continent of Europe—beginning with the France, Holland, and Belgium of the Pereires' day. The Pereires' imitators then founded the "business banks" of Germany, Switzerland, Austria, Scandinavia, and Italy that became the main agents for the industrial development of their countries. After the American Civil War the idea crossed the Atlantic. The American bankers who developed American industry—from Jay Cooke and the American Crédit Mobilier that financed the transcontinental railroad, to J. P. Morgan—were all imitators of the Pereires, whether they knew it or not. So were the Japanese Zaibatsu, the great banker-industrialists who built the economy of modern Japan.

The basic entrepreneurial idea may merely be imitation of something that works well in another country or in another industry. When Thomas Bata, a Slovak shoemaker, returned to Europe from the United States after World War I, he had the idea that everybody in Slovakia and the Balkans could have shoes to wear as everybody had in the United States. "The peasant goes barefoot," he is reported to have said, "not because he is too poor, but because there are no shoes." What was needed to make this vision of a shod peasant come true was a supply of cheap and standardized, but well-designed and durable, footwear as there was in America. On this analogy Bata built in a few years Europe's largest shoe business and one of Europe's most successful companies.

CREATIVITY

To make the future happen one need not, in other words, have a creative imagination. It requires *work rather than genius*—and therefore is accessible in some measure to everybody. The man of creative imagination will have more imaginative ideas, to be sure. But that the more imaginative idea will actually be more successful is by no means certain. Pedestrian ideas have at times been successful; Bata's idea of applying American methods to making shoes was not very original in the Europe of 1920, with its tremendous interest in Ford and his assembly line. What mattered was his *courage* rather than his *genius*.

To make the future happen one has to be willing to do something new. One has to be willing to ask, "What do we really want to see happen that is quite different from today?" One has to be willing to say, "This is the right thing to happen as the future of the business. We will work on making it happen."

Lack of "creativity," which looms so large in present discussions of innovation, is not the real problem. There are more ideas in any organization, including businesses, than can possibly be put to use. *What is lacking, as a rule, is the willingness to look beyond products to ideas.* Products and processes are only the vehicle through which an idea becomes effective. And, as the illustrations should have shown, the specific future products and processes can usually not even be imagined.

When DuPont started the work on polymer chemistry out of which nylon eventually evolved, it did not know that manmade fibers would be the end product. DuPont acted on the assumption that any gain in man's ability to manipulate the structure of large, organic molecules—at that time in its infancy—would lead to commercially important results of some kind. Only after six or seven years of research work did manmade fibers first appear as a possible major result area.

Moreover, the manager often lacks the courage to commit resources to such an idea. The resources that should be invested in making the future happen should be small, but they must be of the best. Otherwise nothing happens.

However, the greatest lack of the manager is a touchstone of validity and practicality. An idea has to meet rigorous tests if it is to be capable of making the future of a business.

It has to have *operational validity*. Can we take action on this idea? Or can we only talk about it? Can we really do something right away to bring about the kind of future we want to make happen?

To be able to spend money on research is not enough. It must be research directed toward the realization of the idea. The knowledge sought may be general, as was that of DuPont's project. But it must at least be reasonably clear that if available, it would be applicable knowledge.

The idea must also have *economic validity*. If it could be put to work right away in practice, it should be able to produce economic results. We may not be able to do what we would like to for a long time, perhaps never. But if we could do it now, the resulting products, processes, or services would find a customer, a market, an end-use; should be capable of being sold profitably; should satisfy a want and a need.

The idea itself might aim at social reform. But unless an organization can be built on it, it is not a valid entrepreneurial idea. The test of the idea is not the votes it gets or the acclaim of the philosophers. It is *economic performance* and *economic results*. Even if the rationale of the business is social reform rather than business success, the touchstone must be the ability to perform and to survive as a business.

Finally, the idea must meet the test of *personal commitment*. Do we *really believe in the idea?* Do we really want to be that kind of people, do that kind of work, run that kind of business?

To make the future demands courage. It demands work. But it also demands faith. To commit ourselves to the expedient is simply not practical. It will not suffice for the tests ahead. For no such idea is foolproof—nor should it be. The one idea regarding the future that must inevitably fail is the apparently "sure thing," the "riskless idea," the one "that cannot fail." The idea on which tomorrow's business is to be built must be uncertain; no one can really say as yet what it will look like if and when it becomes reality. It must be risky: it has a probability of success but also of failure. If it is not both uncertain and risky, it is simply not a practical idea for the future. For the future itself is both uncertain and risky.

Unless there is personal commitment to the values of the idea and faith in them, the necessary efforts will therefore not be sustained. The manager should not become an enthusiast, let alone a fanatic. She should realize that things do not happen just because she wants them to happen—not even if she works very hard at making them happen. Like any other effort, the work on making the future happen should be reviewed periodically to see whether continuation can still be justified both by the results of the work to date and by the prospects ahead. Ideas regarding the future can become investments in managerial ego too, and need to be carefully tested for their capacity to perform and to give results. But the people who work on making the future also need to be able to say with conviction, "This is what we really want our business to be."

It is perhaps not absolutely necessary for every organization to search for the idea that will make the future. A good many organizations and their managements do not even make their present organizations effective—and yet the organizations somehow survive for a while. The big business, in particular, seems to be able to coast a long time on the courage, work, and vision of earlier managers.

But tomorrow always arrives. It is always different. And then even the mightiest company is in trouble if it has not worked on the future. It will have lost distinction and leadership—all that will remain is big-company overhead. It will neither control nor understand what is happening. Not having dared to take the risk of making the new happen, it perforce took the much greater risk of being surprised by what did happen. And this is a risk that even the largest and richest organization cannot afford and that even the smallest one need not run.

To be more than a slothful steward of the talents in one's keeping, the manager has to accept responsibility for making the future happen. It is the willingness to tackle this purposefully that distinguishes the great organization from the merely competent one, and the organization builder from the manager-suite custodian.

SUMMARY

In human affairs it is pointless to try to predict the future. But it is possible and fruitful to identify major events that have already happened irrevocably and that will have predictable effects in the next decade or two. It is possible, in other words, to *identify* and *prepare* for the future *that has already happened.*

A dominant factor for organizations in the next few decades is going to be *demographics.* The key factor for business will not be *over*population that we have been warned of for many years but *under*population of the developed countries—Japan, South Korea, and the nations of Western Europe.

11

Strategic Planning: The Entrepreneurial Skill

Practically every basic management decision is a long-range decision—ten years is a rather short time span these days. Whether concerned with research or with building a new plant, designing a new marketing organization or a new product, every major management decision takes years before it is really effective. And it has to be productive for years thereafter to pay off the investment of people and money. Managers, therefore, need to be skilled in making decisions with long futurity on a systematic basis.

Management has no choice but to anticipate the future, to attempt to mold it, and to balance short-range and long-range goals. It is not given to mortals to do well any of these things. But lacking divine guidance, management must make sure that these difficult responsibilities are not overlooked or neglected.

The idea of long-range planning—and much of its reality—rests on a number of misunderstandings. The present and the immediate short range require strategic decisions fully as much as the long range. The long range is largely made by short-run decisions. Unless the long range is built into, and based on, short-range plans and decisions, the most elaborate long-range plan will be an exercise in futility. And conversely, unless the short-range plans, that is, the decisions on the here and now, are integrated into one unified plan of action, they will be expedients, guesses, and misdirection.

"Short range" and "long range" are not determined by any given time span. A decision is not short range because it takes only a few months to carry it out. What matters is the time span over which it has to be effective. A decision is not long range because in early 2008 we resolve on making it in 2012; this is not a decision but an idle diversion. It has as much reality as the eight-year-old boy's plan to be a fireman when he grows up.

The idea behind long-range planning is that the question, "What *should* our business be?" can and should be worked on and decided by itself, independent of the thinking on "What *is* our business" and "What *will* it be?" There is some sense to this. It is necessary in strategic planning to *start separately* with all three questions: What *is* the business? What *will* it be? What *should* it be? These are, and should be, separate conceptual approaches. With respect to what the business *should* be, the first assumption must be that it will be different.

Long-range planning should prevent managers from uncritically extending present trends into the future, from assuming that today's products, services, markets, and technologies will be the products, services, markets, and technologies of tomorrow, and, above all, from dedicating their resources and energies to the defense of yesterday.

Planning what *is* our business, planning what *will* it be, and planning what *should* it be have to be integrated. What is short range and what is long range is then decided by the *time span* and *futurity* of the decision. Everything that is *planned* becomes immediate *work* and commitment.

The skill we need is not long-range planning. It is *strategic decision making*, or perhaps *strategic planning*.

General Electric calls this work "strategic business planning." The ultimate objective of the activity is to identify the new and different businesses, technologies, and markets that the company should try to create long range. But the work starts with the question, "What *is* our present business?" Indeed, it starts with the questions, "Which of our present businesses should we abandon? Which should we play down? Which should we push and supply new resources?"

WHAT STRATEGIC PLANNING IS *NOT*

It is important for the manager to know what strategic planning is *not:*

1. *It is not a box of tricks, a bundle of techniques.* It is analytical thinking and commitment of resources to action.

Many techniques may be used in the process—but, then again, none may be needed. Strategic planning may require a computer, but the most important questions—What *is* our business? or What *should* it be?—cannot be quantified and programmed for the computer. Model building or simulation may be helpful, but they are not strategic planning; they are tools for specific purposes and may or may not apply in a given case.

Quantification is not planning. To be sure, one uses rigorous logical methods as far as possible—if only to make sure that one does not deceive oneself. But some of the most important questions in strategic planning can be phrased only in terms such as "larger" or "smaller," "sooner" or "later." These terms cannot easily be manipulated by quantitative techniques. And some equally important areas—such as those of political climate, social responsibilities, or human (including managerial) resources—cannot be quantified at all. They can be handled only as restraints or boundaries but not as factors in the equation itself.

Strategic planning is *not* the application of scientific methods to business decision. It is the application of *thought, analysis, imagination,* and *judgment.* It is *responsibility,* rather than *technique.*

2. *Strategic planning is not forecasting.* It is not masterminding the future. Any attempt to do so is foolish; the future is unpredictable. We can only discredit what we are doing by attempting it.

If anyone suffers from the delusion that the human being is able to forecast beyond a very short time span, look at the headlines in yesterday's paper and ask which of them anyone could possibly have predicted a decade or so ago. For example, could we, in 1960, in the waning days of the Eisenhower administration, have forecast the almost explosive growth of the black middle class in America, which by 1970, had raised two-thirds of black families above the poverty line and had given the African-American family an average income well above the average income of affluent Great Britain? And could we also have predicted that this unprecedented achievement would only make more acute and pressing the problem of the one-quarter of African-Americans remaining in poverty?

We must start out with the premise that forecasting is not a respectable human activity and not worthwhile beyond the shortest of periods. *Strategic planning is necessary precisely because we cannot forecast.*

Another, even more compelling, reason why forecasting is not strategic planning is that forecasting attempts to find the most probable course of events or, at best, a range of probabilities. But the entrepreneurial problem is the unique event that will change the possibilities; the entrepreneurial universe is not a physical but a social universe. Indeed, the central entrepreneurial contribution, which alone is rewarded with a profit, is to bring about the unique event or innovation that changes the economic, social, or political situation.

This was what Xerox Corporation did in the 1950s when it developed and marketed photocopying machines. This is what the entrepreneurs in mobile housing did in the 1960s, when the trailer became the new, permanent, and immobile home and took over practically the entire U.S. low-cost housing market. The unique event of Rachel Carson's book *Silent Spring,* in the 1950s, changed the attitude of a whole civilization toward the environment. On the social and political scene, this is what the leaders of the civil rights movement did in the 1960s, and what the leaders in women's rights did at the start of the 1970s.

Since the entrepreneur upsets the probabilities on which predictions are based, forecasting does not serve the purposes of planners who seek to direct their organizations to the future. It certainly is of little use to planners who would innovate and change the ways in which people work and live.

3. *Strategic planning does not deal with future decisions. It deals with the futurity of present decisions.* Decisions exist only in the present. The question that faces the

strategic decision maker is not what the organization should do tomorrow. It is, "What do we have to do today to be ready for an uncertain tomorrow?" The question is not what will happen in the future. It is, "What futurity do we have to build into our present thinking and doing, what time spans do we have to consider, and how do we use this information to make a rational decision now?"

Decision making is a time machine that synchronizes into a single time—the present—a great number of divergent time spans. We are learning this only now. Our approach still tends toward making plans for something we will decide to do in the future, which may be entertaining but is futile. We can make decisions only in the present, and yet we cannot make decisions *for* the present alone; the most expedient, most opportunistic decision—let alone the decision not to decide at all—may commit us for a long time, if not permanently and irrevocably.

4. *Strategic planning is not an attempt to eliminate risk.* It is not even an attempt to minimize risk. Such an attempt can lead only to irrational and unlimited risks and to certain disaster.

Economic activity, by definition, commits present resources to the future, that is, to highly uncertain expectations. To take risks is the essence of economic activity. An important principle of economics (Boehm-Bawerk's Law) proves that existing means of production will yield greater economic performance only through greater uncertainty, that is, through greater risk.

WHAT STRATEGIC PLANNING *IS*

While it is futile to try to eliminate risk, and questionable to try to minimize it, it is essential that the risks taken be the right risks. The end result of successful strategic planning must be the capacity to take a greater risk, for this is the only way to improve *entrepreneurial* performance. To extend this capacity, however, we must understand the risks we take. We must be able to choose rationally among risk-taking courses of action rather than plunge into uncertainty on the basis of hunch, hearsay, or experience, no matter how carefully quantified.

We can now attempt to define what strategic planning is. *It is the continuous process of making present risk-taking decisions systematically with the greatest knowledge of their futurity; organizing systematically the efforts needed to carry out these decisions; and measuring the results of these decisions against the expectations through organized, systematic feedback.*

SLOUGHING OFF YESTERDAY

Planning starts with the objectives of the business. In each area of objectives, the question needs to be asked, "What do we have to do now to attain our objectives tomorrow?" The first thing to do to attain tomorrow is to slough off yesterday. Most plans concern themselves only with the new and additional things that have to be done—new products, new processes, new markets, and so on. But the key to doing something different tomorrow is getting rid of the no-longer-productive, the obsolescent, and the obsolete.

The first step in planning is to ask of any activity, any product, any process or market, "If we were not committed to this today, would we go into it?" If the answer is no, one says, "How can we get out—fast?"

Systematic sloughing off of yesterday is a plan by itself—and adequate in many businesses. It will force thinking and action. It will make available people and money for new things. It will create the willingness to act.

The plan that provides only for doing additional and new things without provision for sloughing off old and tired ones is unlikely to have results. It will remain plan and never become reality. Yet getting rid of yesterday is the decision that most long-range plans in business (and even more in government) never tackle— which may be the main reason for their futility.

WHAT NEW THINGS DO WE HAVE TO DO—WHEN?

The next step in the planning process is to ask, "What *new* and different things do we have to do, and when?"

In every plan there will be areas where all that is needed—or appears to be needed—is to do more of what we already do. It is prudent, however, to assume that what we already do is never adequate to the needs of the future. But, "What do we need?" is only half the question. Equally important is, "When do we need it?" for it fixes the time for beginning work on the new tasks.

There is indeed a "short range" and a "long range" to every decision. The five years between the commitment to a course (building a steel mill) and the earliest possible moment for results (getting finished steel) is the short range of a decision. And the twenty years or more it takes before we get back with compound interest the money invested in the steel mill is the long range. The long range is the time during which the initial decision must remain reasonably valid—as to markets, process, technology, plant location, etc.—to have been the right decision originally.

But it is meaningless to speak of short-range and long-range plans. There are plans that lead to *action today*—and they are true plans, true strategic decisions. And there are plans that talk about *action tomorrow*—they are dreams, if not pretexts for nonthinking, nonplanning, nondoing. The essence of planning is to make present decisions with knowledge of their futurity. It is the *futurity* that determines the time span, and not vice versa.

Results that require a long gestation period will be obtained only if initiated early enough. Hence, long-range planning requires knowledge of futurity: "What do we have to do today if we want to be in some particular place in the future? What will not get done at all if we do not commit resources to it today?"

To repeat an oft-used illustration: If we know that it takes ninety-nine years to grow Douglas firs in the Northwest to pulping size, planting seedlings today is the only way we can provide for this pulp supply in ninety-nine years. Someone may well develop a speeding-up hormone; but we cannot bank on it if we are using pulp from Douglas firs to make paper. If paper plants depend on Douglas fir, planning cannot confine itself to twenty years, but must consider ninety-nine years.

For other decisions, even five years would be absurdly long. If our business is buying up distress merchandise and selling it at auction, next week's clearance sale is the long-range future; anything beyond is largely irrelevant to us. Thus, the nature of the business and the nature of the decision determine the time spans of planning.

Time spans are neither fixed nor "given." The time decision itself is a risk-taking decision in the planning process. It largely determines the allocation of resources and efforts. It largely determines the risks taken. One cannot repeat too often that to postpone a decision is in itself a risk-taking and often irrevocable decision. The time decision largely determines the character and nature of the business.

To sum up: What is crucial in strategic planning is, first, that systematic and purposeful work on attaining objectives be done; second, that planning start out with sloughing off yesterday and that abandonment be planned as part of the systematic attempt to attain tomorrow; third, that we look for new and different ways to attain objectives rather than believe that doing more of the same will suffice; and finally, that we think through the time dimensions and ask, "When do we have to start work to get results when we need them?"

EVERYTHING DEGENERATES INTO WORK

The best plan is only good intentions unless it leads into work. What makes a plan capable of producing results is the commitment of key people to work on specific tasks. The test of a plan is whether management actually commits resources to action that will bring results in the future. Unless such commitment is made, there are only promises and hopes, but no plan.

A plan needs to be tested by asking managers, "Which of your best people have you put on this work today?" The manager who comes back (as most of them do) and says, "But I can't spare my best people now; they have to finish what they are doing now before I can put them to work on tomorrow" is simply admitting that he or she does not have a plan. But this manager also proves that a plan is needed, for it is precisely the purpose of a plan to show where scarce resources—and the scarcest is good people—should be working.

Work implies not only that somebody is supposed to do the job, but also accountability, a deadline, and, finally, the measurement of results—that is, feedback from results on the work and on the planning process itself.

In strategic planning, measurements present very real problems, especially conceptual ones. Yet precisely because what we measure and how we measure determine what will be considered relevant, and, thereby, determine not just what we see, but what we—and others—do, measurements are all-important in the planning process. Above all, unless we build expectations into the planning decision—including a fair understanding of what are significant deviations both in time and in scale—in such a way that we can find out early whether they are actually fulfilled or not, we cannot plan. We have no feedback, no way of self-control from events back to the planning process.

The manager cannot decide whether he or she wants to make risk-taking decisions with long futurity; making such decisions defines the role of manager. All that is within a manager's power is to decide whether he or she wants to make them responsibly or irresponsibly, with a rational chance of effectiveness and success, or as a blind gamble against all odds. And both because the decision-making process is essentially a rational process and because the effectiveness of the entrepreneurial decisions depends on the understanding and voluntary efforts of others, the approach will be more responsible and more likely to be effective if it is rational, organized, and based on knowledge, not prophecy. The end result, however, is not knowledge but strategy. *Its aim is action now.*

Strategic planning does not substitute facts for judgment, does not substitute science for the manager. It does not even lessen the importance and role of managerial ability, courage, experience, intuition, or even hunch—just as scientific biology and systematic medicine have not lessened the importance of these qualities in the individual physician. On the contrary, the systematic organization of the planning job and the supply of knowledge to it strengthens the manager's judgment, leadership, and vision.

SUMMARY

Strategic planning prepares today's business for the future. It asks, What *should* our business be? It asks, What do we have to do today to deserve the future? Strategic planning requires risk-taking decisions. It requires an organized process of abandoning yesterday. It requires that the work to be done to produce the desired future be clearly defined and clearly assigned. The aim of strategic planning is *action now.*

Part III

Performance in
Service Institutions

The public-service institutions—government agency and hospital; school, college, and university; armed service and professional association—have been growing much faster than business in recent decades. They are the growth sector of a modern society. Yet their performance has not kept up with their growth or importance. What explains the lag in performance in the public-service institutions? How can public-service institutions be managed for performance? And within business, service staffs often grow faster than operating units. Yet the performance of service staffs represents a challenge to management.

12

Managing Service Institutions in the Society of Organizations

Business enterprise is only one of the institutions of modern society, and business managers are by no means our only managers. Service institutions are equally institutions and, therefore, equally in need of management. Some of the most familiar of these institutions are government agencies, the armed services, schools, colleges, universities, research laboratories, hospitals and other health-care institutions, unions, professional practices such as the large law firm, and professional, industry, and trade associations. They all have people who are paid for doing the management job, even though they may be called *administrators, commanders, directors,* or *executives,* rather than *managers.*

THE MULTI-INSTITUTIONAL SOCIETY

We are a multi-institutional society. Public-service institutions are supported by the economic surplus produced by economic activity. They are social overhead. The growth of the public service institution in the twentieth and twenty-first centuries is the best testimonial to the success of business in discharging its economic task—producing economic surplus.

Yet, unlike the early nineteenth-century university, the service institutions are not a luxury or an ornament. They are essentials of a modern society. They *have* to perform if society and business are to function. These service institutions are the main expense of a modern society. Approximately half of the gross national product of the United States (and of most of the other developed countries) is spent on public-service institutions. Every citizen in the developed, industrialized, urbanized societies depends for survival on the performance of the public-service institutions. These institutions also embody the values of developed societies. Education, health care, knowledge, and mobility—not just more food, clothing, and shelter—are the fruits of our society's increased economic capacities and productivity.

Yet the evidence for performance in the service institutions is not impressive, let alone overwhelming. Colleges, hospitals, and universities have grown larger than an earlier generation would have dreamed possible. Their budgets have grown even faster. Yet everywhere they are in crisis. A generation or two ago their performance was taken for granted. Today they are attacked on all sides for lack of performance. Services that the nineteenth century managed success-fully with little apparent effort—the postal service, for instance, or the railroads—are today deep in the red and require enormous subsidies. National and local government agencies are constantly being reorganized for efficiency. Yet in every country citizens complain loudly of growing bureaucracy in gov-ernment. What they mean is that the government agency is being run more for the convenience of its employees than for *contribution* and *performance*. This is mismanagement.

ARE SERVICE INSTITUTIONS MANAGED?

The service institutions themselves have become "management conscious." In-creasingly they turn to business to learn management. In all service institutions, manager development, management by objectives, and many other concepts and tools of business management are now common.

This is a healthy sign, but it does not mean that the service institutions under-stand the problems of managing themselves. It only means that they begin to real-ize that at present they are not being managed.

BUT ARE THEY MANAGEABLE?

There is another and very different response to the performance crisis of the service institutions. A growing number of critics have come to the conclusion that service institutions are inherently unmanageable and incapable of performance. Some go so far as to suggest that they should, therefore, be dissolved. But there is not the slightest evidence that today's society is willing to do without the contributions the service institutions provide. The people who most vocally attack the shortcom-ings of the hospitals want more and better health care. Those who criticize public schools want better, not less, education. The voters bitterest about government bureaucracy vote for more government programs.

We have no choice but to learn to manage the public-service institutions for performance.

And they can be managed for performance.

MANAGING PUBLIC-SERVICE INSTITUTIONS FOR PERFORMANCE

Different classes of service institutions need different structures. But all of them need first to impose on themselves discipline of the kind imposed by leaders of the institutions in the examples in the previous chapters.

1. They need to define "what our business is and what it should be." They need to bring alternative definitions into the open and consider them carefully. They should perhaps even work out some balance between the different and conflicting definitions of mission (as did the presidents of the emerging American universities—see later in this chapter).

2. They must derive *clear objectives* and *goals* from their definition of *function* and *mission*.

3. They then must *set priorities* that enable them to *select targets,* to *set standards* of accomplishment and performance—that is, to define the *minimum acceptable results,* to set *deadlines,* to go to work on *results,* and to make someone *accountable for results.*

4. They must *define measurements of performance*—customer-satisfaction measurements for the performance of Medicare services, or the number of households supplied with electric power (a quantity much easier to measure).

5. They must use these measurements to feed back on their efforts. That is, they must build *self-control by results* into their system.

6. Finally, they need an organized review of objectives and results, to *weed out those objectives* that no longer serve a purpose or have proven unattainable. They need to identify unsatisfactory performance and activities that are outdated or unproductive, or both. And they need a mechanism for dropping such activities rather than wasting money and human energies where the results are poor.

The last requirement may be the most important one. Without a market test, the service institution lacks the built-in discipline that forces a business eventually to abandon yesterday—or else go bankrupt. Assessing and abandoning low-performance activities in service institutions, outside and inside business, would be the most painful but also the most beneficial improvement.

As the examples have shown, no success is "forever." Yet it is even more difficult to abandon yesterday's success than it is to reappraise a failure. A once-successful project gains an air of success that outlasts the project's real usefulness and disguises its failings. In a service institution particularly, yesterday's success becomes "policy," "virtue," "conviction," if not holy writ. The institution must impose on itself the discipline of thinking through its mission, its objectives, and its priorities, and of building in feedback control from results and performance on policies, priorities, and action. Otherwise, it will gradually become less and less effective. We are in such a welfare mess today in the United States largely because the welfare program of the 1930s was such a success. We could not abandon it and, instead, misapplied it to the radically different problem of the inner-city poor.

To make service institutions perform, it should by now be clear, does not require great leaders. *It requires a system.* The essentials of this system are not too different from the essentials of performance in a business enterprise, but the application will be quite different. The service institutions are not businesses; performance means something quite different in them.

The applications of the essentials differ greatly for different service institutions. As our later examples will show, there are *at least three different kinds of service institutions*—institutions that are not paid for performance and results, but for efforts and programs.

THE THREE KINDS OF SERVICE INSTITUTIONS

There is first the *natural monopoly.* It produces economic goods and services, or at least, it is supposed to. Yet it cannot be paid for out of results and performance precisely because it is a monopoly.

The economist defines as natural monopolies those businesses that must have exclusive rights in a given area—the electric power or water utility service. But the research laboratory of a chemical company may also be a natural monopoly within its business.

Lilienthal and the TVA

The Tennessee Valley Authority, the public utility and public works complex in the south central United States built mainly in New Deal days, today is no longer controversial.* It is just another large power company, but *one owned by the government rather than by private investors.* But in its early days, seventy-five years ago, the TVA was more: it was a slogan, a battle cry, a symbol. Some, friends and enemies alike, saw government ownership of the TVA as the opening wedge for the *nationalization* of electric energy in the United States. Others saw it as a boon to the Tennessee Valley region, providing cheap power and free fertilizer to a largely agricultural area. Others, still, were primarily interested in flood control and navigation. There was such a conflict in expectations that TVA's first head, Arthur Morgan, floundered completely. Unable to think through what the business of the TVA should be and how varying objectives might be balanced, he accomplished nothing. Finally, President Franklin Roosevelt replaced him with an almost totally unknown young lawyer with little previous experience as an administrator, David Lilienthal.

---

* The TVA is now (2007) the nation's largest public power company, with 33,000 megawatts of dependable generating capacity. Through 158 locally and publicly-owned distributors, TVA provides power to about 8.7 million residents of the Tennessee Valley and is self-financed: http://www.tva.gov/abouttva/index.htm.

Lilienthal faced up to the need to define TVA's business. He concluded that the first objective was to build truly efficient electric plants and to supply an energy-starved region with plentiful and cheap power. All the rest, he decided, hinged on attaining this first need. Today TVA has accomplished many other objectives as well: flood control, navigable waterways, fertilizer production, and even balanced community development. But it was Lilienthal's insistence on a clear definition of TVA's business and on setting priorities that explains why TVA is now taken for granted, even by those who, forty years ago, were its enemies.

The next group of service institutions are those that have to be paid for out of a *budget allocation*. While all of these share a common character, their individual purpose and the specific way in which they try to accomplish it need not be uniform. Their priorities can—and indeed often should—be quite diverse.

The American university is one example.

The American University

The building of the modern American university from 1860 to World War I also illustrates how service institutions can be made to perform. The American university as it emerged during that period is primarily the work of a small number of men: Andrew W. White (president of Cornell University, 1868–1885); Charles W. Eliot (president of Harvard University, 1869–1909); Daniel Coit Gilman (president of Johns Hopkins University, 1876–1901); David Starr Jordan (president of Stanford University, 1891–1913); William Rainey Harper (president of the University of Chicago, 1892–1904); and Nicholas Murray Butler (president of Columbia University, 1902–1945).

These men all had one basic insight in common: the traditional college—essentially an eighteenth-century seminary to train preachers—had become totally obsolete, sterile, and unproductive.

It was dying fast; America in 1860 had far fewer college students than it had had forty years earlier with a much smaller population. The men who built the new universities shared a common objective: to create a new institution, a true university. They all realized, however, that while European universities had much to offer as examples, these new universities had to be American institutions.

Beyond these shared beliefs, though, they differed sharply on what a university should be and what its purpose and mission were.

Eliot, at Harvard, saw the purpose of the university as educating a leadership group with a distinct style. His Harvard was to be a national institution rather than the preserve of the "proper Bostonian," for whom Harvard College had been founded. But its function was also to restore to New England the leadership of a moral elite, such as had been held by the Federalist leaders in the early days of the

Republic. Butler at Columbia—and to a lesser degree, Harper at Chicago—saw the function of the university as the systematic application of rational thought and analysis to the basic problems of a modern society—education, economics, government, and foreign affairs. Gilman at Johns Hopkins saw the university as the producer of advanced knowledge. Originally Johns Hopkins was to confine itself to advanced research and was to give no undergraduate instruction. White at Cornell aimed at producing an educated public, and so on.

Each of these men knew that he had to make compromises. Each knew that he had to satisfy a number of constituencies and publics, each of whom saw the university differently. Eliot and Butler, for instance, had to build their new universities on existing, old foundations without alienating existing alumni and existing faculty. The others could build from the ground up. They all had to be exceedingly conscious of the need to attract and hold financial support.

It was Eliot, with all his insistence on "moral leadership," who invented the first placement office and set out to find for Harvard graduates well-paid jobs, especially in business. Butler, conscious that Columbia was a latecomer and that the millionaire philanthropists of his day had already been snared by his competitors, invented the first public relations office in a university. It was designed—and most successfully—to reach the merely well-to-do and get their money.

Each of these men gave priority to his definition of the university's purpose and mission. *These definitions did not outlive the founders.* Even during the lifetimes of Eliot and Butler, for instance, their institutions escaped their control, began to diffuse objectives and to confuse priorities. In the twentieth century all these universities—and many others like the University of California and other major state universities—have converged toward a common type.

Today it is hard to tell one "multiversity" from another. Yet the imprint of the founders has still not been totally erased. It is hardly an accident that Roosevelt's New Deal chose primarily faculty members from Columbia and Chicago as high-level advisers and policy makers. The New Deal, like these universities, was committed to the application of rational thought and analysis to public policies and problems. Thirty years later when the Kennedy administration came in with an underlying belief in the style of an elite, it naturally turned to Harvard. *The original clear commitment to purpose and to mission* that made these institutions effective is still visible—though only faintly—in their faculty and graduates.

Each of the six university presidents was concerned with higher education. Each was out to build a university on the ruins of the old, decayed eighteenth-century seminary. They all saw alternative missions and functions. Each tried to structure his university to give different emphasis among these alternatives of "what our business is or should be," and each set different priorities. They knowingly and deliberately built competing institutions with the same structure: trustees, an administration, faculty and students, and similar courses leading to the same degrees.

Finally, the third kind of service institution is the service institution in which means are as important as ends and which, therefore, must be structured and operated uniformly. In this class belongs the administration of justice and defense.

THE INSTITUTIONS' SPECIFIC NEED

What does each of these institutions need?

The natural monopoly needs the least structure. Even though it is not directly paid for results, it is close to them. It just needs to do what any business should be doing anyhow, but to do it more systematically.

This, incidentally, is a strong argument in favor of keeping natural monopolies under public regulation rather than under public ownership. An unregulated natural monopoly will inevitably exploit, in addition to being ineffective and inefficient. A government-owned monopoly may not exploit, but the customer has no redress against inefficiency, poor service, high rates, and disregard of his or her needs. An independently managed monopoly under public regulation is likely to be far more responsive to customer dissatisfactions and consumer needs than either the unregulated private or the government-owned monopoly. The regulated but independently managed monopoly stays in touch with its performance through the regulatory agencies. By their control of rates and profits, these agencies express, at least in theory, public opinion on the performance of the monopoly.

In the late 1960s, the operating efficiency of the American telephone system declined in some areas, notably New York City, and waiting periods for service or for repair grew from days to weeks or months. Customers could and did take effective action. They began immediately to oppose requests from the telephone company for rate increases—and a more effective means of disciplining a monopoly is hard to imagine. The American telephone system has now been deregulated and is subject to intense market competition.

The French telephone customer, on the other hand, who enjoys about the worst telephone service in any developed country, can only grumble. Telephone service there is a government-owned monopoly, against which the consumer is powerless.

In addition, government regulatory agencies can provide the means for building into the structure of monopolies the self-discipline that leads to systematic performance.

With respect to the monopoly that the research laboratory represents in a business, top management can and should demand the discipline of thinking through objectives, setting goals and priorities, measuring performance, and sloughing off the unproductive. This is the only way to make the monopoly research laboratory productive and responsive to the company's needs.

One of the most effective research managers—himself a scientist of world renown—makes it his practice to ask, "What have you in this research lab contributed to the company's vision, knowledge, and results during the last three to five years?" And then he asks, "What do you expect to contribute to the company's vision, knowledge, and results during the next five years?" He reports that he never gets an answer the first time he asks the question. But after asking the question for a few years, he begins to get answers; and a few years later, he even gets research results.

SOCIALIST COMPETITION IN THE SERVICE SECTOR

The second kind of service institution is exemplified by schools, universities, and hospitals. Most of the service staffs within business organizations belong here too. Service institutions of the second kind are characteristic of a developed society.

Monopolies and institutions of government—the service institutions of the first and third categories—dominate undeveloped societies. But the service institution of the second category becomes central in the process of economic and social development. Its performance is crucial to modern developed society. And in developed societies, or developed businesses, it is this service institution that most closely touches the daily life of the citizen—or of the manager.

Customers of this kind of service institution are not really customers. They are more like taxpayers. They pay for the service institution whether they want to or not, out of taxes, levies such as compulsory insurance, or overhead allocations. The products of these institutions do not supply a want. They supply a need. School, hospital, and the typical service staff in business supply what everybody should have, ought to have, must have, because it is "good for them," or good for society.

We talk of the "right of every child to an education" and of the "right of every citizen to decent health care." Yet we already have compulsory education and are well on the way toward compulsory health care.

And when the focus shifts to preventive medicine for large numbers of people, as is likely to happen soon, we will demand that everybody avail themselves of health care facilities. In other words, we will make health care compulsory.

Utilization of the service staff is compulsory in many businesses. The marketing managers in the divisions of a decentralized company are not asked, as a rule, whether they want to attend the marketing seminars put on by the central marketing staff. They are told to come.

Service institutions of this second type need a system like Oskar Lange's socialist competition. The objective—the overall mission—must be general for this kind of service institution. There must be minimum standards of performance and results. But for the sake of performance, it is highly desirable that these institutions have managerial autonomy and not be run by government even if they are supervised and regulated by it. There should also be a fair amount of consumer choice between different ways of accomplishing the basic mission, between different priorities and different methods.* There should be enough competition for these institutions to hold themselves to performance standards.

We talk about and experiment in the United States with a voucher system for elementary and high school education under which the government pays to whatever accredited school the child attends an amount equal to the cost of teaching a child in the public schools. No matter how much latitude schools are given under such a voucher plan, surely no school is considered accredited under it unless it promises to teach at least the basic skills, such as reading, writing, and arithmetic. We may leave it up to the school what method it uses—there is room for the traditional classroom and for the open classroom, or some combination of both—but fundamental goals and minimum standards are, and should be, insisted upon. There is no choice as to whether children of school age go to school or not—they will go whether they and their parents like it or not—but parents or child will exercise the consumer's option in choosing which school to attend. (On additional options for elementary and secondary education, see chapter 14.)

The same approach is already being applied to service staffs in major businesses. One large multinational company, primarily producing and selling branded consumer goods, defines its business as "marketing." With such a definition, one would expect to find a large marketing services staff in the company. But the staff is remarkably small. The marketing services staff has a small budget that pays for such activities as training the marketing services personnel, research in the marketing field, the library, and so on, but not for marketing services to the company's businesses. Every one of the forty to fifty decentralized and autonomously managed businesses of the company located in more than thirty countries is held responsible for its marketing performance and marketing results. To help their businesses reach these results, the local general managers may use the marketing services staff, but they are under no compulsion to do so. They are entitled to use outside consultants of their choice, or they may act as their own marketing consultants. Only if a manager does use the marketing services staff does his or her unit pay for marketing

---

* Lange's model provides for public ownership of the means of production, thus eliminating the capitalist. But it also provides for autonomous businesses, under their own managements, competing in a market economy and getting paid for results. What Lange said, in other words, is that socialist doctrine demands that ownership be socialized. But the allocation of resources has to be done by performance and results, that is, on the basis of the market test, if an economy is to allocate its resources rationally and be capable of performance.

services. The marketing staff, however, evaluates the marketing standards and marketing performance of every unit. When last heard of, eighteen or twenty of the divisional and territorial managers of the company used the marketing services staff. Eleven or twelve used outside consultants. Another dozen used no service staff inside or outside the company. The marketing results of these managers show no correlation to their methods. Among the best and among the poorest performers are divisions that use the company's marketing staff, divisions that use outside consultants, and divisions that do not use any marketing staff at all. Even the poor performers in this company have high standards and good marketing results. And the marketing services staff is among the best I know, in its effectiveness, in its performance, and in its spirit and enthusiasm.

THE INSTITUTIONS OF GOVERNANCE

Service institutions of the third category are, by and large, the traditional government activities—the administration of justice and defense, and all the activities concerned with policy making. These institutions do not provide public goods in the economist's sense of the term; they govern.

Here managerial autonomy is not possible. Competition, if possible at all, would be most undesirable. These institutions have to be under direct government control and directly government operated, yet their activities require the *discipline of objectives, priorities,* and *measurement of results.*

Such institutions require, therefore, an organized, independent review of their promises, the assumptions on which they base themselves, and their performance. There is no way of building feedback from results into these institutions. The only discipline, therefore, to which they can be subjected, is analysis and review.

Now that service institutions have become so central, so important, and so costly, we need an auditor-general of objectives and performance. We need to force ourselves to look at proposed government policies, laws, and programs—but also at the policies, programs, and activities of service staffs—and ask, "Are the objectives realistic? Are they attainable or just slogans? How do they relate to the needs they are supposed to satisfy? Have the right targets been set? Have priorities been thought through? And do results relate to promises and expectations?"

We need to go further and accept as a basic premise that every governmental agency and every act of the legislature is to be considered impermanent. A new activity, a new agency, a new program, should be enacted for a specific time, to be extended only if the results prove the soundness of the objective and of the means chosen. Outside of government, in other service institutions—including those that should be autonomous even though public (school or hospital, e.g.)—this way of thinking will also have to become standard. Society is becoming too dependent on the performance and results of service institutions to tolerate the traditional system forever.

Failure to drop nonperforming programs accounts for many of our worst problems. It underlies the failure of the U.S. and the Common Market farm programs; it underlies the "welfare mess" that continues to threaten and destroy our cities; and it underlies the frustration with our international development programs.

Without feedback from results, our efforts to protect the environment are unlikely to succeed. Results are badly needed, but so far we have neither thought through what we are after nor set priorities. Nor have we organized a feedback from results on the direction, the priorities, and the efforts of the environmental crusade. Predictably, this can only mean no results and rapid disenchantment.

What the service institutions need is not to be more businesslike. They need to be subjected to performance tests—if only to that of "socialist competition"—as much as possible. They need to be more *hospital-like, university-like, government-like, church-like,* and so on. In other words, they need to think through their own specific functions, purposes, and missions.

What the service institutions need is not better people. They need people who do the management job systematically and who focus themselves and their institution purposefully on performance and results. They do need efficiency—that is, control of costs—but above all, they need effectiveness—emphasis on the right results.

Few service institutions today suffer from having too few administrators. Most of them are overadministered and suffer from a surplus of procedures, organization charts, and management techniques. What we have to learn is to manage service institutions for performance. This may well be the most important management task of the twenty-first century.

SUMMARY

To make service institutions and service staffs perform does not require genius. It requires, first, clear objectives and goals. Next, it demands priorities on which resources can be concentrated. It requires, further, clear measurements of accomplishment. And finally, it demands organized abandonment of the obsolete. And these four requirements are just as important for the service staff of a business as for the service institution in society.

13

What Successful and Performing Nonprofits Are Teaching Business

The Girl Scouts, the Red Cross, the pastoral churches—nonprofit organizations—are becoming America's management leaders. In two areas, strategy and the effectiveness of the board, they are practicing what most American businesses only preach. And in the most crucial area—the motivation and productivity of knowledge workers—they are truly pioneers, working out the policies and practices that business will have to learn tomorrow.

Few people are aware that the nonprofit sector is by far America's largest employer.* Approximately 80 million plus people work as volunteers, each giving on average nearly five hours a week to one or several nonprofit organizations. This is equal to 10 million full-time jobs. And volunteer work is changing fast. To be sure, what many do requires little skill or judgment: collecting in the neighborhood for the Community Chest one Saturday afternoon a year, chaperoning youngsters selling Girl Scout cookies door-to-door, driving old people to the doctor. But more and more volunteers are becoming "unpaid staff," taking over the professional and managerial tasks in their organizations.

Not all nonprofits have been doing well, of course (on the management challenges for many nonprofit institutions, see chapter 12). A good many community

---

* Approximately one-hundred nonprofit organizations are created every day and foundations are being formed at the rate of approximately 3,000 each year in the United States. Volunteerism in America recently hit a 30-year high; with 27 percent of Americans claiming that they volunteer on a regular basis. Charitable giving has hit approximately $300 billion, up from $120 billion a few years ago. Source: "Creating the Future of Nonprofits: Opportunity and Innovation in the Social Sector," Keynote address by Thomas Tierney at a conference sponsored by the Drucker Institute and Leader to Leader Institute, November 19, 2007, New York City. Thomas Tierney is chairman of the Bridgespan Group, a nonprofit organization designed to provide general management consulting services to foundations and other nonprofits. Tierney is the former CEO of Bain & Co.

hospitals are in dire straits. Traditional churches and synagogues of all persuasions—liberal, conservative, evangelical, fundamentalist—are still steadily losing members. Indeed, the sector overall has not expanded in the last twenty or twenty-five years, either, in terms of the number of volunteers. Yet in its productivity, in the scope of its work, and in its contribution to American society, the nonprofit sector has grown tremendously in the last three decades.

A COMMITMENT TO MANAGEMENT

The Salvation Army Correctional Services is the largest provider of misdemeanor probation services in Florida, meeting judicial and county government needs since 1975.*

People convicted to their first prison term in Florida, mostly very poor black or Hispanic youths, are now paroled into the Salvation Army's custody—approximately 25,000 each year. Statistics show that if these young men and women go to jail, the majority will become habitual criminals. But the Salvation Army has been able to rehabilitate 80 percent of them through a strict work program run largely by volunteers.† And the program costs a fraction of what it would to keep the offenders behind bars.

Underlying this program and many other effective nonprofit endeavors is a *commitment to professional management*. Twenty years ago, "management" was a dirty word for those involved in nonprofit organizations. It meant *business*, and nonprofits prided themselves on being free of the taint of commercialism and above such sordid considerations as the bottom line. Now most of them have learned that nonprofits need management even more than business does, precisely because they lack the discipline of the bottom line. The nonprofits are, of course, still dedicated to "doing good." But the most effective ones realize that good intentions are no substitute for organization and leadership, for accountability, performance, and results. Those require management, and that, in turn, begins with the organization's mission.

Starting with the mission and its requirements may be the first lesson business can learn from *successful nonprofits*. It focuses the organization on action. It defines the specific strategies needed to attain the crucial goals. It creates a disciplined organization. It alone can prevent the most common degenerative disease of organizations, especially large ones: splintering their always limited resources on things that are *interesting* or look *profitable* rather than concentrating them on a *very small number of productive efforts*.

---

* Sourced July 25, 2007, at http://www.cbsnews.com/stories/2007/01/30/national/printable2412890
.shtml
† See Robert A. Watson & Ben Brown, *Leadership Secrets of The Salvation Army* (New York: Crown Business, 2001) pp. 153–154.

The best nonprofits devote a great deal of thought to defining their organization's mission. They avoid sweeping statements full of good intentions and, instead, focus on objectives that have clear-cut implications for the work their members perform—staff and volunteers both. For example: The Salvation Army's mission is *"to turn society's rejects—alcoholics, criminals, derelicts—into citizens."* *"The Girl Scouts help youngsters become confident, capable young women who respect themselves and other people."* *"The Nature Conservancy preserves the diversity of nature's fauna and flora."* Successful nonprofits also start with the environment, the community, the customers to be; they do not, as American businesses often do, start with the inside—that is, with the organization or with financial returns.

Willow Creek Community Church in South Barrington, Illinois, outside Chicago, has become one of the nation's largest churches, approximately 15,000 in weekly attendance in 2007. Bill Hybels, in his early twenties when he founded the church in 1970, chose the community because it had relatively few churchgoers, though the population was growing fast and churches were plentiful. He went from door to door asking, "Why don't you go to church?" Then he designed a church to answer the potential customers' needs: for instance, it offers full services on Wednesday evenings because many working parents need Sunday to spend with their children. Moreover, Hybels continues to listen and react. The pastor's sermon is taped while it is being delivered and instantly reproduced so that parishioners can pick up a cassette when they leave the building, because he was told again and again, "I need to listen when I drive home or drive to work so that I can build the message into my life." But he was also told, "The sermon always tells me to change my life but never how to do it." So now every one of Hybels's sermons ends with specific action recommendations.

A well-defined mission serves as a constant reminder of the need to look outside the organization not only for "customers" but also for measures of success. The temptation to content oneself with the "goodness of our cause"—and thus to substitute good intentions for results always exists in nonprofit organizations. It is precisely because of this that the successful and performing nonprofits have learned to define clearly *what changes outside the organization constitute "results" and to focus on them.*

The experience of one large Catholic hospital chain in the Southwest shows how productive a clear sense of mission and a focus on results can be. Despite the sharp cuts in Medicare payments and hospital stays during the previous eight years, this chain increased revenues by 15 percent (thereby managing to break even) while greatly expanding its services and raising both patient care and medical standards. It has done so because the nun who was its CEO understood that she and her staff are in the business of delivering health care (especially to the poor), not running hospitals.

As a result, when health-care delivery began moving out of hospitals, for medical rather than economic reasons, the chain promoted the trend instead of fighting it. It founded ambulatory surgery centers, rehabilitation centers, X-ray and lab networks, HMOs, and so on. The chain's motto was: "If it's in the patient's interest, we have to promote it; it's then our job to make it pay." Paradoxically, the policy has filled the chain's hospitals; the freestanding facilities are so popular they generate a steady stream of referrals.

This is, of course, not so different from the marketing strategy of successful Japanese companies. But it is very different indeed from the way most Western businesses think and operate. And the difference is that the Catholic nuns—and the Japanese—start with the mission rather than with their own rewards, and with what they have to make happen outside themselves, in the marketplace, to deserve a reward.

Finally, a clearly defined mission will foster innovative ideas and help others understand why they need to be implemented—however much the ideas fly in the face of tradition. To illustrate, consider the Daisy Scouts, a program for five-year-olds that the Girl Scouts initiated a few years back. For ninety years, first grade had been the minimum age for entry into a Brownie troop, and many Girl Scout councils wanted to keep it that way. Others, however, looked at demographics and saw the growing number of working women with "latchkey" kids. They also looked at the children and realized that they were far more sophisticated than their predecessors a generation ago (largely thanks to TV).

Today the Daisy Scouts are 100,000 strong and growing fast. It is by far the most successful of the many programs for preschoolers that have been started these last twenty years, and far more successful than any of the very expensive government programs. Moreover, it is so far the only program that has seen *these critical demographic changes* and children's exposure to long hours of TV viewing as an *opportunity*.

EFFECTIVE USE OF THE BOARD

Many nonprofits now have what is still the exception in business—a functioning board. They also have something even rarer: a CEO who is clearly accountable to the board and whose performance is reviewed annually by a board committee. And they have what is rarer still: a board whose performance is reviewed annually against preset performance objectives. Effective use of the board is thus a second area in which business can learn from the nonprofit sector.

In U.S. law, the board of directors is still considered the "managing" organ of the corporation. Management authors and scholars agree that strong boards are essential and have been writing to that effect for more than thirty-five years, beginning with Myles Mace's pioneering work.* Nevertheless, the top managements

---

* Myles Mace, "The President and the Board of Directors," *Harvard Business Review* (March–April 1972) p. 37.

of our large companies have been whittling away at the directors' role, power, and independence for more than half a century. In every single business failure of a large company in the last few decades, the board was the last to realize that things were going wrong. To find a truly effective board, you are much better advised to look in the nonprofit sector than in our public corporations.

In part, this difference is a product of history. Traditionally, the board has run the shop in nonprofit organizations—or tried to. In fact, it is only because nonprofits have grown too big and complex to be run by part-time outsiders, meeting for three hours a month, that so many have shifted to professional management. The American Red Cross is probably the largest nongovernmental agency in the world and certainly one of the most complex. It is responsible for worldwide disaster relief; it runs thousands of blood banks as well as the bone and skin banks in hospitals; it conducts training in cardiac and respiratory rescue nationwide; and it gives first-aid courses in thousands of schools. Yet it did not have a paid chief executive until 1950, and its first professional CEO came only with the Reagan era.

But however common professional management becomes—and professional CEOs are now found in most nonprofits and all the bigger ones—nonprofit boards cannot, as a rule, be rendered impotent the way so many business boards have been. No matter how much nonprofit CEOs would welcome it—and quite a few surely would—nonprofit boards cannot become their rubber stamp. Money is one reason. Few directors in publicly held corporations are substantial shareholders, whereas directors on nonprofit boards very often contribute large sums themselves, and are expected to bring in donors as well. But also, nonprofit directors tend to have a personal commitment to the organization's cause. Few people sit on a church vestry or on a schoolboard unless they deeply care about religion or education. Moreover, nonprofit board members typically have served as volunteers themselves for a good many years and are deeply knowledgeable about the organization, unlike outside directors in a business.

Precisely because the nonprofit board is so committed and active, its relationship with the CEO tends to be highly contentious and full of potential for friction. Nonprofit CEOs complain that their board "meddles." The directors, in turn, complain that management "usurps" the board's function. This has forced an increasing number of nonprofits to realize that neither board nor CEO is "the boss." They are colleagues, working for the same goal, but each having a different task. And they have learned that it is the CEO's responsibility to define the tasks of each, the board's and his or her own.

The key to making a board effective, as this example suggests, is not to talk about its function but to organize its work. More and more nonprofits are doing just that, currently among them half a dozen fair-sized liberal arts colleges, a leading theological seminary, and some large research hospitals and museums.

The weakening of the large corporation's board would, many of us predicted (beginning with Myles Mace), weaken management rather than strengthen it. It would diffuse management's accountability for performance and results; and indeed, it is the rare big-company board that reviews the CEO's performance against preset business objectives. Weakening the board would also deprive top management of effective and credible support if it were attacked. These predictions have been borne out amply in the recent rash of takeovers.

To restore management's ability to manage, we will have to make boards effective again—and that should be considered a responsibility of the CEO. A few first steps have been taken. The audit committee in most public companies now has a real rather than a make-believe job responsibility. A number of companies have a small board committee on succession and executive development, which regularly meets with senior executives to discuss their performance and their plans. But few companies do what the larger nonprofits now do routinely: put a new board member through systematic training.

TO OFFER MEANINGFUL ACHIEVEMENT

Nonprofits used to say, "We don't pay volunteers, so we cannot make demands upon them." Now they are more likely to say, "Volunteers must get far greater satisfaction from their accomplishments and make a greater contribution precisely because they do not get a paycheck." The steady transformation of the volunteer from well-meaning amateur to trained, professional, unpaid staff member is the most significant development in the nonprofit sector—as well as the one with the most far-reaching implications for tomorrow's businesses.

A midwestern Catholic diocese may have come furthest in this process. It now has fewer than half the priests and nuns it had only fifteen years ago. Yet it has greatly expanded its activities—in some cases, such as help for the homeless and for drug abusers, more than doubling them. It still has many traditional volunteers like the Altar Guild members who arrange flowers. But now it is also being served by some 2,000 part-time unpaid staff that run the Catholic charities, perform administrative jobs in parochial schools, and organize youth activities, college Newman Clubs, and even some retreats.

This development is by no means confined to religious organizations. The American Heart Association has chapters in every city of any size throughout the country. Yet its paid staff is limited to those at national headquarters, with just a few traveling troubleshooters serving the field. Volunteers manage and staff the chapters, with full responsibility for community health education as well as fund-raising.

These changes are, in part, a response to need. With close to half the adult population already serving as volunteers, their overall number is unlikely to grow. And with money always in short supply, the nonprofits cannot add paid staff. If they want to add to their activities—and needs are growing—they have to make volunteers more productive, have to give them more work and more responsibility. But the need for productivity aside, the major impetus for the change in the volunteer's role has actually come from the volunteers themselves.

More and more volunteers are educated people in managerial or professional jobs—some retirement men and women in their sixties, even more baby boomers who are reaching their mid-fifties. These people are not satisfied with being helpers. They are knowledge workers in the jobs in which they earn their living, and they want to be knowledge workers in the jobs in which they contribute to society—that is, their volunteer work. If nonprofit organizations want to attract and hold them, they have to put their competence and knowledge to work. They have to offer meaningful achievement.

TRAINING, TRAINING, TRAINING

Many nonprofits systematically recruit for such people. Seasoned volunteers are assigned to scan the newcomers—the new member in a church or synagogue, the neighbor who collects for the Red Cross—to find those with leadership talent and persuade them to try themselves in more demanding assignments. Then senior staff (either a full-timer on the payroll or a seasoned volunteer) interviews the newcomers to assess their strengths and place them accordingly. Volunteers may also be assigned both a mentor and a supervisor with whom they work out their performance goals. These advisers are two different people, as a rule, and both, ordinarily, volunteers themselves.

The Girl Scouts, which employs 986,000 volunteers and only 6,000 paid staff for 3.7 million girl members, works this way.* A volunteer typically starts by driving youngsters once a week to a meeting. Then a more seasoned volunteer draws her into other work—accompanying Girl Scouts selling cookies door-to-door, assisting a Brownie leader on a camping trip. Out of this step-by-step process evolve the volunteer boards of the local councils and, eventually, the Girl Scouts governing organ, the national board. Each step, even the very first, has its

---

* "Girl Scout national headquarters is located in New York City, with over 400 employees dedicated to supporting the Girl Scout Movement. In partnership with more than 300 local Girl Scout councils or offices, 236,000 troops/groups, 986,000 adult volunteers, our National Board of Directors, and countless corporate, government, and individual supporters, Girl Scouts is helping today's girls become tomorrow's leaders." Sourced July 25, 2007, at http://www.girlscouts.org/who_we_are/.

own compulsory training program, usually conducted by a woman who is herself a volunteer. Each has specific performance standards and performance goals.

What do these unpaid staff people themselves demand? What makes them stay?—and, of course, they can leave at any time. Their first and most important demand is that the nonprofit have a *clear mission,* one that drives everything the organization does. A senior vice president in a large regional bank has two small children. Yet she just took over as chair of the state chapter of Nature Conservancy, which finds, buys, and manages endangered natural ecologies. "I love my job," she said, when I asked her why she took on such heavy additional work, "and of course the bank has a creed. But it doesn't really know what it contributes. At Nature Conservancy, I know what I am here for."

The second thing this new breed requires, indeed demands, is training, training, and more training. And, in turn, the most effective way to motivate and hold veterans is to recognize their expertise and use them to train newcomers. Then, these knowledge workers demand responsibility—above all, for thinking through and setting their own performance goals. They expect to be consulted and to participate in making decisions that affect their work and the work of the organization as a whole. And they expect opportunities for advancement, that is, a chance to take on more demanding assignments and more responsibility as their performance warrants. That is why a good many nonprofits have developed career ladders for their volunteers.

Supporting all this activity is *accountability.* Many of today's knowledge-worker volunteers insist on having their performance reviewed against preset objectives at least once a year. And increasingly, they expect their organizations to remove nonperformers by moving them to other assignments that better fit their capacities or by counseling them to leave. "It's worse than the Marine Corps boot camp," says the priest in charge of volunteers in the midwestern diocese, "but we have 400 people on the waiting list." One large and growing midwestern art museum requires of its volunteers—board members, fund-raisers, docents, and the people who edit the museum's newsletter—that they set their goals each year, appraise themselves against these goals each year, and resign when they fail to meet their goals two years in a row. So does a fair-sized Jewish organization working on college campuses.

These volunteer professionals are still a minority, but a significant one—perhaps a tenth of the total volunteer population. And they are growing in numbers and, more important, in their impact on the nonprofit sector. Increasingly, nonprofits say what one minister in a large pastoral church says, "There is no laity in this church; there are only pastors, a few paid, most unpaid."

A WARNING TO BUSINESS

This move from nonprofit volunteer to unpaid professional may be the most important development in American society today. We hear a great deal about the decay and dissolution of family and community and about the loss of values. And, of course, there is reason for concern. But the nonprofits are generating a powerful countercurrent. They are forging *new bonds of community*, a new commitment to active citizenship, to social responsibility, to values. And surely what the nonprofit contributes to the volunteer is as important as what the volunteer contributes to the nonprofit. Indeed, it may be fully as important as the service—whether religious, educational, or welfare related—that the nonprofit provides in the community.

This development also carries a clear lesson for business. Managing the knowledge worker for productivity is the challenge ahead for American management. The nonprofits are showing us how to do that. It requires a clear mission, careful placement, continuous learning and teaching, management by objectives and self-control, high demands but corresponding responsibility, and accountability for performance and results (on increasing the productivity of knowledge workers, see chapter 19).

There is also, however, a clear warning to American business in this transformation of volunteer work. The students in the program for senior and middle-level executives in which I taught worked in a wide diversity of businesses: banks and insurance companies, large retail chains, aerospace and computer companies, real estate developers, and many others. But most of them also served as volunteers in nonprofits—in a church, on the board of the college they graduated from, as scout leaders, with the YMCA or the Community Chest or the local symphony orchestra. When I asked them why they did it, far too many gave roughly the same answer: "Because in my job there isn't much challenge, not enough achievement, not enough responsibility; and there is no mission, there is only expediency."

SUMMARY

The first lesson business executives can learn from successful nonprofits is to begin with *mission*. Successful nonprofits such as the Salvation Army avoid bland mission statements and focus their mission statement on specific strategies and action: "to turn society's rejects—alcoholics, criminals, derelicts—into citizens." Successful mission statements focus on the outside—the community and the customer. They look outside for what are considered *meaningful results*.

Many nonprofits have what is still rare in business, a *functioning board* with clear duties and responsibilities and measures of both CEO and board effectiveness. Nonprofit boards often serve as volunteers and contributors to the organization and feel commitment toward the mission and active involvement in the actual operations of the organization. As a result, they know more about operations of the organization than their business counterparts.

Finally, successful nonprofits know how to manage volunteers. Managing volunteers requires a clear mission (or score), high demands, accountability, and training. These requirements for effective volunteers are very close to the requirements for leading *knowledge workers* in other sectors of the economy.

14

The Accountable School

A *technological revolution*—desktop computers and satellite transmission directly into the classroom—is engulfing our schools. It will transform the way we learn and the way we teach within a few decades. It will change the economics of education. From being almost totally labor-intensive, schools will become highly capital-intensive.

But more drastic still—though rarely discussed as yet—will be the changes in the social position and role of the school. Though long a central institution, it has been "of society" rather than "in society." It concerned itself with the young, who were not yet citizens, not yet responsible, not yet in the workforce. In the knowledge society, the school becomes the institution of the adults as well, and especially of highly schooled adults. Above all, in the knowledge society, the school becomes accountable for performance and results.

These specifications call for a school as different from the one that exists now as the "modern" school for which the Czech educator and theologian John Amos Comenius drew up the specifications 350 years ago differed from the school that existed before the printed book.

Here are the new specifications:

- The school we need has to provide universal literacy of a high order—well beyond what "literacy" means today.

- It has to imbue students on all levels and of all ages with the motivation to learn and with the discipline of continuing to learn.

- It has to be an open system, accessible both to highly educated people and to people who, for whatever reason, did not gain access to advanced education in their early years.

- It has to impart knowledge both as substance and as process—what the Germans differentiate as *Wissen* and *Können*.

- Finally, schooling can no longer be a monopoly of the schools. Education in

the postcapitalist society has to permeate the entire society, employing organizations of all kinds—businesses, government agencies, nonprofits—
which must become institutions of learning and teaching as well. Schools,
increasingly, must work in partnership with employers and employing organizations.

THE NEW PERFORMANCE DEMANDS

Universal literacy of a very high order is the first priority—it is the foundation.
Without it, no society can hope to be capable of high performance in the postcapitalist world and in its knowledge society. To equip individual students with the
tools to perform, to contribute, and to be employable is also the first social duty of
any educational system.

The new technology of learning will have its first impact on universal literacy.
Most schools throughout the ages have spent endless hours trying to teach things
that are best learned, rather than taught, that is, things that are learned behaviorally
and through drill, repetition, and feedback. Here belong most of the subjects taught
in elementary school, but also a good many of the subjects taught in later stages of
the educational process. Such subjects—whether reading and writing, arithmetic,
spelling, historical facts, biology, and even such advanced subjects as neurosurgery,
medical diagnosis, and most of engineering—are best learned through a computer
program. The teacher motivates, directs, encourages. The teacher, in fact, becomes a
leader and a resource.

In the school of tomorrow, the students will be their own instructors, with a
computer program as their own tool. Indeed, the younger the students are, the
more the computer appeals to them, the more successfully it guides and instructs
them. Historically, the elementary school has been totally labor-intensive. Tomorrow's elementary school will be heavily capital-intensive

Yet, despite the available technology, the goal of universal literacy poses tremendous challenges. The traditional concepts of literacy no longer suffice. Reading, writing, arithmetic, will be needed just as they are today, but literacy now has
to go well beyond these foundations. It requires numeracy; it requires a basic understanding of science and of the dynamics of technology; it requires an acquain-
tance with foreign languages. It also requires learning how to be effective as a
member of an organization, as an employee.

Universal literacy implies a clear commitment to the priority of schooling. It
demands that the school—especially the school of the beginners, the children—
subordinate everything else to the acquisition of foundation skills. Unless the
school successfully imparts these skills to the young learner, it has failed in its
crucial duty: to give beginners self-confidence, to give them competence, and to

make them capable, a few years hence, of performing and achieving in the post-capitalist society, the knowledge society.

This requires a reversal of the prevailing trend in modern education and especially in American education. Having, as we thought, achieved universal literacy in the United States by the end of World War I or, at the latest, by the end of World War II, American education reversed its priorities. Instead of being a learning agency first, it put being a social agency first. In the 1950s and 1960s, when we in the United States made this decision, it was probably an inevitable one. The severity and extent of the racial problem we faced forced us to make the school the agent of racial integration; the legacy of the sin of slavery has been the central American challenge for 150 years and is likely to remain the central American challenge for at least another fifty or hundred years.

But the schools could not do this social job. Like every other organization, the schools are good only at *their own special-purpose task*. Subordinating learning to social goals may have actually impeded racial integration and the advancement of African-American people—as more and more achieving blacks now assert. Yet putting social ends ahead of the goal of learning became a major factor in the decline of American basic education. Upper- and middle-class children still acquire traditional literacy, but the ones who need it most—the children of the poor, especially of poor blacks, and the children of immigrants—do not.

What we have to do now is to reassert the original purpose of the school. *That purpose is not social reform or social amelioration;* it has to be *individual learning*. The most hopeful developments in U.S. education may well be that this is increasingly being asserted by achieving African-Americans and Latinos themselves, such as the black woman legislator in Milwaukee, Wisconsin, who pushed through a "voucher plan" against the strident opposition of the educational establishment. This plan enables parents to choose for their child a school that focuses on, indeed demands, learning.

This will be attacked by liberals and progressives as an elitist position. But the most elitist school, the Japanese school, has created the most egalitarian society. Even those who do not shine in the intensely competitive educational race in Japan still acquire what by any traditional standard is extremely high literacy and an extremely high ability to achieve and perform in modern society. Yet in the Japanese school, literacy is put first, and everything else is subordinated to it. But there are also enough American schools around by now in which the most disadvantaged children learn because it is expected of them and demanded of them.

LEARNING TO LEARN

"Literacy" traditionally meant subject knowledge, for example, the ability to do multiplication or a little knowledge of American history. But the knowledge society equally needs process knowledge—something the schools have rarely even tried to teach. *In the knowledge society, people have to learn how to learn.* Indeed, in the knowledge society, subjects may matter less than the students' capacity to continue learning and their motivation to do so. *Knowledge society requires lifelong learning.* For this, we need a *discipline of learning.*

Actually, we do know what to do. In fact, for hundreds, if not thousands, of years we have been creating both the motivation for continuing to learn and the needed discipline. The good teachers of artists do it; the good coaches of athletes do it; so do the good "mentors" in business organizations of which we hear so much these days in the literature of management development. They lead their students to achievements so great that it surprises the achiever and creates excitement and motivation—especially the motivation for rigorous, disciplined, persistent work and practice that continued learning requires.

There are few things more boring than practicing scales. Yet the greater and the more accomplished pianists are, the more faithfully do they practice their scales, hour after hour, day after day, week after week. Similarly, the more skilled surgeons are, the more faithfully do they practice tying sutures, hour after hour, day after day, week after week. Pianists do their scales for months on end for an infinitesimally small improvement in technical ability. But this then enables them to achieve the musical result they already hear in their inner ear. Surgeons tie sutures for months on end for an infinitesimally small improvement in their finger dexterity, but this then enables them to speed up an operation and thus save a life. *Achievement is addictive.*

But such achievement does not mean doing a little less poorly what one is not particularly good at. The achievement that motivates is doing exceptionally well what one is already good at. Achievement has to be based on the student's strengths—as has been known for millennia by every teacher of artists, every coach of athletes, and every mentor. In fact, *finding the student's strengths and focusing them on achievement* is the best definition of the goal of teaching. It is the definition in the "Dialogue on the Teacher" by one of the greatest teachers of the Western tradition, Saint Augustine of Hippo (354–430).

Schools and schoolteachers know this too, of course. But they have rarely been allowed to focus on the strengths of students and to challenge them. Instead, they have perforce had to focus on weaknesses. Practically all the time spent in traditional Western classrooms—at least until graduate school at the university—is spent on remedying weaknesses. It is spent on producing respectable mediocrity.*

---

* The popularity of the magnet schools within public school districts in the United States, which offer specialized courses and curricula, is a promising trend for encouraging students to develop their strengths.

Students do need to acquire minimal competence in core skills; they do need remedial work. They do need to acquire mediocrity. But in the traditional school, there is practically no time for anything else. The proudest products of the traditional school, "the all-around 'A' students," are the ones who satisfy mediocre standards across the board. They are not the ones who achieve; they are the ones who comply. But, to repeat, the traditional school had no choice. To give every student adequacy in the foundation skills is the first task. This could only be accomplished—even in a small class—by focusing on the weaknesses of students and then remedying them.

Here, the new technologies might make the greatest difference. They free teachers from spending most, if not all, of their time on routine learning, remedial learning, and repetitive learning. Teachers will still need to lead in these activities. But most of their time has traditionally been spent on "follow-up"; teachers, in an old phrase, spend most of their time being "teaching assistants." And that the computer does well, indeed, better than a human being. Teachers, we can hope, will thus increasingly have the time to identify the strengths of individuals, to focus on them, and to lead students to achievement. They will, we can expect, have the time to teach.

THE SCHOOL IN SOCIETY

The school has been a central social institution for a long time—in the West at least since the Renaissance, even longer in the Orient. But it has traditionally been "of society" rather than "in society." It has been a separate institution that rarely, if ever, combined with any other institution. The earliest schools in the West, the Benedictine monasteries of the early Middle Ages, primarily trained future monks rather than the laity. The school was not for grown people; the root of the word "pedagogy"—*paidos*—is the Greek word for "boy."

That the school will now increasingly be in society may, therefore, be as radical a change as any change in teaching and learning methods, in subject matter, or in the teaching and learning process. School will continue to teach the young. But with learning becoming a lifelong activity rather than something one stops upon becoming "grown-up," schools will have to be organized for lifelong learning. Schools will have to become "open systems."

Schools almost everywhere are organized on the assumption that a student has to enter every stage at a given age, with a prescribed and standardized preparation. One starts kindergarten at age five, elementary school at age six, middle school at age twelve, high school at age fifteen, college or university at age eighteen, and so on. If one misses one of these steps (except kindergarten), one is forever out of step and rarely permitted back in.

For the traditional school, this is a self-evident axiom, almost a law of nature. But it is incompatible with the nature of knowledge and with the demands of the knowledge society. What is needed now is a new axiom: "The more schooling a person has, the more often he or she will need further schooling."

In the United States, doctors, lawyers, engineers, business executives, are increasingly expected to go back to school every few years lest they become obsolete. Outside of the United States, however, the return of adults to formal schooling is still the exception—and particularly the return of adults to advanced schooling in the very fields in which they have already acquired substantial knowledge and an advanced degree. In Japan, this phenomenon is still almost unknown; but so it is in France, in Italy, and by and large in Germany, Great Britain, and Scandinavia as well. It will have to become standard in all developed countries.

Even more novel is the need to make the educational system open-ended, that is, to allow people to enter its stages at any age.

Even in countries like the United States and Japan, in which very large numbers of young people go on to the university, many more stop their schooling by the time they are sixteen or eighteen. There is no reason to believe that most of these people lack the intellectual endowment for knowledge work. All our experience proves the opposite. What distinguishes them from the young people who go on to the university is often only lack of money. Also a fair number of very bright young people do not go on to the university because they are mature at age eighteen and want to be adults rather than continue in the cocoon of adolescence. Ten years later, many want to resume their education. Then—as everyone who has taught them will testify—they become challenging students, if only because of their superior motivation. They now *want* to take on advanced work; the nineteen-year-olds do so because they are told to do it.

But even more important, keeping open access to advanced education regardless of age or prior educational credentials is a social necessity.

Individuals must be able at any stage in their lives to continue their formal education and to qualify for knowledge work. Society needs to be willing to accept people into whatever work they are qualified for, regardless of their age.

Schooling will no longer be what schools do. It will increasingly be a joint venture, in which schools are partners rather than monopolists. In many areas, schools will also be only one of several available teaching and learning institutions, in competition with other purveyors of teaching and learning.

School, as has been said before, has traditionally been where you learn; job has been where you work. Increasingly, the line will become blurred. Increasingly, school will be the place where adults continue learning even though they are working full time. They will come back to school for a three-day seminar; for a weekend course; for an intensive three-week stint; or to take courses on two evenings each week for several years until they acquire a degree.

Yet the job will equally be where adults continue learning. Training is of course nothing new, but it used to be restricted to the beginner. Increasingly, training in one form or another will also become lifelong. The adult—and especially the adult with advanced knowledge—will be as much trainer as trainee, as much teacher as student. In the United States, employers already spend almost as much money on training adult employees as the country spends on educating the young in its formal schools.

What is yet to come is a formal partnership between schools and employing institutions. The Germans, in their apprenticeship programs, have had schools and employers working together for more than 150 years training the young. But increasingly, schools and employing institutions will have to learn to work together in the advanced education of adults as well. This task—whether the advanced education of highly educated people or makeup education for people who, for one reason or another, failed to gain access to higher education in the early years—will be carried out in all kinds of partnerships, alliances, internships, in which schools and other organizations work together. The schools need the stimulus of working with adults and employing organizations fully as much as the adults and their employing organizations need the stimulus of working with schools.

THE ACCOUNTABLE SCHOOL

We talk of "good schools" and "poor schools," of "prestige schools" and "also-rans." In Japan, a few universities—Tokyo, Kyoto, Keio, Waseda, Hitotsubashi—largely control access to careers in major companies and government agencies. In France, the Grandes Écoles enjoy a similar position of power and prestige. And while no longer Academia's absolute monarchs, Oxford and Cambridge are still the superpowers of English higher education.

We also go in for all kinds of measurements: the proportion of graduates of a particular liberal arts college who go on to acquire a doctorate; the number of books in a college library; the number of graduates of an American suburban high school who get accepted by the college of their first choice; the popularity of different universities among students. But we have barely begun to ask, *What are the results in this school? What should they be?*

These questions would have come up anyhow. In the twenty-first century, education is much too expensive not to be held accountable. Expenditures on the school systems in developed countries skyrocketed from 2 percent of the GNP around 1913 to 10 percent eighty years later.

But schools have also become much too important not to be held accountable—for thinking through what their results should be, as well as for their performance in attaining these results. To be sure, different school systems will give different answers to these questions. But every school system and every school will soon be required to ask them, and to take them seriously. We will no longer accept the schoolteacher's age-old excuse for malperformance: "The students are lazy and stupid." With knowledge the central resource of society, lazy students or poor students are the responsibility of the school. *There are then only schools that perform and schools that do not perform.*

The schools are already losing their monopoly as providers of schooling.

But increasingly the competition will be between schools and "nonschools," with different kinds of institutions entering the field, each offering a different approach to schooling.*

As knowledge becomes the key resource of the knowledge society, the social position of school as "producer" and "distributive channel" of knowledge, and its monopoly, are both bound to be challenged. And some of the competitors are bound to succeed.

What will be taught and learned, how it will be taught and learned, who will make use of schooling, and the position of the school in society—all of this will change greatly during the ensuing decades. Indeed, no other institution faces challenges as radical as those that will transform the school.

But the greatest change—and the one we are least prepared for—is that the school will have to commit itself to *results*. It will have to establish its "bottom line," the *performance for which it should be held responsible and for which it is being paid.* The school will finally become *accountable.*

SUMMARY

The knowledge society and knowledge workers require high levels of literacy, strengths-based education, and continuous learning. The school is one of the primary institutions of society in which basic literacy and development of one's strengths can take place. Yet, the public schools in the United States have been handicapped by multiple missions that limit their ability to fulfill the educational needs of a knowledge-based society. Numerous alternatives have sprung up both within and outside of the public school system. Charter schools and magnet schools are direct competitors of the public school within the public school system. Both have singular missions and are results driven. Private schools and home schooling are also movements that have proceeded apace outside of the public schools. The demand for basic literacy and for strengths-based education requires that primary and secondary schools be held accountable for their results, which, in turn, requires a clear mission and measurable results.

---

* Opportunities for innovation in primary and secondary education in the U.S. are being encouraged by the development and growth of charter schools within the public school system. The charter school movement within the United States is an attempt, with various degrees of measurable success, to organize new schools that challenge traditional views on public education and to provide choice. "Nearly 3,000 new schools have been launched since state legislatures began passing charter legislation in the 1990s." Sourced on July 25, 2007, at http://www.uscharterschools.org/pub/uscs_docs/o/movement.htm.

15

Rethinking "Reinventing Government"

Vice President Al Gore's promise to *reinvent government*,* proclaimed with great fanfare in the first year of the Clinton administration, produced only a nationwide yawn. There was no lack of publicity about the Gore initiative afterward. Press release after press release announced the reinvention of yet another agency or program; big conferences, one chaired by the president himself, were convened, and any number of TV appearances made. Of all the domestic programs of the Clinton administration, this was one of the few from which there have actually been *results* and not just speeches. Yet neither the public nor the media showed much interest. And election results of 2000 were hardly a vote of confidence in the administration's performance at reinventing government.

There are good reasons for this. In any institution other than the federal government, the changes being trumpeted as reinventions would not even be announced, except perhaps on the bulletin board in the hallway. They are the kinds of things that a hospital expects floor nurses to do on their own; that a bank expects branch managers to do on their own; that even a poorly run manufacturer expects supervisors to do on their own—without getting much praise, let alone any extra rewards.

Here are some past government examples—sadly, fairly typical ones:

- In Atlanta, Georgia, six separate welfare programs, each traditionally with its own office and staff, consolidated their application process to give "one-stop service." The reinvented program actually got phone calls answered, and on the first try.

---

* Vice President Gore headed the National Partnership for Reinventing Government, which started its work on April 15, 1993, and ended early in January 2001 (see http://govinfo.library.unt.edu/npr/index .htm). The project was staffed mostly by approximately 1,300 career professionals from various agencies of federal government. Reported by Stephen Barr, "Members of Campaign to Reinvent Government Packing up, Not Giving up," *Washington Post,* January 14, 2001, p. c2 (http://www.washingtonpost.com/).

- In Ogden, Utah, and Oakland, California, among other places, the Internal Revenue Service experimented with treating the taxpayers as customers and with one-stop service, in which each clerk, instead of shuffling taxpayers from one office to another, had the information to answer their questions.

- The Export-Import Bank was "reinvented." It is now expected to do what it was set up to do all of sixty years ago: *help small businesses get export financing.*

- The U.S. Geological Survey office in Denver was supposed to sell maps of the United States to the public. But it was almost impossible to find out what maps to order and how and where to order them, since the catalog was carefully hidden. And the very fact that a map was in demand by the public all but guaranteed that it would be unobtainable. It could not be reprinted simply because the public wanted to buy it; another government agency had to order it for internal use. If the map sold well, it immediately went out of print. What's more the warehouse was so poorly lit that when an order for a map in print came in, the clerks could not find the map. The task force that the Geological Survey created to reinvent all this only succeeded in putting more lights in the warehouse and making a few other minor improvements.

For the future, however, more ambitious things were promised:

- The Department of Agriculture proposed to trim its agencies from forty-two to thirty, to close more than 1,000 field offices, and to eliminate 11,000 jobs, for savings of about $3.6 billion over five years.

- Of the 384 recommendations of ways to reinvent government identified by the vice president in 1993, about half were proposed in the budget for fiscal year 1995. If all these recommendations had been accepted by Congress, they would have resulted in savings of about $12.5 billion over two years.

But neither the trimming of the Department of Agriculture nor the vice president's 384 recommendations were new. We have long known that a great many agricultural field offices are in cities and suburbs, where few if any farmers are left. Closing them was first proposed in the Eisenhower years. And a good many, perhaps the majority, of Gore's 384 recommendations had been made *ten years earlier,* in the Grace Report, under President Ronald Reagan.

Even if all of these proposals had been enacted, the results would have been trivial. The proposed Agriculture Department saving of $3.6 billion over five years works out to about $720 million a year—or around 1 percent of the department's 1995 annual budget of almost $70 billion. Surely the only way to describe the results of Gore's efforts is with the old Latin tag "The mountains convulsed in labor only to give birth to a ridiculous, teensy-weensy mouse."

RESTRUCTURING

The reason most often given for this embarrassment of nonresults is "resistance by the bureaucracy." Of course, no one likes to be reinvented by fiat from above. But actually, one positive result of Gore's program was the enthusiastic support it received from a great many people in the government's employ—especially the low-level people who were in daily contact with the public and were thus constantly frustrated by red tape and by such inane rules as the one that prevented their selling the beautiful Geological Survey maps, of which they are justly proud.

Nor was lack of effort the explanation. Some of the most dedicated people in Washington met week after week to produce these embarrassing nonresults. They included the deputy secretaries of the major government departments. Vice President Gore—an unusually energetic man—pushed and pushed. And the driving force behind the whole endeavor was the most knowledgeable of all Washington insiders, Alice Rivlin, formerly the director of the Congressional Budget Office, and then director of the Office of Management and Budget.

These were able people who got nowhere fast because their basic approach was wrong. They were trying to *patch* and to *spot-weld,* here, there, and yonder—and that never accomplishes anything. There will be no results unless there is a radical change in the way the federal government and its agencies are managed and paid. The habit of *continuous improvement* has to be built into all government agencies, and has to be made self-sustaining.

Continuous improvement is considered a recent Japanese invention—the Japanese call it *kaizen.* But, in fact, it was used almost eighty years ago, and in the United States. From World War I until the early 1980s, when it was dissolved, the Bell Telephone System applied "continuous improvement" to every one of its activities and processes, whether it was installing a telephone in a home or manufacturing switch gear. For every one of these activities, *Bell defined results, performance, quality, and cost.* And for every one, it set an annual improvement goal. Bell managers weren't rewarded for reaching these goals, but those who did not reach them were out of the running and rarely given a second chance.

What is equally needed—and is also an old Bell Telephone invention—is *benchmarking:* every year comparing the performance of an operation or an agency with the performances of all others, with the best becoming the standard to be met by all the following year.

Continuous improvement and benchmarking are largely unknown in the civilian agencies of the U.S. federal government. They would require radical changes in policies and practices that the bureaucracy, the federal employees' unions, and Congress would all fiercely resist. They would require that every agency—and every bureau within every agency—*define its performance objective, its quality objective,* and *its cost objective.* They would require defining the results that the agency is supposed to produce. However, continuous improvement and benchmarking each need different incentives. An agency that did not improve its performance by a preset minimum would have its budget cut—which was Bell Telephone's approach. And a manager whose unit consistently fell below the benchmark set by the best performers would be penalized in terms of compensation or—more effective—in terms of eligibility for promotion. Nonperformers would ultimately be demoted or fired.

But not even such changes, though they would be considered radical by almost anybody in Congress or the federal bureaucracy, would warrant being called a reinvention of government.

Any organization, whether biological or social, needs to change its basic structure if it significantly changes its size. Any organization that doubles or triples in size needs to be restructured. Similarly, any organization—whether a business, a nonprofit, or a government agency—needs to rethink itself once it is more than forty or fifty years old. It has outgrown its policies and its rules of behavior. If it continues in its old ways, it becomes ungovernable, unmanageable, uncontrollable.

The civilian part of the U.S. government has outgrown its size and outlived its policies. It is now far larger than it was during the Eisenhower administration. Its structure, its policies, and its rules for doing government business and for managing people go back even further than that. They were first developed under William McKinley after 1896, and were pretty much completed under Herbert Hoover from 1929 to 1933.

In fact, there is no point in blaming this or that president for the total disarray of our government today. It is the fault neither of the Democrats nor of the Republicans. Government has outgrown the structure, the policies, and the rules designed for it and still in use.

RETHINKING

The first reaction in a situation of disarray always is to do what Vice President Gore and his associates tried to do—*patching*. It always fails. The next step is to rush into *downsizing*. Management picks up a meat-ax and lays about indiscriminately. In the late 1980s and early 1990s, one big American company after another did this—among them IBM, Sears, and GM. Each first announced that laying off 10,000 or 20,000 or even 50,000 people would lead to an immediate turnaround. A year later there had, of course, been no turnaround, and the company laid off another 10,000 or 20,000 or 50,000—again without results. In many if not most cases, downsizing has turned out to be something that surgeons for centuries have warned against: amputation before diagnosis. The result is always a casualty.

But there have been a few organizations—some large companies (GE, for instance) and a few large hospitals (Beth Israel in Boston, for instance)—that quietly, and without fanfare, did turn themselves around, by *rethinking themselves.* They did not start out by downsizing. In fact, they knew that to start by reducing expenditures is not the way to get control of costs. The starting point is to identify the activities that are productive, that should be strengthened, promoted, and expanded. Every agency, every policy, every program, every activity, should be confronted with these questions: *"What is your mission?" "Is it still the right mission?" "Is it still worth doing?" "If we were not already doing this, would we go into it now?"* This questioning has been done often enough, in all kinds of organizations—businesses, hospitals, churches, and even local governments—that we know it works.

The overall answer is almost never, "This is fine as it stands; let's keep on." But in some—indeed, a good many areas—the answer to the last question is, "Yes, we should go into this again, but with some changes. We have learned a few things."

An example might be the Occupational Safety and Health Administration, created in 1970. OSHA runs on the assumption that an unsafe environment is the primary cause of accidents, and it therefore tries to do the impossible: create a risk-free universe. Of course eliminating hazards is the right thing to do. But it is only one part of safety, and probably the lesser part. In fact, by itself it achieves next to nothing. The most effective way to produce safety is to eliminate unsafe behavior.

OSHA's definition of an accident—*when someone gets hurt*—is inadequate. To cut down on accidents the definition has to be *a violation of the rules of safe behavior, whether anyone gets hurt or not.* This is the definition under which the United States has been running its nuclear submarines. Anyone in a nuclear submarine, whether the commanding officer or the most junior seaman, is punished for the slightest violation of the rules of safe behavior, even if no one gets hurt. As a result, the nuclear submarine has a safety record unmatched by any industrial plant or military installation in the world; and yet a more unsafe environment than a crowded nuclear sub can hardly be imagined.

OSHA's program should, of course, be maintained. But it needs to be refocused.

This analysis will consider a number of agencies whose mission is no longer viable, if it ever was—agencies that we would definitely not start now if we had the choice. The mission may have been accomplished, for instance. One example is that most sacred of cows, the Veterans Administration, which now operates 1,400 hospitals, clinics, and nursing homes.* When they first became accredited hospitals, around 1930, competent hospitals were scarce in the rural areas and small towns where many veterans lived. Today a competent hospital is easily accessible to a veteran almost anywhere. Medically, most VA hospitals are at best mediocre; financially, they are costly to the government. Worst, they are not neighborhood facilities, and thus veterans—especially elderly, chronically ill ones—have to travel far from their communities and their families just when they most need community and family support. The VA hospitals and nursing homes long ago accomplished what they were set up to do. Except perhaps those VA facilities dedicated to treating current war-related psychological and physical issues, they should be closed and the job contracted out to local hospitals and HMOs.

Or there may be no mission left. For example, would we now establish a separate Department of Agriculture? A good many Americans would answer with a loud *no*. Now that farmers are no more than 3 percent of the population, and productive farmers are half that, a bureau at Commerce or Labor is probably all we need.

Continuing with activities that we would not now choose to begin is wasteful. They should be abandoned. One cannot even guess how many government activities would be found to be worth preserving. But my experience with many organizations suggests that the public would vote against continuing something like two-fifths, perhaps even half, of all civilian agencies and programs. And almost none of them would win a vote—that is, be deemed to be properly organized and operating well—by a large margin.

ABANDONING

Together the qualified yeas and nays are likely to be awarded in any organization to some three-fifths or two-thirds of programs and activities. The thorny cases are the programs and activities that are unproductive or counterproductive without our quite knowing what is wrong, let alone how to straighten it out.

Two major and highly cherished U.S. government programs belong in this category. The welfare program is one highly visible example. When it was designed in the late 1930s it worked beautifully. But the needs it then tackled were different from those it is supposed to serve today: the needs of unwed mothers and fatherless children, of people without education, skills, or work experience. Whether it actually does harm is hotly debated. But few claim that it works or that it even alleviates the social ills it is supposed to cure.

---

* Reported Sunday, August 27, 2006, "How Veterans' Hospitals Became the Best in Health Care," by Douglas Waller, *Time*, in partnership with CNN. http://www.time.com/time/magazine/article/0,9171, 1376238,00.html. Reprinted in *Time* September 4, 2006.

And then there is that mainstay of U.S. foreign policy during the Cold War years: military aid. If it is given to an ally who is actually engaged in fighting, military aid can be highly productive: consider *Lend-Lease* to Great Britain in 1940–1941, and military aid to an embattled Israel. But military aid is counter-productive if it is given in peacetime to create an ally—a principle that Plutarch and Suetonious accepted as proved. Surely our recent foreign-policy messes—Panama, Iran, Iraq, and Somalia are prime examples—were caused by our giving military aid to create an ally. Little, if any, military aid since the beginning of the Cold War has actually produced an ally. Indeed, it usually produced an enemy—as did Soviet military aid to Afghanistan.

The favorite prescription for such programs or activities is to reform them. President Clinton's welfare reform was one example, as was the welfare reform proposed by the subsequent Republican majority. Both were quackery. To reform something that malfunctions—let alone something that does harm—without knowing why it does not work can only make things worse. The best thing to do with such programs is to abolish them.

Maybe we should run a few—a very few—controlled experiments. In welfare, for instance, we might try, in some carefully chosen places across the country, to privatize retraining and placing long-term welfare recipients. Indianapolis Mayor Stephen Goldsmith achieved promising results in this area. In health care, we might try several different approaches in different states: for example, managed competition in California, home of the strong and experienced health-care wholesaler Kaiser Permanente; single-payer health care after the Canadian model in New Jersey, where there has been support for it; and in Oregon, rationing on the basis of medical expectations, which is being tried.

But in areas where there are no successes to be tested, for example, military aid, we should not even experiment. There are no hypotheses to test. We should abandon.

Rethinking will result in a list that has activities and programs that should be strengthened at the top, ones that should be abolished at the bottom, and between them activities that need to be refocused or in which a few hypotheses might be tested. Some activities and programs should, despite an absence of results, be given a grace period of a few years before they are put out of their misery.

Rethinking is not primarily concerned with cutting expenses. It leads above all to a tremendous increase in performance, in quality, in service. But substantial cost savings—sometimes as much as 40 percent of the total—always emerge as a by-product. In fact, rethinking could produce enough savings to eliminate the federal deficit within a few years. The main result, however, would be a change in basic approach. For where *conventional policy making ranks programs and activities according to their good intentions, rethinking ranks them according to results.*

AN EXCEPTION FOR CRUSADES

Anyone who has read this far will exclaim, "Impossible. Surely no group of people will ever agree on what belongs at the top of the list and what at the bottom." But amazingly enough, wherever rethinking has been done, there has been substantial agreement about the list, whatever the backgrounds or the beliefs of the people involved. The disagreements are rarely over what should be kept or strengthened and what should be abandoned. They are usually over whether a program or activity should be axed right away or put on probation for two or three years. The programs that people do not agree on are the ones concerned not with results but with "moral imperatives."

The best American example is the War on Drugs. After many years it had little effect on substance abuse and addiction, and much of the effect it had was deleterious. But it underlies the destruction of our cities in that addicts are prostituting themselves, mugging, robbing, or killing to earn enough for the fix that the War on Drugs has made prohibitively expensive. All the War on Drugs actually did, in other words, was enrich drug dealers and penalize and terrorize nonusers, especially in the inner city. But the War on Drugs was a crusade. What was behind it was not logic but outrage. Stopping the War on Drugs, no matter how beneficial, was seen as "immoral."

The smart thing to do is to exclude such crusades from the rational analysis involved in rethinking. Fortunately, there are never a lot of them. As for the rest—more than 90 percent of all programs and activities—rethinking will in all probability produce substantial agreement.

GOVERNMENT THAT'S EFFECTIVE

Surely, it will be argued, even total agreement among highly respected people will be futile. Congress will not accept anything like this. Neither will the bureaucracy. And lobbyists and special interests of all persuasions will be united in opposition to anything so subversive.

Perfectly true: action on rethinking is impossible today. But will it be impossible tomorrow? In the presidential election of 1992, almost one-fifth of the electorate voted for Ross Perot, the man who promised to get rid of the deficit by slashing government expenditures. A substantial number—perhaps another fifth—agreed with his aims even though they could not bring themselves to vote for him. Once the deficit begins again to grow explosively, then the demand for cutting the deficit may become irresistible and overwhelm Congress, the bureaucracy, and the lobbyists. If no rational rethinking of government performance has yet occurred, we will in all likelihood do what so many large companies have done—apply the meat-ax and downsize. We will then destroy performance, but without decreasing the deficit. In fact, it is predictable that the wrong things will then be cut—the things that perform and should be strengthened.

But if we have a plan that shows how and where the government needs to be rethought, we have a chance. In a crisis, one turns to people who have thought through in advance what needs to be done. Of course, no plan, no matter how well thought through, will ever be carried out as written. Even a dictator has to make compromises. But such a plan would serve as the ideal against which the compromises are measured. It might save us from sacrificing things that should be strengthened, in our effort to maintain the obsolete and the unproductive. It would not guarantee that all—or even most—of the unproductive things would be cut, but it might maintain the productive ones.

In fact, we may already be very close to having to reinvent government. The theory on which all governments in the developed world have operated since at least the Great Depression ("Tax and Tax, Spend and Spend," Harry Hopkins, Franklin Delano Roosevelt's adviser, called it) *no longer delivers results*. It no longer even delivers votes. The "nanny state"—a lovely English term—is a total failure. Government everywhere—in the United States, the United Kingdom, Germany, Russia—has been proved unable to run community and society. And everywhere voters revolt against the nanny state's futility, bureaucracy, and burdens. But the counter-theory that preaches a return to pre–World War I government has also not proved out—the theory that was first formulated in 1944 in Friedrich von Hayek's *The Road to Serfdom* and that culminated in neoconservatism. Despite its ascendancy in the 1980s, despite Ronald Reagan and Margaret Thatcher, the nanny state has not shrunk.

Instead, we will have to find out what government programs and activities in community and society do serve a purpose. What results should be expected of each? What can governments—federal, state, local—do effectively? And what nongovernmental ways are there to do worthwhile things that governments do not and cannot do effectively?

For example, the city of West Hollywood, California, outsources a staggering array of services previously performed by the city. These include public safety, sheriff duties, firefighting, three million dollars of social services, city line shuttle busses, trash hauling, and traffic-flow monitoring and computer systems.

At the same time, as President Clinton learned in his first two years, government cannot opt out of the wider world and become domestic only, as he so very much wanted it to be. Foreign brush fires—in Bosnia, in Rwanda, in the former Soviet Union—have to be attended to, because they have a nasty habit of spreading. And the reality of international terrorism, as a weapon by outlaw governments and by terrorist networks, will surely require more government involvement in foreign affairs, including military matters, and more international cooperation.

By now it has become clear that a developed country can neither extend big government, as the (so-called) liberals want, nor abolish it and go back to nineteenth-century innocence, as the (so-called) conservatives want. The government we need will have to transcend both groups. The megastate that the twentieth century built is bankrupt, morally as well as financially. It has not delivered. But its successor cannot be "small government." There are far too many tasks, domestically and internationally. We need *effective* government—and that is what the voters in all developed countries are actually clamoring for.

For this, however, we need something we do not have: a theory of what government can do. No major political thinker—at least not since Machiavelli, almost 500 years ago—has addressed this question. All political theory, from John Locke on through *The Federalist Papers* and down to the articles published by today's liberals and conservatives, deals with the process of government: with constitutions, with power and its limitations, with methods and organizations. None deals with the substance. None asks what the proper functions of government might be and could be. None asks what results government should be held accountable for.

Rethinking government, its programs, its agencies, its activities, would not by itself give us this new political theory. But it would give us the factual information for it. And so much is already clear: the new political theory we badly need will have to rest on an analysis of *what does work* rather than on *good intentions* and *promises* of what should work because we would like it to. Rethinking will not give us the answers, but it might force us to ask the right questions.

"Reinventing government" is an empty slogan so far. Yet what the slogan implies is what free government needs—and desperately.

POSTSCRIPT

In 1994, the Heritage Foundation—a think tank of radical Republicans linked to Newt Gingrich—published a new proposal entitled *Rolling Back Government: A Budget Plan to Rebuild America*. Far from celebrating its victory, it completely ignored the "Contract with America." Instead it took the approach this chapter advocates: it systematically asked of every government agency, every government service, every government program, *If we didn't do this already, would we now go into it?* Its conclusions went a good deal further than anything I would have proposed.

The Heritage Foundation proposed getting rid of not only the Department of Agriculture—something that's mentioned in this chapter—it also proposed getting rid of the majority of other cabinet departments such as Commerce, Energy, Environment, Housing, Veterans Affairs, and to limit the Cabinet to five departments: State, Treasury, Defense, Justice, and Health (Health, by the way, is the only one that was not already a cabinet department under George Washington).

The proposal was equally radical in its treatment of government policies and pro-grams. The very fact that such a proposal was seriously put forward guarantees that "really reinventing government" will remain a central and urgent political "hot button" in the United States—and in all developed countries—for years to come.

SUMMARY

Rethinking government should start by requiring each agency to immediately *define its performance objective, its quality objective,* and *its cost objective.* This should be followed by the adoption of the formal processes of *continuous improvement* and *benchmarking.*

Next, every agency, every policy, every program, every activity, should be con-fronted with these questions: *"What is your mission?" "Is it still the right mission?" "Is it still worth doing?" "If we were not already doing this, would we go into it now?"* If the answer to the last question is no, then the next question is, *"What do we do about it?"* Continuing to carry out activities that we would not now start is wasteful and they should be abandoned.

Rethinking activities and programs will result in identifying those that should be strengthened and those that should be abolished. It will also result in activities where alternative pilot projects should be carried out in specific locations where there is the capability and desire to do so.

The objective of this rethinking policy exercise is to rank programs according to their results not according to good intentions.

16

Entrepreneurship in the Public-Service Institution

Public-service institutions—such as government agencies, labor unions, churches, universities and schools, hospitals, community and charitable organizations, professional and trade associations, and the like—need to be entrepreneurial and innovative fully as much as any business does. Indeed, they may need it more. The rapid changes in today's society, technology, and economy are simultaneously an even greater threat to them and an even greater opportunity.

Yet public-service institutions find it far more difficult to innovate than does even the most "bureaucratic" company. The "existing" seems to be even more of an obstacle for them. To be sure, every service institution likes to get bigger. In the absence of a profit test, size is the one criterion of success for a service institution, and growth a goal in itself. And then, of course, there is always so much more that needs to be done. But stopping what has "always been done" and doing something new are equally anathema to service institutions, or at least excruciatingly painful to them.

Most innovations in public-service institutions are imposed on them either by outsiders or by catastrophe. The modern university, for instance, was created by a total outsider, the Prussian diplomat Wilhelm von Humboldt. He founded the University of Berlin in 1809, when the traditional university of the seventeenth and eighteenth century had been all but completely destroyed by the French Revolution and the Napoleonic wars. Sixty years later, the modern American university came into being, when the country's traditional colleges and universities were dying and could no longer attract students.

Similarly, all basic innovations in the military in the twentieth century, whether in structure or in strategy, have followed on ignominious malfunction or crushing defeat: the reorganization of the American army and of its strategy by a New York lawyer, Elihu Root, Teddy Roosevelt's secretary of war, after its disgraceful performance in the Spanish-American War; the reorganization, a few years later, of the British army and its strategy by Secretary of War Lord Haldane, another civilian, after the equally disgraceful performance of the British in the Boer War; and the rethinking of the German army's structure and strategy after the defeat of World War I.

And in government, one of the greatest examples of innovative thinking in recent political history, America's New Deal of 1933–1936, was triggered by a Depression so severe as to almost unravel the country's social fabric.

Critics of bureaucracy blame the resistance of public-service institutions to entrepreneurship and innovation on "timid bureaucrats," on time-servers who "have never met a payroll," or on "power-hungry politicians." It is a very old litany—in fact, it was already hoary when Machiavelli chanted it almost 500 years ago. The only thing that changes is who intones it. At the beginning of the twentieth century, it was the slogan of the so-called liberals and now it is the slogan of the so-called neoconservatives. Alas, things are not that simple, and "better people"—that perennial panacea of reformists—is a mirage. The most entrepreneurial, innovative people behave like the worst time-serving bureaucrat or power-hungry politician six months after they have taken over the management of a public-service institution, particularly if it is a government agency.

The forces that impede entrepreneurship and innovation in a public-service institution are inherent in it, integral to it, inseparable from it. The best proof of this are the internal staff services in businesses, which are, in effect, the "public-service institutions" within business corporations. These are typically headed by people who have come out of operations and have proven their capacity to perform in competitive markets. And yet, the internal staff services are not notorious as innovators. They are good at building empires—and they always want to do more of the same. They resist abandoning anything they are doing. But they rarely innovate once they have been established.

There are three main reasons why the existing enterprise presents so much more of an obstacle to innovation in the public-service institution than it does in the typical business enterprise.

1. First, the public-service institution is based on a "budget" rather than on being paid out of its results. It is paid for its efforts and out of funds somebody else has earned, whether the taxpayer, the donors of a charitable organization, or the company for which a human resource department or the marketing services staff work. The more efforts the public-service institution engages in, the greater its budget will be.

And "success" in the public-service institution is defined by getting a *larger budget* rather than obtaining results. Any attempt to slough off activities and efforts, therefore, diminishes the public-service institution. It causes it to lose stature and prestige. Failure cannot be acknowledged. Worse still, the fact that an objective has been attained cannot be admitted.

2. A service institution is dependent on a multitude of constituents. In a business that sells its products on the market, one constituent, the consumer, eventually overrides all the others. A business needs only a very small share of a small market to be successful. Then it can satisfy the other constituents, whether they are shareholders, workers, the community, and so on. But precisely because public-service institutions—and that includes the staff activities within a business corporation—have no "results" out of which they are being paid, any constituent, no matter how marginal, has, in effect, a veto power. A public-service institution has to satisfy everyone; certainly, it cannot afford to alienate anyone.

The moment a service institution starts an activity, it acquires a "constituency," which then refuses to have the program abolished or even significantly modified. But anything new is always controversial. This means that it is opposed by existing constituencies without having formed, as yet, a constituency of its own to support it.

3. The most important reason, however, is that public-service institutions exist, after all, to "do good." This means that they tend to see their mission as a moral absolute rather than as economic and subject to a cost-benefit calculus. Economics always seeks a different allocation of the same resources to obtain a higher yield. Everything economic is therefore relative. In the public-service institution, there is no such thing as a higher yield. If one is "doing good," then there is no "better."

Indeed, failure to attain objectives in the quest for a "good" only means that efforts need to be redoubled. The forces of evil must be far more powerful than expected and need to be fought even harder.

For thousands of years the preachers of all sorts of religions have held forth against the "sins of the flesh." Their success has been limited to say the least. But this is no argument as far as the preachers are concerned. It does not persuade them to devote their considerable talents to pursuits in which results may be more easily attainable. On the contrary, it only proves that their efforts need to be redoubled. Avoiding the "sins of the flesh" is clearly a "moral good," and thus an absolute, which does not admit to any cost-benefit calculation.

Few public-service institutions define their objectives in such absolute terms. But even company human resource departments and manufacturing service staffs tend to see their mission as "doing good," and therefore as being moral and absolute instead of being economic and relative.

This means that public-service institutions are out to *maximize* rather than to *optimize*. "Our mission will not be completed," asserts the head of the Crusade Against Hunger, "as long as there is one child on the earth going to bed hungry." If he were to say, "Our mission will be completed if the largest possible number of children that can be reached through existing distribution channels get enough to eat not to be stunted," he would be booted out of office. But if the goal is maximization, it can never be attained. Indeed, the closer one comes to attaining one's objective, the more efforts are called for. For, once optimization has been reached (perhaps between 75 and 80 percent of theoretical maximum), additional costs go up exponentially while additional results fall off exponentially. The closer a public-service institution comes to attaining its objectives, therefore, the more frustrated it will be and the harder it will work on what it is already doing.

It will, however, behave exactly the same way the less it achieves. Whether it succeeds or fails, the demand to innovate and to do something else will be resented as an attack on its basic commitment, on the very reason for its existence, and on its beliefs and values.

These are serious obstacles to innovation. They explain why, by and large, innovation in public services tends to come from new ventures rather than from existing institutions.

The most extreme example around these days may well be the labor union. It was probably the most successful institution of the twentieth century in the developed countries. It has clearly attained its original objectives. There can be no more "more" when the labor share of gross national product in Western developed countries is close to 90 percent. Yet the labor union is incapable of even thinking about new challenges, new objectives, and new contributions. All it can do is repeat the old slogans and fight the old battles. For the "cause of labor" is an absolute good. Clearly, it must not be questioned, let alone redefined.

The university, however, may not be too different from the labor union, and in part for the same reason—a level of growth and success in the twentieth century second only to that of the labor union.

Still there are enough exceptions among public-service institutions (including government agencies) to show that public-service institutions, even old and big ones, can innovate.

A number of Roman Catholic archdioceses in the United States, for instance, have brought in lay people to run the diocese, including married lay women and former executive officers of corporations. Everything that does not involve dispensing sacraments and ministering to congregations is done by lay professionals and managers. Although there is a shortage of priests throughout the American Catholic Church, this policy leaves available priests to move forward aggressively to build congregations and expand religious services.

One of the oldest of scientific societies, the American Association for the Advancement of Science, redirected itself between 1960 and 1980 to become a "mass organization" without losing its character as a leader. It totally changed its weekly magazine, *Science,* to become the spokesman for science to the public and government, and to be the authoritative reporter on science policy. And it created a scientifically solid yet popular mass-circulation magazine for lay readers.

A large hospital on the West Coast recognized, as early as 1965 or so, that health care was changing as a result of its success. Where other large city hospitals tried to fight such trends as those toward hospital chains or freestanding ambulatory treatment centers, this institution has been an innovator and a leader in these developments. Indeed, it was the first to build a freestanding maternity center in which the expectant mother is given a motel room at fairly low cost, yet with all the medical services available should they be needed. It was the first to go into freestanding surgical centers for ambulatory care. But it also started to build its own voluntary hospital chain, in which it offers management contracts to smaller hospitals throughout the region.

Beginning around 1975, the Girl Scouts of the U.S.A., a large organization dating back to the early years of the twentieth century with several million young women enrolled, introduced innovations affecting membership, programs, and volunteers—the three basic dimensions of the organization.

It began to actively recruit girls from the new urban middle classes, that is, African-Americans, Asians, Latinos. It recognized that with the movement of women into professions and managerial positions, girls need new programs and role models that stress professional and business careers rather than the traditional careers as homemaker or nurse. The Girl Scouts management people realized that the traditional sources for volunteers to run local activities were drying up because young mothers were no longer sitting at home searching for things to do. But they recognized, too, that the new professional, the new working mother, represents an opportunity and that the Girl Scouts have something to offer her; and for any community organization, volunteers are the critical constraint. They therefore set out to make work as a volunteer for the Girl Scouts attractive to the working mother as a good way to have time and fun with her child while also contributing to her child's development. Finally, the Girl Scouts realized that the working mother who does not have enough time for her child represents another opportunity: they started Girl Scouting for preschool children. Thus, the Girl Scouts reversed the downward trend in enrollment of both children and volunteers, while the Boy Scouts—a bigger, older, and infinitely richer organization—is adrift.

These are all American examples, I fully realize. Doubtless, similar examples are to be found in Europe or Japan. But I hope that these cases, despite their limitations, will suffice to demonstrate the entrepreneurial policies needed in the public-service institution to make it capable of innovation.

1. First, the public-service institution needs a clear definition of its *mission*. What is it trying to do? Why does it exist? It needs to focus on objectives rather than on programs and projects. *Programs* and *projects* are *means to an end*. They should always be considered as temporary and, in fact, short-lived.

2. The public-service institution needs a *realistic* statement of goals. It should say, "Our job is to assuage famine," rather than, "Our job is to eliminate hunger." It needs something that is genuinely attainable and therefore a commitment to a realistic goal, so that it can say eventually, "Our job is finished."

There are, of course, objectives that can never be attained. To administer justice in any human society is clearly an unending task, one that can never be fully accomplished even to modest standards. But most objectives can and should be phrased in optimal rather than in maximal terms. Then it is possible to say, "We have attained what we were trying to do."

Surely, this should be considered with respect to the traditional goal of the schoolmaster: to get everyone to sit in school for long years. This goal has long been attained in developed countries. What does education have to do now?—that is, What is the meaning of "education" as against mere schooling?

3. Failure to achieve objectives should be considered an indication that the objective is wrong or at least defined wrongly. If an objective has not been attained after repeated tries, one has to assume that it is the wrong one. It is not rational to consider failure a good reason for trying again and again. Failure to attain objectives is a *prima facie* reason to question the validity of the objectives—the exact opposite of what most public-service institutions believe.

4. Finally, public-service institutions need to build into their policies and practices the constant search for innovative opportunity. They need to view change as an opportunity rather than a threat.

Even in government, innovation is possible if simple rules are obeyed. Here is one example. Lincoln, Nebraska, 140 years ago, was the first city in the Western world to take into municipal ownership public services such as public transportation, electric power, gas, water, and so on. As early as the mid-1970s, under a woman mayor, Helen Boosalis, it began to privatize such services as garbage pickup, school transportation, and a host of others. The city provided the money, with private businesses bidding for the contracts; there were substantial savings in cost and even greater improvements in service.

What Helen Boosalis saw in Lincoln was the opportunity to separate the "provider" of public services, that is, government, and the "supplier." This made possible both high service standards and the efficiency, reliability, and low cost that competition can provide.

The four rules outlined above constitute the specific policies and practices the public-service institution requires if it is to make itself entrepreneurial and capable of innovation. In addition, however, it also needs to adopt those policies and practices that any existing organization requires in order to be entrepreneurial, the policies and practices, discussed in chapters 34–37, suitable to the entrepreneurial business.

THE NEED TO INNOVATE

Why is innovation in the public-service institution so important? Why can we not leave existing public-service institutions the way they are and depend on new institutions for the innovations we need in the public-service sector, as historically we have always done?

The answer is that public-service institutions have become too important in developed countries, and too big. The public-service sector, both the governmental one and the nongovernmental but not-for-profit one, has grown faster during the twentieth century than the private sector—maybe three to five times as fast. The growth has been especially fast since World War II.

To some extent, this growth has been excessive. Wherever public-service activities can be converted into profit-making enterprises, they should be so converted. This applies to not only the kind of municipal services the city of Lincoln, Nebraska, now *privatizes*. The move from nonprofit to profit has already gone very far in the American hospital. It may become a stampede in professional and graduate education. To subsidize the highest earners in developed society—the holders of advanced professional degrees—can hardly be justified.

A central economic problem of developed societies is *capital formation*. We therefore can ill afford to have activities conducted as "nonprofit"—that is, as activities that devour capital rather than form it—if they can be organized as activities that form capital, as activities that make a profit.

But the great bulk of the activities that are being discharged in and by public-service institutions will still remain public-service activities, and will neither disappear nor be transformed. Consequently, they have to be made producing and productive. Public-service institutions will have to learn to be innovators, to manage themselves entrepreneurially. To achieve this, public-service institutions will have to learn to look upon social, technological, economic, and demographic shifts as opportunities in a period of rapid change in all these areas.

Otherwise, they will become obstacles. Such public-service institutions will increasingly become unable to discharge their mission as they adhere to programs and projects that cannot work in a changed environment, and yet they will not be able or willing to abandon the missions they can no longer discharge. Increasingly, they will come to look the way the feudal barons came to look after they had lost all social function around 1300: as parasites, functionless, with nothing left but the power to obstruct and to exploit. They will become self-righteous while increasingly *losing their legitimacy*. Clearly, this is already happening to the apparently most powerful among them, the labor union. Yet a society in rapid change, with new challenges, new requirements and opportunities, *needs* public-service institutions.

The public school in the United States exemplifies both the opportunities and the dangers. Unless it takes the lead in innovation, it is unlikely to survive, except as a school for the minorities in the slums as parents of middle- and high-income families send their children to private and parochial schools.

For the first time in its history, the United States faces the threat of a class structure in education in which all but the very poor remain outside of the public school system—at least in the cities and suburbs where most of the population lives. And this will squarely be the fault of the public school itself, because what is needed to reform the public school is already known.

Many other public-service institutions face a similar situation. The knowledge is there. The need to innovate is clear. They now have to learn how to build entrepreneurship and innovation into their own system. Otherwise, they will find themselves superseded by outsiders who will create competing entrepreneurial public-service institutions and so render the existing ones obsolete.

The late nineteenth century and early twentieth century was a period of tremendous creativity and innovation in the public-service field. Social innovation during the seventy-five years until the 1930s was surely as much alive, as productive, and as rapid as technological innovation, if not more so. But in these periods the innovation took the form of creating new public-service institutions. The need for social innovation may be even greater now, but it will very largely have to be social innovation within the existing public-service institution. To build entrepreneurial management into the existing public-service institution may thus be the foremost political task of this generation.

SUMMARY

For a society to prosper, it must have engines of capital formation. Service institutions are paid out of the surplus of wealth-creating institutions. A developed society cannot afford to have its service institutions waste capital. As a result, public-service institutions must be made to perform and to innovate. One way to do this is to privatize whatever activities a service institution can outsource and convert from a nonprofit to a for-profit activity. This single step will make service activities more effective so long as their missions are clear.

The bulk of service activities performed in social-sector and governmental organizations cannot be privatized. These institutions must go to work to eliminate the obstacles to innovation. There are many successful examples to point the way, including the Girl Scouts of the U.S.A., the American Association for the Advancement of Science, and cities such as Lincoln, Nebraska.

There are four requirements for successful innovation in the public-service institution:

1. Provide a clear definition of mission.

2. Establish goals that are attainable and stated in terms of the optimum rather than the theoretical maximum.

3. Probe objectives that are not being attained after repeated attempts. Failure to obtain objectives after repeated attempts means either that the objectives should be redefined or that the objectives should be abandoned.

4. Build into public-service institutions entrepreneurial policies and practices that have been demonstrated to work in other sectors of the economy.

Part IV

Productive Work and Achieving Worker

Making work productive and the worker achieving is the second major aspect of the management task. We do not know enough about it. Folklore and old wives' tales abound, but solid, tested knowledge is scarce. We do know that work and the workforce are undergoing greater changes today than at any time since the beginning of the industrial revolution two centuries ago. We do know that, at least in the developed countries, radically new approaches are needed—approaches to *analysis, synthesis,* and *control* of *work*; to *job structure, work relationships*, and the *structure of rewards* and *power relations*; to making workers *responsible*. We do know that we have to move from managing "personnel" as a "cost center" and a "problem" to the *leadership of people*.

17

Making Work Productive and the Worker Achieving

Few words in the language evoke as much ambivalence as "work," or are as emotion-laden. In the pairing "work and rest," "rest" is clearly good. But whether "retirement" is better than "work" is already questionable. And work is definitely preferable to "idleness." Being "out of work" is far from good—is, indeed, a catastrophe.

In "work and play," "play" carries a favorable connotation. But "playing at being a surgeon" is not good at all. Work can be high achievement, as in the phrase "an artist's life work." Or it can be sheer drudgery, backbreaking, and utter boredom.

There is "work" and there is "working." They are totally dependent on each other. Unless someone is working, no work gets done. And where there is no work, there is also no working.

Yet work and working are quite different. Work is impersonal, and objective. It is "something." Not all work can be weighed or measured. But even the most intangible piece of work is outside and independent of the worker.

What distinguishes work from play is an old question that has never been answered satisfactorily. Work and play may be the very same activity; down to the smallest detail, wood finishing is work when done by a furniture factory worker and play when done by a weekend hobbyist. Psychologically and socially, the two are quite different. The distinction may well be that work, unlike play, is impersonal and objective. The purpose of play lies in the player; the purpose of work lies with the user of the end product. Where the end product is not determined by the player but by others, we do not speak of play, we speak of work.

Working is done by a human being, a worker. It is a uniquely human activity. Working, therefore, is *physiology* and *psychology, society* and *community, personality, economics,* and *power.* As the old human relations tag has it, "One cannot hire a hand; the whole man always comes with it."

Work and working, therefore, follow different rules. Work belongs to the realm of objects. It has its own impersonal logic. But working belongs to the realm of human beings. It has dynamics. Managers always have to manage both work and working. They have to make *work productive* and the *worker achieving*. They have to integrate work and working.

WORK AND WORKER IN RAPID CHANGE

Both work and worker are in a period of rapid change, as was described in chapter 4. The changes that dominated the end of the twentieth century—and will probably dominate most of the twenty-first century as well—are the most radical changes since the beginning of the industrial revolution, more than two centuries ago.

Over the last two centuries, work has shifted away from the home and from people working alone to a society of employees, working in organizations. At the same time the center of gravity of the workforce is shifting from the manual worker to the knowledge worker. A larger and larger proportion of the labor force in all developed countries does not work with its hands but with ideas, concepts, theories. The output of these workers is not physical objects, but *knowledge* and *information*. Half a century ago knowledge work was performed by a few independent professionals working either alone or in very small groups. The bulk of the labor force was manual workers.

THE CRISIS OF THE MANUAL WORKER

These changes have produced a crisis with respect to manual workers and to their specific organization, the union.

For two hundred years the manual worker in industry, the child of the industrial revolution, has been struggling to gain economic security, status, and power in industrial society. During the ninety years since the end of World War I, the workers' progress was dazzling. In most developed countries the manual worker, once a "proletarian" scratching a bare living at the margin of subsistence, acquired substantial economic security, an income level higher than that of the upper middle class of yesterday, and increasing political power.

With the rise of the knowledge worker, the manual workers are endangered again. Their economic security is threatened. And their social position and status are rapidly diminishing. In the developed countries, industrial workers see themselves as severely deprived. They are defeated, losers, before they even start. This is not a result of managerial actions, but of social developments and of the pressures they have generated.

Increasingly, in all developed societies, the able, intelligent, and ambitious members of the working class stay in school beyond the point at which they are eligible for manual work. All the pressures of society—family and neighbors, community and school—push youngsters toward more schooling. The ones who leave school at the age at which they once would have graduated into the manual workforce—fifteen or so—are dropouts, failures, rejects.

The manual workers in the developed countries today have little self-respect. This inevitably makes them bitter, suspicious, distrustful of themselves, as well as of organization and management, and resentful. They are not revolutionaries, like their parents, grandparents, and great-grandparents, for it is obvious to them that revolution cannot alter the fundamental conditions. But they are likely to become militant as the center of social gravity keeps shifting toward knowledge work and the knowledge worker.

The rhetoric of workers' parties and movements still attacks the profit system. But the true class war is increasingly being fought between the hard hats—manual workers—and the middle-class knowledge workers. During most of this century it has been the coalition of manual and knowledge workers that has dominated politics in the developed world—in America's New Deal as well as in the social democratic and labor parties of Europe. The major political event for the early part of the twenty-first century may well be the growing split between these two groups.

THE CRISIS OF THE UNION

The status changes of the manual worker that attend the shift in emphasis to knowledge work and knowledge worker not only create a new class distinction, but also create severe difficulties for the manual worker's own institution, the union.

Perhaps the most visible sign of this is the sharp drop in the quality of trade-union leadership—a change that is largely the result of the educational explosion. Yesterday, union leadership was the career opportunity for the able and ambitious young worker forced out of school early by a lack of money. In the developed countries today, almost any able and ambitious youngster can stay in school—and may go on to a graduate degree. As a result, he moves into the professional and managerial ranks. His sympathies may still be with labor, but his leadership qualities are lost to the working class. The leaders who are moving into the vacuum this creates are likely to be men and women driven by resentment rather than by ambition, of far lower ability, and, above all, without self-confidence. They are weak leaders—and the worst situation for an industry to be in is to have to deal with weak union leadership.

At the same time, the fact that young workers see themselves as "losers" makes them resist and resent the very union leaders they put into office. The moment a worker gains an important leadership position in the trade union, he or she automatically becomes "establishment." Union leaders consort with the mighty, whether in government or in business. They exercise power. They have the trappings of power—the big office, the retinue of aides and assistants, the multiple computers on the desk, and so on. In order to be effective, the union leader has to become one of "them" and ceases to be one of "us." Yesterday's workers looked upon union power as representing them. They were proud of the fact that the union leader had become a person of authority. Today's young workers, feeling keenly that they are losers and rejects, resist the union leader's authority even more than they resist the rest of the bosses. As a result, union leaders are increasingly losing control over their own members, are repudiated by them, resisted by them, and disavowed by them. This, in turn, makes the union increasingly weak. For a union is powerless if it cannot deliver the union members' vote and behavior, cannot guarantee observance of a contract agreement, and cannot count on the members' support for the leader's position and actions.

There is little doubt that collective bargaining—whether between an individual company and a trade union or (as in Western Europe and Japan) between an industry and industry-wide union—is in trouble. Whether the civilized industrial warfare of collective bargaining—a major achievement of the early years of the twentieth century—can even survive is questionable. If it doesn't, there is no hint of what might be an effective replacement.

UNIONS AND THE KNOWLEDGE WORKERS

An organ for the representation of workers in their dealings with management is needed—by the workers, but also by society. Management is and has to be a power. Any power needs restraint and control—or else it becomes tyranny. The union is a very peculiar, an almost unprecedented, organ of restraint on the power of management. It is an opposition party that can never become the governing party. Yet within its limited scope, it serves an essential function in society. Unfortunately, it is increasingly becoming incapable of discharging this function.

The opposition function of the union will be needed more in the future than it ever was in the past. Manual workers are beginning to feel—rightly—that they can no longer depend on a political party and its appeal to a majority. That is the consequence of the gradual failure of the New Deal marriage between worker and liberal. Increasingly, also, the power that needs restraint is not that of the bosses or the capitalists but of the educated managerial middle class of knowledge workers. They are not greatly interested in profits, but they are interested in power. The most bitter power conflicts are not those that erupt in private enterprise or in business; they are conflicts between janitors and schoolboards, medical orderlies and hospital administrators, teaching assistants and graduate faculties, or, as in the Swedish steel industry, between workers and their staunchly socialist bosses in a nationalized industry. They are conflicts between workers and the public interest. In such conflicts, political parties, which aim at mass support and at attracting a majority of the voters, are almost bound to side with the bosses, if only because no amount of rhetoric can conceal that the price of a settlement will be paid, not out of profits, but surely out of prices or taxes.

Public-service institutions may face a much more difficult industrial-relations problem than business and are much less prepared for it. Hospitals, schools, government agencies, and so on have all become increasingly unionized. In these institutions, the manual worker—or the lower-ranking service worker—feels even more "dispossessed" and even more confined to second-class citizenship than does the manual worker in manufacturing or service industries.

The unions themselves are incapable of thinking through their own future role and developing new approaches to their own structure and function. One reason is that the new leaders who replace the dying or retiring pioneers are so often individuals of lesser ability, lesser maturity, and lesser competence. But as important is the fact that the new leaders can keep their slender grip on the membership only by opposing everything. The new leaders dare not even ask questions, let alone come up with answers. They dare not lead but must fight hard even to stay in place.

We need new policy in labor relations. In all developed and developing countries, executives in business and in public-service institutions will have to think through the future of the union, its role, its function, and its position, both within the institution and in society. This is a major *social responsibility* of management. It is also a *business responsibility* of management.

The future of business, of the economy, and of society will be influenced greatly by the way we solve or fail to solve the growing crisis of the unions.

To think through the role and function of the union is also self-interest for management. To believe that union weakness means management strength is sheer self-delusion. Unionization is a fact of life in all developed noncommunist countries. And a weak union—that is, one without established role, function, and authority, and without strong, secure, and effective leadership—means strife, irresponsible demands, and increasing bitterness and tension. It does not mean management strength; it means management frustration.

MANAGING THE KNOWLEDGE WORKER: THE NEW CHALLENGE

Managing knowledge work and the knowledge workers is essentially a new task. We know even less about it than we know about the management (or mismanagement) of the manual worker. It is, therefore, the more difficult task. But because it is new, it is not burdened with a long history of bitterness, of mutual suspicion, and of outdated restrictions, rules, and regulations. Managing knowledge work and knowledge worker therefore can focus on developing the right policies and practices. It can focus on the future rather than on undoing the past, on the opportunities rather than on "problems."

Managing knowledge work and the knowledge worker will require exceptional imagination, exceptional courage, and leadership of a high order. In some ways it will be a far more demanding task than managing the manual worker. The weapon of fear—fear of economic suffering, fear of job security, physical fear of company guards or of the state's police power—which for so long substituted for managing manual work and the manual worker, simply doesn't work at all for knowledge work and knowledge workers.

Knowledge workers, except at the very lowest levels, are not productive under the spur of fear; only *self-motivation* and *self-direction* make them productive. They have to be *achieving* in order to produce at all.

The productivity of every developed society depends increasingly on *making knowledge work productive* and the *knowledge worker achieving*. This is a central social problem of the new, the knowledge society. There are no precedents for the management of knowledge work. Knowledge work traditionally has been carried out by individuals working by themselves or in small groups. Now knowledge work is mostly carried out in large, complex, managed institutions. The knowledge workers are not even the successor to yesterday's "knowledge professionals." They are the successors to yesterday's skilled workers.

Worse, we cannot truly define, let alone measure, productivity for most knowledge work. One can define and measure it for the salesclerk in the retail store. But productivity is already a murky term with respect to the field salesperson of a manufacturing business. Is it total sales? Or is it the profit contribution from sales, which might vary tremendously with the product mix an individual salesperson sells? Or is it sales (or profit contribution) related to the potential of a sales territory? Perhaps a sales representative's ability to hold old customers should be considered central to his or her productivity. Or perhaps it should be the ability to generate new accounts. These problems are far more complex than the definition and measurement of the productivity of even the highly skilled manual worker. There one can almost always define and measure productivity in terms of the quantity of output—for example, the number of pairs of shoes produced per hour, per day, or per week, subject only to a quality standard.

Achievement for knowledge workers is much harder to define. No one but the knowledge workers themselves can come to grips with the question of what in work, job performance, social status, and pride constitutes the personal satisfaction that makes a knowledge worker feel that she contributes, performs, serves her values, and fulfills herself. (On the management of knowledge work and worker, see chapter 19.)

THE SEGMENTATION OF THE WORKFORCE

Manual workers and knowledge workers are not the only workforce segments, however. For example, the *service worker* who is a "production" worker without being a machine worker is a distinct and important group. Equally important is the fact that the workforce in all developed countries is segmenting itself according to gender.

Until fairly recently, women employees were essentially either temporary, working in the interlude between school and marriage, or distinctly lower class. Wives of "respectable" workers did not work outside the home. Such upper-class women as worked were largely independent professionals, doctors, lawyers, and university teachers. The rest were schoolteachers and hospital nurses.

In all developed countries, this has changed drastically. It might well be the sign of a developed country that a large portion of its women work as employees. The married middle-class woman is increasingly becoming the typical woman employee. With family size decreasing and with housework greatly reduced, more and more middle- and upper-class women are joining the workforce. The trend is likely to continue. (On the trend of increasing women participation rates, see chapter 5.) The driving forces are *economic, social,* and *psychological.*

The working woman often requires a different job structure appropriate to her realities and conditions. Women with children, for example, often need part-time work or flexible hours.

Various segments of the workforce also have different needs with respect to benefits. When it comes to cash wages, the standard of value is about the same for all. But when it comes to retirement pay, housing or educational allowances, health and other benefits, their needs and expectations vary greatly with sex, age, and family responsibilities, with the stage in their own life cycle and that of their families, and so on.

The two main challenges to managing work and working are *the changed psychological and social position of the manual worker* (better educated and often better paid, he still sees himself as moving down from yesterday's self-respecting working class into second-class citizenship); and *the emergence of knowledge work and the knowledge worker* as the economic and social center of what is the postindustrial, knowledge society.

THE NEW BREED

It is these changes that explain the arrival of a new breed of worker. These are the young people, especially the well-educated young people, who are challenging the traditional economic and power relationships as well.

This challenge to the old wisdom is often attributed to affluence. This is far too simple an explanation. To be sure, affluence is new. Throughout all of human history the great majority of people have always lived at the margin of subsistence. The great majority never knew where their next meal was going to come from. Now, in the developed countries, the great majority are economically secure, at least in traditional terms. But there is no sign that the great majority—or any but the tiniest of minorities—have lost their appetite for economic rewards, whether material or immaterial. On the contrary, the great majority, now that they have tasted some of the fruits of productivity, are clearly eager for more—much more than the economy can produce so far, and possibly more than the limited resources of our planet can produce.

The shifting structure and character of work has created a demand that work produce more than purely economic benefits.

Making a living is no longer enough. *Work also has to make a life.* This means that it will be more important than ever to make work both productive and achieving. At the same time, both manual workers (with their deep psychological insecurity) and knowledge workers (with their new status) expect work to provide nonmaterial psychological and social satisfactions. They do not necessarily expect work to be enjoyable, but they do expect it to be achieving.

SUMMARY

The main challenges to managing work and working are the changed psychological and social position of the manual worker; the crisis of the traditional role and function of the union as a result of its success; and the emergence of knowledge work as the economic and social center of the postindustrial, knowledge society. Work is changing—but so is the workforce, especially as more and more married women of all classes are working in the developed countries.

18

Managing the Work and Worker in Manual Work

The most important, and indeed the truly unique, contribution of management in the twentieth century was the fiftyfold increase in the productivity of the *manual worker* in manufacturing.

The most important contribution management needs to make in the twenty-first century is similarly to increase the productivity of *knowledge work* and the *knowledge worker*.

The most valuable assets of a twentieth-century company were its production equipment. The most valuable asset of a twenty-first-century institution, whether business or nonbusiness, is its knowledge workers and their productivity.

THE PRODUCTIVITY OF THE MANUAL WORKER

First: a look at where we are.

It was only a little over a hundred years ago that for the first time an educated person actually looked at manual work and manual worker, and then began to study both. Great poets, the Greek Hesiod (sixth century BC) and, five hundred years later, the Roman Virgil (at the end of the first century BC), sang about the work of the farmer. Theirs are still among the finest poems in any language. But neither the work they sang about nor their farmers bear even the most remote resemblance to reality or were meant to have any. Neither Hesiod nor Virgil ever held a sickle in his hands, ever herded sheep, or even looked at the people who did, either. And when, nineteen hundred years after Virgil, Karl Marx (1818–1883) came to write about manual work and manual workers, he, too, never looked at either, nor had he ever as much as touched a machine. The first man to do both, that is, to work as a manual worker and then to study manual work, was Frederick Winslow Taylor (1856–1915).

Throughout recorded history—and actually well before any history was recorded—there have been, of course, steady advances in what we today call "productivity." But they were the result of new tools, of new methods, of new technology; they were advances in what the economist calls "capital." There were few advances throughout the ages in what the economist calls "labor," that is, in the productivity of the worker. It was axiomatic throughout history that workers could produce more only by working harder or by working longer hours. The nineteenth-century economists disagreed as much about most things as economists do today. But they all agreed— from David Ricardo (1772–1823) through Karl Marx—that there are enormous differences in skill among workers, but there are none in respect to productivity other than between hard workers and lazy ones, or between physically strong workers and weak ones. Productivity did not exist.

Within a decade after Taylor first looked at work and studied it, the productivity of the manual worker began its unprecedented rise. Since then it has been going up steadily at the rate of 3.5 percent per annum—which means it has been raised fiftyfold since Taylor. On this achievement rests all the economic and social gains of the twentieth century. The productivity of the manual worker has created what we now call "developed" economies. Before Taylor, there was no such thing—all economies were equally "underdeveloped." An underdeveloped economy today—or even an "emerging" one—is one that has not, or at least has not yet, made the manual worker productive.

THE PRINCIPLES OF MANUAL-WORK PRODUCTIVITY

Taylor's principles sound deceptively simple.

The first step in making the manual worker productive is to look at the task and to *analyze its constituent motions.* The next step is to *record each motion,* the physical effort it takes and the time it takes. Then motions that are not needed can be eliminated—and whenever we have looked at manual work, we have found that a great many of the traditionally most hallowed procedures turn out to be waste and do not add anything. Next, each of the motions that remain as essential to obtaining the finished product is set up so as to be done the *simplest way,* the easiest way, the way that puts the least physical and mental strain on the operator, the way that requires the least time. Then these motions are put together into a "job" that is in a *logical sequence or system,* including provision of appropriate information necessary to *control* the direction, quantity, quality, and acceptable range of exceptions. Finally, the *tools* needed to do the motions are redesigned. And whenever we have looked at any job—no matter for how many thousands of years it has been performed—we have found that the traditional tools are totally wrong for the task. This was the case, for instance, with the shovel used to carry sand in a foundry— the first task Taylor studied. It was the wrong shape, it was the wrong size, and it had the wrong handle.

Taylor's principles sound obvious—effective methods always do. But it took Taylor twenty years of experimentation to work them out.

Over these last hundred years there have been countless further changes, revisions, and refinements. The name by which the methodology goes has changed, too, over the century. Taylor himself first called his method *task analysis* or *task management.* Twenty years later it was rechristened *scientific management.* Another twenty years later, after World War I, it came to be known as *industrial engineering* in the United States, the United Kingdom, and Japan, and as *rationalization* in Germany. To proclaim that one's method "rejects" Taylor or "replaces" him is almost standard "public relations." For what made Taylor and his method so powerful has also made them unpopular. What Taylor saw when he actually looked at work violated everything poets and philosophers had said about work from Hesiod and Virgil to Karl Marx. They all celebrated "skill." Taylor showed that in manual work there is no such thing. There are only simple, repetitive motions. What makes them productive is knowledge, that is, the way the simple, unskilled motions are put together, organized and executed. In fact, Taylor was the first person to apply knowledge to work.*

This also earned Taylor the undying enmity of the labor unions of his time, all of which were craft unions and based on the *mystique* of craft skill and their monopoly of it.

Moreover, Taylor advocated—and this is still anathema to a labor union—that workers be paid according to their productivity, that is, for their output, rather than for their input, for example, for hours worked. But Taylor's definition of work as a series of operations also largely explains his rejection by the people who do not do any manual work: the descendants of the poets and philosophers of old, the literati and intellectuals. Taylor destroyed the romance of work. Instead of a "noble skill," it becomes a series of simple motions.

And yet every method during these last hundred years that has had the slightest success in raising the productivity of manual workers—and with it their real wages—has been based on Taylor's principles, no matter how loudly the protagonists proclaimed their differences with Taylor. This is true of "work enlargement," "work enrichment," and "job rotation"—all of which use Taylor's methods to lessen the worker's fatigue and thereby to increase the worker's productivity. It is true of such extensions of Taylor's principles of task analysis and industrial engineering to the entire manual work process as Henry Ford's assembly line (developed after 1914, when Taylor himself was already sick, old, and retired). It is just

---

* For work in the oldest knowledge profession, that is, in medicine, Taylor's close contemporary William Osier (1849–1919) did what Taylor did and at the same time—in his 1892 book *The Principles and Practice of Medicine* (arguably the best textbook since Euclid's *Geometry* in the third century BC). Osier's work has rightly been called the application of scientific management to medical diagnosis. And, like Taylor, Osier preached that there is no "skill," there is only method.

as true of the Japanese "quality circle," of "continuous improvement" ("*kaizen*"), and of "just-in-time delivery."

The best example, however, is W. Edwards Deming's (1900–1993) "total quality management." What Deming did—and what makes total quality management effective—is to analyze and organize the job exactly the way Taylor did. But then he added, around 1940, "quality control" based on a statistical theory that was only developed ten years after Taylor's death. Finally, in the 1970s, Deming substituted closed-circuit television and computer simulation for Taylor's stopwatch and motion photos. But Deming's "quality control analysts" are the spit and image of Taylor's "efficiency engineers" and function the same way.

Whatever his limitations and shortcomings—and he had many—no other American, not even Henry Ford (1863–1947), has had anything like Taylor's impact. *Scientific management* (and its successor, *industrial engineering*) is the one American philosophy that has swept the world—more so even than the Constitution and the Federalist Papers. In the last century there has been only one worldwide philosophy that could compete with Taylor's: Marxism. And in the end, Taylor has triumphed over Marx.

In World War I, scientific management swept through the United States—together with Ford's Taylor-based assembly line. In the 1920s, scientific management swept through Western Europe and began to be adopted in Japan.

In World War II, both the German achievement and the American achievement were squarely based on applying Taylor's principles to training. The German General Staff, after having lost World War I, applied "rationalization," that is, Taylor's scientific management, to the job of the soldier and to military training. This enabled Hitler to create a superb fighting machine in the six short years between his coming to power and 1939. In the United States, the same principles were applied to the training of an industrial workforce, first tentatively in World War I, and then, with full power, in World War II. This enabled the Americans to outproduce the Germans, even though a larger proportion of the U.S. than of the German male population was in uniform and thus not in industrial production. And then training-based scientific management gave the U.S. civilian worker more than twice—if not three times—the productivity of the workers in Hitler's Germany and in Hitler-dominated Europe. Scientific management thus gave the United States the capacity to outnumber both Germans and Japanese on the battlefield and yet to outproduce both by several orders of magnitude.

Economic development outside the Western world since 1950 has largely been based on copying what the United States did in World War II, that is, on applying scientific management to making the manual worker productive. All earlier economic development had been based on technological innovation—first in France in

the eighteenth century, then in Great Britain from 1760 until 1850, and finally in the new economic "Great Powers," Germany and the United States, in
the second half of the nineteenth century. The non-Western countries that
developed after World War II, beginning with Japan, eschewed technological
innovation. Instead, they imported the training that the United States had
developed during World War II based on Taylor's principles, and used it to
make highly productive, almost overnight, a still largely unskilled and preindustrial workforce. (In Japan, for instance, almost two-thirds of the working
population were still, in 1950, living on the land and unskilled in any work
except cultivating rice.) But, while highly productive, this new workforce was
still—for a decade or more—paid preindustrial wages so that these countries—
first Japan, then Korea, then Taiwan and Singapore—could produce the same
manufactured products as the developed countries, but at a fraction of their
labor costs.

THE FUTURE OF MANUAL-WORKER PRODUCTIVITY

Taylor's approach was designed for manual work in manufacturing, and at first applied only to it. But even within these traditional limitations, it still has enormous
scope. It is still going to be the organizing principle in countries where manual
work, and especially manual work in manufacturing, is the growth sector of society and economy, that is, "Third World" countries with very large and still growing numbers of young people with little education and little skill.

But, as will be discussed in the next chapter, there is a tremendous amount of
knowledge work—including work requiring highly advanced and thoroughly theoretical knowledge—that includes manual operations. And the productivity of
these operations also requires industrial engineering.

Still, in developed countries, the central challenge is no longer to make manual
work productive—we know, after all, how to do it. The central challenge will be
to make knowledge workers productive. Knowledge workers are rapidly becoming
the largest single group in the workforce of every developed country. They already
comprise one-third of the U.S. workforce—and a smaller but rapidly growing proportion of the workforce of all other developed countries. It is on their productivity, above all, that the future prosperity and indeed the future survival of the
developed economies will increasingly depend.

SUMMARY

The realization that *skill and knowledge are in the working rather than in the work is
the key to making work productive.* The generic nature of work implies that work
can be studied systematically, if not scientifically. Until recently the study of
work has been confined to manual work for the reason that this was the main

work around. But the same principles and approaches apply to any other production work, such as most service work. They apply to the processing of information, that is, to most clerical work. They even apply to most knowledge work. Only the applications and the tools vary. Making work productive requires four separate activities, each with its own demands. Because work is objective and impersonal and a "something"—even if it is intangible, like information or knowledge—making work productive has to begin with the end product, the output of work. It cannot start with the input, whether craft skill or formal knowledge. Skills, information, knowledge, are tools; and what tool is to be applied when, and for what purpose, must always be determined by the desired end product. The end product determines what work is needed. It also determines the synthesis into a process, the design of the appropriate controls, and the specifications for the tools needed.

19

Managing the Work and Worker in Knowledge Work

WHAT WE KNOW ABOUT KNOWLEDGE-WORKER PRODUCTIVITY

Work on the productivity of the knowledge worker has barely begun. In terms of actual work on knowledge-worker productivity, we are, in the year 2007, roughly where we were in the year 1900, a century ago, in terms of the productivity of the manual worker. But we already know infinitely more about the productivity of the knowledge worker than we did then about that of the manual worker. We even know a good many of the answers. But we also know the challenges to which we do not yet know the answers, and on which we need to go to work.

Six major factors determine knowledge-worker productivity:

1. Knowledge-worker productivity demands that we ask the question, "What is the task?"

2. It demands that we impose the responsibility for their productivity on the individual knowledge workers themselves. Knowledge workers have to manage themselves. They have to have autonomy.

3. Continuing innovation has to be part of the work, the task and the responsibility of knowledge workers.

4. Knowledge work requires continuous learning on the part of the knowledge worker, but equally continuous teaching on the part of the knowledge worker.

5. Productivity of the knowledge worker is not—at least not primarily—a matter of the quantity of output. Quality is at least as important.

6. Finally, knowledge-worker productivity requires that the knowledge worker is both seen and treated as an "asset" rather than a "cost." It requires that

knowledge workers want to work for the organization in preference to all other opportunities.

Each of these requirements—except perhaps the last one—is almost the exact opposite of what is needed to increase the productivity of the manual worker.

In manual work quality also matters. But lack of quality is a restraint. There has to be a certain minimum quality standard. The achievement of "total quality management," that is, of the application of twentieth-century statistical theory to manual work, is the ability to cut (though not entirely to eliminate) production that falls below this minimum standard.

But in most knowledge work, quality is not a minimum and a restraint. Quality is the essence of the output. In judging the performance of a teacher, we do not ask how many students there can be in his or her class. We ask how many students learn anything—and that's a quality question. In appraising the performance of a medical laboratory, the question of how many tests it can run through its machines is quite secondary to the question of how many test results are valid and reliable. And this is true even for the work of the file clerk.

Productivity of knowledge work therefore has to aim first at obtaining quality—and not minimum quality but optimum if not maximum quality. Only then can one ask, "What is the volume, the quantity of work?"

This not only means that we approach the task of making productive the knowledge worker from the quality of the work rather than the quantity. It also means that we will have to learn to define quality.

WHAT IS THE TASK?

The crucial question in knowledge-worker productivity is the first one: *What is the task?* It is also the one most at odds with manual-worker productivity. In manual work the key question is always, *How should the work be done?* In manual work the task is always a given. None of the people who work on manual-worker productivity ever asked, "What is the manual worker supposed to do?" Their only question was, "How does the manual worker best do the job?"

This was just as true of Frederick W. Taylor's "scientific management" as of the people at Sears, Roebuck or the Ford Motor Company who first designed the assembly line, or of W. Edwards Deming's "total quality control."

But in knowledge work the key question is, "What is the task?"

One reason for this is that knowledge work, unlike manual work, does not program the worker. The worker on the automobile assembly line who puts on a wheel is programmed by the simultaneous arrival of the car's chassis on one line and of the wheel on the other line. The farmer who plows a field in preparation for planting does not climb out of his tractor to take a telephone call, to attend a meeting, or to write a memo. What is to be done is always obvious in manual work.

But in knowledge work the task does not program the worker.

A major crisis in the hospital—for example, when a patient suddenly goes into coma—does, of course, control the nurse's task and programs her. But otherwise, it is largely the nurse's decision whether to spend time at the patient's bed or whether to spend time filling out papers. Engineers are constantly being pulled off their task by having to write a report or rewrite it, by being asked to attend a meeting, and so on. The job of the salesperson in the department store is to serve the customer and to provide the merchandise the customer is interested in or should become interested in. Instead, the salesperson spends an enormous amount of time on paperwork, on checking whether merchandise is in stock, on checking when and how it can be delivered, and so on—all things that take salespeople away from the customer and do not add anything to their productivity in doing what salespeople are being paid for, which is to sell and to satisfy the customer.

The first requirement in tackling knowledge work is to find out what the task is so as to make it possible to concentrate knowledge workers on the task and to eliminate everything else—at least as far as it can possibly be eliminated. But this, then, requires that the knowledge workers themselves define what the task is or should be. And only the knowledge workers themselves can do that.

Work on knowledge-worker productivity, therefore, begins with asking the knowledge workers themselves, *What is your task? What should it be? What should you be expected to contribute? and What hampers you in doing your task and should be eliminated?*

Knowledge workers themselves almost always have thought through these questions and can answer them. Still, it then usually takes time and hard work to restructure their jobs so that they can actually make the contribution they are already being paid for. But asking the questions and taking action on the answers usually doubles or triples knowledge-worker productivity, and quite fast.

This was the result of questioning the nurses in a major hospital. They were actually sharply divided as to what their task was, with one group saying "patient care" and another one saying "satisfying the physicians." But they were in complete agreement on the things that made them unproductive—they called them "chores": paperwork, arranging flowers, answering the phone calls of patients' relatives, answering the patients' bells, and so on. And all—or nearly all—of these could be turned over to a nonnurse floor clerk, paid a fraction of a nurse's pay. The productivity of the nurses on the floor immediately more than doubled, as measured by the time nurses spent at the patients' beds. Patient satisfaction more than doubled. And turnover of nurses, which had been catastrophically high, almost disappeared—all within four months.

And once the *task* has been defined, the next requirements can be tackled—and will be tackled by the knowledge workers themselves. They are

1. Knowledge workers' responsibility for their own contribution—the knowledge worker's decision as to what he or she should be held accountable for in terms of quality and quantity, with respect to time and with respect to cost. Knowledge workers have to have autonomy, and that entails responsibility.

2. Continuous innovation has to be built into the knowledge worker's job.

3. Continuous learning and continuous teaching have to be built into the job.

But one central requirement of knowledge-worker productivity is, then, still left to be satisfied. We have to answer the question: **What is quality?**

In some knowledge work—and especially in some work requiring a high degree of knowledge—we already measure quality. Surgeons, for instance, are routinely measured, especially by their colleagues, by their success rates in difficult and dangerous procedures—for example, by the survival rates of their open-heart surgical patients or the full-recovery rates of their orthopedic-surgery patients. But by and large we have, so far, mainly judgments rather than measures regarding the quality of a great deal of knowledge work. The main trouble is, however, *not the difficulty of measuring quality*. It is the difficulty—and more particularly the sharp disagreements—*in defining what the task is and what it should be*.

The best example I know is the American school. As everyone knows, public schools in the American inner cities have become disaster areas. But next to them—in the same location and serving the same kind of children—are private (mostly Christian) schools in which the kids behave well and learn well. There is endless speculation to explain these enormous quality differences. But a major reason is surely that the two kinds of schools define their tasks differently. The typical public school defines its task as "helping the underprivileged"; the typical Christian school (and especially the parochial schools of the Catholic Church) define their task as "enabling those who want to learn, to learn." One therefore is governed by its scholastic failures, the other one by its scholastic successes.

But similarly, there are two research departments of major pharmaceutical companies that have totally different results because they define their tasks differently. One sees its task as not having failures, that is, in working steadily on fairly minor but predictable improvements in existing products and for established markets. The other one defines its task as producing "breakthroughs" and therefore courts risks. Both are considered fairly successful—by themselves, by their own top managements, and by outside analysts. But each operates quite differently and quite differently defines its own productivity and that of its research scientists.

To define quality in knowledge work and to convert the definition into knowledge-worker productivity is thus to a large extent a matter of defining the task. It requires the difficult, risk-taking, and always controversial defining of what "results" are for a given enterprise and a given activity. We, therefore, actually know how to do it. Still, the question is a totally new one for most organizations, and also for most knowledge workers. And to answer it requires controversy, requires dissent.

THE KNOWLEDGE WORKER AS CAPITAL ASSET

In no other area is the difference greater between manual-worker productivity and knowledge-worker productivity than in their respective economics. Economic theory and most business practice see manual workers as a cost. To be productive, knowledge workers must be considered a capital asset.

Costs need to be controlled and reduced. Assets need to be made to grow.

In managing manual workers, we learned fairly early that high turnover—that is, losing workers—is very costly. The Ford Motor Company, as is well known, increased the pay of skilled workers threefold, to $5 a day, in January 1914. It did so because its turnover had been so excessive as to make its labor costs prohibitively high; it had to hire 60,000 people a year to keep 10,000. Even so, everybody, including Henry Ford himself (who had at first been bitterly opposed to this increase), was convinced that the higher wages would greatly reduce the company's profits. Instead, in the very first year, profits almost doubled. Paid $5 a day, practically no workers left—in fact, the Ford Motor Company soon had a waiting list.

But, short of the costs of turnover, rehiring or retraining, and so on, the manual worker is still being seen as a cost. This is true even in Japan, despite the emphasis on lifetime employment and on building a "loyal," permanent workforce. And short of the cost of turnover, the management of people at work, based on millennia of work being almost totally manual work, still assumes—with the exception of a few highly skilled people—one manual worker is like any other manual worker.

This is definitely not true for knowledge work.

Employees who do manual work do not own the means of production. They may, and often do, have a lot of valuable experience. But that experience is valuable only at the place where they work. It is not portable.

But knowledge workers own the means of production. It is the knowledge between their ears. And it is a totally portable and enormous capital asset. Because knowledge workers own their means of production, they are mobile. Manual workers need the job much more than the job needs them. It may still not be true for all knowledge workers that the organization needs them more than they need the organization. But for most of them, it is a symbiotic relationship in which the two need each other in equal measure.

Management's duty is to preserve the assets of the institution in its care. What does this mean when the knowledge of the individual knowledge worker becomes an asset and, in more and more cases, the main asset of an institution? What does this mean for personnel policy? What is needed to attract and to hold the highest-producing knowledge workers? What is needed to increase their productivity and to convert their increased productivity into performance capacity for the organization?

THE TECHNOLOGISTS

So far we have discussed the productivity of knowledge workers doing knowledge work. But a very large number of knowledge workers do both knowledge work and manual work. I call them "technologists."

This group includes people who apply knowledge of the highest order.

Surgeons preparing for an operation to correct a brain aneurysm before it produces a lethal brain hemorrhage spend hours in diagnosis before they cut—and that requires specialized knowledge of the highest order. And then again, during the surgery, an unexpected complication may occur that calls for theoretical knowledge and judgment, both of the very highest order. But the surgery itself is manual work—and manual work consisting of repetitive manual operations in which the emphasis is on speed, accuracy, uniformity. And these operations are studied, organized, learned, and practiced exactly as any other manual work is, that is, by the same methods Taylor first developed for factory work.

But the technologist group also contains large numbers of people within whose work knowledge is relatively subordinate—though it is always crucial.

The file clerk's job—and that of her computer-operator successor—requires knowledge of the alphabet that no experience can teach. This knowledge is a small part of an otherwise manual task. But it is the foundation and absolutely crucial.

Technologists may be the single biggest group of knowledge workers. They may also be the fastest-growing group. They include the great majority of health-care workers: lab technicians; rehabilitation technicians; technicians in imaging such as X ray, ultrasound, and magnetic-resonance; and so on. They include dentists and all dental support people. They include automobile mechanics and all kinds of repair and installation people. In fact, the technologist may be the true successor to the nineteenth- and twentieth-century skilled worker.

Technologists are also the one group in which developed countries can have a true and long-lasting competitive advantage.

When it comes to truly high knowledge, no country can any longer have much of a lead, the way nineteenth-century Germany had through its university. Among theoretical physicists, mathematicians, economic theorists, and the like, there is no "nationality." And any country can, at fairly low cost, train a substantial number of high-knowledge people. India, for instance, despite her poverty, has been training fairly large numbers of first-rate physicians and first-rate computer programmers. Similarly, there is no "nationality" with respect to the productivity of manual labor. Training based on scientific management has made all countries capable of attaining, overnight, the manual-worker productivity of the most advanced country, industry, or company. Only in educating technologists can the developed countries still have a meaningful competitive edge, and for some time to come.

The United States is the only country that has actually developed this advantage—through its, so far, unique nationwide systems of community colleges. The community college was actually *designed* (beginning in the 1920s) to educate technologists who have both the needed theoretical knowledge and the manual skill. On this, I am convinced, rests both the still huge productivity advantage of the American economy and the—so far unique—American ability to create, almost overnight, new and different industries. Nothing quite like the American community college exists anywhere else yet. The famous Japanese school system produces either people prepared only for manual work or people prepared only for knowledge work. Only in the year 2003 was the first Japanese institution devoted to training technologists started. Even more famous is the German apprenticeship system. Started in the 1830s, it was one of the main factors in Germany's becoming the world's leading manufacturer. But it focused—and still focuses—primarily on manual skills and slights theoretical knowledge. It is thus in danger of rapidly becoming obsolete.

But these other developed countries should be expected to catch up with the United States fairly fast. Other countries—"emerging ones" or "Third World" ones—are, however, likely to be decades behind—in part because educating technologists is expensive, in part because in these countries people of knowledge still look down with disdain, if not with contempt, on working with one's hands. "That's what we have servants for," is still their prevailing attitude. In developed countries, however—and again, foremost in the United States—more and more manual workers are going to be technologists. In increasing knowledge-worker productivity, increasing the productivity of the technologists, therefore, deserves to be given high priority.

The job was actually done in the mid-1920s by the American Telephone and Telegraph Company (AT&T) for its technologists, the people who installed, maintained, and replaced telephones, whether in the home or in the office.

By the early 1920s the technologists working outside the telephone office and at the customer's location had become a major cost center—and at the same time a major cause of customer unhappiness and dissatisfaction. It took about five years or so, from 1920 until 1925, for AT&T—which had by that time acquired a near monopoly on providing telephone service in the United States and in parts of Canada—to realize that the task was not installing, maintaining, repairing, and replacing telephones and telephone connections. The task was to create a satisfied customer. It then became fairly easy to organize the job. It meant, first, that the technicians themselves had to define what "satisfaction" meant. The results were standards that established that every order for a new telephone or an additional telephone connection would have to be satisfied within at most forty-eight hours, and that every request for repair would have to be satisfied the same day if made before noon, or by noon the following day.

Then it became clear that the individual service people—in those days all men—would have to be active participants in such decisions as whether to have one person installing and replacing telephones and another one maintaining and repairing them, or whether the same people had to be able to do all jobs—which in the end turned out to be the right answer. These people had to be taught a very substantial amount of theoretical knowledge—and in those days, few of them had more than six years of schooling. They had to understand how a telephone works. They had to understand how a switchboard works. They had to understand how the telephone system works. These people were not qualified engineers or skilled craftsmen. But they had to know enough electronics to diagnose unexpected problems and to be able to cope with them. Then they were trained in the repetitive manual operation or in the "one right way"—that is, through the methods of scientific management. And they made the decisions, for example, as to where and how to connect the individual telephone to the system and what particular kind of telephone and service would be the most suitable for a given home or a given office. They had to become salesmen in addition to being servicemen.

Finally, the telephone company faced the problem of how to define *quality*. The technologist had to work by himself. He could not be supervised. He, therefore, had to define quality and had to deliver it. It took several more years before that was answered. At first the telephone company thought that this meant a "sample check" that had supervisors go out and look at a sample—maybe every twentieth or thirtieth job done by an individual service person—and check it for quality. This very soon turned out to be the wrong way of doing the job, annoying both servicemen and customers alike. Then the telephone company defined quality as "no complaints"— and soon found out that only extremely unhappy customers complained. It then had to redefine quality as "positive customer satisfaction." And this then meant in the end that the serviceman himself controlled quality—for example, by calling up a week or ten days after he had done a job and asking the customer whether the work was satisfactory and whether there was anything more the technician could possibly do to give the customer the best possible and most satisfactory service.

I have intentionally gone into considerable detail in describing this early example because it exemplifies the three elements for making effective the worker who is *both a knowledge worker and a manual worker.*

1. There is, first, the answer to the question, "What is the task?"—the key question in making every knowledge worker productive. As the example of the Bell System shows, this is not an obvious answer. And as the Bell System people learned, the only people who know the answer to this are the technologists themselves. In fact, until the company asked the technologists, it floundered. But as soon as the technologists were asked, the answer came back loud and clear: a satisfied customer.

2. Then the technologists had to take full responsibility for giving customer satisfaction, that is, for delivering quality. This then showed what formal knowledge the technologist needed. And then, only then, could the manual part of the job be organized for manual-worker productivity.

3. Above all, this example shows that technologists have to be treated as knowledge workers. No matter how important the manual part of their work—and it may take the bulk of their time, as it did in the case of the AT&T installers—the focus has to be on making the technologist *knowledgeable, responsible, productive as a knowledge worker.*

KNOWLEDGE WORK AS A SYSTEM

Productivity of the knowledge worker will almost always require that the work *itself* be restructured and be made part of a *system.*

One example is servicing expensive equipment, such as huge and expensive earth-moving machines. Traditionally, this had been seen as distinct and separate from the job of making and selling the machines. But when the U.S. Caterpillar Company, the world's largest producer of such equipment, asked, "What are we getting paid for?" the answer was, "We are not getting paid for machinery. We are getting paid for what the machinery does at the customer's place of business. That means keeping the equipment running, since even one hour during which the equipment is out of operation may cost the customer far more than the equipment itself." In other words, the answer to "What is our business?" was "Service." This then led to a total restructuring of operations all the way back to the factory, so that the customer can be guaranteed continuing operations and immediate repairs or replacements. And the service representative, usually a technologist, has become the true "decision maker."

The same principle is demonstrated in another, seemingly very different, example. A group of about twenty-five orthopedic surgeons in a midwestern U.S. city have organized themselves as a "system" to produce the highest-quality work: by using optimally the limited and expensive resources of operating and recovery rooms; by using optimally the supporting knowledge of people such as anesthesiologists or surgical nurses; by building continuous learning and continuous innovation into the work of the entire group and of its every member; and finally, by minimizing costs. Each of the surgeons retains full control of his or her practice. He or she is fully responsible for obtaining and treating the individual patient. Traditionally, surgeons schedule surgeries early in the morning. Hence, operating rooms and recovery rooms are standing empty most of the time. The group now schedules the use of operating and recovery rooms for the entire group so that this scarce and extremely expensive resource is used ten hours a day. The group, as a group, decides on the standardization of tools and equipment so as to obtain the highest quality at the lowest cost. Finally, the group has also built quality control into its system. Every three months, three different surgeons are designated to scrutinize every operation done by each of the members—*the diagnosis, the surgery, the after-treatment.* They then sit down with the individual surgeons and discuss their performance. They suggest where there is need for improvement. But they may also recommend that a certain surgeon be asked to leave the group, as his or her work is not satisfactory. And each year the quality standards that these supervising committees apply are discussed with the whole group and are raised, and often substantially. As a result, this group now does almost four times as much work as it did before. It has cut the costs by 50 percent, half of it by cutting back on the waste of operating and recovery rooms, half by standardizing tools and equipment. And in such measurable areas as success rates in knee replacements or shoulder replacements, or in recovery after sports injuries, it has greatly improved its results.

What to do about knowledge-worker productivity is thus largely known. So is *how* to do it.

BUT HOW TO BEGIN?

Making knowledge workers productive requires changes in basic attitude—whereas making the manual worker more productive only required telling the worker how to do the job. And these changes in attitude are required, not only on the part of the individual knowledge worker, but on the part of the whole organization. They therefore have to be "piloted"—as any major changes should be. (On piloting changes, see chapter 37.) The first step is to find an area in the organization or a group of knowledge workers who are receptive. The orthopedic surgeons, for instance, first had their new ideas tried out by four physicians—one an older man, three younger people—who had long argued for radical changes. Then there is a need to work consistently, patiently, and for a considerable length of uninterrupted time in this small area or with this small group. For the first attempts, even if greeted with great enthusiasm, will almost certainly run into all kinds of unexpected problems. It is only after the productivity of this small group of knowledge workers has been substantially increased that the new ways of doing the work can be extended to a larger area, if not to the entire organization. And by then we will also have learned where the main problems are; where, for example, resistance can be expected (e.g., from middle management), or what changes in task, organization, measurements, and attitude are needed for full effectiveness. To try to jump the pilot stage—and there is always pressure to do so—only means that the mistakes become public, while the successes stay hidden. It only means discrediting the entire enterprise. But if the changes are properly piloted, we can already do a great deal to improve—and drastically—knowledge-worker productivity.

Knowledge-worker productivity is the biggest of the management challenges of the twenty-first century. In the developed countries, it is their first survival requirement. In no other way can the developed countries hope to maintain themselves, let alone to maintain their leadership and their standards of living.

In the twentieth century, this leadership very largely depended on making the manual worker productive. Any country, any industry, any business, can do that today—using the methods that the developed countries have worked out and put into practice in the 125 years since Frederick Winslow Taylor first looked at manual work. Anybody today, anywhere, can apply those policies to training, to the organization of the work, and to the productivity of workers, even if they are barely literate, if not illiterate, and totally unskilled.

Above all (as discussed in chapter 5), the supply of young people available for manual work will be rapidly shrinking in the developed countries—in the West and in Japan very fast, in the United States somewhat more slowly—whereas the supply of such people will still grow fast in the emerging and developing countries, at least for another thirty or forty years. *The only possible advantage developed countries can hope to have is in the supply of people prepared, educated, and trained for knowledge work.* There, for another fifty years, the developed countries can expect to have substantial advantages, both in quality and in quantity.

But whether this advantage will translate into performance depends on the ability of the developed countries—and of every industry in them, of every company in them, of every institution in them—to raise the productivity of the knowledge worker and to raise it as quickly as the developed countries, in the last hundred years, have raised the productivity of the manual worker.

The countries and the industries that have emerged as the leaders in the last hundred years in the world are the countries and the industries that have led in raising the productivity of the manual worker: the United States first, Japan and Germany second. Fifty years from now—if not much sooner—the leadership in the world economy will have moved to the countries and to the industries that have most systematically and most successfully raised knowledge-worker productivity.

THE GOVERNANCE OF THE CORPORATION

What does the emergence of the knowledge worker and of knowledge-worker productivity mean for the governance of the corporation? What do they mean for the future and structure of the economic system?

In the last fifteen to twenty years, pension funds and other institutional investors became the main share owners of the equity capital of publicly owned companies in all developed countries (as discussed several times in this book). This has triggered in the United States a furious debate on the governance of corporations (on this, see also chapters 6 and 44). For with the emergence of pension funds and mutual funds as the owners of publicly owned companies, power has shifted to these new owners.

Similar shifts in the definition both of the purpose of such economic organizations as the business corporation and of their governance can be expected to occur in all developed countries.

We are now facing the change that will have to be made in the governance of the corporation caused by the emergence of knowledge work just as we did before with the emergence of shareholder capitalism. We will have to redefine the purpose of the employing organization and of its management as both satisfying the legal owners, such as shareholders, and satisfying the owners of the human capital that gives the organization its wealth-producing power—that is, satisfying the knowledge workers. For increasingly the ability of organizations—and not only of businesses—to survive will come to depend on their *comparative advantage* in making the knowledge worker productive. And the ability to attract and hold the best of the knowledge workers is the first and most fundamental precondition.

Can this be *measured,* however? Or is it purely an "intangible"? This will surely be a central problem—for management, for investors, for capital markets. What does *capitalism* mean when knowledge governs—rather than money? And what do "free markets" mean when knowledge workers—and no one else can "own" knowledge—are the true assets? Knowledge workers can be neither bought nor sold. They do not come with a merger or an acquisition. In fact, though the greatest "value," they have no "market value"—that means, of course, that they are not an "asset" in the traditional accounting sense.

These questions go far beyond the scope of this book. But it is certain that the emergence of the knowledge worker and of the knowledge worker's productivity as key questions will, within a few decades, bring about *fundamental changes in the very structure and nature of the economic system.*

SUMMARY

For thousands of years no one thought that manual work could be made more productive. Even the term "productivity" was not known until around World War II. But as soon as Frederick W. Taylor, in 1881, looked critically at how the manual worker did his job, manual-worker productivity rose dramatically. In the century after 1880, productivity grew steadily at 3 to 4 percent compound per year, and that meant a fiftyfold growth in a hundred years.

In manual work the task is always a given. The machine or the assembly line program the factory worker. The manual worker's productivity is thus never a question of *what to do*. The question is always *how to do it*. And for the great majority of manual workers the employer owns and controls the means of production and the workers' tools. With knowledge work, however, *what to do* becomes the first and decisive question. For knowledge workers are not programmed by the machine or by the weather. They largely are in control of their own tasks and must be in control of their own tasks. For they, and only they, own and control the most expensive of the means of production—their education—and their most important tool—their knowledge. This is not just true of the people who apply high and advanced knowledge. It's just as true of the computer service technician who comes to fix a problem; of the technician in the hospital lab who makes a bacterial culture; of the trainee who oversees a market test of a new product in the supermarket. *The how* in knowledge work comes only after *the what* has been answered.

There are a number of steps to improve knowledge-worker productivity. They include

- Define the task

- Focus on the task

- Define results

- Define quality

- Grant autonomy to the knowledge worker

- Demand accountability

- Build into tasks continuous learning and teaching

The only true competitive advantage for a company or a nation will increasingly be the productivity of its knowledge workers. This will have a future impact on the governance of the corporation.

Part V

Social Impacts and Social Responsibilities

The quality of life is the third major task area for management. Managements of all institutions are responsible for their by-products, that is, the impacts of their legitimate activities on people and on the physical and social environment. They are increasingly expected to anticipate and to resolve social problems. They need to think through and develop new policies for the relationship of business and government, which is rapidly outgrowing traditional theories and habits. What are the tasks? What are the opportunities? What are the limitations? And what are the ethics of leadership for the manager who is a leader but not a master?

20

Social Impacts and Social Responsibilities

Social responsibilities—whether of a business, a hospital, or a university—may arise in two areas. They may emerge out of the social impacts of the institution. Or they arise as problems of the society itself. Both are of concern to management, because the institution that managers manage lives of necessity in society and community. But otherwise the two areas are different. The first deals with what an institution does *to* society. The second is concerned with what an institution can do *for* society.

The modern organization exists to provide a specific service to society. It therefore has to be in society. It has to be in a community, has to be a neighbor, has to do its work within a social setting. Also it has to employ people to do its work. Its *social impacts* inevitably go beyond the specific contribution it exists to make.

The purpose of the hospital is not to employ nurses and cooks. It is patient care. But to accomplish this purpose, nurses and cooks are needed. And in no time at all, they form a work community with its own community tasks and community problems.

The purpose of a ferroalloy plant is not to make noise or to release noxious fumes. It is to make high-performance metals that serve the customer. But in order to do this, it produces noise, creates heat, and releases fumes.

These impacts are incidental to the purpose of the organization. But in large measure they are inescapable by-products.

Social problems, such as a deteriorating educational system, by contrast, are dysfunctions of society rather than impacts of the organization and its activities.

Since the institution can exist only within the social environment and is indeed an organ of society, such social problems affect the institution. They are of concern to it even if, as in the ferroalloy company's case, the company had no role in producing the decline in the education system.

A healthy business, a healthy university, a healthy hospital cannot exist in a sick society. Management has a self-interest in a healthy society, even though the cause of society's sickness is not of management's making.

RESPONSIBILITY FOR IMPACTS

One is responsible for one's impacts, whether they are intended or not. *This is the first rule for the ferroalloy company.* There is no doubt regarding management's responsibility for the social impacts of its organization. They are management's business.

It is not enough to say, "But the public doesn't object." It is, above all, not enough to say that any action to come to grips with such a problem is going to be "unpopular," is going to be "resented" by one's colleagues and one's associates, and is not required. Sooner or later society will come to regard any such impact as an attack on its integrity and will exact a high price from those who have not responsibly worked on eliminating the impact or on finding a solution to the problem.

Here is an example. In the late 1940s and early 1950s, one American automobile company tried to make the American public safety-conscious. Ford introduced cars with seat belts. But sales dropped catastrophically. The company had to withdraw the cars with seat belts and abandoned the whole idea. When, fifteen years later, the American driving public became safety-conscious, the car manufacturers were sharply attacked for their "total lack of concern with safety" and for being "merchants of death." And the resulting regulations were written as much to punish the companies as to protect the public.

The first job of management is, therefore, to identify and to anticipate impacts—coldly and realistically. The question is, "Is what we do right, in the best interest of the customer and society?" And if our social impacts are not right, it is the responsibility of the company to educate the customer and society so that the negative impact can be eliminated.

HOW TO DEAL WITH IMPACTS

Identifying the incidental impacts of an institution is the first step. But how does management deal with them? The objective is clear: impacts on society, the economy, the community, and the individual that are not in themselves the purpose and mission of the institution should be kept to the minimum and should preferably be eliminated altogether. The fewer such impacts the better, whether the impact is within the institution, on the social environment, or on the physical environment.

Wherever an impact can be eliminated by dropping the activity that causes it, this is therefore the best—indeed, the only truly good—solution.

However, in most cases the activity cannot be eliminated. Hence there is need for systematic work at eliminating the impact—or at least at minimizing it—while maintaining the underlying activity itself.

The ideal approach is to make the elimination of impacts into a profitable business opportunity. One example is the way Dow Chemical, one of the leading U. S. chemical companies, has for almost twenty years tackled air and water pollution.

Dow decided, shortly after World War II, that air and water pollution was an undesirable impact that had to be eliminated. Long before the public outcry about the environment, Dow adopted a zero-pollution policy for its plants. It then set about systematically developing the polluting substances it removes from smokestack gases and watery effluents into salable products and creating uses and markets for them.

A variant is the Du Pont Industrial Toxicity Laboratory. In the 1920s, Du Pont became aware of the toxic side effects of many of its industrial products and set up a laboratory to test for toxicity and to develop processes to eliminate the poisons. Du Pont started out to eliminate an impact that at the time every other chemical manufacturer took for granted. But then Du Pont decided to develop toxicity control of industrial products into a separate business, the Industrial Toxicity Laboratory, where products could be tested not only for Du Pont but for a wide variety of customers for whom it developed compounds. Again, an impact was eliminated by turning it into a business opportunity.

WHEN REGULATION IS NEEDED

Turning elimination of an impact into a business opportunity should always be attempted. But it cannot be done in many cases. More often eliminating an impact means increasing the costs. What was an "externality" for which the general public paid becomes business cost. It therefore becomes a competitive disadvantage unless everybody in the industry accepts the same rule. And this, in most cases, can be done only by regulation—that means by some form of public action.

Whenever an impact cannot be eliminated without an increase in cost, it becomes incumbent upon management to think ahead and work out the regulation that is most likely to solve the problem at the minimum cost and with the greatest benefit to public and business alike. And it is then management's job to work at getting the right regulation enacted.

Management—and not only business management—has shunned this responsibility. The traditional attitude has always been that "no regulation is the best regulation." But this applies only when an impact can be made into a business. Where elimination of an impact requires a restriction, regulation is in the interest of business, and especially in the interest of responsible business. Otherwise it will be penalized as "irresponsible," while the unscrupulous, the greedy, the stupid, and the chiseler cash in.

And to expect that there will be no regulation is willful blindness.

The fact that today the public sees no issue is not relevant. Indeed, it is not even relevant that today the public—as it did in every single one of the examples above—actively resists any attempts on the part of farsighted business leaders to prevent a crisis. In the end, there is the scandal.

Any solution to an impact problem requires trade-offs. Beyond a certain level, elimination of an impact costs more in money or in energy, in resources or in lives, than the attainable benefit. A decision has to be made on the optimal balance between costs and benefits. This is something people in an industry understand, as a rule. *But no one outside does—and so the outsider's solution tends to ignore the trade-off problem altogether.*

Responsibility for social impacts is a management responsibility—not because it is a social responsibility, but because it is a business responsibility. The ideal is to make elimination of such an impact into a business opportunity. But wherever that cannot be done, the design of the appropriate regulation with the optimal trade-off balance—and public discussion of the problem and promotion of the best regulatory solution—is management's job

SOCIAL PROBLEMS AS BUSINESS OPPORTUNITIES

Social problems are dysfunctions of society and—at least potentially—degenerative diseases of the body politic. They are ills. But for the management of institutions and, above all, for business management, they represent challenges. They are major sources of opportunity. For it is the function of business—and to a lesser degree of the other main institutions—to satisfy social need and at the same time serve their institution, by making resolution of a social problem into a business opportunity.

It is the job of business to convert change into innovation, that is, into new business. And it is a poor executive who thinks that innovation refers to technology alone. Social change and social innovation have, throughout business history, been at least as important as technology. After all, the major industries of the nineteenth century were, to a very large extent, the result of converting the new social environment—the industrial city—into a business opportunity and into a business market. This underlay the rise of lighting, first by gas and then by electricity, of the streetcar and the interurban trolley, of telephone, newspaper, and department store—to name only a few.

The most significant opportunities for converting social problems into business opportunities may, therefore, not lie in new technologies, new products, and new services. They may lie in *solving* the social problem, that is, in social innovation that then directly and indirectly benefits and strengthens the company or the industry.

The success of some of the most successful businesses is largely the result of such social innovation. Here is an American example:

The years immediately prior to World War I were years of great labor unrest in the United States, growing labor bitterness, and high unemployment. Hourly wages for skilled men ran as low as 15 cents in many cases. It was against this background, as seen in chapter 19, that the Ford Motor Company, in the closing days of 1913, announced that it would pay a guaranteed $5-a-day wage to every one of its workers. James Couzens, the company's general manager, who had forced this decision on his reluctant partner, Henry Ford, became convinced that the workmen's sufferings and hence turnover were so great that only radical and highly visible action could have an effect. Couzens also expected that Ford's actual labor cost, despite the tripling of the wage rate, would go down—and events soon proved him right. Before Ford changed the whole labor economy of the United States with one announcement, labor turnover at the Ford Motor Company had been so high that, in 1912, 60,000 men had to be hired to retain 10,000 workers. With the new wage, turnover almost disappeared. The resulting savings were so great that despite sharply rising costs for all materials in the next few years, Ford could produce and sell its Model T at a lower price and yet make a larger profit per car. It was the saving in labor cost produced by a drastically higher wage that gave Ford market domination. At the same time Ford's action transformed American industrial society. It established the American workingman as fundamentally middle class.

Social problems that management action converts into opportunities cease to be problems. The others, however, are likely to become "chronic complaints," if not "degenerative diseases." Not every social problem can be resolved by making it into an opportunity for contribution and performance. Indeed, the most serious of such problems tend to defy this approach.

What, then, is the social responsibility of management for these social problems that become chronic or degenerative diseases?

They are management's problems. The health of the enterprise is management's responsibility. *A healthy business and a sick society are hardly compatible.* Healthy businesses require a healthy, or at least a *functioning,* society. The health of the community is a prerequisite for successful and growing business.

And it is foolish to hope that these problems will disappear if only one looks the other way. Problems go away because someone does something about them.

To what extent should business—or any of the other special-purpose institutions of our society—be expected to tackle a problem that did not arise out of its impact and that cannot be converted into an opportunity for performance of the institution's purpose and mission? To what extent should these institutions—business, university, or hospital—even be permitted to take responsibility? (These questions are more fully the subject of chapter 21.)

Are there limits to social responsibility? And what are they?

THE LIMITS OF SOCIAL RESPONSIBILITY

The manager is a servant. His master is the institution he manages, and his *first* responsibility must therefore be to it. His first task is to make the institution, whether business, hospital, school, or university, perform the function and make the contribution *for the sake of which* it exists. The executive who uses his position at the head of a major institution to become a public figure and to take leadership with respect to social problems *while his company or his university erodes through neglect is not a statesman. He or she is irresponsible and false to their trust.*

The institution's performance of its specific mission is also *society's first need and interest.* Society does not stand to gain but stands to lose if the performance capacity of the institution in its own specific task is diminished or impaired. *Performance of its function is the institution's first social responsibility.* Unless it discharges its performance responsibly, it cannot discharge anything else. A bankrupt business is not a desirable employer and is unlikely to be a good neighbor in a community. Nor will it create the capital for tomorrow's jobs and the opportunities for tomorrow's workers. A university that fails to prepare tomorrow's leaders and professionals is not socially responsible, no matter how many "good works" it engages in.

Above all, management needs to know the *minimum profitability* required by the risks of the business and by its commitments to the future. It needs this knowledge for its own decisions. But it needs it just as much to explain its decisions to others—the politicians, the press, the public. As long as managements remain the prisoners of their own ignorance of the objective need for, and function of, profit (i.e., as long as they think and argue solely in terms of the "maximization of shareholder wealth"), they will be able neither to make rational decisions with respect to social responsibilities, nor to explain those decisions to others inside and outside the business.

Whenever a business has disregarded the limitation of economic performance and has assumed social responsibilities that it could not support economically, it has soon gotten into trouble.

The same limitation on social responsibility applies to noneconomic institutions. There, too, the manager's first duty is to preserve the performance capacity of the institution in his care. To jeopardize it, no matter how noble the motive, is irresponsibility. These institutions, too, are capital assets of society on whose performance society depends.

This, to be sure, is a very unpopular position to take. But managers, and especially managers of key institutions of society, are not being paid to be heroes to the popular press. They are being paid for performance and responsibility.

To take on tasks for which one lacks competence is irresponsible behavior. It is also cruel. It raises expectations that will then be disappointed. An institution, and especially a business enterprise, has to acquire whatever competence is needed to take responsibility for its impacts. But in areas of social responsibility other than impacts, right and duty to act are limited by *competence* (on this matter see chapter 21 for amendments to this argument).

In particular, an institution better refrain from tackling tasks that do not fit into its value system. Skills and knowledge are fairly easily acquired. But one cannot easily change personality. No one is likely to do well in areas that he or she does not respect. If a business or any other institution tackles such an area because there is a social need, it is unlikely to put its good people on the task or to support them adequately. It is unlikely to understand what the task involves. It is almost certain to do the wrong things. As a result, it will do damage rather than good.

Management therefore needs to know at the very least what it and its institution are truly *incompetent* for. Business, as a rule, will be in this position of absolute incompetence in an "intangible" area. The strength of business is *accountability* and *measurability*. It is the discipline of market test, productivity measurements, and profitability requirement. Where these are lacking, businesses are essentially out of their depth. They are also out of fundamental sympathy, that is, outside their own value systems. Where the criteria of performance are intangible—such as "political" opinions and emotions, community approval or disapproval, mobilization of community energies, and structuring of power relations—business is unlikely to feel comfortable. It is unlikely to have respect for the values that matter. It is, therefore, most unlikely to have competence.

In such areas it is, however, often possible to define goals clearly and measurably for specific *partial tasks*. It is often possible to convert parts of a problem that, by itself, lies outside the competence of business into work that fits the competence and value system of the business enterprise.

No one in America has done very well in training hard-core unemployed African-American teenagers for work and jobs. But business has done far less badly than any other institution: schools, government programs, community agencies. This task can be identified. It can be defined. Goals can be set. And performance can be measured. And then business can perform.

THE LIMITS OF AUTHORITY

The most important limitation on social responsibility is the limitation of authority. The constitutional lawyer knows that there is no such word as "responsibility" in the political dictionary. The term is "responsibility *and* authority." Whoever claims authority thereby assumes responsibility. But, likewise, whoever assumes responsibility thereby claims authority. The two are but different sides of the same coin. To assume social responsibility therefore always means to claim authority.

Again, the question of authority as a limit on social responsibility does not arise in connection with the impacts of an institution. For the impact is the result of *an exercise of authority,* even though purely incidental and unintended. And then *responsibility follows*.

But when business or any other institution of our society of organizations is asked to assume social responsibility for one of the problems or ills of society and community, management needs to think through whether the authority implied in the responsibility is legitimate. Otherwise, it is usurpation and irresponsible.

Every time the demand is made that business take responsibility for this or that, one should ask, "Does business have the authority and should it have it?" If business does not have and should not have authority—and in a great many areas it should not have it—then responsibility on the part of business should be treated with great care. It may not be responsibility; rather it may simply be a lust for power.

Ralph Nader, the American consumerist, sincerely considers himself a foe of big business and is accepted as such by business and by the general public. Insofar as Nader demands that business take responsibility for product quality and product safety, he is surely concerned with legitimate business responsibility, that is, with responsibility for performance and contribution.

Management must resist responsibility for a social problem that would compromise or impair the performance capacity of its business (or its university or its hospital). It must resist when the demand goes beyond the institution's competence. It must resist when responsibility would, in fact, be illegitimate authority. But then, if the problem is a real one, it better think through and offer an alterative approach. If the problem is serious, something will ultimately have to be done about it.

Managements of all major institutions, including business enterprise, need to concern themselves with serious ills of society. If at all possible they should convert solution of these problems into an opportunity for performance and contribution. At the least they can think through what the problem is and how it might be tackled. *They cannot escape concern; for this society of organizations has no one else to be concerned about real problems. In this society, executives of institutions are the leadership group.*

But we also know that a developed society needs performing institutions with their own autonomous management. It cannot function as a totalitarian society. Indeed, what characterizes a developed society—and indeed makes it a developed one—is that most of its social tasks are carried out in and through organized institutions, each with its own autonomous management. These organizations, including most of the agencies of our government, are special-purpose institutions. They are organs of our society for specific performance in a specific area. The greatest contribution they can make, their greatest social responsibility, is performance of their function. The greatest social irresponsibility is to impair the performance capacity of these institutions by having them tackle tasks beyond their competence or usurp authority in the name of social responsibility.

THE ETHICS OF RESPONSIBILITY

Countless sermons have been preached and printed on the ethics of business or the ethics of the executive. Most have nothing to do with business and little to do with ethics.

One main topic is plain, *everyday honesty*. Executives, we are told solemnly, should not cheat, steal, lie, bribe, or take bribes. But nor should anyone else. Men and women do not acquire exemption from the ordinary rules of personal behavior because of their work or job. Nor, however, do they cease to be human beings when appointed vice president, city manager, or college dean. And there have always been a number of people who cheat, steal, lie, bribe, or take bribes. The problem is one of moral values and moral education—of the individual, of the family, of the school. But neither is there a separate ethics of business, nor is one needed.

All that is needed is to mete out stiff punishments to those—whether business executives or others—who yield to temptation.

The other common theme in the discussion of ethics in business has nothing to do with ethics.

Such things as the employment of call girls to entertain customers are not matters of ethics but matters of aesthetics. "Do I want to see a pimp when I look at myself in the mirror while shaving?" is the real question.

It would indeed be nice to have fastidious leaders. Alas, fastidiousness has never been prevalent among leadership groups, whether kings and counts, priests or generals, or even "intellectuals" such as the painters and humanists of the Renaissance or the "literati" of the Chinese tradition. All a fastidious man or woman can do is withdraw personally from activities that violate his or her self-respect and his or her sense of taste.

Lately, these old sermon topics have been joined, especially in the United States, by a third one: managers, we are being told, have an "ethical responsibility" to take an active and constructive role in their community, to serve community causes, give of their time to community activities, and so on.

Such activities should, however, *never be forced on them nor should managers be appraised, rewarded, or promoted according to their participation in voluntary activities.* Ordering or pressuring managers into such work is abuse of organizational power and illegitimate.

But, while desirable, community participation of managers has nothing to do with ethics, and not much to do with responsibility. It is the contribution of an individual in his capacity as a neighbor and citizen.

A problem of ethics that is peculiar to the executive arises from the fact that the executives of institutions are *collectively* the leadership groups of the society of organizations. But *individually* a manager is just another fellow employee.

It is therefore inappropriate to speak of managers as leaders. They are "members of the leadership group." The group, however, does occupy a position of visibility, of prominence, and of authority. *It therefore has responsibility.*

But what are the responsibilities, what are the ethics of the individual executives, as a member of the leadership group?

Essentially being a member of a leadership group is what has traditionally been meant by the term "professional." Membership in such a group confers status, position, prominence, and authority. It also confers duties. To expect every manager to be a leader is futile. There are, in a developed society, thousands, if not millions, of managers—and leadership is always the rare exception and confined to a very few individuals. But as a member of a leadership group, a manager stands under the demands of professional ethics—the demands of an ethic of responsibility.

NOT KNOWINGLY TO DO HARM

The first responsibility of a professional was spelled out clearly, 2,400 years ago, in the Hippocratic oath of the Greek physician: *Primum non nocere*—"above all, not knowingly to do harm." No professional, be he doctor, lawyer, or manager, can promise that he will indeed do good for his client. All he can do is try. But he can promise that he will not knowingly do harm. And the client, in turn, must be able to trust the professional not knowingly to do the client harm. Otherwise the client cannot trust him at all. The professional has to have autonomy. He cannot be controlled, supervised, or directed by the client. He has to be private in that his knowledge and his judgment have to be entrusted with the decision. But it is the foundation of his autonomy, and indeed its rationale, that he see himself as "affected with the public interest." A professional, in other words, is private in the sense that he is autonomous and not subject to political or ideological control. But he is public in the sense that the welfare of his client sets limits to his deeds and words. And *primum non nocere*, "not knowingly to do harm," is the basic rule of professional ethics, the basic rule of an ethics of public responsibility.

The manager who, because it would make him "unpopular in the club," fails to think through and work for the appropriate solution to an impact of his business knowingly does harm. He or she knowingly abets a cancerous growth. That this is stupid has been said. That this always in the end hurts the business or the industry more than a little temporary "unpleasantness" would have hurt has been said too. But it is also a gross violation of professional ethics.

But there are other areas as well. American executives, in particular, tend to violate the rule not knowingly to do harm with respect to

- executive compensation

- the use of benefit plans to impose "golden fetters" on people in the company's employ

- their profit rhetoric

Their actions and their words in these areas tend to cause social disruption. They tend to conceal healthy reality and to create disease, or at least social abnormality. They tend to misdirect and to prevent understanding. And this is grievous social harm.

The facts of increasing income inequality in U.S. society are quite clear. It destroys mutual trust between groups that have to live together and work together. It can only lead to political measures that, while doing no one any good, can seriously harm society, the economy, and the manager as well.

A second area in which the manager of today does not live up to the commitment of *primum non nocere* is closely connected with compensation. Retirement benefits, bonuses, and stock options are all forms of compensation. From the point of view of the enterprise—but also from the point of view of the economy—these are "labor costs," no matter how they are labeled. They are treated as such by managements when they sit down to negotiate with the labor union. But increasingly these benefits are being used to tie an employee to his employer. They are being made dependent on staying with the same employer, often for many years. And they are structured in such a way that leaving a company's employ entails drastic penalties and actual loss of benefits that have already been earned and that, in effect, constitute wages relating to past employment.

Golden fetters do not strengthen the company. People who know that they are not performing in their present employment—that is, people who are clearly in the wrong place—will often not move but stay where they know they do not properly belong. But if they stay because the penalty for leaving is too great, they resist and resent it. They know that they have been bribed and were too weak to say no. They are likely to be sullen, resentful, and bitter the rest of their working lives. Pension rights, performance bonuses, participation in profits, and so on, have been "earned" and should be available to the employee without restricting his or her rights as a citizen, an individual, and a person. And executives will have to work to get any tax law changes that are needed to permit this to happen.

Managers, finally, through their rhetoric, make it impossible for the public to understand economic reality. This violates the requirement that managers, being leaders, not knowingly do harm. This is particularly true in the United States but also in Western Europe. For in the West, managers still talk constantly of the profit motive. And they still define the goal of their business as the maximization of shareholder wealth. *They do not stress the objective function of profit.* They do not talk of risks—or very rarely. They do not stress the need for capital. They almost never even mention the cost of capital, let alone that a business has to produce enough profit to obtain the capital it needs at minimum cost.

Managers constantly complain about the hostility to profit. They rarely realize that their own rhetoric is one of the main reasons for this hostility. For, indeed, in the terms management uses when it talks to the public, there is no possible justification for profit, no explanation for its existence, no function it performs. There is only the profit motive, that is, the desire of some anonymous capitalists—and why that desire should be indulged in by society any more than bigamy, for instance, is never explained. But profitability is a crucial *need* of economy and society.

Primum non nocere may seem tame compared to the rousing calls for "statesmanship" that abound in today's manifestos on social responsibility. But, as the physicians found out long ago, it is not an easy rule to live up to. Its very modesty and self-constraint make it the right rule for the ethics managers need, the ethics of responsibility.

SUMMARY

Central to the issue of social responsibility are first the negative social impacts that are by-products of the legitimate and necessary conduct of business (or institution) and consequences of the fact that the institution exists in a community and has authority over people. Such impacts should always be eliminated or at least minimized. If their elimination cannot be made into an opportunity, there is need for regulation; and it is the responsibility of business to think through and work for the appropriate regulation before there is a scandal. Then there is the issue of the responsibility of business for the ills of society. And finally there is the leadership function of managers in a society in which executives of institutions have become the leadership group.

The individual manager, even the chief executive of a giant corporation, has become anonymous, unassuming—just another employee. But together the managers of our institutions—businesses, universities, schools, hospitals, and government agencies—are the leadership groups in the modern society of organizations. As such, they need an ethics, a commitment, and a code. The right one is the code developed more than 2,000 years ago for the first professional leadership group, physicians: "Above all, not knowingly to do harm."

21

The New Pluralism: How to Balance the Special Purpose of the Institution with the Common Good

Society in all developed countries has become pluralist and is becoming more pluralist day by day. It is splintering into a myriad of institutions, each more or less autonomous, each requiring its own leadership and management, each having its own specific task.

This is not the first pluralist society in history. But all earlier pluralist societies destroyed themselves because no one took care of the *common good*. They abounded in *communities* but could not sustain *community,* let alone create it. If our modern pluralist society is to escape the same fate, the leaders of *all* institutions will have to learn to be *leaders beyond the walls.* They will have to learn that it is not enough for them to lead their own institutions—*though that is the first requirement.* They will also have to learn to become leaders in the community. In fact, they will have to learn to create community. This is going beyond what we have been discussing as *social responsibility* in chapter 20. Social responsibility is usually defined as doing *no harm* to others in the pursuit of one's own interest or of one's own task. The new pluralism requires what might be called *civic responsibility: giving to the community in the pursuit of one's own interest or of one's own task.*

There is no precedent in history for such civic responsibility among institutional leaders. But there are, fortunately, signs that the leaders of our institutions in all sectors are beginning to wake up to the need to become leaders beyond the walls.

A BRIEF VIEW BACK

The last pluralist society in the West existed during the early and high Middle Ages. The Roman Empire had tried, quite successfully, to create a unitary state in

which Roman law and the Roman legions created political uniformity throughout
the empire while cultural diversity was preserved. But after the collapse of the Roman Empire, this unity splintered completely. In its stead arose a congeries of autonomous and semiautonomous institutions: political, religious, economic, craft
oriented, and so on. There was the medieval university, autonomous and a law unto
itself. But there were also the free cities, the multinationals of the medieval economy. There were the craft guilds, and there were the all-but-autonomous major
orders and great abbeys of the church.

There were any number of landowners, from small squires to great dukes, each
all but independent. Next to them were autonomous bishoprics, paying at best lip
service to both the pope in Rome and the local prince. At its height, medieval
pluralism in western and northern Europe alone must have been embodied by several thousands of such autonomous institutions, ranging from small squires to
great landowners, and from small craft guilds and equally small local universities
to transnational religious orders. Each of these pluralist institutions was concerned
only with its own welfare and, above all, with its own aggrandizement. Not one of
them was concerned with the community beyond its walls.

Statesmen and political philosophers tried throughout the Middle Ages to recreate community. It was one of the main concerns of the Middle Ages' greatest
philosopher, Saint Thomas Aquinas, in the early thirteenth century. And it was
equally the concern of the Middle Ages' greatest poet, Dante, in his late-thirteenth-
century work *De Monarchia*. Both preached that there should be two independent
spheres: the secular one, centralized in and governed by the emperor, and the religious one, centralized in and governed by the pope. But by 1300 it was much too
late to restore community. Society had collapsed into chaos.

Beginning in the fourteenth century and enduring for 500 years, the trend
was toward abolishing pluralism. This tendency underlied all modern social and
political theory, all of which preached that there can be only one power in society:
a centralized government. And one by one, over 500 years, government either
suppressed the autonomous institutions of pluralism—such as the free cities of
the Middle Ages and the craft guilds—or it converted them into organs of government. This assumption of power is what is meant by *sovereignty*—a term
coined in the late sixteenth century, by which time, in most of Europe, government had already become the dominant though not yet the only power. By the
end of the Napoleonic Wars following the French Revolution, there were no autonomous institutions left on the European continent. The clergy had become
civil servants everywhere. The universities had become governmental institutions
everywhere. By the mid-1800s, there was one organized power, the government,
and there was a society consisting of individual molecules, without political or
social power.

By the middle of the nineteenth century, political theory and political practice in Europe—and in the West altogether—proclaimed that the task of centralization of power in government, begun 500 years earlier, had been accomplished. Government, to be sure, was subject to severe limitations on its use of power. But nobody else had any power; all institutions with power had either been abolished or had been made government agencies.

But just then a *new pluralism* began.

The first new institution that was not part of government was the large business enterprise, made possible around 1860 to 1870 by the two new technologies of transportation and information. The large business enterprise was not subordinated to government, and it had to have substantial autonomy and substantial power. Since then, modern society has become totally pluralistic again. Even institutions that are legally governmental now have to be autonomous, have to be self-governing, have to have substantial power.

The attempt to preserve the total monopoly of power by one institution, the government, still dominated the first half of the twentieth century. The totalitarian regimes, whether Nazism in Germany or Stalinism in the Soviet Union, can be seen as the last, extreme attempts to maintain the unity of power in one central institution and to integrate all institutions—down to the local chess club—into the centrally controlled power structure. Mao in China tried to do exactly the same with a major effort to destroy the prime autonomous power in Chinese society, the extended family.

Even in the United States the trend was toward increasing centralization of power, with the peak reached in the Kennedy and Johnson years of the 1960s. By that time, prevailing ideology in the United States had come to believe that government could and should take care of every problem and every challenge in the community—a thesis that clearly no one believes anymore but that only forty years ago was almost universally accepted.

By now we know that government cannot take care of community problems. We know that business and the free market also cannot take care of community problems. We have now come to accept that there has to be a third sector, the *social sector* of (mostly nonprofit) community organizations. But we also know that all institutions, no matter what their legal status, have to be run autonomously and have to be focused on their own tasks and their own mission. We know, in other words, that it is almost irrelevant whether a university is private or is tax supported and owned by the state of California. However funded, it functions like other universities. We know that it makes little difference whether a hospital is a nonprofit institution or owned by a profit-making corporation. It has to be run the same way, that is, as a hospital. And the reality in which every modern society lives is therefore one of rapidly increasing pluralism, in which institutions of all kinds, sizes, values, missions, and structures constitute society. But we also know that this means that *no one is taking care of the community*. In fact, the same degenerative tendencies that led to the revolt against pluralism in the fourteenth century are clearly at work in developed societies today. In every single developed country, single-cause interest groups are dominating the political process and are increasingly subordinating the common good to their own values, their own aggrandizement and power. And yet, we need pluralism.

WHY WE NEED PLURALISM

There is one simple reason why the last 150 years have been years in which one institution after the other has become autonomous: the task-centered and autonomous institution is the only one that *performs*. Performance requires clear focus and narrow concentration. Multipurpose institutions do not perform. The achievements of the last 150 years in every single area are achievements of narrow focus, narrow concentration, and parochial self-centered values. All performing institutions of modern society are specialized. All of them are concerned only with their own task. The hospital exists to cure sick people. The fire department exists to prevent and to extinguish fires. The business enterprise exists to satisfy economic wants. The great advances in public health have largely been the result of freestanding organizations that focus on one disease or on one part of the human body and disregard everything else (consider the American Cancer Society, the American Heart Association, the American Lung Association the American Mental Health Society, and so on).

Whenever an institution goes beyond a narrow focus, it ceases to perform. Hospitals that tried to go beyond sickness care into "health education" and "illness prevention" have been miserable failures. There are many reasons why the American public school is in trouble. But surely the one reason that stands out is that we have, of necessity, tried to make the school the agent of social and racial reform and social and racial integration. Schools in all other countries, including countries that have serious social problems of their own (e.g., France, with its large immigrant population), have stuck to the single goal of teaching children to read. And they are still successful in this single endeavor. One may argue (as I have) that the present concentration on "creating shareholder value" as the sole mission of the publicly owned business enterprise is too narrow and, in fact, may be self-defeating. But it has resulted in an improvement in these enterprises' financial performance beyond anything an earlier generation would have thought possible—and way beyond what the same enterprises produced when they tried to satisfy multiple objectives, that is, when they were being run (as I have to admit I advocated for many years) in the "best balanced interests" of all the stakeholders, that is, shareholders, employees, customers, plant communities, and so on.

A striking social phenomenon of the last thirty years in the United States, the explosive growth of the new "mega-churches," rests on these institutions' dedication to a single purpose: the spiritual development of the parishioners. The decline of their predecessors, the liberal Protestant churches of the early years of the twentieth century, can be traced largely to their trying to accomplish too many things at the same time—above all, in their trying to be organs of social reform as well as spiritual leaders.

The strength of the modern pluralist organization is that it is a single-purpose institution. And that strength has to be maintained. But at the same time, the community has to be maintained—and in many cases it has to be rebuilt. How to balance the two, the *common good* and the *special purpose of the institution* is the question we must answer. If we cannot accomplish this integration, the new pluralism will surely destroy itself, the way the old pluralism did 500 years ago. It will destroy itself because it will destroy community. But if at the same time institutions abandon their single purpose or even allow that purpose to weaken, the new pluralism will destroy itself through lack of performance.

LEADERSHIP BEYOND THE WALLS

We know that this integration can be achieved. In fact there are already a good many success stories.

- What is needed is for leaders of *all* institutions to take leadership responsibility beyond the walls.

- They have to lead their own institutions and lead them to performance.

- This requires single-minded concentration on the part of the institution.

- But at the same time the members of the institution—and not just the people at the top—have to take community responsibility beyond the walls of their own institution.

THREE DIMENSIONS TO THIS INTEGRATION

1. There is a *financial* dimension to this integration: the financial support of autonomous community organizations by both government and business.

2. There is a *performance* dimension to it: the organization of partnerships for common tasks among various types of institutions.

3. There is a *personal* dimension to it:

    a. Work as volunteers in community organizations by the people of institutions

    b. Development of second careers by successful people who in middle age switch from, for example, being division controller in a big company to being controller in a nonprofit hospital

    c. Development of parallel careers by people who in the second half of their life take on a major task and a major assignment outside while keeping on with their original work

ABOVE ALL: TWO RESPONSIBILITIES

But above all, there is need for a *different mind-set*. There is need for the acceptance by leaders in every single institution and in every single sector that they, as leaders, have *two responsibilities:*

1. They are responsible and accountable for the *performance of their institutions,* and that requires them and their institutions to be concentrated, focused, limited.

2. They are responsible also, however, for the *community as a whole*. This requires commitment.

    a. It requires a willingness to accept that other institutions have different values, respect for those values, and willingness to learn what those values are.

    b. It requires hard work.

    c. But above all, it requires commitment, conviction, and dedication to the common good. Yes, each institution is autonomous and has to do its own work, the way each instrument in an orchestra plays only its own part. But there is also the *score,* the community. And only if each individual instrument contributes to the score is there music. Otherwise there is only noise. And this chapter is about *the score.*

SUMMARY

In our society of pluralistic institutions, each institution must focus on its narrow mission if it is to achieve results and meet the minimum test of social responsibility. But then, who looks out for the common good? The answer is no one unless executives of society's institutions take on a second responsibility that looks beyond the borders of their institution to the common good. This can be done by making *financial contributions* to social-sector organizations; by encouraging employees to *volunteer* their time and effort to community causes; and by encouraging the leadership group to volunteer their time and resources to help solve the problems of society. A society of pluralistic organizations must be one that consists of leadership groups who look beyond the walls of the institution and take on *civic responsibility* without shirking their primary responsibility, which is to their institution's specific and narrowly defined mission.

Part VI

The Manager's Work and Jobs

It is *responsibility for contributing to the results of the enterprise,* not "responsibility for the work of others" that makes a manager. It is responsibility for his or her own work. There is a distinct "work of the manager"; there are distinct "managerial jobs." There is a distinct way to manage managers: by objectives and self-control. As we move from "middle management" to the "knowledge organization," there are new and different requirements. Most important, managers have to be managed in a way that engenders a spirit of performance in them.

22

Why Managers?

Managers are the basic resource of the organizational enterprise. In a fully automated factory there may be almost no rank-and-file employees. But there will be managers.

Managers are the most expensive resource in most organizations—and the one that depreciates the fastest and needs the most constant replenishment. It takes years to build a management team, but it can be depleted in a short period of misrule. The investment that each manager represents is increasing steadily. Parallel with this goes an increase in the demands of the enterprise on its managers. These demands have multiplied in every generation, and there is no reason to expect the trend to slow during the next decades.

Managers everywhere have subjected themselves to a steady barrage of speeches and programs in which they tell each other that their job is to manage the people under them, urge each other to give top priority to this responsibility, and furnish each other with copious advice and expensive gadgets for "downward communications." Yet, I have yet to sit down with a manager, whatever his or her level or job, who was not primarily concerned with upward relations and upward communications. (See also chapter 30, "Managerial Communications.") Every vice president feels that relations with the president are the real problem. And so on down to the first-line supervisors, who are quite certain that they could get along with their people if only the "boss" and human resource department left them alone.

This is not a sign of the perversity of human nature. Upward relations are properly a manager's first concern. To be a manager means sharing in the responsibility for the performance of the enterprise. Anyone who is not expected to take this responsibility is not a manager.

These problems of upward relations that worry the manager—the relationship to the boss, doubts as to what is expected in terms of performance, difficulty in getting the department's point across or programs accepted, concern that one's activity be given full weight, relations with other departments and with knowledge specialists, and so forth—are all problems of managing managers.

THE RISE, DECLINE, AND REBIRTH OF FORD—A CONTROLLED EXPERIMENT IN MISMANAGEMENT

The story of Henry Ford, his rise and decline, and of the revival of his company under his grandson, Henry Ford II, has been told so many times that it has passed into folklore:

Henry Ford, starting with nothing in 1905, had fifteen years later built the world's largest and most profitable manufacturing enterprise. The Ford Motor Company, in the early 1920s, dominated and almost monopolized the American automobile market and held a leadership position in most of the other important automobile markets of the world. In addition, it had amassed, out of profits, cash reserves of a billion dollars or so.

Yet only a few years later, by 1927, this seemingly impregnable business empire was in shambles. Having lost its leadership position and barely a poor third in the market, it lost money almost every year for twenty years or so, and remained unable to compete vigorously right through World War II. In 1944, the founder's grandson, Henry Ford II, then only twenty-six years old and without training or experience, took over, then two years later ousted his grandfather's cronies in a palace coup, brought in a totally new management team, and saved the company.

It is not commonly realized that this dramatic story is far more than a story of personal success and failure. It is, above all, what one might call a *controlled experiment in mismanagement*.

The first Ford failed because of his firm belief that a business did not need managers and management. All it needed, he believed, was the owner-entrepreneur with his "helpers." The only difference between Ford and most of his contemporaries in business was that, as in everything he did, Henry Ford stuck uncompromisingly to his convictions. He applied them strictly, firing or sidelining any one of his "helpers," no matter how able, who dared act as a "manager," make a decision, or take action without orders from Ford. The way he applied his theory can only be described as a test, one that ended up by fully disproving Ford's theory.

In fact, what makes the Ford story unique and important is that Ford *could* test the hypothesis. This was possible in part because he lived so long and in part because he had a billion dollars to back his convictions. Ford's failure was not the result of personality or temperament. It was first and foremost the result of his *refusal to accept managers and management as necessary*, as a necessity based on task and function rather than "delegation" from the "boss."

GM—THE COUNTER TEST

In the early 1920s, while Ford was trying to prove that managers are not needed, Alfred P. Sloan, Jr., the newly appointed president of General Motors, put the opposite thesis to the test. GM at that time was almost crushed by the towering giant of the Ford Motor Company. It was barely able to survive as a weak number two. Little more than a haphazard financial speculation, GM had been stitched together out of small failing automobile companies sold because they could not stand up to Ford's competition. GM had not one winning car in its line, no dealer organization, and no financial strength. Each of the former company owners had stayed on and had been allowed to mismanage his former business his own way, as if it had been his own personal property. When Sloan became president of GM, he thought through what the business and structure of GM should be and converted his undisciplined barons into a management team. Within five years GM had become the leader in the American automobile industry.

When Henry Ford's grandson put Sloan's hypothesis to the test again twenty years later, the Ford Motor Company was nearly bankrupt. The entire billion dollars of cash assets it had held in the early 1920s had been poured into paying for the deficits since. As soon as young Henry Ford II took over in 1946, he set out to do for his company what Sloan had done for GM two decades earlier. He created a management structure and a management team. Within five years the Ford Motor Company regained its potential for growth and profit, both at home and abroad. It became the main competitor to General Motors and even outstripped GM in the fast-growing European automobile market.

THE LESSON OF THE FORD STORY

The lesson of the Ford story is that managers and management are the specific need of the enterprise, its specific organ and its basic structure. *Enterprise clearly cannot do without managers.* One cannot argue that management does the owner's job by delegation. Management is needed, not because the job is too big for any one individual, but because managing an enterprise is essentially different from managing one's own property.

Henry Ford failed to see the need to change to managers and management because he believed that a large and complex business enterprise "evolves" organically from the small one-man shop. Of course, Ford started small. But growth brought more than a change in size. At some point quantity turned into quality. At some point Ford became a *business enterprise,* that is, an organization requiring different structure and different principles—an organization requiring managers and management.

Management did not evolve out of the small owner-managed firm as a result of its growth. It is a concept, designed for enterprises that are large and complex to begin with.

The large American railroad of the nineteenth century—which wrestled with the engineering task of building a rail bed, the financial task of raising very large sums of capital, and the political-relations tasks of obtaining charters, land grants, and subsidies—was the first enterprise that can be said to have been "managed." Indeed, the management structure designed shortly after the Civil War for the first long-distance American railroads remains today essentially unchanged.

It was not until thirty or forty years later that the concept of management was transferred from the enterprise that *started out large* to the enterprise that *had grown large*. Andrew Carnegie and John D. Rockefeller, Sr., introduced management into the steel and petroleum industries, respectively. A little later still, Pierre S. du Pont restructured the family chemical company (E. I. du Pont de Nemours & Co.) and gave it a management, both to make it capable of growth and to preserve family control. The management structure Pierre du Pont built in his family company between 1915 and 1920 became, a few years later, the starting point for the General Motors structure of "professional management" after the du Ponts had acquired control of the near-bankrupt and floundering automotive conglomerate and made Sloan president.

MANAGEMENT AS A "CHANGE OF PHASE"

The change from a business that the owner-entrepreneur can run with "helpers" to a business that requires a management is what the physicists call a *change of phase*—an abrupt change from one state of matter, from one fundamental structure, to another, such as the change from water to ice. Sloan's example shows that it can be made within one and the same organization. But Sloan's restructuring of GM also shows that the job can be done only if *basic concepts, basic principles, and individual vision are changed radically.*

Henry Ford wanted no managers. The result was that he misdirected managers, set up their jobs improperly, created a spirit of suspicion and frustration, disorganized his company, and stunted or broke management people. The only choice managers have in these areas is whether management jobs will be done well or badly. But the jobs themselves will exist, because there is an enterprise to be managed. And whether the jobs are done right or not will determine largely whether the enterprise will survive and prosper or decline and ultimately fail.

SUMMARY

Managers are not helpers and their jobs are not delegated. Their jobs are autonomous and grounded in the needs of the enterprise. The only choice is between doing the managerial jobs well or badly—but the jobs exist because there is an enterprise that has to be managed.

23

Design and Content of Managerial Jobs

A manager's job should always be based on a task necessary to attain the company's objectives. It should always be a real job—one that makes a visible and, if possible, measurable contribution to the success of the enterprise. It should have the broadest, rather than the narrowest, scope and authority. Managers should be directed and controlled by the objectives of performance rather than by their bosses.

The activities that have to be performed and the contributions that have to be made to attain the company's objectives should always determine what managerial jobs are needed. A manager's job exists because the task facing the enterprise requires it—and for no other reason. The job has to have its own authority and its own responsibility. For managers must manage.

The job should always have managerial scope and proportions. Since a manager is someone who takes responsibility for, and contributes to, the final results of the enterprise, the job should always embody the maximum challenge, carry the maximum responsibility, and make the maximum contribution.

COMMON MISTAKES IN DESIGNING MANAGERIAL JOBS

There is no formula that will guarantee the right job design for a managerial job. Yet six common mistakes that impair the effectiveness of the manager and managerial organization can be avoided.

1. *The too-small job.* The most common mistake is to design the job so small that a good manager cannot grow. Any managerial job may turn out to be a terminal job—that is, a job that the incumbent will stay on until he or she retires.

The number of jobs at the top is inevitably far smaller than the number of jobs at the bottom. If a job is designed so small that the incumbent can learn everything about it in a few years, most managers will be frustrated, bored, and will stop really working. They will "retire on the job." They will resist any change, any innovation, any new idea, for change can only be a change for the worse for them and threaten their security. Knowing very well that they are not actually contributing anymore, they are fundamentally insecure.

Managerial jobs should, therefore, be designed to allow a person to grow, to learn, and to develop for many years to come. There is little harm, as a rule, in a job that is designed too big. This mistake shows up soon and can easily be corrected. A job that is too small, however, is an insidious, slow poison that paralyzes both the manager and the organization.

All managerial jobs should be designed to provide satisfaction through performance. The job itself should challenge and reward. If the main satisfaction of the job is promotion, the job itself has lost significance and meaning. And since the majority in managerial positions are bound to be disappointed in their hopes for promotion—by arithmetic rather than by organization politics—it is unwise to focus on promotion. The emphasis should always be on the job itself rather than on the next job.

In fact, *there are few things quite as dangerous as an organization in which promotions are so rapid as to become the accepted reward for doing a decent job.*

An extreme historical example was the situation in some of the large New York commercial banks. Very few young people were hired in the banking industry in the 1930s and 1940s, when commercial banks in New York were shrinking rather than expanding. When the banking business expanded again after World War II, a series of mergers actually created a surplus of managers. By the early 1950s, however, large numbers of the men who had started before 1929 reached retirement age, and the banks began to hire large numbers of young people, fresh out of college or graduate business school. Within seven or eight years, many of them rose to positions of substantial pay and exalted title such as vice president and senior vice president. Before they were thirty, large numbers of these "young comers" had reached, in other words, what must be their terminal position. Yet—in large part because these young people had not had much experience—these jobs, whatever the big title and the good salary, were quite limited in scope and authority. And by the time they were forty, many of these people had become bored, cynical, frustrated, and no longer excited about the job and its challenge.

A company that is expanding rapidly is well-advised to bring into important positions a few seasoned and older outsiders who have made a career elsewhere. Otherwise, it is bound to create expectations among its own young managers, which, a few years later, it must frustrate.

Another important reason why jobs and a job structure focused on rapid promotion are to be avoided is that they result in an unbalanced age structure. Both an age structure that is overbalanced on the side of youth and one overbalanced on the side of age create serious organizational turbulence.

The management structure needs *continuity* and *self-renewal*. There must be continuity so that the organization does not have to suddenly replace a large number of experienced but old managers with new and untried ones. And there has to be enough "managerial metabolism" that new ideas and new faces can assert themselves. A management group that is all of the same age is a management group headed for crisis.

2. *The nonjob.* Worse even than the job that is too small is the job that is not really a job, the job of the typical "assistant to."

The managerial job must have specific objectives and a specific purpose and function. A manager must be able to make a contribution that can be identified. The manager must be accountable.

But the typical assistant does not have a job that can make a contribution. He or she cannot be held accountable, and his function, purpose, and objectives cannot be identified. He is a "helper" who does whatever the boss thinks needs to be done or whatever the assistant can "sell" to the boss. Such a job corrupts. The holder becomes either a wire-puller who abuses his influence with an important executive or a toady who tries to make his career by licking his boss's boots. The assistant position also corrupts the organization. No one ever knows what the role, authority, and actual power of the assistant are. As a rule, other managers will flatter him, use him, and exploit his insecurity of tenure.

3. *Failing to balance managing and working.* Managing is work. But it is not, by itself, full-time work. The way to design a managerial job is to combine "managing" with "working," that is, responsibility for a specific function or job of one's own. As a rule, *the manager should be both a manager and an individual career professional.*

A manager should have enough to do—otherwise he or she is likely to try to do the subordinates' work for them. The common complaint that managers do not "delegate" usually means that managers do not have enough to do and therefore take on the job the subordinate should be doing. But also, it is rather frustrating not to have work of one's own—especially for people who have grown up in the habit of work. And it is not particularly desirable for a manager not to have a job of his or her own. He or she soon loses the sense of workmanship and the respect for hard work without which a manager is likely to do more harm than good. A manager should be a "working boss" rather than a "coordinator."

4. *Poor job design.* As far as possible, a manager's job should be designed so that it can be done by one person working alone and with the people in the unit that he or she manages. It is a mistake to design a job so that it requires continuous meetings, continuous cooperation and coordination, including by electronic media. There is no need, especially not in managerial jobs, to inflict extra human relations. The job by its very nature requires more human relations than most people are capable of. And one can either work or meet. One cannot do both at the same time.

Another mistake that is fairly common—and usually unnecessary—is to design a job in which the incumbent has to spend a great deal of time traveling. Just as one cannot meet and work at the same time, one cannot travel and work at the same time. Person-to-person and face-to-face meetings with colleagues, associates, subordinates, customers, and superiors are absolutely essential. There is no real substitute. But it is far better to spend a substantial amount of time once every two years with the managers and the main customers of a subsidiary company than to "commute"—that is, leave New York on Tuesday, spend Wednesday in Paris, and be back on the job in New York on Thursday. This means only that no work gets done for four days: one needs, after all, at least one day to recover from this futile attempt to be in two places at once.

5. *Titles as rewards*. Titles should never be used as rewards, let alone to cover up lack of function. Titles "in lieu of a raise" are not nearly as bad, nor as common, as titles "in lieu of a job."

An example is the large commercial bank, both in the United States and in Germany. In the United States everybody has to be a vice president or at least an officer. In Germany everybody has to be a *Herr Direktor*. There are reasons for this. The customers of a bank, say the head of a small business, will not discuss their financial problems with anybody but an officer. But this also deforms. It makes dissatisfied those who do not get the title, perhaps because their job does not entail close customer contact. It adds greatly to the dissatisfaction of people who reach the exalted title of vice president at an early age and then find that they are locked into the same humdrum routine for the rest of their working lives.

The rule should be: For first-rate work we pay—and pay well. But we change title only when function, position, and responsibility change. Titles do create expectations. They do imply rank and responsibility. To use them as empty gestures—that is, as substitutes for rank and responsibility—is asking for trouble.

6. *The widow-maker job*. Finally, jobs that are "widow-makers" should be rethought and restructured. In the heyday of the great sailing ships, around 1850, just before the coming of steam, every shipping company had a widow-maker on its hands once in a while. This was a ship that, for reasons nobody could figure out, tended to get out of control and kill people. After it had done this a few times a prudent shipowner pulled the ship out of service and broke it up, no matter how much money he had invested in it. Otherwise, he soon found himself without captains or mates.

In many companies there are jobs that manage to defeat one good manager after another—without any clear reason why. These jobs seem to be logical, seem to be well constructed, seem to be doable—yet nobody seems to be able to do them. If a job has defeated, in a row, two individuals who in their previous assignments had done well, it should be restructured. It then usually becomes clear, though only by hindsight, what was wrong with the job in the first place.

The widow-maker job is sometimes the result of accident. One person, who somehow combined in himself or herself temperamental characteristics that are not usually found in one person, created the job and acquitted herself well. In other words, what looked like a logical job was an accident of personality rather than the result of a genuine function. But one cannot replace personality.

The widow-maker phenomenon will be discussed further in chapter 29.

JOB STRUCTURE AND PERSONALITY

The abuse of titles and the widow-maker job relate closely to one of the most hotly debated issues with respect to managerial jobs and managerial structure: Should the organization be structured so that jobs fit people? Or should the organization be "functional," with people fitted to jobs?

As commonly propounded, this is not a real problem. Quite obviously, people have to fill the jobs, and therefore jobs have to fit people. We will indeed have to design jobs that really fit people, answer their needs, and fulfill their expectations. We increasingly see "organization planning" in large companies, that is, attempts to make jobs fit people.

Yet organization structure has to be impersonal and task focused. Otherwise it is impossible to have continuity and to have people succeed each other. If the job is designed for an individual rather than for a task, it has to be restructured every time there is a change in the incumbent. And, as experienced managers know, one cannot restructure *one* job. There is a true "domino effect," a true chain reaction. Restructuring a job usually means restructuring a score of jobs, moving people around, and upsetting everybody. And for this reason, jobs have to be designed to fit a task, rather than a particular person.

There is one exception: the exceedingly rare, truly exceptional person for whose sake the rule should be broken.

Alfred P. Sloan, Jr., the architect of General Motors, was adamant that jobs had to be impersonal and task focused. But he made one exception to accommodate one of the great inventors of our century, Charles F. Kettering. Kettering was an exceedingly difficult man, and he was a man who disregarded every single organizational rule. Yet his inventions, from the self-starter to the redesign of the diesel engine, were of major importance. Sloan offered to set up Kettering as an independent researcher. But Kettering wanted to be vice president and a "big businessman." Sloan gave in, but the moment Kettering retired, the job was redesigned—from "resident genius" to manager of a large research laboratory.

The design of a job has to start out with the task, but it also has to be a design that can accommodate people with different temperaments, habits, and behavior patterns. This is a major reason why managerial jobs ought to be designed big rather than small. A job has to be big enough to provide satisfaction and achievement to a good manager, working in his or her own way.

"A job should be small enough so that a good manager can get his arms around it" is a common saying. *It is the wrong rule.* "A job should be specific enough so that a good manager can go to work on it, but so big that the manager can't get his or her arms around it" *is the right rule.*

"Style" should never be a consideration, either in designing a managerial job or in filling it. The only requirement of a managerial job, and the only test of the incumbent, is performance. Every organization needs a clear understanding of the kind of behavior that is unacceptable. There must be a clear definition of the non-permissible action, especially toward people, whether inside the business, employees, or outside, suppliers and customers. But within these limits a manager should have the fullest freedom to do the job the way it best suits individual temperament and personality.

"Style" is packaging. The only substance is performance.

THE SPAN OF MANAGERIAL RELATIONSHIPS

In discussing how big a manager's job should be, the textbooks often start out with the observation that one person can supervise only a very small number of people—the so-called span of control. This, in turn, has led to that managerial atrocity: levels upon levels, which impede cooperation and communication, stifle the development of tomorrow's managers, and erode the meaning of the management job.

In the first place, the principle of the span of control is rarely cited properly. It is not how many people report to a manager that matters. *It is how many people who have to work with each other report to a manager.* What counts are *the number of relationships,* not the number of individuals.

The president of a company who has reporting to her a number of senior executives, each concerned with a major function, should indeed keep the number of direct subordinates to a fairly low number—between eight and twelve is probably the limit. These subordinates—the chief financial officer, the head of manufacturing, the head of marketing, and so on—have to work every day with each other and with the company's president. If they do not work together, they do not work at all. Therefore, the president is engaged in *a great many relationships* even though the number of direct subordinates may be quite small.

By contrast, a regional vice president of Wal-Mart can, and does, have several hundred store managers report to her. Each store is separate. There is no need whatever for interaction between two different stores. All the stores do the same kind of work and have the same job. They can all be appraised and measured by the same yardsticks. Theoretically, there is no limit to the number of store managers a regional vice president of Wal-Mart can manage and supervise. The limit may be set by geography but not by the span of control.

The second shortcoming of the span-of-control argument is that it assumes that a manager's main relationship is downward. But this is only one dimension. The manager, in the traditional definition as someone responsible for the work of other people, has a downward relationship, to be sure. But every manager and every career professional also has a superior. Indeed, many managers, no matter what the organization chart says, have more than one boss. And the upward relationship to the superior is at least equal in importance to the downward relationship to the subordinates. Most important, however, managers and career professionals always have sideways relations, relationships with people who are neither their subordinates nor their superiors and, indeed, stand in no relationship of authority and responsibility to them. Yet these relationships are crucial, both for the manager's own ability to do the work and for the effectiveness of that work.

What is needed, therefore, is to replace the concept of the span of control with another and more relevant concept: *the span of managerial relationships.*

We do not know how wide this span can be. Certainly, there are limits. We do know, however, that the span of managerial relationships is crucial in the design of a managerial job.

In the first place, these relationships define the place of the manager in the managerial structure. Second, they largely define what his or her job is—for these relationships are crucial and essential parts of the job content. Finally, they do set limits—since a job that is all "relationships" and no "work" is not a job at all. In designing managerial jobs, it is just as important to think through the managerial relationships and to make sure that they do not exceed an individual's grasp as it is to think through the specific function.

Again it is better to make the span of managerial responsibilities too wide rather than too narrow. This goes for the number of subordinates with whom a manager works and who constitute the unit and the team. It goes also for upward relationships. The only area where I would strongly counsel to keep rather tight limits on the span of managerial relationships are the sideways relationships. A managerial job, ideally, should have few sideways relationships—every one of them of prime importance, both for the functioning of the entire organization and for the achievement of the manager's own function and objectives. It is not only that these are time-consuming relationships. If there are too many, they will be treated superficially, will not be thought through, and will not be worked at. And the common weakness of many organizations is, by and large, the lack of adequate concern for, and adequate work on, sideways relationships.

DEFINING A MANAGER'S JOB

A manager's job is defined in four ways.

1. There is first the *specific function,* the job itself. This should always be a permanent, continuing job, one expected to be needed for a good long time to come. An example would be manager of market research or an operations manager. Both obviously are jobs that will have to be done for the foreseeable future.

2. But the functional definition of the job, which is what is expressed in the typical job description or position guide, does not define the *specific contribution* that a specific manager is expected to make. While the function is, at least in intent, permanent, there are *assignments* "here and now" that are what the enterprise and the manager's boss should hold the manager accountable for. They contribute the second definition of a managerial position and job.

Managers should ask themselves at least once a year, and always when taking on a new job, "What specific contribution can my unit and I make that, if done really well, would make a substantial difference to the performance and results of my company?"

The position guide and job description are, so to speak, the *mission* statement of a managerial job. They correspond to the definition of "what our business is and what it should be" for the enterprise as a whole. The assignments are the *objectives and goals.* They need, therefore, specific targets, a deadline, a clear statement of who is accountable, and a built-in measurement by feedback from results.

It is the mark of a performing manager that these assignments always exceed the scope of the job as outlined in the job description. A job description usually represents what has already been done; what needs to be done to make the future always exceeds and goes beyond what has been done in the past.

3. A managerial job is defined by *relationships*—upward, downward, and sideways.

4. It is finally defined by the *information needed* for the job and by a manager's place in the *information flow.*

All managers should ask themselves, "What information do I need to do my job and where do I get it?" They should make sure that whoever has to provide that information understands the manager's needs—in terms of not only what is needed but also how it is needed.

Managers need to think through the question "and who depends on information from me, and in what form, upward, downward, and sideways?"

These four definitions, which together describe a manager's job, are the manager's own responsibility. He or she should be expected to write his own job description; to work out his own proposal for the results and contributions for which he and the unit should be accountable; to work out and think through his relationships; and finally, to define both his information needs and the information contribution. Indeed, responsibility for thinking through the four dimensions of the job is a manager's first responsibility, of which he should never be relieved. A superior has both the duty and the responsibility to approve or disapprove what the individual manager proposes. But the responsibility for thinking and proposing is the manager's. *There is no difference in this respect between a "managing" job—that is, one with direct responsibility for the work of other people—and a job as knowledge professional.*

THE MANAGER'S AUTHORITY

Saying that each manager's job must be given the broadest possible scope and authority is just rephrasing the rule that decisions be pushed down the line as far as possible and be made as close as possible to the action to which they apply. In its effects, however, this requirement leads to sharp deviations from the traditional concept of delegation from above.

Top management decides what activities and tasks the enterprise requires. The analysis begins with the desired end product: the objectives of business performance and business results. From these the analysis determines step-by-step what work has to be performed.

But in organizing the manager's job, we have to work from the bottom up. We have to begin with the activities on the "firing line"—the jobs responsible for the actual output of goods and services, for the final sale to the customer, for the production of blueprints and engineering drawings.

The managers on the firing line have the basic management jobs—the ones on whose performance everything else ultimately rests. Seen this way, the jobs of higher management are aimed at helping the first-line managers do their job. Viewed structurally and organically, it is the first-line managers in whom all authority and responsibility center; only what they cannot do themselves passes up to higher management.

Obviously there are real limits to the decisions the first-line managers can or should make, and to the authority and responsibility they should have. A first-line manager is limited as to the extent of his authority. An operations supervisor has no business changing a salesman's compensation, and a regional sales manager has no authority in somebody else's region. A manager is also limited with respect to the kind of decision she can make. Clearly, she should not make decisions that affect other managers. She should not alone make decisions that affect the whole business and its spirit. It is only elementary, for instance, not to allow any manager to make alone and without review a decision on the career and future of one of her subordinates.

First-line managers should not be expected to make decisions that they cannot make. A person responsible for immediate performance does not have the time, for instance, to make long-range decisions. An operations person lacks the knowledge and competence to work out a pension plan or a medical program. These decisions certainly affect the manager and her operations. She should know them, understand them, and, indeed, participate as much as is humanly possible in their preparation and formulation. But she cannot make them. Hence, she cannot have the authority and responsibility for them; for authority and responsibility should always be task focused. This is the rule throughout the management hierarchy up to the chief executive officer.

There is one simple rule for setting limitations on the decisions a manager is authorized to make. The management charter of a division should paraphrase the U.S. Constitution, by stipulating the *reservation of authority:* "All authority not expressly and in writing reserved to higher management is granted to lower management." This is the opposite of the old Prussian idea of a citizen's rights: "Everything that is not expressly commanded is forbidden." In other words, the decisions that a manager is not entitled to make within the extent of the task should always be spelled out; for all others, he or she should be supposed to have authority and responsibility.

MANAGERS, THEIR SUPERIORS, THEIR SUBORDINATES, AND THE ENTERPRISE

The manager's relationships to superiors and subordinates are two-way relationships. Both are formal and informal relationships of authority as well as of information. *Both are relationships of mutual dependence.*

The manager has responsibilities downward, to subordinates. He or she has to first make sure that subordinates know and understand what is demanded of them. He has to help them set their own objectives. Then he has to help them to reach these objectives. He is responsible for their getting the tools, the staff, the information, they need. He has to help them with advice and counsel and, if need be, to teach them how to do better. A one-word definition of this downward relationship might be "assistance."

The objectives of a managerial unit should always consist of the performance that it has to contribute to the success of the enterprise. Objectives should always focus upward.

But the objectives of the manager who heads the units include what he himself has to do to help subordinates attain their objectives. The vision of a manager should always be upward—toward the enterprise as a whole. But his responsibility runs downward as well—to the people on his team. Seeing his relationship toward them as *duty* toward them and as *responsibility for making them perform and achieve* rather than as "supervision" is a central requirement for organizing the manager's unit effectively.

The final duty of the manager is toward the enterprise. A manager's job and function are grounded in the real needs of the enterprise rather than in title or delegation of power.

Each manager, therefore, has to derive from the objectives of the enterprise the definition of his or her own objectives and those of the unit he or she heads.

The discussion in this chapter has focused on the manager in the business enterprise. But everything said here applies just as much to managers in the public-service institution, and especially to managers in the government agency. They need jobs big enough for a good manager to grow in. They need satisfaction through performance rather than through promotion or title. Their jobs need to be designed around job and position, assignments, relationships, and information needs. They need authority to do their tasks. And they have to derive their own objectives from those of the institution they serve.

The manager in a public-service institution needs proper job design, proper job content, and proper job structure even more than the manager in a business. The design of truly managerial jobs is the first—but may also be the biggest—step toward improving both performance and morale in public-service institutions.

SUMMARY

A manager's job should always be based on a necessary task. It should be a real job that makes a visible (if not a measurable) contribution toward the objectives of the entire enterprise. It should have the broadest scope and authority possible. Managers should be directed and controlled by the objectives of performance rather than by their superior. In designing managerial jobs, six specific mistakes are to be avoided. There is a need to design the span of managerial responsibility—and there are four ways of defining a managerial job. Managers are mutually dependent on superiors and subordinates. Their final duty is toward the enterprise.

24

Developing Management and Managers

The years since 1950 have seen a boom in management development within the wider boom in management as a whole. In the mid-1940s, when I first became interested in this subject, I could find only two companies that had given serious thought to the development of managers: Sears, Roebuck in America and Marks & Spencer in England. At that time there were only three university programs in America for the continuing advanced education of managers: the Sloan Program at MIT, the programs at New York University for the continuing education of managers and young professionals in banking and finance, and the Advanced Management Program at Harvard.

Ten years later, in the mid-1950s, the number of companies with specific management-development programs ran to some three thousand. And a great many universities in the United States offered all kinds of advanced management programs.

Today, it is impossible to count the number of companies that, one way or another, work on the development of management and managers. The large company that does not make specific provision for such work and does not have a management-development staff of its own is the exception. And so is the university-level business school without some form of management-development program. In addition, many outside organizations—trade associations, consulting firms, and so on—have gone into management-development work.

WHY MANAGEMENT DEVELOPMENT?

Basic organizational decisions require an increasingly long lead time. Since no one can foresee the future, management cannot make rational and responsible decisions unless it selects, develops, and tests the men and women who will have to take care of these decisions—the executives of tomorrow.

The demand for executives is steadily growing. A developed society increasingly replaces manual skill with theoretical knowledge and the ability to organize and to lead—in short, with managerial ability. In fact, ours is the first society in which the basic question is not, "How many educated people can society spare from the task of providing subsistence?" It is, "How many uneducated people can we afford to support?"

But management development is also necessary to discharge an elementary responsibility that an enterprise owes to society. Continuity, especially of the big business enterprise, is vital. Our society cannot afford to see such wealth-producing resources jeopardized through lack of competent successors to today's executives.

The members of a modern society look to their work for more than a livelihood. They look to it also for satisfactions that go beyond the economic, that is, for pride, self-respect, and achievement. Management development is just another name for making work and organizations more than a way of making a living. By offering challenges and opportunities for the individual development of each manager to his or her fullest ability, the enterprise discharges, in part, the obligation to make a job in organizations a "good life."

And if we know one thing today, it is that managers are made and not born. There has to be systematic work on the supply, the development, and the skills of tomorrow's management. It cannot be left to luck or chance.

WHY MANAGER DEVELOPMENT?

Individual managers need development just as much as company and society do. A manager should, first, keep alert and mentally alive. He or she needs to stay challenged. The manager must acquire today the skills that will be effective tomorrow. He also needs an opportunity to reflect on the meaning of his own experience and—above all—he needs an opportunity to reflect on himself and to *learn to make his strengths count*. And then he needs *development as a person* even more than he needs development as a manager (on this see chapters 45–48).

One of the strengths, but also one of the weaknesses, of knowledge workers is their expectation of satisfaction and stimulation from work. In that respect, the knowledge workers are badly spoiled during their early formative years.

Knowledge workers, and especially highly accomplished knowledge workers, are likely to find themselves in a spiritual crisis in their early or mid-forties. By that time the majority will have reached, inevitably, their terminal positions. Perhaps they will also have reached what, within their business, is their terminal function—whether this be market research, cost accounting, or metallurgy. Suddenly their work will not satisfy them anymore. After fifteen or twenty years in market research in their industry, they know all there is to know about it. What was tremendously exciting when the job was new is boring and humdrum fifteen years later.

Managers have to be able, in other words, to develop lives of their own, outside the organization, before they are in their mid-forties.

They need this for themselves, but they need it also for the organization. For the manager who, at age forty-five, "retires on the job" because he has no more interest in life is not likely to make any further contribution to the organization. He owes it to himself—and to the business—to develop himself as a person, so that he can build his own life and not depend entirely upon the organization or further promotion or on new and different work. He needs to focus on his own personality, on his own strengths, and on his own interests.

We will have to learn to develop second careers for accomplished professional and managerial people when they reach their late forties or so. We will have to make it possible for people who have worked for twenty years or so in an organization and in a function—that is, for most managers—to find new challenge, new opportunity, and new contribution in doing something different, or at least in being effective in different surroundings and in a different institution.

But what do we really mean by the terms "management development" and "manager development"? Undoubtedly, there have been as many fads as there have been sound ventures.

WHAT MANAGEMENT DEVELOPMENT IS *NOT*

For these reasons, it is best to start by spelling out what management and manager development are not.

1. It is not taking courses. Courses are a tool of management development. But they are not management development.

Any course—whether it is a three-day seminar in a special skill or a two-year "advanced" program three evenings a week—has to fit the development needs of a management group or the development needs of an individual manager. But the job, the superior, and the development planning of both company and individual are far more important developmental tools than is any course or courses.

Indeed, some of the most popular courses are of questionable value. I have come to doubt, for example, the wisdom of courses that take a manager away from the job for long periods of time. The most effective courses, in my experience, are those that are done on the manager's own time and after hours—the evening "executive management" programs now offered by a multitude of universities, for instance. And the most effective full-time courses alternate periods at school with periods at work; a manager spends a week or two off the job in an intensive learning experience, after which he or she is immediately reinforced by going back to work and applying the things that were learned.

Managers are action focused; they are not philosophers and should not be. Unless they can right away put into action the things they have learned, the course will not "take." It will remain "information" and never become "knowledge."

Pedagogically, it is unsound not to have action to strengthen learning—that is, not to be able to put into practice on Monday what one has learned the preceding Friday. Finally, managers who have been away thirteen weeks on an advanced course may well find themselves "displaced persons" and homeless when they get back to work after such a long absence.

2. Manager development and management development are not promotion planning, replacement planning, or finding potential. These are useless exercises. They may even do harm.

The worst thing a company can do is try to develop the "comers" and leave out the others. If the others have not developed themselves to the point where they can understand, accept, and put into action the vision of the few "comers," nothing will happen. The eight out of every ten who were not included in the program will, understandably, feel slighted. They may end up by becoming less effective, less productive, less willing to do new things, than they were before.

The attempt to find "potential" is altogether futile. It is less likely to succeed than simply choosing every fifth person. Performance is what counts, and the correlation between promise and performance is not a particularly high one. Five out of every ten "high potential" young workers turn out to be nothing but good talkers by the time they reach forty. Conversely, five out of every ten young employees who do not look "brilliant" and do not talk a good game will have proven their capacity to perform by the time they are in their early forties.

Also, the idea that the purpose of management development is to find "replacements" negates the entire reason for the activity. We need management development precisely because tomorrow's jobs and tomorrow's organizations are going to be different from today's jobs and today's organizations. If all we had to do was replace yesterday's and today's jobs, we would be training people as apprentices under their present bosses.

The worst kind of replacement planning is the search for a "crown prince." Either a crown prince has a legal right to succeed, or else having been chosen crown prince is likely to destroy him. No matter how carefully concealed, picking a crown prince is an act that the whole organization very rapidly recognizes. And then all the other possible contenders unite against the crown prince and work to bring him down—and they usually succeed.

3. Finally, management development and manager development are not means to "make people over" by changing their personalities. Their aim is to make people effective. Their aim is to enable people to use their strengths fully, and to make them perform the way they are, rather than the way somebody thinks they ought to be.

An employer has no business with a subordinate's personality. Employment is a specific contract calling for specific performance, and for nothing else. Any attempt of an employer to go beyond this is immoral as well as an intrusion on privacy. It is abuse of power. An employee owes no "loyalty," no "love," and no "attitudes"—he owes performance and nothing else.

Management and manager development deal with the skills people need. They deal with the structure of jobs and of management relations. They deal with what an employee needs to learn to make his or her strengths effective. They should concern themselves with changes in behavior likely to make a person more effective. They do not deal with who the person is—that is, with personality or emotional dynamics.

Attempts to change a mature individual's personality are bound to fail, in any event. By the time he or she comes to work, personality is set. *The task is not to change personality, but to enable a person to achieve and to perform.*

THE TWO DIMENSIONS OF DEVELOPMENT

Development is not one but two related tasks that affect each other. One task is that of developing management. Its purpose is the health, survival, and growth of the enterprise. The other task is manager development. Its purpose is the health, growth, and achievement of the individual, both as a member of the organization and as a person. *Management* development is a function and activity of the organization—no matter how it is being discharged. *Manager* development is the responsibility of the individual, though company and superior have important parts to play.

Management development starts out with the question, "What kind of managers and knowledge professionals will this organization need tomorrow in order to achieve its objectives and to perform in a different market, a different economy, a different technology, a different society?"

Management development concerns itself with questions such as the age structure of the management group or the skills that managers should acquire today to qualify for tomorrow. It also focuses on the organizational structure and the design of managerial jobs to satisfy the needs and aspirations of tomorrow's "career customer," that is, tomorrow's young manager or young career professional. The market for jobs and careers has become a genuine mass market. Every organization, therefore, needs to design a "career product" that will attract and satisfy the career customer of tomorrow.

Whether management development requires a separate staff depends on the size and complexity of the business. It is certainly not an activity that should require a great many people and run a great many programs. But it does need power and prestige, for its object is to change the basic planning of the company, the structure of its organization, and the design of managerial jobs. At the core of the task are planning the market, designing the product, and obsolescing existing jobs and existing organizational structures. Management development, seen this way, is *an innovator, a disorganizer, a critic*. Its function is to ask with respect to the company's human organization, "What is our business and what should it be?"

The development of a manager focuses on the person. Its aim is to enable an individual to develop his or her abilities and strengths to the fullest extent and to find individual achievement. The aim is excellence.

No one can motivate a person toward self-development. Motivation must come from within. But a person's superior and the company can do a good deal to discourage even the most highly motivated and to misdirect his or her development efforts. The active participation, the encouragement, the guidance, from both superior and company, are needed for manager-development efforts to be fully productive.

The starting point for any manager-development effort is a performance appraisal focused on what the manager does well, what she can do well, and what limitations to her performance capacity she needs to overcome to get the most out of her strengths. Such an appraisal, however, should always be a joint effort. It requires work on the part of the employee herself; it has to be self-appraisal. But it also requires active leadership by the manager.

In appraising themselves, people tend to be either too critical or not critical enough. They are likely to see their strengths in the wrong places and to pride themselves on nonabilities rather than on abilities.

There is, typically, the first-class engineer who judges himself to be a good manager because he is "analytical" and "objective." Yet, to be a manager equally requires empathy, the ability to understand how others do their work, and a keen sense of such "nonrational" factors as personality. There is the sales manager who considers her strengths to lie in "strategy"—in reality, she is a shrewd negotiator, and what she means by *strategy* is "next week's bargain sale." Only too frequently there is the good analyst and adviser who does not realize that he lacks the emotional courage to make hard and lonely decisions.

An appraisal should be based on the performance objectives that the managers set for themselves in cooperation with their superiors. It should start with their performance against these objectives. It should never start out with "potential." It should ask, "What has this manager done well—not once, but consistently?" This should lead to recognition of the manager's strengths and of the factors that prevent him or her from making these strengths fully effective. But a self-development appraisal should also ask, "What do I want from life? What are my values, my aspirations, my directions? And what do I have to do, to learn, to change, to make myself capable of living up to my demands on myself and my expectations of life?" This question, too, is much better asked by an outsider, by someone who knows her, respects her, but at the same time can have the insight that most of us do not possess about ourselves.

Self-development may require learning new skills, new knowledge, and new manners. But above all, it requires new experience. The most important factors in self-development, apart from insight into one's own strengths, are experience on the job and the example of the superior. Self-appraisal, therefore, should always lead to conclusions regarding the needs and opportunities of a person, both with respect to what he himself has to contribute and with respect to the experiences he needs. The question should always be asked, "What are the right job experiences for this person so that his strengths can develop the fastest and the furthest?"

Development is always self-development. For the enterprise to assume responsibility for the development of a person is idle boast. The responsibility rests with the individual, her abilities, her efforts. No business enterprise is competent, let alone obligated, to substitute its efforts for the self-development efforts of the individual. To do this would not only be unwarranted paternalism, it would be foolish pretension.

It is a necessity for the spirit, the vision, and the performance of today's executives that they be expected to develop those who will manage tomorrow. Just as no one learns as much about a subject as the person who is forced to teach it, no one develops as much as the person who is trying to help others to develop themselves. Indeed, no one can develop himself or herself unless he or she works on the development of others. It is in and through efforts to develop others that executives raise their demands on themselves. The best performers in any profession always look upon the people they have trained and developed as the proudest monument they can leave behind.

And again, developing both management and managers is as needed—and requires the same approaches—in the public-service institution as in business enterprise.

But above all, today's manager and knowledge professional has a responsibility to develop themselves. It is a responsibility they have toward their institution, as well as toward themselves.

We hear a great deal today about the alienation of people in organizations. I doubt seriously whether there is more alienation today than in earlier societies. The classic diagnosis of alienation, after all, was not derived from a study of the modern corporation but was made in a thoroughly agrarian preindustrial society: the Denmark in which Soren Kierkegaard lived and wrote in the early nineteenth century. But whether conformity and spiritual despair are greater or lesser today than they used to be, the one effective counterforce to both is the individual's commitment to self-development, the individual's commitment to excellence.

SUMMARY

Management development is based on the genuine needs of organizations and managers alike. But, it is as yet rarely understood that there is *management* development, tied to the needs of the organization, and *manager* development, tied to the needs of the individual—and that the two are different. Manager development is *self-development*, although the superior and the organization can encourage or stifle it. And the aim of manager development is excellence.

25

Management by Objectives and Self-Control

Each member of the enterprise contributes something different, but all must contribute toward a common goal. Their efforts must all pull in the same direction, and their contributions must fit together to produce a whole—without gaps, without friction, without unnecessary duplication of effort.

Every job in the company must be directed toward the objectives of the whole organization if the overall goals are to be achieved. In particular, each manager's job must be focused on the success of the whole. The performance that is expected of managers must be directed toward the performance goals of the business. Results are measured by the contribution they make to the success of the enterprise. Managers must know and understand what the business goals demand of them in terms of performance, and their superiors must know what contribution to demand and expect. If these requirements are not met, managers are misdirected and their efforts are wasted.

Management by objectives requires major effort and special techniques. In a business enterprise managers are not automatically directed toward a common goal. On the contrary, organization, by its very nature, contains four factors that tend to misdirect: the specialized work of most managers, the hierarchical structure of management, the differences in vision and work and the resultant isolation of various levels of management, and the compensation structure of the management group.

To overcome these obstacles requires more than good intentions. It requires policy and structure. It requires that management by objectives be purposefully organized and be made the living law of the entire management group.

THE SPECIALIZED WORK OF MANAGERS

An old story tells of three stonecutters who were asked what they were doing. The first replied, "I am making a living." The second kept on hammering while he said, "I am doing the best job of stonecutting in the entire country." The third one looked up with a visionary gleam in his eyes and said, "I am building a cathedral."

The third man is, of course, the true manager. The first man knows what he wants to get out of the work and manages to do so. He is likely to give a "fair day's work for a fair day's pay." But he is not a manager and will never be one. It is the second man who is the problem. Workmanship is essential—an organization demoralizes if it does not demand of its members the highest workmanship they are capable of. But there is always a danger that the true workman, the true professional, will believe that he is accomplishing something when, in effect, he is just polishing stones or collecting footnotes. Workmanship must be encouraged in the business enterprise. But it must always be related to the needs of the whole.

Most managers and career professionals in any business enterprise are, like the second man, concerned with specialized work. A person's habits as a manager, his vision and values, are usually formed while he does functional and specialized work. It is essential that the functional specialist develop high standards of workmanship, that he strive to be "the best stonecutter in the country." For work without high standards is dishonest; it corrupts the worker and those around him. Emphasis on, and drive for, workmanship produces innovations and advances in every area of management.

That managers strive to do the best job possible—to do "professional human resource management," to run "the most up-to-date plant," to do "truly scientific market research"—must be encouraged. But this striving for professional workmanship in functional and specialized work is also a danger. It tends to divert the manager's vision and efforts from the goals of the business. The functional work becomes an end in itself. In far too many instances the functional managers no longer measure their performance by its contribution to the enterprise but only by professional criteria of workmanship. They tend to appraise subordinates by their craftsmanship and to reward and to promote them accordingly. They resent demands made for the sake of organizational performance as interference with "good engineering," "smooth production," or "hard-hitting selling." The functional manager's legitimate desire for workmanship can become a force that tears the enterprise apart and converts it into a loose association of working groups. Each group is concerned only with its own craft. Each jealously guards its own "secrets." Each is bent on enlarging its own domain rather than on building the business. *The remedy is to counterbalance the concern for craftsmanship with concern for the common goal of the enterprise.*

MISDIRECTION BY HIERARCHY

The hierarchical structure of management makes the danger even greater. Because of his rank, whatever the boss does and says—his most casual remarks, his habits, even his mannerisms—tend to appear to his subordinates as calculated, planned, and meaningful. "All you ever hear around the place is human-relations talk; but when the boss calls you on the carpet, it is always because overtime is too high; and when it comes to promoting a guy, the plums always go to those who do the best job filling out accounting-department forms." This is one of the most common tunes, sung with infinite variations, at every level of management. It leads to poor performance—even in cutting overtime. It also expresses loss of confidence in, and absence of respect for, the company and its management.

Yet the manager who misdirects subordinates in this way does not intend to do so. He genuinely considers human relations to be the most important task of his plant managers. But he talks about overtime because he feels that he has to establish himself with his men as a "practical man," or because he thinks that he shows familiarity with their problems by talking "shop" with them, by expressing concern for their workload. He stresses the accounting-department forms only because they annoy him as much as they do his men—or he may just not want to have any more trouble with the controller than he can help. But to his subordinates these reasons are hidden; all they see and hear is the question about overtime, the emphasis on forms.

The solution to this problem requires a structure of management that focuses the eyes of managers and their bosses on what the job—rather than the boss—demands. To stress style and manner is likely, instead, to worsen the problem. Indeed, everyone familiar with organizations today has seen situations in which a manager's attempt to avoid misdirection through changing his style has converted a fairly satisfactory relationship into a nightmare of embarrassment and misunderstanding. The manager himself becomes so self-conscious as to lose all easy relationship with his people. And his people, in turn, react with, "So help us, the old man has read a book; we used to know what he wanted of us, now we have to guess."

Misdirection can result from a difference in concern between various levels of management. This problem, too, cannot be solved by attitudes and good intentions; for it is rooted in the structure of any enterprise. Nor can it be solved by "better communications," for communications presuppose common language, and it is precisely that which is usually lacking.

It is no accident that the old story of the blind men meeting up with an elephant on the road is so popular among management people. Each level of management sees the same "elephant"—the business—from a different angle of vision. The supervisor in operations, like the blind man who felt the elephant's leg and decided that a tree was in his way, tends to see only the immediate operations problems. Top management—the blind man touching the trunk and deciding a snake bars his way—tends to see only the enterprise as a whole. It sees shareholders, financial problems, altogether a host of highly abstract relations and figures.

Operating management—the blind man feeling the elephant's belly and thinking himself up against a landslide—tends to see things functionally.

Each level needs its particular vision; it could not do its job without it. Yet, these visions are so different that people on different levels talking about the same thing often do not realize it—or, as frequently happens, believe that they are talking about the same thing when in reality they are poles apart.

MISDIRECTION BY COMPENSATION

The most serious force for misdirection within the management group may be the pay structure. At the same time, it is the hardest one to remove. Somehow management people have to be paid, but every compensation system is liable to misdirect.

Compensation is cost to the enterprise and income to the recipient. It also always expresses status, both within the enterprise and in society. It entails judgments on the managers' worth as much as on their performance. It is emotionally tied to all our ideas of fairness, justice, and equity. Money is, of course, quantitative. But the money in any compensation system expresses the most intangible, but also the most sensitive, values and qualities. For this reason, there can be no truly simple or truly rational compensation system.

Any compensation system determines a person's place within the group. How one's pay relates to the pay of others, and especially to the pay of one's peers, is always more important than the absolute amount of the salary. Compensation must always try to balance recognition of the individual with stability and maintenance of the group. No attempt at a "scientific formula" for compensation can, therefore, be completely successful. The best possible compensation plan is of necessity a compromise among the various functions and meanings of compensation, for the individual as well as for the groups. Even the best plan will still misdirect, as well as direct and encourage the wrong as well as the right behavior.

Yet, there is hardly a more powerful signal for managers than compensation and compensation structure. Its importance to them goes far beyond the economic meaning of money. It conveys to them the values of their top management and their own worth within the management group. It expresses in clear and tangible form a manager's position, rank, and recognition within the group. At today's tax rates, a little more money means, as a rule, very little to senior managers. But the status symbol of a little more money and its emotional impact are incalculable.

The most damaging misdirection may result from those apparently eminently "fair" compensation systems that relate a manager's pay directly to performance. Performance is often measured by return on investment during the current year. If we want to *measure* performance, there is no other way. Yet, if return on investment or current profits are overemphasized, the managers of a decentralized business will be misdirected toward slighting the future in favor of the present.

An able management team heading one of the major divisions of a chemical company failed for years to develop a badly needed new product. Year after year, they reported to their top management that the new product was not yet quite ready. Finally, when the division manager was asked bluntly why he was stalled on a project that was clearly vital to the success of his business, he answered, "Have you looked at our compensation plan? My management group and I are compensated primarily on the basis of return-on-investment. The new product is the future of this business. But for five or eight years there will be only investment and no return. I know we are three years late. But do you really expect me to unjustly penalize my closest associates by reducing their compensation?" This story had a happy ending. The compensation plan was changed—somewhat in line with the plan Du Pont has had for years with respect to new developments. Du Pont does not put the cost of a development into the investment base of a division or a subsidiary until the new product has been introduced on the market.

And within a year or two the new product was out and selling.

The preference should be for simple compensation systems rather than for complex ones. It should be for compensation systems that allow judgment to be used and that enable pay to be fitted to the job of the individual rather than imposing one formula on everybody. But I would be the last person to claim that a "fair," let alone a "scientific," system can be devised. All one can do, to repeat, is to watch lest the compensation system reward the wrong behavior, emphasize the wrong results, and direct people away from performance for the common good.

WHAT SHOULD THE OBJECTIVES BE?

Just as "eternal vigilance is the price of freedom," constant effort is needed to prevent misdirection. The superior needs to understand what to expect of subordinate managers. The subordinates, in turn, need to be able to know what results they should hold themselves accountable for. Without special effort, superior or subordinate will not know and understand this, and their ideas will not be compatible, let alone identical.

Each manager, from the "big boss" down to the operations supervisor, needs clearly spelled-out objectives. Otherwise confusion can be guaranteed. These objectives should lay out what performance each managerial unit is supposed to achieve. They should lay out what contribution a manager and his or her unit are expected to make to help other units obtain their objectives. Finally, they should spell out what contribution the manager can expect from other units toward the attainment of these objectives. Right from the start, in other words, emphasis should be on teamwork and team results.

These objectives should always derive from the goals of the business enterprise. A statement of his own objectives based on those of the company and of the operations department should be demanded even of the first-line supervisor. The company may be so large as to make the distance between the individual operations supervisor and the company's total output enormous. Yet the supervisor must focus on the objectives of the company and needs to define his or her results in terms of the unit's contribution to the whole of which it is a part.

The objectives of every manager should spell out his or her contribution to attainment of company goals in all areas of the business. Obviously, not every manager has a direct contribution to make in every area. The contribution that marketing makes to productivity, for example, may be indirect and hard to define. But if a manager's unit is not expected to contribute toward one of the areas that significantly affect prosperity and survival of the business, this fact should be clearly brought out. For managers must understand that business results depend on a balance of efforts and results in a number of areas. This is necessary both to give full scope to the craftsmanship of each function and specialty, and to prevent the empire-building and jealousy of the various functions and specialties. It is necessary also to avoid overemphasis on any one key area.

This is particularly important for service staffs and for highly specialized groups such as the people in information technology. They may not always be able to relate their work directly to organizational objectives and organizational results. But unless they try to, they are likely to direct their work away from organizational objectives and organizational results.

To obtain balanced efforts, the objectives of all managers on all levels and in all areas should also be keyed to both short-range and long-range considerations. And, of course, all objectives should always contain both the tangible business objectives and such "intangible" objectives as manager development, worker performance and attitude, and social responsibility. Anything else is shortsighted and impractical.

MANAGEMENT BY DRIVES

Proper management requires balanced emphasis on objectives, especially by top management. It avoids the all-too-common business malpractice—management by crisis and drives.

That things always revert to their original state three weeks after a drive is over, everybody knows and apparently expects. The only result of an economy drive is likely to be that messengers and typists get fired, and that six-figure executives are forced to do clerical work typing their own letters—and doing it badly. And yet many managements fail to draw the obvious conclusion that drives are, after all, not the way to get things done.

Over and above its ineffectiveness, management by drive misdirects. It puts all emphasis on one phase of the job to the detriment of all other aspects. "For four weeks we cut inventories," one hardened veteran of management-by-crisis once summed it up. "Then we have four weeks of general cost-cutting, followed by four weeks of human relations. We just have time to push customer service and courtesy for a month. And then the inventory is back where it was when we started. We don't even try to do our job. All top management talks about, thinks about, preaches about, is last week's inventory figure or this week's customer complaints. How we do the rest of the job, they don't even want to know."

In an organization that manages by drives, people either neglect their job to get on with the current drive or silently organize to sabotage the drive in order to get the work done. In either event, they become deaf to the cry of "wolf." And when the real crisis comes, when all hands really should drop everything and pitch in, they treat it as just another case of management-created hysteria. Management-by-drive is a sure sign of confusion. It is an admission of incompetence. It is a sign that management does not think. Above all, it is a sign that the company does not know what to expect of its managers and that, not knowing how to direct them, it misdirects them.

HOW SHOULD OBJECTIVES BE SET AND BY WHOM?

The goals for the jobs of all managers must be defined by the contribution they have to make to the success of the larger unit of which they are a part. The objectives of the direct sales manager's job should be defined by the contribution she and her district sales force have to make to the sales department; the objectives of the project engineer's job, by the contribution he and his engineers and technologists make to the engineering department. The objectives of the general manager of a decentralized division should be defined by the contribution the division has to make to the objectives of the parent company.

Higher management must reserve the power to approve or disapprove these objectives. But their development is part of a manager's responsibility; indeed, it is the manager's first responsibility. It means, too, that every manager should responsibly participate in the development of the objectives of the higher unit of which he is a part. To "give a *sense* of participation" is not only not enough. It is the wrong thing. Being a manager means *having* responsibility. Precisely because his aims should reflect the objective needs of the business—rather than merely what the boss, or the manager himself, wants—he must be committed to the objectives with a positive act of assent. Managers must know and understand the ultimate business goals, what is expected of them and why, and what they will be measured against and how. There must be a meeting of minds within the entire management of each unit. This can be achieved only when all the contributing managers are required to think through what the unit objectives are and are led to participate actively and responsibly in the work of defining them. And only if lower managers participate in this way can the higher managers know what to expect of them and make exacting demands.

This is so important that some of the most effective managers I know go one step further. They have each of their subordinates write a *manager's letter* twice a year. In this letter to the superior, managers first define the objectives of the superior's job and of their own job, as they see them. They then set down the performance standards that they believe are being applied to them. Next, they list the things they must do to attain these goals and the things within their own units they consider the major obstacles. They list the things the superiors and the company do that help them and the things that hamper them. Finally, they outline what they propose to do during the next year to reach their goals. If their superiors accept this statement, the manager's letter becomes the charter under which the manager operates.

This device, like no other I have seen, brings out how easily the unconsidered and casual remarks of even the best boss can confuse and misdirect. One large company has used the manager's letter for ten years. Yet almost every letter still lists as objectives and standards things that baffle the superior to whom the letter is addressed. And whenever she asks, "What is this?" she gets this sort of answer, "Don't you remember what you said last spring going down in the elevator with me?"

The manager's letter also brings out whatever inconsistencies there are in the demands made on a person by his or her superior and by the company. Does the superior demand both speed and high quality when she can get only one or the other? And what compromise is needed in the interest of the company? Does the boss demand initiative and judgment of her people but also that they check back with her before they do anything? Does the superior ask for ideas and suggestions but never uses them or discusses them? Does the company expect of a small engineering force that it be available immediately whenever something goes wrong in the plant and yet bend all its efforts to the completion of new designs? Does it expect managers to maintain high standards of performance but forbid them to remove poor performers? Does it create the conditions under which people say, "I can get the work done as long as I can keep the boss from knowing what I am doing"?

As the manager's letter illustrates, managing managers requires special efforts not only to establish common direction, but to eliminate misdirection. Mutual understanding can never be attained by "communications down," can never be created by talking. It results only from "communications up." It requires both the superior's willingness to listen and a tool especially designed to make lower managers heard.

SELF-CONTROL THROUGH MEASUREMENTS

The greatest advantage of management by objectives is perhaps that it makes it possible for managers to control their own performance. Self-control means stronger motivation: a desire to do the best rather than do just enough to get by. It means higher performance goals and broader vision. Even if management by objectives were not necessary to give the enterprise the unity of direction and effort of a management team, it would be necessary to make possible management by self-control.

Indeed, one of the major values of management by objectives is that it enables us to substitute management by self-control for management by domination.

To control their own performance, managers need to know more than what their goals are. They must be able to measure their performance and results against the goal. Managers must have clear and common measurements in all key areas of an organization. These measurements need not be rigidly quantitative nor need they be exact. But they have to be clear, simple, and rational. They have to be reliable—at least to the point where their margin of error is acknowledged and understood. And they have to be self-explanatory, understandable without complicated interpretation or philosophical discussion.

All managers should have the information they need to measure their own performance, and they should receive it soon enough to make any changes necessary for the desired results. This information should go to the managers themselves, and to their superiors. It should be the means of self-control, not a tool of control from above.

This needs particular stress today, when the ability to obtain such information is growing rapidly as a result of technological progress in information gathering, analysis, and synthesis. In the past, information on important facts was either not obtainable at all or could only be assembled so late as to be of little use. This was not an unmixed curse. It made effective self-control difficult; but it also made domination of a manager from above difficult. In the absence of information with which to control him, the manager had to be allowed to work as he saw fit.

The new ability to assemble measuring information will make possible effective self-control. If used properly, it will lead to a tremendous advance in the effectiveness and performance of management. But if this ability is abused to impose control on managers from above, the new information technology will inflict incalculable harm by demoralizing management and by seriously lowering the effectiveness of managers.

SELF-CONTROL AND PERFORMANCE STANDARDS

Management by objectives and self-control asks for self-discipline. It forces the managers to make high demands on themselves. It is anything but *permissive*. It may well lead to demanding too much rather than too little. This has, indeed, been the main criticism leveled against the concept. (See chapter 7, especially the discussion of Abraham Maslow's criticism of Theory Y.)

Management by objectives and self-control assumes that people want to be responsible, want to contribute, want to achieve. That is a bold assumption. Yet we know that people tend to act as they are expected to act.

A manager who starts out by assuming that people are weak, irresponsible, and lazy will get weakness, irresponsibility, and laziness. A manager who assumes strength, responsibility, and desire to contribute may experience a few disappointments. But the first task of managers is to make effective the strengths of people. And this they can do only if they start out with the assumption that people—and especially managers and professional contributors—want to achieve.

Above all, they must make this assumption with regard to the young educated people of today who will be tomorrow's managers. These young people may not know exactly what they mean when they demand to be allowed to "make a contribution." *But their demand is the right one.* They are right also that management, as it has been practiced so far, does not act on the assumption that the young educated people want to make a contribution. Such people need to be subjected—and to subject themselves—to the discipline and the demands of management by objectives and self-control.

A PHILOSOPHY OF MANAGEMENT

What the business enterprise needs is a principle of management that will give full scope to individual strength and responsibility, as well as common direction to vision and effort, one that will establish teamwork and harmonize the goals of the individual with the common good. Management by objectives and self-control makes the interest of the enterprise the aim of every manager. In place of control from outside, it substitutes the stricter, more exacting, and more effective control from inside. It motivates managers to action, not because somebody tells them to do something or talks them into doing it, but because the objective task demands it. They act not because somebody wants them to but because they themselves decide that they have to—they act, in other words, as free men and women.

I do not use the word "philosophy" lightly. Indeed, I prefer not to use it at all; it's much too big a word. But management by objectives and self-control may properly be called a philosophy of management. It rests on a concept of the *job* of management. It rests on an analysis of the specific *needs* of the management group and of the *obstacles* it faces. It rests on a concept of *human action, behavior, and motivation.* Finally, it applies to *every manager,* whatever his or her level and function, and to any organization, whether large or small. It ensures performance by converting *objective needs into personal goals.* And this is *genuine freedom.*

SUMMARY

Each member of the enterprise contributes something different; but all must contribute toward a common goal, a common performance. Each should strive toward workmanship in his or her work. Yet professional excellence is a means toward a common objective. By its very nature, the organization tends to misdirect away from the common objective. Organizations therefore require management by objectives so as to integrate individual efforts into common performance. Managers' objectives need to be set by themselves. And they should be used for self-control. Management by objectives and self-control can truly be called *a philosophy of management for free men and women.*

26

From Middle Management to Information-Based Organizations

The typical large business of today has fewer than half the levels of management of its counterpart in 1988, and no more than a third the managers. In its structure, and in its management problems and concerns, it bears little resemblance to the typical manufacturing company circa 1950. Instead, it is far more likely to resemble organizations that neither the practicing manager nor the management scholar pays much attention to, in those respects, today: the hospital, the university, the symphony orchestra.

For like them, today's typical business will increasingly be knowledge-based, an organization composed largely of specialists *who direct and discipline their own performance through organized feedback* from colleagues, customers, and headquarters. For this reason, it increasingly will be what I call an *information-based organization*.

Businesses, especially large ones, have little choice but to become information-based. Demographics, for one, demand the shift. The center of gravity in employment is moving fast, from manual and clerical workers, to knowledge workers who resist the command-and-control model that business took from the military over one hundred years ago. Economics also dictates change, especially the need for large businesses to innovate and to be entrepreneurial. But above all, information technology demands the shift.

INFORMATION TECHNOLOGY

Advanced information technology isn't necessary to create an information-based organization, of course. As we shall see, the British built just such an organization in India when "information technology" meant the quill pen and barefoot runners were the "telecommunications" system. But as advanced technology becomes more and more prevalent, we have to engage in analysis and diagnosis—that is, in "information"—even more intensively, or risk being swamped by the data we generate.

As soon as a company takes the first tentative steps from data to information, its decision processes, management structure, and even the way its work gets done begin to be transformed. In fact, this has been happening, quite fast, in a number of organizations throughout the world.

We can readily see the first step in this transformation process when we consider the impact of information technology on capital-investment decisions. We have known for a long time that there is no one right way to analyze a proposed capital investment. To understand it, we need at least six analyses: the expected rate of return; the payout period and the investment's expected productive life; the discounted present value of all net returns through the productive lifetime of the investment; the risk in not making the investment or deferring it; the cost and risk in case of failure; and finally, the opportunity cost. Every managerial accounting student is taught these concepts. But before the computer advances in information-processing capacity, the actual analyses would have taken man-weeks of clerical toil to complete. Now anyone with spreadsheet software should be able to do them in a few hours.

The availability of this information transforms the capital-investment analysis from opinion into diagnosis, that is, into the rational weighing of alternative assumptions. Then the information transforms the capital-investment decision from an opportunistic, financial decision governed by the numbers into a business decision based on the probability of alternative strategic assumptions. So the decision both presupposes a business strategy and challenges that strategy and its assumptions. What was once a budget exercise becomes an analysis of policy.

The second area that is affected when a company focuses its advanced technology on producing information is its organization structure. Almost immediately, it becomes clear that both the number of management levels and the number of managers can be sharply cut. The reason is straightforward: it turns out that whole layers of management neither make decisions nor lead. Instead, their main, if not their only, function is to serve as "relays"—human boosters for the faint, unfocused signals that pass for communication in the traditional preinformation organization.

One of America's largest defense contractors made this discovery when it asked what information its top corporate and operating managers needed to do their jobs. Where did it come from? What form was it in? How did it flow? The search for answers soon revealed that whole layers of management—perhaps as many as six out of a total of fourteen—existed only because these questions had not been asked before. The company had data galore. But it had always used its copious data for control rather than for information.

FROM DATA TO INFORMATION

Information is data endowed with relevance and purpose. Converting data into information thus requires knowledge. And knowledge, by definition, is specialized. (In fact, truly knowledgeable people tend toward overspecialization, whatever their field, precisely because there is always so much more to know.)

The information-based organization requires far more specialists overall than the command-and-control company. Moreover, the specialists are found in operations, not at corporate headquarters. Indeed, the operating organization tends to become an organization of specialists of all kinds.

Information-based organizations need central operating work such as legal counsel, public relations, and labor relations as much as ever. But the need for service staffs—that is, for people without operating responsibilities who only advise, counsel, or coordinate—shrinks drastically. In its central management, the information-based organization needs few, if any, specialists.

Because of its flatter structure, the large, information-based organization more closely resembles the businesses of a century ago than today's big companies. Back then, however, all the knowledge, such as it was, lay with the very top people. The rest were helpers or hands, who mostly did the same work and did as they were told. In the information-based organization, the knowledge is primarily at the bottom, in the minds of the specialists, who do different work and direct themselves. An organization phase in which knowledge tends to be concentrated in service staffs, is an attempt to infuse knowledge from the top rather than obtain information from below.

Finally, a good deal of work is done differently in the information-based organization. Traditional departments serve as guardians of standards, as centers for training and the assignment of specialists; they aren't where the work gets done. That happens largely in task-focused teams.

This change is well under way in what used to be the most clearly defined of all departments—research. In pharmaceuticals, in telecommunications, in papermaking, the traditional sequence of research, development, manufacturing, and marketing is being replaced by synchrony: specialists from all these functions work together as a team, from the inception of research to a product's establishment in the market.

The need for a task force, its assignment, its composition, and its leadership will have to be decided on *case by case*. So the organization that is being developed goes beyond the matrix. One thing is clear, though: it requires greater self-discipline and even greater emphasis on individual responsibility for relationships and for communications than does the matrix organization where functional managers supply personnel to projects for specific tasks.

To say that information technology is transforming business enterprises is simple. What this transformation requires of companies and top managements is much harder to decipher. That is why I find it helpful to look for clues in other kinds of information-based organizations, such as the hospital, the symphony orchestra, and the British administration in India.

A fair-sized hospital of about four hundred beds will have a staff of several hundred physicians and twelve-hundred to fifteen-hundred paramedics divided among some sixty medical and paramedical specialties. Each specialty has its own knowledge, its own training, its own language. In each specialty, especially the paramedical ones like the clinical lab and physical therapy, there is a head person who is a working specialist rather than a full-time manager. The head of each specialty reports directly to the top, and there is little middle management. A good deal of the work is done in ad hoc teams as required by an individual patient's diagnosis and treatment.

A large symphony orchestra is even more instructive, since for some works there may be a few hundred musicians on stage playing together. According to traditional organization theory then, there should be several group vice president conductors and perhaps a half-dozen division VP conductors. But that's not how it works. There is only the conductor—CEO—and every one of the musicians plays directly to that person without an intermediary. And each is a high-grade specialist, indeed an artist.

But the best example of a large and successful information-based organization and one without any middle management at all, is the British civil administration in India.*

The British ran the Indian subcontinent for two hundred years, from the middle of the eighteenth century through World War II, without making any fundamental changes in organization structure or administrative policy. The Indian civil service never had more than one thousand members to administer the vast and densely populated subcontinent—a tiny fraction (at most 1 percent) of the legions of Confucian mandarins and palace eunuchs employed next door to administer a not-much-more populous China. Most of the Britishers were quite young; a thirty-year-old was a survivor, especially in the early years. Most lived alone in isolated outposts with the nearest countryman a day or two of travel away, and for the first hundred years there was no telegraph or railroad.

The organization structure was totally flat. Each district officer reported directly to the "COO," the provincial political secretary. And since there were nine provinces, each political secretary had at least one hundred people reporting directly to

---

* The standard account is Philip Woodruff, *The Men Who Ruled India*, especially the first volume, *The Founders* (New York: Shocken, 1964). How the system worked day by day is charmingly told in *Sowing* (New York: Harcourt Brace Jovanovich, 1962), volume one of the autobiography of Leonard Woolf (Virginia Woolf's husband).

him, many times what the "doctrine of the span of control" would allow. Nevertheless, the system worked remarkably well, in large part because it was designed to ensure that each of its members had the information he needed to do his job.

Each month the district officer spent a whole day writing a full report to the political secretary in the provincial capital. He discussed each of his principal tasks—there were only four, each clearly delineated. He put down in detail what he had expected would happen with respect to each of them, what actually did happen, and why, if there was a discrepancy, the two differed. Then he wrote down what he expected would happen in the ensuing month with respect to each key task and what he was going to do about it, asked questions about policy, and commented on long-term opportunities, threats, and needs. In turn, the political secretary "minuted" every one of those reports—that is, he wrote back a full comment.

On the basis of these examples, what can we say about the requirements of the information-based organization? And what are its management problems? Let's look first at the requirements. Several hundred musicians and their CEO, the conductor, can play together because they all have *the same score*. It tells both flutist and timpanist what to play and when. And it tells the conductor what to expect from each and when. Similarly, all the specialists in the hospital share a *common mission:* the care and cure of the sick. The diagnosis is their "score"; it dictates specific action for the X-ray lab, the dietitian, the physical therapist, and the rest of the medical team.

Information-based organizations, in other words, require clear, simple, common objectives that translate into particular actions. At the same time, however, as these examples indicate, information-based organizations also need to concentrate on one objective or, at most, on a few.

Because the "players" in an information-based organization are specialists, they cannot be told how to do their work. There are probably few orchestra conductors who could coax even one note out of a French horn, let alone show the horn player how to do it. But the conductor can focus the horn player's skill and knowledge on the musicians' *joint performance*. And this focus is what the leaders of an information-based organization must be able to achieve.

Yet a business has no "score" to play by except the score it writes as it plays. And whereas neither a first-rate performance of a symphony nor a miserable one will change what the composer wrote, the performance of a business continually creates new and different scores against which its performance is assessed. So an information-based business must be structured around *goals* that clearly state management's performance expectations, for the enterprise and for each part and specialist, and around *organized feedback* that compares results with these performance expectations, so that every member can exercise self-control.

The other requirement of an information-based organization is that everyone take information responsibility. The bassoonist in the orchestra does so every time she plays a note. Doctors and paramedics work with an elaborate system of reports and an information center, the nurse's station on the patient's floor. The district officer in India acted on this responsibility every time he filed a report.

The key to such a system is that everyone asks, "Who in this organization depends on me for what information? And on whom, in turn, do I depend?" Each person's list will always include superiors and subordinates. But the most important names on it will be those of colleagues, people with whom one's primary relationship is coordination. The relationship of the internist, the surgeon, and the anesthesiologist is one example. But the relationship of a biochemist, a pharmacologist, the medical director in charge of clinical testing, and a marketing specialist in a pharmaceutical company is no different. It, too, requires each party to take the fullest information responsibility.

Information responsibility to others is increasingly understood, especially in middle-sized companies. But information responsibility to oneself is still largely neglected. That is, everyone in an organization should be constantly thinking through what information he or she needs to do the job and to make a contribution.

This may well be the most radical break with the way even the most highly computerized businesses are still being run today. There, either people assume the more data, the more information—a perfectly valid assumption when data were scarce, but which leads to data overload and information blackout now that data are plentiful—or they believe that the information specialists know what data executives and professionals need in order to have information. But information specialists are toolmakers. They can tell us what tool to use to hammer upholstery nails into a chair. We need to decide whether we should be upholstering a chair at all.

Executives and professional specialists need to think through what information is for them, what data they need: first, to know what they are doing; then, to be able to decide what they should be doing; and finally, to appraise how well they are doing. Until this happens, departments of information technology are likely to remain cost centers rather than become the result centers they could be.

Most large businesses have little in common with the examples we have been looking at. Yet to remain competitive—maybe even to survive—they will have to convert themselves into information-based organizations, and quickly. They will have to change old habits and acquire new ones. And the more successful a company has been, the more difficult and painful this process is apt to be. It will threaten the jobs, status, and opportunities of a good many people in the organization, especially the long-serving, middle-aged people in middle management, who tend to be the least mobile and to feel most secure in their work, their positions, their relationships, and their behavior.

The information-based organization also poses its own special management problems. I see as particularly critical:

1. Developing rewards, recognition, and career opportunities for specialists

2. Creating unified vision in an organization of specialists

3. Devising the management structure for an organization of task forces

4. Ensuring the supply, preparation, and testing of top management people

Bassoonists presumably neither want nor expect to be anything but bassoonists. Their career opportunities consist of moving from second bassoon to first bassoon and perhaps of moving from a second-rank orchestra to a better, more prestigious one. Similarly, many medical technologists neither expect nor want to be anything but medical technologists. Their career opportunities consist of a fairly good chance of moving up to senior technician and a very slim chance of becoming lab director. For those who make it to lab director, about one out of every twenty-five or thirty technicians, there is also the opportunity to move to a bigger, richer hospital. The district officer in India had practically no chance for professional growth except possibly to be relocated, after a three-year stint, to a bigger district.

Career opportunities for specialists in an information-based business organization should be more plentiful than they are in an orchestra or hospital, let alone in the Indian civil service. But as in these organizations, they will primarily be opportunities for advancement within the specialty, and for limited advancement, at that. Advancement into "management" will be the exception, for the simple reason that there will be far fewer middle-management positions to move into. This contrasts sharply with the traditional organization, where, except in the research lab, the main line of advancement in rank is out of the specialty and into general management.

In the 1950s, General Electric tackled this problem by creating "parallel opportunities" for "individual professional contributors." Many companies have followed this example. But professional specialists have largely rejected it as a solution. To them and to their management colleagues, the only meaningful opportunities are promotions into management. And the prevailing compensation structure in practically all businesses reinforces this attitude, because it is heavily biased toward managerial positions and titles.

There are no easy answers to this problem. Some help comes from looking at large law and consulting firms, where even the most senior partners tend to be specialists and associates who will not make partner are outplaced fairly early on. But whatever scheme is eventually developed, it will work only if the values and compensation structure of business are drastically changed.

The second challenge that management faces is giving its organization of specialists a common vision, *a view of the whole.*

In the Indian civil service, the district officer was expected to see the "whole" of his district. But to enable him to concentrate on it, the government services that arose one after the other in the nineteenth century (forestry, irrigation, the archaeological survey, public health and sanitation, roads) were organized outside the administrative structure and had virtually no contact with the district officer. This meant that the district officer became increasingly isolated from the activities that often had the greatest impact on—and the greatest importance for—his district. In the end, only the provincial government or the central government in Delhi had a view of the "whole," and it was an increasingly abstract one, at that.

A business simply cannot function this way. It needs the view of the whole and the focus on the whole to be shared among a great many of its professional specialists, certainly among the senior ones. And yet it will have to accept, indeed will have to foster, the individual pride and professionalism of its specialists—if only because, in the absence of opportunities to move into middle management, their motivation must come from that pride and professionalism.

One way to foster professionalism, of course, is through assignments to task forces. And the information-based business will use more and more smaller self-governing units, assigning them tasks tidy enough for "a good man to get his arms around," as the old phrase has it. But to what extent should information-based businesses rotate performing specialists out of their specialties and into new ones? And to what extent will top management have to accept as its top priority making and maintaining a common vision across professional specialties?

Heavy reliance on task-force teams assuages one problem. But it aggravates another: the management structure of the information-based organization. Who will the business's managers be? Will they be task-force leaders? Or will there be a two-headed monster—a specialist structure, comparable, perhaps, to the way attending physicians function in a hospital, and an administrative structure of task-force leaders?

The decisions we face on the role and function of the task-force leaders are risky and controversial. Is theirs a permanent assignment, analogous to the job of the supervisory nurse in the hospital? Or is it a function that changes as the task does? Is it an assignment or a position? Does it carry any rank at all? And if it does, will the task-force leaders become, in time, what the product managers have been at Procter & Gamble: the basic units of management and the company's field officers? Might the task-force leaders eventually replace department heads and vice presidents?

Evidence of every one of these developments exists, but there is neither a clear trend nor much understanding as to what each entails. Yet, each would give rise to a different organizational structure from those we are familiar with.

Finally, the toughest problem will be to ensure the supply, preparation, and testing of top management people. This is, of course, an old and central dilemma as well as a major reason for the general acceptance of decentralization in large businesses in the last sixty years. But many existing business organizations have a great many middle management positions that are supposed to prepare and test a person. As a result, there usually are a good many people to choose from when filling a senior management slot. With the number of middle management positions sharply cut, where will the information-based organization's top executives come from? What will be their preparation? How will they have been tested?

Decentralization into autonomous units will surely be even more critical than it is now. Perhaps we will even copy the German *Gruppe,* in which the decentralized units are set up as separate companies with their own top managements. The Germans use this model precisely because of their tradition of promoting people in their specialties, especially in research and engineering; if they did not have available commands in near-independent subsidiaries to put people in, they would have little opportunity to train and test their most promising professionals. These subsidiaries are thus somewhat like the farm teams of a major-league baseball club.

We may also find that more and more top management jobs in big companies are filled by hiring people away from smaller companies. This is the way that major orchestras get their conductors—a young conductor earns his or her spurs in a small orchestra or opera house, only to be hired away by a larger one. And the heads of a good many large hospitals have had similar careers.

Can business follow the example of the orchestra and hospital, where top management has become a separate career? Conductors and hospital administrators come out of courses in conducting or schools of hospital administration respectively. We see something of this sort in France, where large companies are often run by men who have spent their entire previous careers in government service. But in most countries this would be unacceptable to the organization (only France has the *mystique* of the Grandes Écoles). And even in France, businesses, especially large ones, are becoming too demanding to be run by people without firsthand experience and a proven success record.

Thus the entire top-management process—preparation, testing, succession—will become even more problematic than it already is. There will be a growing need for experienced businesspeople to go back to school. And business schools will surely need to work out what successful professional specialists must know to prepare themselves for high-level positions as business executives and business leaders.

Since modern business enterprise first arose, after the Civil War in the United States and the Franco-Prussian War in Europe, there have been two major evolutions in the concept and structure of organizations. The first took place in the ten years between 1895 and 1905. It distinguished management from ownership and established management as work and task in its own right. This happened first in Germany, when Georg Siemens—the founder and head of Germany's premier bank, Deutsche Bank—saved the electrical apparatus company his cousin Werner had founded, after Werner's sons and heirs had mismanaged it into near collapse. By threatening to cut off the bank's loans, he forced his cousins to turn the company's management over to professionals. A little later, J. P. Morgan, Andrew Carnegie, and John D. Rockefeller, Sr., followed suit in their massive restructurings of U.S. railroads and industries.

The second evolutionary change took place twenty years later. The development of what we see as the modern corporation began with Pierre S. du Pont's restructuring of his family company in the early 1920s and continued with Alfred P. Sloan's redesign of General Motors a few years later. This introduced the command-and-control organization of today, with its emphasis on decentralization, central service staffs, personnel management, the whole apparatus of budgets and controls, and the important distinction between policy and operations. This stage culminated in the massive reorganization of General Electric in the early 1950s, an action that perfected the model most big businesses around the world (including Japanese organizations) later followed.*

Now we are in a third period of change: the shift from the command-and-control organization, the organization of departments and divisions, to the information-based organization, the organization of knowledge specialists. We can perceive, though still somewhat dimly, what this organization will look like. We can identify some of its main characteristics and requirements. We can point to central problems of values, structure, and behavior. But the job of actually building the information-based organization is still ahead of us—it is the managerial challenge of the future.

SUMMARY

There have been three distinct phases in the evolution of the structure and information systems in business organizations. The first was the separation of ownership from the day-to-day management of the firm. The second was the development of the command-and-control structure and system. We have now entered the third phase, which may be called the information-based organization. It is an organization of knowledge specialists with many fewer managerial layers.

---

* Alfred D. Chandler, Jr., has masterfully chronicled the process in his two books *Strategy and Structure* (Cambridge: MIT Press, 1962) and *The Visible Hand* (Cambridge: Harvard University Press, 1977)—surely the best studies of the administrative history of any major institution. The process itself and its results were presented and analyzed in two of my books: *The Concept of the Corporation* (New York: John Day, 1946) and *The Practice of Management* (New York: Harper Brothers, 1954).

Using examples from the modern complex hospital and the symphony orchestra, it is possible to determine the requirements for successful operation of an information-based organization. First, there should be agreement on the overall mission (or score) and the mission should be widely shared throughout the organization. Second, for the information-based organization to function properly, everyone in it must take responsibility for the information the specialist owes to others and the information the specialist requires from others. Third, alternative compensation and career paths must be developed within the specialties, since the opportunities to move into management are becoming more limited. Finally, there will be the need for an organization to train and develop its top management. Examples of how this might be done are present in hospitals and in consulting and law firms.

27

The Spirit of Performance

The purpose of an organization is to enable ordinary human beings to do extraordinary things. It is a means to make strengths productive and weaknesses irrelevant.

No organization can depend on genius; the supply is always scarce and unreliable. It is the test of an organization to make ordinary people perform better than they seem capable of, to bring out whatever strength there is in its members, and to use each person's strength to help all the other members perform. It is the task of organization at the same time to neutralize the individual weaknesses of its members. The test of an organization is the spirit of performance.

The spirit of performance requires that there be full scope for individual excellence. The focus must be on the strengths—on what people can do rather than on what they cannot do.

"Morale" in an organization does not mean that "people get along together." The test is performance. Human relations that are not grounded in the satisfaction of good performance in work are actually poor human relations. There is no greater indictment of an organization than that the strength and ability of the outstanding individual threatens the group and that his or her performance becomes a source of difficulty, frustration, and discouragement for the others.

"Spirit of performance" in a human organization means that its energy output is larger than the sum of the efforts put in. It means the creation of energy. This cannot be accomplished by mechanical means. A machine cannot deliver more energy than is put into it. To get out more than is being put in is possible only in the moral sphere.

By morality I do not mean preachments. Morality, to have any meaning at all, must be a principle of action. It must not be speeches, sermons, or good intentions. *It must be practices.* Specifically:

1. The focus of the organization must be on *performance*. The first requirement of the spirit of performance is high performance standards, for the group as well as for each individual. The organization must cultivate in itself the habit of achievement.

2. The focus of the organization must be on *opportunities* rather than on problems.

3. The *decisions that affect people*—their placement and their pay, promotion, demotion, and severance—must express the values and beliefs of the organization. They are the true controls of an organization (see chapter 31, page 329).

4. Finally, in its people decisions, management must demonstrate that it realizes that *integrity* is one absolute requirement of managers, the one quality that they must bring with them and cannot be expected to acquire later on.

THE DANGER OF SAFE MEDIOCRITY

The constant temptation of every organization is safe mediocrity. The first requirement of organizational health is a *high demand on performance*. Indeed, one of the major reasons for demanding that management be by objectives and that it focus on the objective requirements of the task is the need to have managers set high standards of performance for themselves.

This requires that performance be understood properly. Performance is not hitting the bull's-eye with every shot—that is a circus act that can be maintained only over a few minutes. Performance is rather the consistent ability to produce results over prolonged periods of time and in a variety of assignments. A performance record must include mistakes. It must include failures. It must reveal a person's limitations as well as strengths.

And there are as many different kinds of performance as there are different human beings. One person will consistently do well, rarely falling far below a respectable standard, but also rarely excel through brilliance or virtuosity. Another will perform only adequately under normal circumstances but will rise to the demands of a crisis or a major challenge and then perform like a true "star." Both are "performers." Both need to be recognized. But their performances will look quite different.

The one person to distrust, however, is the person who never makes a mistake, never commits a blunder, and never fails in what he tries to do. Either he is a phony, or he stays with the safe, the tried, and the trivial.

A management that does not define performance as a balance of success and failure over a period of time is a management that mistakes conformity for achievement, and absence of weaknesses for strengths. It is a management that discourages its organization. The better a person is, the more mistakes she will make—for the more new things she will try.

The person who consistently renders poor or mediocre performance should be removed from the job for his or her own good. People who find themselves in a job that exceeds their capacities are frustrated, harassed, anxiety-ridden people. One does not do people a service by leaving them in a job they are not equal to. Not to face up to failure in a job is cowardice rather than compassion.

One also owes it to the manager's subordinates not to tolerate poor performance in their boss. They have a right to be managed with competence, dedication, and achievement. Subordinates have a right to a boss who performs, for otherwise they themselves cannot perform.

One owes it, finally, to all the people in the organization not to put up with a manager who fails to perform. The entire organization is diminished by the manager or career professional who performs poorly or not at all. It is enriched by the one who performs superbly.

At first sight the Japanese seem to violate this rule. For few, if any, people are ever fired for nonperformance in the Japanese organization. Actually, the Japanese organization may be as demanding and even as competitive as any in the West. The poor or mediocre performer is not fired. He is quickly sidetracked and assigned to activities that are, in effect, "made work." And both he and the organization know it. Moreover, while everyone advances in pay and title according to seniority, there is a day of reckoning at or around age forty-five, when the very few who will become top management are chosen over the many others who will, ten years later, retire as section managers or department directors.

The only thing that is proven by a person's not performing in a given assignment is that management has made a mistake in giving him or her that assignment. It is a mistake that managers cannot avoid, no matter how carefully they work on the placement of people. "Failure" in such a case may mean only that a first-rate career knowledge professional has been miscast as a manager. It may mean that someone excellent at running an existing operation has been miscast as an innovator and entrepreneur. Or it may mean the opposite: that a person whose strength lies in doing new and different things has been miscast to head a continuing, well-established, and highly routinized operation.

Failure to perform on the part of an individual who has a record of proven performance is a signal to think hard about the person and the job. And sometimes, of course (see the discussion of the "widow-maker" job in chapter 23), it is the job rather than the person that is at fault.

George C. Marshall, chief of staff of the U.S. Army in World War II, was an uncompromising and exacting boss who refused to tolerate mediocrity, let alone failure. "I have a duty to the soldiers, their parents, and the country, to remove immediately any commander who does not satisfy the highest performance demands," Marshall said again and again. But he always asserted, "It was my mistake to have put this or that man in a command that was not the right command for him. It is therefore *my* job to think through where he belongs." Many of the men who emerged in World War II as highly successful commanders in the U.S. Army were once in the course of their careers removed by Marshall from an early assignment. But then Marshall thought through the mistake *he* had made—and tried to figure out where that man belonged. And this explains, in large measure, why the American army, which had gone into World War II without a single one of its future general officers yet in a command position, produced an outstanding group of leaders in a few short years.

"CONSCIENCE" DECISIONS

The toughest cases, but also the most important ones, are those of people who have given long and loyal service to the company but who have outlived their capacity to contribute.

There is, for instance, the bookkeeper who started when the company was in its infancy and grew with it until, at age fifty or so, she finds herself controller of a large company and totally out of her depth. The woman has not changed—the demands of the job have. She has given faithful service. And where loyalty has been received, loyalty is due. But still, she must not be allowed to remain as controller. Not only does her inability to perform endanger the company, her inadequacy demoralizes the entire management group and discredits management altogether.

What can be done with such a person? Many executives would "kick her upstairs." Yet this only buys trouble if you put a person into a bigger job for which she is even less competent. So she must be removed, but thirty years of service creates its obligations. So one must both get her out and treat her right. A creative solution is required. One option is to identify whatever strengths she has and either find a position in which she can be effective or provide substantial assistance to her to start a new career in another organization.

Such cases—fortunately they are not too numerous—challenge the conscience of an organization. To keep the controller in her job would be a betrayal of the enterprise and of all its people. But to fire a person who has given thirty years of faithful service is also betraying a trust. And to say, "We should have taken care of this twenty-five years ago," while true, is not much help.

The decision in such cases must be objective, that is, focused on the good of the company: the person must be removed from the job. Yet the decision is also a human decision that requires utmost consideration, true compassion, and an acceptance of obligations. That Henry Ford II could revive the moribund Ford Motor Company after World War II was in large measure the result of his understanding the crucial importance of these "conscience cases."

At that time, none of the nine management people in one key division were found to be competent to take on the new jobs created in the course of reorganization. Not one was appointed to these new jobs. Yet, for these nine men, jobs as technicians and experts were found within the organization. It would have been easy to fire them. Their incompetence as managers was undisputed. But they had also served loyally through very trying years. Henry Ford II took the line that no one should be allowed to hold a job without giving superior performance, but he also held that no one should be penalized for the mistakes of the previous management. The company owed its rapid revival largely to the strict observance of this rule.

The frequent excuse in a conscience case, "We can't move him; he has been here too long to be fired," is bad logic and rarely more than a weak-kneed alibi. It harms the performance of management people, their spirit, and their respect for the company.

But to fire such a manager is equally bad. It violates the organization's sense of justice and decency. It shakes its faith in the integrity of management. "There, but for the grace of God, go I" is what everybody will say—even though they would be quick to criticize if management left an incompetent in a position of importance. What is done with such a person will largely determine whether you have an organization or not.

A management that is concerned with the spirit of the organization therefore takes these cases exceedingly seriously. They are not too common, as a rule—or at least they should not be. But they have an impact on the spirit of the organization way beyond their numbers. How they are handled tells the organization both whether management takes itself and its job seriously, and whether it takes the human being seriously.

FOCUS ON OPPORTUNITY

An organization will have a high spirit of performance if it is consistently directed toward opportunity rather than toward problems. It will have the thrill of excitement, the sense of challenge, and the satisfaction of achievement if its energies are put where the results are, and that means on the opportunities.

Of course, problems cannot be neglected. But the problem-focused organization is an organization on the defensive. It is an organization that feels that it has performed well if things do not get worse.

A management that wants to create and maintain the spirit of achievement therefore stresses opportunity. But it will also demand that opportunities be converted into results.

A management that wants to make its organization focus on opportunity demands that opportunity be given pride of place in the objectives and goals of each manager and career professional. "What are the opportunities that, if realized, will have the greatest impact on performance and results of the company and of my unit?" should be the first topic to which managers and knowledge professionals address themselves in their performance and work plan.

Every product, for example, should be looked at about once a year or so to make sure the organization doesn't put its efforts and resources where there are no results. And there are at least six classes into which products fall:

1. Yesterday's breadwinners. These are the products we all love because we grew up with them. And now they are over the hump and going down fast, and all we can do by defending them is allow them to die a little more slowly. They ought to be deprived of all resources fast.

2. Today's breadwinners. These products are at or near their peaks, and now the job is to make sure we don't put more resources into them.

3. Tomorrow's breadwinners. This is where people should go and where promotion, sales, and technical efforts should go.

4. Specialties. These specialties can be numerous. Here the test is, Do we get paid well for them? Or are they defended by the sales manager on grounds that "we have to have them to have a full product line" and the controller says, "We have to have them because they absorb overhead"?

5. The sleeper product. This is the product that is doing so much better than anybody ever expected, but nobody pays attention to it; this is the product to run with.

6. The investment in managerial ego. The product that everybody loves; the product that everybody knows is the best quality; the product everybody knows is going to set the world on fire next year, but next year never comes. That is the product that bleeds a company to death, and yet it is the most difficult thing to face up to and get rid of, because everybody has got such an emotional investment in it

One has got to face up to a very simple, very brutal, very harsh rule—*one starves the problems and one feeds the opportunities.* And above all, one puts the resources into tomorrow, where the results are, and not into yesterday, where the memories are.

"PEOPLE" DECISIONS—THE CONTROL OF AN ORGANIZATION

An organization that wants to build a high spirit of performance recognizes that "people" decisions—on placement and pay, on promotion, demotion, and firing—are the true "control" of an organization. They, far more than the accountant's figures and reports, model and mold behavior. For the people decisions signal to every member of the organization what it is that management really wants, really values, really rewards.

The company that preaches, "Our first-line supervisors are expected to practice human relations" but that always promotes the supervisor who gets paperwork in on time, neatly done, will not get "human relations." Even the dumbest supervisor will learn very soon that what the company really wants is neat paperwork.

Indeed, an organization tends to overreact to the people decisions of management. What to top management may look like an innocuous compromise to remove an obstacle or to solve a political impasse may well be a clear signal to the organization that management wants one kind of behavior while preaching another.

Placement and promotion are the most crucial people decisions. They, above all, require careful thinking and clear policy and procedures with high standards of fairness and equity. They should never be made on the basis of opinions or on a person's potential. They should always be based on a factual record of performance against explicit goals and objectives.

But the best placement and promotion procedures do not by themselves ensure that these crucial decisions strengthen the spirit of the organization rather than impair it. For this, top management must build itself into the promotion process. Above all, it must make sure that it participates in the key decisions on promotion, the decisions that spell out to the organization what management's values and beliefs really are and at the same time determine—often irrevocably—the top management of tomorrow.

All top managements take an active role in the decisions on promotion to the jobs directly below or in the top-management group: promotion into the position of general manager of major divisions or into the position as the head of major functional areas, such as operations or marketing. But few top managements, especially in larger businesses, take much interest in the promotion decisions just below the top group, that is, into such jobs as head of market research, operations manager, or even marketing manager of a division. They leave these decisions to the top people in the respective functions or divisions. Yet these upper-middle-management jobs are truly *the* management to the organization. People further down, and especially the younger managers and career professionals, know very well that their own careers depend on these upper-middle people rather than on the big boss. And it is the decision on filling these upper-middle spots that, in effect, determines who, a few years hence, will be eligible for a top-management assignment.

Above all, these promotional decisions have great symbolic value. They are highly visible and signal to the entire organization, "This is what this company wants, rewards, and recognizes." For this reason, old and experienced organizations, such as the U.S. Army and the Catholic Church, focus their main concern on upper-middle-management promotions—in the army, on promotion to the rank of colonel, and in the Catholic Church, on selecting an auxiliary bishop.

INTEGRITY, THE TOUCHSTONE

The final proof of the sincerity and seriousness of an organization's management is uncompromising emphasis on integrity of character. This, above all, has to be symbolized in *management's people decisions*. For it is through character that leadership is exercised; it is character that sets the example and is imitated. Character is not something managers can acquire; if they do not bring it to the job, they will never have it. It is not something one can fool people about. A person's coworkers, especially the subordinates, know in a few weeks whether he or she has integrity or not. They may forgive a great deal: incompetence, ignorance, insecurity, or bad manners. But they will not forgive a lack of integrity. Nor will they forgive higher management for choosing such a person.

Integrity may be difficult to define, but what constitutes lack of integrity of such seriousness as to disqualify a person for a managerial position is not. Someone whose vision focuses on people's weaknesses rather than on their strengths should never be appointed to a managerial position. The manager who always knows exactly what people cannot do, but never sees anything they can do, will undermine the spirit of the organization. A manager should, of course, have a clear grasp of the limitations of subordinates, but should see these as limitations on what they can do, and as challenges to them to do better. A manager should be a realist; and no one is less realistic than the cynic.

A person should not be appointed if he or she is more interested in the question, "Who is right?" than in the question, "What is right?" To put personality above the requirements of the work is corruption and corrupts. To ask, "Who is right?" encourages one's subordinates to play it safe, if not to play politics.

Management should not appoint anyone who considers intelligence more important than integrity. This is immaturity—and usually incurable. It should never promote a person who has shown that he or she is afraid of strong subordinates. This is weakness. It should never put into a management job a person who does not set high standards for his own work. For that breeds contempt for the work and for management's competence.

A man might himself know too little, perform poorly, lack judgment and ability, and yet not do too much damage as a manager. But if he lacks in character and integrity—no matter how knowledgeable, how brilliant, how successful—he destroys. He destroys people, the most valuable resource of the enterprise. He destroys spirit. And he destroys performance.

This is particularly true of the people at the head of an enterprise. For the spirit of an organization is created from the top. If an organization is great in spirit, it is because the spirit of its top people is great. If it decays, it does so because the top rots; as the proverb has it, "Fish rot from the head down." No one should ever be appointed to a senior position unless top management is willing to have his or her character serve as the model for subordinates.

LEADERSHIP AND THE SPIRIT OF PERFORMANCE

This chapter has to this point talked of "practices." It has not talked of *leadership*. This was intentional. There is no substitute for leadership. But management cannot create leaders. It can only create the conditions under which potential leadership qualities become effective—or it can stifle potential leadership. The supply of leadership is much too uncertain for it to be depended on to create the spirit that the enterprise needs to be productive and to hold together.

Practices, though seemingly humdrum, can always be practiced, whatever a person's aptitudes, personality, or attitudes. Practices require no genius—only application. They are things to do rather than to talk about.

And the right practices should go a long way toward bringing out whatever potential for leadership there is in the management group. They should also lay the foundation for the right kind of leadership. For leadership is not magnetic personality—that can just as well be a glib tongue. It is not "making friends and influencing people"—that is flattery.

Leadership is lifting a person's vision to higher sights, the raising of a person's performance to a higher standard, the building of a personality beyond its normal limitations. Nothing better prepares the ground for such leadership than a spirit of management that confirms in the day-to-day practices of the organization strict principles of conduct and responsibility, high standards of performance, and respect for individuals and their work.

Yet, "leadership qualities" are all the rage just now!

LEADERSHIP "QUALITIES"?

"We'd want you to run a seminar for us on how one acquires charisma," the human-resources VP of a big bank said to me on the telephone—in dead earnest. Books, articles, and conferences on leadership and on the "qualities" of the leader abound. Every CEO, it seems, has to be made to look like a dashing Confederate cavalry general or a boardroom Elvis Presley.

Leadership, as we have just described, is something different from what is now touted under this label. It has little to do with "leadership qualities" and even less to do with "charisma." It is mundane, unromantic, and boring. Its essence *is performance*.

In the first place, leadership is not by itself good or desirable. Leadership is a *means*. Leadership *to what end is, thus, the crucial question*. History knows no more charismatic leaders than the twentieth century's triad of Stalin, Hitler, and Mao—misleaders who inflicted as much evil and suffering on humanity as have ever been recorded.

THE UNDOING OF LEADERS

Effective leadership doesn't depend on charisma. Dwight Eisenhower, George Marshall, and Harry Truman were singularly effective leaders, yet none possessed any more charisma than a dead mackerel. Nor did Konrad Adenauer, the chancellor who rebuilt West Germany after World War II. No less charismatic personality could be imagined than Abe Lincoln of Illinois, the raw-boned, uncouth backwoods man of 1860. And there was amazingly little charisma to the bitter, defeated, almost broken Winston Churchill of the interwar years; what mattered was that he turned out, in the end, to have been right.

Indeed, *charisma may become the undoing of leaders. It may make them inflexible, convinced of their own infallibility, unable to change.* This is what happened to Stalin, Hitler, and Mao, and it is a commonplace in the study of ancient history that only Alexander the Great's early death saved him from becoming an ineffectual failure.

Indeed, charisma does not, by itself, guarantee effectiveness as a leader. Nor are there any such things as "leadership qualities" or a "leadership personality." Franklin D. Roosevelt, Winston Churchill, George Marshall, Dwight Eisenhower, Bernard Montgomery, and Douglas MacArthur were all highly effective—and highly visible—leaders during World War II. No two of them shared any "personality traits" or any "qualities."

Leadership is work—something just stressed, and stressed again and again by the most effective leaders: Julius Caesar, for instance, or General MacArthur and Field Marshal Montgomery, or, to use an example from business, Alfred Sloan, the man who built and led General Motors from 1920 to 1955, and most recently Level 5 leaders in Jim Collins's *Good to Great.*

The foundation of effective leadership is first, *thinking through the organization's mission,* defining it and establishing it, clearly and visibly. The leader sets the goals, sets the priorities, and sets and maintains the standards. He makes compromises, of course; indeed, effective leaders are painfully aware that they are not in control of the universe. (Only misleaders—the Stalins, Hitlers, Maos—suffer from that delusion.) But before accepting a compromise, the effective leader has thought through what is right and desirable. The leader's *first task* is to be the trumpet that sounds a clear sound.

What distinguishes effective leaders from misleaders is their goals. Whether the compromise a leader makes with the constraints of reality—which may involve political, economic, financial, or people problems—is compatible with his mission and goals or leads away from them determines whether he is an effective leader. And whether he holds fast to a few basic standards (exemplifying them in his own conduct) or "standards" for him are what he can get away with determines whether the leader has followers or only hypocritical time-servers.

The second requirement is that the effective leader sees leadership as *responsibility rather than as rank and privilege*. Effective leaders are rarely "permissive." But when things go wrong—and they always do—they do not blame others. If Winston Churchill is an example of leadership through clearly defining mission and goals, General George C. Marshall is an example of leadership through responsibility. Harry Truman's folksy "The buck stops here" is still as good a definition as any.

But precisely because an effective leader knows that she, and no one else, is ultimately responsible, she is not afraid of strength in associates and subordinates. Misleaders are; they always go in for purges. But an effective leader wants strong associates; she encourages them, pushes them, indeed glories in them. Because she holds herself ultimately responsible for the mistakes of her associates and subordinates, she also sees the triumphs of her associates and subordinates as her triumphs, rather than as threats. A leader may be personally vain—as General MacArthur was to an almost pathological degree. Or he may be personally humble—both Lincoln and Truman were so almost to the point of having inferiority complexes. But all three wanted able, independent, self-assured people around them; they encouraged their associates and subordinates, praising and promoting them. So did a very different person: Ike Eisenhower, when supreme commander in Europe.

An effective leader knows, of course, that there is a risk in this: able people tend to be ambitious. But he realizes that it is a much smaller risk than being served by mediocrity would be. He also knows that the gravest indictment of a leader is for the organization to collapse as soon as he leaves or dies, as happened in Russia the moment Stalin died and as happens all too often in companies. An effective leader knows that the ultimate task of leadership is to *create human energies and human vision*.

EARNING TRUST IS A MUST

The final requirement of effective leadership is to *earn trust*. Otherwise there won't be any followers—and the only definition of a leader is someone who has followers. To trust a leader, it is not necessary to like him. Nor is it necessary to agree with him. Trust is the conviction that the leader means what he says. It is a belief in integrity. A leader's actions and a leader's professed beliefs must be congruent, or at least compatible. Effective leadership—and again this is very old wisdom—is not based on being clever; it is based primarily on being consistent.

After I had said these things on the telephone to the bank's human-resources VP, there was a long silence. Finally she said, "But that's no different at all from what we have known for years are the requirements for being an effective manager."

Precisely!

SUMMARY

The purpose of organization is to enable ordinary human beings to do extraordinary things. The test of an organization's leadership is, therefore, the spirit of performance. This requires specific *practices* rather than preachment or charisma. It requires, above all, the realization that integrity is the one absolute requirement of managers and leaders.

Part VII

Managerial Skills

Managing is specific work. As such, it requires specific skills. Among them are the abilities of

- effective decision making

- making successful people-decisions

- communicating within and without the organization

- properly using controls and measurements

- skill in budgeting and planning

- skill in using modern tools and concepts of information technology

No manager is likely to master all these skills. But every manager needs to understand what they are, what they can do for him or her, and what, in turn, they require of him or her.

28

The Elements of Effective Decision Making

Good decision makers don't make *many* decisions. They make decisions that *make a difference.* And they know when a decision is necessary. Then they don't procrastinate. Good decision makers know that the most important, and most difficult, part of decision making is not making the decision. That's often quite easy. The most difficult and most important part is to make sure that the decision is about the right problem. Few things can do as much damage as right decisions to wrong problems.

Good decision makers know how to define the problem. They ask, "What does the decision have to do to be appropriate to the problem?" Good decision makers don't even think about what is acceptable to whom and what compromises have to be made until they have thought through what the right decision is. But good decision makers know that, in all likelihood, they will have to make compromises in the end. And they know the difference between the right compromise and the wrong compromise.

Good decision makers know that they haven't finished making a decision until they build its implementation and effectiveness into it. Until then it's not a decision— it's only a good idea. They also know that a decision is a commitment to action. And almost always it's action to be taken by other people. Hence, as most good decision makers have learned the hard way, the actions required must fit the capacities, the understanding, the knowledge, the values, and the language of the people who will have to do the action.

Above all, good decision makers know that decision making has its own process and its own clearly defined elements and steps. Every decision is risky: it is a commitment of present resources to an uncertain and unknown future. Ignore a single element in the process and the decision will tumble down like a badly built wall in an earthquake. But if the process is faithfully observed and if the necessary steps are taken, the risk will be minimized and the decision will have a good chance of turning out to be successful.

Let's get into the elements of decision making.

THE ELEMENTS OF DECISION MAKING

You minimize risk by following seven elements of effective decision making, which are

- Determine whether a decision is necessary.

- Classify the problem.

- Define the problem.

- Decide on what is right.

- Get others to buy the decision.

- Build action into the decision.

- Test the decision against actual results.

DETERMINE WHETHER A DECISION IS NECESSARY

Unnecessary decisions not only waste time and resources, but they also threaten to make all decisions ineffectual. When decision makers fail to distinguish between necessary and unnecessary decisions, their organization can quickly become snowed under and turn cynical about all decisions. Even the most necessary and most important ones will soon be seen as mere busyness.

And few things so damage an organization's ability to make changes or to take effective action as a lot of unnecessary decisions. They lead to the organization's sitting on its hands no matter what the decision. Therefore, it is important that you be able to distinguish between necessary and unnecessary decisions. Surgeons provide perhaps the best example of effective decision making, as they have had to make risk-taking decisions on a daily basis for thousands of years now. Since there is no such thing as risk-free surgery, unnecessary operations must be avoided. The rules surgeons use to make their determinations are very old; they go back to the Father of Medicine, the Greek Hippocrates, 2,400 years ago.

The Rules Used by Surgeons to Make Decisions

Rule one: In a condition that is likely to cure itself or to stabilize itself without risk or danger or great pain to the patient, you put it on watch and check regularly. But you don't cut. To do surgery in such a condition is an unnecessary decision.

Rule two: If the condition is degenerative or life threatening and there is something you can do, you do it—fast and radically. It is a necessary decision, despite the risk.

Rule three: The condition that falls between Rule One and Rule Two is no doubt the largest single category: the condition that is not degenerative and not life threatening but still not self-correcting and quite serious. This is where the surgeon has to weigh *opportunity* against *risk*. It's also where he or she has to make a decision. And it is this decision that distinguishes the first-rate surgeon from the also-ran.

These old rules leave out one important case where a decision has to be made: *the recurring crisis*. If a crisis happens—say a cash crunch, or an inventory buildup, or an accident in a particular location or activity—the first time it happens, one fixes it. But if it happens again, then one finds out the cause and fixes it so that the crisis never happens again.

Quite often, the solution to the crisis is so simple that everybody afterward says, "Why didn't we think of this ourselves?"

All of us, for instance, take for granted that our address is printed on our bank checks. But actually addresses were not printed there until well after World War II. Before the war, only a minority of Americans had bank checking accounts; and after the war, suddenly everybody had one.

And then every bank had an enormous number of accounts of people with the same or very similar names. And, pronto, these accounts got mixed up. Banks spent loads of money; they hired large numbers of people at enormous expense to compare the account number on a check with the account number on a monthly statement. And still, names and accounts and checks got more and more tangled up, to the understandable annoyance of depositors.

And then someone had the simple but bright idea to have addresses on the checks. And all that's needed is to compare the address on the check with the address on the monthly statement. And the problem disappeared almost overnight.

Now let's see how to classify the problem.

CLASSIFY THE PROBLEM

Executives face four basic types of problems:

1. Generic events that are common within the organization and throughout the industry

2. Generic events that are unique for the organization but uncommon throughout the industry

3. Truly unique events

4. Events that appear to be unique but are really the first appearance of a new generic problem

All but the truly unique event require a generic solution. Generic problems can be answered with standard rules and practices. Once the right principle has been developed, all manifestations of the same generic event can be handled by applying the standard principle. All the executive must do is adapt the principle to the concrete circumstances of the specific problem.

Unique events, however, require unique solutions and must be treated individually. The executive cannot develop rules for unforeseen exceptional events.

Truly unique events are quite rare; someone else has already solved virtually every problem an organization faces. Thus the effective decision maker should carefully examine the problem to determine whether it is generic or truly unique. Applying a standard rule or principle can solve most types of problem.

DEFINE THE PROBLEM

The next key element is defining the problem. This has never occurred to most people. Aren't problems obvious?

This may be the most important element in making effective decisions—and the one managers pay the least attention to. They try to cure the symptom rather than the disease, to use a medical analogy.

One can almost take it for granted that what a problem appears to be is not what it really is. And yet—it cannot be said too often—nothing does as much damage as the right answer to the wrong problem. A wrong answer to the right problem can, as a rule, be repaired and salvaged. You know soon enough when events don't follow your expectations, and then you know that it was not the right answer.

But the right answer to the wrong problem, that's very difficult to fix—if only because it's so difficult to diagnose. What effective decision makers have learned is to start out with the assumption that the way the problem looks, in all likelihood, is not what it really is. And then they work until they understand the right problem.

Precisely this principle underlies the insistence of math teachers that students spend time setting up their equations correctly, because if they make mistakes in arithmetic, they can find them and correct them. It's very easy to find a mistake in the manipulation and to correct it if the equation is right. But if the equation is wrong and a student does the arithmetic right, it is much more difficult to make necessary adjustments and to arrive at the right answer. Likewise, if you correctly define the problem and you get the wrong, unexpected result, you can correct the outcome, especially if you build in feedback so that you quickly find out whether you are getting the expected result. It is much more difficult to attain a desired result if one finds the right answer to the wrong problem and then tries to correct it by using a different alternative.

How do effective decision makers determine what the right problem is? Effective decision makers ask

- "What is this all about?"

- "What is pertinent here?"

- "What is key to this situation?"

Questions such as these are not new, yet they are of critical importance in defining the problem. The problem must be considered from all angles to ensure that the right problem is being tackled.

Here is an example from practice:

The management of one of America's largest manufacturing companies prided itself on its safety record. The company had the lowest number of accidents per 1,000 employees of any company in its industry and one of the very lowest of any manufacturing plant in the world. Yet its labor union constantly berated it for its horrendous accident rate, and so did the Occupational Safety and Health Administration (OSHA).

The company thought this was a public-relations problem and spent large sums of money advertising its near-perfect safety record. And yet the union attacks continued. And every public-opinion survey showed that the American people thought the company was a truly unsafe place to work and felt that the company was callous about its workers' safety.

A good statistician would recognize this as "typical of problems caused by false aggregation."

By aggregating all accidents and showing them as accidents per 1,000 workers, they simply hid the places where there was a high accident rate. And true enough, once the company segregated its accidents and reported them in a number of categories—places that had *no* accidents at all, places that had fewer than the average number, places that matched the average, places that had more than the average—it found, almost immediately, that there were a very small number of places, about 3 percent of all units, that had above-average accident rates. And an even smaller number of places had very high accident rates. And these typically were places that would not be considered to have accident dangers and had no dangerous machinery; with the result that no one in safety and accident-prevention ever paid attention to them.

But they were the places the union got its complaints from, the places whose accidents got into the papers and into OSHA reports. It took very little time and almost no money to fix them, and both union complaints and OSHA complaints disappeared. But not until the company realized that the problem was not accidents—the problem was accident reports—and then the real problem could be tackled.

The one way to make sure that the problem is correctly defined is to check it against the observable facts. Until the problem definition explains and encompasses all observable facts, the definition is either still incomplete or, more likely, the wrong definition.

But once the problem has been correctly defined, the decision itself is usually pretty easy. In fact, effective decision makers use very few of the very complex decision models and decision trees. Once the problem has been specified, effective decision makers must next decide what the right decision is.

DECIDE ON WHAT IS RIGHT

When beginning to form the decision, the decision maker must start out with what is right. Most of us, and especially those who work in an organization, tend to start out by asking questions like

- "What is acceptable to the boss?"

- "I know that the financial people won't like that, but how I can make the decision palatable to them?"

- "I know that contradicts what all of us were brought up to believe. How can we start small and slow so as not to shock too many people?"

Every effective decision maker is different, but every one of them can make every conceivable compromise, and compromises are necessary in the end. But there are *right compromises* and *wrong compromises;* each is captured by an old saying. The right compromise is expressed by the proverb "Half a loaf is better than no bread at all." Half a loaf still quenches hunger for one day, and it still enables a person to work or a soldier to fight for one day, even though it is only half of what an adult needs for a day's nutrition. The wrong compromise comes from the biblical story of the Judgment of Solomon: "Half a baby is worse than no baby at all." Half a baby is a corpse and not half a growing and living child.

The effective decision maker thinks through—and well in advance—what compromises are still "half a loaf" and acceptable, and what compromises are "half a baby" and worse than no decision at all.

The way to think through what is the right compromise is to

1. Go back to the definition of the problem and write down the specifications for an effective decision.

2. Ask, "What does the decision have to be able to do to satisfy the definition of the problem?"

- A solution that does this but not perfectly is a right compromise.

- A solution that does not satisfy the problem's definition is the wrong compromise and is likely to do harm. Don't compromise on "what is right" until you must.

3. Think through all the compromises so that you know what you can accept as a right compromise and what you have to fight as the wrong compromise. But, don't tell people the compromises ahead of time. Tell them only what the right decision is. That's the rule for all negotiations.

- People often accept what you were absolutely sure they would never accept, and this will surprise you often.

- Secondly, as in every negotiation, there is tit-for-tat. You make a concession; the other side makes a concession. If you start by making the concession, you have simply lost bargaining position, and quite unnecessarily so. Also, the people who oppose this or that part of the decision are far more likely to accept it and, indeed, even to support it if they can say, "Dick and Mary didn't accept this, but at least they made this concession [or changed that] because we persuaded them."

GET OTHERS TO BUY THE DECISION

Unless the organization has "bought" the decision, it will remain ineffectual; it will remain a good intention. And for a decision to be effective, being bought has to be built into it from the start of the decision-making process. If you wait until you have made the decision and then start to "sell" it, it's unlikely to ever become effective. Here are two examples of effective "buy in" processes:

1. Japanese Decision-Making Process

This is one lesson to learn from Japanese management. As soon as the decision-making process starts, and long before the final decision is made, Japanese management sells the decision. Japanese decisions *are not* being made by "consensus"; that's a mistranslation of the Japanese term. The correct translation would be something like "common understanding."

Everyone who is likely to be affected by a decision—say, to go into a joint venture with a Western company or to acquire a minority stake in a potential U.S.

distributor—is asked to write down how such a decision would affect his work, job, and unit. He is expressly forbidden to have an opinion or to recommend or to object to the possible move. But he is expected to think it through. Top management, in turn, then knows where each of these people stands. Then top management makes the decision from the top down.

There isn't much of "participatory management" in Japanese organizations. But everyone who will be affected by the decision knows what it is all about—whether he likes it or not—and is prepared for it. There is no need to sell it—it's been sold.

2. Franklin Roosevelt's Decision Process

Here is an even better illustration of effective decision making. It is how Franklin D. Roosevelt made his decisions effective.

Whenever Roosevelt tackled a problem, he would ask three, sometimes four, of his cabinet members each to think through the problem and come to him individually with a recommended decision. In this way, he first made sure that the people who would have to carry out the decision, this or that cabinet member, would have thought it through. He also learned which of these cabinet members, and they were independent and self-confident people, would be most in tune with the decision and would therefore be most likely to put it into practice.

And, finally, he got dissent. He got three or four pretty bright and experienced people to think through the decision. Each could be expected to come up with a different definition of the problem. Each had his and her own ideology, his and her own prejudices, his and her own constituents, and his and her own interests. That meant that the same problem was seen, studied, and analyzed from different dimensions.

And then he made his decision from the top down.

FDR's method did not make for a harmonious cabinet, but FDR probably didn't want one anyhow. But it made for superb decisions and, above all, for highly effective ones. For unless one has considered alternatives, one has a closed mind. Executive decisions are not made well by acclamation. They are made well only if they are based on the clash of conflicting views, the dialogue between different points of view, the choice between different judgments. The first rule in decision making is that one does not make a decision unless there is disagreement.

And now we come to the penultimate step—moving from decision to action.

BUILD ACTION INTO THE DECISION

A decision is a commitment to action. Until the right thing happens, there has been no decision. And one thing can be taken for granted: the people who have to take the action are rarely the people who have made the decision.

Converting a Decision to Action

No decision has, in fact, been made until carrying it out has become somebody's work assignment and responsibility—and with a deadline. Until then, it's still only a hope.

And, unfortunately, far too many decisions remain just that—a hope. Good people work for two years to develop a new policy. It's unveiled with great fanfare in a big meeting with overhead projectors, PowerPoint slides, spreadsheets, and what have you. The big boss appears and blesses it. "It has my full support," he solemnly says. Everybody gets a policy memorandum, which he or she duly files, in the bottom drawer. And that's the last we hear about it.

But the effective decision doesn't need all this drama. Instead, it is made into action. A decision will not become effective unless needed actions have been built into it from the start.

Converting a decision into action requires answering several questions:

- Who has to know of this decision?

- What action has to be taken?

- Who is to take it?

- What does the action have to be so that the people who have to do it can do it?

The action must be appropriate to the capacities of the people who have to carry it out. This is especially important if people have to change their behavior, habits, or attitudes for the decision to become effective. If this is the case, the decision maker must make sure that the measurements, standards for accomplishment, and incentives are changed as well.

Let's look at two effective decisions, one that was lost during the implementation stage and one that was implemented very successfully.

A very large company, still the world's leader in its industry, organized a high-level team that was going to put quantitative methods into the company. It was a wonderful team, some top-level engineers, some first-rate mathematicians, and some top-flight manufacturing people.

The team's first assignment was to rationalize production in the company's largest division, one that made small-horsepower motors and sold a large volume of them every year. It had been doing so for nearly sixty years and every customer, needless to say, had always wanted a slightly different design. As a result, the division had about 8,500 model numbers, and production was in total chaos.

In fact, despite the enormous volume and the very good prices the division was able to charge, the division barely broke even because the chaos in design raised manufacturing costs.

The team then worked for approximately eighteen months and succeeded in getting these 8,500 possible motor specs reduced to some ninety or so production models. The division president and his manufacturing vice president were ecstatic. But, of course, these small motors went into any number of appliances and machines around the world. And no customer would scrap a $100,000 machine just because the customer couldn't get a replacement for a $1,000 motor the company wasn't going to make any longer.

The company offered all customers who had bought motors within the last fifteen years the option to reorder within the next two years the motors they had bought, after which the company would discontinue production. In its entire sixty-year history the division had never had anything like the business it had during the next two years.

But when the two years were up and those 8,500 models were discontinued, there were enough parts for every one of them in the company's inventory for another five years of full normal production. They had to be written off at enormous expense and loss. The reason: the purchasing clerks had kept on ordering spare parts for the old models in the way they had always ordered them—they had continued to order spare parts against new incoming orders.

The team thought they had taken care of that problem. They had brought the purchasing clerks into the meetings in which they explained the decision. Management had issued any number of policy letters. But nobody had even thought of talking to the purchasing clerks about actions they would have to take as a result of the decision.

But at least the team learned from the fiasco. Their next assignment in the same company was with a then-small division that made medical and analytical instruments. These instruments required a good deal of service, and the team's assignment was both to redesign the instruments so that they were easy to service and to work out a methodology for servicing them. All the service people in the field were engineers.

But then someone on the team said, "What about the end-users? They are the actual service people. The company's service people come into play only when the users themselves cannot service the product." And so the team went out and looked at the users: lab assistants, maintenance supervisors, hospital nurses—not one engineer or mathematician in the lot.

They got together what now would be called focus groups, and they drafted the instructions. And suddenly, within three months, calls for the company's service people went down by something like 60 percent, because the users could now fix most service problems. That division is now a very big business and the world leader in its industry, despite powerful competition, including from a very large German company and an equally large Japanese company.

The products of these competitors are sometimes better than those of the company and they never cost more. Yet the customers still buy from the organization and the organization still has groups of users who write the instructions whenever a product is changed or a new product is introduced.

TEST THE DECISION AGAINST ACTUAL RESULTS

The results of an important decision are usually in the future, and often quite a few years in the future. Hence monitoring and reporting have to be built in to the decision to provide continuous testing of expectations against actual events.

To this end, effective decision makers build detailed organized feedback into their decisions, including reports, charts, figures, and studies. Yet, far too many decisions fail despite all of this feedback. This is because even the best-organized formal feedback is only an abstraction; while it can provide some useful information, it cannot present the complete picture of actual events.

Effective decision makers know this and follow a rule, which the military developed long ago. The commander who makes a decision does not rely on reports to see how it is being carried out. Instead, the commander goes out and looks for himself or herself.

Failure to go out and look at actual results is the leading reason for persisting in a course of action long after it has ceased to be appropriate or even rational. This is because without actual firsthand knowledge of results, the decision maker will become increasingly divorced from reality.

Reports are only abstractions. While they often provide useful information, it is impossible to capture the complete story in written feedback.

In summary, the effective decision maker follows seven steps to minimize the risks inherent in every decision. These steps are

- Determine whether a decision is necessary.

- Classify the problem.

- Define the problem.

- Decide on what is right.

- Get others to buy the decision.

- Build action into the decision.

- Test the decision against actual results.

BUILDING CONTINUOUS LEARNING INTO EXECUTIVE DECISIONS

In no area is it more important than in decision making to build continuous learning into the executive's work. And the way to do this is to feed back from results of the decision to the expectations for the decision when it was being made.

Whenever an executive makes an important decision—whether on capital appropriation; or on a strategic change, an innovation, or a redesign of a product or service; or on entry into a new market; or on people—he or she puts down in writing what results are expected and when. And then the executive, nine months or a year later, begins to feed back from the actual results to the expected ones, and keeps on doing this as long as the decision is in force. So in an acquisition, for example, an executive compares the actual results to the expected ones for the two to five years it takes fully to integrate an acquisition.

It's amazing how much executives learn by doing this, and how fast. What amazes executives the most, however, is what they learn. For example, some executives learn their greatest weakness in making important decisions is simply impatience. They expect results to happen much faster than they do. And as a result, they are prone to consider a decision a failure and to start fiddling with it when, in fact, it was doing fine and only needed more time. Their lesson disciplines them to give the decision far more time than they initially think reasonable. And their batting average in decision making improves.

On the other had, one brilliant and highly successful executive, found out the opposite about himself. He tends to be much too patient and to wait too long. A decision is very much like a diagnosis in medicine. And physicians have been taught since Hippocrates in Greece, 2,400 years ago, to write down what course they expect a patient's condition to take as a result of the treatment the physician prescribes, that is, as a result of the physician's decision. And that, as every experienced physician will tell you, is what makes even moderately endowed doctors into competent practitioners within a few years. It also makes even moderately endowed managers into competent decision makers.

SUMMARY

Decision making is only one of the tasks of a manager. It usually takes but a small fraction of his or her time. But to make the important decisions is the *specific managerial* task. Only a manager makes such decisions. An *effective* manager makes these decisions in a systematic process with clearly defined elements and in a distinct sequence of steps. Indeed, to be expected (by virtue of position or knowledge) to make decisions that have significant and positive impact on the entire organization, its performance, and its results characterizes the work of an effective manager.

Decision making is not a mechanical job. It is risk taking and a challenge to judgment. The "right answer" (which usually cannot be found anyway) is not central. Central is understanding the problem. Decision making is not an intellectual exercise. It mobilizes the vision, energies, and resources of the organization for effective action. At the end, it is an exercise in *courage* and *responsibility*.

29

How to Make
People Decisions

There are no more important decisions within an organization than people decisions: staffing a job, placing people into jobs and into assignments, promoting people, letting them go, and so on.

No matter how carefully organizations *hire people,* they won't perform if put into the jobs that are the wrong ones for them. No matter how brilliant and clever top-management decisions are regarding a company's business or its strategy, its products, or its services, they will not produce results *if the company's people decisions do not work out.*

Alfred Sloan, the man who built GM into the world's largest and most profitable manufacturing enterprise, once said to me, "If the assistant plant manager of a minor division doesn't perform, all our clever top-management decisions won't produce results."

That's obvious, everybody will say, yet the batting average in most organizations—and the batting average of most managers making people decisions—is just plain *dismal.* Results of people decisions—whether in a business, large or small; in a non-profit; in a government agency—fall into three categories:

1. Those that actually work out

2. Those that are outright failures

3. Those that are *non-failures and non-successes*

Category three is like a nagging backache. You don't die of it, but it drags down the entire organization's performance capacity, it is a burden on all the other people who have to support the "almost-performer," and it demoralizes the entire organization. Unfortunately these non-failures and non-successes are a significant portion of the results of the people decisions in an organization.

It is sheer nonsense to explain away that dismal record with such slogans as "Everybody reaches the level of his or her incompetence." That's a copout. In no other area would we tolerate a record as poor as that of most organizations and most managers in making people decisions. And by the way, the worst record is that of people who pride themselves on being "good judges of people."

This horrible record is totally unnecessary. There is no excuse for it at all. We know how to make people decisions with an overwhelming probability of success. We have loads of examples of managers—in business, in nonbusiness, in government—whose people decisions are perfect or nearly so. It isn't even terribly difficult.

To start with, it just means taking people decisions seriously. And then it requires a few fairly simple and, indeed, practically obvious steps. It requires observing a few equally clear ground rules. There is probably no other area in business and in the work of a manager where performance and success can be raised faster than learning how to make people decisions so that they are successful practically every time.

In this chapter we explain

- the *five decision steps* in making people decisions

- the *five ground rules* in making people decisions

- how to raise your *batting average* in making successful people decisions

Before we begin with the five decision steps, let's look at two examples of successful people decisions. The first successful example was how the United States Army achieved success in making people decisions during World War II; and the second example, how Alfred P. Sloan, Jr., built General Motors into what was the world's largest manufacturing company and, for fifty years, also its most profitable one.

When the United States entered World War II, in 1941, virtually every single one of its senior officers was beyond retirement age and no longer fit for command. Yet when the war was over, four years later, its army had the world's largest ever group of competent and successful general officers, six or seven hundred of them, and there wasn't a single dud among them.

Yet only one of them, Douglas MacArthur, had had any previous experience commanding troops in combat. All the others had only been junior officers until the war broke out. The army was able to achieve such a major turnaround in its commanding officer corps because General George C. Marshall, the army chief of staff and himself already beyond retirement age, picked every single one of the new commanders himself.

MAKING PEOPLE DECISIONS

In making these people decisions, Marshall followed *five simple decision steps*.

The Five Decision Steps

First, Marshall carefully thought through the assignment. Job descriptions may last a long time, but job assignments change all the time, often unpredictably. The job description for a general commanding a division has not changed since the time of Napoleon. But the assignment may be to train a division of raw recruits or it may be to command a division in combat.

Similarly, the job description for Catholic bishops has stayed virtually the same since the thirteenth century; yet the typical bishop's job assignment changes along with the changing needs of his churches and parishioners. *Different assignments require different types of people.* Thinking through the assignment allows you to match the needs of a specific assignment to the strengths of the right people.

Second, Marshall always looked at several qualified people. Formal qualifications—such as those listed in a résumé, in a personnel file, on a job posting, or in a newspaper ad—are no more than a starting point. Their absence disqualifies a candidate. However, the most important qualification is that the person and the assignment fit each other. To find the best fit, you must consider at least three to five candidates.

Third, Marshall studied the performance records of all three to five candidates to find what each did well. He looked for the candidate's strengths. The things a person cannot do are of little importance; instead, you must concentrate on the things they can do and determine whether they are the right strengths for this particular assignment.

Weaknesses are only limitations, and like the absence of formal qualifications, they can rule a candidate out. But performance can be built only on strengths. What matters most is the ability to do the assignment.

Fourth, Marshall discussed the candidates with others who had worked with them. One person's judgment is not enough. By asking for additional opinions, you can learn about strengths that impressed others yet were not noticed by you. But you also are likely to discover weaknesses and limitations you haven't noticed. The best information often comes through informal discussions with a candidate's former bosses and colleagues.

This was the approach used by General Marshall when evaluating candidates for command posts. If he found out that a soldier was the best one at the specific task that needed to be filled, he got the job.

And fifth, once the decision was made, Marshall made sure the appointee understood the assignment. Perhaps the best way to do this is to ask the new person to carefully think over what they have to do to be a success, and then, ninety days or so into the job, have him or her commit it to writing.

Although this is the last step in making people decisions, it may be the most important. If you fail to accept this responsibility of making sure that the appointee understands his or her new job, do not blame the new person if he or she ultimately fails. Blame yourself, for you have failed to do your duty as a manager.

Like General Marshall, Alfred P. Sloan, Jr., achieved a near perfect record in making people decisions over his thirty-year tenure as chairman and CEO of General Motors.

In a career that spanned from 1916 to 1956, Alfred Sloan helped make General Motors the world's largest and most profitable business by carefully defining each job assignment and handpicking each manager. He knew that people decisions were the most important decisions a manager makes and was willing to spend whatever time and effort necessary to find the right fit. He followed, in other words, exactly the same decision process General Marshall followed during World War II.

For example, at a meeting of General Motors' Executive Committee, the entire three hours was taken up by discussing the appointment of a fairly low-level manager, the assistant manufacturing manager of one of the smaller appliance divisions. After the meeting, Sloan was asked by a participant, "How can you justify spending three hours of the time of a dozen important and busy people on such a low-level people decision?"

"The company pays me a very good salary," said Sloan, "and it pays that salary to me to make the important decisions. And what decision could be more important than how to fill a low-level management job? If that assistant manufacturing manager turns out to be incompetent, then it doesn't matter that we at the top are brilliant and clever. Results are achieved at *his* level and not at ours. And, by the way, if he turns out to be incompetent, it will take a great deal more than three hours to undo our mistake."

THE FIVE GROUND RULES

Although General Marshall and Alfred Sloan approached perfection, there is no such thing as a perfect record in making people decisions. Yet, managers who take their people decisions seriously and work hard at getting them right can come close to perfection.

A successful manager also follows *the five ground rules* for making people decisions. First, the manager must *accept responsibility* for any placement that fails. To blame the nonperformer is a cop-out. The manager made a mistake in selecting that particular person. Second, the manager has the responsibility to remove people who do not perform. There is an old military saying, "The soldier has a right to competent command." The incompetent or poor performer, when left in his or her job, penalizes all others and demoralizes the entire organization. And it is also no favor to nonperformers to be allowed to stay in a job they are not right for. They know that they are not performing.

Third, just because a person doesn't perform in the job he or she was put in doesn't mean that that person is a bad worker whom the company should let go. It only means that he or she is in the wrong job.

What, then, is the right job for them? Of the people who get a second chance in a job that fits their strengths—the job they should have been put into in the first place—a very high percentage perform well.

Few managers believe that. So, here are some examples.

CARE

In each country in which CARE (Cooperative for American Relief Everywhere) works, it has a country representative—usually a young man or woman only a couple of years out of college. They are carefully trained and prepared, and yet they are on their own in that foreign country—say, Cambodia or Kenya—and so the failure rate was very high.

For many years, when they came across a nonperformer, CARE brought him or her back home, said "thank you," and then let him or her go. But they simply didn't get enough new people to fill all the country slots. And so, with tremendous misgivings and with a great deal of opposition from within the organization, *CARE put some of these first-rate failures into a second job as a country representative.* And to everybody's tremendous surprise, the great majority of these people succeeded—indeed, quite a few became star performers.

The success rate of the second chance is amazingly high, but one caveat: only one second chance. The person who does not perform twice in a row better go to work for your competition!

Now let's continue with the fourth ground rule. *The manager must try to make the right people decisions for every position.* An organization can perform only to the capacity of its individual workers; thus people decisions must be right. There are dead-end jobs. But there are no unimportant jobs.

And fifth, *newcomers are best put into an established position* where the expectations are known and help is available. New major assignments should mainly go to people whose behaviors and habits are well known and who have already earned trust and credibility. The common practice of hiring somebody from the outside to fill a new job is much too risky. It has an extraordinarily high failure rate.

When placements fail in their new positions, successful managers follow the ground rules for making people decisions. This means that *they accept responsibility for the people decision, remove the nonperformers immediately, and place them in jobs that better match their strengths.*

THE HIGH-RISK PEOPLE DECISIONS

The five decision steps and the five ground rules should guarantee a successful people decision in most cases. But there are some high-risk decisions in which even strict adherence to the rules may not guarantee success, though it will always minimize the risk of failure.

First, *picking managers to head a professional organization* is often a high-risk venture. Professionals such as engineers do not readily accept as their boss someone whose credentials in the field they do not respect. Yet a successful engineer does not necessarily make a successful manager of engineers.

Second, *promoting any high-performing operating person to a staff job where they no longer apply the day-to-day skills that helped make them become a success* is also a high-risk decision. And so is *promoting a high-performing staff person into an operating job.*

There is no reliable way to test or predict whether a person successful in one area can make a successful transition to a different environment. This can be learned only by experience. If such a move does not work out, you must accept that it was a mistake and remove the person immediately.

Return the worker to his or her previous position if it is still available; otherwise place him or her in a role similar to the old one in which he or she was successful. Just because certain people don't work out in challenging new positions doesn't mean that they have to be removed from the organization. If they were productive in their previous positions, they will become productive once again and add to the organization's overall performance.

Most people would call this a "demotion." *It is a demotion.* But contrary to popular myth, a demotion is not only possible; the person very often welcomes it. That person knows perfectly well that he or she isn't performing. Yet few are willing to ask to be relieved. They feel that they have to try to do what they, by now, know perfectly well they can't do.

At first, of course, they feel very bitter. But a few weeks later and he may say, "Thank God, I am back in a job I can do and do well. I sleep again, and my wife says she has a husband again."

However, the smart thing is to build into the high-risk decision right from the start the *exit,* that is, the option to step back into the old job should the new one not work out. This amounts to "risk sharing." One says to the person who moves into such a risky job—say, the top-flight biologist who is asked to become a research manager or the tax specialist asked to become accounting manager, "I am sure you'll succeed and I am sure you will also enjoy the new job. But if it doesn't work out, after six months or a year, you are welcome back in your old job. We can always use a first-rate biologist [or a first-rate tax person]." It gives the new appointee added self-confidence, and with it improves his or her chance of success.

Other than the decision makers *not* following the decision-making steps and the ground rules, the most common cause of failure is also one we already talked about: the new appointee does in the new job what he or she thinks made them successful in the old job. The star salesperson made regional sales manager keeps on selling, the financial manager keeps on accounting, and so on.

After sixty to ninety days into a new assignment, everyone needs to sit down and ask, "What do I have to do now to be successful in this new assignment?" And there is one thing that's predictable: *whatever you did that made you successful in the old assignment is the wrong thing to do to be successful in the new one.*

THE WIDOW-MAKER POSITION

There is also another type of people decision that can be guaranteed to fail. This may be referred to as "the widow maker." This was discussed briefly in chapter 23.

In the business world, a widow maker is a job that defeats two competent people in a row. It will almost certainly defeat a third one, no matter how competent. The only thing to do is to abolish the widow-maker position and restructure the work. Widow makers typically appear when an organization experiences rapid growth or rapid change.

Here is a classic example:

It occurred in the late 1960s and early 1970s when a number of the large New York commercial banks established international branches. Until then, even the biggest American bank had been purely domestic. Each had an international vice president whose job it was to provide routine services to the bank's domestic clients, such as letters of credit or buying foreign currency. Everything else that wasn't domestic was referred to correspondence banks abroad.

Suddenly, almost overnight, the New York banks—but also the big banks in Chicago and San Francisco—developed truly international business and pushed it aggressively. And then the traditional international vice president's job became a widow maker.

When asked about the phenomenon, one of New York's top financial lawyers was asked for an explanation. He said in an interview, "You are talking of widow-makers. There's only one thing to do: abolish the job and restructure."

The widow-maker phenomenon has occurred in many organizations—for example, in a university that within ten years moved from being primarily an undergraduate teaching institution to being a major research university. That killed off two excellent people who took on the presidency as it had been structured the old way, and any number of deans—again, these positions could be filled successfully only *after* the university had restructured itself thoroughly.

BUILD FEEDBACK CONTROL INTO PEOPLE DECISIONS

There is no area in a manager's work and job in which *feedback control* is more important and more productive.

There is nobody without prejudices. There is nobody who doesn't like one person without even knowing why. *There is nobody who is objective about people.* And also, far too often our view of a person is formed by something that happened way in the past and is actually quite trivial—the way that person smiled, for instance, or the way she dressed at our first meeting a number of years ago. And none of us is immune to *flattery.*

Also, there are no "good judges of people"—there are only people who take the people decisions seriously and do them systematically, and then there are all the others. Therefore, it is absolutely imperative to build feedback control into people decisions.

Here is how feedback control is accomplished: Every time you make a decision, you write down what you expect and what your results should be. You appoint, for instance, the star salesman to be regional sales manager in the Midwest. Do you expect, for example, that the new manager will recruit and train a new sales force?

Then make sure that the new manager understands this. But also make sure that *you* keep those written expectations and, after nine months or a year, check results against them. It will show you, very soon, what you are good at in making people decisions, what your problems are, and where you make real mistakes. Doing this is an absolutely essential element in making people decisions.

THE POWER OF MAKING PEOPLE DECISIONS

Making people decisions is the ultimate means of organizational control. No organization can perform better than its people. And it doesn't help to search for "better" people, because there is generally no such thing. There are only people in the right jobs and people in the wrong jobs. People decisions are highly visible. Everyone in the organization will know who has been selected for a certain position.

Employees judge the values and the competency of their management by their people decisions. If people decisions are based on politics rather than merit, everyone in the organization knows it. They will despise management for ignoring performance and either leave out of frustration or, more likely, turn into politicians themselves.

Managers often cannot judge whether a strategic move is a wise one. Nor are they necessarily interested. "I don't know why we are buying this business in Australia, but it won't interfere with what we are doing here in Fort Worth" is a common kind of reaction. But when the same managers read that "Joe Smith has been made controller in the XYZ division," they usually know Joe much better than top management does. These managers should be able to say, "Joe deserves the promotion; he is an excellent choice—just the person that division needs to get the controls appropriate for its rapid growth."

If, however, Joe got promoted because he is a politician, everybody will know it. They will all say, "Okay, that is the way to get ahead in this company." As we have known for a long time, people in organizations tend to behave according to what they see others being rewarded for. And when the rewards go to nonperformance, to flattery, or to mere cleverness, the organization will soon decline into nonperformance, flattery, or cleverness.

Managers who make no effort to get people decisions right risk more than just poor performance: they risk their organization's respect. Yet, there is no reason why managers should make poor people decisions. To succeed, you simply have to follow and apply the five decision steps and five ground rules of people decisions.

SUMMARY

There are the five steps in making people decisions: Carefully think through the assignment. Look at three to five qualified people. Consider each candidate's strengths. Discuss each candidate with his or her colleagues and bosses. And make sure the appointee understands the job and what it requires, and reports back on it once he or she is in the job.

And there are five ground rules for the decision maker: Accept responsibility for any people decision, such as a placement or a promotion that fails. Accept also that people who do not perform must be removed. This is owed to the organization, to the nonperformer, and to his or her coworkers. This does not mean that such a person must be let go; instead, find the position that fits his or her strengths. It is the manager's responsibility to make the right people decision every time and for every position. Newcomers should preferably be put first into an established position, where expectations are known and where they can be helped if necessary.

30

Managerial Communications

We have more attempts at communications today than ever before, that is, more attempts to talk to others, and a surfeit of communications media than were imaginable to the men who, around the time of World War I, started to work on the problems of communicating in organizations. Communications in management has become a central concern to students and practitioners in all institutions—business, the military, public administration, hospital, university, and research. In no other area have intelligent men and women worked harder or with greater dedication than psychologists, human relations experts, managers, and management students have worked on improving communications in our major institutions.

Yet communications has proven as elusive as the unicorn. The noise level has gone up so fast that no one can really listen anymore to all that babble about communications. But there is clearly less and less communicating.

In Plato's *Phaedo,* which, among other things, is the earliest extant treatise on rhetoric, Socrates points out that one has to talk to people in terms of their own experience, that is, one has to use carpenters' metaphors when talking to carpenters, and so on. One can communicate only in the recipient's language or in his terms. And the terms have to be experience-based. It, therefore, does very little good to try to explain terms to people. They will not be able to receive them if they are not terms of their own experience. They simply exceed their perception capacity.

In communicating, whatever the medium, the first question has to be, "Is this communication within the recipient's range of perception? Can he or she receive it?"

The human mind attempts to fit impressions and stimulations into a frame of expectations. It resists vigorously any attempts to make it "change its mind," that is, to perceive what it does not expect to perceive or not perceive what it expects to perceive. It is, of course, possible to alert the human mind to the fact that what it perceives is contrary to its expectations. But this first requires that we understand what it expects to perceive. It then requires that there be an unmistakable signal— "this is different"—that is, a shock that breaks continuity.

Before we can communicate, we must, therefore, know what the recipient expects to see and hear. Only then can we know whether communication can utilize her expectations—and what they are—or whether there is need for the "shock of alienation," for an "awakening" that breaks through the recipient's expectations and forces her to realize that the unexpected is happening.

If communication fits in with the aspirations, values, and purposes of the recipient, it is powerful. If it goes against them, it is likely not to be received at all. At its most powerful, communication brings about "conversion," that is, a change of personality, values, beliefs, and aspirations. But this is the rare event, and one against which the basic psychological forces of every human being are strongly organized. Even the Lord, the Bible reports, first had to strike Saul blind before he could raise him up as Paul. By and large, therefore, there is no communication unless the message can key into the recipient's own values.

Information presupposes communication. Information is always encoded. To be received, let alone to be used, the code must be known and understood by the recipient. This requires prior agreement, that is, some communication.

Communications, in other words, may not be dependent on information. Indeed, the most perfect communications may be purely "shared experiences," without any logic whatever. Perception has primacy rather than information.

DOWNWARD AND UPWARD

What, then, can our knowledge and our experience teach us about communications in organizations, about the reasons for our failures, and about the prerequisites for success in the future?

For centuries we have attempted communication "downward." This, however, cannot work, no matter how hard and how intelligently we try. It cannot work, first, because it focuses on what *we* want to say. It assumes, in other words, that the *emitter* communicates.

This does not mean that managers should stop working on clarity in what they say or write. Far from it. But it does mean that how we say something comes only after we have learned what to say. And this cannot be found out by "talking to," no matter how well it is being done.

But "listening" does not work either. The "human relations school" of Elton Mayo, sixty years ago, recognized the failure of the traditional approach to communications. Its answer was to enjoin listening. Instead of starting out with what "we," that is, the executive, wants to "get across," the executive *should* start out by finding out what subordinates want to know, are interested in, are, in other words, receptive to. To this day, the human relations prescription, though rarely practiced, remains the classic formula.

Of course, listening is a prerequisite to communication. But it is not adequate, and it cannot, by itself, work. Listening assumes that the superior *will* understand what he is being *told*. It assumes, in other words, that the subordinates can communicate. It is hard to see, however, why the subordinate should be able to do what his superior cannot do. In fact, there is no reason for assuming he can.

This is not to say that listening is wrong, any more than the futility of downward communications furnishes any argument against attempts to write well, to say things clearly and simply, and to speak the language of those whom one addresses rather than one's own jargon. Indeed, the realization that communications have to be upward—or rather that they have to start with the *recipient* rather than the emitter, which underlies the concept of listening—is absolutely sound and vital. But listening is only the starting point.

More and better information does not solve the communications problem, does not bridge the communications gap. On the contrary, the more information, the greater is the need for functioning and effective communication. The more information, in other words, the greater is the communications gap likely to be.

MANAGEMENT BY OBJECTIVES

Can we then say anything constructive about communication? Can you do anything? Yes we can.

Management by objectives is a prerequisite for functioning communication. It requires the subordinate to think through and present to the superior his or her own conclusions as to what major contribution to the organization—or to the unit within the organization—he or she should be expected to perform and should be held accountable for.

What the subordinate comes up with is rarely what the superior expects. Indeed, the first aim of the exercise is precisely to bring out the divergence in perception between superior and subordinate. But the perception is focused, and focused on something that is real to both parties. To realize that they see the same reality differently is in itself already communication.

Management by objectives gives to the intended recipient of communication—in this case, the subordinate—access to experience that enables him to understand. He is given access to the reality of decision making, the problems of priorities, the choice between what one likes to do and what the situation demands, and above all, the responsibility for a decision. He may not see the situation the same way the superior does—in fact, he rarely will or even should. But he may gain an understanding of the complexity of the superior's situation and of the fact that the complexity is not of the superior's making, but is inherent in the situation itself.

These are only examples, and rather insignificant ones at that. But perhaps they illustrate the main conclusion to which our experience with communications—largely an experience of failure—and all the work on learning, memory, perception, and motivation point: communication requires shared experience.

There can be no communication if it is conceived of as going from the "I" to the "Thou." Communication works only from one member of "us" to another. Communication in organization—and this may be the true lesson of our communication failure and the true measure of our communication need—is not a *means* of organization. It is the *mode* of organization.

SUMMARY

We know that communication in organizations is perception, is expectations, makes demands, and that communications and information are different, yet interdependent.

We know that downward communications do not work—only upward communications do. And we know that effective communication in organizations requires management by objectives. Communication is not between "me" and "you." It is always from one member of "us" to another.

31

Controls, Control, and Management

In the dictionary of social institutions, the word "controls" is not the plural of the word "control." Not only do more controls not necessarily give more control, but the two words have different meanings altogether. The synonyms for *controls* are "measurements" and "information." The synonym for *control* is "direction." *Controls* pertain to means; *control* to an end. Controls deal with facts, that is, with events of the past. Control deals with expectations, that is, with the future. Controls are analytical, concerned with what was and is. Control is normative and concerned with what ought to be.

We are rapidly acquiring great capacity to design controls because of a great improvement in techniques, especially in the application of logical and mathematical tools and in the ability to process and analyze large masses of data very fast. What does this mean for control? Specifically, what are the requirements for these greatly improved controls to give better control to management? For, in the task of a manager, controls are purely a means to an end. The end is control.

The person in an organization who is charged with producing the controls is the controller. But most executives—including most controllers themselves—would consider it gross misuse and abuse of controllership were this controller to use controls to exercise control in the organization. This, they would argue, would actually make the organization be "out of control" altogether.

The reasons for this apparent paradox lie in the complexity both of human beings and of the social task.

If we deal with a human being in a social institution, controls must become personal motivation that leads to control. Instead of a mechanical system, the control system in a human-social situation is a system based on will. That we know very little about the will is not the central point. A translation is required before the information yielded by the controls can become grounds for action—the translation of one kind of information into another, which we call perception.

In the social institution there is a second complexity, a second "uncertainty principle." It is almost impossible to determine ahead of time the responses appropriate to a certain event in a social situation.

We can, and do, build controls into a machine that slow down the turning speed whenever it exceeds a certain figure. We can do this either by mechanical means or by instrumentation that shows a human operator what the turning speed is and gives him the specific, unambiguous instruction to turn down the speed when the indicator reaches a certain point. But a control-reading "profits are falling" does not indicate, with any degree of probability, the response "raise prices," let alone suggest by how much; the control-reading "sales are falling" does not indicate the response "cut prices," and so on. There are a large number of equally probable responses—so large that it is usually not even possible to identify them in advance. There is also no indication in the event itself which of these responses is even possible let alone appropriate or right. The event itself may not be meaningful. But even if it is, it is by no means certain what it means. And the probability of its *being meaningful* is a much more important datum than *the event itself*—and one that is almost never to be discerned by analyzing the event.

THE CHARACTERISTICS OF CONTROLS

There are three major characteristics of controls in any social institution.

1. *Controls can be neither objective nor "neutral."* When we measure the rate of fall of a stone, we are totally outside the event itself. By measuring we do not change the event; and measuring the event does not change us, the observers. Measuring physical phenomena is both objective and neutral.

In a perceptual situation of the complexity we deal with in organizations, the act of measurement is neither objective nor neutral. It is subjective and, of necessity, biased. It changes both the event and the observer. Events in the social situation acquire value by the fact that they are being singled out for the attention of being measured. No matter how "scientific" we are, the fact that this or that set of events is singled out for being "controlled" signals that it is being considered to be important.

Everybody who ever watched the introduction of a budget system has seen this happen. For a long time—in some organizations, forever—realizing the budget figures becomes more important than what the budget is supposed to measure, namely economic performance. Managers, upon first being exposed to a budget system, often deliberately hold back sales and cut back profits rather than be guilty of "not making the budget." It takes years of experience and a very intelligent budget director to restore the balance. And there are any number of otherwise perfectly sane research directors who act on the conviction that it is a greater crime to get research results for less than the budgeted amount than to not get any research results at all while spending all the "proper" budget money.

Controls in a social institution such as a business are goal-setting and value-setting. They are not "objective." They are, of necessity, moral. The only way to avoid this is to flood the executive with so many controls that the entire system becomes meaningless, becomes mere "noise."

Controls create vision. They change both the events measured and the observer. They endow events not only with meaning but with value. And this means that the basic question is not, "How do we control?" but, "What do we measure in our control system?"

2. *Controls need to focus on results.* Business (and every other social institution) exists to contribute to society, the economy, and the individual. In consequence, results in business exist only on the outside, in the economy, in society, and with the customer. It is the customer who creates a "profit." Everything inside a business—manufacturing, marketing, research, and so on—creates only costs. In other words, the managerial area is concerned with costs alone. But results are entrepreneurial.

We can easily record and therefore quantify efficiency, that is, efforts. We have very few instruments to record and quantify effects. But even the most efficient buggy-whip manufacturer would no longer be in business. It is of little value to have the most efficient engineering department if it designs the wrong product. The Cuban subsidiaries of U.S. companies were by far the best run and, apparently, the most profitable—let alone the least troublesome—of all U.S. operations in Latin America. This was, however, irrelevant to their takeover by the Castro government. And it mattered little, I daresay, during the period of IBM's great expansion, in the 1950s and 1960s, how *efficient* its operations were; its basic entrepreneurial idea was the right, the *effective one.*

The outside, the area of results, is much less accessible than the inside. The central problem of the executive in the large organization is insulation from the outside. This applies to the president of the United States as well as to the president of United States Steel. What today's organization therefore needs is *synthetic sense organs* for the outside. If modern controls are to make a contribution, it would be, above all, here.

3. *Controls are needed for measurable and nonmeasurable events.* Business, like any other institution, has important results that are incapable of being measured. Any experienced executive knows of companies or industries bound for extinction because they cannot attract or hold able people. Every experienced executive also knows that this is a more important fact about a company or an industry than last year's profit statement. Any logician who tried to tell an executive that this statement, being incapable of unambiguous definition, is a "nonstatement" dealing with a "nonproblem," would be quickly—and correctly—dismissed as an ass. The statement cannot be defined clearly, let alone "quantified," but it is anything but "intangible" (as anyone ever having to deal with such a business quickly finds out). It is just nonmeasurable. And measurable results will not show up for a decade.

But business also has measurable and quantifiable results of true meaning and significance. There are all those that have to do with past economic performance. For these can be expressed in terms of the very peculiar measurement of the economic sphere, money.

This does not mean that these are "tangibles." Indeed, many of the things we can measure by money are totally "intangible"—take depreciation, for instance. But they are measurable.

The measurable results are things that happened; they are in the past. There are no facts about the future. Measurable events are primarily inside events rather than outside events. The important developments on the outside, the things that determine that the buggy-whip industry disappears and that IBM becomes a big business, are not measurable until it is too late to have control.

A balance between the measurable and the nonmeasurable is, therefore, a central and constant problem of management and a true decision area. Measurements that do not spell out the assumptions with respect to the nonmeasurable statements that are being made—at least as boundaries or as restraints—misdirect and misinform. Yet the more we can quantify the measurable areas, the greater the temptation to put all emphasis on those. And the greater, therefore, the danger that what looks like better controls will actually mean less control, if not an organization out of control altogether.

SPECIFICATION FOR CONTROLS

To give the manager control, controls must satisfy seven specifications:

- They must be economical.

- They must be meaningful.

- They must be appropriate.

- They must be congruent.

- They must be timely.

- They must be simple.

- They must be operational.

1. *Control is a principle of economy.* The less effort needed to gain control, the better the control design. The fewer controls needed, the more effective they will be. Indeed, adding more controls does not give better control. All it does is create confusion.

The first question the manager therefore needs to ask in designing or in using a system of controls is, "What is the minimum information I need to know to have control?"

The answer may vary for different managers. The company's treasurer needs only to know the total amount invested in inventories and whether it is going up or down. The sales manager needs to know the half dozen products that together account for 70 percent of inventory, but the total inventory amount is not of primary importance to him or her. Neither the treasurer nor the sales manager needs complete inventory figures, except once or twice a year; a fairly small sample should give them all the information they need. But the warehouse manager needs daily figures—and in detail.

The capacity of the computer to spew out huge masses of data does not make for better controls. On the contrary, what gives control is asking the question, "What is the smallest number of reports and statistics needed to understand a phenomenon and to be able to anticipate it?" And then one asks, "What is the minimum of data regarding this phenomenon that gives a reasonably reliable picture?"

2. *Controls must be meaningful.* That means that the events to be measured must be significant either in themselves (e.g., market standing) or as symptoms of at least potentially significant developments (e.g., a sudden sharp rise in labor turnover or absenteeism).

Controls should always be related to the key objectives and to the priorities within them, to "key activities" and to "conscience areas." Controls should, in other words, be based on a company's definition of *what its business is, what it will be,* and *what it should be.*

Controls Follow Strategy

Whatever is not essential to the attainment of a company's objectives should be measured infrequently and only to prevent deterioration. It should be strictly controlled by "exception." A standard should be set, measurement should be periodical and on a sample basis, and only significant shortfalls below the established standard should be reported.

That we can quantify something is no reason for measuring it. The question is, "Is this what a manager should consider important?" Is this what a manager's attention should be focused on? Is this the proper focus for control—that is, for effective direction with maximum economy of effort?"

3. *Controls have to be appropriate to the character and nature of the phenomenon measured.* This may well be the most important specification; yet, it is least observed in the actual design of controls.

Because controls have such an impact, it is important that we select not only the right ones but also the appropriate ones, to enable controls to give right vision and to become the ground for effective action. The measurement must present the events measured in *structurally true form*. Formal validity is not enough.

Formal complaints or grievances coming out of a workforce are commonly reported in this form, "five grievances per thousand employees per month." This is formally valid. But is it structurally valid? Or is it misdirection? The impression this report conveys is, first, that grievances are distributed throughout the workforce in a random manner. And second, the report gives the impression that they are a minor problem, especially if we deal with five grievances per thousand employees per month. This, while formally valid, completely *misrepresents and misinforms*.

Grievances are a social event. And social events are almost never distributed in the "normal distribution" we find in the physical world. In this case, the great majority of departments in the plant, employing 95 percent of the workforce, normally do not have even a single grievance during one year. But in one department, employing only a handful of people, we have a heavy incidence of grievances—so the "five per thousand" may well mean (and in the actual example from which I took these figures, did mean) a major grievance per person per month. If this department happens to be the final assembly through which all the production has to pass, and if the workers in this department go out on strike when their grievances are being neglected by a management that has been misled by its own controls, the impact can be shattering. In this case, it bankrupted the company.

Most measurements of sales performance, whether of the entire sales force or of the individual salesperson, report sales in total dollars. But in many businesses this is an inappropriate figure. The same dollar volume of sales may mean a substantial profit, no profit at all, or a sizable loss—dependent on the product mix sold. An absolute sales figure not related to product mix, therefore, gives no control whatever—neither to the individual salesperson, nor to the sales manager, nor to top management. These are elementary things. Yet few managers seem to know them. The traditional information systems (especially traditional accounting) conceal appropriateness rather than highlight it. Without controls that bring out clearly what the *real structure of events is,* the manager lacks knowledge and therefore will tend to do the wrong things. For all the weight of the daily work pushes him or her toward allocating energies and resources in proportion to the *number* of events. There is a constant drift toward putting energies and resources where they can have the least results, that is, on the vast number of phenomena which, together, account for practically no effects.

4. *Measurements have to be congruent with events measured.* Alfred North Whitehead (1861–1947), the distinguished logician and philosopher, used to warn against the "danger of the false concreteness." A measurement does not become more accurate by being worked out to the sixth decimal when the phenomenon is only

capable of being verified within a range of 50 to 70 percent. This is "false concreteness," and misleading.

It is an important piece of information that this or that phenomenon cannot be measured with precision but can be described only within a range or as a magnitude. To say, "We have 26 percent of the market," sounds reassuringly precise. But it is usually so inaccurate a statement as to be virtually meaningless. What it really means, as a rule, is "We are not the dominant factor in the market, but we are not marginal either." And even then the statement is no more reliable than the definition of the market that underlies it.

It is up to the manager to think through what kind of measurement is appropriate to the phenomenon it is meant to measure. He has to know when *approximate* is more accurate than a firm-looking figure worked out in great detail. He has to know when a range is more accurate than even an approximate single figure. He has to know that *larger* and *smaller, earlier* and *later, up* and *down,* are quantitative terms and often more accurate, indeed more rigorous, than any specific figures or range of figures.

5. *Controls have to be timely.* Frequent measurements and very rapid "reporting back" do not necessarily give better control. Indeed, they may frustrate control. The time dimension of controls has to correspond to the time span of the event measured.

It has lately become fashionable to talk of "real-time" controls, that is, of controls that inform instantaneously and continuously. There are events where "real-time" controls are highly desirable. If a batch of antibiotics in the fermentation tank spoils as soon as temperature or pressure deviate from a very narrow range for more than a moment or two, "real-time" monitoring on a continuous basis is obviously needed. But few events need such controls. And most cannot be controlled by them. "Real time" is the wrong time span for real control.

Children planting a garden are so impatient, it is said, that they tend to pull out the radishes as soon as their leaves show, to see whether the root is forming. This is "real-time" control—misapplied.

Similarly, the attempt to measure research progress all the time is likely to confound research results. The proper time span for research is a fairly long one. Once every two or three years, research progress and results should be rigorously appraised. In between such appraisals, an experienced manager keeps in touch. He or she watches for any indication of major unexpected trouble, and, even more, for any sign of unexpected breakthroughs. But to monitor research in "real time"—as some research labs have been trying to do—is pulling up the radishes.

There is also the opposite danger, of not measuring often enough. It is particularly great with developments that (a) take a fairly long time to have results, and (b) have to come together at a point in the future to produce the desired end result.

6. *Controls need to be simple.* Every major New York commercial bank worked in the 1960s on developing managerial controls, especially of costs and of allocation of efforts. Everyone spent a great deal of time and money on the task and came up with control manuals. In only one of the banks were the manuals being used. When the executive in that bank was asked how he explained this, he did not (as his interviewer expected him to) credit a massive training program or talk about his "philosophy." He said instead, "I have two teenage daughters. They know nothing about banking and are not terribly good at figures. But they are bright. Whenever I had worked out an approach to controlling an activity, I took my intended procedure home in draft form and asked my girls to let me explain it to them. And only when I had it so simple that they could explain back to me what the procedure was intended to accomplish and how, did I go ahead. Only then was it simple enough."

Complicated controls do not work. They confuse. They misdirect attention away from what is to be controlled, and toward the mechanics and methodology of the control. If the user has to know how the control works before he can apply it, he has no control at all. And if he has to sit down and figure out what a measurement means, he has no control either.

7. *Finally, controls must be operational.* They must be focused on action. Action rather than information is their purpose. The action may be only study and analysis. In other words, a measurement may say, "What goes on we don't understand; but something goes on that needs to be understood." But it should never just say, "Here is something you might find interesting."

This then means that controls—whether reports, studies, or figures—must always reach the person who is capable of taking controlling action. Whether they should reach anyone else—and especially someone higher up—is debatable. But their prime addressee is the manager or professional who can take action by virtue of his or her position in the flow of work and in the decision structure. And this further means that the measurement must be in a form that is suitable for the recipient's needs.

Workers and first-line supervisors should receive measurements and control information that enables them to direct their own immediate efforts toward results they can control. Instead, typically, the first-line supervisor receives each month a statement of the quality control results for the entire plant —and the worker receives nothing. And top management usually receives the information and measurements operating middle managers need and can use, and little or nothing of pertinence to their own top-management job.

The reason for this is largely the confusion between control as domination of others and control as rational behavior. *Unless controls are means toward the latter, and this means toward self-control, they lead to wrong action.* They are miscontrol.

THE ULTIMATE CONTROL OF ORGANIZATION

There is one more important thing to be said. There is a fundamental, incurable, basic limitation to controls in a social institution. This lies in the fact that a social institution is both a true entity and a fiction. As an entity, it has purposes of its own, a performance of its own, results of its own—and survival and death of its own. These are the areas of which we have been speaking so far. But a social institution is composed of persons, each with his or her own purpose, ambitions, ideas, and needs. No matter how authoritarian the institution, it has to satisfy the ambitions and needs of its members, and do so in their capacity as individuals, but through institutional rewards and punishments, incentives and deterrents. The expression of this may be quantifiable—such as a raise in salary. But the system itself is not quantitative in character and cannot be quantified.

Yet, here is the real control of the institution, that is, the ground of behavior and the cause of action. People tend to act as they are being rewarded for their actions. To them, this is the expression of the true values of the institution and of its true purpose and role.

A system of controls that is not in conformity with this true, this only effective, this ultimate control of the organization, which lies in its people decisions, will therefore at best be ineffectual. At worst, it will cause never-ending conflict and will push the organization out of control.

SUMMARY

Controls and *Control* are different. Controls are the means; control the needed end. Controls can be neither objective nor neutral in a human organization. They are goal setting and value setting. Controls need to focus on results. Controls are needed for measurable and nonmeasurable events. Controls must satisfy seven specifications for effective control. And people decisions are the ultimate control of an organization.

32

The Manager and the Budget

Next to double-entry bookkeeping and the copying machine, budgets are the most commonly used management tool. Practically every business, large or small, has a budget of some sort. And so has every hospital and every university. Above all, no government agency in the world operates without an annual budget. In fact, budgets are the only management tool that originated in governmental, rather than in business, practice.

The original budget, as it was first developed in its modern form in England during the nineteenth century, listed revenues from taxes, custom duties, and so on one side, and expenses on the other. This showed whether the government's finances would be in surplus or in deficit and, thereby, whether to increase revenues, cut expenditures, or borrow money. It also provided the legal basis for a government department to spend money. Unless authorized in the budget, expenditure was illegal. It was thus the first effective check on the bureaucracy, the first systematic and orderly way of telling the governmental executive how much to spend and for what purpose.

All budgets, no matter how constructed, still serve these original purposes. They enable management—whether of a business, of a hospital, or of a government agency—to pull together its commitments, its plans and projects, and all its costs in one comprehensive document; the budget contrasts total expenditure with the total of expected revenues, thus arriving at a forecast of financial sources and financial requirements for the entire organization. Budgets still establish what planned and authorized expenditures are. And then budgets enable managers on every level to see whether events over the budget period actually follow the course predicted, or whether there is a shortfall of revenues, an excess of cost over the budget, or a significant change in economic performance of an enterprise, department, project, or product.

Almost every business today uses the budget to forecast and to control its financial needs and financial position. In particular, a budget is needed to enable the financial manager to anticipate the cash requirements of the business and to make sure that it obtains the necessary cash resources ahead of time. Every budget process, therefore, develops a "cash flow" budget.

In most businesses there is also a capital budget—usually extending over more than one year—which sets expected needs for capital against the various sources of capital and thus provides the basis for allocation of capital resources among various capital expenditures (e.g., between proposals for expanding capacity and proposals for developing additional markets). At the same time, the capital budget enables management to see whether the plans for obtaining capital are adequate to the capital needs of the business and to take timely action to bring the two into balance.

THE BUDGET IS A MANAGERIAL TOOL

But the budget has grown to be far more than a financial tool. It is, above all, a managerial tool. It is the tool around which an experienced manager organizes all planning. It is the best tool for making sure that key resources, and especially the resource of performing people, are assigned to priorities and to results. It is equally a tool of integration for the entire workforce, and especially a tool of integration for the managers in the organization. And it is a tool that enables the manager to know when to review and revise the plans, either because results are different from what was expected—whether better or worse—or because environment, economic conditions, market conditions, or technologies have changed and no longer correspond to the assumptions of the budget.

The starting point for the budgeting process, especially in a business, should always be *expected results.* What results do we expect to obtain in this business over the course of the next twelve or twenty-four months? What results do we expect in this research department over the course of the next year or the next five years? Only when the expected results have been thought through carefully does one ask, And what *efforts* does this require?

Budgets are expressed in monetary terms. But monetary terms should be seen as symbolic expression—a kind of shorthand—for the actual efforts needed, and should be based on "real values," that is, on people and materials needed, on work needed, on capacity needed. Budgets, in other words, should always be used as a tool to think through the relationship between *desired results* and *available means.* If they are looked at simply as a statement of cost, they soon cease to be the manager's tool for planning and control. Instead they may degenerate into a straitjacket that controls the manager and inhibits correct action.

In particular, it is important to avoid the worst pitfall of budgeting, the pitfall into which government budgets tend to fall. This is the tendency to regard last year's expenditures as being "about right" and to project them into the new budget.

Typically, in this kind of budgeting, the manager starts out with the budget for last year and then either adds 10 percent across the board or cuts 10 percent across the board. This may give her a "symmetrical" budget. But it also means that she has not used the budget as a planning tool and is unlikely to use resources where they are needed.

ZERO-BASED BUDGETING

A remedy against this sort of projected budget is *zero-based budgeting*. Rather than starting with last year's expenditures, the manager starts with the results he or she wants to achieve in a given area and asks, "Is it the right area? Is it a priority area?" And then, "What is really needed to obtain these results?"

In a large and complex enterprise, it is difficult to subject all expenditure areas to these questions every year. Yet it should always be done for major expenditure areas. For less important areas, zero-based budgeting might be done every three years or so, rather than yearly. On such a rotating schedule, zero-based budgeting can, and should, be used in every organization as a tool for the periodic systematic review of all products, markets, and activities. Thus it serves as the tool of *systematic abandonment* of the obsolescent, the unproductive, the unnecessary.

Just as important as zero-based budgeting is the realization that any time period for budgeting is an arbitrary one. A great many of the expenditures for which a manager budgets are, of necessity, geared to much longer periods than one year. This applies particularly to capital expenditures. In the first year of a project—building a new plant, for instance—expenditures might be very low and confined to what is needed to do preliminary engineering and architectural drawings. But this, in effect, commits the business to very large expenditures in subsequent years. And if those are not made because the money is not available, the sums spent the first year are wasted. The same applies to a great many other activities: research work; management and manager development; training, whether of workers in the plant or of salespeople; or sales promotion and advertising. All these activities require continuous efforts over long time periods to have any results. To budget for them on an annual basis is, therefore, self-delusion and likely to lead to waste in subsequent years when it is being discovered that the sums needed to make the activity produce the desired result are not available. These activities require life-cycle budgeting that shows the efforts needed over the life of the project or activity.

TYPES OF COST

Accountants have long distinguished three kinds of cost: One is *variable cost,* that is, cost that should fluctuate with the volume of operations, such as the cost of raw materials needed to produce a certain product, or the cost of direct labor needed in its manufacture. Second is *fixed cost*, that is, cost to which the enterprise is committed by law or by past decisions, such as interest payments on money borrowed to create new capacity, the cost of maintaining capacity, real estate taxes, and insurance premiums. The cost of maintaining an employee pension plan is also a fixed cost. Finally, the accountant speaks of *administered cost*, that is, the cost of such activities as research, advertising and promotion, manager development, activities of the field sales force. These costs are determined neither by the level of operations nor by commitments made in the past, but represent managerial decisions.

LIFE-CYCLE BUDGETING

Accountants debate whether these distinctions are still meaningful ones. Increasingly, for instance, "labor" is becoming a *fixed* rather than a *variable* cost. But for budgeting purposes, the system is still useful. Anything that is likely to be a fixed cost and anything that is an administered cost have, by definition, a time span well beyond one year. Therefore, they should never be budgeted on an annual basis alone. Rather, the budget should start out with the appropriate time cycle. Then it should ask, What portion of the expenditure needed over this time cycle belongs in this current budgeting period?

The best-known example of such life-cycle budgeting is the life-cycle costing that Robert McNamara introduced into the American defense budget while secretary of defense under President Kennedy. Under the budgeting process of the U.S. government, as it had been practiced earlier, the armed services submitted their requests for money for the development of a new weapon, such as a new fighter plane, on an annual basis. In other words, they asked for enough money to get a project started, without disclosing how much money it would take to get the project finished. Then, when the first few hundred million dollars had been spent, they always argued that to abandon a project because its costs were going up sharply (as the new plane moved from drawing board into production) would lead to a waste of money already spent. When the first prototype of the plane rolled off the production line and when it became apparent that there would be need for an expensive and extensive training program, and also for very large sums of money to buy replacement parts for the plane, they could argue that not to provide these sums in the future budget would mean a waste of very large sums already spent. Under life-cycle costing, the armed services are supposed to present total cost estimates over the life of the proposed weapon, including the training expenses and the expense for maintaining, repairing, and replacing equipment. This, in theory at least, enables the secretary of defense, the president, and the Congress to know in advance the size of the commitment and its impact on future budgets.

Life-cycle costing, or some variant thereof, is increasingly becoming standard practice in business as well. In fact, it is poor budgeting to assume that a new project—whether a capital investment or an activity such as an advertising program or a training program—will cost less in the future. Only the unsuccessful program does not require additional money; it can, and should, be abandoned. The plant that turns out not to be needed should be sold. The training program that does not produce trained people should be scrapped. If the product does well in the market, if the plant turns out the right product at the right cost, and if the training program really trains people, it will always require more money in the future—and it should. In budgeting capital expenses, fixed expenses, and administered expenses, the manager should always think through how much more money will be required to run with success. Success commits the organization to increasing the effective support for the program.

OPERATING BUDGET AND OPPORTUNITIES BUDGET

For this reason alone, a great many companies increasingly separate the budget into two major parts. One is the *operating budget*, which deals with all the things that are already being done. The other part is sometimes called the *opportunities budget*; it deals with the new things that might be done, with the products, markets, activities, programs, that represent either something genuinely new or a new way of doing old work. The operating budget tends to be many, many pages thick. The opportunities budget, by contrast, is usually very short. But the manager who has learned how to budget spends just as much time, as a rule, on the brief opportunities budget as on the lengthy operational budget. In analyzing the operational budget, the manager asks, "What is the *minimum* that needs to be done in this area to prevent damage? How much effort and how many resources have to be put into this activity to keep it going? What is the lowest cost to obtain adequate results?" In the terms of economic theory, his approach is one of *satisficing*. He does not try to *maximize*. He does not try to *optimize*. He tries to "satisfice" the minimum requirements needed to prevent unacceptable performance.

In respect to the opportunities budget, the first question is always, Is this the right opportunity? And if the answer is yes, then the question becomes, What is the optimum, in terms of resources and money, this opportunity can absorb at the present level? Can we hope to speed up the development process of a badly needed new product by putting more people to work on it? Will this only create confusion? It is just as dangerous, in the early stages of an opportunity, to oversupply money and resources as it is to undersupply them.

Failure to ask these questions is, in large measure, responsible for the failure of so many of the new government programs in areas of education and health care. They are smothered in money, at a time when they need only a few first-rate people to experiment, develop, learn, and demonstrate. The money brings with it a tremendous bureaucracy that is far too busy with its own internal mechanics to produce results, or even to know when results are being achieved. And the public, led by the lush budgets of these programs, expects immediate breakthroughs, and becomes disenchanted when results are slow in coming—as they have to be in educational or health-care programs, which, by definition, have long lead-times.

BUDGETING HUMAN RESOURCES

In order to budget properly, the manager has to use the budget as a tool for assignment control. Most budgets provide only for money and specify where it should be spent. They do not contain the necessary provisions to make reasonably sure that the *expected results* can indeed be obtained. They do not provide for the only resource that can produce results: accomplished people.

That last, and most crucial, step in the budget process is determining who should be accountable for what activity and for what expected results. Unless the name of a person to do the work is listed against each budget expenditure, this decision has not been made. The only decision that has been made is to spend the money—and that, of course, is the easy part.

In budgeting, a manager starts out with his or her opportunities and priorities. And in respect to each of them, the manager asks, "And whose job is it? Is that the right person? Is he or she capable of producing results? Is that person available to do the job?"

Budgeting, in other words, is not a substitute for effective decisions. It is a tool of planning and decision making. And money is not a substitute for thinking, performance, and competence. People think. People perform. People have competence. They need money, to be sure, but without the people, money will only be wasted.

In addition to being the manager's planning tool, budgeting is also one of the most effective tools for *communication and integration*. Budgeting always tries to present a picture of each part of a business. But it also shows how each part relates to the ends and needs of the whole. Budgeting, therefore, demands that the manager in charge of the whole, and each of the people in charge of the parts, discuss the budget jointly. The manager of each unit needs to take leadership responsibility in the budgeting process. The budget for the entire business is, in essence, the total of the budgets for all its parts. Conversely, the budget for each part is derived from the budget of the whole.

Properly used, therefore, the budget becomes an important communications and integration device for the manager. It should induce effective upward communication, which brings to the manager the point of view, priorities, concerns, and needs of each subordinate unit. It should also provide sideways communication, enabling managers in other areas to understand what their colleagues are trying to accomplish and what they require. And it should be an effective tool of integration that enables the manager to convey to the people who work for him or her an understanding of the needs of the entire business—of the decisions that have to be made, the priorities that have to be set, and, especially, of the personnel assignments that derive from the budget.

A budget authorizes some expenditures and denies others. It highlights and supports some opportunities, but by doing so plays down or denies support to other opportunities and activities. It is a tool for making decisions that affect everybody in the organization. Therefore, the budget can sometimes be seen as a tool to limit managers, or as their own escape from accountability, thus inhibiting motivation. But when properly used, it can become a tool to stimulate and unify, to make understood and comprehensible the common interest, and to motivate even those whose pet projects have had to be denied.

BUDGETING AND CONTROL

The budget is a tool of managerial control. It shows the manager how the organization is performing in each major area. Are we "on budget"? Or are we "under budget"? One look at the figures can show us every month, every three months, every year. And by the same token, the budget also shows when there is a need to revise the forecast—because things go better, worse, or differently than expected.

Businesses typically look upon the budget as an early warning system for danger and lack of performance, and this is an important function. But performance against budget should also be seen as an early warning system for opportunities, that is, for performance that is *better* than expected.

One illustration of a budget control that does both is a very simple color code developed by a large multinational investment firm, operating in emerging markets, that supplies initial capital for new industries and new businesses. The budget for all the investments of the company in any given country is shown on one big wall chart in the conference room in the company's headquarters. Each is coded in one of four colors: green, things are going according to budget; yellow, watch out, there might be trouble; red, there is trouble; and blue, things are going better or faster than expected. Management in this company has learned to spend as much (or more) time on blue areas as on the yellow and red ones.

Suppose a new business finds that its new plant is being built faster than was originally expected. It, therefore, can start marketing its new product a year earlier. What does this mean for hiring people, for building a distributive system, for starting advertising and promotion, for ordering raw materials, and for working capital requirements? If these are not supplied, the opportunity that the unexpected success in building the plant represents will be lost.

Control by the budget enables the manager to disregard all the items that proceed according to budget, while those that significantly deviate from budget, whether on the plus or on the minus side, can easily be identified. In fact, it is sound budget practice to show separately every month or every quarter the items with significant deviation from budget forecast and to have an explanation of the deviation available, so that the manager can decide whether the deviation requires action.

However, different items in the budget obviously differ greatly in their importance, from the most critical to the most trivial. And often, control by exception is not adequate for the most important. Increasingly, therefore, especially in complex operations, a *critical factors budget* is being used. (It was developed first, in the 1920s, by General Motors.)

A critical factors budget asks, for every product, service, and organizational unit, What are the few major items that account together for 75 to 80 percent of the total budget? These items—and all together they may account for only a few hundred items in a budget that numbers thousands, if not millions, of items—are then reported on specifically and in considerable detail. All the other items are reported on only if and when they deviate significantly from preset standards. And the less important the item, either in terms of money or in its impact on strategy and operations, the greater is the range within which fluctuations in performance as against budget are not reported to higher levels of management.

Another important and widely used refinement is the *milestone budget,* which controls disbursements and makes them dependent on achieving preset results. The budget may, for instance, authorize spending on sales promotion and distribution of a new product, subject to the successful completion of market testing by a given time and within a given budget. Until that milestone has been reached, the additional expenditure, while authorized and provided for, cannot be made. Milestone budgeting is particularly important for capital projects, such as a major building, a major research program, or product development and product introduction.

THE GANTT CHART AND NETWORK DIAGRAMS

The budget cuts across the entire organization—whether a whole company, a division, or a department. It controls all its revenues and contrasts them with all its expenditures. It presents, for each time period, a portrayal—or at least an X-ray—of the entire organization and indicates where control is needed. But it does not give the manager the tools for planning and control of individual projects, and especially of complex projects extending over a long period of time.

To build a big oil tanker, a major chemical plant, a new paper mill, or an office skyscraper is a five-year task. The finished product is an integrated whole. But it is the result of a great many different activities and goes through different stages. Some of the activities have to be done in sequence. Electric wiring and plumbing in the office building, for instance, cannot be installed until the frame has been completed. But they must be installed before any work on the interior is done. Other work can be done in parallel. The engine for the tanker and the power train that connects the engine to the propeller will be worked on while the hull is being built and may even have to be begun before work on the hull begins. Yet the contracting firm responsible for building the ship or the skyscraper is committed to a definite completion date and often has to pay heavy penalties if the job is not finished on time. It is also, typically, committed to a definite cost.

The tool to control such projects is the *Gantt chart* (named after the American pioneer of scientific management Henry L. Gantt, 1861–1919, who first developed this tool for the tasks of World War I). The Gantt chart—and its many recent refinements such as the tools of network analysis, including the critical path chart (developed by the DuPont Chemical Company in the 1950s) and PERT (program evaluation and review technique, developed by the U.S. Navy in the late 1950s)— is the most elegant and effective tool of planning and control at the manager's disposal.

Gantt's basic idea was stunningly simple. Traditionally, planning for a major complex job began with the beginning, the first step. And it then went, step-by-step, toward the end. Gantt proposed to start with the end product. "On December 15, 1917," he argued, "we have promised to deliver a finished destroyer, complete and ready to be put into service. What is the last step that has to be done to reach this completion date? And when will that step have to be started so that the ship will actually be ready by the promised delivery date? And what then is the step before, and before that, and before that, all the way back to the beginning?" The results of this analysis are usually shown in a series of parallel bar charts, each of which represents a major activity or effort. There are two types of such bars. One represents efforts that can be made only *after* something else has been done, for example, installing the turbine in the destroyer, which presupposes finishing the hull of the ship. The other bars represent activities that are not dependent on the completion of some other work, such as training the crew or designing the instrument panel. Yet each of these efforts has to be started at a given point if it is to come together in the completed final product at the desired time.

During the 1960s, the Japanese and Swedish shipyards established themselves as the world's leaders and captured the largest shares of the world's shipbuilding business. Their costs for labor and material were not much lower than those of traditional shipyards in Great Britain or the United States. Yet they could underbid traditional shipyards by a substantial margin. They could also promise far shorter delivery dates—and make good on their promises. A major reason was that the Japanese and the Swedes used Gantt charts; other builders had resisted the approach and had continued to plan in the traditional way, that is, step-by-step from the beginning to the end. As a result, traditional shipyards again and again found that needed supplies, subassemblies, or training activities had simply not been planned and provided for, with the result of sharply increasing costs and delaying completion of the finished work.

For extremely complex programs, such as the building of a huge chemical factory complex or of a new weapons system, Gantt charts of greater complexity are required: critical path charts or PERT charts (the differences between these two methods are both minor and purely technical). These are simply methods that enable the manager to stay in control of a great many different efforts that must interlock and interact at many points in time. A starting point for these methods is something Gantt himself understood very well. In every major project, there is one "critical path," that is, one sequence of stages that takes the longest and cannot easily be reduced in size, speeded up, or cut short.

In building the skyscraper office building, for instance, no interior work can be done until the frame, roof, floors, wiring and plumbing, and shafts for elevators have been finished. Once all this has been accomplished, the rest of the work can be scheduled with considerable freedom. The critical path is that of erecting the main structure. The rest of the work has to be organized around it. But renting office space in the skyscraper is also a critical path. Trying to find tenants may well have to begin *before* the ground is broken. And if the building fills up more slowly than was originally expected, finishing the last twenty-five or thirty floors of the building may not have the same urgency it seemed to have when the plans were drawn. There is thus, in building and designing a big office building, both a *critical path to construction* and a *critical path to renting*. And the two have to mesh.

Above all, critical path and PERT methods enable the manager to see what action can be taken to offset unfavorable developments, such as delays in time or increases in costs. Where can resources be switched from less to more critical areas? What must be added or sacrificed to make up for lost time or to speed up a project? How much time might be gained or lost by spending more or less money?

The Gantt chart need not be complicated, except in the case of truly complex systems work. But there should always be a Gantt chart when a project extends over a considerable time period or when a project requires a substantial number of different activities that must come together in time or space. Without a plan that starts from the intended termination point and works backward through the needed stages to the starting point, even simple projects are likely to get out of control with respect to time and cost.

JUDGING PERFORMANCE BY USING THE BUDGET

Managers also need to be able to plan the performance of the human organization and to control it. They need to do this, both in terms of the groups that comprise the organization (divisions, departments, programs, activities) and in terms of the individuals who make up these groups.

The manager needs to know first: What performance is expected from this group or from this person? And then the manager needs to know: What performance has been achieved? The starting point, in other words, is performance planning rather than performance appraisal. The starting point for performance of the human organization, like the starting point in the Gantt chart, has to be the intended result. As has been said many times before in this book, this must be focused on objectives and should be considered a major responsibility of the organizational unit and of the individual manager and professional.

SUMMARY

The budget enables the manager to allocate resources for results, to balance income and expenditures, and to control events in time to take corrective action. The Gantt chart and its various refinements, such as the critical path chart or PERT chart, enable a manager to plan a major project, to allocate resources rationally to the various stages and kinds of work needed to complete the project, and to control progress toward completion of the project, both with respect to the time needed and to the cost incurred. Performance planning for units and individuals and performance appraisal, finally, *enable the manager to make productive the people, the knowledge, the vision, and the motivation of the human organization, to focus human energy on performance, and to make organizational performance, in turn, redound to individual development.*

33

Information Tools and Concepts

Managers require tools to generate the information they need. Some of the tools have been around for a long time, but rarely, if ever, have they been focused on the task of managing an organization. Some are being refashioned; in their original form they no longer work.

Concepts and tools, history teaches again and again, are mutually interdependent and interactive. One changes the other. That is now happening to the concept we call an *enterprise* and to the tools we call *information*. The new tools enable us—indeed, may force us—to see our organizations differently. For some tools that promise to be important in the future, we have so far only the briefest specifications. The tools themselves still have to be designed.

1. FOUNDATION INFORMATION THAT ENTERPRISES NEED

We are just beginning to understand how to use information as a tool. But we can already outline the major parts of the information system enterprises need. In turn, we can begin to understand the concepts likely to underlie the enterprise that managers will have to manage tomorrow.

From Cost Accounting to Result Control

We may have gone furthest in redesigning both enterprise and information in the most traditional of our information systems—*accounting*. In fact, many businesses have already shifted from traditional cost accounting to *activity-based costing*. It was first developed for manufacturing. But it is rapidly spreading to service businesses and even to nonbusinesses, for example, universities. Activity-based costing represents both a different *concept* of the business process and different ways of *measuring*.

The primary techniques of cost accounting that are still in use were designed for mass-production activities. These traditional costing systems emphasize costing products for the purpose of valuing inventory. Inventory costs exclude the costs of many value-producing activities such as technology, marketing, distribution, and service.

When cost accounting was developed over seventy years ago, labor cost in manufacturing was above 50 percent of total manufacturing costs. And manufacturing employment was over 50 percent of employment in U.S. industry. Both assumptions are no longer valid. Yet, traditional cost-accounting techniques continue to enjoy widespread use.

The basic problem is not the *technology* but *mentality*. The ways of thinking about costing under traditional costing and under activity-based accounting are totally different. Traditional costing builds up cost from the *bottom up*—labor, material, and overhead—and concentrates primarily on manufacturing-related direct and support costs, so called "inventoriable costs." Activity-based costing starts from the cost object—the product, service, customer, or distribution channel— and asks, "Which activities and related costs are used in carrying out the complete value-chain activities associated with the cost object?" Users of the technique trace the costs of activities consumed by a product or service according to measures that reflect the quantity of activities used. Activity-based costing may be thought of as *top-down, total costing.*

The cost that matters for competitiveness and profitability is the cost of the total process, and that is what the activity-based costing records and makes manageable. Its basic premise is that business is an integrated process that starts when supplies, materials, and parts arrive at the plant's loading dock and continues even after the finished product reaches the end-user. Service is still a cost of the product, and so is installation, even if the customer pays.

Activity-based costing can substantially lower manufacturing costs. Its greatest impact, however, is likely to be in services. In most manufacturing companies, cost accounting is inadequate. But service industries—banks, retail stores, hospitals, schools, newspapers, and radio and television stations—have practically no accurate *unit cost information*. Activity-based costing shows why traditional cost accounting has not worked for service companies. It is not because the techniques are wrong. It is because traditional cost accounting makes the *wrong assumptions*. Service companies should not start with the cost of individual operations, as manufacturing companies have done under traditional cost accounting. They must start with the assumption that there is only one cost—*that of the total system*. And it is, predominately, a fixed cost over any given time period. By assuming that all costs are fixed, service companies can shift to an emphasis on the customer, in other words to *result control*.

For example, retail discounters, such as Wal-Mart and Costco, must assume that once the shelf space is installed, its cost is fixed, and management consists of maximizing the yield on the space over a given time span. This focus on *result control* has enabled these discounters to increase profitability despite their *low prices* and *low margins*.

Banks for instance, have been trying for several decades to apply conventional cost-accounting techniques to their business—that is, to figure the costs of individual operations and services—with almost negligible results. Now they are beginning to ask, "Which one activity is at the center of costs and of results?" There is one answer: *the customer.* The cost per customer in any major area of banking is a fixed cost. Thus it is the *yield per customer*—both the volume of services a customer uses and the mix of those services—that determines costs and profitability.

Just as the distinction between fixed and variable costs does not make as much sense in services, neither does the basic assumption of traditional cost accounting that *capital* can be substituted for *labor* in knowledge-based work. In fact, in knowledge-based work especially, *additional capital investment is likely to require more rather than less labor.* A hospital that buys a new diagnostic tool will not lay off anybody as a result. But it will have to add four or five people to run the new equipment. Other knowledge-based organizations have had to learn the same lesson.

In some areas, such as research labs, where productivity is difficult to measure, we may always have to rely on assessment and judgment rather than on costing. But for most knowledge-based and service work, we should, within a few years, have developed reliable tools to measure and manage costs and to relate those costs to results.

Thinking more clearly about costing in services and knowledge-based work should yield new insights into the costs of getting and keeping customers in businesses of all kinds.

From Legal Fiction to Economic Reality

Knowing the cost of operations, however, is not enough. To compete successfully in an increasingly competitive global market, a company has to know the costs of its entire *economic chain* and has to work with other members of the chain to manage costs and maximize yield. Companies are, therefore, beginning to shift from costing only what goes on inside their own organizations to costing the entire economic process, in which even the biggest company is just one link.

The legal entity, the company, is a reality for shareholders, for creditors, for employees, and for tax collectors. But economically, it is fiction. Thirty years ago the Coca-Cola Company was a franchiser all over the world. Independent bottlers manufactured the product. Now the company owns most of its bottling operations in the United States. But Coke drinkers—even those few who know that fact—could not care less.

What matters in the marketplace is the economic reality, the costs of the entire process, regardless of who owns what. Again and again in business history, an unknown company has seemingly come from nowhere and in a few short years has overtaken the established leaders without apparently even breathing hard. The explanation always given is superior strategy, superior technology, superior marketing, or lean manufacturing. But in many cases, the newcomer also enjoys a tremendous cost advantage. The reason is often the same: *the new company knows and manages the costs of the entire economic chain rather than its costs alone.*

Toyota is perhaps the best-publicized example of a company that knows and manages the costs of its suppliers and distributors; they are all, of course, members of its keiretsu. Through that network, Toyota manages the total cost of making, distributing, and servicing its cars as one cost stream, putting work where it costs the least and yields the most.

Increasingly managing the economic-cost chain will become a necessity. Indeed, managers need to organize and manage not only the cost chain but also everything else—especially corporate strategy and product planning—as one economic whole, regardless of the legal boundaries of individual companies.

A powerful force driving companies toward economic-chain costing will be the shift from *cost-led pricing* to *price-led costing*. Traditionally, Western companies have started with costs, put a desired profit margin on top, and arrived at a price. They practiced cost-led pricing. Marks & Spencer long ago switched to price-led costing, in which the price the customer is willing to pay determines allowable costs, beginning with the design stage. Until recently, companies that practiced price-led costing were the exceptions. Now price-led costing is becoming more common.

The same ideas apply to outsourcing, alliances, and joint ventures—indeed, to any structure that is built on *partnership* rather than *control*. And such entities, rather than the traditional model of a parent company with wholly owned subsidiaries, are increasingly becoming the models for growth, especially in the global economy.

For many businesses it is painful to switch to economic-chain costing. Doing so requires uniform or at least compatible accounting systems in all companies along the economic chain. Yet, each one does its accounting in its own way. Moreover, economic-chain costing requires information sharing across companies; yet, even within the same company, people tend to resist information sharing.

Whatever the obstacles, economic-chain costing is going to be done. Otherwise, even the most efficient company will suffer from an increasing cost disadvantage.

2. INFORMATION FOR WEALTH CREATION

Enterprises are paid to create wealth, not, primarily, to control costs. Enterprises are not normally run to be liquidated. They have to be managed as going concerns, that is, for wealth creation. To do that requires three additional sets of diagnostic tools: *productivity* information, *competence* information, and *resource-allocation* information. Together with *foundation information,* they constitute the manager's *tool kit* for managing the enterprise.

Productivity Information

The second set of tools includes those that measure the productivity of key resources. The oldest of them—of World War II vintage—measures the productivity of manual labor. Now we are slowly developing measurements for the productivity of knowledge-based and service work. However, measuring only the productivity of workers, whether blue- or white-collar, no longer gives us adequate information about productivity. For that, we require data on *total-factor productivity*.

That explains the growing popularity of *economic-value added* (EVA), even with all its complexities. EVA is based on something that has been known for a long time: what we generally call profits—the money left to service equity—is not profit at all and may be mostly a genuine cost. About this, there is no controversy. Until a business returns a profit that is greater than its cost of capital, it operates at a loss. Never mind that it pays taxes as if it had a genuine profit on its income statement. The enterprise still returns less to the economy than it uses up in resources. It does not cover its full costs unless the reported profit exceeds the cost of capital. Until then, it does not create wealth; it destroys it.

By measuring the value added over all costs, including the cost of capital, EVA measures, in effect, the productivity of all factors of production. It does not, by itself, tell us why a certain product or a certain service does not add value, or what to do about it. But it shows us what we need to find out and that we need to take action. EVA should also be used to find out what works. It does show which products, services, operations, or activities have high economic productivity and add high value. Then we should ask ourselves, "What can we learn from these successes?"

Another widely used tool to obtain productivity information is *benchmarking*—comparing one's performance with the best performance in the industry or, better yet, with the best anywhere in the world. Benchmarking assumes, correctly, that what one organization does, any other organization can do as well. It assumes, correctly, that any business has to be globally competitive. It assumes, also correctly, that being at least as good as the leader is a prerequisite to being competitive. Together, *EVA and benchmarking provide the diagnostic tools to measure total-factor productivity and to manage it.*

Competence Information

A second set of tools for wealth creation deals with competencies. Leadership in an industry rests on being able to do something others cannot do at all or find difficult to do even poorly. It rests on *core competencies* that meld market or customer value with a special ability of the producer or supplier. How does one find out whether one's core competence is improving or weakening? Or whether it is still the right core competence and what changes might be needed?

The discussion of core competencies has largely been anecdotal. But a number of highly specialized, midsized companies—a Swedish pharmaceutical producer and a U.S. producer of specialty tools, to name two—are developing the methodology to measure and manage core competencies.

The first step is to keep careful track of one's own and one's competitors' performance, looking especially for *unexpected successes* and for *unexpected poor performance* in areas where one should have done well. The successes demonstrate what the market values and will pay for. They indicate where the business enjoys a leadership advantage. The nonsuccesses should be viewed as the first indication either that the market is changing or that the company's competencies are weakening.

This analysis allows for the early recognition of opportunities.

By carefully tracking unexpected successes, a U.S. toolmaker found, for example, that small Japanese machine shops were buying its high-tech, high-priced tools, even though it had not designed the tools with them in mind or ever offered these tools to them. That allowed the company to recognize a new core competence: its products were easy to maintain and to repair despite their technical complexity. When that insight was applied to designing products, the company gained leadership in the small-plant and machine-shop markets in the United States and Western Europe, huge markets where it had done practically no business before.

Core competencies are different for every organization; they are, so to speak, part of an organization's personality. But every organization—not just businesses—needs one core competence: *innovation*. And every organization needs a way to record and appraise its *innovative performance*. In organizations already doing that—among them several top-flight pharmaceutical manufacturers—the starting point is not the company's own performance. It is a careful record of the innovations in the entire field during a given period. Which of them were truly successful? How many of them were ours? Is our performance commensurate with our objectives? With the direction of the market? With our market standing? With our research spending? Are our successful innovations in the areas of greatest growth and opportunity? How many of the truly important innovation opportunities did we miss? Why? Because we did not see them? Or because we saw them but dismissed them? Or because we botched them? And how well do we do in converting an innovation into a commercial product? A good deal of that, admittedly, is assessment rather than measurement. It raises rather than answers questions, but it raises the right questions.

Resource-Allocation Information

The last area in which diagnostic information is needed to manage the current business for wealth creation is the allocation of scarce resources—capital and performing people. Those two convert into action all the information that a management has about its business. They determine whether the enterprise will do well or poorly.

Capital appropriation processes are very well developed in today's organizations, yet they are not without defects. Most serious, however, is that the majority of capital-appropriations processes do not even ask for two vital pieces of information:

- What would happen if the proposed investment failed to produce the promised results? Would it seriously hurt the company, or would it be just a fleabite?

- If the investment is successful—and especially if it is more successful than we expect—what will it commit us to?

In addition, a capital-appropriations request requires specific deadlines: when should we expect what results? Then the results—successes, near successes, near failures, and failures—need to be reported and analyzed. There is no better way to improve an organization's performance than to measure the results of capital spending against the promises and expectations that led to its authorization. How much better off would the United States be today had such feedback on government programs been standard practice?

Capital, however, is only one key resource of the organization, and it is by no means the scarcest one. The scarcest resources in any organization are performing people. Since World War II, the U.S. military has learned to test its placement decisions. It now thinks through what it expects of senior officers before it puts them into key commands. It then appraises their performance against those expectations. And it constantly appraises its own process for selecting senior commanders against the successes and failures of its appointments.

In business—but in universities, hospitals, and government agencies as well—placement with specific expectations as to what the appointee should achieve and systematic appraisal of the outcome are virtually unknown. In the effort to create wealth, managers need to allocate human resources as purposefully and as thoughtfully as they do capital. And the outcomes of those decisions ought to be recorded and studied as carefully.

Where the Results Are

Those three kinds of information tell us only about the current business. They inform and direct tactics. For strategy, we need organized information about the environment. Strategy has to be based on information about markets, customers, and noncustomers; about technology in one's own industry and others; about worldwide finance; and about the changing world economy. For that is where the results are.

Inside an organization, there are only cost centers. The only profit center is a customer whose check has not bounced.

Major changes always start outside an organization. A retailer may know a great deal about the people who shop at its stores. But no matter how successful, no retailer ever has more than a small fraction of the market as its customers; the great majority are noncustomers. It is always with noncustomers that basic changes begin and become significant. At least half the important new technologies that have transformed an industry in the past fifty years came from outside the industry itself. Commercial paper, which has revolutionized finance in the United States, did not originate with the banks. Molecular biology and genetic engineering were not developed by the pharmaceutical industry. Though the great majority of businesses will continue to operate only locally or regionally, they all face, at least potentially, global competition from places they have never even heard of before.

Not all of the needed information about the outside is *available,* to be sure, despite the specialty mass magazines. There is no information—not even unreliable information—on economic conditions in most of China, for instance, or on legal conditions in the successor states to the Soviet empire. But even where information is readily available, many businesses are oblivious to it. Many U.S. companies went into Europe in the 1960s without even asking about labor legislation. European companies have been just as blind and ill-informed in their ventures into the United States. A major cause of the Japanese real estate investment debacle in California during the 1990s was the failure to find out elementary facts about zoning and taxes.

A serious cause of business failure is the common assumption that conditions—taxes, social legislation, market preferences, distribution channels, intellectual property rights, and many others—*must* be what we think they are or at least what we think they *should* be.

An adequate information system has to include information that makes managers question that assumption. It must lead them to ask the right questions, not just feed them the information they expect. That presupposes, first, that managers know what information they need. It demands further that they obtain that information on a regular basis. It finally requires that they systematically integrate the information into their decision making.

These are beginnings. These are attempts to organize "business intelligence," that is, information about actual and potential competitors worldwide. Multinationals—Unilever, Coca-Cola, Nestle, some Japanese trading companies, and a few big construction companies, for example—have been working hard on building systems to gather and organize outside information. But in general, the majority of enterprises have yet to start the job. It is fast becoming the major information challenge for all enterprises.

3. INFORMATION THAT MANAGERS NEED FOR THEIR WORK

Information for managers—including all knowledge workers—for their own work may be a great deal more important than *information for the enterprise.* Information increasingly creates the link to their fellow workers and to the organization, and their "network." It is information, in other words, that enables knowledge workers to do their jobs.

By now it is clear that no one can provide the information that knowledge workers need, except knowledge workers themselves. But few managers so far have made much of an effort to decide what they need, and even less, how to organize it. They have tended to rely on the producers of data—IT people and accountants— to provide this information for them. But the producers of data cannot possibly know what data the users need so that such data can become information. Only individual knowledge workers can convert data into information. And only individual knowledge workers can decide how to organize their information so that it becomes their key to effective action.

To produce the information managers need for their work, they have to begin with two questions:

- "What information do I owe to the people with whom I work and on whom I depend? And in what form? And in what time frame?"

- "What information do I need myself? And from whom? And in what form? And in what time frame?"

These two questions are closely connected. But they are different. *What I owe* comes first because it establishes communications. And unless that has been established, there will be no information flow back to the manager.

We have known this since Chester I. Barnard (1886–1961) published his pioneering book *The Functions of the Executive,* in 1938, seventy years ago. Yet, while Barnard's book is universally praised, it has had little practical impact. Communication for Barnard was vague and general. It was human relationships, and personal. However, what makes communications effective at the workplace is that they are focused on something outside the person. They have to be focused on a common task and on a common challenge. They have to be focused on the work.

And by asking, "To whom do I owe information, so that they can do their work?" communications are being focused on the common task and the common work. They become effective. The first question (as in any effective relationship), therefore, is not, "What do I want and need?" It is, "What do other people need from me?" and "Who are these other people?" Only then can the question be asked, "What information do I need? From whom? In what form? In what time frame?"

Managers who ask these questions will soon find that little of the information they need comes out of their own company's information system. Some comes out of accounting—though in many cases the accounting data has to be rethought, reformulated, and rearranged to apply to the manager's own work. But a good deal of the information managers need for their own work will come, as has been said already, from the outside and will have to be organized quite separately and distinctly from the inside information system.

The only one who can answer the question, "What do I owe by way of information? To whom? In what form?" is the other person. The first step in obtaining the information that managers need for their own work is, therefore, to go to everyone with whom they work, everyone on whom they depend, everyone who needs to know what they themselves are doing, and ask them. But before one asks, one has to be prepared to answer. For the other person will—and should—come back and ask, "And what information do you need from me?" Hence, managers need first to think through both questions—but then they start out by going to the other people and asking them first to tell them, "What do I owe you?"

Both questions, "What do I owe?" and "What do I need?" sound deceptively simple. But everyone who has asked them has soon found out that it takes a lot of thought, a lot of experimentation, and a lot of hard work to answer them. And the answers are not forever. In fact, these questions have to be asked again, every eighteen months or so. They also have to be asked every time there is a real change, for example, *a change in the enterprise's theory of the business,* in the individual's own job and assignment, or in the jobs and assignments of the other people.

But if individuals ask these questions seriously, they will soon come to understand both what they need and what they owe. And then they can set about organizing both.

Organizing Information

Unless organized, information is still data. To be meaningful it has to be organized. It is, however, not clear at all in what form certain kinds of information are meaningful, and especially in what form of organization they are meaningful for one's own job. And the same information may have to be organized in different ways for different purposes.

Here is one example: After Jack Welch took over as CEO in 1981, the General Electric Company (GE) created more wealth than any other company in the world. One of the main factors in this success was that GE organized the same information about the performance of every one of its business units differently for different purposes. It kept traditional financial and marketing reporting, the way most companies appraise their businesses every year or so. But the same data were also organized for long-range strategy, that is, to show unexpected successes and unexpected failures, but also to show where actual events differed substantially from what had been expected. A third way to organize the same data was to focus on the innovative performance of the business—which became a major factor in determining the compensation and bonuses of the general manager and of the senior management people of a business unit. Finally, the same data were organized to show how the business unit and its management treated and developed people—which then became a key factor in deciding on the promotion of a manager, and especially of the general manager of a business unit.

No two managers organize the same information the same way. And information *has to be organized the way individual managers work*. But there are some basic methodologies of organizing information.

One is the *key event*. Which events—for it is usually more than one—are the "hinges" on which the rest of my performance primarily depends? The key event may be technological—the success of a research project. It may have to do with people and their development. It may have to do with establishing a new product or a new service with certain key customers. It may be obtaining new customers. What is a key event is very much the manager's individual decision. It is, however, a decision that needs to be discussed with the people on whom the manager depends. It is perhaps the most important thing anyone in an organization has to get across to the people with whom one works, and especially to one's own superior.

Another key methodological concept comes out of modern *probability theory*—it is the concept on which, for instance, total quality management is based. It is the difference between normal fluctuations within the range of normal probability distribution and the exceptional event. As long as fluctuations stay within the normal distribution of probability for a given type of event (e.g., for quality in a manufacturing process), no action is taken. Such fluctuations are data and not information. But the exception, which falls outside the accepted probability distribution, is information. It calls for action.

Another basic methodology for organizing information comes out of the theory of the *threshold phenomenon*—the theory that underlies *perception psychology*. It was a German physicist, Gustav Fechner (1801–1887), who first realized that we do not feel a sensation—for example, a pinprick—until it reaches a certain intensity, that is, until it passes a perception threshold. A great many phenomena follow the same law. They are not actually "phenomena." They are data until they reach a certain intensity, and pass the perception threshold.

For many events, both in one's work and in one's personal life, this theory applies and enables one to organize data into information. When we speak of a "recession" in the economy, we speak of a threshold phenomenon—a downturn in sales and profits is a recession when it passes a certain threshold, for example, when it continues beyond a certain length of time. Similarly, a disease becomes an "epidemic" when, in a certain population, its prevalence passes and exceeds a certain threshold.

This concept is particularly useful in organizing information about personnel events. Such events as accidents, turnover, grievances, and so on become significant when they pass a certain threshold. But the same is true of innovative performance in a company—except that there the perception threshold is the point below which a drop in innovative performance becomes relevant and calls for action. The threshold concept is altogether one of the most useful concepts to determine when a sequence of events becomes a "trend," and requires attention and probably action, and when events, even though they may look spectacular, are by themselves not particularly meaningful.

Finally, a good many managers have found that the one way of organizing information effectively is simply to organize one's being informed about the *unusual*.

One example is the "manager's letter." The people who work with a manager write a monthly letter to him or her, reporting on anything unusual and unexpected within their own sphere of work and action. Most of these "unusual" things can safely be disregarded. But again, and again, there is an "exceptional" event, one that is outside the normal range of probability distribution. Again and again, there is a concatenation of events—insignificant in each reporter's area, but significant if added together. Again and again, the management letters bring out a pattern to which to pay attention. Again and again, they convey information.

NO SURPRISES

No system designed by knowledge workers to give them the information they need for their work will ever be perfect. But, over the years, systems steadily improve. And the ultimate test of an information system is that there are no surprises. Before events become significant, managers have already adjusted to them, analyzed them, understood them and taken appropriate action.

One example is the three or four—very few indeed—American financial institutions that, in the late 1990s, were not surprised by the economic collapse of mainland Asia. They had thought through what "information" means with respect to Asian economies and Asian currencies. They had gradually eliminated all the information they got from within their own subsidiaries and affiliates in these countries—it, they had begun to realize, was just "data." Instead, they had begun early in the 1990s to organize their own financial information about all emerging markets into country risk ratios, going from micro to macro financial and economic information such as foreign debt-to-GDP ratios and debt-service ratios. For example, the ING bank had a very sophisticated risk analysis system for emerging markets, which was made available to client companies of the bank. In addition, in September 1996, the International Monetary Fund issued a report warning about potential problems in financial markets in Southeast Asia.

Long before these economic ratios turned so unfavorable as to make a panic in mainland Asia inevitable, these managers had realized that it was coming. They realized that they had to decide whether to pull out of these countries for short-term growth or to stay for very long-term and very risky strategies. In other words, they had realized what economic data is meaningful with respect to emerging countries, had organized it, had analyzed it, and had interpreted it. They had turned the data into information—and had decided what action to take long before that action became necessary.

By contrast, the overwhelming majority of American, European, and Asian companies doing business on mainland Asia and/or investing in it had relied on what their own people in these countries reported to them. This turned out not to be information at all—in fact, it turned out to be misinformation. But only those managers who had spent several years asking the question, "What information is meaningful with respect to our doing business in Thailand or Indonesia?" were prepared.

Managers have to learn two things: eliminate data that does not pertain to the information they need and organize the data to analyze and interpret it. Then managers must focus on the resulting information and take action. For the purpose of information is not knowledge. It is being able to take the right action.

GOING OUTSIDE

An example of the companies investing in developing countries being surprised by the collapse of the emerging economies of mainland Asia underlines the importance of obtaining meaningful outside information.

For the manager there is, in the end, only one way to get it: that is to go, personally, on the outside. No matter how good the reports, no matter how good the economic or financial theory underlying them, nothing beats personal, direct observation, and in a form in which it is truly outside observation.

The largest hospital-supply company in the United States was built by a chief executive officer who himself spent four weeks a year—two weeks twice a year—taking the place of a salesman on vacation. He demanded that all the company's senior managers do the same. When the regular salesman came back, the customer—for example, the nun who purchases supplies for the Catholic hospital—always more or less said, "What dumb cluck took your place? He always asked why I buy things from other suppliers rather than from you. He was never particularly interested in getting an order for what you sell." But this was precisely the point of the exercise.

And it is a very old observation that few things improve the performance of a physician as much as being a hospital patient for two weeks.

Market research, focus groups, and the like are highly valued, and rightfully so. But still, they always focus on the company's products. They never focus on what the customer buys and is interested in. Only by being a customer oneself, a salesman oneself, a patient oneself, can one get true information about the outside. And even that information is, of course, still limited to one's customers and one's noncustomers. What other information about the outside do managers need, however, to do their work? And how can they get it?

This is one reason why being a volunteer in a nonprofit agency is important not only for preparing oneself for the second half of one's life. It is equally important as a way to get outside information—which is information on how other people, with other jobs, other backgrounds, other knowledges, other values, and other points of view see the world, act and react, and make their decisions. For this reason also, the continuing education of already successful adults will be increasingly important. For in that university course, the forty-five-year-old, successful knowledge worker—business executive, lawyer, university president, minister of a church, and so on—is forced to work with people of different backgrounds and different values. It is one way not only to update one's knowledge but to obtain what managers need: information about the outside.

In the long run, information about the outside may be the most important information managers need to do their work. At the same time, it is the one that still has to be organized. This information is not only the foundation for right action. It is equally the foundation for the challenges discussed in chapter 19, the challenges of knowledge-worker productivity, and in chapter 45, the challenges of managing oneself. Both rely heavily on the knowledge workers' knowing what information they need for their work and what information they owe to others, and on systematically developing the methods that turn the chaos of data in the universe into organized and focused information for the manager's own work and job.

SUMMARY

The manager needs three primary types of information, each with its own concepts and tools. First, there is what goes on *inside the enterprise*. Here we use standard accounting information along with the newer and rapidly evolving techniques of activity-based costing, EVA, and benchmarking. Then, there are the links to be made *across organizations* that are required in alliances and partnerships. Economic-chain accounting is the tool that is needed there. Finally, there is *external informa-*

tion, where major changes usually originate. Business intelligence systems are necessary tools to assist in collecting and organizing this information.

Managers must rely heavily on the information they need for their work, the information they owe to others, and on the methods they use to turn the chaos of data in the universe into organized and focused information for action.

Part VIII

Innovation and Entrepreneurship

In a period of upheavals, such as the one we are living in, change is the norm. To be sure, change is painful and risky, and above all it requires a great deal of very hard work. But unless it is seen as the task of the individual manager and of the leadership group to lead change, the organization—whether business, university, hospital, and so on—will not survive. In a period of rapid structural change, the only ones who survive are those who innovate and create change.

An organization that wants to be able to innovate, wants to have a chance to succeed and prosper in a time of rapid change, has to build into the organization *entrepreneurial management*, that is, entrepreneurial policies and practices. These policies and practices must be applied both *within* the existing enterprise as well as to *new ventures*.

The organization also must apply *entrepreneurial strategies* outside, in the marketplace. Finally, an entrepreneurial organization must do the hard work required to search systematically for innovative *windows of opportunity*, to which it applies its entrepreneurial strategies.

34

The Entrepreneurial Business

"Big businesses don't innovate," says the conventional wisdom. This sounds plausible enough. True, the new, major innovations of the twentieth century did not come out of the old, large businesses of their time. The railroads did not spawn the automobile or the truck; they did not even try. And though the automobile companies did try (Ford and General Motors both pioneered in aviation and aerospace), all of today's large aircraft and aviation companies have evolved out of separate new ventures. Similarly, today's giants of the pharmaceutical industry are, in the main, companies that were small or nonexistent fifty years ago, when the first modern drugs were developed. Every one of the giants of the electrical industry—General Electric, Westinghouse, and RCA in the United States; Siemens and Philips on the Continent; Toshiba in Japan—rushed into computers in the 1950s. Not one was successful.

And yet the all-but-universal belief that large businesses do not and cannot innovate is not even a half-truth; rather, it is a misunderstanding.

In the first place, there are plenty of exceptions, plenty of large companies that have done well as entrepreneurs and innovators. In the United States, there is Johnson & Johnson in hygiene and health care, 3M in highly engineered products for both industrial and consumer markets, and Procter & Gamble in consumer products. Citibank, one of the largest banks in the world, well over a century old, has been a major innovator in many areas of banking and finance. In Germany, Hoechst—one of the world's largest chemical companies, and more than 145 years old by now—has become a successful innovator in the pharmaceutical industry.

Second, it is not true that "bigness" is an obstacle to entrepreneurship and innovation. In discussions of entrepreneurship, one hears a great deal about the "bureaucracy" of big organizations and of their "conservatism." Both exist, of course, and they are serious impediments to entrepreneurship and innovation—but to all other performance just as much. And yet the record shows unambiguously that among existing enterprises, whether business or public-sector institutions, the small ones are least entrepreneurial and least innovative.

Among existing entrepreneurial businesses there are a great many very big ones; the foregoing list could have been enlarged without difficulty to one hundred companies from all over the world, and a list of innovative public-service institutions would also include a good many large ones.

It is not size that is an impediment to entrepreneurship and innovation; it is the existing operation itself, and especially the existing successful operation. And it is easier for a big or at least a fair-sized company to surmount this obstacle than it is for a small one. Operating anything—a manufacturing plant, a technology, a product line, a distribution system—requires constant effort and unremitting attention. The one thing that can be guaranteed in any kind of operation is the daily crisis. The daily crisis cannot be postponed; it has to be dealt with right away. And the existing operation demands high priority and deserves it.

Where the conventional wisdom goes wrong is in its assumption that entrepreneurship and innovation are natural, creative, or spontaneous. If entrepreneurship and innovation do not well up in an organization, something must be stifling them. That only a minority of existing successful businesses are entrepreneurial and innovative is thus seen as conclusive evidence that existing businesses quench the entrepreneurial spirit.

But entrepreneurship is not "natural"; it is not "creative." It is work. Hence, the correct conclusion from the evidence is the opposite of the one commonly reached. That a substantial number of existing businesses—and among them a goodly number of fair-sized, big, and very big ones—succeed as entrepreneurs and innovators indicates that entrepreneurship and innovation can be achieved by any business. But they must be consciously striven for. They can be learned, but it requires effort. Entrepreneurial businesses treat entrepreneurship as a duty. They are disciplined about it, they work at it, they practice it.

STRUCTURES

People work within a structure.

For the existing business to be capable of innovation, it has to create a structure that allows people to be entrepreneurial. It has to devise relationships that center on entrepreneurship. It has to make sure that its rewards and incentives, its compensation, personnel decisions, and policies, all reward the right entrepreneurial behavior and do not penalize it.

1. This means, first, that the entrepreneurial, the new, has to be organized separately from the old and existing. Whenever we have tried to make an existing unit the carrier of the entrepreneurial project, we have failed.

One reason is that (as was said earlier) the existing business always requires time and effort on the part of the people responsible for it, and deserves the priority they give it. The new always looks so puny—so unpromising—next to the reality of the massive, ongoing business. The existing business, after all, has to nourish the struggling innovation. But the "crisis" in today's business has to be attended to as well. The people responsible for an existing business will, therefore, always be tempted to postpone action on anything new, entrepreneurial, or innovative until it is too late. No matter what has been tried—and we have now been trying every conceivable mechanism for thirty or forty years—existing units have been found to be mainly capable of extending, modifying, and adapting what already is in existence. The new belongs elsewhere.

2. This means also that there has to be a special locus for the new venture within the organization, and it has to be pretty high up. Even though the new project, by virtue of its current size, revenues, and markets, does not rank with existing products, somebody in top management must have the specific assignment to work on tomorrow as an entrepreneur and innovator.

This need not be a full-time job; in the smaller business, it very often cannot be a full-time job. But it needs to be a clearly defined job and one for which somebody with authority and prestige is fully accountable.

The new project is an infant and will remain one for the foreseeable future, and infants belong in the nursery. The "adults," that is, the executives in charge of existing businesses or products, will have neither time nor understanding for the infant project. They cannot afford to be bothered.

Disregard of this rule cost a major machine-tool manufacturer its leadership in robotics. The company had the basic patents on machine tools for automated mass production. It had excellent engineering, an excellent reputation, and first-rate manufacturing. Everyone in the early years of factory automation—around 1975— expected it to emerge as the leader. Ten years later it had dropped out of the race entirely. The company had placed the unit charged with the development of machine tools for automated production three or four levels down in the organization, and had it report to people charged with designing, making, and selling the company's traditional machine-tool lines. These people were supportive; in fact, the work on robotics had been mainly their idea. But they were far too busy defending their traditional lines against a lot of new competitors such as the Japanese, redesigning them to fit new specifications, demonstrating, marketing, financing, and servicing them. Whenever the people in charge of the "infant" went to their bosses for a decision, they were told, "I have no time now, come back next week." Robotics was, after all, only a promise; the existing machine-tool lines produced millions of dollars each year.

Unfortunately, this is a common error.

The best, and perhaps the only, way to avoid killing off the new by sheer neglect is to set up the innovative project from the start as a separate business.

The best known practitioners of this approach are three American companies: Procter & Gamble, a very large and aggressively entrepreneurial company; Johnson & Johnson, the hygiene and health-care supplier; and 3M, a major manufacturer of industrial and consumer products. These three companies differ in the details of practice, but essentially all three have the same policy. They set up the new venture as a separate business from the beginning and put a project manager in charge. The project manager remains in charge until the project is either abandoned or has achieved its objective and become a full-fledged business. And until then, the project manager can mobilize all the skills as they are needed—research, manufacturing, finance, marketing—and put them to work on the project team.

3. There is another reason why a new, innovative effort is best set up separately: to keep away from it the burdens it cannot yet carry. Both the investment in a new product line and its returns should, for instance, not be included in the traditional return-on-investment analysis until the product line has been on the market for a number of years. To ask the fledgling development to shoulder the full burdens an existing business imposes on its units is like asking a six-year-old to go on a long hike carrying a sixty-pound pack; neither will get very far. And yet the existing business has requirements with respect to accounting, to personnel policy, to reporting of all kinds, which it cannot easily waive.

The innovative effort and the unit that carries it require different policies, rules, and measurements in many areas.

I learned this many years ago in a major chemical company. Everybody knew that one of its central divisions had to produce new materials to stay in business. The plans for these materials were there, the scientific work had been done, but nothing happened. Year after year there was another excuse. Finally, the division's general manager spoke up at a review meeting, "My management group and I are compensated primarily on the basis of return-on-investment. The moment we spend money on developing the new materials, our return will go down by half for at least four years. Even if I am still here in four years' time when we should show the first returns on these investments—and I doubt that the company will put up with me that long if profits are that much lower—I'm taking bread out of the mouths of all my associates in the meantime. Is it reasonable to expect us to do this?" The formula was changed and the developmental expenses for the new project were taken out of the return-on-investment figures. Within eighteen months the new materials were on the market. Two years later they had given the division leadership in its field, which it has retained to this day. Four years later the division doubled its profits.

THE DON'TS

There are some things the entrepreneurial management of an existing business should not do.

1. The most important caveat is: *Don't mix managerial units and entrepreneurial ones.* Do not ever put the entrepreneurial into the existing managerial component. Do not make innovation an objective for people charged with running, exploiting, optimizing what already exists.

But it is also inadvisable—in fact, almost a guarantee of failure—for a business to try to become entrepreneurial without changing its basic policies and practices. To be an entrepreneur on the side rarely works.

A great many large American companies have tried to go into joint ventures with entrepreneurs. Few of these attempts have succeeded; the entrepreneurs found themselves stymied by policies, by basic rules, by a "climate," they felt was bureaucratic, stodgy, and reactionary. But at the same time, their partners, the people from the big company, could not figure out what the entrepreneurs were trying to do and thought them undisciplined, wild, visionary.

By and large, big companies have been successful as entrepreneurs only if they use their own people to build the venture. They have been successful only when they use people whom they understand and who understand them, people whom they trust and who in turn know how to get things done in the existing business; people, in other words, with whom one can work as partners. But this presupposes that the entire company is imbued with the entrepreneurial spirit, that it wants innovation and is reaching out for it, considering it both a necessity and an opportunity. It presupposes that the entire organization has been made "greedy for new things."

2. Innovative efforts that take the existing business out of its own field are rarely successful. Innovation had better not be "diversification." Whatever the benefits of diversification, it does not mix with entrepreneurship and innovation. The new is always sufficiently difficult not to attempt it in an area one does not understand. An existing business innovates where it has expertise, whether knowledge of market or knowledge of technology. Anything new will predictably get into trouble, and then one has to know the business. Diversification itself rarely works unless it, too, is built on commonality with the existing business, whether commonality of the market or commonality of the technology. Even then diversification has its problems. But if one adds to the difficulties and demands of diversification the difficulties and demands of entrepreneurship, the result is predictable disaster. So one innovates only where one understands.

3. Finally, it is almost always futile to avoid making one's own business entrepreneurial by "buying in," that is, by acquiring small entrepreneurial ventures. Acquisitions rarely work unless the company that does the acquiring is willing and able within a fairly short time to furnish management to the acquisition. The

managers that have come with the acquired company rarely stay around very long. If they were owners, they have now become wealthy; if they were professional managers, they are likely to stay around only if given much bigger opportunities in the new, acquiring company. So, within a year or two, the acquirer has to furnish management to run the business that has been bought. This is particularly true when a nonentrepreneurial company buys an entrepreneurial one. The management people in the new acquired venture soon find that they cannot work with the people in their new parent company, and vice versa.

SUMMARY

A business that wants to be able to innovate, wants to have a chance to succeed and prosper in a time of rapid change, has to build *entrepreneurial management* into its own system. It has to adopt *policies* that create, throughout the entire organization, the desire to innovate and the *habits* of entrepreneurship and innovation. To be a successful entrepreneur, the existing business, large or small, has to be managed as an entrepreneurial business.

35

The New Venture

For the *existing enterprise,* whether business or public-service institution, the controlling word in the term "entrepreneurial management" is "entrepreneurial." For the *new venture,* it is "management." In the existing business, it is the existing that is the main obstacle to entrepreneurship. In the new venture, it is its absence.

The new venture has an idea. It may have a product or a service. It may even have sales, and sometimes quite a substantial volume of them. It surely has costs. And it may have revenues and even profits. What it does not have is a "business," a viable, operating, organized "present" in which people know where they are going, what they are supposed to do, and what the results are or should be. But unless a new *venture* develops into a new *business* and makes sure of being "managed," it will not survive no matter how brilliant the entrepreneurial idea, how much money it attracts, how good its products, nor even how great the demand for them.

Refusal to accept these facts destroyed every single venture started by the nineteenth-century's greatest inventor, Thomas Edison. Edison's ambition was to be a successful businessman and the head of a big company. He should have succeeded, for he was a superb business planner. He knew exactly how an electric power company had to be set up to exploit his invention of the lightbulb. He knew exactly how to get all the money he could possibly need for his ventures. His products were immediate successes and the demand for them practically insatiable. But Edison remained an entrepreneur; or rather, he thought that "managing" meant being the boss. He refused to build a management team. And so every one of his four or five companies collapsed ignominiously once it got to middle size, and was saved only by booting Edison himself out and replacing him with professional management.

Entrepreneurial management in the new venture has four requirements:

It requires, first, *a focus on the market.*

It requires, second, *financial foresight,* and especially planning for cash flow and capital needs ahead.

It requires, third, *building a top management team* long before the new venture actually needs one and long before it can actually afford one.

And finally, it requires of the *founding entrepreneur a decision with respect to his or her own role, area of work, and relationships.*

THE NEED FOR MARKET FOCUS

A common explanation for the failure of a new venture to live up to its promise or even to survive at all is, "We were doing fine until these other people came and took our market away from us. We don't really understand it. What they offered wasn't so very different from what we had." Or one hears, "We were doing all right, but these other people started selling to customers we'd never even heard of and all of a sudden they had the market."

When a new venture does succeed, more often than not it is in a market other than the one it was originally intended to serve, with products or services that are not quite those with which it had set out, bought in large part by customers it did not even think of when it started, and used for a host of purposes besides the ones for which the products were first designed. If a new venture does not anticipate this, organizing itself to take advantage of the unexpected and unseen markets; if it is not totally market-focused, if not market-driven, then it will succeed only in creating an opportunity for a competitor.

A German chemist developed Novocain as the first local anesthetic in 1905. But he could not get doctors to use it; they preferred total anesthesia (they accepted Novocain only during World War I). But totally unexpectedly, dentists began to use the stuff. Whereupon—or so the story goes—the chemist began to travel up and down Germany making speeches against Novocain's use in dentistry. He had not designed it for that purpose!

That reaction was somewhat extreme, I admit. Still, entrepreneurs know what their innovation is meant to do. And if some other use for it appears, they tend to resent it. They may not actually refuse to serve customers they have not "planned" for, but they are likely to make it clear that these customers are not welcome.

This is what happened with the computer. The company that had the first computer, Univac, knew that its magnificent machine was designed for scientific work. And so it did not even send a salesman out when a business showed interest in it; surely, it argued, these people could not possibly know what a computer was all about. IBM was equally convinced that the computer was an instrument for scientific work: their own computer had been designed specifically for astronomical calculations. But IBM was willing to take orders from businesses and to serve them. Ten years later, around 1960, Univac still had by far the most advanced and best machine. IBM had the computer market.

The textbook prescription for this problem is "market research." But it is the wrong prescription. *One cannot do market research for something genuinely new.* One cannot do market research for something that is not yet on the market.

Similarly, several companies who turned down the Xerox patents did so on the basis of thorough market research that showed that printing companies had no use at all for a copier. Nobody had any inkling that businesses, schools, universities, colleges, and a host of private individuals would want to buy a copier.

The new venture therefore needs to start out with the assumption that its product or service may find customers in markets no one thought of, for uses no one envisaged when the product or service was designed, and that it will be bought by customers outside its field of vision and even unknown to the new venture.

To build market focus into a new venture is not in fact particularly difficult. But what is required runs counter to the inclinations of the typical entrepreneur. It requires, first, that the new venture systematically hunt out both the unexpected success and the unexpected failure. Rather than dismiss the unexpected as an "exception," as entrepreneurs are inclined to do, they need to go out and look at it carefully and view it as a distinct opportunity.

Shortly after World War II, a small Indian engineering firm bought the license to produce a European-designed bicycle with an auxiliary light engine. It looked like an ideal product for India; yet it never did well. The owner of this small firm noticed, however, that substantial orders came in for the engines alone. At first he wanted to turn down those orders; what could anyone possibly do with such a small engine? It was curiosity alone that made him go to the actual area the orders came from. There he found farmers were taking the engines off the bicycles and using them to power irrigation pumps that hitherto had been hand-operated. This manufacturer became the world's largest maker of small irrigation pumps, selling them by the millions. His pumps revolutionized farming all over Southeast Asia.

It does not require a great deal of money to find out whether an unexpected interest from an unexpected market is an indication of genuine potential or a fluke. It requires sensitivity and a little systematic work.

Above all, the people who are running a new venture need to spend time outside: in the marketplace, with customers, and with their own salespeople, looking and listening. The new venture needs to build in systematic practices to remind itself that a "product" or a "service" is defined by the *customer,* not by the *producer.* It needs to work continuously on challenging itself with respect to the *utility* and *value* that its products or services contribute to customers.

The greatest danger for the new venture is to "know better" than the customer what the product or service is or should be, how it should be bought, and what it should be used for. Above all, the new venture needs a willingness to see

the unexpected success as an opportunity rather than as an affront to its expertise. And it needs to accept that elementary axiom of marketing: Businesses are
not paid to *reform customers*. They are paid to *satisfy customers*.

FINANCIAL FORESIGHT

Lack of market focus is typically a disease of the "neonatal," the infant new venture. It is the most serious affliction of the new venture in its early stages—and
one that can permanently stunt even those that survive.

The lack of adequate financial focus and the right financial policies is, by contrast, the greatest threat to the new venture in the next stage of its growth. It is,
above all, a threat to a rapidly growing new venture. The more successful a new
venture is, the more dangerous is lack of financial foresight.

Suppose that a new venture has successfully launched its product or service and
is growing fast. It reports "rapidly increasing profits" and issues rosy forecasts. The
stock market then "discovers" the new venture, especially if it is high-tech or in a
field otherwise currently fashionable. Predictions abound that the new venture's
sales will reach a billion dollars within five years. Eighteen months later, the new
venture collapses.

It may not go out of existence or go bankrupt. But it is suddenly awash in red
ink, lays off 180 of its 275 employees, fires the president, or is sold at a bargain
price to a big company. The causes are always the same: lack of cash, inability to
raise the capital needed for expansion, and loss of control, with expenses, inventories, and receivables in disarray. These three financial afflictions often hit together
at the same time. Yet any one of them by itself endangers the health, if not the life,
of the new venture.

Once this financial crisis has erupted, it can be cured only with great difficulty
and considerable suffering. But it is eminently preventable.

Entrepreneurs starting new ventures are rarely unmindful of money; on the
contrary, they tend to be greedy. They therefore focus on profits. But this is the
wrong focus for a new venture, or rather, it should come last rather than first. *Cash
flow, capital, and controls* come much earlier. Without them, the profit figures are
fiction—good for twelve to eighteen months, perhaps, after which they evaporate.

Growth has to be fed. In financial terms, this means that growth in a new venture
demands adding financial resources rather than taking them out. Growth needs
more cash and more capital. If the growing new venture shows a "profit," it is a
fiction—a bookkeeping entry put in only to balance the accounts. And since taxes
are payable on this fiction in most countries, it creates a liability and a cash drain
rather than "surplus." The healthier a new venture and the faster it grows, the
more financial feeding it requires. The new ventures that are the darlings of the

newspapers and the stock market letters, the new ventures that show rapid profit growth and "record profits," are those most likely to run into desperate trouble a couple of years later.

The new venture needs cash flow analysis, cash flow forecasts, and cash management. The fact that America's new ventures of the last few years (with the significant exception of high-tech companies) have been doing so much better than new ventures used to do is largely because the new entrepreneurs in the United States have learned that entrepreneurship demands financial management.

Cash management is fairly easy if there are reliable cash flow forecasts, with "reliable" meaning "worst case" assumptions rather than hopes. There is an old banker's rule of thumb, according to which, in forecasting cash income and cash outlays, one assumes that bills will have to be paid sixty days earlier than expected and receivables will come in sixty days later. If the forecast is overly conservative, the worst that can happen—it rarely does in a growing new venture—is a temporary cash surplus.

A growing new venture should know twelve months ahead of time how much cash it will need, when, and for what purposes. With a year's lead time, it is almost always possible to finance cash needs. But even if a new venture is doing well, raising cash in a hurry and in a "crisis" is never easy and always prohibitively expensive. Above all, it always sidetracks the key people in the company at the most critical time. For several months they then spend their time and energy running from one financial institution to another and cranking out one set of questionable financial projections after another. In the end, they usually have to mortgage the long-range future of the business to get through a ninety-day cash bind. When they are finally able again to devote time and thought to the business, they have irrevocably missed the major opportunities. For the new venture, almost by definition, is under cash pressure when the opportunities are greatest.

The successful new venture will also outgrow its capital structure. A rule of thumb says that a new venture outgrows its capital base with every increase in sales (or billings) on the order of 40 to 50 percent. After such growth, a new venture also needs a new and different capital structure, as a rule. As the venture grows, private sources of funds, whether from the owners and their families or from outsiders, become inadequate. The company has to find access to much larger pools of money by going "public," by finding a partner or partners among established companies, or by raising money from insurance companies and pension funds. A new venture that had been financed by equity money now needs to shift to long-term debt, or vice versa. As the venture grows, the existing capital structure always becomes the wrong structure and an obstacle.

Finally, the new venture needs to plan the financial system it requires to manage growth. Again and again, a growing new venture starts off with an excellent product, excellent standing in its market, and excellent growth prospects. Then suddenly everything goes out of control: receivables, inventory, manufacturing costs, administrative costs, service, distribution—everything. Once one area gets out of control, all of them do. The enterprise has outgrown its control structure. By the time control has been reestablished, markets have been lost, customers have become disgruntled if not hostile, and distributors have lost their confidence in the company. Worst of all, employees have lost trust in management, and with good reason.

Fast growth always makes obsolete the existing controls. Again, a growth of 40 to 50 percent in volume seems to be the critical figure.

Once control has been lost, it is hard to recapture. Yet the loss of control can be prevented quite easily. What is needed is first to think through the critical areas in a given enterprise. In one, it may be product quality; in another, service; in a third, receivables and inventory; in a fourth, operating costs. *Rarely are there more than four or five critical areas in any given enterprise.* Managerial and administrative overhead should, however, always be included. A disproportionate and fast increase in the percentage of revenues absorbed by managerial and administrative overhead means that the enterprise is hiring managerial and administrative people faster than its potential for growth.

To live up to its growth expectations, a new venture must establish today the controls in these critical areas it will need three years hence. Elaborate controls are not necessary, nor does it matter that the figures are only approximate. What matters is that the management of the new venture is aware of these critical areas, is being reminded of them, and can thus act fast if the need arises. Disarray normally does not appear if there is adequate attention to the key areas. Then the new venture will have the controls it needs when it needs them. Financial foresight does not require a great deal of time. It does require a good deal of thought, however. The technical tools to do the job are easily available; they are spelled out in most texts on managerial accounting. But the work will have to be done by the enterprise itself.

BUILDING A TOP MANAGEMENT TEAM

The new venture has successfully established itself in the right market and has then successfully found the financial structure and the financial system it needs. Nonetheless, a few years later it is still prone to run into a serious crisis. Just when it appears to be on the threshold of becoming an "adult," a successful, established, going concern, it gets into trouble nobody seems to understand. The products are first-rate, the prospects are excellent, and yet the business simply cannot grow. Neither profitability nor quality, nor any of the other major areas, performs.

The reason is always the same: a lack of qualified top management. The business has outgrown being managed by one person, or even two people, and it now needs a management team at the top. If it does not have one already in place at the time, it is very late—in fact, usually too late. The best one can then hope is that the business will survive. But it is likely to be permanently crippled or to suffer scars that will bleed for many years to come. Morale has been shattered, and employees throughout the company are disillusioned and cynical. And the people who founded the business and built it almost always end up on the outside, embittered and disenchanted.

The remedy is simple: build a top-management team before the venture reaches the point where it must have one. Teams cannot be formed overnight. They require long periods before they can function. Teams are based on mutual trust and mutual understanding, and this takes years to build up. In my experience, three years is about the minimum.

But the small and growing new venture cannot afford a top-management team; it cannot sustain half a dozen people with big titles and corresponding salaries. In fact, in the small and growing business, a very small number of people do everything as it comes along. How, then, can one square this circle?

Again, the remedy is relatively simple. But it does require the will on the part of the founders to build a team rather than to keep on running everything themselves. If one or two people at the top believe that they, and they alone, must do everything, then a management crisis a few months, or at the latest, a few years down the road becomes inevitable.

Whenever the objective economic indicators of a new venture—market surveys, for instance, or demographic analysis—indicate that the business may double within three to five years, then it is the duty of the founder or founders to build the management team the new venture will very soon require. This is preventive medicine, so to speak.

First of all, the founders, together with other key people in the firm, will have to think through the *key activities* of their business. What are the specific areas upon which the survival and success of this particular business depend? Most of the areas will be on everyone's list. But if there are divergences and dissents—and there should be on a question as important as this—they should be taken seriously. Every activity that any member of the group thinks belongs there should go down on the list.

The key activities are not to be found in books. They emerge from analysis of the specific enterprise. Two enterprises that to an outsider appear to be in an identical line of business may well end up defining their key activities quite differently.

One, for instance, may put operations in the center; the other, customer service. Only two key activities are always present in any organization: there is always the *management of people,* and there is always the *management of money.* The rest has to be determined by the people within looking at the enterprise and at their own jobs, values, and goals.

The next step is, then, for each member of the group, beginning with the founder, to ask, "What are the activities that I am doing well? And what are the activities that each of my key associates in this business is doing well?" Again, there is going to be agreement on most of the people and on most of their strengths. But, again, any disagreement should be taken seriously. (On "activity analysis" for the design of organization structures, see chapter 38.)

Next one asks, "Which of the key activities should each of us, therefore, take on as his or her first and major responsibility because they fit the individual's strengths? Which individual fits which key activity?"

Then the work on building a team can begin. The founder starts to discipline himself or herself not to handle people and their problems if this is not the key activity that fits the founder best. Perhaps this individual's key strength is new products and new technology. Perhaps this individual's key activity is operations, manufacturing, physical distribution, service. Or perhaps it is money and finance, and someone else had better handle people. But all key activities need to be covered by someone who has proven ability in performance.

There is no rule that says, "A chief executive has to be in charge of this or that." Of course, a chief executive is the court of last resort and has ultimate accountability. And the chief executive also has to make sure to get the information necessary to discharge this ultimate accountability. The chief executive's own work, however, depends on what the enterprise requires and on who the individual is. As long as the CEO's work program consists of key activities, he or she does a CEO's job. But the CEO is also responsible for making sure that all the other key activities are adequately covered.

Finally, goals and objectives for each area need to be set. Everyone who takes on the primary responsibility for a key activity—whether product development or people or money—must be asked, "What can this enterprise expect of you? What should we hold you accountable for? What are you trying to accomplish and by what time?" But this is elementary management, of course.

It is prudent to establish the top-management team informally at first. There is no need to give people titles in a new and growing venture, nor to make announcements, nor even to pay extra. All this can wait a year or so, until it is clear that the new setup works, and how. In the meantime, all the members of the team have much to learn: their job, how they work together, and what they have to do to enable the CEO and their colleagues to do their jobs. Two or three years later, when the growing venture needs a top management, it has one.

However, should it fail to provide for a top management before it actually needs one, it will lose the capacity to manage itself long before it actually needs a top-management team. The founder will have become so overloaded that important tasks will not get done. At this point, the company can go one of two ways. The first possibility is that the founder concentrates on the one or two areas that fit his or her abilities and interests. These are key areas, indeed, but they are not the only crucial ones, and no one is then left to look after the others. Two years later, important areas have been slighted and the business is in dire straits. The other, worse, possibility is that the founder is conscientious. He knows that people and money are key activities and need to be taken care of. His own abilities and interests, which actually built the business, are in the design and development of new products. But being conscientious, the founder forces himself to take care of people and finance. Since he is not very gifted in either area, he does poorly in both. It also takes him forever to reach decisions or to do any work in these areas, so that he is forced, by lack of time, to neglect what he is really good at and what the company depends on him for, the development of new technology and new products. Three years later the company will have become an empty shell without the products it needs, but also without the management of people and the management of money it needs.

In the first example, it may be possible to save the company. After all, it has the products. But the founder will inevitably be removed by whoever comes in to salvage the company. In the second case, the company usually cannot be saved at all and has to be sold or liquidated.

Long before it has reached the point where it needs the balance of a top-management team, the new venture has to create one. Long before the time has come at which management by one person no longer works and becomes mismanagement, that one person also has to start learning how to work with colleagues, has to learn to trust people, yet also how to hold them accountable. The founder has to learn to become the leader of a team rather than a "star" with "helpers."

"WHERE CAN I CONTRIBUTE?"

Building a top-management team may be the single most important step toward entrepreneurial management in the new venture. It is only the first step, however, for the founders themselves, who then have to think through what their own future is to be.

As a new venture develops and grows, the roles and relationships of the original entrepreneurs inexorably change. If the founders refuse to accept this, they will stunt the business and may even destroy it.

Every founder-entrepreneur nods to this and says, "Amen." Everyone has horror stories of other founder-entrepreneurs who did not change as the venture changed, and who then destroyed both the business and themselves. But even among the founders who can accept that they themselves need to do something, few know how to tackle changing their own roles and relationships. They tend to begin by asking, "What do I like to do?" Or at best, "Where do I fit in?" The right question to start with is, *"What will the venture need objectively by way of management from here on out?"* And in a growing new venture, the founder has to ask this question whenever the business (or the public-service institution) grows significantly or changes direction or character, that is, changes its products, services, markets, or the kind of people it needs.

The next question the founder must ask is, "What am I good at? What, of all these needs of the venture, could I supply, and supply with distinction?" Only after having thought through these two questions should a founder then ask, "What do I really want to do, and believe in doing? What am I willing to spend years on, if not the rest of my life? Is this something the venture really needs? Is it a major, essential, indispensable contribution?"

But the questions of what a venture needs, what the strengths of the founder-entrepreneur are, and what he or she wants to do might be answered quite differently. Edwin Land, for instance, the man who invented Polaroid glass and the Polaroid camera, ran the company during the first twelve or fifteen years of its life, until the early 1950s. Then it began to grow fast. Land thereupon designed a top-management team and put it in place. As for himself, he decided that he was not the right man for the top management job in the company: what he and he alone could contribute was scientific innovation. Accordingly, Land built himself a laboratory and established himself as the company's consulting director for basic research. The company itself, in its day-to-day operations, he left to others to run.

Ray Kroc, the man who conceived and built McDonald's, reached a similar conclusion. He remained president until he died, well past age eighty. But he put a top-management team in place to run the company and appointed himself the company's "marketing conscience." Until shortly before his death, he visited two or three McDonald's restaurants each week, checking their *quality* carefully, the level of *cleanliness* and *friendliness*. Above all, he looked at the *customers,* talked to them and *listened* to them. This enabled the company to make the necessary changes to retain its leadership in the fast-food industry.

These questions may not always lead to such happy endings. They may even lead to the decision to leave the company.

In one of the most successful new financial services ventures in the United

States, this is what the founder concluded. He did establish a top-management team. He asked what the company needed. He looked at himself and his strengths; and he found no match between the needs of the company and his own abilities, let alone between the needs of the company and the things he wanted to do. "I trained my own successor for about eighteen months, then turned the company over to him and resigned," he said. Since then he has started three new businesses, not one of them in finance, has developed them successfully to medium size, and then quit again. He wants to develop new businesses but does not enjoy running them. He accepts that both the businesses and he are better off divorced from each other.

Other entrepreneurs in this same situation might reach different conclusions. The founder of a well-known medical clinic, a leader in its particular field, faced a similar dilemma. The needs of the institution were for an administrator and money-raiser. His own inclinations were to be a researcher and a clinician. But he realized that he was good at raising money and capable of learning to be the chief executive officer of a fairly large health-care organization. "And so," he says, "I felt it my duty to the venture I had created, and to my associates in it, to suppress my own desires and to take on the job of chief administrator and money-raiser. But I would never have done so had I not known that I had the abilities to do the job, and if my advisers and my board had not all assured me that I had these abilities."

The question, "Where do I belong?" needs to be faced up to and thought through by the founder-entrepreneur as soon as the venture shows the first signs of success. But the question can be faced up to much earlier. Indeed, it might be best thought through before the new venture is even started.

This is what Soichiro Honda, the founder and builder of Honda Motor Company in Japan, did when he decided to open a small business in the darkest days after Japan's defeat in World War II. He did not start his venture until he had found the right man to be his partner and to run administration, finance, distribution, marketing, sales, and personnel. For Honda had decided from the outset that he belonged in engineering and production and would not run anything else. This decision made the Honda Motor Company.

There is an earlier—and even more instructive—example, that of Henry Ford. When Ford decided in 1903 to go into business for himself, he did exactly what Honda did forty years later: before starting, he found the right man to be his partner and to run the areas where Ford knew he did not belong—administration, finance, distribution, marketing, sales, and personnel. Like Honda, Henry Ford knew that he belonged in engineering and manufacturing and was going to confine himself to these two areas. The man he found, James Couzens, contributed as much as Ford to the success of the company. Many of the best-known policies and practices of the Ford Motor Company for which Henry Ford is often given credit—the famous $5-a-day wage of 1913, or the pioneering distribution and service policies, for example—were Couzens's ideas and at first resisted by Ford. So effective did Couzens become that Ford grew increasingly jealous of him and forced him out in 1917. The last straw was Couzens's insistence that the Model T was obsolescent and his proposal to use some of the huge profits of the company to start work on a successor.

The Ford Motor Company grew and prospered to the very day of Couzens's resignation. Within a few short months thereafter, as soon as Henry Ford had taken every single top-management function into his own hands, forgetting that he had known earlier where he belonged, the Ford Motor Company began its long decline. Henry Ford clung to the Model T for a full ten years, until it had become literally unsalable. And the company's decline was not reversed for thirty years after Couzens's dismissal until, with his grandfather dying, a very young Henry Ford II took over the practically bankrupt business.

THE NEED FOR OUTSIDE ADVICE

These last cases point up an important factor for the entrepreneur in the new and growing venture, the need for independent, objective outside advice.

The growing new venture may not need a formal board of directors. Moreover, the typical board of directors very often does not provide the advice and counsel the founder needs. But the founder does need people with whom he can discuss basic decisions and to whom he listens. Such people are rarely to be found within the enterprise. Somebody has to challenge the founder's appraisal of the needs of the venture, and of his own personal strengths. Someone who is not a part of the problem has to ask questions, to review decisions, and, above all, to push constantly to have the long-term survival needs of the new venture satisfied, by building in the market focus, supplying financial foresight, and creating a functioning top-management team. This is the final requirement of entrepreneurial management in the new venture.

The new venture that builds such entrepreneurial management into its policies and practices will become a flourishing large business.

SUMMARY

In so many new ventures, especially high-tech ventures, the techniques discussed in this chapter—*a focus on the market, financial planning, the early need for a top-management team, and the future role of the founding entrepreneur*—are spurned and even despised. The argument is that they constitute "management" and "we are entrepreneurs." But this is not informality; it is irresponsibility. It confuses manners and substance. It is old wisdom that there is no freedom except under the law. *Freedom without law is license,* which soon degenerates into anarchy, and shortly thereafter, into tyranny. It is precisely because the new venture has to maintain and strengthen the entrepreneurial spirit that it needs foresight and discipline. It needs to prepare itself for the demands its own success will make of it. Above all, it needs *responsibility*—and this, in the last analysis, is what entrepreneurial management supplies to the new venture.

36

Entrepreneurial Strategies

Just as entrepreneurship requires entrepreneurial management, that is, practices and policies *within the enterprise,* so it requires *practices and policies outside,* in the marketplace. It requires entrepreneurial strategies.

There are four specifically entrepreneurial strategies:

1. Being "Fustest with the Mostest"

2. "Hitting Them Where They Ain't"

3. Finding and occupying a specialized "ecological niche"

4. Changing the economic characteristics of a product, a market, or an industry

These four strategies are not mutually exclusive. One and the same entrepreneur often combines two, sometimes even elements of three, in one strategy. They are also not always sharply differentiated; the same strategy might, for instance, be classified as "Hitting Them Where They Ain't" or as "Finding and occupying a specialized 'ecological niche.'" Still, each of these four has its prerequisites. Each fits certain kinds of innovation and does not fit others. Each requires specific behavior on the part of the entrepreneur. Finally, each has its own limitations and carries its own risks.

BEING "FUSTEST WITH THE MOSTEST"

Being "Fustest with the Mostest" was how a Confederate cavalry general in America's Civil War explained consistently winning his battles. In this strategy, the entrepreneur aims at leadership, if not at dominance, of a new market or a new industry. Being "Fustest with the Mostest" does not necessarily aim at creating a big business right away, though often this is indeed the aim. But it aims from the start at a permanent leadership position.

Being "Fustest with the Mostest" is the approach that many people consider the entrepreneurial strategy par excellence. Indeed, if one were to go by the popular books on entrepreneurship, one would conclude that being "Fustest with the Mostest" is the only entrepreneurial strategy—and a good many entrepreneurs, especially the high-tech ones, seem to be of the same opinion.

They are wrong, however. To be sure, a good many entrepreneurs have, indeed, chosen this strategy. Yet being "Fustest with the Mostest" is not even the dominant entrepreneurial strategy, let alone the one with the lowest risk or the highest success ratio. On the contrary, of all entrepreneurial strategies, it is the greatest gamble. And it is unforgiving, making no allowances for mistakes and permitting no second chance.

But if successful, being "Fustest with the Mostest" is highly rewarding.

Here are some examples to show what this strategy consists of and what it requires:

Hoffmann-LaRoche of Basel, Switzerland, has for many years been one of the world's largest and one of its most profitable pharmaceutical companies. But its origins were quite humble: until the mid-1920s, Hoffmann-LaRoche was a small and struggling manufacturing chemist, making a few textile dyes. It was totally overshadowed by the huge German dyestuff makers and two or three much bigger chemical firms in its own country. Then it gambled on the newly discovered vitamins at a time when the scientific world still could not quite accept that such substances existed. It acquired the vitamin patents—nobody else wanted them. It hired the discoverers away from Zurich University at several times the salaries they could hope to get as professors, salaries even industry had never paid before. And it invested all the money it had and all it could borrow in manufacturing and marketing these new substances. Sixty-years later, long after all vitamin patents had expired, Hoffmann-LaRoche had nearly half the world's vitamin market, amounting to billions of dollars a year.

DuPont followed the same strategy. When it came up with Nylon, the first truly synthetic fiber—after fifteen years of hard, frustrating research—DuPont at once mounted massive efforts, built huge plants, went into mass advertising (the company had never before had consumer products to advertise) and created the industry we now call plastics.

Not every "Fustest with the Mostest" strategy needs to aim at creating a big business, though it must always aim at *creating a business that dominates its market.* The 3M Company in St. Paul, Minnesota, does not—as a matter of deliberate policy, it seems—attempt an innovation that might result in a big business by itself. Nor does Johnson & Johnson. Both companies are among the most fertile and most successful innovators. Both look for innovations, however, that are dominant in their markets.

Perhaps because "Fustest with the Mostest" must aim at creating something truly new, something truly different, nonexperts and outsiders seem to do as well as the experts, in fact, often better. Hoffmann-LaRoche, for instance, did not owe its strategy to chemists; it owed it to a musician who had married the granddaughter of the company's founder and needed more money to support his orchestra than the company then provided through its meager dividends. To this day, the company has never been managed by chemists, but has always been managed by financial men who have first made their career in a major Swiss bank.

The strategy of being "Fustest with the Mostest" has to hit right on target or it misses altogether. Or, to vary the metaphor, being "Fustest with the Mostest" is very much like a moon shot: a deviation of a fraction of a minute of the arc and the missile disappears into outer space. And once launched, the "Fustest with the Mostest" strategy is difficult to adjust or to correct.

To use this strategy, in other words, requires thought and careful analysis. The entrepreneur of so much of the popular literature or of Hollywood movies, the person who suddenly has a "brilliant idea" and rushes off to put it into effect, is not going to succeed with it.

There has to be one clear-cut goal and all efforts have to be focused on it. And when this effort begins to produce results, the innovator has to be ready to mobilize resources massively.

Then, after the innovation has become a successful business, the work really begins. Then the strategy of "Fustest with the Mostest" demands substantial and continuing efforts to retain a leadership position; otherwise, all one has done is create a market for a competitor. The innovator has to run even harder now that he has leadership than he ran before and continue his innovative efforts on a very large scale. The research budget must be higher after the innovation has successfully been accomplished than it was before. New uses have to be found; new customers must be identified and persuaded to try the new materials. Above all, the entrepreneur who has succeeded in being "Fustest with the Mostest" has to make his product or his process obsolete before a competitor can do it. Work on the successor to the successful product or process has to start immediately, with the same concentration of effort and the same investment of resources that led to the initial success.

Finally, the entrepreneur who has attained leadership by being "Fustest with the Mostest" has to be the one who systematically cuts the price of his own product or process. *To keep prices high simply holds an umbrella over potential competitors and encourages them.*

The strategy of being "Fustest with the Mostest" is indeed so risky that an entire major strategy is based on the assumption that being "Fustest with the Mostest" will fail far more often than it can possibly succeed. It will fail because the will is lacking. It will fail because efforts are inadequate. It will fail because, despite successful innovation, not enough resources are deployed, are available, or are being put to work to exploit success, and so on. While the strategy is, indeed, highly rewarding when successful, it is much too risky and much too difficult to be used for anything but major innovations.

In most cases alternative strategies are available and preferable—not primarily because they carry less risk, but because for most innovations the opportunity is not great enough to justify the cost, the effort, and the investment of resources required for the "Fustest with the Mostest" strategy.

HITTING THEM WHERE THEY AIN'T (CREATIVE IMITATION & ENTREPRENEURIAL JUDO)

Two completely different entrepreneurial strategies are summed up by the words of another battle-winning Confederate general in America's Civil War, who said, "Hit Them Where They Ain't." These strategies might be called *creative imitation* and *entrepreneurial judo,* respectively.

Creative Imitation

"Creative imitation" is clearly a contradiction in terms. What is creative must surely be original. And if there is one thing imitation is not, it is "original." Yet the term fits. It describes a strategy that is "imitation" in its substance. What the entrepreneur does is something somebody else has already done. But it is "creative" because the entrepreneur applying the strategy of creative imitation understands what the innovation represents better than the people who made it and who innovated.

The foremost practitioner of this strategy and the most brilliant one is IBM.

In the early 1930s IBM built a high-speed calculating machine to do calculations for the astronomers at New York's Columbia University. A few years later it built a machine that was already designed as a computer—again, to do astronomical calculations—this time at Harvard. And by the end of World War II, IBM had built a real computer—the first one, by the way, that had the features of the true computer: a "memory" and the capacity to be "programmed." And yet there are good reasons why the history books pay scant attention to IBM as a computer innovator. For as soon as it had finished its advanced 1945 computer— the first computer to be shown to a lay public in its showroom in midtown New York, where it drew immense crowds—IBM abandoned its own design and switched to the design of its rival, the ENIAC, developed at the University of Pennsylvania. The ENIAC was far better suited to business applications such as payroll, only its designers did not see this. IBM structured the ENIAC so that it could be manufactured and serviced and could do mundane "numbers crunching." When IBM's version of the ENIAC came out in 1953, it at once set the standard for commercial, multipurpose, mainframe computers. This is the strategy of creative imitation.

It waits until somebody else has established the new, but only *approximately*. Then it goes to work. And within a short time it comes out with what the new really should be to satisfy the customer, to do the work customers want and pay for. The creative imitation has then set the standard and takes over the market.

When semiconductors became available, everyone in the watch industry knew that they could be used to power a watch much more accurately, much more reliably, and much more cheaply than traditional watch movements. The Swiss soon brought out a quartz-powered digital watch. But they had so much investment in traditional watchmaking that they decided on a *gradual introduction* of quartz-powered digital watches over a long period of time, during which these new timepieces would remain expensive luxuries.

Meanwhile, the Hattori Company in Japan had long been making conventional watches for the Japanese market. It saw the opportunity and went in for creative imitation, developing the quartz-powered digital watch as the standard timepiece. By the time the Swiss had woken up, it was too late. Seiko watches had become the world's best-sellers, with the Swiss almost pushed out of the market.

Like being "Fustest with the Mostest," creative imitation is a strategy aimed at market or industry leadership, if not at market or industry dominance. But it is much less risky. By the time the creative imitator moves, the market has been established and the new venture has been accepted. Indeed, there is usually more demand for it than the original innovator can easily supply. The market segmentations are known or at least knowable. By then, too, market research can find out what customers buy, how they buy, what constitutes value for them, and so on.

Of course, the original innovator may do it right the first time, thus closing the door to creative imitation. There is the risk of an innovator bringing out and doing the right job with vitamins, as Hoffmann-LaRoche did, or with Nylon, as did DuPont. But the number of entrepreneurs engaging in creative imitation, and their substantial success, indicates that perhaps the risk of the *first innovator's preempting the market* by getting it right is not an overwhelming one.

The creative imitator exploits the success of others. Creative imitation is not "innovation" in the sense in which the term is most commonly understood. The creative imitator does not invent a product or service; he *perfects and positions* it. In the form in which it has been introduced, it lacks something. It may be additional product features. It may be segmentation of product or services so that slightly different versions fit slightly different markets. It might be proper positioning of the product in the market. Or creative imitation supplies something that is still lacking.

The creative imitator looks at products or services from the viewpoint of the customer.

All told, creative imitation starts out with markets rather than with products, and with customers rather than with producers. It is both market focused and market driven.

Creative imitators do not succeed by taking away customers from the pioneers who have first introduced a new product or service; they serve markets the pioneers have created but do not adequately service. Creative imitation satisfies a demand that already exists rather than creating one.

The strategy has its own risks, and they are considerable. Creative imitators are easily tempted to splinter their efforts in the attempt to hedge their bets. Another danger is to misread the trend and imitate creatively what then turns out not to be the winning development in the marketplace.

IBM, the world's foremost creative imitator, exemplifies these dangers. It has successfully imitated every major development in the office-automation field. As a result, it had the leading product in every single area. But because they originated in imitation, the products were so diverse and so little compatible with one another that it was all but impossible to build an integrated, automated office out of IBM building blocks. And this risk, *the risk of being too clever,* is inherent in the creative imitation strategy.

Creative imitation is likely to work most effectively in high-tech areas for one simple reason: high-tech innovators are least likely to be *market focused* and most likely to be *technology and product focused.* They therefore tend to misunderstand their own success and to fail to exploit and supply the demand they have created.

Entrepreneurial Judo

The Japanese judo master looks for the strength that is his opponent's pride and joy. He assumes, and does so with high probability, that the opponent bases his strategy on this strength in every fight. And then the judo master figures out where this continuing reliance on a particular strength leaves the opponent *vulnerable* and *undefended.* Then he *turns his opponent's strength into the opponent's fatal weakness that defeats the opponent.* This is the entrepreneurial judo strategy.

In 1947, Bell Laboratories invented the transistor. It was at once realized that the transistor was going to replace the vacuum tube, especially in consumer electronics such as the radio and the brand-new television set. Everybody knew this; but nobody did anything about it. The leading manufacturers—at that time they were all American—began to study the transistor and to make plans for conversion to the transistor "sometime around 1970." Till then, they proclaimed, the transistor "would not be ready."

Sony was practically unknown outside of Japan and was not even in consumer electronics at the time. But Akio Morita, Sony's president, read about the transistor in the newspapers. As a result, he went to the United States and bought a license for the new transistor from Bell Labs for a ridiculous sum, all of $25,000. Two years later, Sony brought out the first portable transistor radio, which weighed less than one-fifth of comparable vacuum tube radios on the market, and cost less than one-third. Three years later, Sony had the market for cheap radios in the United States; and five years later, the Japanese had captured the radio market all over the world.

Of course, this is a classic case of the rejection of the *unexpected success*. The irony is that Americans rejected the transistor because it was "not invented here," that is, not invented by the electrical and electronic companies, RCA and GE. It is also a typical example of pride in doing things the hard way. The Americans were so proud of the wonderful radios of those days, the great *superheterodyne* sets that were such marvels of craftsmanship. Compared to them, they thought silicon chips low-grade, if not indeed beneath their dignity.

But Sony's success is not the real story. How do we explain that the Japanese repeated this same strategy again and again, and always with success, always surprising the Americans? The Japanese, in other words, have again and again been successful in practicing entrepreneurial judo.

But so were MCI and Sprint when they used the Bell Telephone System's (AT&T's) own pricing to take away from the Bell System a very large part of the long-distance business. So was ROLM when it used Bell System's policies against it to take away a large part of the private branch exchange (PBX) market. And so was Citibank when it started a consumer bank in Germany, the Familienbank (Family Bank), which within a few short years came to dominate German consumer finance.

The German banks knew that ordinary consumers had obtained purchasing power and had become desirable clients. They went through the motions of offering consumers banking services. But they really did not want them. Consumers, they felt, were beneath the dignity of a major bank, with its business customers and its rich investment clients. If consumers needed an account at all, they should have it with the postal savings bank.

All these newcomers—the Japanese, MCI, ROLM, Citibank—practiced "entrepreneurial judo." Of the entrepreneurial strategies, especially those strategies aimed at obtaining leadership and dominance in an industry or a market, entrepreneurial judo is by all odds the least risky and the most likely to succeed.

Every policeman knows that a habitual criminal will always commit his crime the same way—whether it is cracking a safe or entering a building he wants to loot. He leaves behind a "signature," which is as individual and as distinct as a fingerprint. And he will not change that signature even though it leads to his being caught time and again.

But it is not only the criminal who is set in his habits. All of us are. And so are businesses and industries. The habit will be persisted in even though it leads again and again to loss of leadership and loss of market. The American manufacturers persisted in the habits that enabled the Japanese to take over their market again and again.

If the criminal is caught, he rarely accepts that his habit has betrayed him. On the contrary, he will find all kinds of excuses—and continue the habit that led to his being captured. Similarly, businesses that are being *betrayed by their habits* will not admit it and will find all kinds of excuses. The American electronics manufacturers, for instance, attributed the Japanese successes to "low labor costs" in Japan. Yet the few American manufacturers *faced up to reality,* for example, RCA and Magnavox in television sets, were able to turn out in the United States products at prices competitive with those of the Japanese, and competitive also in quality, despite their paying American wages and union benefits. The German banks uniformly explain the success of Citibank's Familienbank as the result of its taking risks they themselves would not touch. But Familienbank had lower credit losses with consumer loans than the German banks, and its lending requirements were as strict as those of the Germans. The German banks knew this, of course. Yet they kept on explaining away their failure and Familienbank's success. This is typical. And it explains why the same strategy—the same entrepreneurial judo—can be used over and over again.

There are five fairly common bad habits, in particular, that enable newcomers to use entrepreneurial judo and to catapult themselves into a leadership position in an industry against the entrenched, established companies.

1. The first is what American slang calls NIH ("not invented here"), the arrogance that leads a company or an industry to believe that something new cannot be any good unless they themselves thought of it. And so the new invention is spurned, as was the transistor by the American electronics manufacturers.

2. The second is the tendency to "cream" a market, that is, to get the high-profit part of it. This is basically what Xerox did and what made it an easy target for the Japanese imitators of its copying machines. Xerox focused its strategy on the big users, the buyers of large numbers of machines or of expensive, high-performance machines. It did not reject the others; but it did not go after them. In particular, it did not see fit to give them service. In the end it was dissatisfaction with the service—or rather with the lack of service—Xerox provided for its smaller customers that made them receptive to competitors' machines. "Creaming" is a violation of elementary managerial and economic precepts. It is always punished by loss of market.

3. Even more debilitating is the third bad habit: the belief in "quality." "Quality" in a product or service is not what the supplier puts in. It is what the customer gets out and is willing to pay for. A product is not "quality" because it is hard to make and costs a lot of money, as manufacturers typically believe. That is incompetence.

Customers pay only for what is of use to them and gives them value. Nothing else constitutes "quality."

4. Closely related to both "creaming" and "quality" is the fourth bad habit, the delusion of the "premium" price. A "premium" price is always an invitation to the competitor. What looks like higher profits for the established leader is, in effect, a subsidy to the newcomer who, in a very few years, will unseat the leader and claim the throne for himself. "Premium" prices, instead of being an occasion for joy— and a reason for a higher stock price or a higher price-earnings multiple—should always be considered a threat and a dangerous vulnerability. Yet the delusion of higher profits to be achieved through "premium" prices is almost universal, even though it always opens the door to entrepreneurial judo.

5. Finally, there is a fifth bad habit that is typical of established businesses and leads to their downfall—Xerox provides a good example of this. They *maximize* rather than *optimize*. As the market grows and develops, they try to satisfy every single user through the same product or service. In contrast, when the Japanese came in with their copiers in competition with Xerox, they designed machines that fitted specific groups of users—for example, the small office, whether that of the dentist, the doctor, or the school principal. They did not, as the Xerox people did, try to match the features that they themselves were the proudest of, such as the speed of the machine or the clarity of the copy. They gave the small office what the small office needed most, a simple machine at a low cost. And once they had established themselves in that market, they then moved in on the other markets, each with a product designed to serve optimally a specific market segment.

Sony, similarly, first moved into the low end of the radio market, the market for cheap portables with limited range. Once it had established itself there, it moved in on the other market segments.

Entrepreneurial judo aims *first at securing a beachhead,* one that the established leaders either do not defend at all or defend only halfheartedly—the way the Germans did not counterattack when Citibank established its Familienbank. Once that beachhead has been secured, that is, once the newcomers have an adequate market and an adequate revenue stream, they then move on to the rest of the "beach" and finally to the whole "island." In each case, they repeat the strategy. *They design a product or a service that is specific to a given market segment and optimal for it.* And the established leaders hardly ever beat them to this game. Hardly ever do the established leaders manage to change their own behavior before the newcomers have taken over the leadership and acquired dominance.

Entrepreneurial judo requires some degree of genuine innovation. It is, as a rule, not good enough to offer the same product or the same service at lower cost. There has to be something that distinguishes it from what already exists. It is not enough, in other words, for the newcomer simply to do as good a job as the established leader at a lower cost or with better service. The newcomers have to make themselves distinct.

Like being "Fustest with the Mostest" and creative imitation, entrepreneurial judo aims at obtaining leadership position and eventually dominance. But it *does not do so by competing with the leaders*—or at least not where the leaders are aware of competitive challenge or worried about it. *Entrepreneurial judo* "hits them where they ain't" just as *creative imitation* "hits them where they ain't."

ECOLOGICAL NICHES

The entrepreneurial strategies discussed so far—being "Fustest with the Mostest" and "Hitting Them Where They Ain't," with its two variants, creative imitation and entrepreneurial judo—all aim at market or industry leadership, if not at dominance.

The ecological niche strategy aims at control. The strategies discussed earlier aim at positioning an enterprise in a large market or a major industry. The ecological niche strategy aims at obtaining a *practical monopoly in a small area*. The first two strategies are competitive strategies. The ecological niche strategy aims at making its successful practitioners immune to competition and unlikely to be challenged. Successful practitioners of "Fustest with the Mostest," creative imitation, and entrepreneurial judo become big companies, highly visible, if not household words. Successful practitioners of the ecological niche take the cash and let the acclaim go. They wallow in their anonymity. Indeed, in the most successful of the ecological niche strategies, the whole point is to be so inconspicuous, despite the product's being essential to a process, that no one is likely to try to compete.

There are three distinct niche strategies, each with its own requirements, its own limitations, and its own risks:

- The toll-gate strategy

- The specialty-skill strategy

- The specialty-market strategy

The Toll-Gate Strategy

Alcon Inc. developed an enzyme to eliminate the one feature of the standard surgical operation for senile cataracts that went counter to the rhythm and the logic of the process. Once this enzyme had been developed and patented, Alcon had a "toll-gate" position. No eye surgeon would do without it. No matter what Alcon charged for the teaspoonful of enzyme that was needed for each cataract operation, the cost was insignificant in relation to the total cost of the operation. I doubt that any eye surgeon or any hospital ever even inquired what the stuff cost. The total market for this particular preparation was so small—maybe $50 million a year worldwide—that it clearly would not have been worth anybody's while to try to develop a competing product. There would not have been one additional cataract operation in the world just because this particular enzyme had become cheaper. All that potential competitors could possibly do, therefore, would have been to knock down the price for everybody, without deriving much benefit for themselves.

The toll-gate position is thus in many ways the most desirable position a company can occupy. But it has stringent requirements. *The product has to be essential to a process. The risk of not using it*—the risk of losing an eye, losing an oil well, or spoilage in a tin can—*must be infinitely greater than the cost of the product.* The market must be so limited that whoever occupies it first preempts it. It must be a true ecological niche, which *one species fills completely,* and which at the same time is small and discreet enough not to attract rivals.

Such toll-gate positions are not easily found. Normally they occur only in an incongruity situation. The incongruity, as in the case of Alcon's enzyme, might be an *incongruity in the rhythm or the logic of a process* (on incongruity in a process, see chapter 37).

The toll-gate position also has severe limitations and serious risks. It is basically a static position. Once the ecological niche has been occupied, there is unlikely to be much growth. There is nothing the company that occupies the toll-gate position can do to increase its business or to control it. No matter how good its product or how cheap, the demand is dependent upon the demand for the process or product to which the toll-gate product furnishes an ingredient.

Once the toll-gate strategy has attained its objective, the company is "mature." It can grow only as fast as its end-users grow. But it can go down fast by becoming obsolete if someone finds a different way of satisfying the same end-use.

And the toll-gate strategist must never exploit his monopoly. He must not become what the Germans call a *Raubritter* (the English "robber baron" does not mean quite the same thing), who robbed and raped the hapless travelers as they passed through the mountain passages and river gorges atop of which perched his castle. He must not abuse his monopoly to exploit, to extort, to maltreat his customers. If he does, the users will put another supplier into business, or they will switch to less effective substitutes that they can then control.

The Specialty-Skill Strategy

Everybody knows the major automobile nameplates. But few people know the names of the companies that supply the electrical and lighting systems for these cars, and yet there are far fewer such companies than there are automobile nameplates: in the United States, the Delco Group; in Germany, Robert Bosch; in Great Britain, Lucas; and so on.

But once these companies had attained their controlling position in their specialty-skill niche, they retained it. *Unlike the toll-gate companies, theirs is a fairly large niche; yet it is still unique. It was obtained by developing high skill at a very early time.*

An enterprising German attained so great a hold on one specialty-skill niche that guidebooks for tourists are still called by his name, Baedeker. Karl Baedeker published his first guidebook in 1828, as soon as the first steamships on the Rhine opened tourist travel to the middle classes. He then had the field virtually to himself until World War I made German books unacceptable in Western countries.

As these cases show, timing is of the essence in establishing a specialty-skill niche. It has to be done at the very beginning of a new industry, a new custom, a new market, a new trend.

To attain a specialty niche always requires something new, something added, something that is genuine innovation.

There were guidebooks for travelers before Baedeker, but they confined themselves to the cultural scene—churches, sights, and so on. For practical details—the hotels, the tariff of the horse-drawn cabs, the distances, and the proper amount to tip—the traveling English milord relied on a professional, the courier. But the middle class had no courier, and that was Baedeker's opportunity. Once he had learned what information the traveler needed, how to get at it and to present it (the format he established is still the one many guidebooks follow), it would not have paid anyone to duplicate Baedeker's investment and build a competing organization.

In the early stages of a major new development, the specialty-skill niche offers an exceptional opportunity. Examples abound. For many, many years there were only two companies in the United States making airplane propellers, for instance. Both had been started before World War I.

A specialty-skill niche is rarely found by accident. In every single case, it results from a systematic survey of innovative opportunities. In every single case, the entrepreneur looks for the place where a specialty skill can be developed and can give a new enterprise a unique controlling position.

Robert Bosch spent years studying the new automotive field in order to position his new company where it could immediately establish itself as the leader. Hamilton Standard, for many years the leading airplane propeller manufacturer in the United States, was the result of a systematic search by its founder in the early days of powered flight. Baedeker made several attempts to start a service for the tourist before he decided on the guidebook that then bore his name and made him famous.

The first point, therefore, is that in the *early stages of a new industry, a new market, or a new major trend,* there is the opportunity to search systematically for the specialty-skill opportunity—and then there is usually time to develop a unique skill. The second point is that the specialty-skill niche does require a skill that is both unique and different.

The early automobile pioneers were, without exception, mechanics. They knew a great deal about machinery, about metals, and about engines. But electricity was alien to them. It required theoretical knowledge that they neither possessed nor knew how to acquire. There were other publishers in Baedeker's time, but a guidebook that required on-the-spot gathering of an enormous amount of detailed information, constant inspection, and a staff of traveling auditors was not within their purview.

The business that establishes itself in a specialty-skill niche is, therefore, unlikely to be threatened by its customers or by its suppliers. Neither of them really wants to get into something that is *so alien in skill and in temperament.*

The third point is that a business occupying a specialty-skill niche must constantly work on improving its own skill. It has to stay ahead. Indeed, it has to make itself constantly obsolete.

The automobile companies in the early days used to complain that Delco, in Dayton, and Bosch, in Stuttgart, were pushing them. They turned out lighting systems that were far ahead of the ordinary automobile, ahead of what the automobile manufacturers of the time thought the customer needed, wanted, or could pay for, ahead very often of what the automobile manufacturer knew how to assemble.

While the specialty-skill niche has unique advantages, it also has severe limitations. One is that it inflicts tunnel vision on its occupants. In order to maintain themselves in their controlling position, they have to learn to look neither right nor left, but directly ahead at their narrow area, their specialized field.

A second, serious limitation is that the occupant of a specialty-skill niche is usually dependent on somebody else to bring his or her product or service to market. It becomes a component. The strength of the automobile electrical firms is that the customer does not know that they exist. But this is, of course, also their weakness.

Finally, the greatest danger to the specialty-niche manufacturer is for the specialty to cease being a specialty and to become universal.

The specialty-skill niche, like all ecological niches, is, therefore, limited—in *scope* as well as in *time.* Species that occupy such a niche, biology teaches, do not easily adapt to even small changes in the external environment. And this is true, too, of the entrepreneurial-skill species. But within these limitations, the specialty-skill niche is a highly advantageous position. In a rapidly expanding new technology, industry, or market, it is perhaps the most advantageous strategy.

Very few of the automobile makers of 1920 are still around; many of the electrical and lighting systems makers are. Once attained and properly maintained, the specialty-skill niche protects against competition, precisely because no automobile buyer knows or cares who makes the headlights or the brakes. No automobile buyer is, therefore, likely to shop around for either. Once the name Baedeker had become synonymous with tourist guidebooks, there was little danger that anybody else would try to muscle in, at least not until the market changed drastically.

In a new technology, a new industry, or a new market, the specialty-skill strategy offers an *optimal ratio between opportunity and risk of failure.*

THE SPECIALTY-MARKET STRATEGY

The major difference between the specialty-skill niche and the specialty-market niche is that the former is built around a *product or service* and the latter around *specialized knowledge of a market.* Otherwise, they are similar.

Two medium-sized companies, one in northern England and one in Denmark, supply the great majority of the automated baking ovens for cookies and crackers bought in the non-Communist world.

There is, I am told, nothing very difficult or particularly technical about baking ovens. There are literally dozens of companies around that could make them just as well as those two firms in England and Denmark. But these two know the market: they know every single major baker, and every single major baker knows them. The market is just not big enough or attractive enough to try to compete with these two, as long as they remain satisfactory.

The specialty market is found by looking at a new development with the question: What opportunities are there in this that would give us a unique niche, and what do we have to do to fill it ahead of everybody else?

There was nothing particularly advanced in the early baking ovens. What the two leading firms did was to realize that the act of baking cookies and crackers was moving out of the home and into the factory. They then studied what commercial bakers needed so that they could manufacture the product their own customers—grocers and supermarkets—could, in turn, sell and the housewife would buy. The baking ovens were based not on engineering but on market research; the engineering would have been available to anyone.

The specialty-market niche has the same requirements as the specialty-skill niche: systematic analysis of a new trend, industry, or market; a specific innovative contribution, if only a "twist" like the one that converted the traditional letter of credit into the American Express travelers check; and continuous work to improve the product and especially the service, so that leadership, once obtained, will be retained.

And it has the same limitations. The greatest threat to the specialty-market position is success. The greatest threat is when the specialty market becomes a mass market.

Global banking and the consumer credit card have displaced a significant share of the market for travelers checks.

Perfumes have followed a similar dynamic. A French firm, Coty, created the modern perfume industry. It realized that World War I had changed the attitude toward cosmetics. Whereas before the war only "fast" women used cosmetics—or dared admit to their use—cosmetics had become accepted and respectable. By the mid-1920s, Coty had established itself in what was almost a monopoly position on both sides of the Atlantic. Until 1929 the cosmetics market was a "specialty market," a market of the upper middle class. But then during the Depression it exploded into a genuine mass market. It also split into two segments: a prestige segment, with high prices, specialty distribution, and specialty packaging; and popular-priced, mass brands sold in every outlet including the supermarket, the variety store, and the drugstore. Within a few short years, the specialty market dominated by Coty had disappeared. But Coty could not make up its mind whether to try to become one of the mass marketers in cosmetics or one of the luxury producers. It tried to stay in a market that no longer existed. Finally, through a huge acquisition in 2005, it became the largest manufacturer of mass-market cosmetics.

CHANGING VALUES AND CHARACTERISTICS

In the entrepreneurial strategies discussed so far, the aim is to introduce an innovation. In the entrepreneurial strategy discussed in this section, *the strategy itself is the innovation.* The product or service it changes may well have been around a long time. But the strategy converts this old, established product or service into something new. It changes its *utility,* its *value,* its *economic characteristics. While physically there is no change, economically there is something different and new.*

All the strategies to be discussed in this section have one thing in common. They create a customer—and that is the ultimate purpose of a business, indeed, of economic activity. But they do so in four different ways:

- By creating utility

- By pricing

- By adaptation to the customer's social and economic reality

- By delivering what represents true value to the customer

Creating Customer Utility

Price is usually almost irrelevant in the strategy of creating utility. The strategy works by enabling customers to do what serves *their purpose*. It works because it asks, What is truly a "service," truly a "utility" to the customer?

Every American bride wants to get one set of "good china." A whole set is, however, far too expensive a present, and the people giving her a wedding present may not know what pattern the bride wants or what pieces she already has. So they end up giving something else. The demand was there, in other words, but the utility was lacking. A medium-sized dinnerware manufacturer, Lenox Inc., saw this as an innovative opportunity. Lenox adapted an old idea, the "bridal register," so that it only "registers" Lenox china. The bride-to-be picks one merchant to whom she tells what pattern of Lenox china she wants, and to whom she refers potential donors of wedding gifts. The merchant then asks the donor, "How much do you want to spend?" and explains, "That will get you two coffee cups with saucers." Or the merchant can say, "She already has all the coffee cups; what she needs now is dessert plates." The result is a happy bride, a happy wedding-gift donor, and a very happy Lenox china company.

Again, there is no high technology here, nothing patentable, nothing but a focus on the needs of the customer. Yet the bridal register, for all its simplicity—or perhaps because of it—has made Lenox a favorite "good china" manufacturer.

Pricing

For many years, the best-known American face in the world was that of King Gillette, which graced the wrapper of every Gillette razor blade sold anyplace in the world. And millions of men all over the world used a Gillette razor blade every morning.

King Gillette did not invent the safety razor; dozens of them were patented in the closing decades of the nineteenth century.

Gillette's safety razor was no better than many others, and it was a good deal more expensive to produce. But Gillette did not "sell" the razor. He practically gave it away by pricing it at 55 cents retail or 20 cents wholesale, not much more than one-fifth of its manufacturing cost. But he designed it so that it could use only his patented blades. These cost him less than 1 cent apiece to make: he sold them for 5 cents. And since the blades could be used six or seven times, they delivered a shave at less than 1 cent apiece—or at less than one-tenth the cost of a visit to a barber.

What Gillette did was *to price what the customer buys,* namely, the shave, rather than what the manufacturer sells. In the end, the captive Gillette customer may have paid more than he would have paid had he bought a competitor's safety razor for $5, and then bought the competitor's blades selling at 1 cent or 2 cents. Gillette's customers surely knew this. But Gillette's pricing made sense to them. They were paying for what they bought, that is, for a shave, rather than for a "thing." And the shave they got from the Gillette razor and the Gillette razor blade was much more pleasant than any shave they could have given themselves with that dangerous weapon, the straight-edge razor, and far cheaper than they could have gotten at the neighborhood barber's.

One reason why the patents on a copying machine ended up at a small, obscure company in Rochester, New York, then known as the Haloid Company, rather than at one of the big printing-machine manufacturers, was that none of the large established manufacturers saw any possibility of selling a copying machine. Their calculations showed that such a machine would have to sell for at least $4,000 at that time. Nobody was going to pay such a sum for a copying machine when carbon paper cost practically nothing. Also, of course, to spend $4,000 on a machine meant a capital-appropriations request, which had to go all the way up to the board of directors accompanied by a calculation showing the return on investment, both of which seemed unimaginable for a gadget to help the secretary. The Haloid Company—the present Xerox—did a good deal of technical work to design the final machine. But its major contribution was in *pricing*. At 5 or 10 cents a copy, there is no need for a capital-appropriations request. This is "petty cash," which the secretary can disburse without going upstairs. *Pricing the Xerox machine at 5 cents a copy was the true innovation.*

Most suppliers, including public-service institutions, never think of pricing as a strategy. Yet pricing enables the customer to pay for what he buys—a shave, a copy of a document—rather than for what the supplier makes. What is being paid in the end is, of course, the same amount. But how it is being paid is *structured to the needs and the realities of the consumer.* It is structured in accordance with what the consumer actually buys. And it charges for what represents "value" to the customer rather than what represents "cost" to the supplier.

Adapting to Customer Reality

The worldwide leadership of the General Electric Company (GE) in large steam turbines is based on GE's having thought through, in the years before World War I, what its customers' realities were. Steam turbines, unlike the piston-driven steam engines that they replaced in the generation of electric power, are complex, requiring a high degree of engineering in their design, and skill in building and fitting them. This the individual electric power company simply cannot supply. It buys a major steam turbine maybe every five or ten years when it builds a new power station. Yet the maintenance skill has to be kept in place all the time. The manufacturer, therefore, has to set up and maintain a massive consulting organization.

But, as GE soon found out, the customer cannot pay for consulting services.

Under American law, the state public utility commissions would have to allow such expenditure. In the opinion of the commissions, however, the companies should have been able to do this work themselves. GE also found that it could not add to the price of the steam turbine the cost of the consulting services that its customers needed. Again, the public utility commissions would not have accepted it. But, while a steam turbine has a very long life, it needs a new set of blades fairly often, maybe every five to seven years, and these blades have to come from the maker of the original turbine. GE built up the world's foremost consulting engineering organization on electric power stations—though it was careful not to call this consulting engineering but "apparatus sales"—for which it did not charge. Its steam turbines were no more expensive than those of its competitors. But it put the added cost of the consulting organization plus a substantial profit into the price it charged for replacement blades. Within ten years all the other manufacturers of steam turbines had caught on and switched to the same system. But by then GE had world market leadership.

Much earlier, during the 1840s, a similar design of product and process to fit customer realities led to the invention of *installment buying*. Cyrus McCormick was one of many Americans who built a harvesting machine—the need was obvious. And he found, as had the other inventors of similar machines, that he could not sell his product. The farmer did not have the purchasing power. That the machine would earn back what it cost within two or three seasons, everybody knew and accepted, but there was no banker then who would have lent the American farmer the money to buy a machine. McCormick offered installments, to be paid out of the savings the harvester produced over the ensuing three years. The farmer could now afford to buy the machine—and he did so.

Manufacturers are wont to talk of the "irrational customer." But there are no "irrational customers." As an old saying has it, "There are only lazy manufacturers." The customer has to be assumed to be rational. *His or her reality, however, is usually quite different from that of the manufacturer.*

Delivering Value to the Customer

The last of these innovative strategies delivers what is "value" to the customer rather than what is "product" to the manufacturer. It is actually only one step beyond the strategy of accepting the customer's reality as part of the product and part of what the customer buys and pays for.

A medium-sized company in America's Midwest supplies more than half of all the special lubricant needed for very large earthmoving and hauling machines, the bulldozers and draglines used by contractors building highways, the heavy equipment used to remove the overlay from strip mines, the heavy trucks used to haul coal out of coal mines, and so on. This company is in competition with some of the largest oil companies, which can mobilize whole battalions of lubrication special-ists. It competes by not selling lubricating oil at all. Instead, it sells what is, in effect, insurance. What is "value" to the contractor is not lubrication: it is operat-ing the equipment. Every hour the contractor loses because this or that piece of heavy equipment cannot operate costs him infinitely more than he spends on lu-bricants during an entire year. In all these activities, there is a heavy penalty for contractors who miss their deadlines—and they can get the contract only by cal-culating the deadline as finely as possible and racing against the clock.

What the midwestern lubricant maker does is to offer contractors an analysis of the maintenance needs of their equipment. Then it offers them a maintenance program with an annual subscription price, and guarantees the subscribers that their heavy equipment will not be shut down for more than a given number of hours per year because of lubrication problems. Needless to say, the program al-ways prescribes the manufacturer's lubricant. But this is not what contractors buy. They are buying trouble-free operations, which are extremely valuable to them.

These examples are likely to be considered obvious. Surely, anybody applying a little intelligence would have come up with these and similar strategies? But the father of systematic economics, David Ricardo, is believed to have said once, "Prof-its are not made by differential cleverness, but by differential stupidity." The strat-egies work, not because they are clever, but because most suppliers—of goods as well as of services, businesses as well as public-service institutions—do not think. The strategies work precisely because they are so "obvious." Why, then, are they so rare? For, as these examples show, anyone who asks the question, What does the customer really buy? will win the race. In fact, it is not even a race, since nobody else is running. What explains this?

One reason is the economists and their concept of "value." Every economics book points out that customers do not buy a "product"; they buy what the product does for them. And then, every economics book promptly drops consideration of everything except the "price" for the product, a "price" defined as what the cus-tomer pays to take possession or ownership of a thing or a service. What the prod-uct does for the customer is never mentioned again. Unfortunately, suppliers, whether of products or of services, tend to follow the economists.

It is meaningful to say that "product A costs X dollars." It is meaningful to say that "we have to get Y dollars for the product to cover our own costs of production and have enough left over to cover the cost of capital, and thereby to show an ade-quate profit." But it makes no sense at all to conclude, "and therefore the customer has to pay the lump sum of Y dollars in cash for each piece of product A he buys. Rather, the argument should go as follows: "What the customer pays for each piece of the product has to work out as Y dollars for us. But how the customer pays depends on what makes the most sense to him or her. It depends on what the product does for the customer. It depends on what fits customer reality. It depends on what the customer sees as 'value.'"

Price in itself is not "pricing," and it is not "value." "But this is nothing but elementary marketing," most readers will protest, and they are right. It is nothing but elementary marketing. To start out with the customer's utility, with what the customer buys, with what the realities of the customer are and what the customer's values are—this is what marketing is all about. But, the fact remains that, so far, anyone who is willing to *use marketing as the basis for strategy* is likely to acquire leadership in an industry or a market fast and almost without risk.

SUMMARY

The choice of an entrepreneurial strategy that fits a certain innovation is a high-risk decision. Some entrepreneurial strategies are better fits in given situations, for example, the strategy of entrepreneurial judo, which is the strategy of choice where the leading businesses in an industry persist year in and year out in the same habits of arrogance and false superiority. We can describe the typical advantages and the typical limitations of certain entrepreneurial strategies.

Above all, we know that an entrepreneurial strategy has more chance of success the more it starts out with the users—their utilities, their values, their realities. An innovation is a change in market or society. It produces a greater yield for the user and greater wealth-producing capacity. The test of an innovation is always what it does for the user. Hence, entrepreneurship always needs to be market focused, indeed, market driven.

Still, entrepreneurial strategy remains the decision-making area of entrepreneurship and therefore the risk-taking one. It is by no means a hunch or gamble. But it also is not precisely science. Rather, it is judgment.

37

Systematic Innovation Using Windows of Opportunity

Systematic innovation consists in the purposeful and organized search for changes, and in the systematic analysis of the opportunities such changes might offer for economic or social innovation.

A policy of systematically analyzing *windows of opportunity* for innovation is as important as *entrepreneurial strategies* (chapter 36) and *entrepreneurial management* (chapters 34 and 35). These three topics comprise the most important topics of *innovation and entrepreneurship.*

SEVEN WINDOWS OF OPPORTUNITY

Analyzing windows of opportunity requires a systematic policy of looking, every six to twelve months, for changes that might be opportunities—in the areas called "the windows of opportunity."

The lines between these seven source areas of innovative opportunity are blurred, and there is considerable overlap between them. They can be likened to seven windows, each on a different side of the same building. Each window shows some features that can also be seen from the windows on either side of it. But the view from the center of each is distinct and different.

These seven source areas are:

1. The organization's own *unexpected successes* and *unexpected failures,* but also the unexpected successes and unexpected failures of the organization's competitors.

In the early 1930s, IBM developed the first modern accounting machine, which was designed for banks. But banks in 1933 did not buy new equipment. What saved the company—according to a story that Thomas Watson, Sr., the company's founder and long-term CEO, often told—was its exploitation of an *unexpected success:* The New York Public Library wanted to buy a machine. Unlike the banks, libraries in those early New Deal days had money, and Watson sold more than a hundred of his otherwise unsalable machines to libraries.

The *unexpected failure* may be an equally important source of innovation opportunities. Everyone knows about the Ford Edsel as the biggest new-car failure in automotive history. What very few people seem to know, however, is that the Edsel's failure was the foundation for much of the company's later success. When the Edsel bombed, despite all the planning, market research, and design that had gone into it, Ford realized that something was happening in the automobile market that ran counter to the basic assumptions on which Ford, GM, and everyone else had been designing and marketing cars. No longer was the market segmented primarily by income groups; the new principle of segmentation was what we now call *lifestyles.* Ford's response was the Mustang, a car that gave the company a distinct personality and reestablished it as an industry leader.

2. *Incongruities,* especially incongruities in the process, whether of production or distribution, or incongruities in customer behavior.

Alcon Laboratories was one of the success stories of the 1960s because Bill Conner, the company's cofounder, exploited an incongruity or a dangerous step, in the surgical procedure involving the cataract operation. He allowed surgeons to eliminate this dangerous step by using an enzyme that he discovered. This is an example of using a window of opportunity to apply the *toll-gate entrepreneurial strategy* as illustrated in chapter 36. All Conner did was to add a preservative to this enzyme that gave it a few months' shelf life. The increased shelf life allowed it to be used on demand by eye surgeons. Eye surgeons immediately accepted the new compound, and Alcon found itself with a worldwide monopoly.

Such an incongruity within the logic or rhythm of a process is only one possibility out of which innovation opportunities may arise. Another source is incongruity between economic realities. For instance, whenever an industry has a steadily *growing market but falling profit margins*—as, say, in the steel industries of developed countries between 1950 and 1970—an incongruity exists. The innovative response: the *mini-mill.*

3. Process needs.

In innovations that are based on process need, everybody in the organization always knows that the need exists. Yet usually no one does anything about it. However, when the innovation appears, it is immediately accepted as "obvious" and soon becomes "standard."

Successful process innovation requires the presence of five conditions:

- A self-contained process

- A weak or missing link

- A clear definition of objectives

- Clearly defined specifications for the solution

- Widespread realization that there ought to be a better way

"Program research" is often needed to convert a process from potential into reality. Again, the need must be felt, and it must be possible to identify what is needed. Then the new knowledge has to be produced. The prototype innovator for this kind of process-need innovation was Thomas Edison. For twenty-odd years, everybody had known that there was going to be an "electric power industry." For the last five or six years of that period, it had become abundantly clear what the *missing link* was: the *lightbulb*. Without it, there could be no electric power industry. Edison defined the new knowledge needed to convert this potential electric power industry into an actual one, went to work, and had a lightbulb within two years.

4. Changes in industry and market structures.

One of American business's great success stories in recent decades is the brokerage firm of Donaldson, Lufkin & Jenrette. Sold to E*TRADE in early 2006, it was founded in 1960 by three young men, all graduates of the Harvard Business School, who realized that the structure of the financial industry was changing as institutional investors became dominant. These young men had practically no capital and no connections. Still, within a few years, their firm had become a leader in the move to negotiate commissions and one of Wall Street's stellar performers. It was the first institutional investment company to incorporate and go public.

In a similar fashion, changes in industry structure have created massive innovation opportunities for American health-care providers. During the past twenty-five years or so, independent surgical and psychiatric clinics, emergency centers, and HMOs have opened throughout the country.

Comparable opportunities in telecommunications followed industry upheavals—in transmission (with the emergence of MCI and Sprint in long-distance service), and in equipment (with the emergence of such companies as ROLM in the manufacturing of private branch exchanges).*

Innovations that exploit changes in market structure are particularly effective if one very large manufacturer or supplier dominates the industry and its markets during a period of rapid growth. For example, The U.S. Post Office did not react when United Parcel Service and FedEx took away larger and larger shares of business. What made the Post Office so vulnerable was rapid growth in the demand for urgent delivery of time-sensitive documents and packages.

---

* ROLM was bought by IBM and later was bought from IBM by Siemens AG.

5. Changes in demographics.

Of the outside sources of innovation opportunities, demographics are the most reliable. Demographic events have known lead times; for instance, every person who will be in the American labor force by the year 2020 has already been born. Yet because policy makers often neglect demographics, those who watch them and exploit them can reap great rewards.

The Japanese took an early lead in robotics because they paid attention to demographics. Everyone in the developed countries around 1970 or so knew that there was both a baby bust and an education explosion going on; about half or more of the young people were staying in school beyond high school. Consequently, the number of people available for traditional blue-collar work in manufacturing was bound to decrease and become inadequate by 1990. Everyone knew this, but only the Japanese acted on it, and they took a ten-year lead in robotics.

6. Changes in meaning and perception.

"The glass is half full" and "The glass is half empty" are descriptions of the same phenomenon but have vastly different meanings. Changing a manager's perception of a glass from half full to half empty opens up big innovation opportunities.

All factual evidence indicates, for instance, that in the last forty years, Americans' health has improved with unprecedented speed—whether measured by mortality rates for the newborn, survival rates for the very old, the incidence of cancers, cancer cure rates, successful organ transplantation, or other factors. Even so, a collective hypochondrium grips the nation. Never before has there been so much concern with or fear about health. Suddenly, everything seems to cause cancer or degenerative heart disease or premature loss of memory. The glass is clearly *half empty*.

Rather than rejoicing in great improvements in health, Americans seem to be emphasizing how far away they still are from immortality. This view of things has created many opportunities for innovations: markets for new health-care magazines, for exercise classes and jogging equipment, and for all kinds of health food.

7. And finally: new knowledge.

Among history-making innovations, those that are based on new knowledge—whether scientific, technical, or social—rank high. They are the superstars of entrepreneurship; they get the publicity and the money. They are what people usually mean when they talk of innovation, although not all innovations based on knowledge are important.

Knowledge-based innovations differ from all others in the time they take, in their casualty rates, and in their predictability, as well as in the challenges they pose to entrepreneurs. They have the longest lead time of all innovations. There is a protracted span between the emergence of new knowledge and its distillation into usable technology. Then there is another long period before this new technology appears in the marketplace in products, processes, or services.

To become effective, innovation of this sort usually demands not one kind of knowledge but many.

The computer, to cite another example, required no fewer than six separate strands of knowledge:

- Binary arithmetic

- Charles Babbage's conception of a calculating machine, in the first half of the nineteenth century

- The punch card, invented by Herman Hollerith for the U.S. census of 1890

- The audion tube, an electronic switch invented in 1906

- Symbolic logic, which was developed between 1910 and 1913 by Bertrand Russell and Alfred North Whitehead

- Concepts of programming and feedback that came out of abortive attempts during World War I to develop effective antiaircraft guns

Although all the necessary knowledge was available by 1918, the first operational digital computer did not appear until 1946.

A change in any one of these seven windows of opportunity raises the question, "Is this an opportunity for us to innovate, that is, to develop different products, services, processes? Does it indicate new and different markets and/or customers? New and different technologies? New and different distribution channels?" Innovation can never be risk free. But if innovation is based on *exploiting what has already happened*—in the enterprise itself, in its markets, in knowledge in society, in demographics, and so on—*it is far less risky* than not to innovate by exploiting these opportunities.

Innovation is not "flash of genius." It is hard work. And this work should be organized as a regular part of every unit within the enterprise, and of every level of management.

PILOTING

Enterprises of all kinds increasingly use all kinds of market research and customer research to limit, if not eliminate, the risks of change. But one cannot market research the truly new. Also nothing new is right the first time. Invariably, problems crop up that nobody even thought of. Invariably, problems that loomed very large to the originator turn out to be trivial or not to exist at all. Above all, the way to do the job invariably turns out to be different from what was originally designed.

It is almost a "law of nature" that anything that is truly new, whether product or service or technology, finds its major market and its major application not where the innovator and entrepreneur expected, and not to be the use for which the innovator or entrepreneur has designed it. And that, no market or customer research can possibly discover.

The best example is an early one:

The improved steam engine that James Watt (1736–1819) designed and patented in 1776 is the event that, for most people, signifies the advent of the Industrial Revolution. Actually, Watt until his death saw only one use for the steam engine: to pump water out of coal mines. That was the use for which he had designed it. And he sold it only to coal mines. It was his partner, Matthew Boulton (1728–1809), who was the real father of the Industrial Revolution. Boulton saw that the improved steam engine could be used in what was then England's premier industry, textiles, and especially in the spinning and weaving of cotton. Within ten or fifteen years after Boulton had sold his first steam engine to a cotton mill, the price of cotton textiles had fallen by 70 percent. And this created both the first mass market and the first factory—and together modern capitalism and the modern economy altogether.

Neither studies nor market research nor computer modeling are a substitute for the *test of reality*. Everything improved or new needs, therefore, first to be tested on a small scale, that is, it needs to be *piloted*.

The way to do this is to find somebody within the enterprise who really wants the new. As said before, everything new gets into trouble. And then it needs a champion. It needs somebody who says, "I am going to make this succeed," and who then goes to work on it. And this person needs to be somebody whom the organization respects. This need not even be somebody within the organization. A good way to pilot a new product or new service is often to find a customer who really wants the new, and who is willing to work with the producer on making the new product or the new service truly successful.

If the pilot test is successful—if it finds the problems nobody anticipated but also finds the opportunities that nobody anticipated, whether in terms of design, of market, of service—the risk of change is usually quite small. And it is usually also quite clear where to introduce the change and how to introduce it, that is, what entrepreneurial strategy to employ.

SUMMARY

A policy of systematic innovation produces the mind-set for innovation in an organization. It makes the entire organization see change as an opportunity. As a rule, these are changes that have already occurred or are under way. The overwhelming majority of successful innovations exploit change. To be sure, there are

innovations that in themselves constitute a major change; some of the major technical innovations, such as the Wright Brothers' airplane, are examples. But these
are exceptions, and fairly uncommon ones. Most successful innovations are far
more prosaic; they exploit change. And thus the discipline of innovation is a diagnostic discipline: a systematic examination of the areas of change that typically
offer entrepreneurial opportunities.

The seven sources require separate analysis, for each has its own distinct characteristic. No area is, however, inherently more important or more productive than
the other. Major innovations are as likely to come out of an analysis of symptoms
of change (such as the unexpected success of what was considered an insignificant
change in product or pricing) as they are to come out of the massive application of
new knowledge resulting from a great scientific breakthrough.

Everything new or improved should first be piloted before attempting to introduce the innovation on a large scale.

Part IX
Managerial Organization

Organization structure is the oldest and most thoroughly studied area in management. But we face new needs in organization that the well-known and well-tested structural design of "functional" and "decentralized" organization cannot adequately satisfy. New structural designs are emerging: the task-force team, simulated decentralization, the systems structure. We have learned that organization does not start with structure but with building blocks. There is no one right or universal design; each enterprise needs to design around the key activities appropriate to its mission and its strategies. Three different kinds of work—operating, innovative, and top management—have to be accommodated under the same organizational roof. Organization structure needs to be both task focused and person focused and to have both an authority axis and a responsibility axis.

38

Strategies and Structures

Organization studies leading to the reorganizing of companies, divisions, and functions have been one of the more spectacular "growth industries" of the last few decades. Everybody—whether business, government department or armed service, research laboratory, Catholic diocese, university administration, or hospital—seems to be forever engaged in reorganizing.

There are reasons for this interest in organization and for the underlying conviction that inherited organization structures or structures that "just grew" are unlikely to satisfy the needs of the enterprise. Above all, we have learned the danger of the wrong organization structure. *The best structure will not guarantee results and performances, but the wrong structure is a guarantee of nonperformance.* All it produces are friction and frustration. The wrong organization spotlights the wrong issues, aggravates irrelevant disputes, and makes a mountain out of trivia. It accents weaknesses instead of strengths.

The right organization structure is, thus, a prerequisite of performance.

Until very recently, interest in organization was to be found only in very large businesses. The earlier examples—Alfred P. Sloan's organization structure for General Motors in the early 1920s, for one—all came from large businesses.

Today, we know that organization becomes most critical when a small business grows into a medium-sized one, and a simple business into a complicated one. The small business that wants to grow, even into only a medium-sized business, has to think through and work out the right organization to enable it both to function as a small business and to be able to grow into something bigger. Similarly, the simple one-product, one-market business faces crucial organization problems the moment it adds even a little diversity or complexity.

YESTERDAY'S FINAL ANSWERS

But while we have accepted that organization and management structure are crucial, we are fast outgrowing yesterday's "final answers," as indicated in chapter 7.

Twice in the short history of management we have already had the "final answer" to organization. The first time was around 1910 when Henri Fayol, the

French industrialist, had thought through the functions of a manufacturing company. At that time the manufacturing business was, of course, the truly important organizational problem, and the functions he defined then—such as engineering, manufacturing, and marketing—still apply to manufacturing businesses today.

A generation later one could again say that we "knew." Fayol had given "the answer" for the single-product manufacturing business. Alfred P. Sloan, Jr., in organizing General Motors in the 1920s, made the next step. He found "the answer" for organizing the complex and large manufacturing company. The Sloan approach used Fayol's functional organization for the subunits, the individual departments, but organized the business itself on the basis of *federal decentralization*. This structure is based on *decentralized authority* and *coordinated control*. After World War II, it became the organization model worldwide, especially for larger organizations.

Another generation later, by the early 1950s, it was becoming clear that the General Motors model was no more adequate to new and important challenges in organization than Fayol's model had been adequate to the realities of a very big business that Alfred P. Sloan, Jr., faced when he tackled the task of making General Motors manageable and managed.

Where they fit the realities of an organization, Fayol's and Sloan's models are still unsurpassed. Fayol's functional organization is still the best way to structure a small business, especially a small manufacturing business. Sloan's federal decentralization is still the best structure for the big multiproduct company. None of the new design structures comes nearly as close to fulfilling the design specifications of organization structure as do functional organization and federal decentralization *if and when they fit*. But more and more of the institutional reality that has to be structured and organized does not fit. Indeed, the very assumptions that underlay Sloan's and Fayol's work are not applicable to major organization needs and challenges.

TRADITIONAL ASSUMPTIONS AND CURRENT NEEDS

The best way, perhaps, to show the current needs of organization structure is to contrast the basic characteristics of GM, which Sloan so successfully structured, with the current needs and realities of organization and structure.

1. General Motors was a manufacturing business, producing and selling highly engineered goods. Fayol, too, was concerned with a business producing physical goods, specifically a fair-sized coal-mining company. Today we face the challenge of organizing the large business that is not primarily a manufacturing business. There are not only the large financial institutions and the large retailers. There are worldwide transportation companies, communications companies, companies that, while they do manufacture, are mainly in customer service (such as most computer businesses). Then there are all the nonbusiness service institutions with which

chapters 12 to 16 dealt. These nonmanufacturing institutions are increasingly the true center of gravity of any developed economy. They employ the most people. They both contribute and take the largest share of gross national product. They are the fundamental organization problems today.

2. General Motors was then and is now essentially a single-product, single-technology, single-market business. Most of its sales are automotive. The vehicles that GM sells differ in details, such as size, horsepower, and price, but they are essentially one and the same product.

By contrast, the typical businesses of today are multiproduct, multitechnology, and multimarket businesses. And their central problem is a problem General Motors did not have: *the organization of complexity and diversity.*

3. General Motors was primarily a U.S. company in Sloan's time. It dominated the American automobile industry and loomed very large on the international automobile market. Organizationally, the world outside the United States was still, for GM, *separate* and *outside.*

By contrast, the most rapid growth in the last fifty years has been the multinational company, that is, the company for which a great many countries and a great many markets are all of equal importance, or at least are all of major importance.

General Motors is now multinational with core operations in North America and major overseas operations in three other regions: Europe; Asia Pacific and Latin America; and Africa and the Middle East.

4. Because GM was a one-product and one-country company, information was not a major organizational problem and did not have to be a major organizational concern. Everyone in GM spoke the same language, whether the language of the automotive industry or American English. Everyone fully understood what the other one was doing or should have been doing, if only because, in all likelihood, he had done a similar job himself.

GM was (and still is) organized according to the logic of the marketplace, and the logic of authority and decision. It did not need, in its organization, to concern itself a great deal with the logic and the flow of information.

By contrast, multiproduct, multitechnology, and multinational companies of today do have to concern themselves, in their organizational design and structure, with organization according to the flow of information. They have to be sure that their organization structure does not violate the logic of information. And for this the Sloan model offers no guidance—GM did not have to tackle the problem in Sloan's time.

5. Four out of every five GM employees were production workers, either manual workers or clerks on routine tasks. GM, in other words, employed yesterday's, rather than today's, labor force.

But the basic organization problem today involves knowledge work and knowledge workers. They are the fastest-growing core element in every business.

6. Finally, General Motors was a *managerial* rather than an *entrepreneurial* business—that is, one that started and developed new businesses and products. The strength of Sloan's approach lay in its ability to manage superbly what was already there and known. General Motors had not been innovative; it was an amalgamation of independent automobile companies.

But the challenge is increasingly entrepreneurship and innovation. We need an innovative organization—in addition to a managerial one. And for this, the General Motors model offered no guidance.

But of course we have learned a great deal in the century since Fayol's generation first tackled organization. We know what the job is. We know the major approaches. We know what comes first. We know what will not work—though not always what will. We know what organization structure aims at and, therefore, what the test of successful organization design is.

1. The first thing we have learned is that Fayol and Sloan were right: organization structure will not just evolve. *The only things that develop spontaneously in an organization are disorder, friction, and malperformance.* Nor is the right structure intuitive any more than Greek temples or Gothic cathedrals were. Traditions may indicate where the problems are, but traditions are no help in solving them. *Organization design and structure require thinking, analysis, and a systematic approach.*

2. We have learned that the first step is not designing an organization structure; that is the last step. The first step is identifying and organizing the *building blocks* of organization, that is, the *activities* that have to be built into the final structure and that carry the *structural load* of the final organization.

We now know that building blocks are determined by the kind of *contribution* they make. And we know that the traditional classification of the contributions— *the staff and line concept* of conventional American organization theory—is more of a hindrance to understanding than a help.

3. *Structure follows strategy.* Organization is not mechanical. It is not *assembly*. It cannot be *prefabricated*. Organization is unique to each individual business or institution. For we now know that structure, to be effective, must follow strategy.

Structure is a means for attaining the objectives and goals of an institution. Any work on structure must, therefore, start with objectives and strategy. This is one of the most fruitful new insights we have gained in the field of organization. It may sound obvious, and it is. But some of the worst mistakes in organization building have been made by imposing an ideal or theoretical organization on a living business.

Strategy—that is, the answers to the questions, *"What is our business? What should it be? What will it be?"* determines *the purpose of structure.* Answering those questions determines the key activities in a given business or service institution. Effective structure is the design that makes these *key activities* capable of functioning and of performance. And, in turn, the key activities are the *load-bearing elements* of a functioning structure. Organization design is, or should be, concerned first with the key activities; the rest are secondary.

THE THREE KINDS OF WORK

There are different kinds of work in every organization, however small and simple.

There is first *operating work,* the work of managing what is already in existence and known, building it, exploiting its potential, taking care of its problems.

There is always *top-management work.* And (as will be discussed in chapter 43) it is different work, with its own tasks and requirements.

Finally, there is *innovative work.* It, too, is different work, requiring different things with respect to both operations and top management.

As we shall see later in this part, none of the available design principles can be used to organize all three different kinds of work. Yet each needs to be organized. And they all need to be integrated into one overall organization.

WHAT WE NEED TO UNLEARN

There are also a few things we need to unlearn. Some of the noisiest and most-time-consuming battles in organization theory and practice are pure sham. They pose an *either/or;* yet the right answer is *both*—in varying proportions.

1. The first of these sham battles, which would be better forgotten, is the one between task focus and person focus in job design and organization structure. To repeat what has been said already, *structure,* and *job design* have to be task focused. But *assignments* have to fit both the *person* and the *needs of the situation.* Work, to say it once more, is objective and impersonal; the job itself is done by a person.

2. Somewhat related to this old controversy is the discussion of hierarchical, or scalar, versus free-form organization.

Traditional organization theory knows only one kind of structure, applicable alike to building block and whole buildings, the so-called *scalar organization,* that is, the pyramid of superior and subordinates. Traditional organization theory considers this structure suitable for all tasks.

Today another organization theory is becoming fashionable. It maintains that shape and structure are what we want them to be. They are, or should be, *free-form.* Everything—shape, size, and apparently tasks—derive from interpersonal relations. Indeed, the purpose of the structure is to make it possible for each person to *"do my own thing."*

The first thing to say about this controversy is that it is simply not true that one of these forms is regimentation and the other freedom. The amount of discipline required in both is the same; they only distribute it differently.

A hierarchy does not, as the critics claim, make the superior more powerful. On the contrary, the first effect of hierarchical organization is to protect the subordinate against arbitrary authority from above. It does this by defining carefully the sphere within which the subordinate has the authority, the sphere within which the superior cannot interfere. It protects the subordinate by making it possible for her to say, "This is *my* assigned job." Protection of the subordinate also underlies the scalar principle's insistence that a person have only one superior. Otherwise the subordinate is likely to find herself caught between conflicting demands, conflicting commands, and conflicts of interest as well as of loyalty. "Better one bad master than two good ones," says an old peasant proverb.

At the same time, the hierarchical organization gives the most *individual* freedom. As long as the incumbent does the assigned duties of the position, he or she has done the job. He or she has no responsibility beyond it.

The term *free-form organization* is somewhat misleading. What is meant is organization designed for specific tasks rather than for supposedly eternal purposes. In particular, it means organization of work in small groups and teams.

This (as will be discussed in some detail in later chapters of this part) demands, above all, great self-discipline from each member of the team. Everybody has to do "the team's thing." Everybody has to take responsibility for the work of the entire team and for its performance. Indeed, Abraham Maslow's criticism of Theory Y—for making inhuman demands on that large proportion of people who are weak, vulnerable, timid, impaired—applies with even greater force to free-form organization. The more flexible an organization, the stronger the individual members have to be and the more of the load they have to carry.

Both individual members and the entire organization need some element of hierarchy in any structure. There has to be someone who can make a decision or the organization deteriorates into a never-ending bull session. Knowledge organizations, especially, need to have decision authority and specific, designated "channels" defined with great clarity. Every organization will find itself in a situation of common peril once in a while. And then all perish unless there is clear, unambiguous, designated *command* authority vested in one person.

Just as statesmen long ago learned that both good laws and good rulers are needed for government to function well, so organization builders will have to learn that sound organization structure needs *both* a hierarchical structure of authority and the capacity to organize task forces, teams, and individuals for work both on a permanent and a temporary basis.

3. At bottom these sham battles—between task focus and person-focus and between scalar and free-form organization—reflect the belief of traditional organization theory that one best principle alone is "right" and that it is also *always* "right." There must be *one final answer* (shown to be false in chapter 7).

Instead of the "one right" principle, *three* new major design principles emerged in the thirty years after World War II ended, to join Fayol's functions and Sloan's federal decentralization. These three—the *team, simulated decentralization,* and *systems management*—did not replace the older designs. None of them can lay claim to being a "universal" principle; indeed, all three have serious structural weaknesses and limited applicability. But they are the best answers available for certain kinds of work, the best structures available for certain tasks, and the best approaches to such major organization problems as top management and innovation in many industries.

THE BUILDING BLOCKS OF ORGANIZATION

In designing the building blocks of organization, four questions face the organizer:

1. What should the units of organization be?

2. What components should join together, and what components should be kept apart?

3. What is the best size and shape for the different components?

The traditional approach to identifying the basic units of organization has been to analyze *all* the activities needed for performance in the enterprise. This produces a list of typical functions of a retail, manufacturing, or service organization.

This approach to the typical functions sees organization as mechanical, as an assemblage of functions. Organizations will, indeed, use typical activities—though not necessarily all of them. But how the structure is to be built depends on the results needed. *Organizing has to start out with the desired results.*

THE KEY ACTIVITIES

What we need to know is not all the activities that might conceivably have to be housed in the organization structure. What we need to know are the load-bearing parts of the structure, the *key activities.*

Organization design, therefore, *starts* with these two questions:

- In what area is excellence required to obtain the company's objectives?

- In what areas would nonperformance endanger the results, if not the survival, of the enterprise?

Here are some historical examples of the kind of conclusions these questions lead to:

Sears, Roebuck in the United States and Marks & Spencer in England were in

many ways remarkably similar enterprises, if only because the founders and builders of Marks & Spencer consciously modeled their company on Sears, Roebuck.
But there was a pronounced difference in the organizational placement and role of
the "laboratory" in these two companies. Sears defined its business as being *the
buyer for the American family* and used its laboratory to test the merchandise it
bought. Accordingly, the laboratory, while large, competent, and respected, was
organizationally quite subordinate. Marks & Spencer, on the other hand, defined
its business as developing upper-class goods for the working-class family. As a result, the laboratory was central to Marks & Spencer's organization structure. The
laboratory, rather than the buyer, decided what new products were desirable, developed the new merchandise, designed it, tested it, and then had it produced.
Only then did the buyer take over. As a result, the head of the Marks & Spencer
laboratory was a senior member of management and, in many ways, the chief business planner.

Any company that shows an understanding of success makes the key activities—
and especially those in which excellence is needed to attain business objectives—
the central elements in its organization structure.

But equally important are the questions, "In what areas could *malfunction* seriously hurt us? In what areas do we have major *vulnerability?*" These questions,
however, are seldom asked.

The New York brokerage community, by and large, did not ask them during
the boom years of the 1960s. If it had, it would have realized that malfunction
of the "back office," where customer orders, customer accounts and securities are
handled, could seriously endanger the business. Failure to organize the back office
as a key activity was the single most important cause of the severe crisis that over-
took Wall Street in 1969 and 1970. The one Wall Street firm that asked those
questions, Merrill Lynch, had organized the back office as a *load-bearing key activity*
in its structure. It emerged from the crisis the giant of the brokerage business.

Finally, a third question should be asked, "What are the *values* that are truly
important to us in this company?" It might be product quality. It might be the
ability of the company's dealers to give proper service to the customer. It might be
product or process safety. Whatever the values are, they have to be organizationally based. There has to be an organizational component responsible for them—
and it has to be a key one.

These three questions identify the key activities. And they, in turn, will be the
structural elements of organization. The rest, no matter how important, no matter
how much money they represent, no matter how many people they employ, are
secondary. Obviously, they have to be analyzed, organized, and placed within the
structure. But the first concern must be those activities that are essential to the

success of a business strategy and to the attainment of business objectives. They have to be identified, defined, organized, and centrally placed.

This means that business should always analyze its organization structure when its strategy changes. Whatever the reason—a change in market or in technology, diversification, or new objectives—a change in strategy requires reanalyzing the key activities and adapting the structure to them. Conversely, reorganization that is undertaken without a change in strategy is either superfluous or indicates poor organization to begin with.

THE CONTRIBUTION ANALYSIS

From the earliest days of concern with organization, the most controversial question has been, "What activities belong together and what activities belong apart?"

There are, by and large, four major groups of activities that contribute in different ways:

There are, first, *result-producing activities,* activities that produce measurable results that can be related, directly or indirectly, to the performance of the entire enterprise. Some of these activities are directly revenue-producing.

There are, second, *support activities* that, while needed and even essential, do not by themselves produce results but have results only through the use made of their "output" by other components of the business.

There are, third, activities that have no direct or indirect relationship to the results of the business, activities that are truly ancillary. They are *housekeeping activities.*

Finally, and different in character from any of these, are the top-management activities, which will be discussed separately in chapter 43.

Among the result-producing activities, some directly bring in *revenues.* In service institutions, the comparable activities are those that directly produce "patient care" or "learning." Selling and all the work needed to do a systematic and organized selling job, such as sales forecasting, market research, sales training, and sales management belong in this category. Here also belongs the treasury function, that is, the supply and management of money in the business.

The second group of result-producing activities are those that do not generate revenue but are directly related to the results of the entire business or of a major revenue-producing segment. I call them *result-contributing* rather than *result-producing.*

The operations function is typical of these activities. Training belongs here too, as do recruitment and employment. These are the activities concerned with supplying qualified and trained people to the enterprise. Purchasing and physical distribution are result-contributing but not revenue-producing activities. "Engineering," as the term is normally understood in most organizations, is a result-contributing but not a revenue-producing activity. In a commercial bank "operations," the handling of data and papers, belongs here. In a life insurance company, claims settlement is result-contributing. Labor negotiations and many other similar "relations" activities are result-contributing though not revenue-producing.

The third group of result-producing (or result-contributing) activities are *informational*. They do produce a "finished product" needed by everyone in the system. Yet information, by itself, does not produce any revenue. It is "supply" to revenue and cost centers alike.

First among the *support activities,* which do not by themselves produce a product but are input to others, stand the *conscience activities*. These activities set standards, create vision, and demand excellence in all the key areas where a business needs to strive for excellence. "Conscience" may seem an odd term for this function, but it is a good one. The task of the conscience activities is not to help the organization improve on its present activities. Its task is to hold the organization to its own standards, to remind the organization what it should be, but isn't, doing.

Conscience activities tend to be slighted in most organizations. But every company—and every service institution—needs to provide itself and its managers with vision, with values, with standards, and with some provision for reviewing performance against these standards.

Another support function is *advice* and *teaching*. The contribution is not in what the activity does or can do, but in the impact it has on the ability of others to perform. The "product" is increased performance capacity of the rest of the organization.

A good many of the "relations" activities are also support—the legal staff and the patent department, for example.

The last group of activities defined by their contribution are the *housekeeping activities,* ranging from the medical department to the people who clean the floor, from the plant cafeteria to the management of pension and retirement funds, from finding a plant site to taking care of all the record-keeping requirements imposed on business by government. These functions contribute nothing directly to the results and performance of the business. Their malfunction, however, hurts the enterprise. They serve legal requirements, the morale of the workforce, or public responsibilities. Of all activities, they are the most diverse. And of all activities, they tend to get the shortest shrift in most organizations.

This is a rough classification, and far from scientific. Some activities may belong in one category in one business, in another one in a second business, and in a third company will be left fuzzy and without clear classification at all.

Why classify, then? The answer is that activities that differ in contribution have to be treated differently. *Contribution* determines *ranking* and *placement*.

Key activities should never be subordinated to activities that are not key.

Revenue-producing activities should never be subordinated to any nonrevenue-producing activities.

And support activities should never be mixed with revenue-producing and result-contributing activities. They should be kept apart.

THE "CONSCIENCE" ACTIVITIES

Activities that are the conscience of an organization must never be subordinated to anything else. They also should never be placed with any other activity; they should be clearly separate.

The conscience function of giving vision, of setting standards, and of reviewing performance against standards is basically a top-management function. But it has to work with the entire management group. Every business, even a small one, needs this function. In a small business, it need not be set up as a separate function but can be part of the top-management job. In any business of more than medium size, however, the function usually has to be set up and staffed separately.

However, there should be very few people actually doing the conscience job. It is a job for a single individual rather than a staff. It is a job for a person whose performance has earned the respect of the management group. It is not a job for a "specialist." It is best discharged by a senior member of the management group with a proven performance record who has manifested concern, perception, and interest in the area for which she or he is supposed to act as conscience.

Only those few areas that are vital and central to a company's success and survival should become areas of conscience. Objectives and strategy determine what conscience activities are needed. Managing people is always a conscience area, and so is marketing. The impact of a business on its environment, its social responsibilities, and its relations with the outside community are also basic conscience areas. Innovation (whether technological or social innovation) is likely to be a conscience area for any large business.

Beyond these, however, there is no formula.

The tenure of the few conscience executives should be limited, as a rule. No matter how greatly a conscience executive may be respected, and no matter how successful, he or she will eventually wear out either integrity or welcome. This is a good place for a senior person to end a distinguished career. A younger person in the job should be moved out after a few years—preferably back into a "doing" job.

MAKING SERVICE STAFF EFFECTIVE

There are similarly stringent rules with respect to advisory and teaching activities, that is, with respect to service staffs.

There should be very few of them. They should be set up only in key-activity areas. The secret of effective services work is concentration rather than busyness.

Advisory and teaching staffs should never try to do a little bit of everything. They should zero in on a very small number of crucial areas. Rather than serve everybody, they should select areas within the organization where the managers are receptive and do not have to be "sold," and where success will generate the greatest effect throughout the whole company.

The staffs and their activities should be kept lean.

The supply of people of the right temperament for this kind of work is not large. To do a decent job in an advisory and teaching capacity requires someone who genuinely wants others to get the credit. It requires an individual who starts out with the aim of enabling others to do what they want to do, provided only that it is neither immoral nor insane. It requires, further, someone who has the patience to let others learn rather than does the work single-handed. And finally, it requires someone who will not abuse a position in headquarters close to the seat of power to politick, to manipulate, and to play favorites. People who possess these personality traits are rare. Yet people in services work who lack these qualities can do only mischief.

One basic rule for advisory and teaching staffs is that they abandon an old activity before they take on a new one. Otherwise they will soon start to "build empires" or to produce "canned goods," that is, programs and memoranda, rather than developing the *knowledge and performance capacity* of those whose job it is to produce. They will also otherwise be forced to use second-raters rather than people of outstanding competence. Only if they are required to abandon an old activity before taking on a new one will they be able to put really first-rate people on every job.

Advisory and teaching activities should never "operate." A common weakness of human resource staffs is that they operate. They run the labor negotiations, they do a lot of housekeeping chores such as managing the cafeteria, or they train. As a result, the advisory and teaching work does not get done. The "daily crisis" in operations takes precedence over the work of advice and teaching, which can always be postponed.

Advisory and teaching work should not be a career. It is work to which managers or career professionals should be exposed in the course of their growth. But it is not work that a person should do for long normally. As a career, it corrupts. It breeds contempt for "those dumb operating people," that is, for honest work. It puts a premium on being "bright," rather than on being "right." It is also frustrating work, because one does not have results of one's own but results only at secondhand.

But it is excellent training, excellent development, and a severe test of a person's character and ability to be effective without having the authority of command. It is an experience everyone who rises to the top of an organization should have. But it is an exposure no one should suffer for more than a short time.

THE TWO FACES OF INFORMATION

Information activities present a special organizational problem. They have two faces, two dimensions, and two directions. Unlike most other result-producing activities, they are not concerned with one stage of the process but with the *entire process itself*. This means that they have to be both centralized and decentralized.

The traditional organization chart expresses this in the two different lines that connect an information activity to "bosses." A solid line connects the activity to the head of the unit for which it provides information, and a dotted line connects it to the central information group. A monthly operating statement, for example, might go both to the head of the operating unit and to the company controller.

One conclusion from this is that information work should be kept separate from other kinds of work. American business has typically violated this rule by putting accounting (a traditional *information activity*) into the same component as the treasurer (the *result-producing* operating work of supplying capital and managing money in the business). The justification has been that both "deal with money." But, actually, accounting does not deal with money; it deals with figures. The result of the traditional approach has been to slight financial management.

The tough question with respect to information activities is which of them belong together and which should be kept apart. There is much talk today about "total integrated enterprise information systems." This implies that all—or at least most—information activities should be in one component. Insofar as this means that new and different information activities, such as enterprise resource planning systems, should not be subordinated to traditional accounting, the point is well taken. But should they be coordinated? Or should they be separate?

HOUSEKEEPING

The last group of activities, according to their contribution, are housekeeping activities. They should be kept separate from other work, or else they will not get done. The problem is not that these activities are particularly difficult. Some are. Many others are not. The problem is that they are not even indirectly related to results. Therefore, they tend to be looked down upon by the rest of the organization.

One reason for the tremendous increase in health-care costs in the U.S. is managerial neglect of the "hotel services." The people who dominate the hospital, the doctors and nurses, all know that the hotel services are essential. Patients do not get well unless they are reasonably comfortable, are fed, have their beds changed and their rooms cleaned. But these are not professional activities for a doctor, nurse, or X-ray technician. They are not willing to yield an inch to make it possible for the people in charge of the hotel services to do their jobs. They are not willing to have these activities represented on the upper levels of hospital management. As a result, they are left unmanaged. And this means they are done badly and expensively.

This same sort of neglect extends even to activities in which a great deal of money is at stake. Few companies in the United States for instance have done even an adequate job of managing their employees' pension funds, despite the enormous amount of money involved. It is an activity that does not, it seems, have any relationship to results, and therefore it is an activity that should be outsourced.

One way out is to turn housekeeping activities over to the work community to run. They are activities for the employees, and they are therefore best managed by the employees. Or, such activities may be outsourced to an outside contractor whose business it is to run a pension fund or to manage a cafeteria.

But insofar as a company's management has to do these things itself—and picking a plant site and building a factory is something a company has to do for itself, or at least has to participate in actively—housekeeping activities ought to be kept separate from all other activities. They require different people, different values, and different measurements—and should require little supervision by business management itself.

There is one overall rule: activities that make the same kind of contribution can be combined in one component under one management, whatever their technical specialization. Activities that do not make the same kind of contribution do not, as a rule, belong together.

It is feasible and often best to put all advising and teaching activities, whether they be in human resources, in manufacturing, in marketing, or in purchasing, in one "services" group under one manager. Similarly, in any but large companies, one person might well be the company's conscience in all major conscience areas. *Contribution* rather than skill determines *function*.

DECISION ANALYSIS

Identifying key activities and analyzing their contributions defines the building blocks of organization. But placing the structural units that make up the organization requires two additional pieces of work: an *analysis of decisions* and an *analysis of relations*.

What *decisions are needed* to obtain the performance objectives? What kinds of decisions are they? On what *level* of the organization should they be made?

What *activities* are involved in, or affected by, them? Which managers must, therefore, *participate* in the decisions—at least to the extent of being consulted beforehand? Which managers must be informed after they have been made? The answers to these questions determine where work begins.

In one large company, well over 90 percent of the decisions that managers had to make over a five-year period were found to be "typical," falling in a small number of categories. In only a few cases would it have been necessary to ask, "Where does this decision belong?" had the problem been thought through in advance. Yet, because there had been no decision analysis, almost three-quarters of the decisions had to "go looking for a home." Most of them went to a much higher level of management than was needed. The company's organizational activities had been placed in units so low in the organization structure that key decisions were placed where there was no authority or adequate information to make these decisions.

Four basic characteristics determine the nature of any business decision.

First is the *degree of futurity* in the decision. For how long into the future does it commit the company? And how fast can it be reversed?

Buyers in some retail chains have practically no limit as to the amount to which they can commit the company. Often in these firms, however, no buyer or buying supervisor can either abandon an existing product or add a new one without the approval of the head of the entire buying operation, who, traditionally, is the second or third in command in the entire organization. Similarly, the foreign exchange trader in a major commercial bank traditionally has only the loosest limit on the amounts to which she can commit the bank. But she cannot start trading in a new currency without approval from a high authority in the bank.

The second criterion is the *impact a decision has on other functions,* on other areas, or on the business as a whole. If it affects only one function, it is of the lowest order and should be made fairly low in the organization. Otherwise, either it will have to be made on a higher level, where the impact on all affected functions can be considered, or it must be made in close consultation with the managers of the other affected functions. To use technical language, "optimization" of process and performance of one function must not be at the expense of other functions. This is undesirable "suboptimization."

One example of a decision that looks like a purely "technical" one affecting one area only, but that actually has impact on many areas, is a change in the methods of keeping the parts inventory in a mass-production plant. This affects all manufacturing operations. It makes necessary major changes in assembly. It affects delivery to customers—it might even lead to radical changes in marketing and pricing, such as the abandonment of certain designs and models. The technical problems in inventory-keeping—though considerable—pale into insignificance when compared with the problems that any change in inventory-keeping will produce in other areas. To "optimize" inventory-keeping at the expense of these other areas cannot be allowed. Yet suboptimization will be avoided only if the decision is recognized as being of a fairly high order and handled as one affecting the entire process. Either it has to be reserved for management higher than the plant, or it requires close consultation among all functional managers.

The character of a decision is also determined by the *number of qualitative factors* that enter into it; basic principles of conduct, ethical values, social and political beliefs, and so on. If such value considerations are involved, the decision moves into a higher order. It requires either determination or review at a higher level. The most important and most common qualitative factors are human beings. This, of course, underlies the strong recommendation in chapter 27 for top-management people to play an active part in the decisions on promotion to upper levels of middle management.

Finally, decisions can be classified as *periodically recurrent* or *rare*. The recurrent decision requires establishing a general rule, that is, it requires making a decision in principle. Since suspending an employee deals with a person, the general rule has to be made at a fairly high level in the organization. But the application of the rule to the specific case, while also a decision, can then be placed on a much lower level.

The rare decision, however, has to be treated as a distinct event. Whenever it occurs, it has to be thought through.

A decision should always be made *at the lowest possible level and as close to the scene of action as possible*. However, a decision should always be made at *a level high enough to ensure that all activities and objectives affected are fully considered*. The first rule tells us how far down a decision *should* be made. The second, how far down it *can be* made. It tells us which managers must share in the decision and which must be informed of it. The two together tell us where certain activities should be placed. Managers charged with responsibility for a given decision should be high enough to have the authority to make typical decisions pertaining to their work, and low enough to have the detailed knowledge and the firsthand experience, to be "where the action is."

RELATION ANALYSIS

The final step in designing the building blocks of organization is an analysis of relations. It tells us where a specific component belongs.

The basic rule in placing an activity within the organization structure is to impose on it the smallest possible number of relationships and to make the crucial relations—that is, the relationships on which depend its success and the effectiveness of its contribution—easy, accessible, and central to the unit. The rule is to keep relationships to a minimum and make each count.

This rule explains why functions are not groups of related skills. If we followed the functional principle, we would, for instance, put production planning into a planning component where all kinds of planners would work together. The skills needed in production planning are closely related to all other operational-planning skills. Instead, we put the production planner into operations and as close as possible to both the operations manager and the first-line supervisors. This is where the planner belongs according to *key relationships*.

There is often a conflict between placement according to decision analysis and placement according to relations analysis. By and large, one should try to follow the logic of relations as far as possible.

SYMPTOMS OF POOR ORGANIZATION

There is no perfect organization. At its best, an organization structure doesn't cause trouble. But what are the most common mistakes in designing the building blocks of organization and joining them together? And what are the most common symptoms of serious flaws in organization?

The most common and the most serious symptom of poor organization is an increase in the number of management levels. A basic rule of organization is to build the fewest possible management levels and forge the shortest possible chain of command.

Every additional level makes it more difficult to attain mutual understanding by creating more noise and distorting the message. Every additional level distorts objectives and misdirects attention. Every link in the chain sets up additional stresses and creates one more source of inertia, friction, and slack.

The second most common symptom of poor organization is recurring organizational problems. No sooner has a problem supposedly been "solved" than it comes back again in a new guise.

A typical example in a company is the placement of product development. The marketing people think it belongs to them; the research and development people are equally convinced that it belongs to them. But placing it in either component simply creates a recurring problem. Actually both placements are wrong. In a business that wants innovation, product development is a key, revenue-producing activity. It should not be subordinated to any other activity. It deserves to be organized as a separate component.

Solving the recurrent organization problem requires making the right analyses—the key-activities analysis, the contributions analysis, the decisions analysis, and the relations analysis. An organization problem that comes back more than a couple of times should not be treated mechanically by shuffling little boxes on an organization chart. It indicates lack of thinking, lack of clarity, and lack of understanding.

Equally common and equally dangerous is an organization structure that *puts the attention of key people on the wrong, the irrelevant, the secondary problems*. Organization should put the attention of people on major decisions, on key activities, and on performance and results. If, instead, it puts attention on proper behavior, on etiquette, on procedure, then organization misdirects. Then organization is a bar to performance.

There are several common symptoms of poor organization that, usually, require no further diagnosis. There is, first, the symptom of *too many meetings attended by too many people*.

Whenever executives, except at the very top level, spend more than a fairly small fraction of their time—maybe a quarter or less—in meetings, this is by itself evidence of poor organization. Too many meetings is an indication that jobs have not been defined clearly, have not been structured big enough, have not been made truly responsible. The need for meetings indicates that the decisions and relations analyses either have not been made at all or have not been applied. The rule should be to minimize the need for people to get together to accomplish anything.

An organization in which *people are constantly concerned about feelings and about what other people will or will not like* is not an organization that has good human relations. On the contrary, it is an organization that has very poor human relations. Good human relations, like good manners, are taken for granted. Constant anxiety over other people's feelings is the worst kind of human relations.

An organization that suffers from this—and a great many do—can be said unequivocally to suffer from overstaffing. It might be overstaffed in terms of activities. Instead of focusing on key activities, it tries to do a little bit of everything—especially in advice and teaching activities. Or the individual activities may be overstaffed. It is in crowded rooms that people get on each other's nerves, poke their elbows into each other's eyes, and step on each other's toes. Where there is enough distance, they do not collide. Overstaffed organizations create work rather than performance. They also create friction, sensitivity, irritation, and concern with feelings.

It is a symptom of malorganization *to rely on "coordinators," "assistants,"* and other such whose job it is not to have a job. This indicates that activities and jobs have been designed too narrow, or that activities and jobs, rather than being designed for one defined result, are expected to do a great many parts of different tasks. It usually indicates also that organizational components have been organized according to skill rather than according to their contribution or their place in the process.

Skill always contributes only a part rather than a result. If the organization is by skill, one needs a coordinator to put back together pieces that should never have been separated in the first place.

"ORGANIZITIS" AS A CHRONIC AFFLICTION

A good many organizations, especially large, complex ones, suffer from the disease of "organizitis." Everybody is concerned with organization. Reorganization is going on all the time. At the first sign of any trouble, be it only a spat between a purchasing agent and the people in engineering over a specification, the cry goes up for the "organization doctors," whether outside consultants or inside staff. And no organizational solution ever lasts long. Indeed few organizational arrangements are given enough time to be tested and worked out in practice before another organization study is begun.

In some cases, this does, indeed, suggest malorganization. "Organizitis" will set in if organization structure fails to come to grips with fundamentals. It is brought on especially by not rethinking and restructuring the organization after *a fundamental change in the size and complexity of a business or in its objectives and strategy.*

But just as often "organizitis" is a form of hypochondria. It should, therefore, be emphasized that organizational changes should not be undertaken often and should not be undertaken lightly. Reorganization is a form of surgery, and even minor surgery has risks.

The demands for organization studies or for reorganization as a response to minor ailments should be resisted. No organization will ever be perfect. A certain amount of friction, of incongruity, of organizational confusion, is inevitable. And the test of good organization is not perfection on paper. It is performance at work.

SUMMARY

Twice in the short history of management did we believe we had the right answer to organization. Once was during the time of World War I in Henri Fayol's "functions" and, again, a generation later, in Alfred Sloan's "federal decentralization." If and when they fit, these two designs are still our best answers. But increasingly we have to structure organizations where neither of these two designs fit. Increasingly we have had to develop new and additional design principles: we now have five.

We have learned a great deal about organization in the last one hundred years. We know the specifications for effective organization. We know that we have to organize, in one and the same structure, three distinct kinds of work: operating work, top-management work, and innovating work. We know that structure follows strategy and that structure is therefore not mechanical but must be developed from the purposes, goals, and objectives of an organization, and on the foundation of the key activities needed to attain objectives. We have learned that organizing starts with "building blocks" of organization. We know what activities belong together and what activities should be kept apart. We know the symptoms of poor organization. And we know that there is no one right organization (as shown in chapter 7).

Good organization structure does not guarantee performance. But poor or inappropriate structure impedes performance—and *performance is the test of organization structure.*

39

Work- and Task-Focused Design

The organization architect has available today *five design principles,* five distinct ways of organizing activities and ordering relationships. Two of them are traditional: Henri Fayol's functional structure, and Alfred P. Sloan's federal decentralization.

Three are new: team organization, simulated decentralization, and the systems structure.

Each of these five was developed to meet specific needs. The first impression is, therefore, that they represent expediency rather than design, let alone logic. But in reality, each of these designs expresses a *different design logic.* Each takes *one general dimension* of managerial organization and builds a structure around it.

FORMAL SPECIFICATIONS

Organization structure must satisfy minimum requirements with respect to clarity, economy, the direction of vision, understanding by the individual of his or her own task and the task of the whole, decision making, stability and adaptability, and perpetuation and self-renewal.

1. *Clarity.* All managerial components, and all individuals within the organization, especially all managers, need to know where they belong, where they stand, where they have to go for whatever is needed, whether information, cooperation, or decision. Clarity is by no means the same thing as simplicity. Indeed, structures that look simple may lack clarity. And seemingly complex structures may have great clarity.

A structure in which workers do not know without an elaborate organization manual where they belong, where they have to go, and where they stand creates friction, wastes time, causes bickering and frustration, delays decisions, and is altogether an impediment rather than a help.

2. *Economy.* Closely related to clarity is the requirement of economy. One should be able to control, to supervise, and to coax people to perform with a minimum

effort. Organization structure should make self-control possible and should encourage self-motivation. And the smallest possible number of people, especially people of high-performance capacity, should have to devote time and attention to keeping the machinery going.

In any organization, some of the effort has to be used to keep the organization running and in good repair. Some time will have to be spent on "internal control," "internal communications," and "personal problems." *But the less the input of the organization has to be used to keep it going, the more input can become output.* The organization will be more economical, and more of its "input" can become performance.

3. *The direction of vision.* Organization structure should direct the vision of individuals and of managerial units toward performance, rather than toward efforts. And it should direct vision toward results, that is, toward the performance of the entire enterprise.

Performance is the end that all activities serve. Indeed, organization can be likened to a transmission that converts activities into the one "drive"—performance. Organization is more efficient the more "direct" the transmission is, that is, the less it has to change the speed and direction of individual activities to make them yield performance. The largest possible number of managers should perform as operating people rather than as "experts" or "bureaucrats." As many as possible should be tested against performance and results rather than primarily by standards of administrative skill or professional competence.

4. *Understanding one's own task and the common task.* An organization should enable all individuals, especially all managers and professionals, to understand their own tasks.

But at the same time, an organization should enable everyone to understand the common task, the task of the entire organization. All members of the organization, in order to relate their efforts to the common good, must understand how their tasks fit in with the task of the whole. And, in turn, they must know what the task of the whole implies for their own tasks, their own contributions, their own directions. Communications therefore need to be helped rather than hampered by organizational structure.

5. *Decision making.* None of the available design principles is primarily structured around a "decision model." Yet decisions have to be made, made on the right issues and at the right level, and have to be converted into work and accomplishment. An organization design, therefore, needs to be tested to find whether it impedes or strengthens the decision-making process.

A structure that forces decisions to go to the highest possible level of organization rather than be settled at the lowest possible level clearly hampers decision making. So does a decision structure that obscures the need for crucial decisions, or that focuses attention on the wrong issues, such as jurisdictional disputes.

6. *Stability and adaptability.* An organization needs stability. It must be able to do its work even though the world around it is in turmoil. It must be able to build on its performance and achievement of yesterday. It needs to be able to plan for its own future and continuity.

The individual also needs a "home." Nobody gets much work done in an airport waiting area; no one gets much work done as a transient. The individual needs to belong to a "community" in which he or she knows people and is known by them, and in which his or her own relationship is anchored.

But stability is not rigidity. On the contrary, organization structure requires adaptability. A totally rigid structure is not stable; it is brittle. Only if the structure can adapt to new situations, new demands, new conditions, will it be able to survive.

7. *Perpetuation and self-renewal.* Finally, an organization needs to be able to perpetuate itself. It needs to be able to provide for its self-renewal. These two needs entail a number of demands.

An organization must be capable of producing tomorrow's leaders from within. One minimum requirement for this is that it must not have so many levels of management that an able person, entering a management job early, say at age twenty-five, cannot normally reach the top rungs of the promotion ladder while still young enough to be effective.

One self-renewal requirement is the ability of an organization structure to prepare and test an individual on each level for the next level above. It must especially prepare and test today's junior and middle managers for senior and top-management positions. For perpetuation and self-renewal, an organization structure must also be accessible to new ideas and must be willing and able to do new things.

MEETING THE SPECIFICATIONS

Some of these specifications clearly conflict. No design principle could fully satisfy all of them. Any organization structure capable of performance and continuity will, however, have to satisfy all these specifications to some degree. This means compromises, trade-offs, balancing. It also implies that several design principles rather than one are likely to be used even for simple organization. For if any one of these specifications goes totally unsatisfied, the enterprise will not perform. Organization building therefore requires understanding the available design principles, their requirements, their limitations, and their *fit* against the design specifications.

The first thing to know about the available design principles is their logic. "Functional organization" and "team organization" are organized around *task* and *work*. Both kinds of "decentralization" are organized around *results*. The "systems structure" is organized around *relationships*.

THREE WAYS OF ORGANIZING WORK

All work, physical as well as mental, can be organized in three ways.

It can be organized by *stages in the process*. In building a house, we first build the foundation, then the frame and the roof, and finally the interior.

It can be organized so that *the work moves to where the skill or tool required for each of the steps is located*. The traditional metalworking unique-product plant has rows of reamers and lathes in one aisle, stamping machines in another, heat-treating equipment in a third, with the pieces of metal moving from one set of tools and their skilled operators to another.

Finally, we can organize the work so that *a team of workers with different skills and different tools moves to the work*, which itself is stationary. A moviemaking crew—the director, the actors, the electricians, the sound engineers—"goes on location." Each does highly specialized work, but they work as a team.

Fayol's "functional organization" is commonly described as organizing work into "related bundles of skill." Actually, it organizes work both by stages and by skills. Such traditional functions as manufacturing or marketing involve a very wide variety of unrelated skills—the machinist's skill and the production planner's skill in operations, for example, and the salesperson's skill and the market researcher's skill in marketing. But *manufacturing and marketing are distinct stages in a process*. Other functions, such as accounting and human resources, are, however, *organized by skills*. But in any functional organization the *work* is moved to the *stage* or the *skill*. The *work moves*, while the *position of the worker is fixed*.

In the "team structure," however, *work and task are, so to speak, fixed*. Workers with different skills and different tools are brought together in a team. The team is assigned a piece of work or to a job, whether this is a research project or the architectural design of a new office building.

Both functional and team structures are old designs. The Egyptian pyramid builder organized work functionally. And the organized and permanent team of the "hunting band" goes back even further, to the last ice age.

Work and task have to be structured and organized. Any organization has to apply either functional structure or team structure or both in order to design work and task. Many organizations, as will be discussed later in this chapter, should apply both. And all need to understand both.

THE FUNCTIONAL STRUCTURE

Functional design has the great advantage of clarity. Everybody has a "home." Everybody understands his or her own task. It is an organization of high stability.

But the price for clarity and stability is that it is difficult for people, up to and including the top functional people, to understand the task of the whole and to relate their own work to it. While stable, the structure is rigid and resists adaptation.

It does not prepare people for tomorrow, does not train and test them. On the whole, it tends to make them want to do what they already do a little better, rather than to seek new ideas and new ways of doing things.

The strengths and the limitations of the functional principle give it peculiar characteristics with respect to the economy specification. At its best, functional organization works with high economy. Very few people at the top need to spend much time on keeping the organization running, that is, on organizing, coordination, conciliation, and so on. The rest can do their work. But at its fairly common worst, functional organization is grossly uneconomical. As soon as it approaches even a modest size or complexity, "friction" builds up. It rapidly becomes an organization of misunderstanding, feuds, empires, and Berlin-Wall building. It soon requires coordinators, committees, meetings, troubleshooters, special dispatchers, which waste everybody's time without, as a rule, solving much. And this tendency toward conflict exists not only between different functions. The large functional unit with its subdivisions and subfunctions is also prone to internal inefficiency and also requires more and more managerial effort to keep it running smoothly.

The basic strength as well as the basic weakness of functional organization is its *effort-focus*. Every functional manager considers his or her function the most important one. This emphasizes craftsmanship and professional standards. But it also makes people in the functional unit tend to subordinate the welfare of the other functions, if not of the entire business, to the interests of their unit. There is no real remedy against this tendency in the functional organization. The wish of every function to improve its own standing in the organization is the price paid for the worthy desire of each manager to do a good job.

Communications are fairly good in a small functional organization, but they, too, break down as the size of the organization increases. Even within an individual functional unit—a marketing department, for example—communications weaken if the unit becomes large or complex. People are then increasingly specialists, interested primarily in their own narrow specialty.

As a decision-making structure, functional organization—even if fairly small—works poorly. For decisions in a functional organization cannot, as a rule, be made except at the highest level. No one except the executive at the top sees the entire business. As a result, decisions are easily misunderstood by the organization and are often poorly implemented. And because a functional organization *has high stability* but *low adaptability,* the challenge to do something truly new and different is likely to be suppressed rather than brought out in the open and faced up to.

Functional organization also does poorly in developing, preparing, and testing people. Functional organization puts the major emphasis on a person's acquiring the knowledge and competence that pertain to a particular function. Yet the functional specialist may become narrow in vision, skills, and loyalties. In a functional organization, there is a built-in emphasis on not showing too much curiosity about the work of other functions or specialties. That is, narrow departmentalization is encouraged.

These limitations and weaknesses of functional organization were apparent from the very first. A good deal of thought has, therefore, been given to offsetting them, and to offsetting, in particular, the greatest weakness: the tendency of functional organization to misdirect the vision of functional people from *contribution and results* to *efforts and business.*

ITS LIMITED SCOPE

Even where functional organization applies, its scope is limited to operating work. Top management is work (see chapter 43), but it is not "functional" work. And functional organization is the wrong organization for it. Wherever applied, it has made for a weak top management.

The functional principle is even less applicable to innovating work. In innovation, we try to do something not done before, that is, something we do not yet know. We need the individual skills of the various disciplines in innovation, but we do not yet know where and when they will be needed, for what time, in what degree, or in what volume. The innovative task therefore cannot be organized on the basis of functional organization. It is incompatible with it.

Where Functionalism Works

Functionalism works very well in the kind of business for which it was designed. The model for Henri Fayol's functional design early in this century was the coal-mining company he ran. It was a fairly large business at that time but would be considered rather small today. Except for a few engineers, it employed only manual workers, who all did one kind of work. A coal mine has only one product—and it varies only in size. Coal requires no treatment beyond simple washing and sorting. Coal had, at least at that time, only a few markets—steel mills, railroads and steamships, power plants, and homeowners. But in these markets, it had practically a monopoly, and while the machinery and tools for mining coal were changing rapidly in Fayol's day, the process itself did not change at all. There was not much scope for innovation.

Fayol's company is the kind of business that the functional design principle organizes well. Anything more complex, more dynamic, or more innovative demands performance capacities that the functional principle does not possess. If used beyond the limits of Fayol's model, functional structure rapidly becomes costly in terms of time and effort. It also runs a high risk of directing the energies of the organization away from performance and toward mere busyness. In businesses that exceed Fayol's model, in size, in complexity, or in innovative scope, functional design should be used only as one principle and never as *the* principle. And even in businesses that fit Fayol's model, top-management design and structure require a different design principle.

THE TEAM

A team is a number of people—usually only a few—with different backgrounds, skills, and knowledge, and drawn from various areas of the organization, who work together on a specific and defined task. There is usually a team leader or team captain. The leader is often permanently appointed for the duration of the team's assignment. But leadership at any one time places itself according to the logic of the work and the specific stage in its progress. There are no superiors and subordinates; there are only seniors and juniors.

Every business—and every other institution—has been using teams all along for one-time tasks, but we have only recently recognized what the hunting bands of our nomadic ice age ancestors knew—the team is also a useful principle for *permanent, structural design.* The mission of the team is a specific task: hunting expedition or product development. But the team itself can be permanent. Its composition may vary from task to task. Its base remains, however, fairly constant, even though individual members may scatter between tasks or belong, at one and the same time, to a number of teams.

The hospital may be the clearest example of the team. The structural component in the hospital is a team mobilized from the *services* for the needs of the *individual patient* as defined by the *team captain,* the physician, with the nurse as the executive officer of the group.

In the hospital, everyone directly concerned with patient care, that is, everyone on the team, is supposed to take *personal responsibility* for the success of the whole team's effort. The doctor's orders are law in a hospital. Yet, physical therapists who are told, for instance, to give rehabilitation exercises to a patient are expected to notice when the patient seems to run a fever, to stop the exercises, and to notify the nurse immediately and ask for a temperature reading. *They will not hesitate to countermand a doctor's orders within their own sphere.* The doctor may order an orthopedic patient to be measured for crutches and taught how to use them. The physical therapist may take one look and say, "You don't need crutches; you'll be better off using a cane right away or just walking on your walking cast without any support."

Performance responsibility rests with the whole team. Each nurse as leader draws on the resources of the whole organization as needed. At one stage she brings in X-ray technicians; at another, physical therapists; at another stage, medical laboratory technicians; and so on. The composition of the team may be different for every patient, but the team leader who carries primary responsibility will also tend to work again and again with the same three or four people in each functional area.

The Requirements of Team Design

Team design requires *a continuing mission* in which the specific tasks change frequently. If there is no continuing mission, there might be a temporary task force, but not an organization based on the team as a permanent design. *If the tasks do not change, there is no need for team organization and no point to it.*

A team needs a clear and sharply defined objective. It must be possible all the time to feed back from the objectives to the work and performance of the whole team and of each member.

A team needs leadership. It can be a permanent leader—physician and nurse on the patient-care team in the hospital, or the recognized head of a top-management team. Or leadership can shift with each major phase. But if it does, one person must be clearly designated to decide, at a given stage, who takes team leadership for a particular phase of the task. This is not leadership responsibility for making the decision and giving the command. It is leadership responsibility for deciding who among the team members has the decision and command authority for a particular phase. A team is, therefore, not "democratic." It emphasizes *authority*. But the *authority is task derived and task focused*.

The team as a whole is always responsible for the task. The individual members contribute their particular skills and knowledge. But every individual is always responsible for the output and performance of the entire team rather than for only his or her own work. *The team is the unit.*

Team members need not know each other well to perform as a team. But they do need to know each other's function and potential contribution. "Rapport," "empathy," "interpersonal relations," are not needed. *Mutual understanding of each other's job and common understanding of the common task are essential.*

It is therefore the team leader's first job to establish clarity: clarity of objectives and clarity with respect to everybody's role, including the leader's own.

The Strengths and Limitations of the Team Principles

The team has obvious strengths. Everybody always knows the work of the whole and holds him or herself responsible for it. It is highly receptive to new ideas and new ways of doing things. And it has great adaptability.

It also has great shortcomings. It has clarity only if the team leader creates it. It has poor stability. Its economy is low: a team demands continuing attention to its management, to the relationships of people within the team, to assigning people to jobs, to explanation, deliberation, communication, and so on. Much of the energy of the members goes into keeping things running. Although each person on the team understands the common task, he does not always understand his own specific task. He may be so interested in what others are doing that he pays inadequate attention to his own assignment.

Teams are adaptable. They are receptive to new ideas and to new ways of doing things. They are the best means available for overcoming *functional isolation and narrow interest.* All career professionals should serve on a few teams during their working life.

Still, teams do only a little better than functional organization in preparing people for higher management responsibilities or in testing them in performance. A team structure makes for neither clear communications nor clear decision making. The whole group must work constantly on explaining both to itself and to managers throughout the rest of the organization what it is trying to do, what it is working on, and what it has accomplished. The team must constantly make sure that the decisions that need to be made are brought into the open. There is a real danger, otherwise, that teams will make decisions they should not make—decisions, for instance, that irreversibly commit the whole company.

Team's fail—and the failure rate has been high—primarily because they do not impose on themselves the self-discipline and responsibility required by their high degree of freedom. No task force can be "permissive" and function.

But the *greatest limitation* of the team structure is *size.* Teams work best when there are few members. The hunting band had seven to fifteen members. So do the teams in team sports such as football, baseball, and cricket. If a team gets much larger, it becomes unwieldy. Its strengths—such as flexibility and the sense of responsibility of the members—diminish. Its limitations—lack of clarity, communication problems, overconcern with its internal relationships—become crippling weaknesses.

The Scope of Team Organization

Its size limitation determines the scope of applicability of the team principle of organization.

It is the best available design principle for top-management work. Indeed (as will be discussed in chapter 43), it is probably the only appropriate design principle for top management. The team is also the preferred design principle for innovative work (see chapter 40).

But for most operating work, the team is not appropriate by itself alone as the design principle of organization. It is a complement—a badly needed one—to functional design. It may well be that it is team organization that will make the functional principle fully effective and will enable it to do what its designers had hoped for.

Team Design and the Knowledge Organization

The area where team design as a complement to functional organization is likely to make the greatest contribution is in *knowledge work*. The knowledge organization is likely to balance *function* as a *person's home* with *team* as his or her *place of work* (the technical term for this is *matrix organization*).

Knowledge work by definition is specialized work. *The shift from middle management to knowledge organization therefore brings a host of specialists into the management group as operating people.* The traditional pattern of functions is being replaced by an enormous number of new functions. Of course many of them can, and should, be grouped together. Still, while the tax specialist will often be put together with other financial people, either in accounting or in the treasurer's department, tax work is different and separate. This also applies, for example, to product managers or market managers, who are related alike to the traditional marketing function.

This requires better functional management. The organization must decide what specialties are needed, or it will drown in useless learning. It must think through what the key activities are in which specialized knowledge is needed, and it must make sure that knowledge work in the key areas is provided for in depth and with excellence. Knowledge work in other areas must either not be done at all or be kept in low key.

A specialty or function must be managed to assure that it makes the contribution to the enterprise for the sake of which it has been established. Management must anticipate today the new specialties that will be needed tomorrow and the new demands that will be made tomorrow on existing specialties. There is need for concern, in other words, for developing specialized knowledge, which in chapter 24 is called "management development."

There is great need for concern with, and for management of, the specialists themselves. Do they work on the truly important things, or do they fritter away their time? Do they do over again what they already know how to do, or do they work on creating new potential and new performance capacity? Are they being used productively, or are they just being kept busy? Are they developing both as professionals and as persons?

These are crucial questions that cannot be answered by checking how many hours a person works. They require knowledge of the functional area and genuine functional management.

Much knowledge work will undoubtedly be organized on a strictly functional basis. Much will also be done by individuals who, in effect, are an organizational component by themselves.

An increasing number of knowledge workers, however, will have a functional home but do their work in a team with other knowledge workers from other functions and disciplines. The more advanced knowledge is, the more specialized it has to be. And specialized knowledge is a fragment, if not mere "data." It becomes effective only as input to other people's decisions, other people's work, other people's understanding. It becomes results only in a team.

Knowledge organization will therefore increasingly have two aspects: a functional one, managing the individual and his or her knowledge, and another one, the team, managing work and task. Seen one way, this undermines the functional principle and destroys it. Seen another way, it saves the functional principle and makes it fully effective. It certainly requires strong, professional, effective, functional managers and functional components.

The team is clearly not a cure-all. It is a difficult structure requiring great self-discipline. It has severe limitations and major weaknesses.

But it is also not, as many managers still believe, only a temporary measure for dealing with nonrecurring special problems. *It is a genuine design principle of organization.* It is the best principle for such permanent organizing tasks as top-management work and innovating work. And it is an important and perhaps essential complement to functional structure—in mass-production work, whether manual or clerical, and above all, in knowledge work. It is probably the key to making functional skill fully effective in the knowledge organization through the matrix organization, in which a functional skill-oriented component is one axis and the task-oriented team the other axis.

SUMMARY

There are available to us now *five different design principles*. Each satisfies some of the design specifications, but none satisfies all of them. Each of the design principles has strengths, limitations, and rigorous requirements for effectiveness. And each expresses different design logic. The first two design principles, "functional organization" and "team organization," are organized around the *logic of work and task*. Though often seen as in conflict, they are largely complementary, especially for knowledge work, which is increasingly being organized in matrix organizations, using both functional and team designs.

40

Three Kinds of Teams

Team building has now become a buzzword in American organizations. The results are not overly impressive.

Ford Motor Company began more than twenty years ago to build teams to design its new models. It then reported "serious problems," and the gap in development time between Ford and its Japanese competitors had hardly narrowed. General Motors' Saturn Division was going to replace the traditional assembly line with teamwork in its "factory of the future." But the plant then steadily moved back toward the Detroit-style assembly line. Procter & Gamble launched a team-building campaign with great fanfare. Then P&G began moving back to individual accountability for developing and marketing new products.

One reason—perhaps the major one—for these near failures is the all-but-universal belief among executives that there is just *one kind of team*. There actually are three kinds of teams—each different in its structure, in the behavior it demands from its members, in its strengths, its vulnerabilities, its limitations, its requirements, but above all, in what it can do and should be used for.

The first kind of team is the baseball team. The surgical team that performs an open-heart operation is a *baseball team*. So is the team Detroit traditionally sets up to design a new car.

The players play *on* the team; they do not play *as* a team. They have fixed positions they never leave. The second baseman rarely runs to assist the pitcher; the anesthesiologist rarely comes to the aid of the surgical nurse. "Up at bat, you are totally alone," is an old baseball saying. In the traditional Detroit design team, marketing people rarely saw designers and were never consulted by them. Designers did their work and passed it on to the development engineers, who in turn did their work and passed it on to manufacturing, which in turn did its work and passed it on to marketing.

The second kind of team is the football team. The hospital unit that rallies around a patient who goes into shock at three AM is a "football team," as are Japanese automakers' design teams. The players on the football team like those on the baseball team, have fixed positions. But on the football team *players play as a team*.

The Japanese automakers' design teams, which Detroit and P&G rushed to imitate, are football-type teams. To use engineering terms, the designers, engineers, manufacturing people, and marketing people work in *parallel*. The traditional Detroit team worked *in series*.

The third kind of team is the tennis doubles team—the kind Saturn management hoped would replace the traditional assembly line. It is also the sort of team that plays in a jazz combo, that consists of senior executives who form the "president's office" in big companies, or that is most likely to produce a genuine innovation, such as the personal computer thirty-five years ago.

On the doubles team, players have a *primary rather than a fixed position*. They are supposed to "cover" their teammates, adjusting to their teammates' strengths and weaknesses and to the changing demands of the "game."

Business executives and the management literature have little good to say these days about the baseball-style team, whether in the office or on the factory floor. There is even a failure to recognize such teams as teams at all. But this kind of team has enormous strengths. Each member can be evaluated separately, can have clear and specific goals, can be held accountable, can be measured—as witness the statistics a true aficionado reels off about every major leaguer in baseball history. Each member can be trained and developed to the fullest extent of the individual's strengths. And because the members do not have to adjust to anybody else on the team, every position can be staffed with a "star," no matter how temperamental, jealous, or limelight-hogging each of them might be.

But the baseball team is inflexible. It works well when the game has been played many times and when the sequence of its actions is thoroughly understood by everyone. That is what made this kind of team right for Detroit in the past.

As recently as thirty years ago, to be fast and flexible in automotive design was the last thing Detroit needed or wanted. Traditional mass production required long runs with minimum changes. And since the resale value of the "good used car"—one less than three years old—was a key factor for the new-car buyer, it was a serious mistake to bring out a new design (which would depreciate the old car) more than every five years. Sales and market share took a dip on several occasions when Chrysler prematurely introduced a new, brilliant design.

The Japanese did not invent "flexible mass production"; IBM was probably the first to use it, around 1960. But when the Japanese auto industry adopted it, it made possible the introduction of a new car model in parallel with a successful old one. And then the baseball team did, indeed, become the wrong team for Detroit, and for mass-production industry as a whole. The design process then had to be restructured as a football team.

The football team does have the flexibility Detroit needs. But it has far more stringent requirements than the baseball team. It needs a *score*—such as the play the coach signals to the huddle on the field. The specifications with which the Japanese begin their design of a new car model—or a new consumer-electronics product—are far more stringent and detailed than anything Detroit is used to with respect to style, technology, performance, weight, price, and so on. And they are far more closely adhered to.

In the traditional "baseball" design team, every position—engineering, manufacturing, marketing—does its job its own way. In the football team, there is no such permissiveness. The word of the coach is law. Players are beholden to this one boss alone for their orders, their rewards, their appraisals, their promotions.

The individual engineer on the Japanese design team is a member of his company's engineering department. But he is on the design team because the team's leader has asked for him—not because the chief engineer sent him there. He can consult engineering and get advice. But his orders come from the design-team chief, who also appraises his performance. If there are stars on these teams, they are featured only if the team leader entrusts them with a *solo*. Otherwise, they subordinate themselves to the team.

Even more stringent are the requirements of the *doubles team*—the kind that GM's Saturn Division hoped to develop in its "flexible-manufacturing" plant, and a flexible plant does, indeed need such a team. The team must be quite small, with five to seven members at most. The members have to be trained together and must work together for quite some time before they fully function as a team. There must be one clear goal for the entire team, yet considerable flexibility with respect to the individual member's work and performance. And in this kind of team, only the team "performs"; individual members "contribute."

All three of these kinds of teams are true teams. But they are so different—in the behavior they require, in what they do best, and in what they cannot do at all—that they cannot be hybrids. One kind of team can play only one way. And it is very difficult to change from one kind of team to another.

Gradual change cannot work. There has to be a total break with the past, however traumatic it may be. This means that people cannot report to both their old boss and to the new coach, or team leader. And *their rewards, their compensation, their appraisals, and their promotions must be totally dependent on their performance in their new roles on their new teams.* But this is so unpopular that the temptation to compromise is always great.

At Ford, the financial people were left under the control of the financial staff and report to it rather than to the new design teams. GM's Saturn Division tried to maintain the authority of the traditional bosses—the first-line supervisors and the shop stewards—rather than hand decision-making power over to the work teams. This, however, is like playing baseball and a tennis doubles match with the same people, on the same field, and at the same time. It can only result in frustration and nonperformance. And a similar confusion seems to have prevailed at P&G.

Teams, in other words, are tools. As such, each team design has its own uses, its own characteristics, its own requirements, its own limitations. Teamwork is neither "good" nor "desirable"—it is a fact. Wherever people work together or play together, they do so as a team. *Which team to use for what purpose* is a crucial, difficult, and risky decision that is even harder to unmake. Managements must learn how to make it.

SUMMARY

Teams are very much in vogue. It is, therefore, important to know not only when the team is the appropriate design principle but what kind of team is appropriate for a given task. There are three kinds of teams. First, in the *baseball team,* each player is a specialist, plays mostly as an *individual,* and *rarely leaves a fixed position.* The surgical team is an example of the first kind of team. The second kind is the *football team,* where each person has a specialty but each performs their specialty *in parallel as directed by the coach,* and teamwork is critical to success. The team of professionals that care for patients in a trauma unit is an example of the second team. Finally, the third kind of team is the *tennis doubles team,* where *team members are trained in a number of positions* and *have considerable flexibility with respect to the contribution* they must make to achieve the goal of the team.

41

Result- and Relation-Focused Design

FEDERAL DECENTRALIZATION

In federal decentralization, a company is organized as a number of self-governing businesses. Each unit is responsible for its own performance, its own results, and its own contribution to the total company. Each unit has its own management that, in effect, runs its own autonomous business.

Federal decentralization assumes that the activities within an autonomous business are organized on the functional principle, though, of course, the use of teams is not excluded. The autonomous businesses of a decentralized structure are designed to be small enough to put the strengths of a functional structure to work while neutralizing its weaknesses.

But the starting point of decentralization is different. Functional and team organization start with *work and task*. They assume that the results are the sum total of the efforts. "If only efforts are organized properly, the right results will follow" is the underlying premise. Decentralization, by contrast, starts out with the question, *"What results do we aim for?"* It tries to set up the right business first, that is, the unit that will have the best capacity for results and especially for results in the marketplace. Then the question is asked, "What work, what efforts, what key activities, have to be set up and organized within the autonomous business?"

It is desirable to set up the same, or at least a similar, functional structure for all the autonomous businesses within a company. Almost all major retail chains, have, for instance, a store controller, an operations manager, and department heads for major merchandise areas.

But care should be taken lest this desirable similarity becomes stifling uniformity.

The General Electric reorganization of 1950–1952 provides an example of what not to do. GE decided that the "typical manufacturing business" had five key functions: engineering, manufacturing, marketing, accounting, and personnel. That this did not fit nonmanufacturing businesses such as GE Credit—now General

Electric Financial Services, everyone saw, of course. But two things were not seen—and the result was considerable damage. First, some manufacturing businesses needed additional and different key functions, or at least they needed a different arrangement of the same functional work. For example, in the computer business, product development and customer service are far too important to be subordinated to engineering and marketing. GE's failure in the computer business had many causes, but imposing the functional structure of a typical manufacturing business was a major factor. Second, some businesses that looked like manufacturing businesses were really innovative businesses. These units were genuine businesses and result centers, but they had no "product"; they were set up to develop one. They had no "market" but a research-and-development contract, usually from the U.S. government. They did not "manufacture"; at most, they had a model shop to build a few prototypes. Yet, the functions of a typical manufacturing business were imposed on them. Some of these innovative-development businesses managed to survive by quiet sabotage of the official structure. *Others were seriously damaged—by having to carry a heavy load of functions they did not need and, above all, by misdirection of vision and efforts.*

The Strength of Federal Decentralization

Of all design principles available so far, federal decentralization comes closest to satisfying all the design specifications listed in chapter 39. It also has the widest scope. Both operating work and innovative work can be organized as decentralized autonomous businesses. And while top management obviously cannot be set up as an autonomous business, federal decentralization of the business, if done properly, makes for strong and effective top managements. It frees top management for the top-management tasks.

Federal decentralization has great clarity and considerable economy. It makes it easy for all members of the autonomous business to understand their own tasks and to understand the task of the whole business. It has high stability and yet is adaptable.

It focuses the vision and efforts of managers directly on business performance and results. The danger of self-deception—of concentrating on the familiar but old and tired, rather than on the difficult but new and growing, or of allowing unprofitable lines to be carried on the backs of the profitable ones—is much lessened. Reality is not easily obscured by overhead costs. It is not hidden somewhere in the figures for total sales.

With respect to communications and decisions, the federal organization is the only satisfactory design principle we have.

Since the entire management group, or at least the upper ranks within it, share a common vision and a common perception, they tend to communicate easily. And usually, for that reason, communication between people in different kinds of work is encouraged all the way down the line rather than frowned upon. Decision making is also likely to be placed at the proper level without great effort. The focus tends to be on the right rather than the wrong issue, and on the important rather than the trivial decision.

The greatest strength of the federal principle lies, however, in *manager development*. Of all known principles of organization, it alone prepares and tests people for top-management responsibility at an early stage. This by itself makes it the principle to be used in preference to any other.

In a federally organized structure, the managers are close enough to business performance and business results to focus on them. They are close enough to results to get immediate feedback from performance on their own tasks and work. Because management by objective and self-control becomes effective, the number of people or units under one manager is limited only by the span of managerial responsibility.

Above all, the general managers of the decentralized businesses are truly top management, if only in a small business. They face most of the challenges of the top-management job in an independent company—the one exception being, as a rule, the responsibility for financial resources and their supply. They have to make decisions. They have to build a team. They have to think about markets and processes, people and money, today and tomorrow. As a result, they are being tested in an autonomous command. Yet they are being tested fairly early in their career, and at a reasonably low level. A mistake can, therefore, be unmade without too much damage to the company, and, equally important, without too much damage to the person. No other known principle of organization, whether in business or in any other institution, satisfies the need to prepare and test people for tomorrow's leadership positions nearly as well as the federal principle does.

The search for a system that will prepare and test tomorrow's leaders is the oldest problem of political theory and political practice. No political system has ever solved it adequately. The principle of federal decentralization does not solve it fully. The autonomous manager of a decentralized business is still not faced with the full responsibility, let alone with the full loneliness, of the top position. But the federal principle comes closer to being a solution than any other known design.

The Requirements of Federal Decentralization

Federal decentralization has strict requirements. It also makes very substantial demands for responsibility and self-discipline.

Decentralization must not create a weak center. On the contrary, one of the main purposes of federal organization is to strengthen top management and to make it capable of doing its own work rather than being forced to supervise, coordinate, and prop up operating work. Federal decentralization works only if the top-management job is clearly defined and thought through.

The test of effective federal decentralization is top-management strength. Top management in a decentralized company must, first, accept its responsibility for thinking through "what our business is and what it should be." It must accept the responsibility for setting the objectives for the entire company and for working out the strategies for obtaining these objectives. It must, in other words, accept the responsibility for its own job. A federal structure is a shambles if top management does not live up to the responsibilities of its own tasks.

Top management must think through carefully what decisions it *reserves* for itself. There are decisions that have to do with the entire company, its integrity, and its future. But there are also decisions that should be made on the basis of what is good for an individual autonomous business. To distinguish between the two, and to make each kind of decision correctly, requires somebody who sees the whole and is responsible for the whole.

Specifically, there must be three reserved areas if the organization is to remain a whole rather than splinter into fragments. Top management, and top management alone, can decide *what technologies, markets, and products to go into, what businesses to start and what to abandon,* and *what the basic values, beliefs and principles of the organization are.*

Second, top management must reserve *control of the allocation of the key resource of capital.* Both the supply of capital and its investment are top-management responsibilities that cannot be turned over to the autonomous units of a federal organization.

The other key resource is people. The people in a federally organized company, and especially managers and key professionals, are a resource of the entire company rather than of any one unit. *The company's policies with respect to people and decisions on key appointments* in the decentralized autonomous business are thus the third area for top-management decisions—though, of course, autonomous business managers need to take an active part in them. And a decentralized company must have a strong, respected, and senior executive in top management who is the company's conscience with respect to people.

Federal decentralization requires *centralized controls* and *common measurements.* Whenever a federal organization gets into trouble, the reason is always that the measurements at the disposal of the center are not good enough. As a result, personal supervision has to be substituted. Both the managers of the autonomous businesses and top management must know what is expected of each business, what is meant by "performance," and what developments are important. *To give autonomy, one must have confidence.* And this requires controls that make opinions unnecessary. To manage by objectives, one must know whether goals are being reached or not, and this requires clear and reliable measurements.

A federal structure requires *common vision*. A federal unit of an organization is autonomous, but it is not independent and should not be. Its autonomy is a means toward better performance—for the entire institution. Its managers should regard themselves all the more as members of the greater community, the whole enterprise.

Size Requirements

Federal decentralization was designed in response to a problem of size: the deterioration that begins in functional structures when they reach more than medium size. But federal decentralization also has size requirements. When the federal unit becomes so big that the functional subunits are too large to function well, the whole autonomous business becomes unwieldy, sluggish, and too big to perform. The "brain," that is, the top management of the autonomous unit, may still perform. But the "members," the functional components, turn rigid and bureaucratic and will increasingly serve themselves rather than the common purpose.

DuPont counteracted this, in part, by splitting autonomous businesses in two as they grew bigger and, in part, by setting up small autonomous decentralized businesses within large autonomous decentralized businesses. Another approach is that of Johnson & Johnson, the multinational producer of health-care products ranging from absorbent cotton to birth control pills. J&J for many years tried to limit the size of each business to 250 employees. Each business was run as a separate company with its own complete management, and each reported directly to a small, central parent-company top-management team. While J&J, with current worldwide sales of over 50 billion and a workforce over 100,000, has been forced to accept individual businesses a good deal larger than 250 employees, it still limits the size of each business and will split one rather than permit it to grow large. As a result, functional units are still quite small in most J&J businesses.

But breaking up or subdividing autonomous businesses as they grow to large size is not always possible; or at least it is not always done. And the result is then the emergence of functional empires.

The Chevrolet division of General Motors, for instance, grew so large at one time that it would by itself have been the world's third- or fourth-largest manufacturing company if it had been independent. Chevrolet could have been split up into a number of separate divisions: one, for instance, in charge of the large-truck business; another one, perhaps, in charge of the smaller cars such as compacts and subcompacts; with the original Chevrolet division confined to standard-sized passenger automobiles.

How Small Is Too Small?

But the decentralized autonomous unit also needs to be big enough to support the management it needs.

How small is too small depends on the business. A Marks & Spencer store can be quite small and yet support adequate management. All a small store needs is one manager and a few department heads who actually manage on the selling floor.

In other industries, the mass-production metalworking industry, for example, there is a minimum size. A metalworking business is rarely capable of supporting adequate management and its own engineering, manufacturing, and marketing work unless it sells $20–30 million of merchandise a year. Businesses with a significantly lower sales volume are likely to be understaffed, or staffed with inadequate people.

The decisive criterion is not size but the *scope and challenge* of the management job. A federal unit should always have enough scope so that a good manager can show his or her ability. It should have enough challenge so that the management group in the unit truly has to manage—that is, to think through objectives and plans, to build human resources into an effective team, to integrate the work, and to measure its performance. It should have enough challenge so that management will have to work on all major phases of a business, but also enough challenge that it can really develop a market, a product, or service—and, above all, can truly develop people. The true criterion of size for an autonomous business unit is not economics: *it is managerial scope and challenge, and managerial performance.*

A decentralized organization needs effective "conscience" work. It needs, especially if large and diversified, organized thinking and planning for top management. It needs strong central information and unified controls and measurements. It will have some common operating work, such as the supply and management of money; research; legal counsel; relations with the public, organized labor, and government; and perhaps purchasing. It may have to organize company-wide work on innovation in key activities, whether marketing or managing people.

But the autonomous businesses of a decentralized organization should not have to depend on central service staffs, that is, on advisory and teaching activities operating out of headquarters. The decentralized operating units should be strong enough to stand on their own feet. Dependence on central staff services can only impose on a decentralized organization the weaknesses and vulnerabilities, without giving it the benefits and strengths, of functional design.

What Is a "Business"?

Federal decentralization is applicable only where an organization can truly be organized into a number of genuine businesses. This is its basic limitation.

But what is a "business"? Ideally, of course, a federal unit should be a complete business in its own right.

This idea underlay Alfred P. Sloan, Jr.'s, organization of General Motors in the early 1920s. Each of the automotive divisions did its own design, its own engineering, its own manufacturing, its own marketing, and its own sales. The divisions were limited as to the price range in which they could offer automobiles but were autonomous otherwise. GM's accessory divisions sold a large share of their output to the automotive divisions of their own company. But they were selling an even larger share directly to the outside market and indeed, very often, to General Motors' own competitors. They, too, were businesses in every sense of the word.

So are the autonomous companies into which Johnson & Johnson is organized. Each has its own product lines, its own research and development, its own markets and marketing.

But how much of the reality of a genuine business does there have to be for federal decentralization to work effectively? At a minimum the unit must contribute a profit to the company. Its profit or loss should directly become company profit or loss. In fact, the company's total profit should be the sum total of the profits of the individual businesses.

Perhaps even more important—and the real mark of autonomy—is that the federal unit must have a market of its own. The market may be only a geographic entity—as in the case of Marks & Spencer stores, or in the case of the regional companies into which several large American life insurance companies have divided themselves. But still there has to be a distinct market within which the unit has autonomy.

As long as a business can have full market responsibility and objective comparability of results, it can be an autonomous business, even though it obtains its products from another autonomous unit or from a centralized company-run manufacturing source.

Where, however, no market test exists, we should not speak of an autonomous business. Federal decentralization then does not work.

So far we have been discussing federal decentralization of operating work, that is, of existing and known businesses. A decentralized unit for innovative work is structured and measured differently (see chapter 35). But federal decentralization is also an effective design principle for such work—as long as its performance and results can be objectively measured and as long as innovative teams can be freely formed within the unit. A decentralized innovative unit also has to be a business—or must be capable of becoming one.

SIMULATED DECENTRALIZATION

Whenever a unit can be set up as a business, no design principle can match federal decentralization. We have learned, however, that a great many large companies cannot be divided into genuine businesses. Yet they have clearly outgrown the limits of size and complexity of the functional or of the team structure.

These are the organizations that are increasingly turning to *simulated decentralization* as the answer to their organization problem.

Simulated decentralization forms units that are not businesses but that are still set up as if they were businesses, with as much autonomy as possible, with their own management, and with at least *a simulation of profit-and-loss responsibility*. They buy from and sell to each other using *transfer prices* determined administratively rather than by an outside market. Or their profits are arrived at by internal *allocation of costs* to which then, often, a standard fee (revenue) such as 20 percent of costs is added. Simulated decentralization is the one available design principle that copes with the structural problems of the big materials business, such as a company in the chemical, steel, glass, and oil industries, in which all products come from a common source and out of a common process, but in which there are many different markets for each product.

The most interesting attempts to apply simulated decentralization to very large businesses that could not use federal decentralization are the reorganizations of commercial banks. These bank examples show clearly some of the major problems of simulated decentralization. The head of a small fashion-design business, for instance, will use the local branch bank that *finances her firm* for her personal banking business and for her savings account. She will expect it to act as executor of her will, to be the manager for her investments and the trustee for her firm's pension fund. She does not want to deal with four different branches of the same bank. Whose customer is she, and who gets the credit for her business? These determinations of credits must be identified for profit and loss to be simulated for each branch.

Simulated decentralization is obviously difficult and full of problems. Yet it will be used even more in the future, because simulated decentralization is potentially most useful in the growth areas of the economy and society, process industries, and private and governmental service institutions. In these sectors, neither functional organization nor federal decentralization can do the organizing job. Managers, therefore, need to understand the requirements and limitations of simulated decentralization. What problems can be expected in an organization built on it?

The Problems of Simulated Decentralization

Simulated decentralization is a poor fit with respect to *all* design specifications. It is not clear. It does not make for an easy focus on performance. It rarely satisfies the specification that everyone should be able to know his or her own task. Nor do managers and professionals necessarily understand the job of the whole.

Least satisfactory in simulated decentralization are economy, communications, and decision authority. These weaknesses are unavoidable features of the design.

Because the unit of simulated decentralization is not truly a business, its results are not truly determined by market performance. They are largely the results of internal management decisions. They are decisions on *transfer prices* and *cost allocations*.

Communications are likely to suffer. A tremendous amount of managerial time and energy will be spent working out the lines between different units that supposedly are autonomous; making sure that they cooperate; mediating between them. The smallest adjustment becomes a top-management decision, a trial of strength, and a matter of honor and sacred principle.

Simulated decentralization makes high human demands—on self-discipline; on mutual toleration; on subordinating one's own interest, including the interest in one's own compensation, to arbitration by higher authority; demands to be a "good sport" and a "cheerful loser." These demands are far more difficult and, above all, far more divisive than the big demands that federal decentralization makes on people.

I once heard that a candidate for a very senior position in a big bank was to be turned down because his unit was doing too well at the bank's expense. "He puts the performance of his own unit before everything else." The next man was turned down because "he is too willing to subordinate the performance of his unit to the needs and requirements of other units and, therefore, does not show a good enough performance." Everyone admitted to confusion when I asked, "Are there any guidelines for behavior? Is there any way in which you can tell an executive ahead of time what you consider 'excessive cooperation'?" All admitted that this was the greatest worry of their own subordinates. "You have to play it by ear," the ranking officer finally concluded. But then he stopped himself and added, "But by whose ear?"

In scope, simulated decentralization is limited to operating work. It clearly has no applicability to top-management work. And if innovative work cannot be set up as a federal decentralized unit, it requires either functional or team structure.

Rules for Using Simulated Decentralization

Simulated decentralization is a last resort only. As long as a functional structure—with or without teams added—works, that is, as long as a business is small or fair-sized, simulated decentralization is to be shunned. And beyond such size, federal decentralization is vastly preferable.

Even in the materials company, federal decentralization might be tried first—though it may not work forever. One example of an adaptation of genuine federal decentralization to a materials business is Owens-Illinois in Toledo, Ohio, a very large manufacturer of glass bottles. After World War II, when plastic bottles came into wide use, Owens-Illinois went into plastics to retain its leadership position in the bottle market. The company decided, after long soul-searching, to set up both the glass-bottle business and the plastic-bottle business as separate autonomous "product" businesses, competing with each other for the same customers and in the same markets.

The Owens-Illinois strategy was a brilliant success. The company's growth was very rapid. And yet, fifteen years later, in the early 1970s Owens-Illinois changed over to simulated decentralization. It retained the two divisions but confined them to manufacturing. Marketing of all bottles, glass and plastic, was put into a new marketing division. The reason given was that the customers demanded one source of supply for all their bottles. "Glass" and "plastics" were not meaningful to them; they wanted bottles and not materials.

With all its limitations, weaknesses, and risks, simulated decentralization may, therefore, be the best available principle where constituent parts of the same large business have to work together and yet have to have individual responsibility. This applies especially where the *organizing principle of the market* is incompatible with that of *technology* and *operations*.

A railroad or an airline has by definition no purely "local" business. Hence, these businesses cannot be federally decentralized but have to organize themselves according to functions with, at best, a regional coordinator who intervenes between the functions, mediates, and ensures liaison. The decisions that affect the performance of a transportation system must be made centrally.

They are, above all, decisions on capital use, on the assignment of airplanes, locomotives, and freight cars, for instance. Yet transportation businesses, while incapable of being decentralized except for relatively unimportant tasks, are also clearly far too large to work well under functional organization.

This means, in effect, that there are businesses and service institutions for which we do not possess an adequate principle of organization.

In simulated decentralization, at least we know what to expect. It is therefore a major task of organization theory and organization practice to develop for these large, overcentralized functional structures, such as a railroad system or most government agencies, an organization design that works no worse for them than simulated decentralization works, for instance, for the large materials companies and the large commercial banks. This will probably have to be some application of the principle of simulated decentralization.

THE SYSTEMS STRUCTURE

Of the design principles of organization, only one, Fayol's functions, can be said to have started in a theoretical analysis. The others—the team, federal decentralization, and simulated decentralization—developed as responses to specific challenges and needs of the moment. This is true also of the systems structure.

Systems organization is an extension of the team design principle. But instead of a team consisting of individuals, the systems organization builds the team out of a wide variety of different organizations. They may be government agencies, private businesses, universities and individual researchers, and organizations inside and outside the parent organization. *Systems design uses all the other design principles* as the task demands: functional organizations and teams, federal and simulated decentralization.

Some of the members of the systems structure may have a specific task that does not change throughout the entire life of the venture. Others may change tasks according to the stage of the program. Some will be permanent members. Others may be brought in only for one specific assignment.

Although the National Aeronautics and Space Administration (NASA), in its organization of the U.S. space program in the 1960s, first made the systems structure *visible as a principle of organization design,* it had existed for at least a century. It actually was first developed as a structure for businesses; and its major application is probably in business. The large Japanese company and its suppliers and distributors have for decades worked in a relationship very similar to that in which NASA worked with its *suppliers, subcontractors, and partners.* The Japanese large company sometimes owns its suppliers. More often, it has little or no ownership stake in them. Yet the suppliers are integrated into the system. Similarly, the Japanese company usually depends upon a trading company that is both independent and integrated.

What organizations that use the systems structure have in common is a need to integrate diversity of culture, values, and skills into unity of action. Each component of the system has to work in its own way, be effective according to its own logic and according to its own standards. Or else it will not be effective at all. Yet all components have to work toward a common goal. Each has to accept, understand, and carry out its own role. This can be achieved only by direct, flexible, and tailor-made relationships among people, or groups of people, in which personal bond and mutual trust bridge wide differences in point of view and in what is considered "proper" and "appropriate."

NASA, for instance, faced the problem of divergent values and cultures. NASA, a large government agency, was built of some major units staffed with men and women used to the ways of the U.S. military services, while other units were built and run by German-born and German-trained space scientists like Wernher von Braun, raised in the tradition of the German *Herr Professor.* There were businesses, some large, some small, who were "partners" on the team rather than subcontractors. They did not make and deliver a part to preset specifications but planned, designed, and operated the "nervous systems" of the entire space effort. The Jet Propulsion Laboratory (JPL) in Pasadena, California, is one example. Other team members were individual university scientists working independently in their own laboratories. Yet NASA had to integrate all these traditions, values, and behavior patterns into common performance.

The Difficulties and Problems of the Systems Structure

Like simulated decentralization, systems design is a poor "fit" with respect to *all* design specifications. It lacks clarity. It lacks stability. People find it neither easy to know what their job is nor to understand the job of the whole and their relationship to it. Communications are a continuing problem. It is never clear where a certain decision should be made or, indeed, what the basic decisions are. Flexibility is great, and receptivity to new ideas is almost too great. Yet the structure does not, as a rule, develop people and test them for top-management positions. Above all, the systems structure violates the principle of internal economy.

When NASA first started, the scientists who then dominated it believed that controls, especially computer-based information, would run the system. Their thinking soon changed as they learned the *crucial importance of face-to-face personal relationships,* of constant meetings and bringing people into the decision-making process, even on matters remote from their own assignments. Key executives at NASA spent about two-thirds of their time in meetings, and mostly in meetings on matters not directly related to their own tasks.

Personal relationships are the only thing that prevents breakdown in the systems structure. There is constant need for arbitration of conflicts between various members of the system, on jurisdiction, on direction, on budgets, on people, and on priorities. The most important people, regardless of their job descriptions or assigned tasks, spend most of their time keeping the machinery running. In no other organizational structure is the *ratio between output and effort needed for internal cohesion* as poor as in the systems structure.

The requirements for the systems structure to work at all are exceedingly stringent. It demands absolute *clarity of objectives.* The objectives themselves may well change, but at any one time they must be clear. The objective for the work of each of the members of the system must be derived from the objective of the whole and must be directly related to it. In other words, the systems structure can function only if the job of thinking through "What is our business and what should it be?" is taken seriously and performed with excellence. And then it requires that operational objectives and strategy be developed with great care from the basic mission and purpose. *Get a man on the moon by 1970* is exactly the kind of clear objective that enables a systems structure to work.

Another requirement is a demand for *universal communications responsibility.* Every member of the systems structure, but especially every member of every one of the managing groups, has to make sure that *mission, objective,* and *strategies* are fully understood by everyone, and that the doubts, questions, and ideas of every member are heard, listened to, respected, thought through, understood, and resolved. In projects like the NASA space effort, the communications problem is enormous, involving the need to spread word of any problem, breakthrough, or discovery immediately to hundreds of people.

A third requirement is that each member of the team, that is, each managerial unit, take responsibility far beyond its own assignment. Each member must, in effect, take *top-management responsibility*. To get any results requires, from each member, independent responsibility and initiative. At the same time, each member must try to know what goes on throughout the entire system and to keep the common goal in mind. Executives, especially, must always see their own assignments clearly in the perspective of the whole project.

No wonder that the systems structure has not, on the whole, been an unqualified success. For every successful moon shot (but also with an almost unlimited budget to support it), dozens of systems structures have failed miserably to perform or have performed only through budgetary irresponsibility such as no private business could survive—as in the development of the Anglo-French supersonic plane, the Concorde, for example, and of various weapons systems in Europe as well as in the U.S. The attempt to use systems management to tackle major social problems is almost certain to be a total failure. Social and political complexities that are encountered when we move from outer space (where, after all, there are no voters) into the inner city and its problems, into economic development, or even into something seemingly so purely technical as mass transit are almost certain to overwhelm the fragile cohesion of a systems structure as the Central Tunnel Project (The Big Dig) overwhelmed engineering and social systems in Boston.

But NASA's success in the Apollo Program and the success of systems-organized enterprises in Japan show that the systems structure can be made to work and can be highly effective. *It needs, however, clear goals, high self-discipline throughout the structure, and a top management that takes personal responsibility for relationships and communications.*

For many managers, the systems structure is not of direct personal concern—though any manager in an alliance who wants to function effectively will have to understand it (on the issues involved in managing alliances, see chapter 42). The systems structure is an important structure and one that the organization designer and managers need to know and understand—if only to know that it should not be used where other, simpler and easier structures will do the job.

SUMMARY

Both kinds of decentralization—federal decentralization and simulated decentralization—are organized around results. The systems structure is organized around relationships. Of all known design principles, federal decentralization comes closest to satisfying organization specifications. But it is severely limited in its applicability and has stringent requirements that must be met if it is to function. Otherwise, we have to apply simulated decentralization—complex, unwieldy, difficult, and far from satisfactory, but the only design principle we know for the organization of materials businesses, service businesses such as the very big banks, or government agencies. The systems structure is even more complex and difficult, but necessary to organize such multicultural enterprises as the American space program under NASA.

42

Alliances

Mergers, acquisitions, and divestitures have been around for a long time. Alliances, however, are fairly new. But what makes different the present restructuring of the economy and business is the worldwide trend toward alliances of all sorts: joint ventures, know-how agreements, outsourcing, marketing alliances, research alliances, and many others.

These alliances cross industry lines. They cross national borders. They are alliances between business and business and between nonbusinesses, such as a university and a government agency.

In their totality, they are likely to exceed all the headline-making mergers, acquisitions, and divestitures together. What's equally important is that the most spectacular of the mergers tend to be defensive. They are what business analysts call "strategies of despair." They are intended to slow the decline of an industry, such as commercial banking, or to slow the declining profitability of an industry by cutting overhead costs.

Most alliances, by contrast, are what business analysts call "strategies of hope," aimed at speeding up growth, market share, and profitability. Alliances rarely make headlines. They are rarely even reported in the media. They do not, as a rule, require approval, whether by the government or by shareholders. In many of them no money changes hands.

Yet they are fast changing the world's business landscape. It is becoming a *world economy of networks based on partnership rather than on ownership.* The trend toward alliances is accelerating among big, medium-sized, and small businesses; in high-tech as well as in low-tech or no-tech industries; among multinationals as well as among purely domestic companies. *It is being driven by technology needs, by marketing needs, by people needs.*

Alliances have their own rules and their own dos and don'ts. These are quite different from the rules for managing the traditional business based on ownership and control.

Few businesses and executives yet know these rules, much less observe them. Many alliances start out auspiciously. But just when they are successful economically, they collapse. They fail because the partners do not know and do not observe the rules for managing alliances. Answers to a few questions should shed light on these rules.

Why Do Organizations Enter into Alliances?

Organizations generally enter into alliances for one of five reasons. First, they may want to obtain access to new, distinct *technology*. Large computer-makers buy into small software houses. Large electronics manufacturers buy into small designers of specialty chips. Large pharmaceutical companies buy into genetics start-ups. Large Internet sites buy into or set up a cross-promotional arrangement with smaller online groups.

Second, an alliance may be the way to achieve genuine *synergy* between separate and independent companies. One company, for instance, has the research strength and has developed new and superior products or services. But another company has the manufacturing strength, and yet a third company has the marketing strength.

An alliance gives the needed "push" to the new product line. Or, one company has excess manufacturing capacity while another one has the distribution network but not enough stuff to put through it.

Third, alliances are one way for an organization to get access to *people* with know-how.

Fourth, there are alliances in which an independent company performs basic *supply activities* that are actually integrated into the other company's operations.

And fifth, alliances can be a way for an organization to extend its reach *geographically*. It may even be the only way. Setting up branch offices in foreign countries often runs into legal problems and logistical nightmares. It also means that the organization has to adapt itself to an unfamiliar economy and country. But companies can enter into alliances with foreign counterparts whereby one or both parties agree to represent the other or sell or manufacture its products in its home country.

This kind of alliance is by no means limited to doing business in different countries. Within the U.S. for instance, there are many alliances between one fair-sized company that is strong on the East Coast with another fair-sized company that is strong on the West Coast or in the Midwest. These companies can then work together and get most of the advantages of a national company without giving up their independence and separate ownership.

To summarize, organizations typically enter into alliances for one of these five reasons: to obtain access to new, distinct *technology;* to achieve *synergy* between the strengths of two independent partners; to gain access to *people* with specialized knowledge; to *outsource noncore activities* to specialists; and to extend *geographically* into new markets.

Practically every pharmaceutical company in the world has worked out alliances with small genetics and biomolecular companies so as to get access to new knowl-edge and to new technology. Genetics and biomoleculars produce, in the end, the same kind of products the pharmaceutical companies aim at. But they employ to-tally different knowledges. In fact, they require a different mind-set from that of the biochemist and physician in a pharmaceutical company.

An alliance of synergy was an alliance between Intel, the U.S. example of an mi-crochip giant, and a major Japanese manufacturing company. Intel did the research and development for a new kind of microchip. The Japanese have the uniquely Japa-nese competence in miniaturization. Miniaturization is a legacy of two hundred years of a uniquely Japanese art tradition. The Japanese, therefore, converted the Intel design into something that was manufactured as a microchip. And they manufactured the chip, at least in the beginning. And then both companies, inde-pendently and in competition, marketed the new chip. And this particular alliance was concluded without a single penny changing hands.

The best example of an alliance to gain access to key people is the numerous agreements between businesses and universities. Many types of business pursue such agreements—chemical companies, pharmaceutical companies, materials companies, to name just a few. And they are partnering up with university depart-ments all over the United States and Canada.

The trend is spreading to Europe, too. The business pays to support the very expensive university research, and the university scientists decide what they re-search. In return, the business has the right of first refusal on whatever products come out of the research. Unlike a government grant for research, the business does not control what the university people do and concentrate on. The academi-cians keep their independence.

But unlike the traditional university research, it is not the university or the individual researchers who are in control of commercial exploitation of research results.

The best example of an alliance for *outsourcing* began right after World War II when hospitals and schools turned to outside specialist companies to do cleaning and maintenance. Now one of the fastest-growing areas of outsourcing is data pro-cessing. More and more organizations—the U.S. government may have been the first—turn over their data processing to an independent, specialized data-processing company. And now, companies increasingly outsource their manufacturing.

In fact under e-commerce outsourcing, manufacturing may become the most prevalent outsourcing form and the one that enables a major company with a strong brand, such as a major consumer-goods producer, to sell centrally, through an e-commerce center, but deliver locally, where the customer is.

Among the most visible examples of geographic alliances are the hundreds of joint ventures through which American and European companies got into the Japanese market in the 1960s and 1970s. The market was there and it was growing fast. But first the Japanese government made it very difficult for Westerners to get in without a Japanese partner—though those Westerners who persisted in the face of government foot-dragging eventually did very well, as a rule.

But there were also language difficulties. Few Western firms had Japanese-speaking executives. Above all, it was almost impossible to hire experienced Japanese middle managers and professionals. They had to be supplied by a Japanese joint-venture partner with whom these people enjoyed lifetime employment.

The Different Types of Alliances

Alliances can take many different forms. There is the *joint venture*, where two or more companies agree to work together toward achieving a single goal. There is also the *minority-holdings agreement*, where one or both companies take a small stake in their alliance partner. With the *cross-holdings* alliance, a type of minority-holdings agreement, each partner owns the same small percentage of the other.

But increasingly alliances are being formed without any ownership stake. This was the case in the Intel alliance with the Japanese manufacturer mentioned above. There is the alliance to jointly market a product or service, with each partner serving a different market. There is the *outsourcing alliance,* where the outsourcing operator actually becomes a part of the organization for which it provides a distinctive support function. There is *cross-licensing*.

What all alliances have in common is that two or more organizations, each maintaining its separate identity and management, agree to work together in one area. *They agree to become partners.*

With so many different types of alliances, which ones tend to be most successful, and in what situations? Alas, that's like asking what kind of marriage is likely to be a happy one. There is no answer. But all alliances have four things in common.

First, they are different from the ownership-based organization. They are, in the words of a very old and very famous French novel, "dangerous liaisons"—exceedingly satisfactory when they work, but vulnerable and easily damaged.

Second, they all have the same problems.

Third, they all require the same basic behavior on the part of both partners.

And fourth, and perhaps most important, alliances are usually easy and work well as long as the going is difficult—that is, in their early stages. But unlike the businesses with which most executives are familiar, they tend to get into trouble when they are *successful*.

Common Problems Facing All Alliances and Their Resolution

The success of the alliance can be a problem, for it then usually becomes apparent that the partners have different objectives and expect different things from the alliance. As long as the alliance is struggling, the partners are usually in agreement. Their goal is to make the alliance work. But once that has been accomplished, each partner begins to want something different from the successful alliance.

Here are two examples, both quite typical.

One is of a joint venture between an American and a German chemical company—both quite large, though neither of them giants. They teamed up to establish a pharmaceutical joint venture in Latin America.

It took five years of hard work to develop it into a profitable enterprise. And during that time the two partners worked in harmony. But when the venture became profitable, the Americans wanted to plow back all earnings into the company; they wanted to build a major pharmaceutical company in Latin America. The Germans, on the other hand, badly needed cash to support their research program at home; they wanted to get as much money out of the joint venture as possible, and as fast as possible.

For several years they bickered and bickered. And they could not agree on anything, and finally the venture, once promising, began to go down and quite rapidly. And eventually it was liquidated.

The second example is that of a development company for Southeast Asia formed in the early 1970s by four major banks, two American and two European. The four banks early saw that Southeast Asia would grow and offer excellent investment opportunities. Again the venture worked beautifully until it became successful. It took about four years.

By then it became clear that three of the four partners wanted it to become as successful as possible. And that meant pushing aggressively into commercial banking in Southeast Asia, in direct competition with the parent banks.

The fourth, a major European bank, wanted itself to become a major bank in Southeast Asia. In fact, it had entered the partnership mainly to get entrance into the market and experience in it. It strongly felt that the successful joint venture was becoming an ungrateful brat and needed spanking rather than encouragement or praise. It vetoed the joint venture's going into commercial banking, which in effect killed it.

Again, after several years of bickering, the joint venture had to be liquidated—and just when Southeast Asia really took off.

For an alliance to remain successful and in working order, this problem needs to be anticipated and taken care of before it arises. Before the parties enter into the alliance, they need to think through their objectives and the objectives of their offspring.

Do they want the joint enterprise eventually to grow into a separate, autonomous venture? Do they agree from the start that it will be allowed, perhaps even encouraged, to compete with one or all parents? If so, in what products, services, or markets?

In the marketing alliance where each partner sells to a different market, there needs to be similar clarity about the objectives. Is the agreement to be limited to one particular product or service? Or, if the alliance works, will it eventually be extended to include more of each partner's products or services? Should profits be plowed back into the alliance, or should they be remitted as fast as possible? Should the offspring develop its own research, or should it contract for its research exclusively with one or both parents?

In the research alliance, there needs to be agreement as to who gets to patent the research results. Will patents belong to the university scientist who made the discovery? Or will they belong to the university itself? Or will they belong to the company or companies that are funding the research?

Such objectives should be reviewed and revised every few years, particularly if the alliance succeeds. There also has to be careful thinking about who will manage the alliance. Regardless of what specific form it takes, the alliance has to be managed separately. And the people in charge have to have the incentives to make it successful.

How should the alliance be managed? Should the partners run it by joint committee, or should one of the partners assume full responsibility?

The alliance, whatever its legal form, has to be managed by its own management. *Not a committee—a committee only means that no one is accountable.*

If it's a joint venture, it requires its own separate management; and these people, wherever they come from, are the management of the joint venture and accountable solely for the joint venture's results, and measured solely by the joint venture's performance.

The one thing that *must never be said* about an executive who manages a joint venture: "John doesn't do too well in his assignment. But he sure looks after *our* interests and is no pushover for our partners."

In fact, in a joint venture, one of the management's most important duties is to say *no* to the parents if the management thinks that the parents' demands are not in the best interest of the joint venture.

In the other alliances, too, there has to be clear management responsibility. The woman manager of an outsourcing firm who manages the maintenance and cleaning contract for the hospital is responsible.

Sure, she wants to satisfy the hospital management; after all, maintenance and cleaning expenses are almost 30 percent of the typical hospital's budget, and the standards of maintenance and cleanliness are even more important for the hospital's medical performance. And that woman has to satisfy her own boss at the outsourcing firm. *But it is her job.*

And in the marketing agreement in which each partner sells the products of both partners in its own market, there has to be someone in each company who is responsible for the sales under the alliance. Or perhaps the two companies together appoint one person who is, in effect, a one-person joint venture. That person is then *the alliance.*

The next problem that must be solved by each alliance partner is what kind of relationship the venture should have with its offspring and with the other partners. Even if the joint enterprise is quite subordinate for one of the partners—a small underwriting venture in Luxembourg, for instance, in which a major commercial bank holds a one-sixth interest—its management people must have access to someone in the parent organization who can say yes or no without having to go through channels. The best way, especially in a large organization, is to entrust all such "dangerous liaisons" to one senior executive.

Finally, there has to be prior agreement on how to resolve disagreements. Orders from the top do not work in an alliance. The best way is to agree, in advance of any dispute, on an arbitrator whom all sides know and respect and whose verdict will be accepted as final by all of them.

This arbitrator should be empowered to go beyond the specific issue in dispute. He or she should be able to decide, for instance, that each party is entitled to buy out the other according to a prearranged formula. He or she should also be able to recommend that the joint enterprise be liquidated or that it become a separate business independent of its parents. These are radical measures. But for this reason, arbitration will be seen as a last resort. Such provisions make each party realize how much it has to gain by subordinating its individual interest, opinion, and pride to the perpetuation of the successful alliance.

MANAGING ALLIANCES AS MARKETING PARTNERSHIPS

Alliances are difficult precisely because there is no "boss" in them. *They are partnership.* And partners are equals, by definition. One cannot give orders to a partner. Hence the secret of the successful alliance is to manage it as a *marketing relationship.* In the traditional organization in which command and control are based on ownership, managers start out with the question, "How do we get our people to *accept* what we think they should be doing?"

In a partnership, one considers the other partner as a *customer.* And the first question is not, "What do we want to do?" It is, "What are the partner's goals, the partner's objectives? What is value for the partner? How does the partner work and operate?"

Once this is understood and accepted, the alliance will work.

SUMMARY

Organizations generally enter alliances for one of five reasons: to obtain access to new, distinct technology; to achieve synergy between the strengths of two independent partners; to gain access to people with specialized knowledge; to outsource noncore activities to specialists; and to extend a company's geographic reach.

Many alliances do well in the early stages. But they fall apart when they become successful. To avoid this fate, before they enter into an alliance the partners must think through and take care of four major questions: What are the different objectives for the partners and their alliance? How will the alliance be managed, and who will manage it? What relationship will each partner have with the alliance and with each other? And how will disagreements be resolved?

Alliances are risky. Alliances are difficult. But they are increasingly *necessary* for growth. The traditional means of growth either are becoming too expensive, like most grassroots developments, or are not easily available to existing businesses. They may require access to new and often totally different skills; to different people with different values, such as the values, habits, and policies of academia; or access to different geography and different markets.

Alliances should be managed as marketing relationships.

43

The CEO in the New Millennium

CEOs have ultimate responsibility for the work of everybody else in their institution. But they also have work of their own—and the study of management has so far paid little attention to it. It is the same work regardless of whether the organization is a business enterprise, a nonprofit, a church, a school or university, or a government agency, or whether it is large or small, worldwide or purely local. And it is work only CEOs can do, but also work that CEOs must do.

In any organization, regardless of its mission, the CEO is the link between the *inside*, that is, the organization, and the *outside*, that is, society, the economy, technology, markets, customers, the media, public opinion. *Inside, there are only costs. Results are only on the outside.* Indeed, the modern organization (beginning with the Jesuit Order in 1536) was expressly created to have results on the outside, that is, to make a difference in its society or its economy.

THE TASKS OF THE CEO

- *To define the meaningful outside of the organization.*

To define the *meaningful outside* of the organization is the CEO's first task. The definition is anything but easy, let alone obvious. For a particular bank, for instance, is the meaningful outside the local market for commercial loans? Is it the national market for mutual funds? Or is it major industrial companies and their short-term *credit* needs? All three of these "outsides" deal with money and *credit*. And one cannot tell from the bank's published accounts, for example, its balance sheet, on which of these "outsides" it concentrates. Each of them is a different *business* and requires a different organization, different people, different competencies, and different definitions of results. Even the very biggest bank is unlikely to be a leader in all of these "outsides." And which of these to concentrate on is a highly risky decision and one very hard to change or reverse. Only the CEO can make it. But also the CEO must make it. It is the first task of the CEO.

- *To work on getting information from the "outside" into usable form.*

The second specific task of the CEO is to think through what information regarding the outside is meaningful and needed for the organization and then to work on getting it into usable form. Organized information has grown tremendously in the last hundred years. But the growth has been mainly in "inside" information, for example, accounting. The computer has further accentuated this inside focus. As regards the outside, there has been an enormous growth in data—beginning with Herbert Hoover in the 1920s (to whose work as secretary of commerce we largely owe the data on GNP, on productivity, and on standard of living). But few CEOs, whether in business, in nonprofits, or in government agencies, have yet organized these data into systematic information for their own work (on the methodology for doing this, see chapter 33).

To give one example, every major maker of branded consumer goods knows that few things are as important as the values and the behavior of that great majority of consumers who are not buyers of the company's products, and especially information on major changes in the noncustomers' values and habits. The data are largely available. But so far few consumer-goods manufacturers have converted them into organized information on which to base their decisions (one well-publicized exception is the Shell Petroleum group of companies). Again it is primarily the CEO who needs this information and whose work it is to organize getting it.

Thinking through what is meaningful information on the outside is also a high-risk decision. That U.S. business executives, for instance in the 1950s and 1960s, decided (in many cases quite deliberately) that what was going on in Japan was not particularly meaningful information for them and their companies explains in large part why the Japanese export push caught them so unawares and unprepared.

It is information about the outside that needs the most work. For far too many institutions—and not only businesses—define "outside" in large part as their direct competitors. Toy makers tend to define the "outside" as their toy-maker competitors; a hospital, as the other two competing hospitals in the same suburb; and so on. But the most meaningful competitors for the toy maker are not other toy makers but other claimants on potential customers' disposable dollars. The most meaningful information about the toy maker's outside is therefore what value the toy presents to the potential buyer. (Customer research, in other words, may be more important than market research—but also far more difficult.)

- *To decide what results are meaningful for the institution.*

The definition of the institution's meaningful outside and of the information the institution needs makes it possible to answer the key questions, "What is our business? What should it be? What should it not be?" The answers to these questions establish the boundaries within which an institution operates. And they are the foundation for the specific work of the CEO. Particularly, they enable the CEO to decide *what results are meaningful for the institution.*

Defining results is important, critical, and risky above all for institutions that lack the discipline of the "bottom line," that is, for nonbusinesses. And nonbusinesses constitute a significant number of organizations in every developed society. But even for businesses, the bottom line is not by itself adequate as a definition of results—the same bottom line may have very differing meanings according to how an institution defines "meaningful results." To decide what results a given bottom line represents is a major job of the executive. It is not based on "facts"—there are no facts about the future. It is not made well by intuition. It is a judgment. Again, only the CEO can make this judgment, but also the CEO must make it.

This definition of desirable results invariably requires a "short-term–long-term" judgment. It is so risky that all premodern economies tried to avoid making it. In fact, the one major institutional innovation of the modern economy was to create in large part the systematic risk-taker and risk-sharer, the public corporation, thereby enabling the individual to strictly limit the personal risk of investing in future expectations.

By thus making possible these time decisions in very large numbers and on an enormous scale, the *enterprise* can be said to be the one invention that created the modern economy—far more so than any other invention, whether material or conceptual. With the invention of the enterprise, the manager came into being as a distinct role and function, with one of his or her major tasks being the making of the decision between short-term yields and deferred expectations. Making this decision requires a good deal of very hard work on the part of the CEO. (Both Machiavelli's *Prince* and Shakespeare's *The Merchant of Venice,* two Renaissance masterpieces the background of which is the emergence of the modern economy, are built around the challenge of this decision.)

- *To decide the priorities.*

In any but a dying organization, there are always far more tasks than there are available resources. But results are obtained only by *concentration of resources,* especially by concentration of the scarcest and most valuable resource, people with proven performance capacity.

There is constant pressure on every CEO to do a little bit of everything. That makes everybody happy but guarantees that there are no results. The CEO's most critical job—also the CEO's most difficult job—is to say no. To do so is not just a matter of willpower. It requires an inordinate amount of study and work—work that only the CEO can do, but again work that the CEO must do.

- *To place people into key positions. This, in the last analysis, determines the performance capacity of the institution.*

Every organization says, "We have better people." But this is, of course, impossible. Once an organization grows beyond a handful of people, it is subject to statistics' most ruthless law: the law of the great number, which dictates that there is only "normal distribution." What differentiates organizations is whether they can make common people perform uncommon things—and that depends primarily on whether people are being placed where their strengths can perform or whether, as is only too common, they are being placed for the absence of weakness. And nothing requires as much hard work as "people decisions." The only thing that requires even more time (and even more work) than putting people into a job is unmaking a wrong people-decision. And again, critical people-decisions only the CEO can make.

- *To organize top management.*

The recent failure rate of chief executives in big American companies points in the same direction. A large proportion of CEOs of such companies appointed in the past fifteen years were fired as failures within a year or two. But each of these people had been picked for his proven competence, and each had been highly successful in his or her previous jobs. This suggests that the jobs they took on had become undoable. The American record suggests not human failure but systems failure. *Top management* in big organizations needs a new organization concept.

Some elements of such a concept are beginning to emerge. For instance, Jack Welch at GE built a top-management team in which the company's chief financial officer and its chief human-resources officer were near equals to the chief executive, and both were excluded from the succession to the top job. He also gave himself and his team a clear and publicly announced priority task on which to concentrate. During his twenty-one years in the top job, Mr. Welch had three such priorities, each occupying him for five years or more. Each time he delegated everything else to the top managements of the operating businesses within the GE confederation.

A different approach was taken by Asea Brown Boveri (ABB), a huge Swedish-Swiss engineering multinational. Goran Lindahl, who retired as chief executive in

December 2000, went even further than GE in making the individual units within the company into separate worldwide businesses and building up a strong top-management team of a few nonoperating people. But he also defined for himself a new role as a one-man information system for the company, traveling incessantly to get to know all the senior managers personally, listening to them, and telling them what went on within the organization.

A large financial-services company tried another idea: appointing not one CEO but six. The head of each of the five operating businesses is also CEO for the whole company in one top-management area, such as corporate planning and strategy or human resources. The company's chairman represents the company to the outside world and is also directly concerned with obtaining, allocating, and managing capital. All six people meet twice a week as the top-management committee. This seemed to work well, but only because none of the five operating CEOs wanted the chairman's job; each preferred to stay in operations. Even the man who designed the system, and then took the chairman's job, doubted that the system would survive his tenure.

THE CEO: AN AMERICAN INVENTION AND EXPORT

The CEO is an American invention—designed first by Alexander Hamilton in the Constitution in the earliest years of the Republic, and then transferred into the private sector in the form of Hamilton's own Bank of New York and of the Second Bank of the United States, in Philadelphia. There is no real counterpart to the CEO in the management and organization of any other country. The German *"Sprecher des Vorstands,"* the French *"administrateur délégué,"* the British "chairman," or the Japanese "president" are all quite different in their powers and in the limitations thereon.

The American CEO is, however, fast becoming a major U.S. export. Tony Blair, as Britain's prime minister, and Gerhard Schroeder, as Germany's chancellor, tried to make over their countries' top political job in the image of the U.S. president. In *business,* the CEO model is being adopted even faster all over the world, for example, in the recent restructuring of Europe's largest industrial complex, the German Siemens Group. And what makes the American CEO unique is that he or she has distinct and specific work.

SUMMARY

The CEO in the new millennium has six specific tasks. They are

1. To define the meaningful outside of the organization

2. To think through what information regarding the outside is meaningful and needed for the organization, and then to work on getting it into usable form

3. To decide what results are meaningful for the institution

4. To set priorities for the organization

5. To place people into key positions

6. To organize top management

The concept of the CEO is an American invention and export.

44

The Impact of Pension Funds on Corporate Governance

The rise of pension funds as dominant owners and lenders represents one of the most startling power shifts in economic history. The first modern pension fund was established in 1950 by General Motors. In 2006, pension funds controlled total assets of $4.6 trillion, divided among common stocks, fixed-income securities, hedge funds, private equity, real estate, and so on. Demographics guarantee that these assets will continue to grow aggressively.

America's failure to recognize, let alone address, this power shift accounted in large measure for much of the financial turbulence of the 1980s—the hostile takeovers, the leveraged buyouts, and the general restructuring frenzy. This power shift is also reflected in the more recent and growing influence of institutional investments in private-equity firms.

Two questions, in particular, demand attention: For what should America's new owners, the pension funds, hold corporate management accountable? And what is the appropriate institutional structure through which to exercise accountability?

CAN'T SELL

Pension funds first emerged as the premier owners of the country's share capital in the early 1970s. But for fifteen or twenty years thereafter, the realities of pension fund ownership were ignored. In part, this was because the pension funds themselves did not want to be "owners." They wanted to be passive "investors," and short-term investors, at that. "We do not buy a company," they asserted. "We buy shares that we sell as soon as they no longer offer good prospects for capital gains over a fairly short time." Moreover, the development was totally at variance with American tradition and with what everybody took for granted—and many still take for granted—as the structure of the U.S. economy. Long after pension funds had become the largest holders of equity capital, the United States was still referred to as the country of "people's capitalism," in which millions of individuals each own small pieces of the country's large companies. To be sure, employees have become the owners of America's means of production. But their ownership is exercised through a fairly small number of very large "trustees." For example, a recent study (Millman Consultants and Actuaries, 2007) found that the assets in 100 large U.S. company-defined benefit plans exceeded $1.3 trillion in 2006.

Finally, though, the fog has lifted, the trustees of pension funds, especially those representing public employees, are waking up to the fact that they are no longer investors in shares. An investor, by definition, can sell his holdings. A small pension fund may still be able to do so. There are thousands of such small funds, but their total holdings represent no more than a quarter or so of all pension fund assets. The share holdings of even a midsized pension fund are already so large that they are not easily sold. Or more precisely, these holdings can, as a rule, be sold only if another pension fund buys them. They are much too large to be easily absorbed by the retail market and are thus permanently part of the circular trading among institutions.

The 1 percent holder cannot sell easily. And the more than 30 percent holder, that is, the pension fund community at large, cannot sell at all. It is almost as committed as the German *Hausbank* is to a client company or the Japanese *keiretsu* is to a member company. Thus the large funds are beginning to learn what Georg Siemens, founder of Deutsche Bank and inventor of the *Hausbank* system, said a hundred years ago when he was criticized for spending so much of his and the bank's time on a troubled client company, "If one can't sell, one must care."

Pension funds cannot be managers as were so many nineteenth-century owners. Yet a business, even a small one, needs strong, autonomous management with the authority, continuity, and competence to build and run the organization. Thus pension funds, as America's new owners, will increasingly have to make sure that a company has the management it needs. As we have learned over the last sixty years, this means that management must be clearly accountable to somebody and that accountability must be institutionally anchored. It means that management must be accountable for performance and results, rather than for good intentions, however beautifully quantified. It means that accountability must involve financial accountability, even though everyone knows that performance and results go way beyond the financial "bottom line."

Surely, most people will say, we know what *performance* and *results* mean for business enterprise. We should of course, because clearly defining these terms is a prerequisite both for effective management and for successful and profitable ownership. In fact, there have been two definitions offered in the years since World War II. Neither has stood the test of time.

MANAGEMENT FOR THE STAKEHOLDERS

The first definition was formulated around 1950, at about the same time the modern pension fund was invented. The most prominent of the period's "professional managers," Ralph Cordiner, CEO of the General Electric Company, asserted that top management in the large, publicly owned corporation was a "trustee." Cordiner argued that senior executives were responsible for managing the enterprise "in the best–*balanced interest* of shareholders, customers, employees, suppliers, and plant community cities." That is, what we now call *stakeholders*.

Cordiner's answer, as some of us pointed out right away, still required a clear definition of "results" and of the meaning of "best" with respect to "balance." It also required a clear structure of accountability, with an independent and powerful organ of supervision and control to hold management accountable for performance and results. Otherwise, professional management becomes an enlightened despot— and enlightened despots, whether platonic philosopher kings or CEOs, neither perform nor last.

But Cordiner's generation and its executive successors did not define what *performance* and *results* produce the *best balance,* nor did they develop any kind of accountability. As a result, professional management, 1950s-style, neither performed nor lasted.

The single most powerful blow to Cordiner-style management was the rise of the hostile takeover in the late 1970s. One after the other of such managers has been toppled. The survivors have been forced to change drastically how they manage, or at least to change their rhetoric. No top management I know now claims to run its business as a "trustee" for the "best–balanced interests" of "stakeholders."

Pension funds have been the driving force behind this change. Without the concentration of voting power in a few pension funds and the funds' willingness to endorse takeovers, most of the raiders' attacks and leveraged buyouts would never have been launched. A takeover firm who has to get support from millions of dispersed individual stockholders soon runs out of time and money.

To be sure, pension fund managers have serious doubts about many buyouts and takeovers, about their impact on the companies in play and about their value to the economy. Pension fund managers—especially the moderately paid civil servants running the funds of public employees—also have serious aesthetic and moral misgivings about such things as the "golden parachutes" for executives of acquired firms, and the huge fortune earned by corporate takeover firms, lawyers, and investment bankers. Yet they feel they have no choice but to provide money for takeovers and buyouts and to tender their shares to them.

One reason for their support is that these transactions keep alive the illusion that pension funds can, in fact, sell their shares—that is, that they are "investors" still. Takeovers and buyouts also offer immediate capital gains. And since pension fund managers are evaluated based on returns on the portfolio under management, such gains are most welcome.

What makes takeovers and buyouts inevitable (or at least creates the opportunity for them) is the mediocre performance of management, the management without clear definitions of performance and results and with no clear accountability to somebody. It may be argued that the mediocre performance of so many of America's large corporations from 1960 to 1990 was not management's fault, that it resulted instead from wrongheaded public policies that have kept American savings rates low and capital costs high. But captains are responsible for what happens on their watches. And whatever the reasons or excuses, until recently, the large U.S. company has not done particularly well on professional management's watch—whether measured by competitiveness, market standing, or innovative performance. As for financial performance, it had, by and large over long periods of time, not even earned the minimum acceptable result, a return on assets equal to its cost of capital.

The raiders and buyout firms thus perform a needed function. As an old proverb has it, "If there are no grave diggers, one needs vultures." But takeovers and buyouts are very radical surgery. And even if radical surgery is not life-threatening, it inflicts profound shock. Takeovers and buyouts deeply disturb and indeed alienate middle managers and professionals, the very people on whose motivation, effort, and loyalty a business depends. For these people, the takeover or dismantling of a company to which they have given years of service is nothing short of betrayal. It is a denial of all they must believe in to work productively and with devotion. As a result, a number of the companies that are taken over or sold in a buyout do not perform any better a few years later than they performed under the old dispensation.

Today nearly all CEOs of large U.S. companies proclaim that they run their enterprises "in the interest of the shareholders" and "to maximize shareholder value." This is the second definition of *performance and results* developed since World War II. It sounds much less noble than Cordiner's assertion of the "best-balanced interest," but it also sounds much more realistic. Yet its life span will be even shorter than yesterday's professional management. For most people, "maximizing shareholder value" means a higher share price within six months or a year—certainly not much longer. Such short-term capital gains are the wrong objective for both the enterprise and its dominant shareholders. As a theory of corporate performance, then, "maximizing shareholder value" has little staying power.

Regarding the enterprise, the cost of short-term thinking hardly needs to be argued. The interest of a large pension fund is in the value of a holding at the time at which a beneficiary turns from being an employee, who pays into the fund, to being a pensioner, who gets paid by the fund. Concretely, this means that the time over which a fund invests—the time until its future beneficiaries will retire—is on average thirty years rather than three months or six months. This is the appropriate return horizon for these owners.

There is, however, one group that does—or at least thinks it does—have an interest in short-term gains. These are the employers with "defined-benefit" pension plans. Until now, in a classic case of the tail wagging the dog, the *interests of these employers* have dominated how the pension fund community approaches its role as owner. In a defined-benefit plan, retiring employees receive fixed annual payments, usually a percentage of their wages averaged over the last three or five years on the job. The employer's annual contribution to the fund fluctuates with the value of the fund's assets. If in any given year that value is high (compared with the amount needed on an actuarial basis to cover the fund's future pension obligations), the employer's contribution is cut. If the fund's asset value is low, the contribution goes up.

We owe the defined-benefit trust to mere accident. When General Motors management proposed the pension fund in 1950, several powerful board members resisted it as a giveaway to the union. The directors relented only when promised that under a defined-benefit plan the company would have to pay little or nothing. An ever-rising stock market, so the argument went, would create the assets needed to pay future pensions. Most private employers followed the GM model, if only because they, too, deluded themselves into believing that the stock market rather than the company would take care of the pension obligation.

Needless to say, this was wishful thinking. Some defined-benefit plans have done poorly, precisely because they have been chasing inappropriate short-term gains. The other kind of plan, the "defined-contribution" plan, under which the employer contributes each year a defined percentage of the employee's annual salary or wages, has done better in a good many cases. Indeed, defined-benefit plans are rapidly losing their allure. Because they have not delivered the promised capital gains, a great many are seriously underfunded. From now on, as a result of new accounting standards, such underfunding has to be shown as a liability on the employing company's balance sheet. This means that even in a mild recession (in which both a company's earnings and the stock market are down), a good many companies may actually be pushed to, if not over, the brink of insolvency. And what many of them have done in good years—that is, siphoned off the actuarial surplus in the pension fund and shown it as "net income" in their income statement—is unlikely to be permitted.

Company after company is therefore *getting out of defined-benefit plans*. As a result, short-term gains as an objective for pension decisions for organizations making defined-benefit contributions should no longer dominate. They are already playing second fiddle. Most public-employee funds are defined-benefit plans, and they constitute the majority of the biggest funds. Being independent of corporate management, they, rather than the pension funds of private businesses, are taking the lead and writing the new script.

We no longer need to theorize about how to define performance and results in the large enterprise. We have successful examples. Both the Germans and the Japanese have highly concentrated institutional ownership. In neither country can the owners actually manage. In both countries industry has done extremely well in the years since its near destruction in World War II. It has done well in terms of the overall economy of its country.

How, then, do the institutional owners of German or Japanese industry define performance and results? Though they manage quite differently, they define them in the same way. Unlike Cordiner, they do not "balance" anything. They maximize. But they do not attempt to maximize shareholder value or the short-term interest of any one of the enterprise's stakeholders. Rather, they *maximize the wealth-producing capacity of the enterprise.* It is this objective that integrates short-term and long-term results and that ties the operational dimensions of business performance—market standing, innovation, productivity, and people and their development—to financial needs and financial results. It is also this objective on which all constituencies depend for the satisfaction of their expectations and objectives, whether shareholders, customers, or employees.

To define *performance* and *results* as *maximizing the wealth-producing capacity of the enterprise* may be criticized as vague. To be sure, one doesn't get the answers by filling out forms. Decisions need to be made, and economic decisions that commit scarce resources to an uncertain future are always risky and controversial. When Ralph Cordiner first attempted to define performance and results—no one had tried to do so earlier—maximizing the wealth-producing capacity of the enterprise would indeed have been pretty fuzzy. By now, after decades of work by many people, it has become crisp. All the elements that go into the process can be quantified with considerable rigor and are, indeed, quantified by those arch-quantifiers, by the planning departments of large Japanese companies and by the German banks as well.

The first step toward a clear definition of the concept was probably taken in my 1954 book, *The Practice of Management,* which outlined eight key objective areas for a business (these eight areas are described in chapter 9). These areas (or some variations thereof) are still the starting point for business planning in the large Japanese company. Since then, management analysts have done an enormous amount of work on the strategy needed to convert objectives into performance metrics.

Financial objectives are needed to tie all this together. Indeed, financial accountability is the key to the performance of management and enterprise. Without financial accountability, there is no accountability at all. And without financial accountability, there will also be no results in any other area.

What we have is not the "final answer." Still, it is no longer theory but proven practice. And its results, to judge by German and Japanese business performance, are clearly superior to those that derive from running the enterprise as a "trustee" for stakeholders or to maximize short-term gains for shareholders.

INSTITUTIONAL STRUCTURE FOR ACCOUNTABILITY

The one thing that we in the United States have yet to work out—and we have to work it out ourselves—is how to build the new definition of *management accountability* into an institutional structure.

Even the largest U.S. pension fund holds much too small a fraction of any one company's capital to control it. Law wisely limits a corporate pension fund to a maximum holding of 5 percent of any one company's stock, and very few funds go anywhere near that high. Not being businesses, the funds have limited access to commercial or business information. They are not business focused, nor could they be. They are asset managers. Yet they need the in-depth business analysis of the companies they collectively control. And they need an institutional structure in which management accountability is embedded.

In an American context, the business analysis—call it the business audit—will have to be done by some kind of independent professional agency. Certain management consulting firms already do such work, though only on an ad hoc basis and usually after a company has gotten into trouble, which is rather late in the process. And several firms have recently come into being to advise pension funds—mostly public funds—on the industries and companies in which they invest.

I suspect that in the end we shall develop a formal business-audit practice, analogous perhaps to the financial-audit practice of independent professional accounting firms. For while the business audit need not be conducted every year (every three years may be enough in most cases), it needs to be based on predetermined standards and go through a systematic evaluation of business performance, starting with mission and strategy, through marketing, innovation, productivity, people development, community relations, all the way to profitability. The elements for such a business audit are known and available. But they need to be pulled together into systematic procedures. And that is best done, in all likelihood, by an organization that specializes in audits, whether an independent firm or a new and separate division of an accounting practice.

Thus it may not be too fanciful to expect that a major pension fund will not invest in a company's shares or fixed-income securities unless that company submits itself to a business audit by an outside professional firm. Managements will resist, of course. But in the 1930s managements equally resisted—in fact, resented—demands that they submit themselves to a financial audit by outside public accountants and even more to publication of the audit's findings.

Still, the question remains, Who is going to use this tool? In the American context, there is only one possible answer: *a revitalized board of directors.*

AN EFFECTIVE BOARD

The need for an effective board has been stressed by every student of the publicly owned corporation since the late 1940s. To run a business enterprise, especially a large and complex enterprise, management needs considerable power. But power without accountability always becomes flabby or tyrannical, and usually both. Surely, we know how to make boards effective as an organ of corporate governance. Having better people is not the key; ordinary people will do. Making a board effective requires *spelling out its work, setting specific objectives for its performance and contribution,* and regularly *appraising the board's performance against these objectives.*

We have known this for a long time. But American boards have, on the whole, become less, rather than more, effective. Boards are not effective if they represent good intentions. Boards are effective if they represent strong owners, committed to the enterprise.

In 1933, Adolph A. Berle, Jr., and Gardner C. Means published *The Modern Corporation and Private Property,* arguably the most influential book in U.S. business history. They showed that the traditional "owners," the nineteenth-century capitalists, had disappeared, with the title of ownership shifting rapidly to faceless multitudes of investors without interest in or commitment to the company and concerned only with short-term gains. As a result, they argued, ownership was becoming divorced from control and a mere legal fiction, with management becoming accountable to no one and for nothing. Then, fifteen years later, Ralph Cordiner's *Professional Management* accepted this divorce of ownership from control and tried to make a virtue out of it.

By now, the wheel has come full circle. The pension funds are very different owners from nineteenth-century tycoons. They are owners not because they want to be owners but because they have no choice. They cannot sell. They also cannot become owner-managers. But they are owners, nonetheless. As such, they have more than mere power. *They have the responsibility to ensure performance and results* in America's largest and most important companies.

SUMMARY

Increasingly the modern corporation is owned by employees through their representatives, the pension fund. The size of the holdings of the large U.S. pension fund makes it difficult for trustees to sell shares as normal retail investors do when they are displeased with performance. Therefore, institutional pension investors have actually encouraged takeovers and buyouts as a way of liquidating their shares. The need stems from the lack of corporate performance and from accountability for the needs of the pension fund investor.

Three models of corporate accountability have evolved since the separation of ownership from control became a reality for the modern corporation. The first, proposed by Ralph Cordineer, was to run the corporation "in the best–balanced interest of shareholders." This model failed to produce results for owners and led to hostile takeovers.

The second model that evolved in the U.S. was to run the corporation so as "to maximize shareholder value." This often takes the form of maximizing short-term profits and leads to actions that actually weaken the long-term viability of the corporation. This model does not consider that the interests of employee investors in pension funds are long-term interests with a time frame of at least fifteen years.

Therefore, a model that maximizes the long-term wealth-producing capacity of the corporation, with strong metrics and an effective board of directors to hold top management accountable, seems advisable for U.S. corporations. This model, in force in Japan and Germany, holds promise for enhancing corporate accountability and for serving the best long-term interests of the primary beneficiaries of pension funds, the employees.

Part X

New Demands on the Individual

More and more people in the workforce—and most knowledge workers—will have to *develop themselves*. They will have to place themselves where they can make the greatest contribution; they will have to learn to develop themselves. They will have to learn to stay young and mentally alive during a fifty-year working life. They will have to learn how and when to change what they do, how they do it, and when they do it.

Knowledge workers are likely to outlive their employing organization. Even if knowledge workers postpone entry into the labor force as long as possible—if, for instance, they stay in school till their late twenties to get a doctorate—they are likely, with present life expectancies in the developed countries, to live into their eighties. Their average working life, in other words, is likely to be fifty years.

But the average life expectancy of a *successful business* is approximately thirty years—and in a period of great turbulence such as the one we are living in, it is unlikely to be even as long. Even organizations that normally are long-lived if not expected to live forever—schools and universities, hospitals, government agencies—will see rapid changes in the period of turbulence we have entered. Even if they survive—and a great many surely will not, at least not in their present form—they will change their structure, the work they are doing, the knowledges they require, and the kind of people they employ. Increasingly, therefore, workers, and especially knowledge workers, will outlive any one employer, and will have to be prepared for more than one job, more than one assignment, more than one career.

45

_____

Managing Oneself

This chapter deals with the *new demands on the individual knowledge worker.* The very great achievers, a Napoleon, a Leonardo da Vinci, a Mozart, have always managed themselves. This, in large measure, made them great achievers. But they were the rarest of exceptions. And they were so unusual, both in their talents and in their achievements, as to be considered outside the boundaries of normal human existence. Now even people of modest endowments, that is, average mediocrities, have to learn to manage themselves.

Knowledge workers, therefore, face drastically *new demands:*

1. They have to ask, Who am I? What are my strengths? How do I work?

2. They have to ask, Where do I belong?

3. They have to ask, What is my contribution?

4. They have to take relationship responsibility.

1. WHAT ARE MY STRENGTHS?

Most people think they know what they are good at. They are usually wrong. People more often know what they are not good at—and even there, people are more often wrong than right. And yet, one can perform only with one's strengths. One cannot build performance on weaknesses, let alone on something one cannot do at all.

For the great majority of people, to know their strengths was irrelevant only a few decades ago. One was born into a job and into a line of work. The peasant's son became a peasant. If he was not good at being a peasant, he failed. The artisan's son was similarly going to be an artisan, and so on. But now people have choices. They therefore have to know their strengths so that they can know where they belong.

There is only one way to find out: *feedback analysis.* Whenever one makes a key *decision* and whenever one takes a key *action,* one writes down what one expects will happen. And nine months or twelve months later, one then feeds back from results to expectations.

This is by no means a new method. It was invented sometime in the fourteenth century, by an otherwise totally obscure German theologian. Some 150 years later, John Calvin (1509–1564), father of Calvinism, in Geneva, and Ignatius of Loyola (1491–1556), the founder of the Jesuit Order, quite independent of each other, picked up the idea and incorporated it into their rules for every member of their group—that is, for the Calvinist pastor and the Jesuit priest. This explains why these two new institutions (both founded in the same year, in 1536) had within thirty years come to dominate Europe: Calvinism, the Protestant north; the Jesuit Order, the Catholic south. By that time each group contained so many thousands of clerics that most of them had to be ordinary rather than exceptional. Many of them worked alone, if not in complete isolation. Many of them had to work underground and in constant fear of persecution. Yet very few defected. The routine feedback from results to expectations reaffirmed them in their commitment. It enabled them to focus on performance and results, and with it, on achievement and satisfaction.

Within a fairly short period of time, maybe two or three years, this simple procedure will tell people, first, where their strengths are—and this is probably the most important thing to know about oneself. It will also show them what they do or fail to do that deprives them of the full yield from their strengths. It will show them where they are not particularly competent. And, finally, it will show them where they have no strengths and cannot perform.

Several *action conclusions* follow from the feedback analysis. The *first,* and most important, conclusion: Concentrate on your strengths. Place yourself where your strengths can produce performance and results.

Second: Work on improving your strengths. The feedback analysis rapidly shows where a person needs to improve skills or has to acquire new knowledge. It will show where skills and knowledge are no longer adequate and have to be updated. It will also show the gaps in one's knowledge.

Of particular importance is the *third* conclusion: the feedback analysis soon identifies the areas where intellectual arrogance causes disabling ignorance. Far too many people—especially people with high knowledge in one area—are contemptuous of knowledge in other areas. Feedback analysis soon shows that a main reason for poor performance is the result of simply not knowing enough or the result of being contemptuous of knowledge outside one's own specialty.

First-rate engineers may take pride in not knowing anything about people—human beings are much too disorderly for the good engineering mind. And accountants, too, may think it unnecessary to know about people.

Human resources people, by contrast, often pride themselves on their ignorance of elementary accounting or of quantitative methods altogether. Brilliant executives who are being posted abroad often believe that business skill is sufficient, and dismiss learning about the history, the arts, the culture, and the traditions of the country where they are now expected to perform—only to find that their brilliant business skills produce no results.

One important action conclusion from the feedback analysis is, thus, to overcome intellectual arrogance and work on acquiring the skills and knowledge needed to make one's strengths fully productive.

Another equally important action conclusion is to remedy one's bad habits— things one does or fails to do that inhibit effectiveness and performance. They quickly show up in the feedback analysis.

The analysis may show, for instance, that a planner's beautiful plans die because he or she does not follow through. Like so many brilliant people, he or she believes that ideas move mountains. But bulldozers move mountains; ideas show where the bulldozers have to go to work. The most brilliant planners far too often stop when the plan is completed. But that is when the work begins. Then the planner needs to find the people to carry out the plan, explain the plan to them, teach them, adapt and change the plan as it moves from planning to doing and, finally, decide when to stop pushing the plan.

But the analysis may also show that a person fails to obtain results because he or she lacks manners. Bright people—especially bright young people—often do not understand that good manners are the "lubricating oil" of an organization.

It is a law of nature that two moving bodies in contact with each other create friction. Two human beings in contact with each other therefore always create friction. And then manners are the lubricating oil that enable these two moving bodies to work together, whether they like each other or not—simple things like saying "please" and "thank you" and knowing a person's birthday or name, and remembering to ask after the person's family. If the analysis shows that brilliant work fails again and again as soon as it requires cooperation from others, it probably indicates a lack of courtesy, that is, of manners.

The *next* action conclusion from the feedback analysis is *what not to do*.

Feeding back from results to expectations soon shows where a person should not try to do anything at all. It shows the areas in which a person lacks the minimum endowment needed—and there are always many such areas for any person. Not enough people have even one first-rate skill or knowledge area, but all of us have an infinite number of areas in which we have no talent, no skill, and little chance to become even mediocre. And in these areas a person—especially a knowledge worker—should not take on work, jobs, assignments.

The *final* action conclusion is to waste as little effort as possible on improving areas of low competence. Concentration should be on areas of high competence and high skill. It takes far more energy and far more work to improve from incompetence to low mediocrity than it takes to improve from first-rate performance to excellence. And yet most people—and equally most teachers and most organizations—try to concentrate on making an incompetent person into a low mediocrity. The time, energy, and resources should instead go into making a competent person into a star performer.

How Do I Perform?

How do I perform? is as important a question—especially for knowledge workers—as, What are my strengths?

In fact, it may be an even more important question. Amazingly few people know how they get things done. On the contrary, most of us do not even know that different people work and perform differently. We therefore work in ways that are not our ways—and that almost guarantees nonperformance.

The main reason, perhaps, that so many people do not know how they perform is that schools throughout history insisted, out of necessity, on there being only one way for everybody to do his or her schoolwork. The teacher who ran a classroom of forty youngsters simply did not have the time to find out how each of the students performed. The teacher, on the contrary, had to insist that all do the same work, the same way, at the same time. And so, historically, everybody grew up with one way of doing the work. Here perhaps is where our new technology may have the greatest and most beneficial impact. It should enable even the merely competent teacher to find out how a student learns and then to encourage the student to do the work the way that fits that individual student.

Like one's strengths, how one performs is individual. It is personality. Whether personality derives from "nature" or "nurture," it surely is formed long before the person goes to work. And how a person performs is a "given," just as what a person is good at or not good at is a "given." It can be modified, but it is unlikely to be changed. And just as people produce results by doing what they are good at, people produce results by working according to how they perform.

The feedback analysis may indicate that there is something amiss in how one performs. But rarely does it identify the cause. It is, however, normally not too difficult to find out. It takes a few years of work experience. And then one can ask—and quickly answer—how one performs. For a few common personality traits usually determine how one achieves results.

AM I A READER OR A LISTENER?

The first thing to know about how one performs is whether one is a reader or a listener. Yet very few people even know that there are readers and there are listeners, and that very few people are both. Even fewer know which of the two they themselves are. But a few examples will show how damaging it is not to know.

When he was commander in chief of the Allied Forces in Europe, General Dwight (Ike) Eisenhower was the darling of the press, and attendance at one of his press conferences was considered a rare treat. These conferences were famous for their style, for Eisenhower's total command of whatever question was being asked, and, equally, for his ability to describe a situation or to explain a policy in two or three beautifully polished and elegant sentences. Ten years later, President Eisenhower was held in open contempt by his former admirers. They considered him a buffoon. He never, they complained, even addressed himself to the question asked, but rambled on endlessly about something else. And he was constantly ridiculed for butchering the King's English in his incoherent and ungrammatical answers. Yet Eisenhower had in large measure owed his brilliant earlier career to his virtuoso performance as a speechwriter for General Douglas MacArthur, one of the most demanding stylists in American public life.

The explanation: Eisenhower apparently did not know himself that he was a reader and not a listener. When he was commander in chief in Europe, his aides had made sure that every question from the press was handed in in writing at least half an hour before the conference began. And then Eisenhower was in total command. When he became president, he succeeded two listeners, Franklin D. Roosevelt and Harry Truman. Both men knew this and both enjoyed free-for-all press conferences. Roosevelt knew himself to be so much of a listener that he insisted that everything first be read out loud to him—only then did he look at anything in writing. And when Truman realized, after becoming president, that he needed to learn about foreign and military affairs—neither of which he had ever been much interested in before—he arranged for his two ablest cabinet members, General George Marshall and Dean Acheson, to give him a daily tutorial in which each delivered a forty-minute spoken presentation, after which the president asked questions. Eisenhower, apparently, felt that he had to do what his two famous predecessors had done. As a result, he never even heard the question the journalists asked. And he was not even an extreme case of a nonlistener.

A few years later Lyndon B. Johnson destroyed his presidency, in large measure, by not knowing that he—unlike Eisenhower—was a listener. His predecessor, John F. Kennedy, who knew that he was a reader, had assembled as his assistants a brilliant group of writers such as Arthur Schlesinger, Jr., the historian, and Bill Moyers, a first-rate journalist. Kennedy made sure that they first wrote to him before discussing their memos in person. Johnson kept these people as his staff—and they kept on writing. He never, apparently, got one word of what they wrote. Yet, as a senator, Johnson, only four years earlier, had been superb; for parliamentarians have to be, above all, listeners.

Only a century ago, very few people, even in the most highly developed country, knew whether they were right-handed or left-handed. Left-handers were suppressed. Few actually became competent right-handers. Most of them ended up as incompetent no-handers and with severe emotional damage such as stuttering.

Yet, just as few left-handers became competent right-handers, few listeners can be made, or can make themselves, into competent readers—and vice versa. The listener who tries to be a reader will, therefore, suffer the fate of Lyndon Johnson, while the reader who tries to be a listener will suffer the fate of Dwight Eisenhower. They will underperform or underachieve.

HOW DO I LEARN?

The second thing to know about how one performs is to know how one learns. There things may be even worse than they are with respect to readers and listeners. For schools everywhere are organized on the assumption that there is one right way to learn, and that it is the same way for everybody.

Many first-class writers—Winston Churchill is but one example—do poorly in school, and they tend to remember their school as pure torture. Yet few of their classmates have the same memory of the same school and the same teachers; they may not have enjoyed the school very much, but the worst they suffered was boredom. The explanation is that first-rate writers do not, as a rule, learn by listening and reading. They learn by writing. Since this is not the way the school allows them to learn, they get poor grades. And to be forced to learn the way the school teaches is sheer hell for them and pure torture.

Here are a few examples of different ways in which people learn.

Beethoven left behind an enormous number of sketchbooks. Yet he himself said that he never looked at a sketchbook when he actually wrote his compositions. When asked, "Why, then, do you keep a sketchbook?" he is reported to have answered, "If I don't write it down immediately, I forget it right away. If I put it into a sketchbook I never forget it, and I never have to look it up again."

Alfred Sloan—the man who built General Motors into the world's largest, and for sixty years the world's most successful, manufacturing company—conducted most of his management business in small and lively meetings. As soon as a meeting was over, Sloan went to his office and spent several hours composing a letter to one of the meeting's participants, in which he brought out the key questions discussed in the meeting, the issues the meeting raised, the decisions it reached, and the problems it uncovered but did not solve. When complimented on these letters, he is reported to have said, "If I do not sit down immediately after the meeting and think through what it actually was all about, and then put it down in writing, I will have forgotten it within twenty-four hours. That's why I write these letters."

A chief executive officer who, in the 1950s and 1960s, converted what was a small and mediocre family firm into the world's leading company in its industry, was in the habit of calling his entire senior staff into his office, usually once a week, having them sit in a half-circle around his desk, and then talking at them for two or three hours. He very rarely asked these people for their comments or their questions. He argued with himself. He raised the possibility of a policy move—for instance, acquisition of a small and failing company in the industry that had, however, some special technology. He always took three different positions on every one of these questions: one in favor of the move, one against the move, and one on the conditions under which such a move might make sense. He needed an audience to hear himself talk. It was the way he learned. And again, while a fairly extreme case, he was by no means an unusual one. Successful trial lawyers learn the same way; so do many medical diagnosticians.

There are probably half a dozen different ways to learn. There are people who learn by taking copious notes—the way Beethoven did. But Alfred Sloan never took a note in a meeting, nor did the CEO mentioned above. There are people who learn by hearing themselves talk. There are people who learn by writing. There are people who learn by doing. And in an (informal) survey I once took of professors in American universities who successfully publish scholarly books of wide appeal, I was told again and again, "To hear myself talk is the reason why I teach; because then I can write."

Actually, of all the important pieces of self-knowledge, this is one of the easiest to acquire. When I ask people, "How do you learn?" most of them know it. But when I then ask, "Do you act on this knowledge?" few do. And yet to act on this knowledge is the key to performance—or rather, not to act on this knowledge is to condemn oneself to nonperformance.

"How do I perform?" and "How do I learn?" are the most important first questions to ask. But they are by no means the only ones. To manage oneself, one has to ask, "Do I work well with people, or am I a loner?" And if one finds out that one works well with people, one then asks, "In what relationship do I work well with people?"

Some people work best as subordinates. The prime example is the great American military hero of World War II, General George Patton. He was America's top troop commander. Yet, when he was proposed for an independent command, General George Marshall, the American chief of staff—and probably the most successful picker of men in American history—said, "Patton is the best subordinate the American Army has ever produced, but he would be the worst commander."

Some people work best as team members. Some people work exceedingly well as coaches and mentors, and some people are simply incompetent to be mentors.

Another important thing to know about how one performs is whether one performs well under stress or whether one needs a highly structured and predictable environment.

Also, does one work best as a minnow in a big organization, or best as a big fish in a small organization? Few people work well in both situations. Again and again people who have been very successful in a large organization—for example, the General Electric Company or Citibank—flounder miserably when they move into a small organization. And again and again people who perform brilliantly in a small organization flounder miserably when they take a job with a big organization.

Another crucial question: "Do I produce results as a decision maker or as an adviser?" A great many people perform best as advisers, but cannot take the burden and pressure of the decision. A good many people, by contrast, need an adviser to force them to think, but then they can take the decision and act on it with speed, self-confidence, and courage. This is a reason why the number-two person in an organization often fails when promoted into the top spot. The top spot requires a decision maker. Strong decision makers in the top spot often put somebody whom they trust into the number-two spot as their adviser—and in that position, that person is outstanding. But when then promoted into the number-one spot, the person fails. He or she knows what the decision should be but cannot take decision-making responsibility.

The *action conclusion:* Again, do not try to change yourself—it is unlikely to be successful. But work, and hard, to improve the way you perform. And try not to do work of any kind in a way in which you do not perform or perform poorly.

What Are My Values?

To be able to manage oneself, one has to know, finally, the answer to, "What are my values?" With respect to ethics, the rules are the same for everybody, and the test is a simple one—I call it the "mirror test."

As the story goes, the most highly respected diplomat among all those of the Great Powers in the early years of the twentieth century was the German ambassador in London. He was clearly destined for higher things, at least to become his country's foreign minister, if not German federal chancellor. Yet, in 1906, he abruptly resigned. King Edward VII had then been on the British throne for five years, and the diplomatic corps had been planning to give him a big dinner. The German ambassador, being the dean of the diplomatic corps—he had been in London for close to fifteen years—was to be the chairman of that dinner. King Edward VII was a notorious womanizer and made it clear what kind of dinner he wanted—at the end, after the dessert had been served, a huge cake was going to appear, and out of it would jump a dozen or more naked prostitutes as the lights were dimmed. The German ambassador resigned rather than preside over this dinner: "I refuse to see a pimp in the mirror in the morning when I shave."

This is the mirror test. What ethics requires is to ask oneself, "What kind of person do I want to see when I shave myself [or put on my lipstick] in the morning?" Ethics, in other words, are a clear value system. And they do not vary much—what is ethical behavior in one kind of organization or situation is ethical behavior in another kind of organization or situation.

But ethics are only a part of a value system and only a part, especially, of the value system of an organization.

To work in an organization whose value system is unacceptable to a person or incompatible with the person's own values, condemns that person both to frustration and to nonperformance.

Here are some examples of values people have to learn about themselves.

A brilliant and highly successful executive found herself totally frustrated after her old company was acquired by a bigger one. She actually got a big promotion—and a promotion into doing the kind of work she did best. It was part of her job to select people for important positions. She deeply believed that one hired people from the outside into important positions only after having exhausted all inside possibilities. The company in which she now found herself as senior human-resources executive believed, however, that in staffing an important position that had become vacant, one first looked at the outside, "to bring in fresh blood." There is something to be said for either way (though, in my experience, the proper way is to do some of both). But they are fundamentally incompatible, not as policies, but as values. They bespeak a different view of the relationship between organization and people; a different view of the responsibility of an organization to its people and with respect to developing them; a different view of what is the most important contribution of a person to an enterprise; and so on. After several years of frustration, the human-resources executive quit, at considerable financial loss to herself. Her values and the values of the organization simply were not compatible.

Similarly, the question of whether to try to obtain results in a pharmaceutical company by making constant, small improvements or by occasional, highly expensive and risky "breakthroughs" is not primarily an economic question. The results of either strategy may be pretty much the same. It is at bottom a conflict of values—between a value system that sees the contribution of a pharmaceutical company as helping the already successful physician to do better at what he or she already does well, and a value system that is "science" oriented.

It is, similarly, a value question whether a business should be run for short-term results or for "the long run." Financial analysts believe that businesses can be run for both, simultaneously. Successful businessmen know better. To be sure, everyone has to produce short-term results. But in any conflict between short-term results and long-term growth, one company decides in favor of long-term growth, another company decides such a conflict in favor of short-term results. Again, this is not primarily a disagreement on economics. *It is fundamentally a value conflict regarding the function of a business and the responsibility of management.*

In one of the fastest-growing pastoral churches in the United States, success is being measured by the number of new parishioners. It is believed that what matters is how many people join, and become regular churchgoers, who never before came to church. The Good Lord, this church believes, will then take care of the spiritual needs of a sufficient number of parishioners. Another pastoral, evangelical church believes that what matters is the spiritual experience of people. It will ease out newcomers who join the church but who then do not enter into the spiritual life of the church.

Again, this is not a matter of numbers. At first glance, it appears that the second church grows more slowly. But it retains a far larger proportion of newcomers than the first one does. Its growth, in other words, is far more solid. This is also not a theological problem, or only secondarily so. It is a value problem. One of the two pastors said in a public debate, "Unless you first come to church, you will never find the Gate to the Kingdom of Heaven." "No," answered the other one. "Until you first look for the Gate to the Kingdom of Heaven, you don't belong in church."

Organizations have to have values. But so do people. To be effective in an organization, one's own values must be compatible with the organization's values. They do not need to be the same. *But they must be close enough so that they can coexist.* Otherwise, the person will be frustrated, but also the person will not produce results.

What to Do in a Value Conflict

There rarely is a conflict between a person's strengths and the way that person performs. The two are complementary. But there is sometimes a conflict between a person's values and the same person's strengths. What one does well—even very well—and successfully may not fit with one's value system. It may not appear to that person as making a contribution and something to which to devote one's life (or even a substantial portion thereof).

If I may inject a personal note: I, too, many years ago, had to decide between what I was doing well and successfully, and my values. I was doing extremely well as a young investment banker in London in the mid-1930s; it clearly fit my strengths. Yet I did not see myself making a contribution as an asset manager of any kind. People, I realized, were my values. And I saw no point in being the richest man in the cemetery. I had no money, no job in a deep Depression, and no prospects. But I quit—and it was the right thing.

Values, in other words, are and should be the ultimate test.

2. WHERE DO I BELONG?

The answers to the three questions, "What are my strengths? How do I perform? What are my values?" should enable the individual, and especially the individual knowledge worker, to decide where he or she belongs.

This is not a decision that most people can or should make at the beginning of their careers.

To be sure, a small minority know very early where they belong. Mathematicians, musicians, or cooks, for instance, are usually mathematicians, musicians, or cooks by the time they are four or five years old. Physicians usually decide in their teens, if not earlier. But most people, and especially highly gifted people, do not really know where they belong till they are well past their mid-twenties. By that time, however, they should know where their strengths are. They should know how they perform. And they should know what their values are.

And then they can and should decide where they belong. Or rather, they should be able to decide where they do not belong. The person who has learned that he or she does not really perform in a big organization should have learned to say "no" when offered a position in a big organization. The person who has learned that he or she is not a decision maker should have learned to say "no" when offered a decision-making assignment. A General Patton (who probably himself never learned it) should have learned to say "no" when offered an independent command, rather than a position as a high-level subordinate.

But knowing the answer to these three questions also enables people to say to an opportunity, to an offer, to an assignment, "Yes, I'll do that. But this is the way I should be doing it. This is the way it should be structured. This is the way my relationships should be. These are the kind of results you should expect from me, and in this time frame, because this is who I am."

Successful careers are not "planned." They are the careers of people who are prepared for the opportunity because they know their strengths, the way they work, and their values. For knowing where one belongs makes ordinary people—hardworking, competent, but mediocre otherwise—into outstanding performers.

3. WHAT IS MY CONTRIBUTION?

To ask, "What is my contribution?" means moving from knowledge to action. The question is not, "What do I want to contribute?" It is not, "What am I told to contribute?" It is, "What should I contribute?"

This is a new question in human history. Traditionally, the task was given. It was given either by the work itself—as was the task of the peasant or the artisan. Or it was given by a master or a mistress, as was the task of the domestic servant. And, until very recently, it was taken for granted that most people were subordinates who did as they were told.

The advent of the knowledge worker is changing this, and fast. Knowledge workers will have to learn to address the question, "What should *my* contribution be?" Only then should they ask, "Does this fit my strengths? Is this what I want to do?" And, "Do I find this rewarding and stimulating?"

The best example of this I know of is the way Harry Truman repositioned himself when he became president of the United States, upon the sudden death of Franklin D. Roosevelt at the end of World War II. Truman had been picked for the vice presidency because he was totally concerned with domestic issues. For it was then generally believed that with the end of the war—and the end was clearly in sight—the United States would return to an almost exclusive concern with domestic affairs. Truman had never shown the slightest interest in foreign affairs, knew nothing about them, and was kept in total ignorance of them. He was still totally focused on domestic affairs when, within a few weeks after his ascendancy, he went to the Potsdam Conference after Germany surrendered. There he sat for a week, with Winston Churchill on one side and Joseph Stalin on the other, and realized, to his horror, that foreign affairs would dominate, but also that he knew absolutely nothing about them. He came back from Potsdam convinced that he had to give up what he wanted to do and instead had to concentrate on what he had to do, that is, concentrate on foreign affairs. He immediately put himself into school with General George Marshall and Dean Acheson as his tutors. Within in a few months, he was a master of foreign affairs, and he, rather than Churchill or Stalin, created the postwar world—with his policy of containing Communism and pushing it back from Iran and Greece; with the Marshall Plan that rescued Western Europe; with the decision to rebuild Japan; and finally, with the call for worldwide economic development.

By contrast, Lyndon Johnson lost both the Vietnam War and his domestic policies because he clung to "What do I want to do?" instead of asking himself, "What should my contribution be?"

Johnson, like Truman, had been entirely focused on domestic affairs. He, too, came into the presidency wanting to complete what the New Deal had left unfinished. He very soon realized that the Vietnam War was what he had to concentrate on. But he could not give up what he wanted his contribution to be. He splintered himself between the Vietnam War and domestic reforms—and he lost both.

One more question has to be asked to decide "What should I contribute?"— *"Where and how can I have results that make a difference?"*

The answer to this question has to balance a number of things. Results should be hard to achieve. They should require "stretching," to use the present buzzword. But they should be within reach. To aim at results that cannot be achieved— or can be achieved only under the most unlikely circumstances—is not being "ambitious." It is being foolish. At the same time, results should be meaningful.

They should make a difference. And they should be visible and, if at all possible, measurable.

Here is one example from a nonprofit institution.

A newly appointed hospital administrator asked himself the question, "What should my contribution be?" The hospital was big and highly prestigious. But it had been coasting on its reputation for thirty years and had become mediocre. The new hospital administrator decided that his contribution should be to establish a standard of excellence in one important area within two years. And so he decided to concentrate on turning around the Emergency Room and the Trauma Center—both big, visible, and sloppy. The new hospital administrator thought through what to demand of an Emergency Room, and how to measure its performance. He decided that every patient who came into the Emergency Room had to be seen by a qualified nurse within sixty seconds. Within twelve months that hospital's Emergency Room had become a model for the entire United States. And its turn-around also showed that there can be standards, discipline, and measurements in a hospital—and within another two years, the whole hospital had been transformed.

The decision that answers *"What should my contribution be?"* thus balances three elements. First comes the question, *"What does the situation require?"* Then comes the question, *"How could I make the greatest contribution with my strengths, my way of performing, my values, to what needs to be done?"* Finally, there is the question, *"What results have to be achieved to make a difference?"*

This then leads to the *action conclusions:* what to do, where to start, how to start, what goals and deadlines to set.

Throughout history, few people had any choices. The task was imposed on them either by nature or by a master. And so in large measure was the way in which they were supposed to perform the task. But so also were the expected results—they were given.

To "do one's own thing" is not freedom. It is license. It does not have results. It does not contribute. But to start out with the question, *"What should I contribute?"* gives freedom. It gives *freedom because it gives responsibility.*

4. RELATIONSHIP RESPONSIBILITY

Very few people work by themselves and achieve results by themselves—a few great artists, a few great scientists, a few great athletes. Most people work with other people and are effective through other people. That is true whether they are members of an organization or legally independent. To manage oneself, therefore, requires *taking relationship responsibility.*

There are two parts to it.

The first one is to accept the fact that other people are as much individuals as one is oneself. They insist on behaving like human beings. This means that they, too, have their strengths. It means that they, too, have their ways of getting things done. It means that they, too, have their values. To be effective, one therefore has to know the strengths, the performance modes, and the values of the people one works with.

This sounds obvious. But too few people pay attention to it.

Typical are people who, in their first assignment, worked for a man who is a reader. They, therefore, were trained in writing reports. Their next boss is a listener. But these people keep on writing reports to the new boss—the way President Johnson's assistants kept on writing reports to him because Jack Kennedy, who had hired them, had been a reader. Invariably, these people have no results. Invariably, their new boss thinks they are stupid, incompetent, and lazy. They become failures. All that would have been needed to avoid this would have been to take one look at the boss and ask the question, "How does he or she perform?"

Bosses are not a title on the organization chart or a "function." They are individuals and entitled to do the work the way they do it. And it is incumbent on the people who work with them to observe them, to find out how they work, and to adapt themselves to the way the bosses are effective (a full discussion of "managing the boss" is contained, next, in chapter 46).

There are bosses, for instance, who have to see the figures first—Alfred Sloan at General Motors was one of them. He himself was not a financial person but an engineer with strong marketing instincts. But as an engineer, he had been trained to look first at figures.

Three of the ablest younger executives in General Motors did not make it into the top ranks because they did not look at Sloan—they did not realize that there was no point in writing to him or talking to him until he had first spent time with the figures. They went in and presented their reports. Then they left the figures. But by that time they had lost Sloan.

As said before, readers are unlikely ever to become listeners, and listeners are unlikely ever to become readers. But everyone can learn to make a decent oral presentation or to write a decent report. It is simply the duty of the subordinate to enable the boss to do his or her work. And that requires looking at the boss and asking, "What are his or her strengths? How does he or she do the work and perform? What are his or her values?"

One does the same with all the people one works with. Each of them works his or her way and not my way. And each of them is entitled to work in his or her way. What matters is whether they perform, and what their values are. How they perform—each is likely to do it differently. The first secret of effectiveness is to understand the people with whom one works and on whom one depends, and to make use of their strengths, their ways of working, and their values. For working relations are as much based on the person as they are based on the work.

The second thing to do to manage oneself and to become effective is to take responsibility for communications. After people have thought through what their strengths are, how they perform, what their values are, and, especially, what their contribution should be, they then have to ask, *"Who needs to know this? On whom do I depend? And who depends on me?"* And then one goes and tells all these people—and tells them in the way in which they receive a message, that is, in a memo if they are readers, or by talking to them if they are listeners, and so on.

Most of the "personality conflicts" in organizations arise from the fact that one person does not know *what* the other person does, or does not know *how* the other person does his or her work, or does not know what *contribution* the other person concentrates on and what results he or she expects. And the reason that they do not know is that they do not ask and, therefore, are not being told.

This reflects human stupidity less than it reflects human history. It was unnecessary until very recently to tell any of these things to anybody. Everybody in a district of the medieval city plied the same trade—there was a street of goldsmiths and a street of shoemakers and a street of armorers. One goldsmith knew exactly what every other goldsmith was doing; one shoemaker knew exactly what every other shoemaker was doing; one armorer knew exactly what every other armorer was doing. There was no need to explain anything. The same was true on the land, where everybody in a valley planted the same crop as soon as the frost was out of the ground. There was no need to tell one's neighbor that one was going to plant potatoes—that, after all, was exactly what the neighbor did too, and at the same time.

And those few people who did things that were not "common," the few professionals, for instance, worked alone, and also did not have to tell anybody what they were doing. Today the great majority of people work with others who do different things.

The marketing vice president may have come out of sales and know everything about sales. But she knows nothing about promotion and pricing and advertising and packaging and sales planning, and so on—she has never done any of these things. Those who work under her must make sure that the marketing vice president understands what they are trying to do, why they are trying to do it, how they are going to do it, and what results to expect.

If the marketing vice president does not understand what these high-grade knowledge specialists are doing, it is primarily their fault, and not that of the marketing vice president. They have not told her. They have not educated her. Conversely, it is the marketing vice president's responsibility to make sure that every one of the people she works with understands how she looks on marketing, what her goals are, how she works, and what she expects of herself and of every one of them.

Even people who understand the importance of relationship responsibility often do not tell their associates and do not ask them. They are afraid of being thought presumptuous, inquisitive, or stupid. They are wrong. Whenever anyone goes to his or her associates and says, "This is what I am good at. This is how I work. These are my values. This is the contribution I plan to concentrate on and the results I should be expected to deliver," the response is always, "This is most helpful. But why haven't you told me earlier?"

And one gets the same reaction if one then asks, "And what do I need to know about your strengths, how you perform, your values, and your proposed contribution?"

In fact, a knowledge worker should request of people with whom he or she works—whether as subordinates, superiors, colleagues, team members—that they adjust their behavior to the knowledge worker's strengths and to the way the knowledge worker works. Readers should request that their associates write to them, listeners should request that their associates first talk to them, and so on. And again, whenever that is done, the reaction of the other person will be, "Thanks for telling me. It's enormously helpful. But why didn't you ask me earlier?"

Organizations are no longer built on force. They are increasingly built on trust. Trust does not mean that people like one another. It means that people can trust one another. And this presupposes that people understand one another. Taking relationship responsibility is therefore an absolute necessity. It is a duty. Whether one is a member of the organization, a consultant to it, a supplier to it, a distributor, one owes relationship responsibility to everyone with whom one works, on whose work one depends, and who, in turn, depends on one's own work.

SUMMARY

The workforce has changed fundamentally in its life expectancy, but above all in its composition and work. It has become a knowledge workforce. And therefore to have even a chance of success and achievement, knowledge workers have to do something totally new and totally unprecedented. They have to manage themselves, and this creates new demands on the individual. First, they must understand what they do well—that is, their strengths. Feedback analysis is a tool used by many successful executives to understand their strengths. They must also understand the most effective way in which they work. Once the knowledge worker understands her strengths and work style, the next demand is that she understand her values. One tends to do best when applying one's strengths in areas that one values. Then the knowledge worker is able to determine where to try to place himself or herself as opportunities present themselves.

Once in an organization, the knowledge worker must ask, "Given my strengths and values, where can I make the greatest contribution to the needs of this organization?" Finally, the knowledge worker must take responsibility for the relationships required to make the contribution. Relationship responsibility requires asking and answering the same questions about those with whom one works and adapting oneself to the strengths and work styles of associates.

46

Managing the Boss

Almost everybody has a boss. There are still some individual professionals in solo practice who don't answer to anyone, are not accountable to anyone, and do not have a boss:

- the small-town lawyer in a solo practice
- the physician in a solo practice
- the individual consultant
- perhaps the pastor of a church or the senior professor in a university

But they are a small minority of today's working population.

MOST OF US HAVE MORE THAN ONE BOSS

The human resources person who works on a team has at least two bosses—the human-resources manager who put her on the team and the manager of the team. The division controller in the big company has at least two bosses: the company's chief accounting or financial officer and the division manager.

And the trend is for knowledge workers to have an increasing number of bosses, an increasing number of people on whose approval and appraisal they depend, and whose support they need.

THE BOSS IS KEY TO EFFECTIVENESS

But the boss is not only the key person for pay, promotion, and placement; he or she is also the key person for the knowledge worker's effectiveness.

Whether as an employee or as an outside contractor and supplier, the knowledge worker is dependent on his boss or bosses for effectiveness. No matter how good the knowledge worker's work, if the boss does not act on it, nothing will happen, nothing will get done.

Also—though rarely mentioned in polite society—there are few things quite as helpful to one's own career as a boss who goes places. Everybody knows these things, but almost no one does anything about them.

NEGLECT OF MANAGING THE BOSS

There is a good historical reason for this perverse neglect of managing the boss. Most of the management books and management seminars are still caught in a definition of a manager that has actually been obsolete for decades: the definition of a manager as someone who has subordinates. But we have known for a very long time that this is a totally wrong definition—wrong, and not just inadequate.

WHO IS THE BOSS?

We have known—I'd say since the 1950s—that a manager or executive is somebody who is responsible for the work of all the people besides himself on whom the manager's own performance depends. And surely the first one of these is the boss.

Instinctively most of us know this; we know this through our own experience. When I spoke with people—let's say, the forty-year-old executives in my Executive Management class, for instance, or people in a client organization—and I asked them to tell me something about their work and their company, not one began talking about his or her subordinates. Everyone began by telling me about their boss. And most everybody basically said, "If I only knew how to manage the boss." But we do know. It's actually neither difficult nor complicated.

MANAGING THE BOSS

The following are seven specific keys to success in managing bosses:

1. Making a "boss list"

2. Asking each for his or her input, and giving each your own input

3. Enabling bosses to perform

4. Playing to the bosses' strengths

5. Keeping bosses informed

6. Protecting bosses from surprises

7. Never underrating bosses

1. Making a Boss List

The first thing to do is to make a "boss list." Put down on a piece of paper everyone to whom you are accountable, everyone who can direct you or your people, everyone who appraises you and your work and is expected to have an opinion about you and your performance, everyone on whom you depend to make effective your work and that of your people. And revise that list once a year and always when your job or your assignment changes. It is unlikely to be the same list for longer than a year or so.

The most common mistake people make when they draw up the boss list is to omit from it people who do not officially work for their own organization, that is, people in a joint venture or an alliance or in a client organization. In fact, one of the most common reasons why such alliances or partnerships go sour is that their people are not on the boss list of the partner or client.

One example, a very old one but a telling one: GM (or the American automobile companies altogether) would not be in such trouble today if, in the 1960s, their marketing people had put the most influential of their dealers on their boss lists. They didn't, and as a result they had no idea who these dealers were and what they, as marketers, were doing that caused trouble for their dealers or made life difficult for them. The dealers who sold the most GM cars and were the most profitable ones for GM were the ones who got the most disgruntled.

Altogether, to define a boss in legal terms is much too narrow; the boss list defines a boss in operational terms. A boss is anyone who has the power and anyone who is likely—let alone certain—to be listened to when he or she has an opinion about you, your performance, your work, your competence and qualifications. It is better to have a few more people on the boss list and then take them off than to leave off people who should have been on it.

Each manager should ask, "Who should be on my boss list?" And the list should include not only specific people, but also the roles and types of people who should be on the list.

2. Asking for Input

Go to each of the people on the boss list at least once a year and ask, "What do I do and what do my people do that helps *you* do your job? And what do we do that hampers *you* and makes life more difficult for you?"

This sounds obvious, but it is rarely done. The first person on whom your performance depends is the boss, and the boss is thus the first person for whose performance you have to take responsibility. To do this, you must directly ask each of the people on your boss list, "What do I do to help you or to hamper you?"

Most bosses will be able to answer that question right away. In fact, most have long ago realized what you or your people do that hampers them and, as a rule, have little difficulty telling you what you and your people do that helps them.

And when they have answered that question you say, "Give me a few days so that I can think about it and talk it over with my people. I'll come back then and tell you what I and my people can do to eliminate or downplay the things that hamper you and what I and my people can do to do more of the things that help you."

Be sure to take that promise seriously and don't wait too long to report back. Ten days or so is about all you should allow yourself before you come back to each of the bosses with definite suggestions.

At the same time, you should also prepare a list of the things a boss does that help and hamper you and your people. "This is what *you* do that helps me and my people; and the more you can do of it, the easier it will be for us to do our work. And here are the things you do that hamper us in doing our work. Are these things necessary?"

Aren't people going to be afraid to go to each boss and ask and tell these things? Most people are very hesitant the first time and feel awkward. But when they screw up their courage and actually go to the boss and ask the question, they are then totally surprised. Practically without exception, the boss's reaction is, "Why did it take you so long to ask me?" And when then being told what the boss does that helps or hampers the subordinate, the boss often says, "Why didn't you tell me earlier?"

A good many years ago I worked fairly intensively with one of the world's big bankers. For six or seven years, I met each month with him and his associates for a whole day. A year or two after we began working together, I did go to him and ask him.

He totally surprised me—every time we had met, he had told me how much he valued the report I sent him after every one of our meetings. But when I asked him, he said, "What hampers me, Peter, is that you don't consider how I can use your report for my work with my own associates in the bank. I have to sit down and spend three hours redoing it so that it fits them." From then on, I wrote his reports so that they would be the tools of my boss.

But then I told him that what hampered me in the relationship was that he didn't send me the agenda for their meeting until a day or two before the meeting, and I didn't have enough time to prepare. And he looked at me and said, "So that's the reason why the meetings with my key associates always waste so much time before we really get going. I don't give them the time to prepare themselves. Thanks for telling me. But why didn't you tell me earlier?"

But that's not the end of the story. The man is, of course, long retired and he and I had pretty much lost contact except for the annual Christmas card. But on my ninetieth birthday, in November of 1999, I got a long handwritten letter from him in which he wrote, "The most important contribution you made to me and the bank was when you told me what I did that helped and what I did that hampered you in your work. I date my success in building the bank from that moment."

Each person needs to ask his or her boss, "What do I do that hampers you and your people?"

3. Enabling Bosses to Perform

No two persons work alike, perform alike, or behave alike. Thus, it is important to recognize that each boss has his or her own working style, his or her own way to be comfortable, and his or her own way to be effective. The subordinate's job is not to reform the boss, not to reeducate the boss, not to make the boss conform to what books or business schools say bosses should be like. Instead, it is to enable each of his or her bosses to perform as unique individuals.

This requires thinking through such questions as, "Does this boss want monthly presentations concerning the performance, plans, and problems of my department? Or does this boss want me to come in every time there is something to report, some problem to solve, or some results to analyze? Does this boss prefer written or oral reports? Does this boss want information first thing in the morning, at the end of the day or somewhere in between?"

The variety of questions is endless. What is important is that you accept that it is your responsibility to enable your bosses to perform according to their own unique work styles. To enable your bosses to perform, you must determine their work styles.

4. Playing to the Bosses' Strengths

A manager's task is to make the strengths of people effective and their weaknesses irrelevant, and that applies as much to the manager's bosses as it applies to the manager's subordinates.

Managing the boss means creating a relationship of trust. This requires that your bosses feel comfortable that you are playing to their strengths and safeguarding them from their limitations and weaknesses. This sounds very complicated. How does one find out? Do you have to be a psychoanalyst?

What's wrong with asking? We are not talking about values. We are not talking about motivations. We are talking about habits. Most people know their habits in such matters, and there is no reason to keep them a secret or to be ashamed of them. Sure, you can learn a great deal about a person just by watching them. And often that's all you need.

But the one infallible and simple way is to ask, "How do you want it?" This is the question and not, What kind of a person is he or she? And how a person behaves you had best find out by asking him or her. The *very, very last thing* you want to do is to try to be a psychologist and ask, "Why does a person behave like this?"

5. Keeping Bosses Informed

Your bosses must always know what to expect from both you and your subordinates. This means that they must be kept up-to-date on what your goals and priorities are, as well as what they are not.

It is by no means always necessary that the boss approve; in fact, it is sometimes not even desirable. But the boss must understand what you are up to, must know what to expect and what not to expect.

Bosses, after all, are held responsible by their own bosses for the performance of their people. They must be able to say, "I know what Anne (or Joe) is trying to do." Only if they can say this will they be able to fully trust you.

6. Protecting Bosses from Surprises

In an organization, there is no such thing as a pleasant surprise. To be exposed to a surprise in the organization one is responsible for is humiliation, and usually public humiliation. Thus it is the subordinate's job to protect his or her boss from all surprises. Different bosses want very different warnings of possible surprises. Some may prefer a simple warning, such as a comment that things may turn out differently than expected. Others may demand a full, detailed report even if there is only a slight chance of a surprise. Regardless, all bosses need to be protected from surprises. Otherwise, they will not trust a subordinate, and with good reason.

President John F. Kennedy hated surprises while in office and always demanded a detailed written report if there was even a slight chance of a surprise. Why do you think President Kennedy wanted to be warned of possible surprises? President Kennedy demanded written reports in great detail on possible surprises because he knew that surprises lead to humiliation and that there is no such thing as a pleasant surprise in the workplace.

Kennedy didn't know about the need to be informed and the way *he* needed to be informed when he became president. And the Bay of Pigs fiasco in the first year of his administration was largely the result of Kennedy's not being organized to inform himself about the way *he* needed to be and wanted to be informed. And then, two years later, his greatest success in getting the Soviets to back down over Cuba in the missile crisis was largely because Kennedy by then had his administration organized superbly to anticipate and prevent surprises.

Similarly, the terrible fumbling in the first year of Bill Clinton's administration was largely caused by the new president's not organizing himself and his staff to protect the president from surprises.

Accept it—different people need to be informed differently. And if you don't adjust yourself to the way each of your bosses gets the message, you'll be ineffectual.

Again American presidents are good examples simply because they are so very visible. Franklin Roosevelt wanted the earliest possible warning, and he wanted it orally.

If he got it in a report, it simply didn't register. He was a total listener. Harry Truman didn't want a warning. If the subordinate could handle it, Truman didn't even want to hear about it, though by "handling it" he also meant that it was the staff member's job to keep things out of the paper and off the air. Eisenhower wanted a one-page memo. He was a reader. And he always wanted an action recommendation at the end.

All three, Roosevelt, Truman, Eisenhower, were perfectly normal. They were just different. And in every case, the new staff members whom each of these three presidents came to trust and on whom they came to rely—Harry Hopkins in FDR's case, General George Marshall in Truman's case, John Foster Dulles in Eisenhower's case—were men who asked the president, "How do you want to be informed so as to be shielded from surprises?" They did not guess.

What are the most common mistakes managers and professionals make in keeping a boss informed? There are two in particular. A person's boss changes and that person keeps on informing the new boss the way he or she had informed the last boss. Invariably that leads to disaster. The new boss concludes either that the subordinate is trying to keep things from him or her or, more commonly, that the subordinate is just plain stupid—which, by the way, is true.

If a boss changes, one changes the way one communicates and informs. And to say it again, the best way to do this is to go and ask. One reason why Lyndon Johnson was such a failure as president is that the staff he inherited from John Kennedy kept on communicating to the new president as Kennedy had taught them to communicate— that is, in lengthy, carefully reasoned written reports. And Johnson was a listener, not a reader, and these lengthy, beautifully written reports simply didn't get to him.

The second mistake is to fail to ask, "Have I ever failed to protect a boss from surprises? What could I have done differently to spare him or her the problems associated with being surprised?"

7. Never Underrating Bosses

Finally, never underrate a boss. He or she will either see through your little game and bitterly resent it, or else see in you the same deficiencies as you see in the boss. But there is no risk at all in overrating a boss. At worst, he or she may feel flattered.

SUMMARY

Managing the boss is a fairly simple but important process. All it requires is that you follow the seven keys to success: make a boss list to identify who your bosses are, ask for their input, enable each boss to perform, play to each boss's strengths, keep each boss informed, protect each boss from surprises, and never underrate a boss. All managing the boss requires is a little thinking, a little common sense. But it does require some work. Above all, however, it requires accepting that managing the boss is both a major opportunity and a major responsibility.

47

Revitalizing Oneself—Seven Personal Experiences

How can the individual, especially the individual who is putting knowledge to work, become effective, and how can such a person remain effective over long periods of years, over periods of change, over years of work, and over years of living?

Since this question deals with the individual, it might be appropriate to start with myself. I will begin by talking of seven experiences in my life that taught me how to maintain myself as effective, capable of growth, capable of change—and capable of aging without becoming a prisoner of the past.

I was not yet eighteen when, having finished high school, I left my native Vienna in Austria, and went to Hamburg in Germany, as a trainee in a cotton-export firm. My father was not very happy. Ours had been a family of civil servants, professors, lawyers, and physicians, for a very long time. He therefore wanted me to be a full-time university student, but I was tired of being a schoolboy, and wanted to go to work. To appease my father, but without any serious intention, I enrolled at Hamburg University in the law faculty.

In those remote days, the year 1927, one did not have to attend classes in Austria or Germany to be a perfectly proper university student. All one had to do was to obtain signatures of the professors in the registration book. For this, one did not even have to go to class. All one had to do was to give a small tip to the faculty messenger, who then went and sought the professors' signatures.

The work as a trainee at the export firm was terribly boring, and I learned very little. It began at seven-thirty in the morning, and was over at four in the afternoon on weekdays and at twelve on Saturday. So I had lots of free time.

On weekends, two other trainees—also from Austria, but working in other firms—and I usually went hiking in the beautiful countryside outside of Hamburg, spending the night in a youth hostel, where, being officially students, we could obtain free lodging.

I had five weekday evenings all to myself in Hamburg's famous City Library, which was almost next door to my office. University students were encouraged to borrow as many books as they wanted. For fifteen months, I read, and read, and read, in German and English and French.

EXPERIENCE ONE: GOAL AND VISION TAUGHT BY VERDI

And then, once a week, I went to the opera. The Hamburg Opera was then, as it still is, one of the world's foremost opera houses. I had very little money, as trainees were not paid, but for university students, the opera was free. All one had to do was to go there one hour before the performance. Ten minutes before the performance began, cheap seats remaining unsold were given out free to university students. On one of these evenings I went to hear an opera by the great nineteenth-century Italian composer, Giuseppe Verdi—the last opera he wrote, in 1893, *Falstaff.*

It has now become one of Verdi's most popular operas, but at that time it was rarely performed. Both singers and audiences thought it too difficult.

I was totally overwhelmed by it. I had had a good musical education as a boy, as the Vienna of my youth was an extremely musical city. Although I had heard a great many operas, I had never heard anything like this. I have never forgotten the impression that evening made on me.

When I made a study, I found, to my great surprise, that this opera, with its gaiety, its zest for life, and its incredible vitality, was written by a man aged eighty! To me, then just eighteen, eighty was an incredible age. I doubt that I even knew anyone that old. It was not a common age when life expectancies, even among healthy people, were around fifty or so. Then I read what Verdi himself had written when he was asked why, at his age, a famous man and considered one of the nineteenth-century's foremost opera composers, he had taken on the hard work of writing one more opera, and an exceedingly demanding one. "All my life as a musician," he wrote, "I have striven for perfection. It has always eluded me. I surely had an obligation to make one more try."

I have never forgotten these words—they made an indelible impression on me. Verdi, when he was my age, eighteen, was of course already a seasoned musician. I had no idea what I would become, except that I knew by that time that I was unlikely to be a success exporting cotton textiles. At eighteen, I was as immature, as callow, as naive as an eighteen-year-old can be. It was not until fifteen years later, when I was in my early thirties, that I really knew what I was good at and where I belonged. But I then resolved that, whatever my life's work would be, Verdi's words would be my lodestar. I then resolved that if I ever reached an advanced age, I would not give up, but would keep on. In the meantime, I would strive for perfection, even though, as I well knew, it would surely always elude me.

EXPERIENCE TWO: "THE GODS CAN SEE THEM"—TAUGHT BY PHIDIAS

It was at about the same time, and also in Hamburg during my stay as a trainee, that I then read a story that conveyed to me what "perfection" means. It is a story of the greatest sculptor of ancient Greece, Phidias. He was commissioned around 440 BC to make the statues that to this day, 2,400 years later, still stand on the roof of the Parthenon in Athens. They are considered among the greatest sculptures of the Western tradition. The statues were universally admired, but when Phidias submitted his bill, the city accountant of Athens refused to pay it. "These statues," the accountant said, "stand on the roof of the temple, and on the highest hill in Athens. Nobody can see anything but their fronts. Yet, you have charged us for sculpturing them in the round, that is, for doing their backsides, which nobody can see."

"You are wrong," Phidias retorted. "The gods can see them." I read this, as I remember, shortly after I had listened to *Falstaff,* and it hit me hard. I have not always lived up to it. I have done many things that I hope the gods will not notice, but I have always known that one has to strive for perfection even if only "the gods" notice.

Whenever people ask me which of my books I consider the best, I smile and say, "The next." I do not, however, mean it as a joke. I mean it the way Verdi meant it when he talked of writing an opera at eighty in the pursuit of a perfection that had always eluded him. Though I am older now than Verdi was when he wrote *Falstaff,* I am still thinking and working on two additional books, each of which, I hope, will be better than any of my earlier ones, will be more important, and will come a little closer to excellence.

EXPERIENCE THREE: CONTINUOUS LEARNING—DECISION AS A JOURNALIST

A few years later, I moved to Frankfurt in Germany. I worked first as a trainee in a brokerage firm. Then after the New York stock market crash in October 1929, when the brokerage firm went bankrupt, I was hired on my twentieth birthday by Frankfurt's largest newspaper, as a financial and foreign affairs writer. I continued to be enrolled as a law student at the university, because in those days one could easily transfer from one European university to any other. I still was not interested in the law, but I remembered the lessons of Verdi and of Phidias. A journalist has to write about many subjects, so I decided that I had to know something about many subjects to be at least a competent journalist.

The newspaper I worked for came out in the afternoon. We began work at six in the morning and finished by a quarter past two in the afternoon, when the last edition went to press. So I began to force myself to study afternoons and evenings:

international relations and international law; the history of social and legal institutions; history in the round; finance; and so on. Gradually, I developed a system. I still adhere to it. Every three or four years, I pick a new subject. It may be statistics, it may be medieval history, it may be Japanese art, it may be economics. Three years of study are by no means enough to master a subject, but they are enough to understand it. So, for more than sixty years, I have kept on studying, one subject at a time. This has not only given me a substantial fund of knowledge. It has also forced me to be open to new disciplines and new approaches and new methods—for every one of the subjects I have studied makes different assumptions and employs a different methodology.

EXPERIENCE FOUR: REVIEWING—TAUGHT BY THE EDITOR IN CHIEF

The next experience to report, in this long story of keeping myself intellectually alive and growing, is what was taught by the newspaper's editor in chief, one of Europe's leading newspapermen. The editorial staff consisted of very young people. At age twenty-two, I became one of three assistant managing editors. The reason was not that I was particularly good. In fact, I never became a first-rate daily journalist. But, in those years around 1930, the people who should have held this kind of position—people aged thirty-five or so—were not available in Europe. They had been killed in World War I. Even highly responsible positions had to be filled by young people such as me.

This situation was not too different from what I found in Japan when I first went there ten years after the end of the Pacific War, in the mid- and late 1950s.

The editor in chief, then around fifty, took infinite pains to train and to discipline his young crew. He discussed with each of us every week the work we had done. Twice a year, right after New Year and then again before summer vacations began in June, we would spend a Saturday afternoon and all of Sunday to discuss our work over the preceding six months. The editor would always start out with the things we had done well. Then he would proceed to the things we had tried to do well. Next he reviewed the things where we had not tried hard enough. And finally, he would subject us to a scathing critique of the things we had done badly or had failed to do. For the last two hours of that session, we would then project our work for the next six months: *What are the things on which we should concentrate? What are the things we should improve? What are the things each of us needs to learn?* And a week later, each of us was expected to submit to the editor in chief our new program of work and learning for the next six months.

I tremendously enjoyed the sessions, but I forgot them as soon as I left the paper.

Almost ten years later, and already in the United States, I remembered them. It was then, in the early 1940s, that I became a senior professor in a major faculty, started my own consulting practice, and began to publish major books. Then I remembered what the Frankfurt editor in chief had taught. Since then, I have set aside two weeks every summer in which to review my work during the preceding year, beginning with the things I did well, but could or should have done better, down to the things I did poorly and the things I should have done but did not do. I decide what my priorities should be in my consulting work, in my writing, in my teaching.

I have never once truly lived up to the plan I make each August, but it has forced me to live up to Verdi's injunction "to strive for perfection" even though "it has always eluded me" and still does.

EXPERIENCE FIVE: WHAT IS NECESSARY IN A NEW POSITION—TAUGHT BY THE SENIOR PARTNER

My next learning experience came a few years later. From Frankfurt in Germany, I moved to London in England in 1933, first as a securities analyst in a large insurance company and then, a year later, to a small but fast-growing private bank as the firm's economist and executive secretary to the three senior partners—one, the founder, a man in his seventies; two others, in their mid-thirties. At first I worked exclusively with the two younger men, but after I had been at the firm some three months or so, the founder called me into his office and said, "I didn't think much of you when you came in here and still don't think much of you, but you are even more stupid than I thought you would be, and much more stupid than you have any right to be." Since the two younger partners had been praising me to the skies each day, I was dumbfounded.

And then, the old gentleman said, "I understand you did very good securities analysis at the insurance company. But if we had wanted you to do securities analysis work, we would have left you where you were. You are now the executive secretary to the partners, yet you continue to do securities analysis. What should you be doing now, to be effective in your new job?" I was furious, but still I realized that the old man was right. I totally changed my behavior and my work. Since then, when I have a new assignment, I ask myself the question, "What do I need to do now that I have a new assignment, to be effective?" Every time it is something different.

I have been a consultant, now, for sixty years. I have worked with many organizations and in many countries. The greatest waste of human resources in all the organizations I have seen is the failed promotion. Of the able people who are being promoted and put into a new assignment, not many become true successes. Quite a few are outright failures. A very much larger number are neither successes nor failures, they become mediocrities. A handful only are successes.

Why should people who, for ten or fifteen years have been competent, suddenly become incompetent? The reason in practically all cases I have seen is that people do what I did, seventy years ago in that London bank. They continue in their new assignment to do what made them successful in the old assignment and what earned them the promotion. Then they turn incompetent, not because they have become incompetent, but because they are doing the wrong things.

For many years, I have made it my practice to ask those of my clients who are truly effective people—and especially those who are truly effective executives in large organizations—to what they attribute their effectiveness. Practically always, I am being told that they owe their success, as I do, to a long-dead boss who did what the old gentleman in London did for me: forced me to think through what the new assignment requires. No one, at least not within my experience, discovers this for himself. You need someone to teach you. Once one has learned that, one does not forget it, and then—almost without exception—one is successful in the new assignment. What it requires is not superior knowledge or superior talent. It requires concentration on the things that the new assignment requires, the things that are crucial to the new challenge, the new job, the new task.

EXPERIENCE SIX: WRITING DOWN—TAUGHT BY THE JESUITS AND THE CALVINISTS

Quite a few years later, around 1945, and after I had moved from England to the United States in 1937, I picked for my three-year study subject early modern European history, and especially the fifteenth and sixteenth centuries. There I found that *two* European institutions had become the dominant forces in Europe: the Jesuit Order in the Catholic south and the Calvinist Church in the Protestant north. Both owed their success to the same method. Both were founded independently, in 1536. Both from the very beginning adopted the same learning discipline.

Whenever a Jesuit priest or a Calvinist pastor does anything of significance, for instance, making a key decision, he is expected to write down what results he anticipates. Nine months later, he then feeds back from the actual results to these anticipations. This very soon shows him what he did well and what his strengths are. It also shows him what he has to learn and what habits he has to change. Finally, it shows him what he is not gifted for and cannot do well. I have followed this method for myself—now for fifty years. It brings out what one's strengths are—and this is the most important thing an individual can know about himself or herself. It brings out where improvement is needed and what kind of improvement is needed. Finally, it brings out what an individual cannot do and therefore should not even try to do. To know one's strengths, to know how to improve them, and to know what one cannot do—they are the keys to continuous learning.

EXPERIENCE SEVEN: WHAT TO BE REMEMBERED FOR—TAUGHT BY SCHUMPETER

One more experience, and then I am through with the story of my personal development. At Christmas 1949—I had just begun to teach management at New York University—my father, then seventy-three years old, came to visit us from California, where he had retired a few years earlier. Right after the New Year, on January 3, 1950, he and I went to visit an old friend of his, the famous economist Joseph Schumpeter. Schumpeter, then sixty-six and world-famous, was still teaching at Harvard and very active as president of the American Economic Association.

In 1902 my father had been a young civil servant in the Austrian Ministry of Finance, but also did some teaching in economics at the university. He had come to know Schumpeter, then at age nineteen, the most brilliant of the young students. Two more different people are hard to imagine: Schumpeter was flamboyant, arrogant, abrasive, and vain; my father, quiet, the soul of courtesy, and modest to the point of being self-effacing. Still, the two became fast friends and remained fast friends.

By 1949, Schumpeter had become a very different person. Sixty-six years old and in his last year of teaching at Harvard, he was at the peak of his fame. The two old men had a wonderful time together reminiscing about the old days. Both had grown up and had worked in Austria, and both had eventually come to America, Schumpeter in 1932 and my father, four years later. Suddenly that day, my father asked with a chuckle, "Joseph, do you still talk about what you want to be remembered for?" Schumpeter broke out in loud laughter, and even I laughed. For Schumpeter was notorious for having said, when he was thirty or so and had published the first two of his great economic books, that what he really wanted to be remembered for was to have been "Europe's greatest lover of beautiful women, and Europe's greatest horseman—and perhaps also as the world's greatest economist." Schumpeter said, "Yes, this question is still important to me, but I now answer it differently. I want to be remembered as having been the teacher who converted half a dozen brilliant students into first-rate economists."

He must have seen an amazed look on my father's face because he continued, "You know, Adolph, I have now reached the age where I know that being remembered for books and theories is not enough. One does not make a difference unless it is a difference in the lives of people." One reason my father had gone to see Schumpeter was that it was known that he was very sick and would not live long. Schumpeter died five days after we had visited him.

I have never forgotten that conversation. I have learned from it three things. First, one has to ask oneself what one wants to be remembered for. Second, that should change as one gets older. It should change both with one's own maturity and with the changes in the world. Finally, one thing worth being remembered for is the difference one makes in the lives of people.

THE SAME THING CAN BE LEARNED

I am telling this long story for a simple reason. All the people I know who have managed to remain effective during a long life have learned pretty much the same things I learned. This applies to effective managers and to scholars; to top-ranking military people and to first-rate physicians; to teachers and to artists. Whenever I work with a person—and as a consultant I have been working of course with a great many, in businesses, in governments, in universities, in hospitals, in opera houses, in symphony orchestras, in museums, and so on—I sooner or later try to find out to what the individual attributes his or her success. I am invariably told stories that are remarkably like mine.

And so, my answer to the question, "How can the individual, and especially the individual in knowledge work, maintain his or her effectiveness?" would be, "By doing a few fairly simple things."

The first one is to have the kind of goal or vision that Verdi's *Falstaff* gave me. To keep on striving means that one matures but one does not age.

Second, I have found that the people who maintain their effectiveness take the view Phidias took of his own work: the gods see it. These people are not willing to do work that is only average. They have respect for the integrity of their work. In fact, they have self-respect.

The third thing these people all have in common: They build continuous learning into the way they live. They may not do what I have been doing for more than sixty years now, that is, to become a student of a new discipline every three or four years. They experiment. They are not satisfied with doing what they did yesterday. The very least they demand of themselves is that they do better, whatever they do, and more often, they demand of themselves that they do it differently.

The people who keep themselves alive and growing also build a review of their performance into their work. An increasing number, I have found, do what the Jesuits and Calvinists of the sixteenth century first thought of. They keep a record of the results of their actions and decisions, and compare them with their expectations. Then they soon know what their strengths are, but they also know what they have to improve, to change, to learn. Finally they know what they are not good at, and what they therefore should let other people do.

Again and again, when I ask one of these effective people to tell me the experiences that explain their success, I hear that a long-dead teacher or a boss challenged them and taught them that whenever one changes one's work, one's position, one's assignment, one thinks through what the new job, the new position, the new assignment requires. Always it requires something different from what the preceding job or the preceding assignment required.

ONE'S OWN RESPONSIBILITY

The most important thing that underlies all these practices is that individuals—and especially knowledge people—who manage to keep themselves effective and who manage to keep on growing and changing take responsibility for their development and their placement.

This may be the most novel conclusion. And it may be the one that is most difficult to apply. Today's organization, whether it is a business or a government agency, is still based on the assumption that the organization is responsible for placing the individual and for providing the experiences and challenges that the individual needs. The best example of this I know is the personnel department in the typical, large Japanese company—or the prototype on which it has been modeled or the human-resources department in a traditional army. I know no more responsible group of people than those in the typical Japanese human-resources department. Yet they will, I think, have to learn to change. Instead of being decision makers, they will have to become teachers, guides, counselors, advisers.

The responsibility for the development of the individual knowledge worker, and for his or her placement, will, I am convinced, have to be taken by the individual. It will have to become very much the responsibility of the individual to ask, What kind of assignment do I now need? What kind of assignment am I now qualified for? What kind of experience and what kind of knowledge and skill do I now need to acquire? The decision, of course, cannot be that of the individual alone. It has to be made in contemplation of the needs of the organization. It also has to be made on the basis of an outside appraisal of the strengths, the competencies, the performance of the individual.

SUMMARY

The responsibility for development of the individual has to become responsibility for self-development. Responsibility for placing the individual has to become the responsibility for self-placement. Otherwise, it is unlikely that knowledge people can continue to remain effective and productive and capable of growth over the long span of working life we can now expect.

48

The Educated Person

Knowledge is not impersonal, like money. Knowledge does not reside in a book, a databank, a software program; they contain only information. Knowledge is always embodied in a person; carried by a person; created, augmented, or improved by a person; applied by a person; taught and passed on by a person; used or misused by a person. The shift to the knowledge society therefore puts the person in the center. In so doing, it raises new challenges, new issues, new and quite unprecedented questions, about the knowledge society's representative, the educated person.

In all earlier societies, the educated person was an ornament. He or she embodied *Kultur*—the German term, which in its mixture of awe and derision, is untranslatable into English (even "highbrow" does not come close). But in the knowledge society, the educated person is society's emblem, society's symbol, society's standard-bearer. The educated person is the social "archetype"—to use the sociologist's term. He or she defines society's performance capacity. But he or she also embodies society's values, beliefs, and commitments. If the feudal knight was the clearest embodiment of society in the early Middle Ages, and the "bourgeois" under capitalism, the educated person will represent society in the knowledge society in which knowledge has become the central resource.

This must change the very meaning of "educated person." It must change the very meaning of what it means to be educated. It will, thus, predictably make the definition of an "educated person" a crucial issue. With knowledge becoming the key resource, the educated person faces new demands, new challenges, new responsibilities. *The educated person now matters.*

Since the early 1970s, a vigorous—often shrill—debate has been raging in American academia over the educated person. Should there be one? Could there be one? And what should be considered "education" anyway?

A motley crew of post-Marxists, radical feminists, and other "antis" argues that there can be no such thing as an educated person—the position of those new nihilists, the "deconstructionists." Others in this group assert that there can be only educated persons, with each sex, each ethnic group, each race, each "minority," requiring its own separate culture and a separate—indeed, an isolationist—educated person. Since these people are mainly concerned with the "humanities," there are few echoes as yet of Hitler's "Aryan physics," Stalin's "Marxist genetics," or Mao's "Communist psychology." But the arguments of these antitraditionalists recall those of the totalitarians. And their target is the same: the universalism that is at the very core of the concept of an educated person, whatever it may be called ("educated person" in the West or *bunjin* in China and Japan).

The opposing camp—we might call them the "humanists"—also scorns the present system. But it does so because it fails to produce a universally educated person. The humanist critics demand a return to the nineteenth century, to the "liberal arts," the "classics," the German *gebildete Mensch*. They do not, so far, repeat the assertion made by Robert Hutchins and Mortimer Adler in the 1930s at the University of Chicago that "knowledge" in its entirety consists of a hundred "great books." But they are in direct line of descent from the Hutchins-Adler "Return to Pre-Modernity."

Both sides, alas, are wrong.

AT THE CORE OF THE KNOWLEDGE SOCIETY

The knowledge society must have at its core the concept of the educated person. It will have to be a *universal* concept, precisely because the knowledge society is a society of knowledges and because it is global—in its money, its economics, its careers, its technology, its central issues, and, above all, in its information. The knowledge society requires a unifying force. It requires a leadership group, which can focus local, particular, separate traditions on a common and shared commitment to values, a common concept of excellence, and on mutual respect.

The knowledge society thus needs exactly the opposite of what deconstructionists, radical feminists, or anti-Westerners propose. It needs the very thing they totally reject: a universally educated person.

Yet the knowledge society needs a different kind of educated person from the ideal for which the humanists are fighting. They rightly stress the folly of their opponents' demand to repudiate the Great Tradition and the wisdom, beauty, knowledge, that are the heritage of mankind. But a bridge to the past is not enough—and that is all the humanists offer. The educated person needs to be able to bring his or her knowledge to bear on the present, not to mention molding the future. There is no provision for such ability in the proposals of the humanists, indeed, no concern for it. But without it, the Great Tradition remains dusty antiquarianism.

In his 1943 novel *Das Glasperlenspiel* (*The Glass Bead Game*), Hermann Hesse anticipated the sort of world the humanists want—and its failure. The book depicts a brotherhood of intellectuals, artists, and humanists who live a life of splendid isolation, dedicated to the Great Tradition, its wisdom and its beauty. But the hero, the most accomplished Master of the Brotherhood, decides in the end to return to the polluted, vulgar, turbulent, strife-torn, money-grubbing reality—for his values are only fool's gold unless they have relevance to the world.

What Hesse foresaw in 1943 is now in fact happening. "Liberal education" and *"allgemeine Bildung"* are in crisis today because they have become a *Glasperlenspiel* that the brightest desert for crass, vulgar, money-grubbing reality. The ablest students appreciate the liberal arts. They enjoy them fully as much as did their great-great-grandparents, who graduated before World War I. For that earlier generation, liberal arts and *allgemeine Bildung* remained meaningful throughout their lives, and defined their identity. They still remained meaningful for many members of my generation, which graduated before World War II—even though we immediately forgot our Latin and Greek. But all over the world today's students, a few years after they have graduated, complain that "what I have learned so eagerly has no meaning; it has no relevance to anything I am interested in or want to become." They still want a liberal arts curriculum for their own children—Princeton or Carleton, Oxbridge, Tokyo University, the *lycée,* the *Gymnasium*—though mainly for social status and access to good jobs. But in their own lives, they repudiate such values. They repudiate the educated person of the humanists. Their liberal education, in other words, does not enable them to understand reality, let alone to master it.

Both sides in the present debate are largely irrelevant. The knowledge society needs the educated person even more than any earlier society did, and access to the great heritage of the past will have to be an essential element. But this heritage will embrace a good deal more than the civilization that is still mainly Western, the Judeo-Christian tradition, for which the humanists are fighting. The educated person we need will have to be able to appreciate other cultures and traditions: the great heritage of Chinese, Japanese, Korean paintings and ceramics; the philosophers and religions of the Orient; and Islam, both as a religion and as a culture. The educated person also will have to be far less exclusively "bookish" than the product of the liberal education of the humanists. He or she will need trained *perception* fully as much as *analysis.*

The Western tradition will, however, still have to be at the core, if only to enable the educated person to come to grips with the present, let alone the future. The future may be "post-Western"; it may be "anti-Western." It cannot be "non-Western." Its material civilization and its knowledges all rest on Western foundations: Western science, tools and technology, production, economics; Western-style finance and banking. None of these can work unless grounded in an understanding and acceptance of Western ideas and of the entire Western tradition.

The most profoundly "anti-Western" movement today is not only Fundamentalist

Islam. It is the kind of revolt represented by the "Shining Path" in Peru—the desperate attempt of the descendants of the Incas to undo the Spanish Conquest, to go back to the Indians' ancient tongues of Quechua and Aymara, and to drive the hated Europeans and their culture back into the ocean. But this anti-Western rebellion finances itself by growing coca for the drug addicts of New York and Los Angeles. Its favorite weapon is not the Incas' slingshot; it is the car bomb.

Tomorrow's educated person will have to be prepared for life in a global world. It will be a "Westernized" world, but also increasingly a tribalized world. He or she must become a "citizen of the world"—in vision, in horizon, in information. But he or she will also have to draw nourishment from his or her own local roots and, in turn, enrich and nourish his or her own local culture.

KNOWLEDGE SOCIETY AND SOCIETY OF ORGANIZATIONS

The postcapitalist society is both a knowledge society and a society of organizations, each dependent on the other and yet each very different in its concepts, views, and values. Most, if not all, educated persons will practice their knowledge as members of an organization. The educated person will, therefore, have to be prepared to live and work simultaneously in two cultures—that of the "intellectual," who focuses on words and ideas, and that of the "manager," who focuses on people and work.

Intellectuals see the organization as a tool; it enables them to practice their *techne,* their specialized knowledge. Managers see knowledge as a means to an end of organizational performance. Both are right. They are opposites; but they relate to each other as poles rather than as contradictions. They surely need each other: the research scientist needs the research manager just as much as the research manager needs the research scientist. If one overbalances the other, there is only nonperformance and all-around frustration. The intellectual's world, unless counterbalanced by the manager, becomes one in which everybody "does his own thing" but nobody achieves anything. The manager's world, unless counterbalanced by the intellectual, becomes the stultifying bureaucracy of the "organization man." But if the two balance each other, there can be creativity and order, fulfillment and mission.

A good many people in the knowledge society will actually live and work in these two cultures at the same time. And many more should be exposed to working experience in both cultures, by rotation early in their careers—from a specialist's job to a managerial one, for instance, rotating the young computer technician into project manager and team leader, or by asking the young college professor to work part-time for two years in university administration. And again, working as "unpaid staff" in an agency of the social sector will give the individual the perspective, the balance, to respect both worlds, that of the intellectual and that of the manager.

All educated persons in the postcapitalist society will have to be prepared to understand both cultures.

TECHNES AND EDUCATED PERSON

For the educated person in the nineteenth century, *technes* were not knowledge. They were already taught in the university and had become "disciplines." Their practitioners were "professionals," rather than "tradesmen" or "artisans." But they were not part of the liberal arts or the *allgemeine Bildung,* and thus not part of knowledge.

University degrees in *technes* go back a long way: in Europe, both the law degree and the medical degree as far back as the thirteenth century. And on the Continent and in America—though not in England—the new engineering degree (first awarded in Napoleon's France a year or two before 1800) soon became socially accepted. Most people who were considered "educated" made their living practicing a *techne*—whether as lawyers, physicians, engineers, geologists, or, increasingly, in business (only in England was there esteem for the "gentleman" without occupation). But their job or their profession was seen as a "living," not a "life."

Outside their offices, the *techne* practitioners or technologists did not talk about their work or even about their disciplines. That was "shop talk"; the Germans sneered at it as "*Fachsimpelei.*" It was even more derided in France: anyone who indulged in shop talk there was considered a boor and a bore, and promptly taken off the invitation lists of polite society.

But now that the *techne* or technologies have become knowledges in the plural, they have to be integrated into knowledge. The *technes* have to become part of what it means to be an educated person. The fact that the liberal arts curriculum they enjoyed so much in their college years refuses to attempt this is the reason why today's students repudiate it a few years later. They feel let down, even betrayed. They have good reason to feel that way. Liberal arts and *allgemeine Bildung* that do not integrate the knowledges into a "universe of knowledge" are neither "liberal" nor "*Bildung.*" They fall down on their first task: to create mutual understanding, that "universe of discourse" without which there can be no civilization. Instead of uniting, such disciplines only fragment. We neither need nor will get "polymaths" who are at home in much knowledge; in fact, we will probably become even more specialized. But what we do need—and what will define the educated person in the knowledge society—is the ability to understand the various knowledges. What is each one about? What is it trying to do? What are its central concerns and theories? What major new insights has it produced? What are its important areas of ignorance, its problems, and its challenges?

TO MAKE KNOWLEDGES A PATH TO KNOWLEDGE

Without such understanding, the knowledges themselves will become sterile, will, indeed, cease to be "knowledges." They will become intellectually arrogant and unproductive. For the major new insights in every one of the specialized knowledges arise out of another, separate specialty, out of another one of the knowledges.

Both economics and meteorology are being transformed at present by the new mathematics of chaos theory. Geology is being profoundly changed by the physics of matter; archaeology, by the genetics of DNA typing; history, by psychological, statistical, and technological analyses and techniques. An American, James M. Buchanan (b. 1919), received the 1986 Nobel Prize in Economics for applying recent economic theory to the political process and thereby standing on their heads the assumptions and theories on which political scientists had based their work for over a century.

The specialists have to take responsibility for making both themselves and their specialty understood. The media, whether magazines, movies, or television, have a crucial role to play. But they cannot do the job by themselves. Nor can any other kind of popularization. Specialties must be understood for what they are: serious, rigorous, demanding disciplines. This requires that the leaders in each of the knowledges, beginning with the leading scholars in each field, must take on the hard work of defining what it is they do.

There is no "Queen of the Knowledges" in the knowledge society. All knowledges are equally valuable; all knowledges, in the words of the great medieval saint and philosopher Saint Bonaventura, lead equally to the truth. But making them paths to truth, paths to knowledge, has to be the responsibility of the men and women who own these knowledges. Collectively, they hold knowledge in trust.

Capitalism had been dominant for over a century when Karl Marx in the first volume of *Das Kapital* identified it (in 1867) as a distinct social order. The term "capitalism" was not coined until thirty years later, well after Marx's death. It would, therefore, not only be presumptuous in the extreme to attempt to write *The Knowledge* today; it would be ludicrously premature. All that can be attempted is to describe society and polity as we begin the transition from the Age of Capitalism (also, of course, from the Age of Socialism).

But we can hope that a hundred years hence a book of this kind, if not one entitled *The Knowledge*, can be written. That would mean that we have successfully weathered the transition upon which we have only just embarked. It would be as foolish to predict *The Knowledge* as it would have been foolish to predict in 1776—the year of the American Revolution, of Adam Smith's *Wealth of Nations*, and of James Watt's steam engine—the society of which Marx wrote a hundred years later. And it was as foolish of Marx to predict in mid-Victorian capitalism—and with "scientific infallibility"—the society in which we live now.

But one thing we can predict: The greatest change will be the *change in knowledge*—in its form and content, in its meaning, in its responsibility, and in what it means to be an educated person.

SUMMARY

The knowledge society changes the very idea of what it means to be an educated person. In earlier societies, the educated person was an ornament. Now the educated person is the knowledge society's chief representative and key resource. This brings new responsibilities and new demands on the individual. The person educated in the liberal arts must not only know the great traditions of the past but be able to perceive and come to grips with reality so as to gain mastery over it.

The educated person will have to be able to understand the world's cultures, religions, and traditions and not limit himself or herself only to knowledge of Western civilization. In an age of rapid change and turning points such as the one in which we are now living, the educated person will have to be trained in *perception* fully as much as in *analysis*.

The educated person will have to become familiar with knowledges in multiple disciplines, because changes in one discipline often originate from innovations in another discipline. The integration of knowledges will increasingly be a part of the work of the manager. This requires continuous learning and teaching. Making one's specialized knowledge accessible to those whose specialty is a different discipline will become increasingly necessary for managing knowledge organizations as knowledge splinters further.

Conclusion

The Manager of Tomorrow

Today's student in the college course in management will still be active and working forty-five or fifty years hence—into the third quarter of the twenty-first century.

A century ago, no one could have predicted the world of 1950 or 1960. And no one in the 1960s, when many of today's managers began their college studies or went to work, could have predicted the world of 2008. The one thing one can predict about the politics, society, and economy that lie half a century ahead is that there will be great changes.

Yet one can also predict, with high probability, some important things with respect to the manager of tomorrow—that is, the management student of today. There will surely be new skills and, with them, a need for the manager of tomorrow to organize his or her own self-development and to acquire the habit of *continuous learning*. Yet the three tasks of the manager will be the same. Managers of tomorrow will have, as their first responsibility, the *performance of the institution* for which they work. They will be responsible for *making work productive* and *the worker achieving*. And the task of *managing social impact* and *social responsibilities* will hardly become less important or less demanding. The managers of tomorrow will, in other words, concern themselves with the same tasks as the managers of today, will worry about the same things, will face similar problems and similar demands—though they will be expected to tackle these tasks with more knowledge, more thought, more planning, and greater competence in order to operate in the knowledge society.

First, managers will have to learn how to manage in situations where they do not have command authority, where they are neither controlled nor controlling. That is a fundamental change. Management textbooks still talk mainly about managing subordinates. But one can no longer evaluate an executive in terms of how many people report to him or her. That standard doesn't mean as much as the complexity of the job, the information it uses and generates, the contribution expected, and the different kinds of relationships needed to do the work.

Similarly, business news still refers to managing subsidiaries. But this is the control approach of the 1950s or 1960s. Businesses used to grow in one of two ways: from grassroots up or by acquisition. In both cases, the manager had control. Today businesses often grow through alliances, all kinds of dangerous liaisons and joint ventures, which very few managers understand how to effectively manage. This new type of growth upsets the traditional manager who believes he or she must own or control sources and markets.

Managers will have to make productive people who work for them but are not employees. It is probable that an enterprise will eventually outsource most work that does not have a career ladder up to senior management. To get productivity, you should consider outsourcing activities that lack their own senior management. The trend toward outsourcing has less to do with economizing and a great deal to do with quality.

Managers still talk about the people who "report" to them, but that word should be stricken from management vocabulary. *Information is replacing authority.* A company treasurer with outsourced information technology may have only two assistants and a receptionist, but his or her decisions in foreign exchange can lose—or make—more money in a day than the rest of the company makes all year. A scientist decides which research to do in a big company lab. He doesn't even have a secretary or a title, but his track record means that he is not apt to be overruled. He may have more effect on results than the CEO. In the military, a lieutenant colonel used to command a battalion, but today he may have only a receptionist and be in charge of liaisons with a major foreign country.

One can, however, also anticipate significant expansion in the application of managerial tasks. One of them will surely be a major thrust toward systematic management in the public-service institution—whether government agency, hospital, school, or university. Indeed, the frontier of management in this half of the twenty-first century is likely to be in the public-service institution, just as the frontier of management in the last seventy years was in business enterprise.

But there are also major priorities with respect to each of the major task areas that will, in all likelihood, demand systematic work on the part of the managers of tomorrow. In the first task area—that of the specific *performance* of business and of the public-service institution—the biggest immediate problem is to organize for *systematic abandonment* of the obsolete, the unproductive, the no longer appropriate. We have learned a great deal about innovation as an organized activity. At least we have learned that the making of a different tomorrow is a major responsibility of managers. Now we will have to learn that sloughing off yesterday is also a central managerial task. And this is something that managers in public-service institutions, in particular, have yet to learn. So far, public-service institutions have rarely abandoned the obsolete, and almost never done so systematically.

In the area of *work and working,* the big job ahead is to make the management of human resources within our organizations conform to social reality. Within the last seventy years, the "working class" has changed dramatically in all developed countries. Today's worker is likely to be a "knowledge worker" rather than a "manual worker." Indeed, the "blue collar worker" in manufacturing industry is already a distinct minority in all developed countries, and likely to be a very small segment of the working population by the year 2020. But even the manual worker of today, the blue-collar worker in manufacturing industry, is very different in income and above all in education, from the manual worker of yesterday. The traditional line between "worker" and "owner" is fast disappearing; it is already an anachronism, no matter how strong its emotional hold on our rhetoric. For, through the pension fund, employees (especially in the United States) are fast becoming the true owners of commerce. In the United States today, employee pension funds own about one-third of industry, and a good deal more of the truly big companies. By 2020, pension fund ownership of the share capital of American business will have risen to 50 percent or so—again, considerably more with respect to big business. Other developed countries are reaching the same end through different routes and with different mechanisms.

This will not usher in Utopia in the management of human resources. The old tensions, problems, and conflicts of work and working discussed in this book will remain. But the emergence of the worker as a true owner through pension funds—even though the worker does not directly control business—will make both possible and necessary systematic and purposeful work toward what this book has called "the responsible worker," the worker who, regardless of job, takes a high degree of managerial responsibility for his or her own task, his or her own work group, and for the governance of the work community and its concerns. Not much innovation is required. A good many businesses, for well over a hundred years, have been doing the job. But what has been the isolated exception will have to become general rule. The needed changes will again be greatest in public-service institutions. For in managing work and working, public-service institutions, by and large, are well behind any reasonably well-managed business.

The next change in managing work and working is the need to manage one's own career. Even today, remarkably few Americans are prepared to select jobs for themselves. When you ask, "Do you know what you are good at? Do you know your limitations?" they look at you with a blank stare. Or they often respond in terms of subject knowledge, which is the wrong answer. When they prepare their résumés, they still try to list positions like steps up a ladder. It is time to give up thinking of jobs or career paths as we once did and to think in terms of taking on assignments and acquiring competencies one after the other.

It is a very difficult thing to think through who you are and what you do best. In helping people learn how to be responsible, our educational system is more and more counterproductive. The longer you stay in school, the fewer decisions you have to make. For instance, the decision whether to take French II or Art History may be based on whether one likes to get up early in the morning. And graduate school is much worse.

Most graduates start with big companies because they have not figured out where to place themselves, and companies send in the recruiters. But as soon as the recruits get through training and into a job, they have to start making decisions about the future. Nobody's going to do it for them.

And once they start making decisions, many of the best will move to midsize companies in three to five years, because there they can break through to top management. With less emphasis on seniority, a person can go upstairs and say, "I've been in accounting for three years, and I'm ready to go into marketing."

Strange as it may seem, a knowledge economy's greatest pitfall is in becoming a Mandarin meritocracy. You see creeping credentialism all around. Why should people find it necessary to tell me so-and-so is really a good researcher even though he or she doesn't have a PhD? It's easy to fall into the trap because degrees are black-and-white. But it takes *judgment to weigh a person's contribution*.

You not only have to understand your own competencies, but you also have to learn the strengths of the men and women to whom you assign duties, as well as those of your peers and boss. Too many managers still go by averages. They still talk about "our engineers." And I say, "Brother, you don't have engineers. You have Joe and Mary and Jim and Bob, and each is different." You can no longer manage a workforce. You lead individuals. You have to know them so well you can go and say, "Mary, you think you ought to move up to this next job? Well, then you have to learn not to have that chip on your shoulder. Forget you are a woman; you are an engineer. And you have to be a little considerate. Do not come in at ten minutes to five on Friday afternoon to tell people they have to work overtime when you knew it at nine AM."

The key to the productivity of knowledge workers is to make them concentrate on the real assignment. Do you know why most promotions now fail? Poor fit. The standard case, of course, is the star salesman promoted to sales manager. That job can be any one of four things—a manager of salespeople, a market manager, a brand manager, or a super salesman who opens up an entire new area. But nobody figures out what it is, so the man or woman who got the promotion just tries to do more of whatever led to the promotion. That's the surest way to be wrong.

One of the worst problems in managing knowledge workers is the assumption among knowledge workers that if you are understandable, you are vulgar. When I was growing up, it was taken for granted that economists, physicists, psychologists, leaders in any discipline, would make themselves understood. Einstein spent years with three different collaborators to make his theory of relativity accessible to the layman. Even John Maynard Keynes tried hard to make his economics accessible.

We cannot afford arrogance among knowledge workers. Knowledge is power, which is why people who had it in the past often tried to make a secret of it. In knowledge work, power comes from transmitting information to make it productive, not from hiding it.

That means you have to be intolerant of intellectual arrogance. At whatever level, knowledge people must make themselves understood, and whatever field the manager comes from, he or she must be eager to understand others. This may be the main job of the manager of technical people. He or she must not only be an interpreter but also work out a balance between specializations and exposure.

The productivity of knowledge has both a qualitative and a quantitative dimension. We know executives must be both managers of specialists and synthesizers of different fields of knowledge—really of *knowledges,* plural. This situation is as threatening to the traditional manager, who worries about high-falutin highbrows, as it is to the intellectual, who worries about being too commercial to earn respect in his or her discipline. But in the knowledge-based organization, the highbrow and the lowbrow have to play on the same team.

Finally, with respect to managing social impact and social responsibility, managers will have to learn how to think through systematically and carefully the difficult and risky "trade-offs" between conflicting needs and conflicting rights. At the same time, managers will have to learn to think ahead with respect to the social impacts of the institutions—whether business enterprises, schools and colleges, hospitals, or government agencies; whether the impacts are technological or social; and whether they are impacts on individuals within the organization or on society, community, and the environment outside. This is a leadership responsibility. And in a society of organizations, managers as a group are the leadership—however modest the personal role and individual power of a specific manager might be.

These are new challenges for management and new demands on it. But one can also predict a major change for the individual manager. The manager of tomorrow will increasingly have more than one career. Increasingly, men and women will change their work, their environment, their own role, sometime between the ages of forty and fifty. And the more successful a person is as a manager or professional, the more likely that he or she will make such a career change. It may only be a move from one company to another or a shift from accounting work to sales management.

But it may also be a move from one kind of institution to another. The successful controller of a fair-sized company may move, as administrator, into a hospital, for instance. "Second careers" are by no means uncommon today. However, tomorrow they may well have become the accepted rule, though we still look upon them as an exception. One reason, and by no means the only one, is the employee pension plan—especially the pension plan of businesses. They now give the middle-aged manager and professional a substantial degree of economic security, where hitherto economic uncertainty alone tended to keep people in jobs and employment they had outgrown, had become bored with, and had ceased to feel as challenging and enjoyable. And this, it is safe to predict, will put a high premium on continued learning by managers, on their taking responsibility for self-development as a person and as a manager, and on a thorough knowledge of a manager's work, managerial skills, and managerial tools.

But the most important thing one can predict, with respect to the manager of tomorrow, is that there will be a manager of tomorrow, one defined by *expected contribution*. In all likelihood, there will be more managers tomorrow than there are today, and they will matter more. Unless mankind destroys itself in some such self-inflicted catastrophe as nuclear war, society will continue to be a society of organizations and a knowledge society. And to the degree to which developing nations advance socially and economically, they will increasingly become societies of organizations *too*.

Organizations are far from perfect. As every manager knows, they are very difficult; full of frustration, tension, and friction; clumsy and unwieldy. But they are the only tools we have to accomplish such social purposes as economic production and distribution, health care, governance, and education. And there is not the slightest reason to expect society to be willing to do without these services that only performing organizations can provide. Indeed, there is every reason to expect society to demand more performance from all its institutions, and to become more dependent upon their performance.

And it is managers who make institutions perform.

Author's Note

The revised edition of *Management* is a distillation and synthesis of the writings of Peter F. Drucker on management and society with an emphasis on his published and unpublished writings between 1973, the year of publication of the original edition of *Management: Tasks, Responsibilities, Practices* (*MTRP*), and his death on November 11, 2005. His publications during this period were more extensive than his publications from 1954 to 1973, the time period between publication of *The Practice of Management* (1954) and publication of *MTRP*.

I was a colleague of Peter Drucker from 1979 until his death in 2005. In 1999, Professor Drucker began to reduce his teaching, and I began to develop and teach the graduate course Drucker on Management to MBA and executive students. Peter Drucker gave me advice on teaching that I will never forget: focus on general management and make sure students apply the principles of management either directly to their work or indirectly to cases. He wrote a book of cases precisely for this purpose.

Beginning in early 2001, Peter Drucker offered me the opportunity to collaborate with him on a number of writing projects, including *The Daily Drucker* and *The Effective Executive in Action*. I always felt like I was in the presence of a master. Working with him was a transformative experience for which I will always be grateful. I will never forget the lessons I learned such as: his concern for the dignity and development of the human being; his emphasis on mission and results; and his uncompromising demand for integrity in personal relationships.

I trace the idea for revision of this book back to a conversation I had with Peter Drucker in December 2001. After a wonderful lunch, during which he offered career advice to my son, I drove him home. During the drive I asked him when he was going to revise "the big" management book. "Never" he shouted! Stunned, I boldly asked, "Well, then, how are we going to continue to teach your material?" "Look around" he said, "it's all there."

My work with him on *The Daily Drucker* provided me the opportunity to "look around" at all of his work. It was a humbling exercise; I was amazed at the breadth and depth of his life's work.

On June 8, 2005, I was with Peter Drucker at his home as he reviewed and edited an early draft of *The Effective Executive in Action*. When he finished, he turned to me and said, "I understand you want to revise my book, *The Practice of Management*." He shocked me still again and I said "No, I would like to revise your management book." He said, "There is no such book" to which I said, "*Management: Tasks, Responsibilities, Practices*." "Oh," he said, "that is going to be a lot of work." I nodded, and he said, "Okay."

Now that the revised edition is published, I look back and recognize just how many people have helped me. First and foremost, Peter Drucker and his wife, Doris. They gave me the opportunity. It is my hope that this book captures the heart of Peter Drucker's work on management and extends his influence. He has shown us how to manage organizations to achieve results and to develop people in the process. He has shown us how to be successful and socially responsible at the same time.

Joan Drucker Winstein, co-trustee of the Drucker Literary Trust, worked with Ethan Friedman, senior editor of HarperCollins, to make the book a reality. I am very grateful to Joan and Ethan for their confidence and help.

Sarah Brown, editorial assistant, and Matt Inman, assistant editior, at Harper-Collins provided valuable assistance from the beginning to the end of this project. I thank Sarah and Matt for their help. I also owe a debt of gratitude to Diane Aronson, senior copy chief at HarperCollins, and to Ceci Hunt, the copyeditor of this book.

Emily Trent and Kazumi Sakuhara served as my assistants and helped me to organize the Drucker body of knowledge. They served as able colleagues and friends over a two-year period of time. Jasper Spencer-Scheurich helped me to review the copyedited manuscript and the page proofs. He helped me meet the editorial and production deadlines for the book. These three assistants have my profound thanks.

Jacob High, Drucker Institute archivist, worked with me to identify, obtain and organized all primary source material for the book. My thanks to Jacob.

Dean Ira Jackson of the Peter F. Drucker and Masatoshi Ito Graduate School of Management organized the Drucker Institute. With his help and the help of Rick Wartzman, director, and Zach First, assistant director of the Drucker Institute, projects like this one have become possible. They have my thanks.

My assistant Bernadette Lambeth has assisted me every day. She is calm and positive and created an environment that helped me to be productive. My thanks to Bernadette.

Finally, my wife, Judy, has done it again. Her encouragement and patience with me have allowed me to spend the majority of my time during the past two years working on this book. She has the gift of giving and she is God's gift to me.

Joseph A. Maciariello
December 2007

Bibliography

Management literature has become so voluminous that no one can hope to keep up with it. Even to pick out the "best" books is a fruitless attempt. What we have tried to do is prepare a list of the books that a fairly large number of friends, experienced managers in a number of countries around the world, have found to be stimulating, readable, and worthwhile.

To make the list more useful, the books have been divided into major categories and a title is listed in more than one category if it seemed to deserve mention in several categories.

AMERICAN BOOKS ABOUT PETER F. DRUCKER

Beatty, Jack. *The World According to Peter Drucker*. New York: Free Press, 1998.

Cohen, William A. *A Class with Drucker: The Lost Lessons of the World's Greatest Management Teacher*. New York: AMACOM, November 2007.

Eldersheim, Elizabeth Hass. *The Definitive Drucker*. New York: McGraw-Hill, 2006.

Flannerty, John E. *Shaping the Managerial Mind—How the World's Foremost Management Thinker Crafted the Essentials of Business Success*. San Francisco: Jossey-Bass, 1999.

Tarrant, John J. *Drucker: The Man Who Invented the Corporate Society*. Boston: Cahners Books, 1976.

1. ORIGINS, FOUNDATIONS, AND TASKS OF MANAGEMENT

Chandler, Alfred D., Jr. *Strategy and Structure*. London: MIT Press, 1962.

Chandler, Alfred D., Jr. *The Visible Hand: The Managerial Revolution in American Business*. Cambridge, MA: Belknap Press of Harvard University Press, 1993 (new edition).

Chandler, Alfred D., Jr., and Stephen Salisbury. *Pierre S. DuPont and the Making of the Modern Corporation*. New York: Harper & Row, 1971.

Drucker, Peter F. *Concept of the Corporation*. Rutgers, NJ: Transaction Publishers, 1993. Originally published by John Day Company, NY, 1946.

Drucker, Peter F. *The Future of Industrial Man.* Rutgers, NJ: Transaction Publishers, 1995. Originally published by John Day Company, NY, 1942.

Drucker, Peter F. *The New Society.* Rutgers, NJ: Transaction Publishers, 1993. Originally published by John Day Company, NY, 1950.

Drucker, Peter F. *The Post-Capitalist Society.* New York: HarperCollins, 1993.

Landes, David S. *The Unbound Prometheus: Technological Change and Industrial Development in Western Europe from 1750 to the present.* Cambridge, UK: Cambridge University Press, 1969.

Machlup, Fritz. *The Production and Distribution of Knowledge in the United States,* Princeton, NJ: Princeton University Press, 1962.

Maciariello, Joseph A. "Peter Drucker on Executive Leadership and Effectiveness," in *Leader of the Future 2.* Edited by Frances Hesselbein and Marshall Goldsmith, San Francisco: Jossey-Bass, 2006, pp. 3–27.

Maciariello, Joseph. "Peter F. Drucker on a Functioning Society." *Leader to Leader* (Summer 2005).

McCraw, Thomas K. *Prophet of Innovation: Joseph Schumpeter and Creative Destruction,* Cambridge, MA: Belnap Press of Harvard University Press, 2007.

Nevins, Allan, and Frank E. Hill. *Ford: Decline and Rebirth 1911–1962.* New York: Scribner, 1962, 1963.

Schumpeter, Joseph. *Capitalism, Socialism and Democracy.* London: Allen & Unwin, 1950.

Schumpeter, Joseph. *The Theory of Economic Development.* Cambridge, MA: Harvard University Press, 1934. Original German edition, 1911.

Siemens, George. *Der Wegtler Elektrotechnik: Geschichte des Hawes Siemens.* Freiburg: Alber, 1961.

Sloan, Alfred P., Jr. *My Years with General Motors.* New York: Doubleday, 1963, 1990.

Watts, Steven. *The People's Tycoon: Henry Ford and the American Century.* New York: Knopf, 2005.

Woodruff, Philip. *The Men Who Ruled India.* 2 vols. London: Macmillan, 1954.

2. MANAGEMENT AS A PROCESS AND A DISCIPLINE

Drucker, Peter F. *Management Challenges for the 21st Century.* New York: HarperCollins, 1999.

Drucker, Peter F. *Managing the Nonprofit Organization.* New York: HarperCollins, 1990.

Drucker, Peter F. *The Practice of Management.* New York: HarperCollins, 1993. Originally published by Harper & Row, 1954.

Gantt, Henry. *Gantt on Management.* Edited by Alex W. Rathe. New York: American Management Association, 1961.

Leader to Leader Institute. *The Drucker Foundation Self-Assessment Tool.* 2nd ed. San Francisco: Jossey-Bass, 1998.

Simon, Herbert A. *Administrative Behavior.* 4th ed. New York: Free Press, 1997.

Urwick, Lyndall F., and E.F.L. Brech. *The Making of Scientific Management.* Facsimile edition. Thoemmes Continuum. 2002. Originally published by Pitman, London, 1966.

3. MANAGEMENT IN JAPAN

Liker, Jeffrey K. *The Toyota Way.* New York: McGraw-Hill, 2004.

Womack, James P., Daniel T. Jones, and Daniel Roos. *The Machine That Changed the World: The Story of Lean Production—Toyota's Secret Weapon in the Global Car Wars That Is Now Revolutionizing World Industry.* Paperback ed. New York: Free Press, 2007.

4. MANAGING FOR PERFORMANCE

Collins, Jim. *Good to Great.* New York: HarperCollins, 2001.

Drucker, Peter F. *Managing for Results.* New York: HarperCollins, 1993. Originally published by Harper & Row, 1964.

Drucker, Peter F. "Not Enough Generals Were Killed." Foreword in *The Leader of the Future.* Edited by Frances Hesselbein, Marshall Goldsmith, and Richard Beckhard. San Francisco: Jossey-Bass, pp. xi–xv.

Gerstner, Louis V. *Who Says Elephants Can't Dance: Leading a Great Enterprise through Dramatic Change.* New York: HarperCollins, 2002.

Interviews and Postscript by Joseph A. Maciariello. *The Journal of Management, Spirituality & Religion.* Special issue. *Values and Virtues in Organizations.* Edited by Charles C. Manz, Kim S. Cameron, Karen P. Manz, and Robert D. Marx. Vol. 3, nos. 1 and 2 (2006).

Penrose, Edith R. *The Theory of the Growth of the Firm.* 3rd ed. New York: Oxford University Press, 1995.

Porter, Michael E. "Strategy and the Internet." *Harvard Business Review* (June 2001).

Prahalad, C. K., and V. Hamel. *Competing for the Future.* New York: Free Press, 1995.

Rose, Stuart. "Back in Fashion: How We're Reviving a British Icon," *Harvard Business Review.* May 2007.

Warren, Rick. *Purpose-Driven Church.* Grand Rapids, MI: Zondervan, 1995.

Welch, Jack. *Winning.* New York: HarperCollins, 2005.

Schumpeter, Joseph. *The Theory of Economic Development.* Cambridge, MA: Harvard University Press, 1934.

5. WORK AND WORKER

Davenport, Thomas H. *Thinking for a Living: How to Get Better Performance and Results from Knowledge Workers.* Boston: Harvard Business School Press, 2005.

Friedman, Thomas, L. *The World Is Flat.* New York: Farrar, Straus & Giroux, 2005. Updated and expanded edition, 2006.

Herzberg, Frederick. *Work and the Nature of Man.* London: Staples Press, 1968.

Herzberg, Frederick, B. Mausner, and B. R. Snyderman. *The Motivation to Work.* New York: Wiley, 1959.

Likert, Rensis. *The Human Organization.* New York: McGraw-Hill, 1967.

Malone, Thomas W. *The Future of Work.* Boston: Harvard Business School Press, 2004.

Maslow, A. H. *Eupsychian Management: A Journal.* Burr Ridge, IL: Richard D. Irwin, 1965.

Maslow, A. H. *Motivation and Personality.* London: Harper & Row, 1970.

Mayo, Elton. *The Human Problems of an Industrial Civilization.* Boston: Harvard Business School Press, 1946.

Mayo, Elton. *The Social Problems of an Industrial Civilization.* London: Routledge & Kegan Paul, 1949.

McGregor, Douglas. *The Human Side of Enterprise.* New York: McGraw-Hill, 1960.

Taylor, F. W. *Scientific Management.* New York: Harpers, 1912 (and many editions since).

Wiener, Norbert. *The Human Use of Human Beings.* London: Sphere Books, 1969.

Womack, James P., Daniel T. Jones, and Daniel Roos. *The Machine That Changed the World: The Story of Lean Production—Toyota's Secret Weapon in the Global Car Wars That Is Now Revolutionizing World Industry.* Paperback ed. New York: Free Press, 2007.

6. SOCIAL IMPACTS AND SOCIAL RESPONSIBILITIES

Drucker, Peter F. "What Is Business Ethics?" *The Public Interest* (Spring 1981) pp. 18–36.

Friedman, Milton. "The Social Responsibility of Business Is to Increase Its Profits." *The New York Times Magazine,* September 13, 1970.

7. THE MANAGER'S WORK AND JOB

Barnard, Chester I. *The Functions of the Executive.* Cambridge, MA: Harvard University Press, 1938, reprinted 1968.

Drucker, Peter F. *The Effective Executive.* New York: HarperCollins, 2005. Originally published by Harper & Row, 1966.

Follet, Mary Parker. *Mary Parker Follet Prophet of Management: A Celebration of the Writings from the 1920s.* 1st ed. Edited by Pauline Graham. Boston, MA: Harvard Business School Press, 1995.

Ghoshal, Sumantra. "Bad Management Theories Are Destroying Good Management Practices," *Academy of Management Learning & Education,* Vol. 4 No. 1, 75–91.

McGregor, Douglas. *The Professional Manager.* New York: McGraw-Hill, 1967.

8. MANAGERIAL SKILLS AND MANAGERIAL TOOLS

Allison, Graham, and Phillip Zelikow. *Essence of Decision: Explaining the Cuban Missile Crisis.* 2nd ed. New York: Longman, 1999.

Anthony, Robert N., and Vijay Govindaragan. *Management Control Systems.* 12th ed. New York: McGraw-Hill Irwin, 2007.

Anthony, Robert N., and David W. Young. *Management Control in Nonprofit Organizations.* 6th ed. Burr Ridge, IL: Richard D. Irwin, 1999.

Chandler, Alfred D., Jr. *Scale and Scope: The Dynamics of American Capitalism.* Cambridge, MA: Harvard University Press, 1990.

Cooper, Robin, and Robert S. Kaplan. *The Design of Cost Management Systems.* 2nd ed. Englewood Cliffs, NJ: Prentice Hall, 1998.

Forrester, Jay W. *Industrial Dynamics.* Cambridge, MA: MIT Press, 1961.

Kaplan, Robert S., and David P. Norton. *Alignment: Using the Balanced Scorecard to Create Corporate Synergies.* Boston, MA: Harvard Business School Press, 2006.

Kerr, Steven. "On the folly of rewarding A, while hoping for B." *Academy of Management Executive,* 1995, 9(1): 7–14.

Porter, Michael E. *Competitive Strategy.* New York: Free Press, 1980.

Senge, Peter M. *The Fifth Discipline: The Art and Practice of the Learning Organization.* Rev. ed. New York: Doubleday, 2006.

Solomons, David. *Divisional Performance: Measurement and Control.* Homewood, IL: Richard D. Irwin, 1988.

Stewart, Bennet G. *The Quest for Value.* New York: HarperCollins, 1991.

9. ORGANIZATION DESIGN AND STRUCTURE

Drucker, Peter F. *Concept of the Corporation.* Rutgers, NJ: Transaction Publishers, 1993. Originally published by John Day Company, NY, 1946.

Fayol, Henri. *General and Industrial Management.* London: Pitman, 1967.

Galbraith, Jay R. *Designing Organizations.* San Francisco: Jossey-Bass, 1995.

March, James G., and Herbert A. Simon. *Organizations.* 2nd ed. Boston, MA: Blackwell Publishers, 1993.

Sayles, Leonard R., and Margaret K. Chandler. *Managing Large Systems: Organizations for the Future.* New York: Harper & Row, 1971.

Sloan, Alfred P., Jr. *My Years with General Motors.* New York: Doubleday, 1963, reprinted 1990.

Urwick, Lyndall F. *Notes on the Theory of Organization.* New York: American Management Association, 1953.

Vancil, Richard F. *Decentralization: Management Ambiguity by Design.* Homewood, IL: Dow-Jones-Irwin, 1979.

10. THE TOP-MANAGEMENT JOB

Chandler, Alfred D., Jr., and Stephen Salisbury. *Pierre S. DuPont and the Making of the Modern Corporation.* New York: Harper & Row, 1971.

Cloud, Henry. *Integrity: The Courage to Meet the Demands of Reality.* New York: HarperCollins, 2006.

De Geus, Arie. *The Living Company.* Boston, MA: Harvard Business School Press, 2002.

Schien, Edgar H. *The Corporate Culture Survival Guide.* San Francisco: Jossey-Bass, 1999.

Sloan, Alfred P., Jr. *My Years with General Motors.* New York: Doubleday, 1963, reprinted 1990.

Woodruff, Philip. *The Men Who Ruled India.* 2 vols. London: Macmillan, 1954.

11. STRATEGIES AND STRUCTURE

Chandler, Alfred D., Jr., and Stephen Salisbury. *Pierre S. DuPont and the Making of the Modern Corporation.* New York: Harper & Row, 1971.

Dale, Ernest. *The Great Organizers.* New York: McGraw-Hill, 1960.

Sayles, Leonard R., and Margaret K. Chandler. *Managing Large Systems: Organizations for the Future.* New York: Harper & Row, 1971.

Monks, Robert A. G., and Nell Minow. *Corporate Governance,* 4th ed. West Sussex, England: John Wiley & Sons, 2008.

12. THE MULTINATIONAL CORPORATION

Bartlett, Christopher A., and Sumantra Ghoshal. *Managing Across Borders.* Boston: Harvard Business School Press, 1999.

Hofstede, H. "Motivation, Leadership, and Organizations: Do American Theories Apply Abroad?" *Organizational Dynamics* (summer 1980) pp. 42–63.

Yoshino, Michael Y., and Srinivasa U. Rangan. *Strategic Alliances: An Entrepreneurial Approach to Globalization.* Boston: Harvard Business School Press, 1995.

13. THE INNOVATIVE ORGANIZATION

Argyris, Chris, G. *On Organizational Learning.* 2nd ed. Oxford: Blackwell Publishing, 1999.

Christensen, Clayton M. *The Innovator's Dilemma.* New York: HarperCollins, 2003.

Drucker, Peter F. *Innovation and Entrepreneurship.* New York: HarperCollins, 1993. Originally published by Harper & Row, NY, 1985.

Gendron, George. "Flashes of Genius," *Inc.Com* (May 1996): http://www.inc.com/magazine/19960515/2083.html.

14. THE MANAGER OF TOMORROW

Drucker, Peter F. *The Age of Discontinuity.* Rutgers, NJ: Transaction Publishers, 1992. Originally published by Harper & Row, 1969.

Drucker, Peter F. *Management Challenges for the 21st Century.* New York: HarperCollins, 1999.

Drucker, Peter F. *Managing in the Next Society.* New York: St. Martins, 2002.

Drucker Annotated Bibliography

Below is a complete, annotated bibliography of the major books of Peter F. Drucker.

The End of Economic Man: Transaction Publishers, 1995. Originally published by John Day Company, NY, 1939.

The End of Economic Man is Peter Drucker's first full-length book. It is a diagnostic study of the totalitarian state and the first book to study the origins of totalitarianism. He describes the reasons for the rise of fascism and the failures of established institutions that led to its emergence. Drucker develops an understanding of the dynamics of the totalitarian society and helps us to understand the causes of totalitarianism in order to prevent such a catastrophe in the future. Developing social, religious, economic, and political institutions that function effectively will prevent the emergence of circumstances that frequently encourage the totalitarian state.

The Future of Industrial Man: Transaction Publishers, 1995. Originally published by John Day Company, NY, 1942.

Drucker describes the requirements for a functioning society by developing a social theory of society in general and of the industrial society in particular. In *The Future of Industrial Man,* Drucker presents the requirements for any society for it to be both legitimate and functioning. Such a society must give status and function to the individual. The book addresses the question, "How can individual freedom be preserved in an industrial society in light of the dominance of managerial power and the corporation?" Written before the entrance of the United States into World War II, it is optimistic about post–World War II Europe and reaffirms its hopes and values through a time of despair. The book dared to ask, "What do we hope for the postwar world?"

Concept of the Corporation: Transaction Publishers, 1993. Originally published
by John Day Company, NY, 1946.

This classic book is the first to describe and analyze the structure, policies, and
practices of a large corporation, General Motors. The book looks upon a "business" as
an "organization," that is, as a social structure that brings together human beings in
order to satisfy the economic needs and wants of a community. It establishes the "organization" as a distinct entity, and management of an organization as a legitimate
subject of inquiry. The book represents a link between Drucker's first two books on
society and his subsequent writings on management. Detailed information is provided regarding such management practices as decentralization, pricing, and the
roles of profits and of labor unions. Drucker looks at General Motors' managerial organization and attempts to understand what makes the company work so effectively.
Certain questions are addressed, such as: "What are the company's core principles,
and how do they contribute to the success of the organization?" The principles of organization and management at General Motors described in this book became models for organizations worldwide. The book addresses issues that go beyond the
borders of the business corporation, and considers the "corporate state" itself.

The New Society: Transaction Publishers, 1993. Originally published by Harper
& Row Publishers, NY, 1950.

In *The New Society,* Peter Drucker extends his previous works *The Future of Industrial Man* and *Concept of the Corporation* into a systematic, organized analysis of
the industrial society that emerged out of World War II. He analyzes large business enterprises, governments, labor unions, and the place of the individual within
the social context of these institutions. Following publication of the of *The New
Society,* George G. Higgins wrote in *Commonweal,* "Drucker has analyzed, as brilliantly as any modern writer, the problems of industrial relations in the individual
company or 'enterprise.' He is thoroughly at home in economics, political science,
industrial psychology, and industrial sociology, and has succeeded admirably in
harmonizing the findings of all four disciplines and applying them meaningfully
to the practical problems of the 'enterprise.' " Drucker believes that the interests of
the worker, management, and corporation are reconcilable with society. He advances the idea of "the plant community," in which workers are encouraged to take
on more responsibility and act like "managers." He questions whether unions can
survive in their present form if the worker is encouraged to act as a manager.

The Practice of Management: HarperCollins, 1993. Originally published by Harper
& Row Publishers, NY, 1954.

This classic is the first book to define management as a practice and a discipline, thus establishing Drucker as the founder of the discipline of modern man-

agement. Management has been practiced for centuries, but this book systematically defines management as a discipline that can be taught and learned. It provides a systematic guide for practicing managers who want to improve their effectiveness and productivity. It presents "management by objectives" as a genuine philosophy of management that integrates the interests of the corporation with those of the managers and contributors to an organization. Illustrations come from such companies as Ford; GE; Sears, Roebuck & Co.; GM; IBM; and AT&T.

America's Next Twenty Years: Out of print. HarperCollins, Harper & Row Publishers, NY, 1957.

In this collection of essays, Peter Drucker discusses the issues that he believes will be significant in America, including the coming labor shortage, automation, significant wealth in the hands of a few individuals, college education, American politics, and, perhaps most significant, the growing disparity between the "haves" and the "have-nots." In these essays, Drucker identifies the major events that "have already happened" that will "determine the future." "Identifying the future that has already happened" is a major theme of Drucker's many books and essays.

Landmarks of Tomorrow: Transaction Publishers, 1996. Originally published by Harper & Brothers Publishers, NY, 1959.

Landmarks of Tomorrow identifies "the future that has already happened" in three major areas of human life and experience. The first part of the book treats the philosophical shift from a Cartesian universe of mechanical cause to a new universe of pattern, purpose, and configuration. Drucker discusses the need to organize men of knowledge and of high skill for joint effort, and performance as a key component of this change. The second part of the book sketches four realities that challenge the people of the free world: an educated society, economic development, the decline of the effectiveness of government, and the collapse of Eastern culture. The final section of the book is concerned with the spiritual reality of human existence. These are seen as basic elements in late-twentieth-century society. In his new introduction, Peter Drucker revisits the main findings of *Landmarks of Tomorrow* and assesses their validity in relation to today's concerns.

Managing for Results: HarperCollins, 1993. Originally published by Harper & Row Publishers, NY, 1964.

This book focuses upon economic performance as the specific function and contribution of business and the reason for its existence. The effective business, Peter Drucker observes, focuses on opportunities rather than problems. How this focus is achieved in order to make the organization prosper and grow is the subject of this companion to his classic, *The Practice of Management*. The earlier book was chiefly concerned with how management functions as a discipline and practice; this volume shows what the executive decision maker must do to move his enterprise forward. One of the notable accomplishments of this book is its combining of specific economic analysis with the entrepreneurial force in business prosperity. For though it discusses "what to do" more than Drucker's previous works, the book stresses the qualitative aspect of enterprise: every successful business requires a goal and spirit all its own. *Managing for Results* was the first book to describe what is now widely called "business strategy" and to identify what are now called an organization's "core competencies."

The Effective Executive: HarperCollins, 2005. Originally published by Harper & Row Publishers, NY, 1966.

The Effective Executive is a landmark book that develops the specific practices of the executive that lead to effectiveness. It is based on observations of effective executives in business and government. Drucker starts by reminding executives that the measure of effectiveness is the ability to "get the right things done." This involves five practices: (1) managing one's time, (2) focusing on contribution rather than problems, (3) making strengths productive, (4) establishing priorities, and (5) making effective decisions. A major portion of the book is devoted to the process of making effective decisions and the criteria for effective decisions. Numerous examples are provided of executive effectiveness. The book concludes by emphasizing that effectiveness can be learned and must be learned.

The Age of Discontinuity: Transaction Publishers, 1992. Originally published by Harper & Row Publishers, NY, 1969.

Peter Drucker focuses with great clarity and perception on the forces of change that are transforming the economic landscape and creating tomorrow's society. He discerns four major areas of discontinuity underlying contemporary social and cultural reality: (1) the explosion of new technologies resulting in major new industries, (2) the change from an international to a world economy, (3) a new sociopolitical reality of pluralistic institutions that poses drastic political, philosophical, and spiritual challenges, and (4) the new universe of knowledge work based on mass education, along with its implications. *The Age of Discontinuity* is a fascinating and important blueprint for shaping a future already very much with us.

Men, Ideas, and Politics: Out of print. HarperCollins, Harper & Row Publishers, NY, 1971.

This book is a compilation of thirteen essays addressing the issues of society—people, politics, and thought. Included are essays on Henry Ford, Japanese management, and effective presidents. Two articles in particular show aspects of Drucker's thinking that are especially important. One is an essay on "The Unfashionable Kierkegaard," which encourages the development of the spiritual dimension of humankind. The other is on the political philosophy of John C. Calhoun, describing the basic principles of America's pluralism and how they shape government policies and programs.

Technology, Management, and Society: Out of print. HarperCollins, Harper & Row Publishers, NY, 1970.

Technology, Management, and Society presents an overview of the nature of modern technology and its relationships with science, engineering, and religion. The social and political forces that increasingly impinge on technological development are analyzed within the framework of broad institutional change. Peter Drucker's critical perspective will be welcomed by scholars and students troubled by society's growing reliance on technological solutions to complex social and political problems.

Management: Tasks, Responsibilities, Practices: HarperCollins, 1993. Originally published by Harper & Row Publishers, NY, 1973.

This book is a compendium of Drucker on management. It updates and expands on *The Practice of Management*, and is an essential reference book for executives. *Management* is an organized body of knowledge consisting of managerial tasks, managerial work, managerial tools, managerial responsibilities, and the role of top management. According to Peter Drucker, "This book tries to equip the manager with the understanding, the thinking, the knowledge, and the skills for today's and also tomorrow's jobs." This management classic has been developed and tested during more than thirty years of management teaching in universities, executive programs, seminars, and through the author's close work with managers as a consultant for large and small businesses, government agencies, hospitals, and schools.

The Pension Fund Revolution: Transaction Publishers, 1996. Originally published as The Unseen Revolution, by Harper & Row Publishers, NY, 1976.

In this book, Drucker describes how institutional investors, especially pension funds, have become the controlling owners of America's large companies, and the country's "capitalists." He explores how ownership has become highly concentrated in the hands of large institutional investors, and how, through the pension funds, "ownership of the means of production" has become "socialized" without becoming "nationalized." Another theme of this book is the aging of America. Drucker points to the new challenges this trend will pose with respect to health care, pensions, and social security's place in the American economy and society; and how American politics, altogether, would become increasingly dominated by middle-class issues and with the values of elderly people. In the new epilogue, Drucker discusses how the increasing dominance of pension funds represents one of the most startling power shifts in economic history and examines their present-day impact.

Adventures of a Bystander: John Wiley & Sons, 1997. Originally published by Harper & Row Publishers, NY, 1978.

Adventures of a Bystander is Peter Drucker's collection of autobiographical stories and vignettes, in which he paints a portrait of his life and of the larger historical realities of his time. Drucker conveys his life story—from his early teen years in Vienna through the interwar years in Europe, the New Deal era, World War II, and the postwar period in America—through intimate profiles of a host of fascinating people he's known through the years. Along with bankers and courtesans, artists, aristocrats, prophets, and empire builders, we meet members of Drucker's own family and close circle of friends, among them such prominent figures as Sigmund Freud, Henry Luce, Alfred Sloan, John L. Lewis, and Buckminster Fuller. Shedding light on a turbulent and important era, *Adventures of a Bystander* also reflects Peter Drucker himself as a man of imaginative sympathy and enormous interest in people, ideas, and history.

Managing in Turbulent Times: HarperCollins, 1993. Originally published by Harper & Row Publishers, NY, 1980.

This important and timely book concerns the immediate future of business, society, and the economy. We are, says Drucker, entering a new economic era with new trends, new markets, a global economy, new technologies, and new institutions. How will managers and management deal with the turbulence created by these new realities? This book, as Drucker explains it, "is concerned with action, rather than understanding, with decisions, rather than analysis." It deals with the strategies needed to adapt to change and to turn rapid changes into opportunities, that is, to turn the threat of change into productive and profitable action that contributes positively to our society, the economy, and the individual. An organization must be structured to withstand a blow caused by environmental turbulence.

Toward the Next Economics: Out of print. HarperCollins, Harper & Row Publishers, NY, 1981.

These essays cover a wide-ranging collection of topics on business, management, economics, and society. They are all concerned with what Drucker calls "social ecology" and especially with institutions. These essays reflect "the future that has already happened." The essays reflect Drucker's belief that in the decade of the 1970s there were genuine changes in population structure and dynamics, changes in the role of institutions, changes in the relation between the sciences and society, and changes in the fundamental theories about economics and society, long considered as truths. The essays are international in scope.

The Changing World of the Executive: Out of print. Truman Talley Books, NY, 1982.

These essays from *The Wall Street Journal* explore a wide variety of topics. They deal with changes in the workforce—its jobs, its expectations—with the power relationships of a "society of employees," and with changes in technology and in the world economy. They discuss the problems and challenges facing major institutions, including business enterprises, schools, hospitals, and government agencies. They look anew at the tasks and work of executives, at their performance and its measurement, and at executive compensation. However diverse the topics, these chapters have one common theme, the changing world of the executive—changing rapidly within the organization; changing rapidly with respect to the visions, aspirations, and even characteristics of employees, customers, and constituents; changing outside the organization, as well, economically, technologically, socially, politically.

Innovation and Entrepreneurship: HarperCollins, 1993. Originally published by Harper & Row Publishers, NY, 1985.

The first book to present *innovation and entrepreneurship* as a purposeful and systematic discipline. It explains and analyzes the challenges and opportunities presented by the emergence of the entrepreneurial economy in business and public-service institutions. The book is a major contribution to functioning management, organization, and economy. The book is divided into three main sections: (1) The Practice of Innovation, (2) The Practice of Entrepreneurship, and (3) Entrepreneurial Strategies. The author presents innovation and entrepreneurship as both practice and discipline, choosing to focus on the *actions* of the entrepreneur, as opposed to entrepreneurial psychology and temperament. All organizations, including public-service institutions, must become entrepreneurial to survive and prosper in a market economy. The book provides a description of entrepreneurial policies and windows of opportunity for developing innovative practices in both emerging and well-established organizations.

The Frontiers of Management: Truman Talley Books, 1999. Originally published by Truman Talley Books, NY, 1986.

This book is a collection of thirty-five previously published articles and essays, twenty-five of which have appeared on the editorial page of *The Wall Street Journal*.

In a new introduction, Drucker forecasts the business trends of what was then the next millennium. *The Frontiers of Management* is a clear, direct, lively, and comprehensible examination of global trends and management practices. There are chapters dealing with the world economy, hostile takeovers, and the unexpected problems of success. Jobs, younger people, and career gridlock are also covered. Throughout this book, Drucker stresses the importance of forethought and of realizing that "change is opportunity" in every branch of executive decision making.

The New Realities: Transaction Publishers, 2003. Originally published by Harper & Row Publishers, NY, 1989.

This book is about the "next century." Its thesis is that the "next century" is already here, indeed that we are well advanced into it. In this book, Drucker writes about the "social superstructure"—politics and government, society, the economy and economics, social organization, and the new knowledge society. He describes the limits of government and the dangers of "charisma" in leadership. He identifies the future organization as being information-based. While this book is not "futurism," it attempts to define the concerns, the issues, and the controversies that will be realities for years to come. Drucker focuses on what to do today in contemplation of tomorrow. Within self-imposed limitations, he attempts to set the agenda on how to deal with some of the toughest problems we are facing today that have been created by the successes of the past.

Managing the Non-Profit Organization: HarperCollins, 1992. Originally published by HarperCollins, NY, 1990.

The service, or nonprofit, sector of our society is growing rapidly (with more than 8 million employees and more than 80 million volunteers), creating a major need for guidelines and expert advice on how to lead and manage these organizations effectively. This book applies Drucker's perspective on management to nonprofit organizations of all kinds. He gives examples and explanations of mission, leadership, resources, marketing, goals, people development, decision making, and much more. Included are interviews with nine experts that address key issues in the nonprofit sector.

Managing for the Future: Truman Talley/E.P. Dutton, 1992.

Bringing together the most exciting of Drucker's many recent essays on economics, business practices, managing for change, and the evolving shape of the modern corporation, *Managing for the Future* offers important insights and lessons for anyone trying to stay ahead of today's unremitting competition. Drucker's universe is a constantly expanding cosmos composed of four regions in which he demonstrates mastery: (1) the economic forces affecting our lives and liveli-hoods, (2) today's changing workforce and workplaces, (3) the newest manage-ment concepts and practices, and (4) the shape of the organization, including the corporation, as it evolves and responds to ever-increasing tasks and responsibili-ties. Each of this book's chapters explores a business or corporate or "people" problem, and Drucker shows how to solve it or use it as an opportunity for change.

The Ecological Vision: Transaction Publishers, 1993.

The thirty-one essays in this volume were written over a period of more than forty years. These essays range over a wide array of disciplines and subject matter. Yet they all have in common that they are "Essays in Social Ecology" and deal with the man-made environment. They all, in one way or another, deal with the interac-tion between individual and community. And they try to look on the economy, on technology, on art, as dimensions of social experience and as expressions of social values. The last essay in this collection, "The Unfashionable Kierkegaard," was written as an affirmation of the existential, the spiritual, the individual dimension of the Creature. It was written by Drucker to assert that society is not enough—not even for society. It was written to affirm hope. This is an important and per-ceptive volume of essays.

Post-Capitalist Society: Transaction Publishers, 2005. Originally published by HarperCollins, NY, 1993.

In *Post-Capitalist Society,* Peter Drucker describes how every few hundred years a sharp transformation has taken place and greatly affected society—its worldview, its basic values, its business and economics, and its social and political structure. According to Drucker, we are right in the middle of another time of radical change, from the Age of Capitalism and the Nation-State to a Knowledge Society and a Society of Organizations. The primary resource in the post-capitalist society will be knowledge, and the leading social groups will be "knowledge workers." Looking backward and forward, Drucker discusses the Industrial Revolution, the Productivity Revolution, the Management Revolution, and the governance of cor-porations. He explains the new functions of organizations, the economics of knowl-edge, and productivity as a social and economic priority. He covers the transformation from Nation-State to Megastate, the new pluralism of political systems, and the needed turnaround in government. Finally, Drucker details the knowledge issues and the role and use of knowledge in the post-capitalist society. Divided into three parts—Society, Polity, and Knowledge—*Post-Capitalist Society* provides a searching look into the future as well as a vital analysis of the past, focusing on the challenges of the present transition period and how, if we can understand and respond to them, we can create a new future.

Managing in a Time of Great Change: Truman Talley/E.P. Dutton, 1995.

This book compiles essays written by Drucker from 1991 to 1994 and published in the *Harvard Business Review* and *The Wall Street Journal*. All of theses essays are about change: changes in the economy, society, business, and in organizations in general. Drucker's advice on how managers should adjust to these tectonic shifts centers around the rise of the now-ubiquitous knowledge worker and the global economy. In this book, Drucker illuminates the business challenges confronting us today. He examines current management trends and whether they really work, the implications for business in the reinvention of the government, and the shifting balance of power between management and labor.

Drucker on Asia: Out of print. Butterworth-Heinemann, 1995. First published by Diamond, Inc., Tokyo, 1995.

Drucker on Asia is the result of an extensive dialogue between two of the world's leading business figures, Peter F. Drucker and Isao Nakauchi. Their dialogue considers the changes occurring in the economic world today and identifies the challenges that free markets and free enterprises now face, with specific reference to China and Japan. What do these changes mean to Japan? What does Japan have to do in order to achieve a "third economic miracle"? What do these changes mean to society, the individual company, the individual professional and executive? These are the questions that Drucker and Nakauchi address in their brilliant insight into the future economic role of Asia.

Peter Drucker on the Profession of Management: Harvard Business School Press, 1998. Revised edition published as *Classic Drucker: Wisdom from Peter Drucker from the Pages of Harvard Business Review*. Harvard Business School Press, 2006.

This is a significant collection of Peter Drucker's landmark articles from the *Harvard Business Review*. Drucker seeks out, identifies, and examines the most important issues confronting managers, from corporate strategy to management style to social change. This volume provides a rare opportunity to trace the evolution of great shifts in our workplaces and to understand more clearly the role of managers in the ongoing effort to balance change with continuity—the latter a recurring theme in Drucker's writings. These are strategically presented here to address two unifying themes: the first examines the "Manager's Responsibilities," while the second investigates "The Executive's World." Containing an important interview with Drucker on "The Post-Capitalist Executive," as well as a preface by Drucker himself, the volume is edited by Nan Stone, longtime editor of the *Harvard Business Review.*

Management Challenges for the 21st Century: HarperCollins, 1999.

In his first major book since *The Post-Capitalist Society,* Drucker discusses the new paradigms of management—how they have changed and will continue to change our basic assumptions about the practices and principles of management. Drucker analyzes the new realities of strategy, shows how to be a leader in periods of change, and explains the "New Information Revolution," discussing the information an executive needs and the information an executive owes. He also examines knowledge-worker productivity, and shows that changes in the basic attitude of individuals and organizations, as well as structural changes in work itself, are needed for increased productivity. Finally, Drucker addresses the ultimate challenge of managing oneself while meeting the demands on the individual during a longer working life and in an ever-changing workplace.

Managing in the Next Society: St. Martin's Press, 2002.

In this compilation of essays—culled from published magazine articles, including a lengthy essay appearing in *The Economist* in November 2001, and interviews during the period of 1996 to 2002—Drucker has expertly anticipated our ever-changing business society and ever-expanding management roles. He identifies the reality of the "Next Society," which has been shaped by three major trends: the decline of the young portion of the population, the decline of manufacturing, and the transformation of the workforce (together with the social impact of the Information Revolution). Drucker also asserts that e-commerce and e-learning are to the Information Revolution what the railroad was to the Industrial Revolution, and thus, an information society is developing. He speaks, too, of the importance of the social sector (that is, nongovernmental and nonprofit organizations), because NPOs can create what we now need: communities for citizens and especially for highly educated knowledge workers, who increasingly dominate developed societies.

The Daily Drucker (with Joseph A. Maciariello): HarperCollins, 2004.

The Daily Drucker distills the essence of management from Peter F. Drucker's teachings in an easy-to-access, daily calendar format. It presents in organized form a key statement of Drucker's, followed by a few lines of comment and explanation, on topics ranging across a great many fields of his work: management, business and the world economy; a changing society; innovation and entrepreneurship; decision making; the changing workforce; and the nonprofit and its management. However, the most important part of this book is the blank parts of its pages. They are where the readers will contribute—their actions, decisions, and the results of these decisions. There are 366 readings, each addressing a major topic, one for every day of the year. Each reading starts with a topic and a Drucker proverb, such as "Know Thy Time," capturing the essence of the topic. Then there is a teaching taken directly from the works of Peter Drucker. Next comes the action step, where readers are asked to "think on" the teaching and apply it to themselves and their organization.

The Effective Executive in Action (with Joseph A. Maciariello): HarperCollins, 2005.

The Effective Executive in Action is a companion book to *The Effective Executive*. It provides a step-by-step guide for training oneself to be an effective person, an effective knowledge worker, and an effective executive—for training oneself to get the *right things done*. The book helps develop habits of effectiveness, to apply wisdom to tasks. There are five practices or skills to acquire to be an effective person. These five are (1) managing your time, (2) focusing your efforts on making contributions, (3) making your strengths productive, (4) concentrating your efforts on those tasks that are most important to results, and (5) making effective decisions. This is both a "what to do" and a "how to do it" book. It is also a self-development tool. By using the fill-in sections to record decisions, the reasons underlying them, and the expected results and then checking those against actual results, executives and other professional contributors will fast learn what they do well, what they need to improve on, and what they cannot even do.

ANTHOLOGIES

The Essential Drucker: HarperCollins, 2001.

The Essential Drucker offers, in Peter Drucker's words, "a coherent and fairly comprehensive 'Introduction to Management' and gives an overview of my management work and thus answers the question I've been asked again and again: 'Which writings are Essential?' " The book contains twenty-six selections on management in the organization, management and the individual, and management in society. It covers the basic principles and concerns of management, and its problems, challenges, and opportunities, giving managers, executives, and professionals the tools to perform the tasks that the economy and society of today and tomorrow will demand of them.

A Functioning Society: Transaction Publishers, 2003.

In these essays, Drucker has brought together selections from his vast writings on community, society, and the political structure. Drucker's primary concern is with a functioning society in which the individual has status and function. Parts I and II identify the institutions that could recreate community, the collapse of which produced totalitarianism in Europe. These selections were written during

World War II. Part III deals with the limits of governmental competence in the social and economic realm. This section is concerned with the differences between big government and effective government.

Novels

The Last of All Possible Worlds: Out of print. HarperCollins, 1982.
The Temptation to Do Good: Out of print. HarperCollins, 1984.

Index

About Peter F. Drucker

Peter F. Drucker—writer, management consultant, and university professor—was born in Vienna, Austria, November 19, 1909 and died in Claremont, California, on November 11, 2005.

After receiving his doctorate in public and international law from Frankfurt University in Frankfurt, Germany, he worked as an economist and journalist in London before moving to the United States in 1937.

Peter Drucker published his first book, *The End of Economic Man,* in 1939. He joined the faculty of New York University's Graduate Business School as professor of management in 1950. Since 1971, he had been Clarke Professor of Social Science and Management at the Claremont Graduate University in Claremont, California. The university named its management school after him in 1987.

Peter Drucker wrote thirty-four major books in all: fifteen books deal with management, including the landmark books *The Practice of Management* and *The Effective Executive;* sixteen cover society, economics, and politics; two are novels; and one is a collection of autobiographical essays. His most recent book, *The Effective Executive in Action,* was published in fall 2005.

Peter Drucker also served as a regular columnist for *The Wall Street Journal* from 1975 to 1995 and contributed essays and articles to numerous publications, including the *Harvard Business Review, The Atlantic Monthly,* and *The Economist.* Throughout his sixty-five year career, he consulted with dozens of organizations across the world—ranging from the world's largest corporations to entrepreneurial start-ups and various government and nonprofit agencies.

Experts in the worlds of business and academia regard Peter Drucker as the founding father of the study of management.

For his accomplishments, Peter Drucker was awarded the Presidential Medal of Freedom by President George W. Bush on July 9, 2002. A documentary series about his life and work appeared on CNBC ten times from December 24, 2002, through January 3, 2003.

About the Drucker Institute

The Drucker Institute is a think tank and action tank whose purpose is to advance the ideas and ideals of Peter F. Drucker, the father of modern management. The institute hosts conferences, undertakes research that builds on Drucker's writings, produces material that applies Drucker's work to current events, and offers a curriculum that distills Drucker's decades of leading-edge thinking. The institute also houses Drucker's archives, which are in the process of being digitized for easy online access. The Drucker Institute is a campus-wide resource of Claremont Graduate University and is closely aligned with the Peter F. Drucker and Masatoshi Ito Graduate School of Management, where Peter Drucker taught for thirty-five years and which continues to produce effective managers and ethical leaders for business, government, and civil society.

http://www.druckerinstitute.com